T0335879

Selected Readings on Global Information Technology:
Contemporary Applications

Hakikur Rahman
SDNP, Bangladesh

INFORMATION SCIENCE REFERENCE

Hershey · New York

Director of Editorial Content: Kristin Klinger
Managing Development Editor: Kristin M. Roth
Senior Managing Editor: Jennifer Neidig
Managing Editor: Jamie Snavely
Assistant Managing Editor: Carole Coulson
Typesetter: Lindsay Bergman
Cover Design: Lisa Tosheff
Printed at: Yurchak Printing Inc.

Published in the United States of America by
        Information Science Reference (an imprint of IGI Global)
        701 E. Chocolate Avenue, Suite 200
        Hershey PA 17033
        Tel: 717-533-8845
        Fax: 717-533-8661
        E-mail: cust@igi-global.com
        Web site: http://www.igi-global.com

and in the United Kingdom by
        Information Science Reference (an imprint of IGI Global)
        3 Henrietta Street
        Covent Garden
        London WC2E 8LU
        Tel: 44 20 7240 0856
        Fax: 44 20 7379 0609
        Web site: http://www.eurospanbookstore.com

Library of Congress Cataloging-in-Publication Data

Selected readings on global information technology : contemporary applications / Hakikur Rahman, editor.

        p. cm.

    Includes bibliographical references and index.

    Summary: "This book offers articles focused on key issues concerning the development, design, and analysis of global IT"--Provided by publisher.

    ISBN 978-1-60566-116-2 (hbk.) -- ISBN 978-1-60566-117-9 (ebook)

    1. Information technology. I. Rahman, Hakikur, 1957-

    HC79.I55S445 2009

    303.48'33--dc22

                                    2008026279

British Cataloguing in Publication Data
A Cataloguing in Publication record for this book is available from the British Library.

All work contributed to this book set is original material. The views expressed in this book are those of the authors, but not necessarily of the publisher.

Table of Contents

Section V
Criticial Issues

Section VI
Emerging Trends

Detailed Table of Contents

Section I
Fundamental Concepts and Theories

The development and design of online and mobile devices has begun to change our concept of reality. Within this chapter, speed, virtuality, and networking—the three factors of this change—are discussed. Speed allows information to circulate faster and faster, but this information becomes outdated quickly, so it must be continuously updated. Virtuality, the second of these factors, has become an integral part of our system of relations. Networking, finally, has become a primary method for interpreting our culture. Knowledge, in this context, is not yet a authenticated truth; it is, on the contrary, a social activity, a process quite similar to a conversation where each of the participants is negotiating a point of view. This chapter explores and analyzes knowledge in today's society.

In this chapter, the authors introduce the concept of digital divide, present its multiple definitions, and describe the short history of the problem. The basic figures and facts, which characterize information and communication technologies' usage in different countries and regions, are also given. Basic indicators that allow the monitoring of the country's advancement on the way to bridging the digital divide are stated. The main purpose of this chapter is to show that the digital divide is not only a technical problem, but also a social and political one.

The problem of global digital divide, namely disparity in Internet access and use among the various regions of the world, is a growing concern. Even though, according to some reports, the gap is getting narrower, this does not mean that the problem is disappearing, because the problem does not just consist in getting more people to become "wired," so to speak. This chapter investigates the various relationships among the global digital divide, global justice, cultures and epistemology.

This chapter discusses the digital divide from the perspective of education and culture and highlights the forms in which the problem is presented in Brazil, understanding that it is not exclusive to this context. Given the complex challenges to digital inclusion in the context of globalization, the chapter emphasizes that for children and young people to be able to appropriate new technologies and languages in a significant manner, the promotion of digital literacy should be realized with respect to the concept of multiliteracies. Digital inclusion means much more than access to technologies and is understood as one of the fronts in the struggle against poverty and inequality.

This chapter introduces how culture impacts global knowledge sharing. Effective knowledge sharing (KS), one of the four interdependent dimensions of knowledge management (KM), is particularly important in today's global environment in which national cultural differences are negotiated all the time. Knowledge sharing is described along six dimensions and national culture along four dimensions. A model is presented, which provides guidelines for effectively sharing different types of knowledge within different cultural environments. Using the model as a guide, the authors believe that decision makers will increase the chances that information and knowledge will be shared successfully.

Chapter VI

Jeffrey Roy, University of Ottawa, Canada

The objectives of this chapter are threefold: first, to provide a conceptual framework for understanding e-government as a set of four interrelated dimensions of public sector change; second, to consider the relevance and applicability of this framework for both developed and developing nations; and third, to explore the interface between domestic and transnational governance reforms in an increasingly digital era. The world in the twenty-first century needs a globally federated governance architecture, the design of which must include social, economic, political, and technological considerations.

Section II
Development and Design Methodologies

Chapter VII

M. Aminul Islam, United Nations Development Program, Bangladesh
Elena Murelli, Università Cattolica del Sacro Cuore, Italy
Frederick Noronha, Bytesforall, India
Hakikur Rahman, Sustainable Development Networking Program, Bangladesh

Capacity development initiatives for marginal communities with information and knowledge under the contemporary global scenario perhaps could be one of the effective instruments to make a meaningful change towards sustainable human development in developing countries. This chapter focuses on how capacity development initiatives for marginal communities work with reference toward achieving the Millennium Development Goals (MDGs) in developing countries. It approaches the issues and concerns related with the empowerment of the marginal communities, problems, and apprehensions in human and social capacity development in the information and communications technology (ICT) sector.

Chapter VIII

Martin Schell, New York University, USA

Considering that 347 languages have over 1 million speakers each and account for 94% of the world's population, localization is unsustainable as a strategy for making online courses globally accessible. Writing Web content in Global English is the best way to ensure that people from all linguistic backgrounds have a reasonable chance of comprehending course materials. This chapter shows how to transform native English text into Global English (simpler syntax, less jargon, fewer idioms, no slang). It also discusses e-learning design issues such as cultural perspective and Internet logistics (speed and cost of connection). Finally, it addresses the future of English as a global language, particularly in reference to its supposed "rivalry" with Mandarin.

This chapter presents data from the 2001 Census of Population and Housing to highlight the low levels of computer and Internet usage by indigenous Australians. One possible way of addressing the digital divide between capital city dwellers and other Australians is through the development of community online access centres. Using evidence from the literature and from fieldwork in New South Wales, the chapter considers some factors that are likely to make these centres more successful. These include a strong commitment by the community to the development of a centre and a close integration of the centre with community activities.

Information and knowledge management technologies and globalization have changed how firms in service industries formulate, implement, and sustain competitive advantage. This research project contributes to our understanding of the relationships between global knowledge management technology strategies and competitive functionality from global IT. Based on field research, this study found that global knowledge management technology strategies have a positive impact on competitive advantage from information technology applications functionality from global IT. This study provides recommendations to international engineering, procurement, and construction industry executives regarding the impact of knowledge management strategies and global information technology on competitive advantage of firms in their industry.

Section III
Tools and Technologies

This chapter introduces the concepts of culturally aware systems (CAWAS), a new family of adaptive systems that try to adapt learning contents and pedagogical strategies according to learners' cultural background. CAWAS is based on the notion of cultural intelligence and on the representation of a culture as both a static system, that is, a "relatively stable system of shared meanings, a repository of meaningful symbols..." and a dynamic one, that is, "a process of production of meanings." The aim of this work is to develop systems that will be better accepted by learners and de facto will work more efficiently by showing a cultural proximity with learners during a learning session.

Whether globalisation results in a "métissage" of cultures or the hegemony of one culture will depend
on the analytical and social skills of those who make up our communities. The introduction of new
technologies in education such as laptops, MP3s, and iPods and the new concept of mobile learning
require an examination of the teacher's role in facilitating innovation, conveying culture, and acting as
a conceptual translator. This chapter explores the notion that by modeling and teaching students critical
and social skills, teachers can help tomorrow's citizens to use the new flow of information to meet the
challenges of globalization.

This chapter presents a case study examining the effectiveness and significance of the Internet and
interactive video broadcasting as instructional and communication media in a global virtual learning
system. Differences in students' technology experiences, curriculum, cultures, and access to technology influence learning and student attitude in a technology-based distance education environment are
explored. The research also investigates whether the use of online references and materials is adequate
and appropriate for successful distance learning. The study reveals that students had mixed perceptions
about the effectiveness of technology, with positive attitudes exhibited towards interactive video and
some anxiety and dissatisfaction with the use of the Internet.

The need for more effective communication between people of different countries has increased as
travel and communications bring more of the world's people together. Communication is often difficult
because of both language differences and cultural differences. This chapter presents an approach to
automatically compute cultural differences by comparing databases of common-sense knowledge in
different languages and cultures. GlobalMind provides an interface for acquiring databases of common-sense knowledge from users who speak different languages. It implements inference modules to
compute the cultural similarities and differences between these databases. In this article, the design of
the GlobalMind databases, the implementation of its inference modules, as well as an evaluation of
GlobalMind are described.

Chapter XV

This chapter discusses the challenges in constructing a culture-centric Web site. With business Web sites reaching international audiences, cultural differences are an important issue in interface design. Global Web sites must be culture-centric, taking into account the attitude, technology, language, communication, sensibility, symbolism, and interface usability of targeted communities. Site design and development also should follow the Unicode standard for multilingual support with implementation done on UTF-8-enabled operating systems and applications. Globalization has led many people to become more sensitive to cultural diversity. The author hopes that understanding and awareness of international user needs, limitations, and expectations will lead to global Web sites with improved usability and sensitivity.

Section IV
Utilization and Application

Chapter XVI

Research to date on information technology (IT) adoption has focused primarily on homogeneous, single country samples. This study integrates the Theory of Reasoned Action (TRA) and the Technology Acceptance Model (TAM) with Hofstede's (1980, 1983) Masculinity/Femininity (MAS-FEM) work value dimension to focus instead on post adoption attitudes and behaviors among a mixed gender sample of United States and Canadian users of a specialized supply chain IT. Consistent with the national MAS-FEM scores and contrary to the conventional consideration of the U.S. and Canada as a unitary homogenous cultural unit, the authors found significant differences between U.S. men and women, but not between Canadian men and women. These results support the importance of the MAS-FEM dimension—independent of gender—on user attitudes and help to clarify the relationship between culture and gender effects.

Chapter XVII

This chapter investigates how, and with what success, global organisations design computer-based systems for knowledge sharing, which aim to balance centralised and standardised approaches against more diverse local needs. The empirical basis for the article is provided by an analysis of two different global organisations, each with its own knowledge-sharing infrastructure in place. The contributions from this chapter are twofold. The first is the authors' theoretical lens, where activity theory is applied to the domain of global information systems and their organisational context. The second contribution concerns the theoretical and practical insights this gives on the problems and challenges of achieving a balance between global and local priorities within highly distributed work contexts, and the role of computer-based systems in this arena.

Chapter XVIII

This chapter argues that Information Ethics (IE) can provide a successful approach for coping with the challenges posed by our increasingly globalized reality. After a brief review of some of the most fundamental transformations brought about by the phenomenon of globalization, the chapter distinguishes between two ways of understanding Global Information Ethics, as an ethics of global communication or as a global-information ethics. It is then argued that cross-cultural, successful interactions among micro and macro agents call for a high level of successful communication, that the latter requires a shared ontology friendly towards the implementation of moral actions, and that this is provided by IE.

Chapter XIX

Poor infrastructures in developing countries such as Ethiopia and much of Sub-Saharan Africa have caused these nations to suffer from lack of efficient and effective delivery of basic and extended medical and healthcare services. E-medicine awareness among both governmental policy makers and private health professionals is motivating the gradual adoption of technological innovations in these countries. The particular case of Ethiopia, one such developing country where e-medicine continues to carry significant promises, is investigated and reported in this chapter.

Given the fact that more and more governments invest heavily in e-government design and implementation, e-government has become an evolving and important research area in the IS field. Most, if not all, currently published e-government strategies are based on successful experiences from developed countries, which may not be directly applicable to developing countries. Based on a literature review, this study summarizes differences between developed/developing countries. It identifies key factors for a successful e-government implementation and proposes an implementation framework.

Section V
Criticial Issues

This study attempts to examine empirically how social institutional factors relate to Internet diffusion in 39 countries. Based on nine-year cross-country data, the analytical results show that the rule of law, educational systems, and industrialization significantly influenced the global Internet diffusion, while the economic system did not exert significant impact. Uncertainty avoidance as a national cultural phenomenon significantly inhibited the Internet diffusion. This significant and negative effect is particularly true with less developed countries (LDCs).

This chapter studies the role of international spillover of information and communication technology (ICT) in economic growth. By empirically analyzing the relationship between total factor productivity (TFP) and domestic and foreign ICT investment with time series analysis tools, the authors find limited evidence that there exist international ICT spillovers for a group of countries. Further, possible ICT policies to improve productivity and balance out a win-win situation for both ICT spillover sending and receiving countries are discussed.

ICT mediated learning provides utilities for achieving the goal of education for all, and in turn acts as an enabler in reducing the digital divide, reducing poverty, and promoting social inclusion. However, the integration of ICTs in education deserves considerable investment in time and resources. This chapter critically analyzes the effective role of ICT methods in learning and presents several successful cases of learning mechanisms that assisted in socioeconomic empowerment and, at the same time, provided recommendations for establishing similar endeavors in promising economies.

Chapter XXIV

This chapter presents an interpretive analysis of the key problems and challenges to technology implementation in developing countries, based on a three-year case analysis of an IT project in a city government in Ukraine. Authors employ the concept of technological frames of reference as an analytical tool for articulating the group-level structures related to the implementation context from the perspectives of key stakeholders and examine the degree of conflict between these frames using a Fishbone diagram. Conflict between technological frames held by key stakeholders in large-scale system implementation projects often creates an unexpected, dysfunctional, and politically charged implementation environment, ultimately leading to project failures, even if the project enjoys a high level of financial and management support. This, in turn, creates unique challenges for technology implementation projects in developing countries that are often overlooked in the traditional academic and practitioner literatures based on experiences from developed countries.

Chapter XXV

This chapter discusses cultural diversity challenges in globally distributed software development and the implications for educating and managing the future global information technology workforce. It argues that the work practices of global software development are facing a variety of challenges associated with cultural diversity, which are manifested in and can be analyzed from three dimensions: the work environment of global software development, the globally distributed knowledge workers, and the global software development work. It further articulates how cultural diversity is manifested in these three dimensions and highlights the importance of developing cultural awareness and cultural diversity understanding as important skills for the future information technology workforce.

Section VI
Emerging Trends

Chapter XXVI

This chapter examines the payoffs from e-government in the form of national performance by initially examining the relationship of e-government development with the first order government process efficiency parameters (resource spending efficiency and administrative process efficiency). Subsequently, the authors examine the association of these first order efficiency outcomes with the two second order dimensions of national performance (reduction of social divide and business competitiveness). This analysis reveals significant association of 'e-government development' with both the first order 'government efficiency parameters'. Through this research, the authors make important contributions which have implications for researchers, practitioners, public administrators, and policy makers.

Chapter XXVII

This chapter examines the effects the World Wide Web had on opening the door for many organizations with international ambitions to go global. With the advent of this technology, organizations that did not have a global presence or access to international markets could hence create websites to offer products/services to a new customer base, while companies that were already internationally entrenched could make their products easily accessible. However developing a process to deliver products in a timely fashion and ensuring availability of items remains a prevalent challenge. This chapter explores the impact of telecommunications, customer relationship management (CRM) and supply chain management (SCM) and its impact on meeting customers' expectations regardless of location. Through this examination, the research results address the challenges, the advantages and the future trends in each of these areas. Finally, this chapter provides suggestions to help companies implement strategies that will effectively overcome the challenges of globalization.

This chapter explores how representations of indigenous peoples on the Internet and other media are contextualized according to an outsider worldview, and that much of the information about indigenous peoples accessed through virtual media lack the original context in which to position the information. This means that the information is completely distanced from the indigenous peoples whom the information is purported to represent. With the increase of technology and the race to globalization, symbols are being reconstructed and redefined to connect and create a global identity for indigenous peoples. The consequences of this further the current practices of erasing and reconstructing indigenous history, language, culture and tradition through control and commodification of representations and symbols. Although these misrepresentations continue to frame the discourse for indigenous peoples in Canada, it is time for indigenous peoples to reclaim and resist these representations and for outsiders to stop creating social narratives for indigenous peoples which support western hegemony.

Prologue

The term "Information Technology (IT)" encompasses the methods and techniques used in information handling and retrieval by automatic process. The processes include computers, telecommunications and office systems or any combination of these essential elements[1]. In broader sense, IT encompasses the use of hardware, software and services to create, store, retrieve, transfer, process and present information[2]. In other sense, information technology compromises of all computerized and auxiliary automated information handling, including systems design and analysis, conversion of data, computer programming, information storage and retrieval, voice, video, data communications, requisite systems controls, and simulation[3]. However, information technology, as defined by the Information Technology Association of America (ITAA) is: "the study, design, development, implementation, support or management of computer-based information systems, particularly software applications and computer hardware[4].

In recent years, the contemporary applications of information technology to support and drive globalization of nations, societies and entrepreneurship have received increased attention. Today information technology provides the ability to coordinate the activities of globally dispersed communities, citizens, clients, employees, consumers and suppliers; increase the efficiency and effectiveness of important organizational functions and processes; and manage data, information, and knowledge across borders. A book containing selected readings develops a valuable literature on how global information technology applications are being utilized and influencing global societies deserves attention from all corners of the readers. It is a multi-faceted window to study their implications, perhaps in the longer-term of development perspectives.

Information technology is an ever-expansive domain that includes not only information and data processing but also voice, video and image applications and multimedia systems. In simple sense, concurrent information technology applications incorporate all aspects of computing and communication, as such the hardware and software for: management information system applications, office support, transaction processing systems, decision support and executive information systems, telecommunication networks, Internet, multimedia applications, databases and data mining. Information technology provides the means for the preparation, collection, transfer, retrieval, archival, access, presentation, and transformation of information in all representative forms (voice, graphics, text, video, and image). Global information technology (GIT) applications can be defined as information technology applications that are used across national borders, in two or more countries or regions of the world. This includes IT applications designed to provide a global information infrastructure; global inter-organizational information systems; as well as functional intra-organizational systems used on a global (and regional) basis. These are IT applications that make it possible for any business to be efficient, effective, and competitive in this evolving global environment (Boar, 1994; Palvia, Whitworth, Williams & Aasheim, 2004).

In terms of contemporary application of information technology, it is not only about application of new technology, but also about new ways of doing things by applying information technology in innovative ways. These applications can be seen across the dimension of new developments in the technologies themselves; new innovations, developments within organizations, and development in several working/ business practices; and researches on how quickly and how widely these developments are being taken up in society. The details of the technology are, therefore, less important than the changes that the technology is bringing to the basic structure of society (Hetemäki & Nilsson, 2005).

Furthermore, information technology has increasingly becoming a powerful tool in the fight against world poverty, providing developing countries with an unprecedented opportunity to meet vital development goals, such as poverty reduction, basic health care, environment protection and education, far more effectively than before. The countries that succeed in bridging the digital divide by harnessing the potential of information technology can look forward to enhance their economic growth, and improving human welfare and good governance practices (ADB, 2001; Qureshi & Vogel, 2007a).

In addition to these, while IT is seen in terms of academic aspects, it encompasses diversified dimensions of computing and technology, and the term is more recognizable than ever before. The information technology enclosure can be quite enormous, by enclaving many emerging fields. Not only academics and researchers, but also IT professionals perform a variety of tasks that range from installing applications to design complex computer networks, information databases, information bank (rather knowledge bank) data management, computer networking, computer science, computer engineering, artificial intelligence, human computer interactions and software design, as well as the management and administration of entire systems. When computer and communications technologies are joined together, the result is information technology. In these contexts, information technology incorporates any technology that assists to produce, manipulate, store, communicate, and/or disseminate information in a holistic manner.

This book comprising of sections on Fundamental Concepts and Theories; Development and Design Methodologies; Tools and Technologies; Application and Utilization; Critical Issues; and Emerging Trends in Global Information Technology incorporates the above mentioned issues and aspects depicting their contemporary applications.

CONTEMPORARY APPLICATIONS

Infromation technology has affected nations, societies, communities and their surroundings in numerous ways. In many societies, technology has assisted to develop more advanced economies allowing more synchronized application of it. Despite, many technological processes produce unwanted by-products, as such pollution and depletion of natural resources that are detrimental to the Earth and its environment, and various implementations of new technology influence the values of a society that often raises new ethical questions, contemporary applications of information technology, by far are advancing the entire globe for making a better living place.

Though, philosophical debates have arisen over the present and future use of technology in society, with disagreements over whether technology improves the human condition or worsens it; proponents of ideologies such as transhumanism and techno-progressivism view continued technological progress as beneficial to society and the human condition. In fact, information technology is the bridge that a society may use to eliminate the barriers of development, adopt to accord the society for controlling its own development environments and as a whole, can bridge the digital divide[5].

Generally speaking, information technology application refers to utilization of appropriate tools and techniques to solve real-world problems. The applications will vary from applying for the advancement of society development goals (environment, energy and agriculture to health care and biotechnology), service industry (manufacturing and production control to aviation and tourism), entrepreneurship (small scale industries to corporate business houses), government sectors (government services, non-government counterparts to action of development partners), and human skill development (education, learning to knowledge development and knowledge networking) (Carmel & Tjia, 2005; Kurihara, Takaya & Yamori, 2005; Lacity & Willcocks, 2001; Raisinghani, 2007; GITR, 2004; Tan, 2007). A few of the areas of contemporary applications have been cited in this section before running into challenges of these applications.

DIGITAL MEDIA, ARTS AND ENTERTAINMENT

Incorporating texts, graphics, animation, audio, video and multimedia through various applications like Java[6], php[7], DHTML[8], XML[9] and macromedia, information technology has enclave activities related to leisure, entertainment, arts, culture and edutainment.

Education and Learning

Technology driven learning has improved not only the educational content but also the way of teaching and learning. Learning process is no longer restricted to a unidirectional form of pushing of knowledge content. It is a bidirectional interactive knowledge enhancing process; unrestricted, flexible and open-ended; independent of age, time, location and subject matter. Learning is no more a time bound sequence; rather it is a life long knowledge acquisition process depending on the mode of learning and technology adopted during the learning.

Environment, Energy and Agriculture

Environment comprises of the complex physical, chemical, and biological factors in which human or community exists; while energy is an important concept in science; and agriculture is the science, art, and business of cultivating the soil, producing crops, and raising livestock and farming. These three parameters of social cohesion are intertwined and interlinked in many respects, and information technologies contribute in a large extent for their improved effect on the society resulting in major uplift of livelihood[10].

Financial Services, Insurance and Real Estate

Among the financial services comprised of programs related to planning, managing and providing banking, investment, financial planning, insurance services, and real estate businesses information technology takes a leading role in managing the entire network of operation more efficiently and manageably.

Healthcare and Biomedical Sciences

Application of information technology importantly applies to the techniques and methods for preservation of mental and physical health of all elements of the society by preventing or treating illness through technology mediated services offered by the health profession and experts. It applies simultaneously for advanced application of the principles of the natural sciences to various branches of medicine.

Manufacturing, Production Control and Logistics

Information technology not only improves the flow of production of goods by the application of labor and capital to raw materials and other intermediate inputs, like agriculture, mining, forestry, fishing, and related services, but also improves the procedure of planning, routing, scheduling, dispatching, and expediting the flow of materials, parts, subassemblies, and assemblies within the entire system. Furthermore, it makes the life of the stakeholders easier by making the process of planning, implementing and controlling more efficient, cost effective flow and managed storage of raw materials, and faster in-process inventory[11].

Aviation, Transportation, Tourism, Hospitality and Recreation

Technology has always had important implications for improved tourism (Shultis, 2001), as such interconnectivity among almost all the airlines and tour media (Railway, Bus, Ship and others) through their agents, operators and corporate houses. ICT through utilization of Semantic technologies has advanced the sequences further by incorporating choices of the users to choose among cheap routes, tourist spots, economy hotels, better connection, promotional packages, and other incentives.

Small and Medium Enterprises

The strategic and operational importance of information technology in business sector no longer remains experiments. By the advent of the 21st century, almost all the corporate houses across the world started transforming themselves into global business powerhouses via major investments in global e-business, e-commerce, and other information technology initiatives. Information technology is an essential component of successful entrepreneurship today. At the same time, information technology has created tremendous opportunities for service sector professionals like business managers to understand and manage their organizational functionalities. Thereby, managing the information systems and technologies that support the current business processes in the corporate sector has became a major challenge for both business and information technology managers and professionals (On-line document).

Government and Non-Government Agencies

Information technology contributes tremendously for managing the government-controlled institutions that are responsible for its internal administration and its relationships with other institutions or countries, and at the same time enhances operation and management of non-profit making, voluntary, service-oriented, development oriented grass roots organizations for the benefit of the citizens.

ICT, Productivity and Globalization

ICT has amplified the productivity of the actual production process through automation. At the same time, it has made the internal handling of business within organizations more efficient. Furthermore, ICT has increased the productivity through proper utilization of raw-material, improved procurement process, increased logistic support, and advanced marketing strategy. Finally, adopting ICT any organizations (or nations) have improved their images ranked as an ICT-intensive organization (or country).

Peace and security

Nowadays, conflicts are not restricted to only military intervention, but also to the scale and depth of information penetration to the society. Depending on the adaptability, information may lead to confrontation. Unless necessary measures being taken to restrict unnecessary or misleading information

Development and Poverty Reduction

Poverty, hunger, development and information technology are intricately interlinked. Many countries have adopted methods and processes to empower communities or societies through information technology to eradicate poverty by enhancing development processes and facing elements of hunger. These processes have been made easier and accessible through use of information technology. Utilizing databases and software to monitor food security chains (production, demand, consumption, surplus, deficit, early forecast, available supply link), information technology enabled countries are in better position to combat hunger and reduce poverty (UN, 2001).

Culture and Heritage

Preservation and use of traditional knowledge, that are essential components of society's resources, are also recognized as important aspects of modern day information technology initiatives. Information technologies are increasingly used to support and encourage cultural diversity, to preserve and promote indigenous languages, distinct identities and traditional knowledge of indigenous people, nations and tribes in a manner which they determine the best for their own advancement. The evolution of information and communication societies is founded on the respect and promotion of the rights of indigenous people, nations and tribes and their distinctive and diverse cultures (UNESCO, 2003a; b).

Apart from these, there are a few information technology applications, worthy to mention in terms of academic perspective. These incorporate learning and skill development in;

- **Data management:** Encompassing all the disciplines related to managing data as a valuable resource as per the full data lifecycle needs of an enterprise (data analysis, database management, data modeling, database administration, data warehousing, data movement, data maintenance, data mining, data quality assurance, data security, Meta-data management (data repositories, and their management), and data architecture)[12].
- **Computer networking:** Incorporating theoretical and practical applications of the scientific and engineering discipline concerned with communication between computer systems or related devices (Networking[13], routers, switches, routing protocols, and networking over the public Internet via twisted-pair copper wire cable, coaxial cable, optical fiber, Bluetooth, 3G and various wireless technologies) comprised of sub-disciplines like telecommunications, computer science, information technology and computer engineering.
- **Computer engineering:** Encompassing wider aspects of electrical engineering and computer science (firmware development, software development, hardware-(firmware/software) integration, circuit design, and system-level design and integration) with skill development in the areas of software design and hardware-software integration (incorporating algorithms, computer architecture and organization, computer systems engineering, circuits and signals, digital logic, digital signal processing, human-computer interaction, software engineering, and VLSI design and fabrication).
- **Software design:** A process of problem-solving and planning for software solutions that may include low-level component and algorithm implementation issues as well as the architectural view of the software system (software requirements analysis (SRA), software engineering, and automated user interface design) that may be platform-independent or platform-dependent depending on the technology, demand and operating fund.
- **Systems management:** Refers to enterprise-wide administration of distributed computer systems (incorporating network management, hardware inventories, server availability monitoring and metrics, software inventory and installation, anti-virus and anti-malware management, user's

activities monitoring, capacity monitoring, security management, storage management, network capacity and utilization monitoring), and

- **System administration:** Skill development pertaining to maintainance and operation of a computer system or network (installation, support, maintenance of servers and other components of the computer system, planning for and responding to service outages and other problems like preventive maintenance and/or breakdown maintenance, scripting or light programming, project management, supervising or training computer orinted personnel, and acting to problems beyond the knowledge of technical support staff).

CHALLENGES

Diversified use of information technologies in all spheres of life, including government and entrepreneurship has long been at the center of discussions about the relationships between advances in technologies and the social, business and political significance of communication and information in a particular society (Innis, 1950; Dutton, 1990; Heeks, 2002). However, apart from the aspirations there are a few other schools of thoughts. Among them, lack of in-depth analysis ignoring the real situation, providing mere simple solution to a complex social and political problem, copying solutions from others without looking into the real scenario, confusion in the application of the technology in appropriate form, pushing a new technology without making any pilot experimentation, introducing the new technology without mapping the capability and adaptability of the stakeholders, and dominance of technology rather than the exact solution remain as challenges among many (Bryan, Tsagarousianou & Tambini, 1998; Seneviratne, 1999; Tehranian, 1990; Lievrouw, 1994; Anderson & Danziger, 1995; Khosrow-Pour, 2000).

While separating the issues of practical application and academic analysis, it would be misleading to regard them as clearly demarcated areas during implementation. There are cases where practical applicability defers from empirical studies depending on diverse ground reality. Moreover, as the technology advances, there arises adaptability and managerial issues, especially in public administration sector, and specifically they affect the patterns of organizational change that are being misled in many cases hampering the real development.

In terms of information technology applications in developing countries, several common factors becomes challenging; as such controlling position of governments, total reliance on only the technology transfer, lack of competency at the policy level, not opening up for the private entrepreneurs, and discouraging investment at the grass roots. Despite computers made their first appearance in developing countries in the 60s; in Bangladesh in 1964, Brazil in 1958, China 1958, Egypt in 1962, India 1960, Indonesia 1962, Kenya 1961, and Malaysia 1965; most of the developing countries are yet to come at the forefront of information technology applications (Pendit, 2003)

Henceforth several questions arise. Should we afford to abandon societies lagging in information infrastructures and logistics they require to sustain themselves? Should they been pulled up further through collaboration? Should they be bypassed while initiating decisions related to majority of the population? Should we take this as challenge to reduce the digital gap between the information rich and the information poor?

The increasing globalization of the world economies is being fueled by a number of information technology infrastructure based initiatives and applications. The challenge facing policy makers, practitioners, academics and researchers is how to achieve significant and measurable improvements in addressing development goals through information and communication technology. (Rametsteiner, Vähänen, & Braatz, 2005) According to Duncombe & Heeks (2003) the role of information technology in enabling information and knowledge should cover social and economic development aspects of the society. Furthermore, Qureshi (2005)'s model of information technology for development suggests that the effects of information and communication technology are recurring and, therefore, deserves explicit attention.

Apart from providing better access to information and expertise; ensuring increased competitiveness and access to new markets including global markets; acquiring administrative efficiencies from low transaction costs; increase in labor productivity through skill development; and activities related to direct reduction of poverty (World Bank 2003, UNDP 2003) the following string of questions should also be attended. Should the effects of information technology implementations bring positive results, the cycle of development involves an increase in human development and gross domestic product through the use of better tools and techniques? Should the process lead to an increase in per capita income and perpetuate a positive spiral for social and economic development? (Qureshi & Davis, 2007; Qureshi, & Vogel, 2007a)

In many cases, it has been observed that while information technology implementations were not focused to feed the local needs, digital divides increase, and the reverse can occur and perpetuate a downward spiral. For example, lack of access to information due to lack of access to information reduces the ability of a farmer or merchant to sell goods at the most favorable price, thus reducing income generated by their efforts. Similarly the implementation of information systems that intend to provide better access to government services to citizens can bring about administrative inefficiencies by locking out them without providing any means or ability to use the information system (Giddens, 2003; Qureshi, & Vogel, 2007b).

Historically, development partners comprising of international agencies had to fund information infrastructures and build information hubs during early 90s due to lower motivation from the business community. Even after 20 years of information technology based revolutions, many countries are lagging behind in terms of globally accepted information infrastructure, especially countries with remote and dispersed communities. There remain barriers of social inclusion, telecommunications regulation, government protectionism, huge capital investment, difference of opinion and difference of technology transfer, illiteracy and cultural difference among many (Keen, 2004; Rahman, 2005; Rahman, 2006)

FUTURE RESEARCH

ICT has enhanced the realm of innovation in all spheres of life. Innovation is the creation, development and implementation of a new product, process or service, with the aim of improving efficiency, effectiveness or competitive advantage[14]. Innovation is the process that translates knowledge into economic growth and social well-being. It encompasses a series of scientific, technological, organizational, financial and commercial activities[15], and ICT has perceived as an enabler of innovation, and facilitator of adaptation. In terms of open, incremental, radical, induced or general purpose innovation (Center for Innovation Studies, 2004), ICT has a distinct role as the facilitator. In the very recent years, global information technology has seen the paradigm shift through diversified researches and their applications for the development of communities, societies and nations. At the same time, technological innovation and diffusion are considered as significant component of a country's development platform that includes the advances of information technology applications (Pendit, 2003; Wyun, Whitley, Myers & DeGross, 2002; Palvia, Palvia & Roche, 1996; Khosrow-Pour, 2001a).

Society and culture are the driving factors of adoption window for any new technologies, and information technology can open the possibilities of adoption by transforming the societal benefits to economic benefits. In this context, perhaps the greatest social driver of information technology use is the wish of individuals to upgrade the lifestyle and enhance security for themselves and their families. This drive will result in reallocation of personal time and resources to allow participation in the information society in spite of numerous problems like illiteracy, innumeracy, indebtedness, and lack of basic amenities of day-to-day survival (Roztocki & Weistroffer, 2007; Thomson & Colfer, 2005)

However, there are socio-cultural differences in people's receptiveness to information technology that will affect its future adoption and usage. Specifically, in the third-world nations, economic aspects of relative change are the most important factor, but at the same time social approval is not ignored. Therefore, adoption of information technology remains an opportunity or means to many depending on their culture, society, politics, geography and many other seen or unforeseen factors (Pendit, 2003; Hunter & Tan, 2004). While information technology is perceived as an enabler of development (UNDP, 2001), but, their adoption in the society by majority of its elements are yet to be established. It needs to be attended appropriately, and deserves further research, study and evaluation.

This has been observed that most of the government agencies, especially in the developing and transitional economies are lagging in effective utilization of information technology in their processes and attain measurable advancement. Not only government processes need to be transformed to fit in this new technology arena, but also other innovative technologies can adopted into their systems. They can introduce geographic information system (GIS) based land management, computerized mapping, records management systems for the collection, maintenance, use and storage of huge data; and the emerging citizen public access technologies which cater for both increasing public demand for more information and the eagerness of public offices to promote access to relevant information.

Comprehensive research approaches are needed to be develop in different parts of the world when information systems applications are being implemented looking at the global perspective. Where applicable, traditional research methods may be applied coping with the dynamic changes in this technology, or may not necessarily be applied to other parts of the world if situation at the ground dictates so. The best possible scenario in this aspect is to learn from changes in emerging economies and develop research methods in such ways to enable issues in these economies so that they can be effectively addressed through information technology and more traditional information systems practices can be strengthened. Furthermore, research community in the development sector comprising information technology initiatives should be able to framework and explore new lines of study so that academia can be engaged to respond in finding better opportunities and able to deploy technologies for better accomplishments.

It is natural that new technologies should be drivers of the future. However, just by looking at the new technologies, predicting the future is difficult, and forecasting their impact on the society is more difficult. The interface among nano-science, nano-technology, bio-technology, and information technology may escalate recognizable changes in the society. Nevertheless, without being adopted in successive ways, the rapid introduction of newly evolved technologies could lead to unsettlement and disruption to the common elements of the society. Moreover, it is extremely difficult for both social and political systems to keep track of the positive changes and quantify their ripple effect on the society in a shorter term (Christensen, 2000; Williams & Kuekes, 2001).

Software agents will play a major role in future accompanying information technology based development systems. Time zone and geographic boundaries have already been overcome to serve the communities with specialized software driven solutions. Customized software development, on-line skill development, call centers, VoIP are among them.

World has seen many revolutions in terms of societal development and contemporary application of information technology. If a nation would like to focus on grass root development through utilization of information technology, success of telecenter movement in that country has no alternative. Sustained

Figure 1. Probable components of e-applications (Adopted from Brücher & Gisler, 2002)

Degree of
interactions

E-learning	E-government	E-commerce	E-democracy
Online enrolment, examination, evaluation	Online tax declaration, govt. services	Online bidding, transaction	Online opinion poll, voting
Online content, courses, schedule	Online E-mail contacts, forms, FAQ,	Online marketing, electronic data interchange	Online discussion on voting system
Information on education system	Information on legislation, judiciary, administration	Information on entrepreneurship	Information on political and legal structures

Degree of applications

growth and existence of organized telecenter is another precondition of information technology based society development, and needs intensive observation, attention and research.

There is general conformity that information technology affects all sectors of society and economy. Along this perspective, governments have a major role to play through their investments in information technology research and development. They will also be influential in shaping the future of information technology developments through their national and international policies. However, policies aimed at creating an enabling environment for the development and deployment of information technology at the grass roots need to address issues of trade, investment, industry development, and e-business (Ramet-steiner, Vähänen & Braatz, 2005; Khosrow-Pour, 2001b; Elliott, 2004). The following figure gives an overall picture (though not exhausted) of e-Application platform in a nation or society. As the degree of interaction increases, and degree of application enclaves more features of the society, a comprehensive e-Application platform will emerge.

CONCLUSION

In recent years, several indicators have been developed that can measure relative presence, use and accomplishment of information technology in their countries. However, mere indicators of availability of information technology through access could be a misleading indicator, unless it is not meant to empower the end users (Sciadas, 2002). Moreover, apart from being just familiar with the information technology, skills of the people and individual have to be elevated. In this perspective, adoption of technologies will have to be in such forms that their livelihood could be amalgamated and they could feel from within that the benefits of the technologies are intrinsic. Furthermore, as Hetemäki, & Nilsson

(2005) indicated that, the new technologies offer new capabilities and opportunities for participation. Nevertheless, during the process, ownership of the process and delivery of products are key elements of acceptance of the process outcome.

Contemporary application of information technologies in society is characterized by high level of information interaction in the everyday life of most citizens in most institutions and workplaces. This can be achieved through use of common or compatible technology for a wide range of personal, social, educational and business activities, and via ability to transmit, receive and exchange digital data rapidly between places irrespective of distance. The current trend is to emphasize that intensity of using the e-prefix for everything from shopping to governance, but that distinction may disappear in future as the use of information technology in business, government and daily lives is destined to terminate at a common point (Thomson & Colfer, 2005). In a holistic view, information technology will not spare a single activity of the future society.

On the contrary, tremendous groundwork needs to be performed at the grass roots, especially in transitional or developing economies, where majority of the World population reside. Ignoring social, economic, cultural, political and ethical considerations can result in a high probability of failure of development projects in general and information technology based projects in particular. In developing countries, the communication component of information technology may be the most significant aspect in the short run, but in the longer run, new technologies require new social norms, new legislation and policy, and new institutions. However, to see the impact of information technology at the level of individual element of the society is not a time bound phenomenon. Incrementally, with the availability of positive atmosphere (win-win situation), the new social forces will gradually develop. Future successful information technology dependent development projects will have to be well integrated into communities, planned for optimal use of existing infrastructure, and focused to adequate human intermediaries for longer-term sustainability (Thomson & Colfer, 2005; Pendit, 2003; Qureshi & Vogel, 2007a).

REFERENCES

ADB (2001). *Towards e-Development in Asia and the Pacific: A Strategic Approach for Information and Communication Technology*, Manila: Strategy and Policy Department, Asian Development Bank (ADB).

Anderson, K.V. & Danziger, J.N. (1995). Information technology and the political world: The impacts of it on capabilities, interactions, orientations and values. *International Journal of Public Administration*, 11 (November 1995), p. 1693 - 1724.

Boar, B. H. (1994). *Practical Steps for Aligning Information Technology with Business Strategies*, John Wiley and Sons.

Bryan, C., Tsagarousianou, R. & Tambini, D. (1998). (Eds.) Electronic democracy and the civic networking movement in context. *Cyberdemocracy : Technology, Cities and Civic Networks.*, p. 1-17. London: Routledge.

Brücher, H., and Gisler, M., 2002, E-Government—from the bases to application (von den Grundlagen zur Anwendung), *HMD—Praxis Wirtschaftsinformatik*, 226.

Carmel, E., & Tjia, P. (2005). *Offshoring Information Technology: Sourcing and Outsourcing to a Global Workforce*, Cambridge University Press, 2005.

Center for Innovation Studies (2004). Innovation Study available at http://www.cfsinnovation.com/managed_documents/pobpaper.pdf

Christensen, C.M., 2000, *The Innovator's Dilemma: When New Technologies Cause Great Firms to Fail*, Harperbusiness, New York.

Duncombe, R. and R. Heeks, R. (2003) "An information systems perspective on ethical trade and self-regulation." *Information Technology for Development*, Vol. 10 Issue 2, p123-139, 2003.

Dutton, W.H. (1990). The political implications of information technology: challenge to power. In Berleur, J., Clement, A., Sizer, R. & Diane (Eds.). *The Information Society: Evolving Landscapes*. Edited by Whitehouse, p. 54 - 78. New York: Springer-Verlag.

Elliott, G. (2004). *Global Business Information Technology: An Integrated Systems Approach*, Pearson/Addison Wesley.

Giddens, A. (2003). *Runaway World: How Globalization is Reshaping Our Lives*. Routledge. New York.

GITR (2004). *The Global Information technology Report 2003-2004*, Oxford University Press, Inc. NY.

Heeks, R., 2002, *Failure, Success and Improvisation of Information Systems Projects in Developing Countries,* Development Informatics, Working Paper Series. Paper No. 11. Institute for Development Policy and Management, University of Manchester, UK.

Hetemäki, L., & Nilsson, S. (2005). (Eds.) *Information Technology and the Forest Sector, International Union of Forest Research organizations*, Vienna, 2005.

Hunter, M.G. & Tan, F.B. (2004). *Advanced Topics in Global Information Management*, Idea Group Inc.

Innis, H.A. (1950). *Empire and Communications*. Toronto : University of Toronto Press.

Ken, P. (2004). A Manifesto for Electronic Commerce, a paper presented at the *International Conference on Electronic Commerce*, Bled., Slovenia.

Khosrow-Pour, M. (2000). *Organizational Achievement and Failure in Information Technology*, Idea Group Inc.

Khosrow-Pour, M. (2001a). *Pitfalls and Triumphs of Information Technology Management*, Idea Group Inc.

Khosrow-Pour, M. (2001b). *Managing Information Technology in a Global Economy: 2001*, Idea Group Publishing.

Kurihara, Y., Takaya, S., & Yamori, N. (2005). *Global Information Technology and Competitive Financial Alliances*, Idea Group Inc.

Lacity, M.C. & Willcocks, L. (2001). *Global Information Technology Outsourcing: In Search of Business Advantage*, Wiley.

Lievrouw, L.A. (1994). Information resources and democracy: understanding the paradox. *Journal of the American Society for Information Science*. 45 (July 1994): 350 - 357.

Online document, Accessed April 06, 2008 from http://www.scribd.com/doc/396854/Enterprise-and-Global-Management-of-Information-Technology.

Palvia, P., Palvia, S. & Roche, E. (1996). *Global Information Technology and Systems management: Key Issues and Trends*, Ivy League Publishing.

Palvia, P.C., Whitworth, J.E., Williams, S.R., & Aasheim, C.L. (2004). Using a Trait Approach to Analyze the Impact of Global Information technology Applications, a *Proceeding of the 7th Annual Conference of the Southern Association for Information Systems*, Savannah Marriott Riverfront, USA. February 27-28.

Pendit, P.L. (2003) The use of information technology in public information services : an interpretative study of structural change via technology in the Indonesian Civil Service. In *Proceedings CONSAL XII "Information Resources Empowerment: Enhancing Knowledge Heritage"*, Bandar Seri Begawan (Brunei Darussalam).

Qureshi, S. (2005). "How does Information Technology Effect Development? Integrating Theory and Practice into a Process Model." A *Proceedings of the Eleventh Americas Conference on Information Systems*, Omaha, NE, USA August 11th-14th.

Qureshi, S., and A. Davis, (2007). Overcoming the Digital Divide through Electronic Commerce: Harnessing opportunities in IT for Development, a paper presented at the *40th Annual Hawaii International Conference on System Sciences (HICSS'07)*.

Qureshi, S. & Vogel, D. (2007a). Information technology Drivers for Development, In Qureshi, S. & Vogel, D. (2007). (Eds.). Information Technology Application in Emerging Economies: A Monograph of Symposium at *the Hawaii International Conference on System Sciences (HICSS)*, HICSS 40, January 3-6, 2007 at Hilton Waikoloa Village Resort, Waikoloa, Big Island, Hawaii. pp. 3-6.

Qureshi, S. & Vogel, D. (2007b). (Eds.) Information Technology Application in Emerging Economies: A Monograph of Symposium at *the Hawaii International Conference on System Sciences (HICSS)*, HICSS 40, January 3-6, 2007 at Hilton Waikoloa Village Resort, Waikoloa, Big Island, Hawaii.

Rahman, H. (2005). Social Impact of Virtual Networking, In *Encyclopedia of Virtual Communities and Technologies*, edited by Dr. Subhasish Dasgupta, Idea Group Inc., USA, 2005, pp. 417-423.

Rahman, H. (2006). Community-Based Information Networking in Developing Countries, In *Encyclopedia of Digital Government*, edited by Anttiroiko, A-V & Malkia, M., Idea Group Inc., USA, 2006, pp. 201-207.

Raisinghani, M.S. (2007). *Global Information Technology Management in the Digital Economy*, Idea Group Inc.

Rametsteiner, E., Vähänen, T. & Braatz, S. (2005). ICT and International Governance, In Hetemäki, L., & Nilsson, S. (2005). (Eds.) *Information Technology and the Forest Sector*, International Union of Forest Research organizations, Vienna.

Roztocki, N. & Weistroffer, H.R. (2007). Information Technology Investment Evaluation for Emerging Economies: Tools and a General Framework. In Qureshi, S. & Vogel, D. (2007). (Eds.) Information Technology Application in Emerging Economies: A Monograph of Symposium at *the Hawaii International Conference on System Sciences (HICSS)*, HICSS 40, January 3-6, 2007 at Hilton Waikoloa Village Resort, Waikoloa, Big Island, Hawaii. Pp. 62-75

Sciadas, G., 2002, *Monitoring the Digital Divide,* Orbicom–CIDA Project, National Research Council of Canada.

Seneviratne, S.J. (1999). Information technology and organizational change in the public sector. In *Information Technology and Computer Applications in Public Administration: Issues and Trends.* G. David Garson, (Ed.), p. 41 - 61. Hershey, USA : Idea Group Publishing.

Shultis, J., 2001, Consuming nature: The uneasy relationship between technology, outdoor recreation and protected areas, *The George Wright FORUM*, 18: 56–66.

Tan, F.B. (2007). *Global Information technologies: Concepts, Methodologies, Tools & Applications,* Information Science Reference, USA.

Tehranian, M. (1990). *Technologies of power: information machines and democratic prospect,* Norwood, Ablex Publishing Company.

Thomson, A. & Colfer, C. (2005). ICT and Social Issues, In Hetemäki, L., & Nilsson, S. (2005). (Eds.) *Information Technology and the Forest Sector*, International Union of Forest Research organizations, Vienna.

UN (2001). *Road map Towards the Implementation of the United Nations Millennium Declaration,* Report of the Secretary-General. See http://www.un.org/ documents /ga/docs/56/a56326.pdf

UNDP (2001). *Information Communications Technology for Development,* United Nations Development Programme Evaluation Office, Essentials No. 5.

UNDP (2003). *Human Development report 2003*, Millennium Development Goals: A compact among nations to end human poverty, Oxford University Press, NY.

UNESCO (2003a). *Performance indicators on ICT for education matrix,* available at http://www.unece. org/stats/documents/ces/sem.52/wp.1.e.pdf.

UNESCO (2003b). *Cultural and Linguistic Diversity in the Information Society.* UNESCO Publications for the World Summit on the Information Society, Paris.

Williams, R.S., & Kuekes, P.J. (2001). We've only just begun, in M.C. Roco, and W.S. Bainbridge, (Eds.), *Societal Implications of Nanoscience and Nanotechnology*, National Science Foundation, NSET Workshop Report, pp. 83–87.

World bank (2003). *ICTs and MDGs: A World Bank Perspective*, Global ICT Department, The World bank Group, December.

Wynn, E.H., Whitley, E.A., Myers, M.D. & DeGross, J.I. (2002). (Eds.), *Global and Organizational Discourse About Information Technology*, Springer, 2002.

ENDNOTES

[1] www.nao.org.uk/intosai/edp/directory/misc/glossary.html
[2] www.finance.gov.au/gateway/guidance_glossary.html
[3] sam.dgs.ca.gov/TOC/4800/4819.2.htm
[4] en.wikipedia.org/wiki/Information technology

5   http://en.wikipedia.org/wiki/Technology

6   A programming software developed by Sun Microsystems, Inc.

7   A server-side HTML embedded scripting language

8   Dynamic Hyper Text Markup language

9   Extensible Markup Language

10   Google definitions

11   Google definitions

12   http://en.wikipedia.org/wiki/Data_management

13   local area network (LAN), wide area network (WAN), wireless LANs and WANs (WLAN & WWAN)

14   www.digitalstrategy.govt.nz/templates/Page____60.aspx

15   www.arc.gov.au/general/glossary.htm

About the Editor

Engr. Md. Hakikur Rahman, PhD is the principal, Institute of Computer Management & Science (ICMS), and president of ICMS Foundation. He is currently serving Bangabandhu Sheikh Mujibur Rahman Agricultural University as an adjunct faculty, and the South Asia Foundation Bangladesh Chapter as the secretary. He served Sustainable Development Networking Foundation (SDNF) as its executive director (CEO) from January 2007 to December 2007, the transformed entity of the Sustainable Development Networking Programme (SDNP) in Bangladesh where he was working as the national project coordinator since December 1999. SDNP is a global initiative of UNDP and it completed its activity in Bangladesh on December 31, 2006. Before joining SDNP he worked as the director, Computer Division, Bangladesh Open University. Graduating from the Bangladesh University of Engineering and Technology in 1981, he has done his Master of Engineering from the American University of Beirut in 1986 and completed his PhD in computer engineering from the Ansted University, UK in 2001.

Section I
Fundamental Concepts
and Theories

Chapter I
Knowledge, Culture, and Society in the Information Age

Pier Cesare Rivoltella
Università Cattolica del Sacro Cuore, Italy

ABSTRACT

Informational society, mainly after the development of online and mobile devices, is changing the forms with which we build our image of the reality. Speed, virtuality, and networking are three of the factors of this change. Speed means that information is circulating faster and faster, but also that it becomes aged very soon, with the necessity of being updated. Virtuality, after its first conceptualizations like a parallel dimension in the 1990s, is nowadays an integral part of our system of relations. Networking, finally, is becoming the main category for interpreting our culture, made of multiple dimensions of sociability, inside and outside the net. Knowledge, in this context, is not yet a truth authenticated; it is, on the contrary, a social activity, a process quite similar to a conversation where each of the discussants is negotiating a point of view. This is the scenario into which modern teachers, parents, and youngsters are acting.

INTRODUCTION

Since a few years ago, the research in the field of social and communication sciences has described our time as a transition phase from the industrial age to the information age. This passage is usually seen as a substitution of machines and productive routines with information technologies, but we need to deepen our analysis. Castells (1996) accurately suggests moving the discourse from technology protagonist to the ways in which knowledge is produced and relationships between individuals and systems are constructed within the society. According to this perspective, the industrial age ceases to be identified with Ely Whitney's cotton-gin, Stephenson's locomotive, or the mechanization of labour processes; it rather indicates a particular sort of social organization—based on Taylorism—regarding every single aspect of human activity, from school to family. If Castells' approach is worthwhile, a similar discourse can be promoted in relation to the information age. It cannot be identified with the introduction of information and communication technologies (ICT); better it could be bended with the systematic reorganization that these technologies promote on social level. Rather than talking about information society, the Spanish sociologist prefers to refer to the concept of informational society. In the first case, information is the content of society, while in the second one it defines the nature of society itself. Informational society is a society "made out of information." In the next paragraph, we will better understand how.

The process of rearrangement leading to this society might be interpreted according to at least three meaningful factors:

1. The **speed** of knowledge exchanges and knowledge aging. In fact, the transactions, thanks to network implementation, are not based on goods anymore, but on information. This makes the exchange almost instantaneous (i.e., in the case of tickets release or of home banking). The same speed hits the possibility of individual knowledge, capitalized in initial training through the educational system, to answer properly to the needs of a society adopting an innovative rhythm that is at least double with respect to knowledge updating.

2. **Virtuality**, which means the clearer disconnection between space and time, to which we can refer macrophenomena such as the globalization of industries and markets and micropractices such as teleworking or video conferencing. The separation between space and time means to emancipate information sender and receiver from the need of sharing the same place at the same time. This also means a great flexibility of places and time in information access.

3. **Networking**, which means that the net metaphor becomes a paradigm explaining most of our social practices. Our society is characterized by the need for a collective dimension, even if with evident contradictions: intelligence is collective, work is done in staff, and cooperation and collaboration seem strategic scenarios in different fields, from economy to didactics. The connectivity becomes a cultural macroindicator; the diffusion of the net is participating to a progressive move from the local to the planetary dimension: besides, in the economy development and in political and social macrophenomena (disappearance of the idea of nation, migratory movements, cultural melting pot), *globalization* mainly consists in aiding the circulation of symbolic meanings and this depends on the telematic-based connectivity.

The consequence of this set of so decisive changes, under the perspective of cultural sociology, has been a new importance of knowledge. Its creation, elaboration, and diffusion are nowadays the main source of productivity and power. This means a new protagonist of symbolic goods. Following Baudrillard (1976), in traditional societies goods had a specific value; today the value is represented by the good itself. It is possible to verify that thinking about commercial "objects" as television formats, Internet services, or about other activities such as financial intermediations or advertisement. This emphasis on symbolic goods produces the growth of a new category of "symbolic workers" (Neveu, 1994) who build their professional identity on the production-diffusion of symbolic good (i.e., trainers, PRs, consulting projectionists, marketing experts, etc.). Finally, this means a new need for a new know-how. This is the actual field of education. A field into which the new media competences become the very important thing. digital literacy is the response to this need.

THE INFORMATIONAL SOCIETY AS A SOCIAL CONSTRUCTION

In one of his works, Mattelart (2001, p. 4) states the main coordinates to understand the real meaning of what today is commonly indicated as "Information society." Mattelart's (2001) point of view is clear. He connects the space conquest with Internet diffusion, grasping their common connecting aspect. They are "conquests," using a category proposed by the American sociologists Dayan and Katz (1992), both are accompanied (as always happens with conquests) by a story of emancipation. The main indicators that mark a conquest refer to some elements linked to the exceptionality of the event the conquest represents and to the heroism expressed by men engaged to make it happen. More precisely, a conquest:

•   Refers to a situation that appears unsolvable and to the need for an important action to overcome it
•   Finds in some men's charisma (according to the weberian declination) the instrument to realize this change
•   Thanks to this transition, allows and defines the access of humanity into a new symbolic order

This last definition makes sense of the fact that usually great conquests are accompanied by a story of emancipation. This story, from a social point of view, works as a tool for understanding the event itself, increasing its symbolic value; it is a role that in traditional societies was played by poets and that today is strongly supported through media, particularly through television (Fiske & Hartley, 1978). Just consider Armstrong's and Aldrin's walk on the moon on July 20, 1969, and the meaning it assumed in that specific historical period. Mass media represent and construct it as a story of emancipation in relation to the Cold War and to the need to make humanity free from self destruction and lack of resources.

A close mechanism can be found in relation to the informational society. Similarly we are in front of a conquest and we can effortlessly find out its own structural aspects:

•   The idea of the informational society was climbed in the past decade in a context of great transformations and problems. On a geopolitical level, the fall of ideologies and the overcoming of the logic of opposite blocks produced as a main consequence the multiplication of regional conflicts and the dissemination of nuclear potential even within countries considered politically unstable. Economically speaking, the need to affirm a "human capitalism" becomes even more urgent in order to reduce the lack of balances in riches distribution (this lack can easily turn into new conflicts). Finally, on a demographic level, the inverse growth rhythm between Western and Third World countries, and the following enormous migratory mobility between them, put in evidence the problem of an adequate cohabitation of differences on a social and cultural level. We can affirm that we are now facing a complex and uneasy situation that can only be modified by a great action.

- The informational society has its own heroes. There are forerunners such as Charles Babbage and Norbert Wiener, material builders such as Bill Gates, gurus providing a legitimation with their provisions such as Nick Negroponte and Kevin Warwick. The possibility of finding a good answer to the problems mentioned above passes through these men's' work, a work of implementation and reflection.

- Finally, the informational society represents a new symbolic order able to balance conflicts regionalization with the predisposition of a new arena for dialogue, providing the peaceful cohabitation between market and equality through the promises of new economy, fixing new rules for the democratic game. The Internet in this perspective really becomes a new space of mediation where the reduction of social conflicts could be possible.

From these general lines, it looks evident that the informational society should be considered, more than a fact, as the result of a careful and patient work of social construction (Mattelart, 2000). This work is based on three main "emancipation discourses."

The first discourse is represented by the words of science. Mattelart (2000) very well underlines how the idea of an informational society was theoretically diffused since the first part of the 1960s, linked to the theme of the collapse of ideologies. What was described is the origin of a new model of society marked by the organization (*management society*) and the labour dematerialization, by the substitution of the *labor theory of value* with the *knowledge theory of value*, by the getting over of the central position of companies and business men towards a new centrality of universities and research centres. To define this society we introduced the adjective "postindustrial," then substituted with the category of "information society" in the 1970s. The "fathers" of this society have been found in the main representatives of the organizational theory: Saint-Simon's technocratic utopia and Taylor's organizational paradigm connote the functional society as the fortunate result of development and progress. The net metaphor has been soon indicated as the necessary base for the representation of a decentralized and complex organizational model.

The idea of the net, of a network society, is the focus also of the second category of discourses, the provisional discourses promoted by the futurologists. The last 20 years have seen the origin of the figure and role of the *think tanks*, specialists who transform the ability to foresee the evolutionary future scenarios into a real professional competency (*professional prognosticators*). Among them, besides Herman Kahn, Alvin Toffler, and the already mentioned Nicholas Negroponte, we quote also Zbigniew Brzezinski, councilor for international affairs during the presidency of Jimmy Carter. It is due to Brzezinski that the first intuition of a "net diplomacy" should have gradually replaced the traditional force diplomacy.

We arrive now to the hearth of the third discourse level on informational society, related to the geopolitical situation of the planet, marked by a slow dissolution of the role of the nation, by the multiplication of centers, and by the globalization of processes.

While Brzezinski imagined a world architecture aimed to dominate scientific reason—a real obstacle to technological innovation—the new protagonists of the geo-economy undermined in the name of market reasons the traditional foundations of geopolitics. And the idea of the one world supported by multinational companies was based on the growth of industries and information nets, able to free production managers, consumers, and products from the ties of the borders and to let them interact within one self-regulated market, ordaining in this way the unsustainability of the nation-state and, consequently, the frailness of public policies (Mattelart, 2000, pp. 87-88).

The result of specialists' analysis, of marketing provisions, of international scenarios shared within television imaginary, is represented by the perception of the fact that informational society represents something "indisputable," that thanks to it we entered a new period for economy and history, that nothing can be as before. If the NASDAQ grows, to which extent it depends on the strength of informatics companies or on the faith bouncing from specific reviews and the ideas of opinion makers? The dependence on market mood is an old stock market law, but referring to information society and new economy it gains a new interesting meaning: it becomes the specular image of a society that is exactly made out of information. Here lies the meaning of what we underlined at the beginning of the paragraph.

During our analysis this aspect will be underlined applying the category of the symbolic.

SPEED, VIRTUALITY, NETWORKING

At least according to the perspective proposed, it seems undeniable that the affirmation of the network society is based on a mythological disposal in which it is hard to discern what is the result of a construction process and what is real; but, on the other hand, the main changes in market and production influenced by telematics and its organizational consequences, with the growth of new professions and new social relationships, are undoubtedly real facts. Failing these conditions, we could not talk about the informational society, even in the presence of the construction of a mythology linked to this form of society created and fed up by the media. As suggested in the introduction, we will focus on three main aspects: speed, virtuality, and networking in their substaining effects towards globalization.

Speed

Speed marks the growth of telematic nets and their impact on social organization with three main attentions. First, it produces time compression and distances erosion. Under this point of view, telematic nets represents both a resolute leap and an inversion in the history of communication technologies. As a matter of fact, until now, the pulling down of distances has always passed through the progressing rise of speed: a horse is faster than a walking man, a car is faster than a horse, a plane is faster than vehicles running on the ground. Concretely, pulling down distances meant in these cases to increase speed or to power the conveyance. According to this logic, the Internet affirms itself as the fastest medium since the transfer of speed is almost close to the instant, but this incredible speed only depends on the fact that what is traveling is information. So the maximum speed lies in the absence of movement: everything starts from and goes to where we are. This idea gets a perfect explanation in the image of the "sitted journalism" introduced by media sociology to depict the current model of journalism: a journalism far from the facts and dependent on a few sources of information generally searched through a computer standing on his own desk (Neveu, 2002). Agency dispatches allow the journalist to "deliver" news with no need to move and search them (even if this attitude evidently includes strong repercussions on news construction process, as agrees to the mediation of agencies without verifying facts, as usually occurs in classical inquiry journalism).

Information exchange speed brings about some consequences. The most evident, which will be discussed in the next paragraph, is the virtualization of communication. This means its emancipation from space and time sharing.

It is not yet necessary to share the same room to communicate, with all its advantages and drawbacks. The other two consequences, on the contrary, shape as two different ways to decline speed within information society.

First of all, in a social system where information is required to be moved in very strict time thanks to information technology, speed itself becomes a new fundamental factor referred to as individual cognitive profile. Knowledge elaboration depends not only on the ability to read facts and produce concepts, but also on specific skills necessary for their expression. When we participate to a brainstorming via chat, discussing a project launching, the fact that we are not able to use a computer keyboard appropriately or that we do not manage the environment we are using (icons, buttons, processes) produces the same effect as if we do not exactly understand the language spoken in a foreign country. I can have great ideas but I will not manage to impose my opinion, because my slowness will turn into a reduced visibility on the screen and this slow rhythm will be interpreted as a lack of personal meaningful contributions. Besides this aspect— the ability to interact with interfaces—a specific quickness in feed-back suggestion will be asked. If information runs fast, what is needed is not only a deep rapidity to process it, but also to produce the required answers, because a subsiding in our feed-back implies a general fall in the system speed and this can create serious organization effects (if I do not immediately answer an e-mail that is fundamental to come to a decision, I deeply stop the resolute process) and an economical loss. Anthropologically speaking, this is an important change, as the syncopated rhythm of electronic communication, which proposes to examine quickly really big amounts of information and to react in an even shorter time, are taking over the long term rhythm linked to retrospective analysis (Godman, 1968) typical of the civilization of literacy (before answering I read accurately, then

I read again, I think, I can write a draft, rewrite, and correct, then I can send it). The results are indicated in the substitution of pondered reading with rapid reading practices, the ripening of a synthetic and superficial understanding of reality as to the deep and analytical mode, the information overload. This is one of the most diffused shapes of the impossibility to totalize knowledge, typical of the informational society as observed by Levy (1997). Concerning this topic, Virilio (1998) states that we are facing a real pathology, close to the uneasiness manifested by traditional travelers who suffer car or plane.

The third and last meaning of speed (second effect of the growing of information sharing) refers to knowledge obsolescence. There are two main factors influencing this phenomenon.

On one hand, the speed of technological change imposes a frequent knowledge upgrading. It is a condition well experienced by people working in e-learning market, a case in which it is difficult to exit the experimental phase of a process because when we are about to abandon it in favour of a steady condition, technological innovation radically changes things and imposes to start a new experimental phase, with the common result of a condemnation for the ones who try to interpret innovation, a condemnation that implies the impossibility of reasoning in term of productive routines and vice versa: to be updated means to risk to exit the labour market, always running to innovation; but run to innovation means otherwise to renounce to obtain those productive standards that only allow to recover investments and start to gain profits.

This changing speed, finally, affects knowledge updating also in relation to rapidity in the information exchange processes. We move from a "heavy" knowledge, typical of the pre-electronic age, in which knowledge share and appropriation represented a long term task, to a "light" knowledge that is used in a very short lapse of time. "New knowledges" grow and erase; they are the result of intersections that are often temporary. Speed creates them quickly and soon sweeps them away.

Virtuality

The abundant literature on the term virtuality allows a critical reflection on it, far enough from the futurological (science fictional?) enthusiasms created around it in the first part of the 1990s. Concerning the term virtual, we can distinguish at least three aspects: a punctual meaning (etymological level), the perceptive experience linked to it (technological level), and the significance of its effects (social level).

Concerning the definition of the term, Pierre Levy (1995) is credited with putting order in the debate. On this subject the French philosopher has accurately shown that the term virtual (if we look at its Latin etymology and at the use of the medieval scholastic philosophy) is not opposite to the term "real," but to the term "actual."

The term virtual comes from the medieval Latin virtualis, which derives from virtus, strength, power. For the scholastic philosophy, virtual is what can potentially exist, something which is not in progress. What is virtual tends to come true, nevertheless without being passed through a formal and effective concreteness. A tree is virtually present in the seed. Remaining in the rigorous frame of philosophy, the virtual is not opposed to the real, but to the actual: virtuality and actuality are only two different states of being. (Levy, 1995, p.5)

In this way we can easily get over the ordinary meaning we usually use to refer to virtual, figuring it out as something that does not exist, that is only an illusion. Virtual reality is not "another" world as regards to reality (reality exists, virtual reality does not), but a different manifestation of reality.

Which are, then, the characteristics that inertly define the virtual? Simplifying Levy's (1995) analysis, there are two defining aspects:

*   The **problematic nature**, that is the fact of representing a system of forces which is differently realizable. For example, when we talk about a virtual company, its virtuality consists in the fact that the labour distribution and the localization of its main areas do not refer to something finally and totally solved, but that has to be permanently redefined according to the actual needs (management can be moved from London to New York, while production can slide from Taiwan to Brasil, etc.);
*   The **delocalization**, which refers to the loss of power owned by localization aspects in defining situations. A virtual company is not yet precisely localizable: its elements are nomadic and dispersed, their geographic position has no more value (Levy, 1995). Virilio grasps the meaning of this concept when he says that nowadays we are spectators of the end of geography more than of the end of the history (Virilio, 1998, p. 9).

The explanation of the terms allows us to gain great advantages also on the second level of our analysis, the technological one. For a long time, in fact, virtual has been identified with a specific technology granting immersion and manipulation of and within a synthetic space. Also, from the point of view of social imaginary, virtual reality has been traditionally associated to all those devices—from head mounted displays to datagloves, created to support user's interaction with a computer-generated space as if it was real (and here lies again the contraposition between real and virtual that, thanks to Levy (1995), we have already defined as theoretically passed).

For example, the fact that wearing eye-phone, slipping on a data-glove, and a data-suit we are able to access an illusionary reality and live it as if it was real (or almost real), represents a concrete step in favour of what is explained. Now we are ready to reconnoiter from the inside a reality that appears as the counterfigure of our reality. (Maldonado, 1992, pp. 51-52)

This "strong" meaning of the concept of virtual has fallen into a fast disuse, both because the kind of technology it referred to was too encumbering and because the initial utopia of making virtual reality available for everyone, directly from personal computers, sensationally failed. Actually, technologically, the costs implied to obtain adequate immersion and navigation effects are so high that they allow RV devices purchased only in case of research laboratories. At the same time, with the crisis of the "strong" declination of the virtual, a "weak" meaning of the term has developed and was diffused for its wide social implications, a meaning that joins what is today defined as "culture of virtuality." This culture, which probably finds its origin in the cyber-culture (Benedikt, 1991; Gibson, 1984), is nowadays present in the different forms of virtual communities, form IRCs to Second Life. It confirms the idea according to which the main forms of network existence would be the ones to prefer: more freedom, more possibilities to meet people, more opportunities to create doubles of the self through simulation. A perspective that some authors compared to the different experiences of body escaping promoted by shamanism (Zolla, 1992) or by the platonic tradition.

For instance, the idea of a virtual reality conceived as an escape from reality towards virtuality can be interpreted as an ascendant escape, liberating to the absolute. Above all, when this idea is seen as something happening through a disembodied human sensorial, through a sensorial made autono-

mous as regards to the body, thanks to advanced digital technologies. This clearly reminds us that the plotinian ecstasy, the escape from the sensible to the intelligible. (Maldonado, 1992, p. 56)

Also under this cultural meaning of the term virtual, the contraposition to the real still appears implicit: virtual life is a "life on the screen," to quote the title of the renowned work of Turkle (1995), that has to be seen in antithesis to the "real" life; a perspective that vanishes, on the contrary, if we reflect on what virtuality represents today on a social level. It has to do with all those forms of interaction surrogating physical presence through the mediation of electronic devices. In this way, when we talk about "virtual classroom" within the e-learning field we refer to learning/teaching activities as they are made possible among individuals who do not share the same physical place, thanks to the mediation of a telematic environment such as the current Learning Management Systems. The adjective virtual, in this sense, does not refer to a different dimension where it is possible to experience perceptive simulated situations, nor a world made of fictional interactions supporting masking free play. On the contrary, the term refers to a situation where physical presence resolves into telepresence. So, rather than an alternative place where it is possible to enter, virtual has to be considered as an action scenario conceptualized besides other scenarios: going further with the example of e-learning, it means to consider that, besides personal reading of texts and materials and face to face discussion with colleagues, we can open new scenarios such as forum discussions or chatting with a professor who lives several kilometers away. Both these forms of activity are consistent with the aim of learning, and the only difference is represented by the fact that the first forms require a physical presence, while the others replace it through telepresence (Rivoltella, 2003).

From Networking to Globalization

A society that conceptualizes itself according to the two metaphors of speed and virtuality cannot be anything except a network society. Speed, for instance, comprises always greater possibilities to circulate ideas and knowledges that, on the contrary, would remain local, while virtuality supports the possibility of making a mediate experience of things with no need to move. The main consequence is represented by the origin of new connections point-to-point within the world-system, as properly explained by Mattelart (1996, p. 9):

Progressively extending circulation possibilities, linked both to people and material and symbolic goods, mass media has increased the inclusion of specific societies within wider groups, continuously moving physical, intellectual, and mental borders.

This remark is very interesting and allows us to understand some ideas.

First of all, being connected, or the need to be connected, is not only a fact or a strategic choice within companies, but an effect of technological development. Many years before the advent of the Internet, in fact, the development of rail transport or the diffusion of radio-television frequencies required (imposed) the adoption of common strategies, standards, that progressively supported the growth of an international network among societies and nations.

This fact—the link between media and connection—has become, starting from the Illuminist 18th Century, a guiding topic of those currents that double-locked the possibility of people cohabiting with the realization of a factual network. The configuration of a network society, then, besides being a consequence of technology development, can be read as the founding myth of a certain conceptualization of relationships among individuals and nations.

Finally, network society, technological development, and ideological formulation seem to cross another central category of the current cultural debate, represented by globalization, supporting a new interpretation less focused on economical factors (certainly decisive) and more sensible to cultural logics.

Let us grasp all these suggestions following a unitary path and clarifying in which direction the meaning of networking, as a structural dimension

Table 1. Aspects linked to globalization/networking (Source: personal elaboration)

Items	Globalization outcomes	Networking outcomes
Concentration	Monopoly	Co-ordination
Use practices	Omologation	Circulation of meanings
Access to technologies	Digital divide	Access for everyone
Socio-cultural effects	Occidentalization	Situational appropriation

of informational society, makes it a globalization society as well. Our hypothesis is that what the term globalization tends to evoke negatively (the erosion of cultural specific characters, the growth of planetary poverty, market expansion to the prejudice of the environment, the increase of social differences, Rossi, 2002, pp. 19) finds its positive version in the "mythological" image of the net that Mattelart (2000) precisely described: networking and globalization could then refer to the same phenomenon, declining its opposite implications on the market level and on the second level of individual and social practices.

Two of the main definitions of the term globalization that help explain the current debate on the concept:

The increasing connection among different regions of the world, a process generating complex forms of interaction and interconnection (Thompson, 1995, p. 221)

The process of economical unification of the world and, for extension, of al that refers to the planet. (Mattelart, 1996, p. 95)

Reading attentively these definitions, we can understand that, besides the common "connective" matrix ("interconnection" and "unification" imply a relational process referring to the category of the net), the phenomenon of globalization occupies the same semantic area of other terms with which it is often confused:

- The **transnationalization** (better than multinationalization), considered as the process of polycentric reorganization of the business
- The **internationalization**, that is the progressive reduction—after the Modern Age—of the role of the Nation (the European unification process, but also the new role played by the ONU are a synthomatic example of this aspect)

- The **mondialization**, that is, the final effect of internationalization, or the opening of symbolic negotiation tables among individuals and society to the entire planet (Morin & Kern, 1993), refer to the concept of "planetary age"
- The **homogenization**, conceived as a planetary standardization of tastes and culture (a process that would happen according to the main parameters of the western culture in obedience to the classical thesis of the cultural imperialism, advanced by Herbert Schiller (1969) in his work *Mass Communications and American Empire*)
- The **interculturality**, "good" version of the idea of homogenization, where cultural colonization is replaced by the free integration of different cultures in societies that nowadays are always more multiethnic

Following Thompson's (1995) analysis, every single dimension is part of the phenomenon of globalization without disappearing in it. Concretely, the single ideas we have quickly described can differently refer to the three structural aspects of globalization:

- The placement in a planetary arena (internationalization, mondialization)
- The organization on a global scale (transnationalization)
- The reciprocity and interdependence (interculturality)

These dimensions, as easily evident, are perfectly recognizable in the processes relating to new economy: the planetary market configuration, the partnership logic, and the virtuality of the systems of services production/distribution, the systemic quality of relation forms (something that implies the reversibility of every connection and the co-implication of every element of the system within the transformation processes concerning all the other elements).

Figure 1. Knowledge level implied in business (Source: Eppler, 2002)

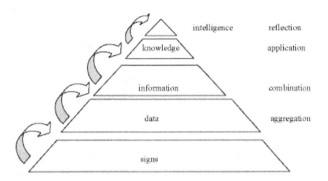

Where is the origin of this sociocultural reality? Where do we find the logics identifying its advent and affirmation?

According to Morin and Kern (1993) and Mattelart (2000), referring to globalization, we can find out (1) a remote genesis, (2) two close cultural matrices, and (3) a recent evolution.

The remote genesis of globalization can be found in the discovery of America that, in 1492, interrupts the Eurocentric orientation of history introducing its first evident globalistic acceleration. The cultivation of potatoes or tomatoes, formerly unknown in the West (as syphilis), are symptomatic of the incipient creolezation of cultures and behaviours, right as measles, previously unknown within the New World, that beat more indios than the Conquerors did.

The close cultural matrices in the 18th Century are represented by the universalistic theories of Illuminism and Liberalism. Both of them developed their own ideology on the creative power of the exchange, intending it obviously under two different points of view. The Illuminists underline its capability to circulate ideas guaranteeing democracy. Under this perspective we can read the revolutionary politics aimed to unify the French language against the outliving of regional idiomatic languages as an answer to the logic of the Ancienne Régime that on the contrary intended to block the circulation of ideas and

to separate people. Concerning Liberalism, its logic could be identified with J.S.Mill's maxim: Producing means moving. It aimed to build a universal mercantile republic, an extended wide economical community of consumers whose free initiatives replace mighty institutions as the one represented by the State.

In relation to the recent evolution of the phenomenon, finally, it tends to coincide with the development of communication technologies starting from the half of the 19th Century and with their political and cultural implications, as already anticipated at the beginning of the paragraph.

On a *technology level*, just think about the birth of the telegraph and about its function to reduce distances, evidently shown in 1851 with the laying of the first telegraphic cable between Calais and Dover and, in 1902, with the completion of the first transpacific line. A tendency progressively sharpened by the advent of radio and television until the current topics of information highways and the World Wide Web.

But this technological tendency primes a similar process also on a *political level*. In 1865 the International Telegraphic Union arose, with the aim of fixing standards, prices, and principles common to all the countries. It is followed in 1874 by the General Postal Union and in 1906 by the International Radio-telegraphic Union. So, technology not only "narrows" the planet, but it causes the dialogue among States, supporting the international coagulum of relations.

This inevitably affects the *cultural level*. Europe, sunk in the crisis followed by the French Revolution and painfully committed to guarantee a political balance among States, finds in communication the salvation utopia able to point out a future of peace for the world.

Universalism, with Saint-Simon above all, becomes a real redeeming ideology that finds in the industry and in Positivism its basic supports and in the huge universal expositions an effective moment for mythological elaboration as Mattelart (1996) suggests.

Temporarily faded at the end of the century with the fall of the Commune of Paris and the collapse of the States system after the French-Prussian conflict, this utopia had a rebirth during the 20th Century finding in Wiener's cybernetic program its refoundation: the current topics of communication society and the planetary village, as pointed out by Breton (1992), largely depends on it.

On the base of this historical landscape, which is today the image of globalization in relation to telematic communication, adapting Thompson's (1995) analysis, we can underline at least four relevant topics about it:

First of all the concentration of sector industries in very few groups. Just reflect on emblematic examples such as Microsoft or AOL-Warner. In the first case, we are in front of a producer who imposes a real monopoly on the software area, dictating the terms even in the hardware market (machines obsolescence is, in fact, largely defined by the technical characteristics required by the running of new releases of Windows or Office—see for example the case of Vista). In the second, we refer to the joint-venture between the biggest provider in the world and the biggest communication holding. On a market level, these tendencies create a general unbalance in the distribution of economical power and, above all, of symbolic power within a wide collective arena.

But if we gain the view of networking rather than about monopolistic instances, we prefer to talk about the logic of partnership that does not comprise a nonlibertarian omologation of markets, but the coordination of productive industries with evident advantages both for the producer and for the consumer.

A second relevant aspect related to the globalization of telematic markets is represented by their own impact in use practices. Network technologies, in fact, clearly dephase national frames in respect to the space of potential global markets they allow to reach. Also in this case, the view seems different according to the perspective of globalization or of networking: the first view underlines the themes of omologation and the loss of cultural identities; the second puts in evidence the topics of free circulation of meaning and the creation of collaborative international networks (the genesis of collective intelligence and of cooperative work lies here).

A third topic particularly useful is the problem of access to technologies. The launch of global context for services distribution and for goods circulation, on one hand, does not appear to cause a balanced access to technologies, that, on the contrary, is based on preference flow on a planetary level (from the leading countries to the rest of the world) or transregional (it is exactly what is happening in Latin America for Mexico and Brasil in relation to the other countries of the subcontinent), but on the other hand it feeds the utopia that connects the constant increase of links with the diffusion of further development possibilities.

The last question concerns the effects of globalization on a socio-cultural level that allows defining in details what we have already forwarded on the impact of globalization on use practices. The thesis dominating the topic for a long time (probably resisting until today) is represented by the idea of cultural imperialism that suggests a progressive cultural colonization of the world, from the Marshall plan on, guided by the American model because the United States always was the main controller of media and communication industry. Following this thesis, then, globalization should be read in terms of an Americanization (more in general, of an occidentalization) of other cultures. Without deepening the analytical critic of this hypothesis, we can anyway put in evidence its main theoretical weakness that consists of an ingenuous explanation of the appropriation process through which an individual assimilates cultural models promoted by the media. This process cannot be seen as a simple mechanic assumption (as the cultural imperialism presumes: I learn consumerism through consumerist programs), but needs to be interpreted as an ermeneuthic model related to the idea that the meaning that people makes to the media messages and the uses they do of them are depending from the contexts of reception and from resources they use in interpretation process.

KNOWLEDGE SOCIETY

The changes described above support a final reflection on the new meaning of knowledge within a market where information represents the priority value. Synthetically we can describe this change referring to a shift from "transmissive" models, where knowledge is owned and moved from someone to someone else, to "sharing" models, where it is basically coconstructed and available for other people who can freely use it.

Towards a New Image of Knowledge

Weinberger (2002) suggests that the evolution of the idea of knowledge can be articulated in four big phases identified by philosophy, science, computer, and the Web. Passing through them lets us understand the single qualities of each phase and, above all, the definition of knowledge nowadays, as now telematic networks have such

vivid effects on the social system that they also contribute to its definition.

Regarding knowledge, the problem of philosophy has always been represented by the issue of certainty, expressed with the search of the forms to be used to fix criteria of knowledge validity. These forms, from Hellenism to Modern Age, have been connoted each time in a different way, even if sharing, generally, the superiority of the rational moment to the sensible one. This aspect is evident in the platonic tradition: according to it the theoretical sight of the reason is the only one able to grasp the idea, understood as an ontological paradigm of reality. It is also confirmed by Aristotle, even in its medieval revisions, for which the real knowledge is the one that goes back to the grounds of reality (*scire est per essentias scire*). This is also connoted by Descartes (and his perspective will be actualized by modern philosophy until Kant and even further on) when he identifies the horizon of reasoning as the only element that can be rescued from the corrosive effects of doubt. The consequence of this formulation has been the progressive contraposition of thought and reality until the extreme limit of their separation. The terms of the problem are already clear with Parmenides. When the Goddess who dictates him the verses of his poem *On nature* appears to Parmenides, he vividly distinguish the indication of the "path of truth" and the indication of the "path of the error." The first is the path of rational reflection; the second is the path of the senses. The error path (according to Parmenides) is the one passed by Heraclitus who suggests that according to the experience everything changes in the world: seasons alternate, night and day follow one another, man grows old and dies. These experiences, passed through the lens of reasoning, are contradictory. In fact, if something exists, it cannot "not exist" at the same time, as recommended by the glimpse of those whom, trusting senses, see that everything unceasingly transforms. Therefore, becoming is a false movement, an illusion of our senses.

Reason clearly shows that what we can have is existence or nonexistence, without transitions (as provokingly proposed by the Italian philosopher Emanuele Severino).

Science, right in the same period when Descartes fixes the coordinates of the *cogito*, shifts the terms of the problem. The philosophy-based rational foundation steps aside in favour of the experimental method that, from Francis Bacon to Galileo and Newton, primarily made two victims: prejudice, which means every subjective thing altering the knowledge of facts as they are, and what is not verified, that is everything that did not pass the prove of experiment (Newton emblematically synthesizes it in his rules of method with the well-known "hypoteses non fingo").

Theorically, science works easily. Scientists collect facts, often through experiments, to isolate causes; then they formulate hypothesis on eventual explanations to these facts and try to prove them. Hypotheses are further elaborated into theories that are defined as solid and certified because their essential components—facts—are adequately proved. In this way, science describes a world based on proofs and immune from personal views (value-free) (Weinberger, 2002, p. 164).

Popper (1963) and the epistemology influenced by his thought (Kuhn, 1970, Lakatos, 1980, and Feyerabend, 1975) will intervene on this model, underlining that the fact on its own does not exist and that for scientific work it acquires a meaning only within a plan founded on theory. But this aspect does not shift the problem, typical of scientific knowledge, of the need to deal with the validity of theories to read facts (and in recent debates we note a clear reassertion of the perspective of Realism—Boghossian, 2006).

ICT revolution and computer advent introduce, besides this two "classical" connotations of knowledge, a third perspective. It is a "mechanical" and computational conception of knowledge well represented by the famous principle of informatics: "Garbage in, garbage out." This means that the quality of computer processes on information depends on information itself, on the correctness of their codification. This knowledge view finds its theoretical legitimation in Shannon and Weaver's (1948) mathematical model. It provided for many years to artificial intelligence scholars the basic model to analyze the analogy between human and artificial mind: the calculation ability, the mechanical elaboration of information.

With the Internet (and particularly with the new tools of Social Network), we face a different connotation of knowledge. To know does not mean to reach rational certainty about a problem (as for philosophy), to check a theory comparing it to facts (as for science), or processing pertinent information (as for information technology), but it means to share our point of view. Again, as Weinberger (2002, p. 176) accurately noted, Knowledge is not a truth authenticated: it is on the contrary a social activity, a process quite similar to a conversation where each of the discussants is negotiating his point of view. The social dimension of this form of knowledge, besides confirming the thesis advanced by recent social and organizational theories, implies some interesting consequences.

First of all, the idea of authority tends to change. In the Web, authority is not determined by official criteria (academic title, position in publishing trade market), but by the visibility and the recognition among a professional community. From this perspective, discussion lists or Bloggers' communities represent a knowledge source that is extraordinarily more effective than the enormous amount of pages recorded on planetary servers. These pages, in fact, are just the online version of paper materials, often already available (even if not easily accessible, this is the origin of Web usefulness); regarding online communities, on the contrary, we refer to experts who are consultable and whose capability in conceptual elaboration is continuously in progress in relation to the issues analyzed through the discussion list.

From this first underlining, we obtain a second fundamental predictor. If accessible knowledge in the Internet strictly depends on social interaction online, this means that the more people are connected, the more we have the possibility to build knowledge. This issue has been developed by Bob Metcalfe, founder of 3Com, one of the most important companies in the field of Net hardware. Following Metcalfe, the Vr value of a net increases with the square of the number of people connected to that net. This mathematical connection is known as *Metcalfe's Law* and it is expressed in the formula: $Vr = n(n-1)$, where n is the number of connected users and $(n-1)$ stays for the fact that when I connect to myself I obtain the engage tone. Therefore the real knowledge value of the Internet does not lie in documents, but in contacts.

David Reed, professor at MIT and later director of Lotus's research lab, turned back to Metcalfe's Law to correct it (or better to integrate it). In fact, this law appears empirically rejectable only if we note that the exponential growth of connected people does not necessarily imply the exponential growth of contacts. In other words, it is not obvious that if users' numbers increase, also the number of my contacts is going to increase exponentially (banally, the fact that more new users get a telephone line does not mean that my personal telephone use is going to increase exponentially). Reed, reasoning on this problem that apparently seems to question Metcalfe's Law, took this remark as a starting point to rearticulate it. The real value of the Internet is not associated with the number of single contacts, but with the fact that these single contacts contemporarily enter in a multiplicity of groups. *Reed's Law* translate this issue in this formula: $2^n - (n-1)$. Besides numbers, Reed's Law furnishes a theoretical justification to the fact that knowledge in the Internet is shared. The knowledge management and the fact that the capital of a business consists in it is based on this fundamental topic.

Intelligence as Business Capital

While affirming that intelligence is the real capital of a business, we connote it as the capability to use knowledge in a proper way according to different contexts.

This implies, first of all, to define the difference between terms such as "intelligence" and "knowledge" and others that are usually considered as synonymous referring to the question of knowledge within the business context, such as "information," or "data."

Technically we can define a datum as a sequence of numeric values that is a set of signs. When we combine two or more data we get information. When this information is interpreted, that means framed in a context and connected to a system of already existing concepts, we have knowledge. Intelligence implies the reflection on this knowledge, its comparison to others' knowledges, the operative and strategic evaluation of what we can presume or plan from it.

So, in organizations, the value is not made of raw or information, but of the possibility to develop knowledges from those data and, finally, to promote its intelligent exploitation.

The fulfillment of this need depends on the control of two levels of factors:

- First, the possibility to make *explicit knowledge* (processes, encoded practices, information) and to support the socialization of *implicit knowledge* (the know-how belonging to experts which is not easily codified into transferable information).
- Second, the capability to fight against the so called "corporate amnesia," the collective autism and the groups resistance to innovation, "groupthink effects," (Eppler, 2002, p. 3; the structure of the entire paragraph refers to this work).

Both conditions find in the ICT an opportunity for development and applicative field.

Concerning explicit knowledge, a system that is oriented to its management—usually an Intranet—needs to include four functions (Eppler, 2002, p. 5):

- **Collaboration:** This function is assured by technologies for *Computer Supported Collaborative Work* (CSCW), through which, for example, different members of the same organization can co-edit a document, and for *Computer Supported Collaborative Learning* (CSCL), the great part of online courses through which it is possible to provide in-service training. These functions can be integrated in more complex learning management systems thanks to which collaborative work is supported through asynchronous communication tools (as discussion boards) and synchronous communication tools (different systems of chat and virtual classroom);

- **Content management:** This function is usually sustained by personal and group agendas of the single user and the access to shared folders. The significance of this service lies in the possibility of solving eventual issues related to different versions of the same document and to obtain a patrimony of materials that can be a common benefit on different levels (personal, of a small group, of the entire company);

- **Visualization and aggregation:** This function is supported by the so-called *knowledge visualizers* that are the real internal portals of the organization generally planned in order to furnish a structured access to resources (through taxonomies related to processes, projects, etc.) and a conceptual shared lexicon (usually with the implementation of an internal glossary or—better—of a web ontology);

- **Search and intelligent extraction:** Through this faction, it is possible to obtain a facilitation for single users in order to access information that can likely be of interest, a result that is usually achieved through the definition of personal users' profiles to help the automatic delivery of information within electronic mail (*push*) or through a profile-guided search process (*pull*).

The socialization of implicit knowledge can also find a strategic support in Intranet technology. In particular, we have again four possible actions:

- **Knowledge creation:** It is specific to communities of practice, groups belonging to the same organization dealing with the same problems. Inside these communities, generally supported by chat or discussion boards, the creation of knowledge can be pursued through different actions: workshops aimed at problem-solving and pushing innovation (*Team Syntegrity*, see Beer, 1993), work spaces designing future scenarios through simulation (*Future Labs*), discussion and reflective activity voted to the development of new ideas and concepts (*Think Tanks*);

- **Knowledge transfer:** It can be obtained in different ways, such as "telematic marketplaces" where different project groups can introduce the main themes they are dealing with and interact with other groups in relation to these themes, and the varied forms of tutoring thanks to which new human resources can be guided by senior experts during the learning phase of their own tasks;

- **Knowledge Application:** Also in this situation, simulation systems are usually employed both to socialize actions and steps generally implied in projects realization (*Project Labs*) and to provide *team training*;

- **Evaluation:** During the implementation of a project, people involved bring along their own tacit knowledges to face problems as they occur. The evaluation phase, in the shape of case study, can help the explicitation of this knowledge capturing them in a specific Intranet area where every member of the organization can find, for every single project, the synthesis of "plus" and "minus."

Evidently in both cases (explicit and implicit knowledge), the support of technological infrastructure is fundamental, but it would be of no help without the facilitation of real relationships. This fact decisively shifts the attention from technology to human resources.

CONCLUSION AND FUTURE TRENDS: THE LEARNING ECONOMY

The comments related to intelligence management can clear that an organization (a company like a school), to be recognized as a *knowledge organization*, does not necessarily have to belong to the IT or to new economy business. The decisive factor is the level of formalization according to which this organization defines the intellectual component as an integrative part of its patrimony, recognizes the central role of the informative system and of knowledge technologies, and evolves as the critical node of management culture and praxis. In particular, this form of organization reveals itself as deeply connected to the capability to learn, in general and from its own performances.

The concept of *learning economy* starts here and connotes, as the term suggests, the fact that the markets of education and learning represent in the information society one of the most relevant expenditure item for organizations. Evidently times and methods of education had to accept the needs of organizations, planning its own actions according to "light" models, consistent with work

time and tasks. So in these last years, the boom in education consisted of the boom in online and mobile education, almost following the logic of identification. The data related to 2007 referred to an increase equivalent to 15-30% in the market of e-learning, with more than $17.5 billion of investments only in the United States: learning economy is actually an e-learning economy and probably it could become a m-learning economy thanks to the diffusion of broad band wireless systems, connected palms, forth generation smart phones.

We have to mark that this is an anomalous economy where knowledge is a particular good, and anomalous is also the market in which it is moved. One reason for this depends on the fact that the benefits deriving from the "purchase" of education are hardly measurable and anyway, even when possible, time passing from the attendance of an online course to the moment when the evaluation of its usefulness to productive capabilities and income is generally very extended. Two examples can explain the topic. The purchase of an online course, designed to help an entrepreneur launch a new innovative production line, could be considered as an unnecessary expense in case that the entrepreneur realized that this choice would involve an unsustainable expense rise. On the same time, a professionist interested in improving his mastery of English could join a collaborative learning community on English, but then the period of time between the conclusion of the course and the experimentation of acquired competencies in English could be too long, risking that when starting to talk he could have lost all the benefits of the online English course previously attended.

A second reason for this anomaly is that, in the case of e-learning, knowledge transfer does not impoverish the one who delivers it: the expertise remains even if shared. The problem is basically different and it can be recognized in the fact that the more knowledges are shared, the more their value tends to decrease. That is why one of the crucial problems in the e-learning market is represented, for the deliverers of education services, by the possibility to sell education without sharing the expertise that allows them to sell. This explains the deep caution shown by corporations in defending their know-how and the relevance assumed within the current debate by the intellectual property and copyright related to processes and good practices.

This new market, with all its anomalies, is at the same time a product and a relevant segment of a new economy. It is a product, as in a new economy, where the need of education, even for senior workers, is definitely higher than in other productive areas, and to fulfill this education the need for *new training* (based on Internet and mobile devices) appears to be as an obliged step. Further, digital learning provides new economy workers those conditions—motivation, performances, collaboration, and innovation—that are an integral part of their profession. The result is represented by the fact that the new economy is an important development factor supporting digital learning, so that it becomes one of its most promising subsegments, even more promising than e-commerce and e-business.

This reciprocity between digital economy and online/mobile education market remarks on and confirms some thesis previously developed.

First of all, digital learning verifies the mythological aspect of information society and its leading factors.

Myth, under the anthropological and functional perspective we have assumed as reference to this chapter, represents a demarcation of reality extensions that is a horizon where men place think to approach and know them. This ordering logic expresses itself through an accompanying narration (*mithologoumenon*) aimed to articulate and radicate it on a social and personal level.

Read under this perspective, digital learning works mythologically because it corresponds to the idea of an information and technology-based society, demonstrating to interpret properly its main characteristics. As a matter of fact, digital learning is an education model that accepts the challenge of speed (connoted both as speed of transference and speed of knowledge updating), it is structurally virtual (emancipating teaching/learning from space and time), it turns the network structure and the global open up into its natural dimensions. Besides this, digital learning also provides an accompanying narration to the myth of the information society. It is a narration about competencies rapidly aging, about information that needs to be at our disposal "everywhere, anytime for everyone," about the collaborative dimension that appears to be effectively possible only in a telematic network.

If we go back to the reciprocity of new economy and e-learning (new economy "pushes" e-learning that, when supported, feeds new economy, promoting it) we easily understand the economical and social origins of the myth and of its accompanying narration: myth feeds economy, through the issue of the need for incessant update it creates a market—the Longlife Education market—destined to extend infinitely, helps the employment of new professional figures.

When knowledge is transformed into a good to share, digital learning confirms also the idea previously advanced, through Baudrillard's (1976) analysis: the fact that information society is connoted by the supremacy of symbolic goods. From this point of view, online education perfectly embodies the third-level of simulacral activities: it plays on secondary needs contemporarily supported; it does not produce goods, but learning, that is something extremely difficult to measure, so that it is not possible to blame only educational actions, when not obtained; it sells competencies to the user, something so immaterial and extremely subjective that can be only embodied by hyperspecialized experts.

So, the learning economy is connoted as a mythological device creating a market on a symbolic good of knowledge and socially legitimating professional figures even more competent in topics that are progressively less decisive. As Panikkar (1990) would say, it is necessary to understand if it is a new starting point, a transitory phase, or only the fulfillment of a destiny. We are in front of a new humanism, or of the despair of finiteness?

REFERENCES

Baudrillard, J. (1976). *L'echange symbolyque et la mort.* Paris: Gallimard.

Beer, S. (1993). *Origins of team syntegrity.* Retrieved October 2, 2007, from http://www.staffordbeer.com/papers/Origins%20Team%20Syntegrity.pdf

Benedikt, M. (1991). *Cyberspace: First steps.* Cambridge, MA: The MIT Press.

Benjamin, W. (1955). *Das kunstwerk in zeitalter seiner technischen reproduzierbarkeit in schriften.* Frankfurt am Main: Suhrkamp Verlag.

Boghossian, P. (2006). *Fear of knowledge: Against relativism and constructivism.* Oxford: Oxford University Press.

Breton, P. (1993). *L'utopie de la communication.* Paris: La Découverte.

Castells, M. (1996). *The rise of the network society.* Malden, MA: Blackwell.

Dayan, D., & Katz, E. (1992). *Media Events: The live broadcasting of history.* Cambridge, MA: Harvard University Press.

Eppler, M.J. (2002). Le savoir dans le contexte de l'entreprise. Individus, systémes et socialisation. *Quaderni dell'Istituto Comunicazione e Formazione,* 5. Retrieved October 2, 2007, from http://www.icief.com.unisi.ch/quaderno5.pdf

Feyerabend, P. (1975). *Against method.* London: Verso.

Fiske, J., & Hartley, J. (1978). *Reading television.* London: Methuen.

Gibson, W. (1984). *Neuromancer.* New York: Ace Books.

Goddman, N. (1968). *Languages of art: An approach to a theory of symbols.* Indianapolis, IN: Bobbs-Merrill.

Kotler, P., Jain, D.C., & Maesincee, S. (2000). *Marketing moves. A new approach to profits, growth and renewal.* Boston: Harvard Business School Press.

Kuhn, T. (1970). The structure of scientific revolutions (2nd ed). Chicago: U Chicago .

Lakatos, I. (1980). The methodology of scientific research programmes. Cambridge, MA: Cambridge University Press.

Levy, P. (1995a). *Qu'est-ce que le virtuel?* Paris: La Découverte.

Levy, P. (1997). *Cyberculture. Raport au conseil de l'Europe.* Paris: Odile Jacob.

Maldonado, T. (1992). *Reale e virtuale.* Milano: Feltrinelli.

Mattelart, A. (1996). *La mondialisation de la communication.* Paris: PUF.

Mattelart, A. (2000). *Histoire de la société de l'information.* Paris: La Découverte.

Morin, E., & Kern, A.B. (1993). *Terre-patrie.* Paris: Editions de Seuil.

Neveu, E. (1994). *Une société de la communication?* Paris: Montchrestien.

Neveu, E. (2002). Profession : Journaliste. *Sciences Humaines, 129*(7), 22-25.

Panikkar, R. (1979). The myth of pluralism: The Tower of Babel. A meditation on non-violence. *Cross Currents, 29,* 197-230.

Popper, K.R. (1963). *Conjectures and confutations: The growth of scientific knowledge.* London: Routledge and Kegan Paul.

Rivoltella, P.C. (2003). *Costruttivismo e pragmatica della comunicazione on line. Socialità e didattica in Internet*. Trento: Erickson.

Rossi, A. (2002). *Il mito del mercato*. Troina: Città aperta.

Schiller, H. I. (1969). *Mass communications and American empire*. New York: M. Kelley.

Shannon, C., Weaver, W. (1948). *The Mathematical theory of communication*. Urbana: University of Illinois Press.

Thompson, J.B. (1995). *The media and the modernity. A social theory of the media*. Cambrdige: Polity Press.

Turkle, S. (1995). *Life on the screen. Identity in the age of Internet*. New York: Simon & Schuster.

Virilio, P. (1998). *La bombe informatique*. Paris: Galilée.

Weinberger, D. (2002). *Small pieces looseley joined*. New York: Perseus Books.

Zolla, E. (1992). *Uscite dal mondo*. Milano: Adelphi.

This work was previously published in Digital Literacy: Tools and Methodologies for Information Society, edited by P. Rivoltella, pp. 1-25, copyright 2008 by IGI Publishing, formerly known as Idea Group Publishing (an imprint of IGI Global).

Chapter II
Digital Divide:
Introduction to the Problem

Liudmila Burtseva
Academy of Sciences of Moldova Institute of Mathematics and Computer Science, Moldova

Svetlana Cojocaru
Academy of Sciences of Moldova Institute of Mathematics and Computer Science, Moldova

Constantin Gaindric
Academy of Sciences of Moldova Institute of Mathematics and Computer Science, Moldova

Galina Magariu
Academy of Sciences of Moldova Institute of Mathematics and Computer Science, Moldova

Tatiana Verlan
Academy of Sciences of Moldova Institute of Mathematics and Computer Science, Moldova

ABSTRACT

In this chapter the authors introduce the digital-divide concept to the reader, bring its different definitions, and describe the short history of the problem. The basic figures and facts, which characterize the information and communication technologies' usage in different countries and regions, are given as well. Also, basic indicators that allow the monitoring of the country's advancement on the way to bridging the digital divide are stated. The main purpose for the authors was to show that the digital divide is not only (and not as much) a technical problem, but rather a social and politi-cal one. Hence, the approaches to this problem decision, both in the world community as a whole and in separate countries, are described.

INTRODUCTION

"The future belongs not so much to those peoples who have achieved today a high standard of well-being, as to those ones which can induce new ideas in the field of high technologies and in their relations with the Nature. The erudition is necessary for this purpose, and not of separate people, but of the nation as a whole. And this circumstance imposes the special responsibility on a governing body of the state and on the intelligentsia." (N. N. Moiseev, "Universum. Information. Society." Moscow, 2001)

"It is not the gap that divides, but the difference of levels." (Stanislaw J. Lec, "Unkempt Thoughts")

The problem of the digital divide has probably only now begun to be perceived as it deserves. Practically any society can face it. Its manifestations are so various in different countries that it is actually impossible to offer common recipes for its solution. As the problem is basically social rather than technological, the ways of its overcoming depend on the degree of the democratization of a society, on the standard of living of a population, on the level of population erudition, and on cultural and ethnic features of the specific community of people. Certainly, the presence of an ICT infrastructure is necessary, but this is only the necessary condition. This chapter contains a brief history of the problem and various relevant definitions. On the basis of statistical data, the state of the art in the world is shown, the various countries are compared, and some basic ideas of the Genoa action plan are stated.

The necessary steps, without which the solution of the digital-divide problem is impossible, are brought. Positive experiences of the European Union (EU) and other countries are confirmed by examples. Basic indicators of the digital divide that allow the monitoring of the problem solution are brought as well.

A SHORT HISTORY OF THE PROBLEM

The end of the 20th century and the beginning of the 21st were marked by the rapid development of information and communication technologies, which has led to the avalanche growth of

digital information. However, any progressive phenomenon, as a rule, is accompanied also by negative by-products. In this case, alongside the overcoming of existing temporal, spatial, and social borders when using information, society has also received a new problem, the so-called digital divide. There are a lot of definitions of this term, which as a matter of fact are reduced to the following: "the term 'digital divide' describes the fact that the world can be divided into people who do and people who don't have access to—and the capability to use—modern information and communication technology" (*Digital Divide*, 1999).

The world community started talking about the problem of the digital divide and the "have-nots" at the end of the last century (Brown, Barram, & Irving, 1995). The *Oxford English Dictionary Online* (2004) considers that the term digital divide was used for the first time in 1995 in an article of Ohio's daily newspaper *Columbus Dispatch* and gives the following explanation as the commonly accepted meaning of this term: "the gulf between those who have ready access to current digital technology (esp. computers and the Internet) and those who do not; (also) the perceived social or educational inequality resulting from this." At that time, many people refused to take this problem seriously and even spoke about it as a far-fetched problem that promoted further enrichment of computer and telecommunication corporations. By the end of the '90s, the stable concept of the digital divide appeared as the serious, recognized problem that is regularly being studied and periodically being discussed by people all over the world today.

In 1999, in its third survey *Falling Through the Net: Defining the Digital Divide*, the USA National Telecommunications and Information Administration (NTIA) noted that the digital divide became "one of America's leading economic and civil rights issues" (1999, p. xiii).

With time, many international organizations and agencies (United Nations [UN], European Union, World Bank, United Nations Development

Program [UNDP], Organization for Economic Cooperation and Development [OECD], International Telecommunications Union [ITU], United Nations Educational, Scientific, and Cultural Organization [UNESCO], Economic and Social Council [ECOSOC]) began to express growing concern that the deepening of the digital divide problem may leave many nations far behind, producing growing disparities between advanced, industrialized countries and developing societies. Therefore, they give a lot of attention, force, and means for studying decisions regarding this problem. The international community carries out international conferences and summits (the Digital Divide Summit by the United States Department of Commerce in 1999, and the World Summit on the Information Society [WSIS] in Geneva in 2003 to Tunis in 2005), organizes various forums, creates specialized sites on the digital-divide problem (http://www.pbs.org/digitaldivide/, http://www.digitaldivide.net, http://cbdd.wsu.edu/, http://europa.eu.int/information_society/eeurope/i2010/digital_divide/index_en.htm), and launches various programs and initiatives. They study the experiences of various countries in overcoming this problem. Their discussions have come to a level of development on which practical recommendations are giving for bridging digital inequality both within an international scope and between separate states as well.

DEFINING THE CONCEPT OF DIGITAL DIVIDE

There are a lot of terms to describe the concept of digital divide—digital gap, digital inequality, and rarely, information inequality—but all of them reflect the inequality of access to digital or information technologies.

However, before speaking about the problem of digital inequality, and for easier understanding of its essence and origin, it is necessary to pay attention to inequality in general. The following

discussion is widespread and absolutely true. Inequality takes place in all spheres of social life from the moment of the beginning of a society. This is the inequality in access to vital resources (food, raw power, and now to information as well), workplaces, education, medical services, and cultural heritage. The distinctions of people regarding social status, the amount of available money resources, level of education, age, residence, and so forth lay in the basis of inequality. Inequality is the reason for conflicts and social cataclysms of various scales. Therefore, the world community, first of all the advanced countries, makes efforts for the neutralization of threats to global and local stability caused by various sorts of inequality.

In this way. the ensuring of equal access to social, economic, cultural, educational, and technological opportunities is offered for all people and for all states. Thus, they get the potential opportunity to reach an equal social status. However, it is an opportunity only, not the solution of the problem. In fact, certain limited resources (financial and especially human resources), even in the presence of political will, cannot be the sole determining factor as they do not allow the removal of inequality. If the opportunities exist already, then it is the will and efforts of people that will determine whether the actual inequality will proceed or will be eliminated. The consciousness of the person influences his or her will. The comprehension of inequality is already a powerful stimulus for social transformations, and for the development of separate people, social groups, and states as a whole. Therefore, discussion of the problem and the popularization of the necessity of overcoming inequality at all levels—internationally, nationally, and in governmental circles and various social groups—are very important.

Now let us turn to the digital-inequality problem, or as it is put more often, the digital-divide problem.

The attention of researchers of the problem at first was usually focused on the inequality in access to technical equipment. Even the definition given in the UN review (UN, 2003) fixes this position: The digital divide is "the fact that poor people in the industrialized world and almost all in the developing world are excluded from modern (information and communication) technologies" (p. 25).

However, this definition is too elementary to characterize the problem, which, actually, is much deeper and extensive. For today, we may consider, among others, the following aspects of the digital divide as basic ones:

- Property
- Age
- Education
- Territory
- Gender
- Culture

In addition, all these aspects are manifested differently in various countries, irrespective of their well-being and ICT infrastructure development level. From practical experience it becomes obvious that the idea "the more computers, the less digital divide" is narrow.

Irvine M. Warschauer (2002), a professor at California University, analyzed three examples of projects concerning ICT promotion. The conclusion was that providing access to ICT is not enough for bridging the digital divide. Analogously, taking into account each of the factors of the digital division (social factors, age, etc.) separately does not determine the problem. The problem needs to be considered in a complex way, taking into account all relevant factors.

For an illustration, let us examine these projects.

- **Example 1. (Warschauer, 2002, "A Slum 'Hole in the Wall'"):** This project was established in 2000 by the New Delhi government in collaboration with an information-technology corporation. A computer kiosk was

set up in one of New Delhi's poorest slums. Five computers were inside a booth, and monitors were placed in holes in the walls. Specially designed joysticks and buttons were provided instead of computer mice and keyboards. Dial-up, 24-hour Internet access was available. There were no teachers in accordance to the concept of minimally invasive education. The idea was to allow children to learn by their own desire and capabilities.

Researchers and government officials appreciated this project as it was one that offered a model for how to bring India's and the world's urban poor into the computer age. However, as M. Warschauer (2002) noted, visits to the computer kiosk indicated a rather different reality. Internet access was of little use since it seldom functioned. There were no special educational programs and no special content in Hindi, the only language the children knew. Children did learn to manipulate the joystick and buttons, but almost all their time was spent drawing with paint programs or playing computer games.

Parents had ambivalent feelings. Some saw the kiosk as a welcome initiative, but most expressed concern that the lack of organized instruction took away from its value. In short, the community came to realize that minimally invasive education was, in practice, minimally effective education.

- **Example 2. (Warschauer, 2002, "An Information Age Town"):** In 1997, Ireland's national telecommunications company held a national competition "Information Age Town." Towns of 5,000 people and more across Ireland were invited to compete by submitting proposals detailing their vision of an information-age town and how they could become one. Four towns were chosen as finalists, and then Ennis, a small, remote town of 15,000 people, was selected as the winner. The prize consisted of over $1,200 per resident, a huge sum for a struggling Irish town.

The proposal planned for the following:

- An Internet-ready personal computer (PC) for every family
- An ISDN (integrated services digital network) line for every business
- A Web site for every business that wanted one
- Smart-card readers for every business, and smart cards for every family

Ennis was strongly encouraged to implement these plans as quickly as possible.

Meanwhile, each of three other towns received consolation prizes of about $1.5 million. These towns were not limited by time.

Three years later, Ennis had little to show for its money. Training programs had been run, but they were not sufficiently accompanied by awareness programs. People were not prepared to use advanced technology. In some cases, well-functioning social systems were broken.

The unemployed had received computers and Internet connections at home so that they could sign in and receive electronic payments via the Internet, thus the necessity to visit the labor registry office fell away. However, these people lost the important social function to overcome isolation. More over, they could not use the equipment, and most others saw no reason to do so. Thus, a good number of those computers were sold.

Meanwhile, the other three towns with far fewer resources were forced to carefully plan the usage of their funds rather than spend them for massive amounts of equipment. Community groups, small businesses, and labor unions participated in the planning process. Much greater effort and money were spent on developing awareness, planning and implementing effective training, and setting up processes for sustainable change. The towns built on already existing networks

among workers, educators, and businesspeople to support basic uses of technology. As a result, these three towns actually achieved more success than the winner.

- **Example 3. (Warschauer, 2002, "A Model Computer Lab"):** An international donor project funded by the United States Agency for International Development decided to donate a computer laboratory to the College of Education at a major Egyptian university. The purpose was to establish a model teacher-training program using computer-assisted learning in one of the departments of the college. State-of-the-art equipment was selected, including more than 40 computers, an expensive video projection system, several printers and scanners, and expensive educational software. To guarantee that the project would be sustainable, the Egyptian university would be required to manage all the ongoing expenses and operations, including paying for Internet access, maintaining the local area network (LAN), and operating the computer laboratory.

Before the equipment was installed, it became clear that the college would have difficulty in making use of such a huge and expensive donation. Other departments within the college became envious because of the fact that a single department would have such modern and expensive equipment. The college and university could not easily justify spending the money. No money was available to engage an outside LAN manager or provide Internet access at the proper level. Due to all these difficulties, the expensive state-of-the-art computers sat in boxes in a locked room for more than a year before they were even installed, thus losing about one third of their economic value.

These experiences confirm the idea expressed by Bridges.org that states:

providing access to technology is critical, but it must be about more than just physical access. Computers and connections are insufficient if the technology is not used effectively because it is not affordable; people do not understand how to put it to use, or they are discouraged from using it; or the local economy cannot sustain its use. ("Spanning the Digital Divide," 2001, p. 5)

Thus, we come to the wider definition: "digital inequality is a going deep inequality in access to social, economic, educational, cultural and other opportunities owing to unequal access to information and communication technologies" (Baranov, 2003).

FIGURES AND FACTS

A lot of analysis and research was carried out to compare the state of the art in the world. The results allow for the assessment of disparities existing in the access to and use of ICT between different countries (international digital divide) and groups within countries (domestic digital divide).

The existence of the digital-divide problem is recognized already by one and all. However, to compare the problem in different countries and at various times, it is necessary to measure it somehow. There are three basic parameters that are frequently used for measuring the digital divide: the number of ICT users, number of computer users, and number of Internet users.

According to data from the Digital Opportunity Task Force (DOT Force, 2001), 70% of the world's poor live in rural and remote areas, and very often they have scarce access even to a telephone, not speaking about ICT in general. Thus, one third of the world population has never made a telephone call.

In its *Human Development Report* of 1998, the UNDP drew attention to the fact that 109 million primary-school-age children (22% of

those in the world) were out of school, 885 million adults (age 15 and above) were illiterate, and 4 copies of daily newspapers were circulated per 100 people in developing countries, in contrast to 26 in industrial countries.

Other impressive comparative statistics include the following:

* On the entire continent of Africa, there are only 14 million phone lines—less than the number in either Manhattan or Tokyo (Nkrumah, 2000).
* Wealthy nations make up only 16% of the world population but possess 90% of Internet host computers (Nkrumah, 2000).
* Sixty percent of world Internet users reside in North America, but only 5% of the world population reside there (Nkrumah, 2000).
* One in two Americans is online as opposed to 1 in 250 Africans ("Falling through the Net?" 2000).

In digital-divide studies, Internet-usage numbers are most often cited to describe the divide. Nua Internet Surveys ("How Many Online?," 2002) offers an estimate of the global Internet-user population based on an extensive examination of surveys and reports from around the world. Nua's data on how many people have used the Internet show a clear division. In 2001 in the world as a whole, there were 407.1 million Internet users; by 2002, the online users numbered 605.6 million. The leading regions were Europe (190.91 million), Asia and the Pacific (187.24 million), and Canada and the USA (182.67 million). A comparison with similar data on Latin America (33.35 million), Africa (6.31 million), and the Middle East (5.12 million) impresses.

Internet World Stats (2005), an International Web site, shows up-to-date 2005 worldwide Internet-usage and population statistics for over 233 countries and world regions. See Table 1[1] for world-regions data. These data as well as Nua's

("How Many Online?," 2002) show the identical world tendency: Asia, Europe, and North America remain leaders in Internet usage.

However, one can notice that in 2002, Europe was the leader by the absolute amount of Internet users (though its population makes up only 11.4% of the world's population); in 2005, Asia was the leader in the world (see Figure 1). Nevertheless, speaking about the percent of the country's population using the Internet (see Internet penetration in Figure 1), Asia, the population of which makes up 56.4% of the world's population, is still far behind (8.9%), and Northern America is the absolute leader (68%), though its population makes up only 5.1% of the world's population. By examining the dynamics of Internet users' growth inside each region for 2000 to 2005, one can see that the largest progress during these 5 years was made by the nonmembers of the EU (377.6%); the Middle East follows with 311.9%. However, penetration inside these regions remains at only 17.5% and 8.3%, accordingly. The tendency is characteristic for countries of Latin America and the Caribbean (277.1%), Africa (258.3%), and Asia (183.2%) as well, where the penetration parameter is equal to 12.5%, 1.8%, and 8.9%, respectively. Let us compare the same parameters for North America, with a penetration rate of 68%. In this region for the same period, Internet users' growth was only 106.7%.

That is, during the last several years, less developed countries of the Middle East, East Europe, the Asian-Pacific region, and Latin America showed a constant increase in the active Internet audience, but not the USA, Japan, and countries of Western Europe. Insignificant growth of the number of Internet users in countries where penetration is already high is quite clear. Additionally, it is not only saturation, but probably an insuperable part of the digital divide that will remain in each society, at least in the near future.

According to the statistics in Table 1, on July 23, 2005, only 14.6% of the world population used the Internet. The reasons for which the other 85.4% are nonusers are interesting. Numerous reviews specify the following reasons: poverty, a badly advanced ICT infrastructure, a lack of education, a misunderstanding of the benefits of ICT usage, bad content, the absence of interesting e-services, and so forth. However, the factor of motivation in using or not using ICT, the Internet in particular, is not less important. The report (Kalkun & Kalvet, 2002) prepared at the order of the Estonia state chancellery contains an analysis of motivation regarding Internet nonuse. Some ideas of this analysis are appropriate for the discussion below.

This report indicates that Internet nonusers constitute about 58% of the Estonian population in the age group of 15 to 74 (February 2002). Every second nonuser acknowledges one or many benefits of computers or the Internet, while one half of the nonusers cannot point out any benefits of Internet.

One third of Internet nonusers are motivated to use the Internet. They have access to the Internet due to ongoing projects. This is because they have a more open attitude to learning new skills on the one hand, and an ability to overcome any barriers to Internet use that may arise on the other hand.

New projects should pay special attention to those two thirds of Internet nonusers who do not associate the possibilities of Internet use with their lives. There are two distinct categories in this group: retired persons and workers, or, as they are called in this report, "passive people" and "blue collars."

- **Passive people** (28% of nonusers)
  - About 60% of people in this group are of 50 or older.
  - They have relatively little interest in matters outside their daily life.
  - They have a very weak relation to the Internet or computers; they see no benefits in the Internet and have no need to use it.

- They prefer to use traditional media (even if the Internet were cheaper and more convenient); besides a lack of interest, they have a language barrier and are incapable of handling the user interfaces of computers. They are also relatively less able to learn and memorize new things, and are unwilling to change their habits.
- **Blue collars** (27% of nonusers)
  - They are mainly unskilled and skilled workers who do not use computers in their work.
  - About half of people in this group see no benefits in the Internet and would not very willingly change their daily routines as the Internet is unattractive for them.
  - A personal monetary gain would make the Internet attractive for them.
  - There are social and psychological barriers (fear of new technologies, no perception of the need for lifelong learning, a fear of demonstrating their lack of skills to others), skill barriers (lack of computer and ignorance of foreign languages), and economic barriers (income per family member is low).

These groups have not realized a relation between their lives and the Internet yet. That is why the important task is to motivate them, to introduce Internet services adjusted to the habits of these target groups, and to develop suitable Internet services where necessary. It is also important to pay attention to the Internet-skills and Internet-access problems of the passive people and blue collars groups. The rest of the nonusers already have the motivation to use the Internet.

It may be said with fair certainty that the sociodemographic characteristics of the population segments that do not use information technologies are similar to those of other countries. The problem of motivation regarding ICT use arises in many

countries, both in the developing and advanced. For example, in Scotland, where the technical base exists and is at a high-enough level, the question about the necessity of projects for the motivation to use ICT arises for those who do not use them (nonusers). Viviane Reding, member of the European Commission, states the same idea. She notes that governments need to encourage the use of new technologies, saying that the public will find new technologies "beneficial but guidance will be needed. The infrastructure exists but is underused: broadband is available on 80% of the European network but has been taken up by only 7% of users" (Raven, 2004).

The authors of the Estonian review fairly remark that if the problems of nonusers are ignored, a part of the population would effectively be excluded from actively participating in economic activities. This implies a decrease in the number of consumers, lower labor quality for the private sector, and, in the worst case scenario, the generation of an army of unemployed for the public sector, which in turn may cause extensive social problems (Kalkun & Kalvet, 2002).

SOLUTIONS FOR THE DIGITAL DIVIDE PROBLEM

In July 2000, the summit of the Great 8 (G8) was held in Kyushu-Okinawa, Japan. At this summit, the leaders from G8 countries adopted the *Okinawa Charter on Global Information Society* (2000). This charter established the DOT Force to integrate "efforts into a broader international approach" (p. 5). The DOT Force presented the report *Digital Opportunities for All: Meeting the Challenge* (2001) at the G8 summit held in Genoa in 2001. In that report, a nine-point action plan (Genoa Plan of Action) was proposed as well as a theory of ICT utilization to activate social and economic development.

Since then, the recipes for overcoming the digital inequality in and among countries have found reflection also in a lot of other world community documents ("Spanning the Digital Divide," 2001; UN ECOSOC, 2000). Today, the European Union is aimed to become the most dynamic knowledge-based economy and considers closing the digital divide as a key goal. This idea is reflected in such fundamental EU documents as the conclusion of the European Council in Lisbon 2000 (Lisbon European Council, 2000), the *eEurope 2002 Action Plan* (Council of the European Union & Commission of the European Communities [CEU & CEC], 2000), the *eEurope Benchmarking Report* (CEC, 2002b), and the *eEurope 2005 Action Plan* (CEC, 2002a).

There are many initiatives in the world directed to the digital-divide reduction.

However, it is necessary to understand the idea ("Spanning the Digital Divide," 2001) that solutions that are successful in developed countries cannot simply be copied in the environments of developing countries. The solutions must take into consideration the local needs and conditions. As UN review (UN, 2003) stated, "The UN Millennium Declaration mentions the digital divide issue as one of the symbols of deepening developmental inequality in the world and indeed, finding a comprehensive solution to it belongs to world-making efforts" (p. 26).

Also, the analysis of relevant documents allows drawing a conclusion that the solution to the digital-inequality problem demands a balanced, nationwide-system approach that concentrates on the following basic directions: (a) policy, (b) access, (c) services, (d) content, (e) knowledge and skills, and (f) motivation.

In the Genoa Plan of Action (DOT Force, 2001), special attention is given to the coordination of strategies produced by less developed countries, as well as to involving in the work representatives of both private and state sectors. The states should produce these strategies by themselves, and the strategies' presence in itself is already important for less developed countries. With that,

it is necessary to formulate the strategy in strict conformity with national interests.

The many areas of human activity where ICTs can be applied and the many reasons for the digital divide assume many directions to operate and many various forces to involve for its overcoming. In what proportion, when, and what should be preferred depends on features of the specific country. The problem should be solved in a complex way, taking into account and coordinating the actions directed on the elimination of the separate reasons and overcoming any separate barrier. To embrace the basic aspects of the digital divide and to take into account the fact that each society has its own economical, political, social, and historical peculiarities, the following level of reality is necessary to be achieved.

- Physical access (infrastructure, computers, availability of necessary information in the language required on the Net)
- Comprehension of necessity and desire for ICT advantages
- Sufficient degree of society democratization
- Certain literacy level and opportunity for training
- Legislative base (electronic signatures, electronic documents, rights of access to information and protection of confidential information)
- Commercial-structures participation
- Sufficient financing
- State support (political will)

Having in view the objective of achieving this level, experts emphasize the following steps for overcoming the digital divide that are necessary to undertake in the directions listed previously.

1. Formation of national strategy, international and internal policy, and a favorable legislative, public, and economic atmosphere in the fields of informatisation and of ICT use

2. Maintenance of the potential opportunity for the population to access ICT everywhere due to the association of efforts of the state and private sectors of the economy on the development of an information infrastructure

3. Assistance to increase the variety and amount of services for the population and business by means of ICT

4. Concentration of efforts of the state and society for the creation of public electronic information resources (content) on the basis of national, world, political, economic, cultural, religious, and other types of aspects of development

5. Ensuring the possibility to get knowledge and skills in ICT use while getting basic special and higher education, and also the creation of conditions for obtaining initial knowledge and skills in this area for all layers of the population

6. Creation of a system of motivations for ICT application and use, aimed at the formation of wide demand for the use of such technologies in all spheres of society life

In these directions, a variety of avenues have been taken to bridge the digital divide in the world in general and in the EU particularly. Primarily, there have been efforts to promote e-government, encourage technological innovation and the use of existing technologies, guarantee more people Internet access, and advocate media pluralism and creativity. Many of these plans are interesting and noteworthy, but it will take a great deal of political will to accomplish them.

Lately, many high-ranking officials in the EU in their statements express their readiness to undertake the necessary actions to bridge the digital divide. British prime minister Tony Blair, in his speech to the Labour Party Conference in Brighton (Blair, 2004), promised a broadband Britain by 2008. Also, member of European parliament and former French minister of culture and communication Catherine Trautman stated, "Europe must allocate resources for equity of access but also in equipment and in education" (as cited in Raven, 2004). These intentions of high-ranking officials agree with the *eEurope 2005 Action Plan* (CEC, 2002a), which is based on two complementary groups of actions: "On the one hand, it aims to stimulate services, applications and content, covering both online public services and e-business; on the other hand it addresses the underlying broadband infrastructure and security matters" (p. 3).

According to information presented in *People's Daily Online* ("280 Mln U.S Dollars Spent to Eliminate Digital Divide in HK," 2001), the Hong Kong secretary for information technology and broadcasting, Carrie Yau, emphasized that in spite of the fact that the digital-divide problem is not so sharp for Hong Kong as for other countries, the government had formulated clear policies in tackling the issue. She outlined a series of measures taken to bridge the gap or avoid the emergence of a potential gap between various sectors of the community. These include providing education and training, creating a favorable environment for technology diffusion in the community, enhancing knowledge and awareness, and developing e-government. By 2001, the Hong Kong government already expended $282 million to strengthen the community for the exploitation of opportunities in the digital world. Yau noted that a substantial proportion of the local population already had the opportunity to access ICT and the Internet. Half of the households have installed computers. One third of the population are Internet users. The mobile-phone penetration rate has reached nearly 80%.

The new-coming technologies of information transmission are currently applied to bridge the technology and media clusters of the digital divide. The EU's action plan for 2005 includes a thesis for carrying out a cost-benefit analysis of various technological options including space-based ones (CEC, 2002a). In the summer of 2004, the eEurope Advisory Group published *Work Group No.1: Digital Divide and Broadband Territorial Coverage*. The main idea of this paper is that fast data exchange can supply citizens with e-services and help in bridging technological and other clusters of the digital divide. The paper presents recommendations to public authorities for selecting proper and effective technologies that correspond to local conditions. Satellite technologies are proposed for low-density rural areas because of "service costs dependent on the average bit rate usage, and investment costs dependent on peak bit rates" (p. 7). WiFi (wireless fidelity), DSL (digital subscriber line), and fibre technologies are recommended in the case of a medium-density village. High-density rural and urban areas are supposed to be covered by ADSL/VDSL and fibre or cable. The eEurope Advisory Group has examined other alternative technologies such as third-generation mobile/UMTS, power-line communications, broadband wireless access, and digital terrestrial TV, but found out that these technologies are more expensive or offer insufficient bit rates and interactivity as compared with other solutions.

According to these recommendations, "public authorities could also encourage the creation of Public Access Points (libraries, community centres, schools) in order to extend broadband access as much as possible into rural areas" (p. 10).

In particular, WiFi is currently widespread. Several projects based on this technology started during the last 3 years. Both inter-European projects, for example, TWISTER (Terrestrial Wireless Infrastructure Integrated with Satellite Telecommunications for E-Rural; European Space Policy, 2004), and national projects, for example, the Spanish program Rural Public Access Points (Diputacion de Badajoz, 2005), have begun.

Included in the framework of the EU action plan of 2005 was the forum on the digital divide (http://www.techsoup.org/fb). Through this forum, any concerned person can exchange opinions, ask about possible solutions to a problem, or share a solution.

Although the digital-divide problem has become apparent all over the world, it has its own manifestations in each country because of different experiences according to the situation in the respective country.

ABOUT BASIC INDICATORS CHARACTERIZING THE DIGITAL DIVIDE PROBLEM

The sets of indicators for digital-divide assessment differ when mentioned by different organizations. These sets sometimes have some common elements, and sometimes they differ in their composition; however, they are not contradicting in essence, but supplement each other. Even in the evolution of these sets, we can track some consecution and regularity. Thus, at the first stages of studying the digital-divide problem, more attention was paid to the technological aspects. In the course of time, the world community became conscious that this problem is also of human and social character, and that is why the indicators characterizing this problem began to reflect these parts of human activity as well.

Thus, inasmuch as the digital divide was in the first place directly connected with ICT penetration into society life, for digital-divide monitoring and assessment it will be efficient to evaluate ICT development using a range of indicators to benchmark connectivity, access, ICT policy, and overall ICT diffusion. In the Geneva *Plan of Action* (WSIS, 2003), in the section "Action Lines," it is stated, "In the context of national e-strategies, devise appropriate universal access policies and strategies, and their means of implementation, in line with the indicative targets, and develop ICT connectivity indicators." In the section "Follow-Up and Evaluation," the following is stipulated:

Appropriate indicators and benchmarking, including community connectivity indicators, should clarify the magnitude of the digital divide, in both its domestic and international dimensions, and keep it under regular assessment, and tracking global progress in the use of ICTs to achieve internationally agreed development goals, including those of the Millennium Declaration...

All countries and regions should develop tools so as to provide statistical information on the Information Society, with basic indicators and analysis of its key dimensions. Priority should be given to setting up coherent and internationally comparable indicator systems, taking into account different levels of development.

So, each country should develop its own basic indicators to characterize the state of the art of ICT development in it, and to be able to evaluate the development or reduction of the digital divide. Nevertheless, there is a core list of ICT indicators that was developed and is adopted by international organs; it is recommended to be followed, not excluding the indicators elaborated to stress the specific country's peculiarities. Thus, the WSIS Thematic Meeting on "Measuring the Information Society," held in Geneva in February 2005, published the recommended core list of ICT indicators and its broad evolvement ("Final Conclusions," 2005). So, not to overload the space in this chapter but to give an idea of their details, we give the core list of ICT indicators and only some of its subindicators given in the document.

Core List of ICT indicators:

- Infrastructure and access core indicators (CIs)
- CI on access and ICT use by households and individuals
- CI on access and ICT use by businesses

Infrastructure and access CIs (basic core):

- Fixed telephone lines per 100 inhabitants
- Mobile cellular subscribers per 100 inhabitants
- Computers per 100 inhabitants
- Internet subscribers per 100 inhabitants
- Broadband Internet subscribers per 100 inhabitants (fixed and mobile)
- International Internet bandwidth per inhabitant
- Population percentage covered by mobile cellular telephony
- Internet-access tariffs
- Mobile-cellular tariffs
- Percentage of localities with public Internet-access centres by number of inhabitants (rural/urban)

Certainly, the problem of digital-divide evolution is a rather specific one. This problem differs to some extent from the problems of ICT evolution and of information-society evolution. Perhaps it should take into account some specific trends, but these basic trends are useful for assessment, too. Therefore, the indicators mentioned above are taken as the components for the calculation of more complex indicators that take into account the human factor as well. These are e-readiness, e-government, and e-ranking. They were calculated in analytical UN reports during last decade to estimate the level of society informatisation.

For example, we show the structure of the e-government indicator according to its explanation presented in the UN report (American Society for Public Administration & United Nations Division for Public Economics and Public Administration [ASPA & UNDPEPA], 2002).

a. **Presence on the Internet**
b. **Infrastructure of telecommunications**
   - Number of PCs per 100 persons
   - Number of Internet hosts per 10,000 persons

- Percentage of population using Internet
- Number of telephone lines per 100 persons
- Number of mobile telephones per 100 persons
- Number of TV sets per 1,000 persons

c. **Human resources**
- Human-development index
- Index of access to information
- Ratio between urban and rural population

Tracking all of these indicators is useful for digital-divide monitoring and comparative analysis. These indicators' are indicative for every country, too.

The mentioned indicators for any range of countries or population groups allow carrying out comparative analysis, but do not allow expressing numerically the unevenness of the researched resource distribution between these groups. In the UN report *The Digital Divide: ICT Development Indices 2004* (2005), the authors propose to use Gini coefficients and Lorenz curves in the fields of telephone main lines, mobile subscribers, Internet hosts, PCs, and Internet users for the measurement of digital-divide unevenness.

The Gini coefficient is a measure of inequality. It is usually used to measure income inequality, but can be used to measure any form of uneven distribution. The Lorenz curve was developed as a graphical representation of income distribution and is used to calculate the Gini coefficient. These tools are very visual and can be calculated simply enough, having the values of the researched indicators for the chosen set of countries or groups of population.

In the same report, the calculated Gini coefficients are presented (UN, 2005). These data show changes that occurred during the period from 1995 until 2002 in the fields of telephone main lines, mobile subscribers, Internet hosts, PCs, and

Internet users. For example, for telephone main lines, the value of the Gini coefficient in 1995 was equal to 0.688 for 200 measured countries, and it became equal to 0.551 in 2002 for 188 measured countries. For mobile subscribers, these values were 0.822 (195 countries) and 0.609 (194 countries), correspondingly. In other words, the inequality of these resources' distribution between countries had decreased. The same tendency was seen for PCs and Internet users. However, for Internet hosts, the picture is different: In 1995, the value was 0.910 (199 countries), and in 2002, it was 0.913 (204 countries). In this field, the inequality had increased instead of decreased. Perhaps this can be explained by the fact that this resource is the most expensive and requires a strategic approach.

Summarizing all discussed above about digital-divide estimation, we can recommend the use of the simple and complex (e-readiness, e-government) indicators as well as Gini coefficients for digital-divide monitoring and assessment.

In this chapter, the authors described the history of the problem, showed the situation in the world and the large-scale and magnitude of the problem, and set out the traditional, generally accepted views and trends for its solution. Every time, before giving a thesis, the authors endeavored to choose demonstrative examples from the world practice and then, on their basis, to make generalizations and conclusions.

Now, when benchmarking is made, it would be logical and useful to show the application of these judgments and recommendations for specific situations in the example of a typical, average country that is not distinguished by anything. The authors examine the application of these judgments for a specific country in the next chapter of this book. Being an agrarian country with a transition economy (from planned to market), in which the digital-divide problem is especially manifested, Moldova was chosen as such a country.

CONCLUSION

The analysis of the situations in some countries, made in this chapter, shows that the digital-divide problem has a set of common aspects irrespective of country's development level or other (geographical, demographical, etc.) characteristics. Moreover, this problem is not so much technological as it is even more social and political. Therefore, its solution needs not only technological measures, but social and political ones as well.

- Creation of a system of motivation for ICT usage in everyday life
- Creation by the state and society of national electronic, informational resources, available for the population
- Elaboration of national strategy for information-society development, supported by a system of laws that provide (ensure) the creation of a favorable climate for nondiscriminated access to information for all citizens, for economic activity, and for social progress

REFERENCES

280 mln U.S dollars spent to eliminate digital divide in HK. (2001). *People's Daily Online.* Retrieved July 8, 2005, from http://english.people-daily.com.cn/english/200106/07/eng20010607_71990.html

American Society for Public Administration & United Nations Division for Public Economics and Public Administration (ASPA & UNDPEPA). (2002). *Benchmarking e-government: A global perspective.* Retrieved February 29, 2004, from http://www.itpolicy.gov.il/topics_egov/docs/benchmarking.pdf

Baranov, A. (2003). Nad "tsifrovoi propast'yu." *Zerkalo Nedeli, 2*(427). Retrieved July 8, 2005, from http://www.zerkalo-nedeli.com/nn/show/427/37343/

Blair, T. (2004). *Full text of Blair's speech.* Retrieved July 15, 2005, from http://news.bbc.co.uk/1/hi/uk_politics/3697434.stm

Brown, R. H., Barram, D. J., & Irving, L. (1995). *Falling through the Net: A survey of the "have nots" in rural and urban America.* Retrieved July 1, 2005, from http://www.ntia.doc.gov/ntiahome/fallingthru.html

Commission of the European Communities (CEC). (2002a). *eEurope 2005: An information society for all. Action plan.* Retrieved August 5, 2005, from http://europa.eu.int/information_society/eeurope/2002/news_library/documents/eeurope2005/eeurope2005_en.pdf

Commission of the European Communities (CEC). (2002b). *eEurope benchmarking report.* Retrieved August 5, 2005, from http://europa.eu.int/eur-lex/en/com/cnc/2002/com2002_0062en01.pdf

Council of the European Union & Commission of the European Communities (CEU & CEC). (2000). *eEurope 2002 action plan.* Retrieved August 5, 2005, from http://europa.eu.int/information_society/eeurope/2002/action_plan/pdf/actionplan_en.pdf

Digital divide. (1999). Retrieved April 20, 2005, from http://searchsmb.techtarget.com/sDefinition/0,290660,sid44_gci214062,00.html

Digital Opportunity Task **(DOT) Force. (2001).** *Digital opportunities for all: Meeting the challenge.* **Retrieved March 25, 2005, from** http://www.labi-berlin.nubb.dfn.de/bibliothek/position-spapiere/dot_force.htm

Diputacion de Badajoz. (2005). *Convocatoria publica para la participacion de los entes locales de la diputacion de Badajoz en el programa "Puntos de Acceso Publico a Internet Ii" (Telecentros. Es).* Retrieved August 2, 2005, from http://www.

dip-badajoz.es/municipios/internet_rural/inetru-ral_convocatoria2005_diputacion.pdf

eEurope Advisory Group. (2004). *Work Group No.1: Digital divide and broadband territorial coverage.* Retrieved August 2, 2005, from http://europa.eu.int/information_society/eeurope/2005/doc/wg1_digi_divide_written_recs_290904.pdf

European Space Policy. (2004). *TWISTER: New project moves to close "digital divide."* Retrieved August 2, 2005, from http://europa.eu.int/comm/space/news/article_730_en.html

Falling through the Net? (2000). *The Economist.* Retrieved April 12, 2005, from http://www.economist.com/surveys/displayStory.cfm?Story_id=375645

Final conclusions. (2005). *WSIS Thematic Meeting on "Measuring the Information Society."* Retrieved November 28, 2005, from http://www.itu.int/wsis/docs2/thematic/unctad/final-conclusions.pdf

Internet World Stats. (2005). Retrieved July 25, 2005, from http://www.internetworldstats.com/stats.htm

Kalkun, M., & Kalvet, T. (2002). *Digital divide in Estonia and how to bridge it.* Retrieved July 1, 2005, from http://unpan1.un.org/intradoc/groups/public/documents/UNTC/UNPAN018532.pdf

Lisbon European Council. (2000). *Presidency conclusions.* Retrieved August 4, 2005, from *http://ue.eu.int/ueDocs/cms_Data/docs/press-Data/en/ec/00100-r1.en0.htm*

National Telecommunications and Information Administration (NTIA). (1999). *Falling through the Net: Defining the digital divide.* Retrieved July 18, 2005, from http://www.ntia.doc.gov/ntiahome/fttn99/contents.html

Nkrumah, G. (2000). Digital divide. *Al-Ahram Weekly, 492.* Retrieved April 12, 2005, from http://www.ahram.org.eg/weekly/2000/492/in3.htm

How many online? (2002). *Nua Internet Surveys.* Retrieved March 18, 2005, from http://www.nua.com/surveys/how_many_online/index.html

Okinawa charter on global information society. (2000). Retrieved July 20, 2005, from http://lacnet.unicttaskforce.org/Docs/Dot%20Force/Okinawa%20Charter%20on%20Global%20Information%20Society.pdf

Oxford English dictionary online. (2004). Retrieved June 14, 2005, from http://dictionary.oed.com

Raven, F. (2004). *The European Union on the digital divide.* Retrieved July 15, 2005, from http://www.digitaldivide.net/articles/view.php?ArticleID=41

Spanning the digital divide: Understanding and tackling the issues. (2001). Retrieved April 3, 2005, from http://www.bridges.org/spanning/download.html

United Nations (UN). (2003). *World public sector report 2003: E-government at the crossroads.* Retrieved March 25, 2004, from http://www.unpan.org/dpepa_worldpareport.asp

United Nations (UN). (2005). *The digital divide: ICT development indices 2004.* Retrieved November 26, 2005, from http://www.unctad.org/en/docs/iteipc20054_en.pdf

United Nations Development Program (UNDP). (1998). *Human development report 1998: Consumption for human development.* Retrieved March 17, 2005, from http://hdr.undp.org/reports/global/1998/en/

United Nations Economic and Social Council (UN ECOSOC). (2000). *Development and international cooperation in the twenty-first century: The role of information technology in the context of a knowledge-based global economy.* Retrieved July 13, 2005, from http://www.un.org/documents/ecosoc/docs/2000/e2000-l9.pdf

Warschauer, M. (2002). Reconceptualizing the digital divide. *First Monday, 7*(7). Retrieved July 19, 2005, from http://firstmonday.org/issues/issue7_7/warschauer/index.html

World Summit on the Information Society (WSIS). (2003). *Plan of action*. Retrieved February 4, 2005, from http://www.itu.int/wsis/documents/doc_multi.asp?lang=en&id=1160|0

ENDNOTE

[1]   Here and further on, the most recent data available at the moment of this chapter's writing are presented. For example, the data for year 2004 for Moldova are taken when possible from a preliminary report issued in 2005 by the National Bureau for Statistics. If the table or diagram lacks some data for year 2004 for Moldova, it means that the data were not presented in 2004's report and in the preliminary 2005 report. Also, it may be that corresponding data from the preliminary 2005 report were calculated by a different method and disagree with similar data for previous years from the 2004 report.

This work was previously published in Information Communication Technologies and Human Development: Opportunities and Challenges, edited by M. Gasco-Hernandez, F. Equiza-Lopez, and M. Acevedo-Ruiz, pp. 57-76, copyright 2007 by IGI Publishing, formerly known as Idea Group Publishing (an imprint of IGI Global).

Chapter III
Global Digital Divide, Global Justice, Cultures, and Epistemology

Soraj Hongladarom
Chulalongkorn University, Thailand

ABSTRACT

The problem of global digital divide, namely disparity in Internet access and use among the various regions of the world, is a growing concern. Even though, according to some reports, the gap is getting narrower, this does not mean that the problem is disappearing, because the problem does not just consist in getting more people to become "wired," so to speak. This chapter investigates the various relationships among the global digital divide, global justice, cultures and epistemology. Very briefly stated, not getting access to the Internet constitutes an injustice because the access is a social good that can lead to various other goods. Furthermore, as informa-tion technology is a second-order technology, one that operates on meaning bearing symbols, access to the technology is very much an issue of social epistemology, an attempt to find out the optimal way to distribute knowledge across the social and cultural domains.

INTRODUCTION

The digital divide has been one of most talked about phenomena in recent years. Trying to bridge the gap has been on the agenda of virtually all public policy makers since the products of infor-mation and communication technologies started to become more common not too long ago. It is recognized almost universally that the digital divide, basically a gap in access to and use of information technology and the global network that access makes possible, and especially the *global* digital divide, represent a significant policy problem that governments at various levels in all countries feel the need to address. The amount of attention and, more importantly, of physical and intellectual resources devoted to the issue has been really staggering. It has been so intensive in recent years that the World Bank announced a little while ago that the global digital divide is indeed disappearing (*Digital divide closing fast*, 2005).

Hence it might seem that the topic of this chapter is beginning to be outmoded. After all, if the digital divide is really closing, then why should we be concerned with its ethical or social implications? The exercise may cease to be relevant for current public policy formulation and may indeed become one of history—what kind of social and ethical implications arose when the digital divide prevailed? However, I do not believe that discussing the ethical dimensions of the digital divide would become irrelevant; nor do I believe that we would cease talking about the phenomenon, even if it really is the case that it is indeed disappearing. For reasons that will be made clear in this chapter, the sheer fact that more and more households in the world are equipped with computer technology and are getting wired to the Internet does not automatically translate to the realization of all the goals and visions that characterized attempts to close the digital divide. Simply having a tool does not always mean that one uses it in the way that was originally intended. We are now just beginning to see how the tools of information and communication technologies are going to be used in the various localities around the world.

What I would like to do in this chapter is to begin to explore the relations between the global digital divide, global justice, cultures and epistemology. This is pertinent to the discussion earlier because attempts to bridge the global digital divide, I would like to argue, are a species of attempts to bring about global justice and that the attempts need first to start from an appreciation of local cultures and how these cultures view their own epistemic practices, which are invariably part and parcel of their own cultures. Nevertheless, I can do no more than present a brief sketch of the relations here, because to do justice to each of the aspects of the relations would take us further afield than the space of this chapter allows. The sketch is also intended as an invitation to further research. The World Bank report that the digital divide is disappearing everywhere may be convincing, but it does not lessen the urgency of making an effort to understand how these factors are related to one another. This is so because simply providing the population with hardware and software and access to the Internet seldom suffices to realize the kind of "utopian" information society that the earlier pioneers and evangelists of information technology had in their visionary eyes.

NARROWING OF THE GLOBAL DIGITAL DIVIDE AND THE PERSISTENCE OF OLD PROBLEMS

It was just only slightly more than two decades ago that personal computers started to make their way into our lives; and the Internet started to appear on the scene little more than a decade ago. Yet these seem to most of us like ages ago. This points to the extreme speed at which the technology is evolving and spreading throughout the world. When it was in its infancy, proponents of information technology usually hailed it as a harbinger of a time when time itself and distance were eliminated. A result of this would be, in their view, a complete merging of ideas and information in such a way that every piece of information would be at everybody's fingertips. Ideas such as democracy and freedom would float around the world and enter the consciousness of the people who would presumably take these ideas as a basis for changes in their own communities and societies. Knowledge would be readily available and the whole world will be blessed with better-informed and knowledgeable global citizens.

However, it seems that even as the digital divide is closing, these visions have not been fulfilled in many parts of the world. Universal knowledge, for example, is still a dream, as the near universal attempts at promoting the use of ICTs in schools can attest. Entz and Hongladarom (2004) argue that simply providing hardware and software to people seldom suffices in bringing about any kind of desired change in their worlds and communities. In the late 1990s the Thai government tried to bridge the digital divide problem in the country through a direct injection of hardware and software to villages. Computers were provided to village schools free of charge. What happened, however, was that many of the computers were not used to their full potential, and not in a way that would bring about any kind of universal knowledge or flow of information; many were not used at all. In many areas there was no electricity; in others there was a lack of qualified personnel who could operate computers reasonably well. Giving away computers in this case became a symbolic act of the powerful and centralized government, acting on its own without consultation with the village schools (Entz & Hongladarom, 2004).

The problems remain because there is no simple equation between possession of hardware and software on the one hand, and being able to use that software and hardware to their full potential on the other. Furthermore, it is difficult to say precisely what actually constitutes "using the computers to their full potential." This alone requires much more conceptual and empirical study. Thus, one should not take the World Bank Report that the global digital divide is closing as evidence that the problems are disappearing. It may be the case that the World Bank Report does not specifically refer to the Thai case or similar ones, because they may already have factored in the conditions that would make computer access and use a real possibility before they announced that the gap is indeed closing. Thus, they might not have counted the Thai case as an example of the divide closing. Nonetheless, even if the scenario they are reporting is true, even if a proportionally large number of people, say in Africa and Asia, are actually using computers that are wired to the Internet, that by itself does not mean that the utopian dream is automatically realized. The old problems, of poverty, inequality and so on, seem to persist even in the face of the virtually total diffusion of ICTs.

To see how this is the case let us look at the utopian dream in more detail. Early proponents of diffusion of information technology have pointed out that ICTs could facilitate and engender rapid development in various areas, such as education, health care, finance and taxation, and many more. It was envisaged that the diffusion, in integrating data and information scattered in many places, would result in eradicating poverty in rural areas through providing needed information to the rural poor so that they could build up their capabilities and rise above the poverty line. The Ministry of Information and Communication Technology of Thailand (www.mict.go.th/), established in 2003, also subscribed to the idea, and has as one of its prime missions to facilitate development through bridging the digital divide within the country. In 2003 the Ministry had a plan of selling low-cost computers to the Thai population, and it contracted a number of hardware manufacturers to produce machines according to its own specifications in huge numbers so that the economy of scale would drive the price down to make the machines become more affordable. The operating system was originally set to be a version of localized Linux developed by a research arm of the Ministry. However, the buyer could also choose to have Microsoft Windows XP installed in these systems after Microsoft offered to sell their products at a much reduced price (Entz & Hongladarom, 2004). In early March 2005, the Ministry of Information and Communication Technology again declared a policy of providing 250,000 computers, together with broadband Internet connection, to schools nationwide. The stated target is one computer for 20 students and funds from the national budget are to be used. (*Lofty plans for schools*, 2005).

Despite these efforts, however, the promise of the information society has not been fulfilled. Of course empirical research on the local Thai context here is necessary to substantiate the claim, but as the Thai examples alluded to earlier show, providing hardware and software alone does not seem adequate. To date there have been no systematic studies to measure the effectiveness of these measures, and we can see the same line of thinking behind these policies, viz. centralized government acting as if the entire country were a pliant mold that they can shape whatever way they want. In any case, many researchers have pointed out that attempts to bridge the digital divide require much more than hardware and software. In a background report to the InfoDev Symposium in Switzerland, Kerry McNamara says:

The presence or absence of ICTs (the "digital divide") is a symptom, not a cause. And the underlying causes of persistent poverty often have little to do, except indirectly, with the supply or absence of ICTs. By focusing on the "digital divide" (another in a long series of gaps that international development agencies have identified and sought to bridge over the past several decades) the proponents of ICT-for-development often misdirected their energies and weakened their own cause. (McNamara, 2003, p. 4)

Lisa Servon argues that one needs to change one's thinking about the digital divide and broaden the concept to more than the simple provision of hardware and software because when "we provide people with computers, we find that not much changes. IT on its own does not function as a ladder out of poverty" (Servon, 2002, p. 6). She

indicates dimensions of the digital divide problem other than access, which have to do with training and content (Servon, 2002, pp. 7-8). Her findings indicate that access is an "incomplete solution" and that "tech-fix is a myth" (Servon, 2002, pp. 222-223). Even though the gap is narrowing, this does not necessarily show that the problem is disappearing, for she found that many who are using the computer a lot are actually performing low-level tasks such as data input or other secretarial tasks (Servon, 2002, p. 222). In addition, it seems that the technology provides resources, freedom, flexibility and opportunities for the already powerful group in society (Servon, 2002, p. 223). It seems, then, that the old problems of social inequality still persist, even in a supposedly "information-intensive" society where the global digital divide and the divide within countries are fast disappearing.

Much more, then, is needed to close the digital gap. It is, however, surprising that many policy initiatives still aim at doing nothing more than providing hardware and software infrastructure and hoping that they alone can do the trick. In an attempt to reformulate how the digital divide problem should be conceptualized, Mark Warschauer sees the issue as a problem of social inclusion rather than a divide, which he regards as too restrictive and as presupposing a binary opposition between the "haves" and "have-nots" which is not supported by the facts (Warschauer, 2003). According to Warschauer, the main aim of is not to narrow or to close the digital divide, but to find ways for marginalized groups to be included in sharing the benefits that information and communication technologies can bring about (Warschauer, 2003, p. 211). He spells out the need for thorough analyses of the social structures, problems, organizations and relations involved, which naturally are different from one context to another, as an important factor in any attempt to formulate policies in that context. Moreover, the capabilities of individuals need to be promoted (Warschauer, 2003, p. 211). It is clear that Warschauer, too, does not see sheer provision of hardware and software as sufficient.

GLOBAL DIGITAL DIVIDE AND GLOBAL JUSTICE

The disparity between the amount of access to and usage of information technology among the nations of the world, to the extent that it exists in a form that constitutes inequality, is thus an issue of global justice. Many discussions of global justice by social and political philosophers have typically tended to focus on the more abstract aspects of the issue centered around the justification of global justice. Onora O'Neill focuses on the more theoretical aspect of global justice, arguing that Rawls's conception of justice is too restrictive and calling for the international organizations to play their part, even though these organizations do not, as a rule, have the kind of power needed to ensure justice in a "bounded" society (O'Neill, 2000). Andrew Hurrell argues that international organizations have a moral role to play in ensuring global economic justice and that they are "dense" enough to do the job. However, they "constitute a deformed political order," namely in distribution of advantages and disadvantages, in who sets the rules, in the capacity of states themselves to adjust to the economy, and in the "limited capacity of international laws and institutions to constrain effectively the unilateral and often illegal acts of the strong" (Hurrell, 2001, p. 43). Furthermore, Thomas Pogge argues that the Western nations have often put their priorities regarding global justice in the wrong place. He deeply criticizes the new global economic order led by the United States, which he sees to be responsible for mass poverty in the developing world. In her Olof Palme lecture, Martha Nussbaum calls for a new alternative theory of global justice to the dominant contractarian and Rawlsian one, or the one favored by Pogge, which attempts to broaden Rawls's

conception across national borders (Nussbaum, 2004). She would like to base consideration of global justice on certain fixibility of outcomes, rather than on fair procedure as is prominent in the contractarian theories. Following Amartya Sen, Nussbaum argues for a "human capabilities approach" of global justice that focuses more on facilitating the realization of certain human capabilities rather than on sheer provision of economic goods. Hence, narrowing the digital gap might presumably be included in the list of Nussbaum's list of capabilities also. Fred Dallmayr seems to be one of the rather limited number of philosophers who take up the gap in knowledge as a factor contributing to global injustice. Dallmayr (2002) issues a "plea for global justice," an action that is needed as a result of globalization and its consequent social and economic inequality across the globe. He indicates three areas of global inequality, viz. power, wealth and knowledge (Dallmayr, 2002). It is especially inequality in knowledge that is of particular concern in Dallmayr's paper and the next section of this chapter will be devoted to this.

What these philosophers share in common here is that they look at global justice from a wider perspective, emphasizing not only the actual contents of justice, but also the theoretical foundation—how a particular version of global justice is to be justified. Pogge, for example, argues that Western nations are morally bound to rethink their priorities in ensuring global justice. He does not spend much time in his paper detailing what a particular developing nation, such as Thailand or Cambodia, might need in order to achieve a kind of parity in terms of information and communication technologies that presumably would alleviate the problem. Nussbaum offers an alternative theory of global justice, but her paper does not focus specifically on how information technology itself should figure in an attempt to delineate the list of capabilities that should be fulfilled. Consequently, the time has come for an investigation of how the discussions on the global digital divide should have any bearing on those on global justice.

Taking the digital divide as an issue of global justice would mean that access to the benefits of information and communication technologies is a good—something, like health and opportunities, that should be equally shared among the population in the community. However, as it is by no means clear what actually constitutes the benefits of access to the information and communication technologies, more work still needs to be done to clarify this point. On the one hand, access to ICTs and the Internet should in itself be considered as a good, because, presumably, having it enables one to realize one's own goals and desires, just as being in possession of good health enables one to enjoy one's life and to perform activities that one could not do had one not been healthy. On the other hand, there are many people nowadays who choose not to get connected and not to use the computers at all, but these people are not considered unequal to others because they have other social and economic goods, such as an adequate level of income, education, welfare and so on. But there are not very many who would deny having good health. Hence it seems that having access to ICTs alone is not the answer. Moreover, we have seen in the last section that hardware and software alone are not enough to achieve the kind of parity that would qualify for there to be justice. Someone might counter that those who chose not to get connected did not get connected out of their own choice. They are not unequal to their peers, as mentioned, since they could easily get connected as soon as they wanted to, whereas those who are denied access, such as the rural poor in Thailand, would not get access to ICTs, even if they really wanted to. But this only shows that access to ICTs may not be a primary good, but a secondary good. A primary good is one that satisfies some basic need of those in possession of the good. Thus health is a primary good because just about everybody desires it for its own sake, as Aristotle said. Access to ICTs,

on the other hand, appears to be more secondary, since having it enables one to enjoy other kinds of goods, such as information (in an age where information itself is considered a *good*) or income (through e-commerce). This points to the extreme importance of the content of the flow of data facilitated by the network. In some way the content being transmitted through the network is itself a primary good, and the network is then a secondary good because it enables the former to be distributed to where it is needed. Thus, if one wants to tie this up with the global justice issue, one would then need to elaborate upon what it is that the possession of would reduce global inequality. Here knowledge, or epistemic practices, and culture have a very important role to play, and attempts to bridge the global digital divide effectively would not be successful if these are not taken into consideration.

Talking about the global digital divide as an instance of global justice is a step down toward the more specific from the often highly abstract papers on theories that the literature offers. It seems that taking the digital divide as an issue of justice would need a special set of vocabulary, because of the technical nature of the phenomenon. Most policy analysts and researchers on diffusion of ICTs in Thailand are bureaucrats working for the government. Most of them have a technical background and usually regard their jobs to be technical tasks of studying and conceiving policies in a rather formulaic manner. In Thailand it is usually the case that policy researchers on a technical issue consist of technicians in that area. Thus, it is mostly medical doctors who formulate the country's health care policy and it is usually engineers and computer scientists who propose policies to the government in the areas of information technology and the digital divide. This may stem from the Thais' belief that in technical matters, including policy studies on those matters, things are better left to the technicians or experts in question, since they know best about their own field. Hence, discourse on these topics is often couched in technical language and jargon, which further deepens the public's attitude toward such matters as being purely technical requiring technical solutions. Talks about the digital divide, in Thailand at least and presumably in other developing countries as well, are often couched in the technical jargon of computer scientists and network specialists. Thus a knowledge gap that is already in existence between the educated urban elites and the less educated majority in the countryside is exacerbated. The digital divide then becomes a symptom of a wider divide between the elites who seem to have everything and the poor who do not seem to have anything. And the use of specialist jargons by the authorities has become a symbol of power for them against the local villagers. If there is to be a solution to the digital divide problem, then language has to be considered too; and, as we shall see in this chapter, language is but one of the aspects of culture that needs to be taken into consideration in any attempt to solve the problem.

At any rate, the issue of the use of computer and specialist jargon in policy formation and deliberation is related to another, more theory-oriented, issue of which set of vocabulary is most suitable for discussion of the philosophical and ethical components of the digital divide problem. In fact, one might make the case that talking about the digital divide in this context does not require a special set of vocabulary, that is specific to the technology in question and that makes its discussion different from talking about other goods, such as income and education. In this sense, taking the global digital divide as an issue of global justice is no different in principle from taking the global divide in health care as an issue in global justice. Since what is being emphasized here is the provision of health care to the world's population in a just and equitable manner, so too the provision of access to information and communication technologies should be in the same vein. No special vocabulary needs to be involved. However, the issue of which set of vocabulary is

suitable is a very complicated one and cannot be treated in full detail in this chapter.

While this position is plausible, it is nonetheless the case that there are different levels of abstraction when one discusses global justice and its content, and these different levels make it necessary for there to be at least two sets of vocabulary to work with. This difference is not the same as that of the policy formulators mentioned in the previous paragraph. On the one hand, there is the general vocabulary that discusses global justice; this is often found in the literature on the topic among social and political philosophers. On the other, there is the special set of vocabulary that pertains to information and computer technologies in particular. This set is not the exactly the same as that of the technicians discussed earlier, for it focuses not on the technical nature of the technology, but on the more conceptual problem of how the diffusion of information technology is related to the goals and values of a community and the life-world of a people. Thus this latter set is more in tune with the conceptual resources found in philosophy of technology. In this sense, a case could perhaps be made that discussion of the global digital divide as an issue of global justice requires some set of vocabulary that is specific to the issue.

This set of vocabulary can be found, for example, in the works of philosophers of technology when they analyze the role technology plays in human life. One of the chief problems in philosophy of technology concerns technological determinism—the view that infusion of technology in society invariably brings about certain changes in the attitudes and structures of that society. It is well-known that this view is subscribed to by such philosophers as Martin Heidegger and Jacques Ellul. In the context of the global digital divide, the issue is whether the infusion of the technology, which is the aim of proponents of attempts to narrow the divide, would bring in certain changes which are inevitable. The early proponents alluded earlier in the chapter argued that the infusion would certainly bring about desirable changes, and it is clear that the belief is based on technological determinism. However, technological determinism is being challenged from many angles. Charles Ess and Fay Sudweeks (1998, 2000, 2001, 2002, 2004) have shown that the belief that computer-mediated communication will bring about certain inevitable changes in any culture where it is practised is unfounded empirically. This is mainly because cultures usually have within their resources the capability of "co-opting" these influences to make them their own. Thus, it has not been shown to be the case that all cultures will change in the same way as a result of their participating in the Internet and in the global communication network (Hongladarom, 2000, 2001a).

If this is indeed the case, then it is ultimately up to the cultures themselves to determine their course of action regarding the Internet. The implication for the global digital divide issue is that, at the very least, a special set of vocabulary, that of philosophy of technology and analyses of computer-mediated communication and culture, pioneered by Ess and Sudweeks, should be of value in aiding us to understand the complexities surrounding the global digital divide and global justice better.

INFORMATION TECHNOLOGY, EPISTEMOLOGY AND CULTURE

Ess and Sudweeks have done a lot to show that information technology, computer-mediated communication and cultures are interrelated to a great extent. We have already seen that information and communication technologies can indeed be considered a good, albeit in a secondary manner, and that social inequality can indeed happen when one section of a population has more of their products and benefits than another section. In addition to these aspects, information and communication technologies do have their own special quality,

which merits a separate type of discussion apart from the usual one in political and social philosophy when social inequality is discussed. Another reason for this is that information and communication technologies, including the Internet, are pliable and can be used in daily life in very diverse ways, and it is here that the technologies have an intimate relation with culture. While older technological products, such as the tractor or the plough, can only be used in a limited number of ways, computers can be programmed to do many tasks, as many are, no doubt, familiar. Operating a tractor or a plough does not seem to require as much knowledge and skill as one needs to work a computer efficiently.

In this sense, the computer can be seen as a *second-order* technology, as opposed to the *first-order* technologies exemplified by the tractor or the toaster oven. First-order technology, like the toaster, operates on a chunk of concrete reality. But computers do not directly do so, as they operate on binary digits acting as symbols capable of referring to anything, including non-existent things in future plans. It is true that computers do actually operate on chunks of reality, namely the electronic signals representing ones or zeroes, but these do not mean anything and the binary digits always refer to something other than themselves. An older tool such as an abacus can actually do the same kind of work that a computer can do, though much more slowly. In this case the abacus can be considered a second-order technology also. But the immense speed and power of computers to operate on these electronic signals seems to make them a breed apart from the older tools, even from the electronic calculator. Computers can be used in many ways, from playing video games to speculating on the stock market. The toaster or the automobile, as first-order technologies, can do only limited things.

The epistemological implication of this is that, as a second-order technology, the computer's capability in manipulating symbols makes it, in a real sense, an extension of the cognitive power of human beings. Traditionally, epistemologists are concerned with the normative problems of knowledge—what counts as knowledge, how a piece of information should be justified so that it becomes a piece of knowledge, and so on. However, with the influx of the information technology, these problems have expanded quite significantly in range. Goldman, for example, is calling for a revamp in how epistemology is done in that he calls for a "social epistemology" that takes into account the societal aspects of knowledge (Goldman, 1999). He writes:

In what respects is social epistemology social? First, it focuses on social paths or routes to knowledge. That is, considering believers taken one at a time, it looks at the many routes to belief that feature interactions with other agents, as contrasted with private or asocial routes to belief acquisition. This "social path" dimension is the principal dimension of sociality that concerns me here. Second, social epistemology does not restrict itself to believers taken singly. It often focuses on some sort of group entity—a team of co-workers, a set of voters in a political juris-diction, or an entire society—and examines the spread of information or misinformation across that group's membership. Rather than concentrate on a single knower, as did Cartesian epistemol-ogy, it address the distribution of knowledge or error within the larger social cluster. Even in this second perspective, however, the knowing agents are still individuals. Third, instead of restricting knowers to individuals, social epistemology may consider collective or corporate entities, such as juries or legislatures, as potential knowing agents. This third approach will occasionally be taken in this volume, but only rarely. (1999, pp. 4-5)

It is these aspects of social epistemology mentioned by Goldman, especially the one on distribution of knowledge across a group of popu-lation and societies, that most concern us here. Basically what Goldman has done is to relocate

the focus of epistemology from the exclusive attention toward the individual knower to the wider array of individuals in groups and societies. Nonetheless, the normative interest of epistemol-ogy still remains. It is relocated in new problems concerning how the best approach in knowledge distribution across groups of individuals is to be effected, for example. Goldman's rough answer to this problem is that the distribution should be such that the amount of knowledge across the array of groups is maximized, where he defines knowledge roughly as "true belief" (Goldman, 1999, pp. 3-7). I have no quarrel with Goldman's proposal in this chapter (that was an occasion for another of my papers (Hongladarom, 2002), but I agree with his social epistemology project, especially on the normative problem of knowledge distribution, and it is this that is most relevant to the topic of this chapter.

The digital divide exacerbates the knowledge distribution problem in many ways. First of all, the divide clearly shows that knowledge distribution is skewed. As in individualistic epistemology, where the concern is on how to find the best route toward knowledge for an individual. Here the concern is also on how to find such a route for a society. The computer's role as the symbol manipulation tool for the modern age—its role as a second-order technology—makes it the key player in knowledge distribution. Secondly, when the discussion turns toward the global digital divide, the focus then is on knowledge distribution across nations; hence the issue becomes intertwined with those in political philosophy. Thirdly, discussions of culture further complicate the issue because, as I will elaborate further in this chapter, culture could be regarded as the sum total of the beliefs and practices of a group of people who have stayed together for a long time sharing a system of symbols, meanings and traditions together. Thus epistemic practice, which is the practice of a culture regarding production, dissemination and evaluating knowledge, plays an obvious role in knowledge distribution and digital divide problems. A social epistemology that seeks to illuminate the digital divide problem needs to pay serious attention to cultures and their epistemic practices.

The computer's capacity to operate on anything that human beings can think of or talk about make it a very powerful tool. In this case computers can even operate on non-existent things like future plans and fictional works. As the works of Ess and Sudweeks show, culture permeates the use and design of information technology, and the second-order nature of information technology means that it functions as more of a transparent medium through which *content* is transmitted, stored and processed. Since content depends largely on the goals and agenda of all who are communicating through the medium, it is a perfect means by which the cultural traits of the people communicating with one another emerge.

The capacity of computers to operate on symbols makes it a very powerful cultural tool. "Culture" is taken here in the anthropological sense that refers to the sum total of a group of humans' symbolic and meaning-giving activities. Thus language is definitely part of human culture, as well as all activities that have symbolic meaning attached to them, such as religions and ways of greeting. In this sense the computer can be regarded as a tool that facilitates and extends human symbol production and manipulation, in much the same way as pencil and paper, or charcoal and cave wall in the past. So there is a strong connection between computers and cultures. On the one hand, computers are a symbol manipulation tool *par excellence,* and human culture is nothing if not production and interpretation of symbolic representations. What Ess and Sudweeks have found is that computers and computer-mediated communication have largely been co-opted into the worlds of local cultures. Instead of computer use dictating how a particular local culture produces its own content and in what manner the computer itself is being used, computers and information technology have become integrated to local cultures in such a way that the technol-

ogy itself, the symbols being produced, and their meanings, are all included within the horizon of that culture.

Technological determinists may object to this, saying that it may be too simplistic to say that information technology is a transparent medium. After all, so the argument goes, operating a computer requires one to change many of one's habits. Firstly a stable source of electricity has to be installed; then the user has to have learned the skills needed to work on the computer; and then the computer requires one to work on it in a certain way which, in a way, limits the freedom of the user, because one has to follow the prescribed rules and choices of the operating system which means that the user seems to have no choice other than what is dictated them by the software. However, this does not necessarily mean that the user is constrained to the extent that her creative talents or her distinctive cultural traits are not possible at all. Nowadays members of all cultures in the world do use pencil and paper as a matter of course, and this older technology is so pervasive that one hardly pauses to think about it. Yet it does not seem that the identity of a particular culture does change as a result of the culture's adoption of pencil and paper. Furthermore, there is no denial that the culture itself also changes as a result of their adoption of the technology. The determinists do, in fact, have a point—only that technology and culture seem to determine each other, since one is part and parcel of the other, rather than one determining the other externally, so to speak (Warschauer, 2003, pp. 199-216).

This distinctiveness on the part of computers makes it the case that running it effectively requires much more knowledge and skill than is required for running the first-order technologies. Much more is needed before those who have not found a place for computers and the network in their lives can be fully "computer literate" and function in a way that alleviates the inequality exemplified by the divide. Education is, of course, important. The second-order characteristic of computer technology makes it the case that one needs to factor in epistemological considerations in a kind of philosophical endeavor to make sense of the whole phenomenon, and in any attempt to lay a foundation for a workable and effective policy for solving the digital divide problem. This is so because, in addition to the fact that one needs to possess a certain amount of knowledge and skill in order to operate a computer relatively well, the second-order characteristic, the one that enables computers to work on symbols capable to referring to anything whatsoever, makes them prime epistemic tools which could prove instrumental in bridging the knowledge and information gap that undoubtedly exists in the world. And, in this sense, looking for ways to solve the digital divide should go hand in hand with solving the knowledge and information divide too. Furthermore, as the problem takes on a global dimension, the epistemological considerations become global, too, and in the same manner, the digital/knowledge/information gap becomes global, which adds another dimension to the whole discussion. It is here that discussions on global/local epistemic practices have a role (Hongladarom, 2002).

THE DIGITAL DIVIDE AND THE KNOWLEDGE GAP

Fred Dallmayr (2002) points out that there are three main areas of global inequality, namely power, wealth and knowledge. Thus he raised the knowledge distribution issue mentioned earlier as a serious problem facing the world today. The discussion on knowledge is the more interesting, since disparities in power and wealth are rather commonplace. According to Dallmayr, the global knowledge gap is exemplified by the fact that more than four-fifths of the world's output in science and technology comes from the West, that the vast majority of scientific and technological experts reside in the West, and that there exists in the West a policy guarding knowledge and information as a

highly precious commodity (Dallmayr, 2002, pp. 148-149). This gap is a result of the "expertocracy" and "Europeanization of the earth" (Dallmayr, 2002, p. 148). Dallmayr argues that the rise of globalization and ICTs has made it possible for the few who possess the technical know-how to rule over the majority of the world's cultures and population. These few who hold the power are the ones who manipulate the images and content of the mass media that is distributed via the global network, including satellite television, the print media and the Internet. The power exists through a manipulation of symbols and images through these media in such a way that the ordinary citizens of the world have become "image consumers and pliant tools of telegenic politicians and pundits ruling over a televisual or phantom democracy" (Dallmayr, 2002, pp. 149-150).

The technological determinist bent in Dallmayr's paper here is unmistakable. Taking a rather pessimistic stance, Dallmayr views the contemporary infusion of information and communication technologies as a system of control by which the world's population is mesmerized and virtually enslaved by the few manipulators of images and symbols who hold the real power. If the hold on the consciousness of the people through the "information revolution" is a strict causal relation, then there are only two ways out—either abandon all information revolution altogether and build a protective shield around the people so as to prevent the effects of the technology from harming them, or stage another revolution and take the power of manipulating symbols and images to the people themselves. Following the first course sounds like one is trying to turn back the clock. Even today there are people who choose not to get connected to the outside world; but I think this is no longer a viable option for most people. The second alternative is a radical one. Looking at the mass media regime as a seat of political and psychological power and trying to destroy that power would mean that the people take the power of producing and distributing media images themselves. In fact this is already happening in the case of the Internet. The problem is only that the images and stories being produced and disseminated are so huge in volume that the effects tend to cancel one another out. When there are billions of Web sites to turn to, the power that one particular Web site can hold on to someone's imagination is minimal indeed. More importantly, the technological determinist thesis is that it is the technology itself that is to blame; thus sharing the technology with a large number of population would just spread the blame to all over the place, and this does not seem to be a good solution.

The implication of Dallmayr's idea here on the global digital divide problem is that he reiterates the need for a critical stance on the media regime of today. He reminds us that there still exists a huge knowledge gap between the West and the rest of the world in terms of production of scientific and technological output and other related measures, and that attempts to bridge the divide should proceed in an equitable and democratic manner. Bridging the divide, wiring the remote villages so that they have access to the Internet, should not be tantamount to ensnaring these people with centrally produced media images so that they are forever addicted to them. Instead providing access to the Internet to the remote villagers should proceed in such a way that the technology needs to become integrated into the lives of the villagers themselves. According to Dallmayr, this does not seem possible because the premise of his argument is that the Internet is a kind of symbolic manipulation on a grand scale by a few "expertocrats." But it is very important that the villagers, those on the receiving end of the divide, be helped so that they can stand on their own feet and take the Internet as yet another of the long list of tools that they rely on to make their living.

Another point is that Dallmayr seems to think that most knowledge comes from the West. The knowledge gap in modern science and technology may be the case, but this does not preclude

there being systems of knowledge and technology that are indigenous to the local cultures. As I also pointed out in another paper, the digital divide problem can be solved partly through recognizing the knowledge potential in local communities and seeking ways to make such knowledge and information "transparent"—meaning making it easier for local knowledge and information to become a productive force (Hongladarom, 2001b). It is possible that such systems now lie dormant without their potential being tapped fully. As philosophers and scholars in science studies, such as Sandra Harding (1998) and Susantha Goonatilake (1998), have pointed out, there is a vast store of indigenous knowledge systems in the world's cultures, to which modern science itself owes its origins. Furthermore, locals have relied on these systems for centuries in their lives. It is only because of the mindset, influenced by Western colonialism that regards modern, Western science and technology as the only possible knowledge and technological system, that the potential of these systems have not been tapped. Moreover, Harding has also argued that Western science as it is currently practised contributes to global inequality (Harding, 2002). Hence, an account of how to bridge the knowledge gap should also include a recognition of the important role of indigenous systems, and, as Goonatilake has argued, such systems can indeed be "mined" so that their treasures are revealed to the local people and the world at large (Goonatilake, 1998). In this sense, bridging the digital divide effectively also includes improving local knowledge systems and the means by which the content of these systems can be effectively retrieved.

CONCLUSION

Some conclusions can be made from the previous discussion. Firstly, it is clear that the global digital divide is an issue of global justice. This is clearly a truism, but an implication is that deliberations on global justice need also to pay attention to how the global digital divide problem is to be addressed. More specifically, one needs to find out exactly how the fruits of information and communication technologies are to contribute to global justice. If provision of hardware and software is not enough, then what could be adequate? Are training and content sufficient? What kind of content? How should the training be developed? And what aim should the training be geared to achieve? These questions are all important, and obviously they cannot be answered satisfactorily in this chapter. Much more work needs to be done.

Secondly, discussion of the normative aspects of the digital divide should also pay attention to the fact that computer technology is a second-order device, which makes it distinct from other first-order social goods. The second-order nature of computer technology makes it the case that cultural epistemological considerations do have an important and necessary role to play; hence, policy deliberations on the global digital divide need to pay attention to the role played by the epistemological considerations.

That is, the deliberation needs to consider the specificities of the culture and their epistemic practices. Hence, I agree with Anthony Wilhelm's idea of the Digital Nation, especially when he says, "a Digital Nation is much more than industrial policy; it drives the social agenda as information, skills and knowledge become building blocks of a learning culture" (2004, p. 131). What this means is that a policy aiming at solving the digital divide problem first of all should start from the ground up. The locals themselves should be the ones who decide which kind of technology they will be using and according to what agenda. For example, in a rural village in Thailand, which is experiencing a host of changes and has become ever more tightly integrated with the world economy, attempts should be made toward computer literacy as well as installing the necessary infrastructure. But, more importantly, it is the emphasis on their own agenda, beliefs and values,

that should take precedence. The villagers have their goals and their aspirations, as does everyone else. The problem is how to find a way, through the attempt to solve the digital divide problem, for their goals and aspirations to be realized. A necessary condition for that to happen is, I believe, that computers should be integral to their lives and not something foreign to them.

REFERENCES

Dallmayr, F. (2002). Globalization and inequality: A plea for global justice. *International Studies Review, 4*, 137-156.

Digital divide closing fast—World Bank. (2005). Retrieved March 24, 2005, from http://xtramsn. co.nz/news/0,,11965-4145138,00.html

Entz, A., & Hongladarom, S. (2004). Turning digital divide into digital dividend: Anticipating Thailand's demographic dividend. In K. Wong-bunsin (Ed.), *Six last golden years of economic competitiveness: Results of demographic change* (pp. 135-146). Bangkok: Thailand Research Fund [in Thai].

Ess, C., & Sudweeks, F. (Eds.). (1998). *Proceedings of the International Conference on Cultural Attitudes Toward Technology and Communication.* Sydney, Australia: Key Centre for Design and Computing, University of Sydney.

Ess, C., & Sudweeks, F. (Eds.). (2000). *Proceedings of the International Conference on Cultural Attitudes Toward Technology and Communication 2000.* Perth, Australia: School of Information Technology, Murdoch University.

Ess, C., & Sudweeks, F. (Eds.). (2001). *Culture, technology, communication: Towards an intercultural global village.* Albany, NY: SUNY Press.

Ess, C., & Sudweeks, F. (Eds.). (2002). *Proceedings of the International Conference on Cultural Attitudes Toward Technology and Communication*

2002. Perth, Australia: School of Information Technology, Murdoch University.

Ess, C., & Sudweeks, F. (Eds.). (2004). *Proceedings of the International Conference on Cultural Attitudes Toward Technology and Communication 2004*. Perth, Australia: School of Information Technology, Murdoch University.

Goldman, A. J. (1999). *Knowledge in a social world*. Oxford: Oxford University Press.

Goonatilake, S. (1998). *Toward a global science*. Bloomington: Indiana University Press.

Harding, S. (1998). *Is science multicultural?* Bloomington: Indiana University Press.

Harding, S. (2002). Must the advance of science advance global inequality? *International Studies Review, 4*(2), 87-105.

Hongladarom, S. (2000). Negotiating the global and the local: How Thai culture co-opts the Internet. *First Monday, 5*(8). Retrieved July 26, 2005, from http://www.firstmonday.dk/issues/issue5_8/hongladarom/

Hongladarom, S. (2001a). Global culture, local cultures and the Internet: The Thai example. In C. Ess & F. Sudweeks (Eds.), *Culture, technology, communication: Towards an intercultural global village* (pp. 305-324). Albany, NY: SUNY Press.

Hongladarom, S. (2001b). Making information transparent as a means to close the global digital divide. *Minds and Machines, 14*(1), 85-99.

Hongladarom, S. (2002). Cross-cultural epistemic practices. *Social Epistemology, 16*(1), 83-92.

Hurrell, A. (2001). Global inequality and international institutions. *Metaphilosophy, 32*(1/2), 34-57.

Lofty plans for schools. (2005, March 6). *Bangkok Post*.

McNamara, K. S. (2003, December 9-10). Information and Communication Technologies, Poverty and Development: Learning from Experience: A Background Paper for the infoDev Annual Symposium, Geneva, Switzerland. Washington, DC: World Bank.

Nussbaum, M. C. (2004). Beyond the social contract: Capabilities and global justice. Olof Palme lecture, delivered in Oxford, UK, on June 19, 2003. *Oxford Development Studies, 32*(1), 3-18.

O'Neill, O. (2000). *Bounds of justice*. Cambridge, UK: Cambridge University Press.

Pogge, T. (2001). Priorities of global justice. *Metaphilosophy, 32*(1/2), 6-24.

Servon, L. (2002). *Bridging the digital divide: Technology, community, and public policy*. Oxford, UK: Blackwell.

Warschauer, M. (2003). *Technology and social inclusion: Rethinking the digital divide*. Cambridge, MA: MIT Press.

Wilhelm, A. G. (2004). *Digital nation: Toward an inclusive information society*. Cambridge, MA: MIT Press.

This work was previously published in Information Technology and Social Justice, edited by E. Rooksby and J. Weckert, pp. 93-111, copyright 2007 by Information Science Publishing (an imprint of IGI Global).

Chapter IV
Digital Literacy and Cultural Mediations to the Digital Divide

Monica Fantin
Universidade Federal De Santa Catarina (UFSC), Brazil

Gilka Girardello
Universidade Federal De Santa Catarina (UFSC), Brazil

ABSTRACT

This chapter discusses the digital divide from the perspective of education and culture and highlights the forms in which the problem is presented in Brazil, understanding that it is not exclusive to this context. Given the complex challenges to digital inclusion in the context of globalization, the chapter emphasizes that for children and young people to be able to appropriate new technologies and languages in a significant manner, the promotion of digital literacy should be realized with respect to the concept of multiliteracies. Digital inclusion means much more than access to technologies and is understood as one of the fronts in the struggle against poverty and inequality. The authors propose that the understanding of the digital divide be enriched with the valorization of cultural mediations in the construction of digital literacy. In this sense, a culturalist perspective of media education can promote digital inclusion that is an experience of citizenship, belonging, and critical and creative participation of children and young people in the culture.

INTRODUCTION

In the early days of the popularization of personal computers in the 1980s, many people spoke of the infinite potential of the information highway that promised egalitarian and multidirectional communication among all peoples, groups, and nations. But another metaphor, critical of the naive optimism of the early years, did not take long to appear: that of the digital divide. How can the abyss that separates the digitally literate from the digitally illiterate—commonly understood as those excluded from the technological promise—be gapped? What other image could represent this tension in an alternative form, not as an unpassable chasm but as a space to be traversed? A river, which both separates and unites? A sea of currents that at once flow together and apart? How can this river be crossed, this sea be navigated?

This chapter proposes to discuss this problem—the distance between those who have and those who do not have complete access to the archives of culture made available by the media and the possibilities of recreating them critically. We focus on the new configurations that the problem takes with the intensification of the presence of digital technologies in education and culture. Our discussion seeks to identify possible contributions to the dilemmas of media education and of digital literacy that emerge from the Brazilian scene—a country of continental dimensions, where the pulsation of globalized media culture co-exists with a strong and sometimes preliterate popular culture, often in the same city and just a few blocks away. Our anchor in the problems as they are presented in Brazil does not mean, however, that we see the Brazilian or Latin American context as exclusive.

The diversity of semiotic practices and dislocations resulting from the forms by which industrial culture was incorporated into local contexts has challenged Brazilian thinkers for a number of decades. Concepts such as syncretism and cultural anthropophagy marked sociological, anthropological, and literary thinking in the country during the past century, in the search to understand the tensions between the "local" and "global" images and narratives, tensions that are at times generative and at times paralyzing. Paulo Freire's

(2000) proposal for a pedagogy of liberation, with its emphasis on a dialogical methodology that would be a space for a radical and micropolitical criticism of oppression, continues to inspire a large number of educational experiences, in and outside of schools. Nevertheless, although these conceptual proposals are on the horizon of an increasing number of media education practices, they are rarely explicit.

This chapter identifies a number of theoretical themes and concepts that have been instigating and challenging the field of media education in Brazil. The digital divide will be understood as the contradiction between digital exclusion and inclusion, recognizing however, that one is not always opposed to the other. We will focus on concepts associated with practices that strive to establish a digital inclusion that transcends a merely operational access to machines and programs, that is, inclusion that is also political, social, and cultural—and thus meets the broad needs of education.

It is first necessary to locate the place from where we write, both from a theoretical as well as a geographic perspective. Our reflection about this theme is based on the Brazilian condition, although we believe that many of the issues that we will discuss here are analogous to those found in other countries at the periphery of capitalism. We are both professors and researchers working at the interface between education and communication in a large federal, public university. For this reason we feel comfortable speaking about the issue of the digital divide, since it would be impossible to consider the relationship between the media and education in our country without recognizing the social inequality, made evident in statistical data presented below. It is also necessary to recognize that exclusion is far from the only theme discussed in Brazilian or Latin American academic spaces that work with media education. We will thus attempt to consider the material precariousness in our country and the challenges that it creates for digital education, while highlighting those ideas, themes, and processes that, being fruit of the cultural singularity of our context, can contribute in a positive way to considering digital literacy and the digital divide.

CONSIDERING INCLUSION IN EDUCATION AND CULTURE

Digital exclusion is not to be without a computer or a cell phone. It is to remain incapable of thinking, or creating and organizing new more just and dynamic forms of production and distribution of symbolic and material wealth. (Schwartz, 2000)

When we speak of digital inclusion, one immediately tends to think in the expansion of access to computers. Another way of thinking of the issue, however, is to give importance precisely to that which resists being done with computers, which tends to remain outside technological rationality. For Latin Americans, by taking simulation to the extreme, the new communication technologies "make visible the non-digestible, non-simulative, *remains* that from cultural alterity resists generalized homogenization" (Martín-Barbero, 2004, p.183). These "remains,", which resist media dilution, are related to the existence of popular culture, an expression that on our continent designates not the pop universe or the museum, but a space for symbolic exchanges and tensions that are still very much alive in society.

In this context many authors in our field highlight the importance of resistance to the model of technological and economic acceleration that is dominant in contemporary Western society and "that appears to condemn all other societies to an integration to its paradigm or to disappearance," as Santos (2003) warns. He adds that resistance to this model includes the maintenance of the diversity of cultures and societies, particularly of the "diversity of temporalities and of rhythms that are not annihilated by the imperative of total acceleration" (Santos, 2003, p.28).

Thus, a first presumption of this chapter is the need to consider the access to digital culture dialectically, abandoning any naïve enlightenment ideas or welfare-type programs that merely distribute equipment. We also seek a distance from the logic of globalized integration and the dichotomy between backwardness and modernity, which impels entire populations to the quest for the latest electronic gadgets. To think of digital inclusion in countries considered peripheral, requires paying attention to the cultural manifestations that take place outside of cyberspace. The absence of the latest technology is not necessarily understood as backwardness, a form of symbolic poverty or incompetence, but perhaps as a situation that composes a valuable and eloquent difference—a possible space for creative and critical constitution. It also requires paying attention to public policies for teacher education, as well as special educational and cultural programs. We consider it to be important to have this cultural perspective as a horizon, to assure that the democratization of digital access signifies the broadening of the social and cultural participation of various sectors of the population and not only a new form of ceding to old modes of discrimination and domination.

To think dialectically of digital inclusion in Latin America thus requires a careful look at the relationship between education and communication. Once again, it is Martín-Barbero who indicates that schools push young people to social-cultural marginalization, by encouraging passivity, redundancy, uniformity, anachronism, and provinciality, which contrast so strongly with the activity, diversity, curiosity, currentness, and opening of frontiers that mark the world of communication (2004, p. 350). The most grave consequence of this contradiction, according to the author, is that schools deny the poorest portion of the population the strength of orality found in their original culture, at the same time in which the poor are not introduced to the grammars of the new media. For the author, the cultural specificity of Latin American modernity lies in the complicity and interpenetration between oral and visual cultures.

The productive co-existence, whether marked by tension or partnership, between different cultures and imaginaries in Latin America, has been the object of analysis of a long critical tradition, exactly because this co-existence highlights the most eloquent of artistic and literary expression on the continent. To cite only two examples, we can begin with the "antropophagy" movement of the Brazilian modernist vanguard of the 1920s: "Tupi, or not Tupi, that is the question. I am only interested in what is not mine," Oswald de Andrade declared in his celebrated manifesto of 1928, permeated by nationalist references to the joy and creative potential of cultural syncretism. A second reference that is equally important is the concept of "hybrid cultures" developed by the Argentine García Canclini, which had wide academic circulation in the 1990s throughout South America. Based on this concept, the author discusses the new and original uses that each local community makes of videogames, videocassettes, and copying machines, emphasizing the egalitarian vitality of the singular mixes between the academic, the popular and the mass culture that the technologies favor.

These interactions allow the relativization of fundamentalisms, whether "religious, political, national, ethnic or artistic, which hold as absolute certain patrimonies and discriminate against the others," said Canclini (1998, p. 307). In relation to education, a fragmentary relationship with texts, books and annotations can also, Canclini suggests, induce "more fluid ties among the texts, among the students and knowledge" (1998, p. 308). In addition to these interesting aspects, however, he also points to the inequality in cultural capital and therefore the differences among the meanings constructed by youths for technologies in various social contexts. Appropriation of technologies is not the same for "poor adolescents who go

to video-game arcades and for middle and upper class youth who have them in their homes." (Canclini, 1998). In addition, large sectors of Brazilian society pass from the traditional oral culture directly to audiovisual culture, or to the media orality, without passing through written culture. This evidently interferes in the various types of relationships with the new media products—given that the meanings of the technologies depend on the way that they are inserted in daily life—and how culture appropriates and then transforms them.

To dialectically consider digital inclusion in Latin America also requires paying attention to the relations between education and popular cultures. In Brazil, a large variety of manifestations linked to different traditions are still very much alive. Dramas and ritual and or religious festivals, musical narratives, and poetic repertoires are relatively easy to access, even in urban centers. As Azevedo (2006) said,

If for students of the middle and upper classes, children and grandchildren of literate people, the discourse of the school appears to make sense, for students coming from an oral tradition – the large mass of the Brazilian population, it presents an authoritarian, prejudicial, discriminatory and exclusionary character.

The prejudice of the school against traditional oral culture, Azevedo (2006) adds, leaves many children without references, because of the institutional disdain for the knowledge and values of their parents and thus with a difficulty in identifying with the educational "truth." The result, we can say, deepens the sociocultural marginalization to which we referred earlier.

A reflection that clearly and critically locates the relationship between education and social exclusion in Brazil is conducted by Muniz Sodré. He begins by recalling that we educate not only for what is viable today, but for what is possible tomorrow.

To educate means establishing an (ethical) distance from the animal condition and preparing for complete citizenship, which presupposes knowledge by the subject, in addition to that of technical-operative instrumentation, of the political and administrative processes of its *Polis*, that is, of its Human City. (Sodré, 2002, p. 87)

The dominant change of paradigm and new forms of labor organization have provoked alterations in pedagogical relationships at various levels of schooling, in the forms of teaching and learning and in curricular content. Moreover, in the new social-cultural order, he explains, common knowledge, or knowledge about the self, is in crisis. The transmission of information in media space has become characterized by persuasion or fascination and this fascination with the media wonders can result in an ideological practice that attributes to technological innovation itself a "magic power to resolve problems (…) generating a *technical temptation*" (Sodré, 2002, p. 99-100). Muniz Sodré maintains that this ideology is instilled not on an ethical but on a corporate horizon, in the framework of a private-sector oriented educational matrix.

Many projects with this technocratic and private sector focus can have consequences that can misguide educational policy, because they are based on market interests, Brazilian, and foreign, often, but not always, imbedded in the guidelines of international agencies.[1] In many programs said to promote digital inclusion, "the real intention to promote business competition with support for the implantation of electronic commerce, new security policies and other government objectives was camouflaged by the official discourse as 'digital literacy' and public education" (Sodré, 2002, p.104). More than transforming the real conditions in which the old educational structures are placed, Sodré maintains that these programs intend to include the largest possible number of people, qualifying them for the labor market as "cybernetic simulacros for 'inclusion of everyone in the Web', in other words, there is no reflection of a collective desire, but only an adaptation to a techno-bureaucratic scenario" (idem).

By emphasizing technical instruction, education abandons the socialization of knowledge linked to human values and enters the market for goods and services. According to Sodré this perspective cannot understand that what is most important in terms of education "is not in the technical means and the disciplinary content (knowledge and information) but in the *cultural form* by which the knowledges are incorporated and the pertinent connections are promoted among them" (2002, p.106) Thus, when programs for inclusion said to be innovative emphasize only access to equipment, they understand the school merely as a physical place and not as a cultural form.

These ideas establish a reference horizon that allows us to consider the challenges of digital inclusion in the complex scenario in which we live. These include developing: a capacity to pay attention to cultural—and not merely technical—dimensions of the relationship of children and youth with the technologies; a dialectical understanding of the relationship between school, media, and popular cultures; a focus on the local uses of the medias and a recognition of the possibility that the critical and creative tensions of the repertoires and languages that occur there can point to routes for the mediation, even if circumstantial, of digital exclusion.

GLOBALIZATIONS AND CONTEXTS OF INEQUALITY

The fight against exclusion is part of the rhetoric of the "information society" in the context of the dream of a "second Renaissance" based on creativity, scientific discovery, cultural development, and community cohesion, as proposed by the European Forum for the Information Society. The concern for inclusion was also recommended in the 1990s by the G7, which sought a transition to the "information society" including: global interaction of broadband networks, transcultural education, support for libraries, museums, and electronic art galleries, environmental management, natural resources, and healthcare, interconnection of public administration and a global multimedia inventory of projects and studies for the development of the Global Information Society (Cadimo, 2004, p. 4).

Certain experiences have shown that the new communication and experiential paradigm present real opportunities for the democratization of media and messages and for citizens to overcome their condition as consumers and or spectators and transform themselves into reflexive and participative subjects. However, in general, what we find is not only a growing distance between the info-rich and the info-poor, but also the production of a new type of illiteracy, digital illiteracy.

There is considerable regional disparity in the reach of the Internet, given that the most highly developed countries, with nearly 15% of the world's population, in 1998, accounted for 88% of all Internet users. In Latin America, 90% of the users are in the highest income groups as Castells (2006, p. 433) notes. "The spatial inequality in the access to the Internet is one of the most impressive paradoxes of the information era, due to the characteristic supposedly independent from the space of the technology " he maintains (Castells, 2006, p. 434). "Globalization acts selectively, including and excluding segments of economies and societies from networks of information, wealth and power that characterize the new dominant system" and for Castells "the new information technologies are the instrument of this global storm of accumulation of wealth and diffusion of poverty", that relegates entire peoples and territories to irrelevance from the perspective of the dominant interests of global informational capitalism (Castells, 2002, p. 191-192).

In this light, the situation in Brazil is concerning: 54% of Brazilians have never used a computer and only 14% of all homes have Internet access.[2] Three percent of school age children (6-14) are out of school, corresponding to 1.5 million children.[3]

Of the 162,000 public schools in Brazil, 129,000 do not have Internet access, 40,000 do not have a library, 25,000 do not have electricity, and 1,000 do not have a bathroom.

This data reinforces the certainty that the digital divide truly cannot be understood only as a question of access to technologies, because it involves much broader questions of a cultural, political, and social order.

At the same time in which we seek the universalization of schooling, reading and writing, for the first time in the history of humanity enormous changes are taking place within a single generation and no longer from one generation to another. In a country of continental scope such as Brazil, problems also take on enormous proportions: the challenge of digital inclusion coexists with these social challenges that have been resolved in other locations. For these reasons, this is a time of searching for paths and alternatives given the complexity of the problems that are not only related to education.

Another question that we must keep in mind when we speak of digital exclusion is its dynamic character, requiring that countries that are not at the vanguard of technological production develop a critical capacity for analysis of technological trends. At the minimum, "it is necessary to discuss the technology politically and get to know the possible technological options to avoid that they are not presented as inexorable and that we swallow them whole" (Santos, 2003, p. 33). Although it is common for us to hear that poor countries can "skip certain phases" of development, absorbing more advanced technologies, this development is continuous and moved by competition. Thus, each "last generation" of devices is quickly surpassed and becomes obsolete and "the highly dynamic character of the new technologies is a constantly renewed barrier to the capacity to approximate the poorest countries to the wealthiest ones" (Sorj, 2003, p.61). Considering that a large portion of the Brazilian population does not have physical access to the new technologies, in order for the country to begin to participate more broadly in the cyber-culture, public policies are needed that guarantee access, software development, the work of educational-cultural mediation and the training for citizenship through these technologies.

Thus, the access to communication technologies and technical knowledge provided by digital inclusion programs is not sufficient to construct an experience of citizenship, since it can be oriented towards critical as well as passive uses. It is necessary to promote conditions for the development of autonomy in the interaction with the media, in order to favor the critical formation of citizens, not only of users. This includes an ability to develop search criteria, to encourage technological fluency means to critically use information and communication technologies, interact with words, graphics, images, and sounds, locate, select and critically evaluate information, and know and have command of the rules of the social practice of communication supported by the media, in a search for significant, autonomous, and continuous learning, as Almeida (2005) affirmed. This facilitates the production of knowledge that is needed to improve living conditions, thus creating and organizing social relationships, communicative interactions, and cultural participation. This perspective of digital literacy as a social practice goes beyond learning about codes or technology. It implies the attribution of meanings to information that comes from different texts, as Almeida (2005) proposed. That is, it is a perspective aimed at the production and representation of knowing oneself, the others and the world.

DIGITAL LITERACY AND MULTILITERACIES

Demographic data also present disturbing statistics indicating low literacy rates[4] forcing us to think of a new form of *dual illiteracy*: the functional and the digital. Is the complete computerization of

schools the solution to this problem? The question does not have a single response, but we can say that the distribution of computers in schools would not be sufficient if there is no teacher training policy aimed at cultural and artistic enrichment so that the use of the equipment can gain social meaning. Dual illiteracy creates a dual challenge—or perhaps a multiple one, if we consider the need for literacy in multiple languages—to promote digital inclusion and digital literacy as public policies that confront the inheritance of functional illiteracy and at the same time combat technological apartheid. To believe that it is first necessary to eradicate one and later confront the other would be a fundamental error, as Silveira (2001) emphasizes. Without a policy to invest in writing there would be a continuous production of inequality in digital literacy, since this requires a command of writing.

In the early 1960s, Paulo Freire recognized that the reading of the world preceded the reading of the word. In the 1980s, Emília Ferreiro and Ana Teberosky emphasized that children already have contact with written language before they enter school and highlight the importance of the social function of writing and learning to read and write as a form of representation, more than as a simple acquisition of an alphabetic code. Even so, in Brazil and in other countries, the word that designates learning to read and write "alfabetização" refers primarily to the process of acquisition of an alphabetic system. The word literacy "letramento" is used to emphasize the social function of writing.

In various countries such as Brazil, it is found that many children, although they know how to read and write, do not practice the social use of reading and writing. This is the other reason for the distinction in our context, between the terms "alfabetização" and "letramento," which, although they are interrelated, have specific meanings. Implicit in the concept of literacy, "is the idea that writing has social, cultural, political, economic, cognitive, and linguistic consequences, whether for the social group in which it is introduced, or for the individual that learns to use it," said Soares (2005, p. 17).

From this perspective, literacy can be understood as a condition that the individual acquires in virtue not only of knowing how to read and write, but of having appropriated the social dimension of writing, incorporating it into their life, and transforming oneself, as Soares (2002) emphasizes. The author uses the term in the plural, literacies, recognizing that different writing technologies create and require different literacies, above all since the introduction of cyberculture.

Some scholars even broaden this concept to that of multiliteracies, in order to include the audiovisual and digital grammars that involve a certain level of understanding of reading and production in all these dimensions. There is an interesting aspect in this notion of multiliteracies, which is the need that we have today to circulate in other types of representation of reality that transcend writing and involve the visual, musical, corporal, digital, and other forms of representation. It is important to work with these dimensions in a transdisciplinary manner, with an emphasis on circulation, transit, and interaction, involving scientific, literary, aesthetic, and cultural literacy.

The notion of digital literacy is related to print literacy in Buckingham's (2003) analogy:

As with print, children also need to be able to evaluate and use information critically if they are to transform it into knowledge. (...) As with older media, children need to be empowered to make informed choices on their own behalf, and to protect and regulate themselves. And just as print literacy involves writing as well as reading, digital literacy must involve creative production in new media as well as critical consumption. (Buckingham, 2003, p. 177)

In this perspective, digital literacy is associated to play, art and narrative, as languages that are essential for children to be able to express and communicate their feelings, ideas, and experiences. The specificities of each language should be considered, given that different abilities are required, for example, to write words, take photos, watch a film, or make a video-clip.[5] An articulation between the different languages and contents involves a collaborative work of experimentation, creation, and discovery. It also involves dialogue, negotiation, polyphony, openness, flexibility, criticism, and collaboration. In this process, the languages of different fields of knowledge can be understood based on different perspectives: as forms of expression of the subject and of the culture, as a means of communication, as a form of interaction and human development, and also as a social-cultural object of knowledge. This perspective requires that the initial and on-going education of teachers also considers their own experience with expression and creation, based not only on scientific knowledge, but also on the recovery of their experiences with languages that at times are dormant (artistic, performatic, literary).

It is through the different languages that children use, verbal and nonverbal, that they express their wealth of imagination and produce culture. In this perspective, speech, crying, gesture, observing, silence, play, sciences, arts, and experiences with media are part of a network of symbolic systems that is the context of a plural literacy. This leads us to reconsider what it means to be literate. For the teacher today it is not enough to have information from books, to dominate codes of writing and understand them as a form of representation of speech. To what degree is an individual literate if he or she is not capable of seeing, interpreting, and questioning TV images, watching and understanding films, critically analyzing advertising and news, using a computer, conducting research, navigating the Web or creating and inserting texts and images in the flow of social circulation? And to what degree are we as teachers literate in these languages and are we working in a suitable manner with the multiple literacies?

In sum, to be literate in the 21st Century involves multiple literacies, including digital literacy, which also concerns the construction of real and virtual citizenship and the possibility of effectively participating in society. For this reason, the media can no longer be excluded from the literacy process. Even if it seems obvious, this idea has still not been sufficiently adopted and converted into a transformative practice in many social-cultural contexts.

The concept of multiliteracies as a new understanding of the appropriation of the social practices of reading and writing, demands considering the theoretical bases that are its foundation and giving it legitimacy. In this sense, the multiliteracies can be understood as a repertoire of related capacities, some generic and others specifically related to the media and other areas, as Bazalgette (2005) emphasizes. This concept is related to media education, particularly to an ecological approach to media education (Rivoltella, 2002), understood as the interface between the various fields of knowledge, involving science, art, and literature.

Three elements have been identified that sustain this approach to media education: culture, as the expansion of and opportunities created by various cultural repertoires, criticism, as the capacity to analyze, reflect, and evaluate, and creation, as the creative capacity of expression, communication, and construction of knowledge. To these three words that begin with the letter C,[6] we propose adding the C of citizenship, thus establishing the "4 Cs" of media education: culture, criticism, creation, and citizenship, which must be present to make possible transformative work in the schools (Fantin, 2006).

CITIZENSHIP AND DIGITAL INCLUSION OF CHILDREN AND YOUTH

Based on the conceptual fluidity of the concept of citizenship, Rivoltella (2005, p. 155) identifies some dimensions that qualify citizenship and the citizen: civil law, political citizenship, social citizenship, and cultural citizenship. Relating these dimensions of citizenship with media education, Rivoltella emphasizes what he calls the "dual exercise of citizenship" or the combination of *citizenship of belonging* with *instrumental citizenship*. On one hand media education can call the attention of civil society and political power to the values of citizenship, and on the other, through its specificity, media education contributes to building this citizenship. It involves "a dual exercise of citizenship, which is active and passive, composed of solicitation of rights and of a set of efforts to build them" (Rivoltella, 2005, p. 156).

For Rivoltella (2005), to educate for citizenship involves an inclusionary education based on the recognition of universal rights, the formal and legal factors of citizenship as well as social and cultural rights, school education that conducts transversal work among the disciplines, considering the implicit and explicit curriculum, and an education that seeks solidarity. It also implies favoring interaction with territory, developing multiple and complex identities, and promoting a sense of belonging to the local, national, and global context. This perspective of educating for citizenship strives to favor: *the acquisition of knowledges* (knowledge of the world and the cultural, social, and economic reality in which we live, as well as of the laws, institutions, and their functioning); the *acquisition of social competencies* (knowing how to perform the role of citizen, to cooperate, construct and realize common projects, to assume responsibilities, resolve conflicts and intervene in a political debate); and the *acquisition of ethical and interpersonal abilities* (knowing how to express solidarity, to be open to difference, etc.).[7]

By encouraging this type of education, schools would be taking on new responsibilities in society and could contribute to the construction of a new form of cultural mediation, integrating with the communication media in order to reduce the asymmetries on the plane of cognitive and participatory capacities of individuals, as Morcellini (2004) emphasizes. Upon transposing this idea to the concern for the digital divide, we note that the term "digital inclusion" cannot always be understood as the opposite of exclusion, given that it often only describes programs that propose alternatives to the problems presented by social inequality. In order to struggle against the forms of domination and control caused by the digital divide, the public calls for digital inclusion began to appear, with the impact of the Internet on the world in the 1990s. To be inserted digitally comes to be a condition for citizenship and a right of individuals for their existence in the world of information and communication.

The debate about the forms of insertion of Brazilian society in this scenario is even more important when we analyze the data from the "Map of Digital Exclusion" which indicates that 85% of the Brazilian population is excluded from the information society (Néri, 2003). Although the federal government has invested in various digital inclusion programs, data indicates unequal growth among the regions of the country. From 2000-2004, Brazil had a 286.2% growth in the number of Internet users, becoming the country with the tenth most users in the world, with nearly 19 million people navigating the Internet. This growth is incomparably greater than that of the other means of communication.[8] Nevertheless, the penetration of the Internet in the country is unequal, concentrated in the upper classes. According to the map of digital exclusion, 79% of Brazilians never touched a computer and 89% never accessed the Internet. According to a study conducted in Latin America, only 10% of the poorest 40% of the Brazilian population have Internet access. Among Argentina, Brazil, Chile,

and Mexico, Brazilians pay the most to have a computer (IBOPE).[9] This reveals that Brazil still has much to do to gap the digital abyss.[10]

While from a simplistic perspective the recipe to transpose the digital divide would be to make technology available, we see that this is important but not sufficient, and we must consider the many complexities of the problem. We can ask what is the significance of including and what are the forms of inclusion, since the digital divide can be examined from its social, economic, cultural, technological, and/or intellectual dimensions, and based on its technical, subjective, or economic specificities. What does it mean to include? What rights does technological access to the use of the computer promote if this access is not accompanied by literacy in the multiple languages? Is to access a computer without being literate allowing its use without assuring the rights to citizenship it makes possible? Is digital inclusion a right of citizenship or a market necessity? While much of the international literature about the digital divide emphasizes the technical nature of inclusion, the questions above seek to point to the cultural and social aspects of inclusion, which seem fundamental from a Latin American perspective.

The term inclusion today, in some public debates, appears to have become a consensual politically correct label, immune to reflection and discussion. The principle that society must be included in the information era is accepted without questioning, and the question "who will be included and what will he or she do with this new tool?" appears to have little importance. Without guarantees of employability, without real opportunities to use digital tools to participate in decision making about their communities and schools and in formulating and accessing public policies and services for healthcare, education, housing and so forth, and given the speed of technological change, it appears that the discourse of digital inclusion is satisfying to only a few companies, NGOs, and technocrats who sell this ideology as one more technological novelty.[11] In this context, to include appears to mean in most cases to offer material conditions (skill and access to the Internet) to manipulate technologies. More than developing critical and questioning cognitive processes, it appears that in this vision, to include is to merely adapt pre-existing procedures to current technologies.

If to include is to give access to proprietary computers with primitive software and mechanically train people to use them efficiently at work, as is implicit in most of the inclusion projects,[12] Lemos (2003) asks why should society be included? For whom and for what does inclusion serve? In societies such as ours, where basic rights are still not assured, inclusion appears to be a goal and a utopia in some social fields such as healthcare, education, housing, and public safety. Is it possible to evaluate digital inclusion by the number of computers, people navigating, and other similar statistics, Lemos (2003) asks, highlighting that in this perspective, to include appears basically to adapt and mold. But to include is much more than to adapt to a technocratic logic. After all, it is by participating and acting in the world that we construct ourselves and "it is in the *insertion* in the world and not in the *adaptation* to it that we become historic and ethical beings, capable of choosing deciding and overcoming" said Freire (2000, p. 90).

Digital inclusion must include social, cultural, technological, and intellectual dimensions, in order to favor forms of belonging and assure the effective participation of people in the culture. Thus, the policies of digital inclusion should also encourage the deconcentration of power and local, regional, and national autonomy and not subordination to monopolies and imprisonment to private networks. This is the position taken by numerous authors, such as Silveira (2003), who see the open software movement as an important route to autonomy and a possibility for a creative mediation of the digital divide. In his analysis, "the open software movement is an authentic expression of this potential of the network and the

great model for consolidation of shared solutions before complex questions, based on multiethnic, multinational and multicultural interaction" (Silveira, 2003, p. 38). He understands the open software model as an economically viable option, which is technologically innovative and stable, and explains that an extensive use of open software in Brazil would not only save money in royalties, but also establish the country as an important producer and distributor of solutions in open code. This use of open software can exemplify imaginative alternatives to the monopolistic tendencies of technological globalization. As Boaventura Souza Santos affirms, "it is through the imagination that citizens are disciplined and controlled by States, markets and other dominant interests, but it is also from the imagination that citizens develop collective systems of dissidence and new designs for collective life" (2002, p. 46).

Now we can examine some implications of these developments in the cultural lives of children and young people.

CHILDHOOD, YOUTH, AND CONTEMPORARY DIALOGUES

How can we consider the possibilities of citizen participation of children and youth in contemporary society? If on one hand technological developments offer certain forms of interaction and participation, above all in networks, many authors indicate that on the other hand technological interactions with the most immediate local context become more difficult. The matter is still open to debate. Could it be that the exacerbation of individualism in the society of consumption also offers possibilities for overcoming this individualism through the contradictions that are revealed? Can children and young people, through educational mediation and by interacting with technologies, transcend the limits created by individualism and build other dimensions of participation? To think of forms of participation only as a reproduction of the usual form of conducting politics would be an insufficient contribution to democracy and to the questioning of cultural standards. It is necessary to think of social and digital inclusion as a form of participation in culture and as a possibility for change in the forms of seeing and relating to society. We will discuss some of the many challenges this poses.

Children and young people are increasingly present on the public scene. In addition to their recognition as consumers and citizens, it is recognized that they are particularly vulnerable to social changes. Although child labor is generally restricted to peripheral countries, children are targeted as consumers in borderless campaigns by globalized marketing. Cultural products aimed at children, video, television, cinema, cartoons, computer games, children's literature, and other products for children, fashion, candy, school supplies, recreational services, and so forth, constitute one of the most important segments in the consumer market. In this sense, the child is seen more as a consumer than as a citizen.

In this process, childhood comes to share the same media repertoires, often by developing a "single taste." We know that in each context there is an active reinterpretation of cultural products, in a process in which globalized cultures cross and recombine with local cultures.[13] But it is important to explore the possibilities for autonomy of childhood, in a context in which economic and cultural globalization operate in a complex and contradictory form on the status of childhood.[14] On one hand, hegemonic forces lead to the use of children's labor, to an increase in poverty, social inequality, and to the constitution of a global children's market, with effects on behavior, lifestyles, and the cultures of childhood. On the other hand, contrahegemonic globalization promotes the rights of children and strives to establish a political agenda that focuses on childhood.

Tensions between *heterogenous living conditions* and *homogenizing pressures* contribute to the formation of fragmentary and changing

identities, and the contemporary social space of (re)institutionalization of childhood can also imply a possibility for alternative paradigms. Given this situation, schools can be seen as one of the important faces of counter-hegemonic globalization.[15] While the school is the institution that has contributed most to the definition of the social status of children, Brazil's deep educational problems challenge the structure and symbolic order of school's as well as public educational policies, questioning the meaning of educational actions. Therefore, schools cannot remain divorced from the movement to construct rights for children, including the right to digital citizenship. As a public service, schools cannot be merely a preparatory space devoted to the aim that one day each individual can become a citizen. They must be places where citizenship is a reality even in childhood.

In order to accomplish this goal, education must consider the complexities of being a young person today, especially in its subjective aspects, which also depend on the sociocultural context. A recent study[16] revealed that Latin American children and youth say they are happier, more nationalist, and live closer to their families than boys and girls in developed countries. In contradiction, this same group occupies the worst position in well-being, due to their concerns for public safety. According to the study, these children and youth are concerned about losing their parents, with physical appearance, education, and in getting a job. This survey revealed two distinct worlds: "In the developed countries, young people are rich, but pessimistic about the future. In the developing world, children and adolescents are optimistic and hopeful, despite the fact that they confront large daily challenges."[17] The study also shows that more than 70% of youth and 80% of children in Argentina and Mexico said that they are happy, in contrast with the data obtained in the United States and England, where less than 30% of youth and less than 50% of the children say they are happy.[18]

This data confirms the degree to which subjective production is involved in the identity of young people and consequently in the perspectives that they have for the future. The data shows, once again, how important it is for digital inclusion to go beyond mere technical access and achieve towards cultural inclusion. This indicates the need to promote digital inclusion, while considering the specificity of memories, traditions, aims, values, fears, and hopes of youth in each culture. Projects designed from top to bottom (or from the "center" to the "periphery") in which there is no space for the emergence of different responses to these subjective and differing realities, will certainly have limited results from the perspective of participation and citizenship.

Another theme that is obviously part of the situation that we are examining is the relationship between adults and children in the scenario of digital culture. The emergence of a new type of subjectivity in the new generations, as a result of complex factors, has been identified by researchers in various fields. Others argue that the vision of a *deficiency* of new generations—that identifies their cognitive and cultural poverty—should be substituted by a vision based on *difference*. Based on theories that consider the combination of technological identity with human identity, Green and Bigum (1995), for example, have provocatively suggested that if a moralist panic tends to see children and youth today as aliens—a culture that is "designed, motivated and constructed differently," (Green & Bigum, 1995, p. 212)—on the other hand, it is adults who should be increasingly seen as aliens, given that it is "youth that inherit the earth" (Green & Bigum, 1995).

If we accept the provocation of these authors and admit that we as adults are increasingly *alien*, foreign, and—from the cultural perspective of children and young people, it is not for this reason that we are exempt from responsibility. We need to sharpen our tools for understanding, invest in the transformation of languages, contents, and contexts of reception, and on improving our capacity to understand the needs and desires of the young. In fact, we find ourselves today at the edge of various abysses—between generations, cultures, classes with unequal access to material and immaterial goods. At the same time, the new cultural forms are also means for bridging these gaps. Faced with the creation of this new culture, we need to adapt ourselves to new ways of seeing, reading, thinking, learning, interacting, and intervening in reality; but at the same time we need to continue to demand the presence of oral, written, and audiovisual culture in the school space. The various forms of production of knowledge that emerge among us can only dialog with each other if we give potential to the diversity of experiences in different social spaces.[19]

Thus, it is important to promote an *intergenerational dialogue*: children, young people, and adults of all ages need to hear one another. In addition, it is also necessary to have more *intragenerational dialogue* and promote forms of perceiving what exists in common between the challenges and rights of each generation. This is one more reason for an understanding of digital inclusion as more than a mere technical issue, or as a method to expand old forms of sociability and of teaching-learning. Digital inclusion should not be about using media in the schools to mitigate the tedium of education. Digital inclusion should involve a new form of insertion of children, young people, and adults in the complex processes of communication of society today.[20]

Education mediated by technology can favor the recovery of a playful dimension in the production of knowledge. We can say that in this game, one generation can contribute something to the other. On one hand, children and young people continue learning from adults that history, memory, and cultural inheritance are the foundations of current experience. On the other hand, there are many indications that adults have learned from youth the playful dimension of the use of digital technologies. It can be said that to play with or against these machines is a form of recovering liberty in a world programmed by technology, as Flusser (1998) suggests.

A sociocultural redefinition of the school can lead it to incorporate the new technologies, reaffirming the specific trait of education in modernity, which is that of basing the socialization of knowledge on technologies of intelligence. This is discussed by Sodré (2002), who suggests that the use of the computer in classrooms could be understood as a new form of arts and crafts, in a playful approach to software production. The *bricolage* offered by the culture of simulation allow the appearance of new forms of learning and of resolution of problems that emphasize concrete thinking in relation to the abstract and an exploratory approach to the conceptual, approximating the modes of production of knowledge of adults and children.

Culture and education can be "spaces of emancipation and not only of reproduction, domination and hegemony," observes Belloni (2006, p. 22). This author adds that this perspective for integration of technologies in educational practices in schools can be based on two elements: "the category of *generation*, [which] allows us to perceive the importance of the young, of the new generations, as actors in the construction of the future and of change" and *media education*, that "appears as an unescapable route for the basic education of all children to become complete citizens"(Belloni, 2006, p. 17).

MEDIA EDUCATION AND A CULTURAL PERSPECTIVE OF DIGITAL INCLUSION

For digital inclusion to be implemented in a way that it provides more than simple access to a model of technical education in which students learn to use software and navigate the Internet, an ecological perspective of media education (Rivoltella, 2000) can contribute to another perspective of digital inclusion.

The ecological paradigm of media education presents an integrated concept, which calls for using all the media and technologies available: computers and the Internet in addition to photography, cinema, video, books, and CDs, and for articulating educational proposals with the demands of the communication environment based on each technological innovation in order to integrate them to each other.[21] As much as the computer, Internet, and the World Wide Web are important today, and can even be considered necessary conditions for social insertion and participation, media education is not limited to them. As we have suggested above, it is essential to analyze the needs of each group, project, and context. In this perspective, the objective of media educational work in school is not only the use of the computerized classroom or multimedia laboratory, but for children to act in these and other spaces to establish interactions and build relations and meanings. This mediation should be thought of as a form of affirming corporality—gesture, voice, movement, look—and relationships with nature as essential dimensions for the construction of meanings.

The different forms of citizenship—civil, political, social, and cultural—are challenged by new media in contemporary society, requiring new forms of thinking of education and social inequality. In relation to media education, new emphases are being thought of: one, on a *new media* education, another on a new *media education* (Rivoltella, 2006). The first perspective accentuates that the new media create new educational demands, and that children and young people need other forms of education (medialiteracy, cyberliteracy). The second perspective highlights that with the change in the social role of the media in our society, the paradigm of media education must also change, based on an integrating and nonexclusionary perspective, which seeks responses to the challenges of a society in which the media play central, and not secondary, roles. A new media education aware of these challenges would have to go beyond functionalism and criticism towards, again, a culturalist perspective. For Rivoltella (2006), this hypothesis should depart from technologies of production and of signs to reach the *technologies of self*,[22] in a scenario in which every educator would have to be a media-educator and citizenship would be a central factor.

In the field of media education, the confrontation of the digital divide thus implies proposals for mediation that assure the possibility for a critical and creative appropriation of the technologies, oriented towards the development of authorship in children and young people, their insertion and participation in the culture.

PARTICIPATION IN THE CULTURE AS MEDIATION OF THE DIGITAL DIVIDE

When we emphasize the role of cultural participation in a media education concerned with inclusion we need to make clear what mean by *participation*, since it is a polysemous concept. We think of participation, here: as action of the individual in society, as autonomy and authorship in the political exercise of citizenship. Participation also connotes diversity, plurality, and liberty. It is a strong and politicized word, colored by various values and interests, and for this reason has been subject to different uses or simplifications.

Thinking of participation from the perspective of marginality—as we are doing—we cannot forget that in heteronomous societies such as ours, the excluded are symbolically included, because they are always an implicit or explicit reference, whether present or absent, *participating* in and integrating the same shared imaginary, or that is, the same culture. In this sense, the nonparticipant is paradoxically, a participant. The "outsider" is "inside."

The reconfiguration center-periphery is central to understanding the dynamics of cultural participation in Brazil today. The production of art and culture with the use of digital technologies in poor neighborhoods of large Brazilian cities has taken on increasing social, aesthetic, and economic importance in recent years. According to anthropologist Hermano Vianna, "the most important novelty of Brazilian culture in the past decade was the appearance of the voice straight from the periphery speaking up throughout the country" (2004, p.8-9). This voice is clearly related to the technological possibilities for its amplification and reproduction, which make it a bit more accessible to poor artist communities and collectives, and which are thus able to hear their own music, see their dance, film their stories and histories. A respected analyst of Brazilian culture, Vianna is an enthusiast of *telecentros*[23] (centers of free community Internet access): "the telecenters," he said, "can both produce community and citizen pride in the peripheries as well as connect all these peripheries to each other and to the world, not allowing these conquests to be coopted by political-cultural systems from "outside" or criminal organizations from "within" who only want to make the periphery more peripheral"(Vianna, 2004). He describes how more than 100 telecenters in the city of São Paulo are constantly full of young people, who lose their fear of the computer "treating it as a toy" and, as soon as they become intimate with the machines, come to program them. Since these telecenters work with open-source software, programming is encouraged. "The machines do not have secrets, their codes are open, and whoever wants to investigate the core of its operating system can do so" Vianna explains, reporting a representative example:

This opening led people like Cléber Santos, 18 (whose father is a recently unemployed construction worker –and mother a maid who earns the minimum wage), to frequent the telecenter in the city of Tiradentes (the first inaugurated by the municipal government in 2001), who made various open code programs with the programming resources that he learned totally on his own.

Cléber, who is now a monitor at the telecenter in his "city" (and the fact that he participates in a pioneer project produced his pride of living there), speaks as if it is completely normal to know and have exchanged ideas with Richard Stallman, the father of the world's open-source software movement, the principal creator of this new concept of liberty. I never get tired of admiring this direct connection between the poorest periphery of São Paulo (the telecenters were installed in places with the lowest Human Development Indexes in the city) with the political, cultural, and economic movement that I consider to be the vanguard and most important taking place in the world today. Any other political movement, of antiglobalization or the landless movement, will prove to be inefficient in light of the conquests of free software. Any cultural movement, from punk to Luther Blissett, seems like a "childhood disease" in face of the free software ideology. (Vianna, 2004, p.8-9)

Vianna maintains that the movement has a revolutionary meaning, although it is taking place in near silence.

We can of course question the importance Vianna (2004) attributes to the free software movement, or, at least, await greater evidence of its results. Nevertheless, we cannot ignore that what the author calls "a revolution" is based in fact on a "collaborative and decentralized regime, with no political party in command, but with pieces of code in different computers spread across the planet, commanded by people who work not to get rich, but for the common good" (Vianna, 2004). This is certainly important from the perspective of inclusion. The effervescent production of youth at the Brazilian telecenters, is also highlighted by their public and visible character, an alternative to what is seen as one of the obstacles to the democratization of technologies, which is their invisible and individual use.[24]

Enthusiasm for the telecenters is not unanimous in Brazil, although they are part of most digital inclusion projects.[25] Lemos, for example,

criticizes the idea of the telecenters, arguing that although they are seen as the "new panacea of inclusion" they are nothing more than a palliative to the problem of access and education, because the trend is toward generalized dissemination of the network to all areas (schools, squares, entire cities) "where each citizen, whether they want to or not, will have to deal with connected communication machines" (Lemos, 2003, p. 2). Whatever may be the political form of implantation of technologies in communities, however, the aspect that we want to highlight is the opportunity for artistic and cultural creation, and for participation in social life, that they make possible.[26]

It is in this sense that the digital culture can be understood as a new concept, because "it is based on the idea that the digital technology revolution, is in essence, cultural," according to Gil (2004). This is because the use of digital technology changes the ways people interact socially. Technology is no longer considered simply as a tool, it becomes part of a person's personality and identity. In this perspective, the complete use of the Internet and of free software, for example, creates great opportunities to democratize access to information and knowledge, broaden the potential of cultural goods and services, expand the values that form our common repertoire and therefore, our culture, and also give potential to cultural production, even create new forms of art, Gil (2004) adds. This occurs because the technology itself, as a means for social inclusion, takes on a new form, "not only as incorporation to the market, but as incorporation to citizenship and to the market" when it assures access to information and the reduction of costs of the multimedia means of production, which can broaden the creative potential of the citizen. Considering that this citizen is also a consumer, broadcaster, and receiver of knowledge and information, who has relative autonomy and who is connected in networks, which are a new form of collectivity, this process can redimension his or her participation in the culture.

In the field of education, participation is related to the need for decentralization and democratization of school management, to the social rights of children, adolescents, and youth and to certain concepts of teaching-learning, making it a central concept in recent years based on the perspective of education for citizenship. If the dimension of participation necessarily involves the "other," promoting participation in the school or outside of it implies working on the formation of groups; this brings us to the importance of the group and of situations of cooperative work from the perspective of digital inclusion within the framework of media education.

We can situate this perspective from the social rights of children and adolescents, both the "passive rights" linked to *protection* and *provision*, as well as the "active rights" of *participation*. In order to better elaborate on this theme, we can explore the possible tensions between these 3 Ps and their forms of mediation. How can we protect children's privacy and security while encouraging them to participate in open networks? Will the provision of access to sites, software, and new technologies be done in a restricted way that controls this access or that creates real opportunity to participation in these new media? Is it possible that encouraging the forms of participation of children in the culture involves anticipating certain responsibilities? What are the gains and losses of the different forms of participation of the children in the culture? Are there requirements and presumptions for promotion of participation of children at an active and visible level? How can the participation of children be guaranteed in such a way that there is personal action, self-expression and the establishment of another relationship with time that is less alienated and production-oriented than that which guides the daily life of contemporary urban societies?

A number of educational contexts have sought to support the playful-expressive *participation* of children through teaching-learning games and various opportunities found in daily ac-

tivities. We are speaking here of other modes of participating in society: those in which children interact, communicate, plan, propose, share ideas, intervene, produce, create dialogue, and conduct experiences (Fantin, 2006a). A central objective of these actions is the promotion of agency and of the authorship of children. When we defend the participation of children from a perspective of digital inclusion, it is important to recognize that there are different realms of participation, whether in the space of the global society, social movements, communities, schools, and other cultural institutions or in the intimacy of domestic space. Each of these realms can be a space for critical and creative use of the digital media that promote inclusion.

The participation of children at school, our priority focus, gives new dimension to the paradigms of learning. A new paradigm has emerged in contemporary society: some authors affirm that while the production of knowledge had been principally defined either as acquisition from experience (empiricism) or as construction (constructivism), it can now be understood as participation. Although this thesis may be debatable from an epistemological point of view, since participation is not separated from acquisition and construction, it reconfigures some questions for educational mediation: to go beyond "knowing by doing" and "working cooperatively" a vision of "learning by participating" arises.[27]

Thus, for digital inclusion projects—thought of from their social, economic, technological, aesthetic, and cultural dimensions—be truly inclusive, they need to be linked_to a perspective for cultural-educational mediation, based on interactivity, on citizenship, on access, and on critical and creative appropriation. Although this emphasis may be part of the rhetoric of many projects, most of the programs still appear to be too highly centered on the economic needs. From the concept of participation that we are discussing, and with a cultural understanding of technology access and digital inclusion, educational mediation can make viable some situations of participation, whether in classrooms, laboratories, workshops, or other cultural spaces that the relationship with technology encourages.

One precaution that should be taken in this sense is not to demean the cultural production of children and of young people through the media, qualifying it simply as "social inclusion" actions. It is common, for example, for videos and home pages produced in school and cultural projects in poor regions to be appreciated principally for what they represent in terms of the construction of "self-esteem" of their authors and not for their own merits as forms of art, communication and language. This paternalist posture contradicts the true sense of inclusion, according to which not only do young and poor children have the right to express their vision of the world, but that the entire society has the right to hear what these young people and children have to say. In the Brazilian case, many of the most interesting aesthetic innovations and the most vigorous analyses of the social situation come precisely from "alternative" uses of technological resources invented by groups in impoverished regions from the very lack of more advanced material resources.

The educational proposals that are made to overcome the digital divide will depend on what is understood by a digitally literate person. If only the technical capacity to use the computer is considered, access to computers would be enough. But if a broader concept is adopted, from the perspective of media education and of citizen participation in the culture, which also involves a development of multiple languages, we can propose a few fundamental objectives of the educational and cultural mediations:

1. Competence in reading and writing of various texts and images and their use as social practice.
2. The education of critical and creative subjects who are able to appropriate, read, and write in various media languages through

public access to the multimedia and the Internet in schools and communities.
3. Initial and continued education of teachers for media education. This is essential so that digital inclusion projects are not only palliative measures and episodic campaigns, because without investment in the school perspective and teacher training, the digital divide will continue to be produced.
4. Integration between digital media and the traditional systems of access to cultural production (museums, libraries, film clubs , and artistic workshops) to approximate different generations and trajectories and stimulate the linking of different cultures, broadening the concept of inclusion, with emphasis on the perspective of participation in culture.

It is clear that all of these objectives require specific policies and financing, with an emphasis on the education of and respect for teachers.

Given these objectives, the proposals for digital inclusion from a cultural and educational perspective involve the production of art, knowledge, subjectivity, politics, information, research, and memory, which encourage different types of participation.

In the realm of the classroom they include:

- Various types of peer-interaction (those who know/with those who don't know; those who are eager/ with those who are resistant);
- Different forms of communication between groups (using the various languages and both traditional and new technologies);
- Various forms of organizations of work groups (spontaneous, casual and directed);
- Different spatial contexts, in the classroom and outside of it (to explore the spatial configuration of the classroom; to extend pedagogical encounters to other cultural spaces, such as workshops, museums,

theaters, squares, communities; to explore possibilities for virtual spaces);

- Situations that involve different attitudes (active, passive, critical, collaborative, resistant, indifferent, concentrated, moved);
- Different types of interaction with knowledge and with culture (critical, instrumental, productive);
- Different theoretical-methodological tools for research (observation, interview, video-recording, photography, participant-observation);
- Possibilities for reflection and socialization of the observations made, reflecting on the representations observed;
- Different forms of navigation, interaction and audiovisual production(creation of sites, screenplays, blogs).

In broader realms of participation they include:

- Action in the school: student clubs, meetings for evaluation and class councils, parent, teacher and student associations, management of places for play in the schools;
- Action in the community: resident associations, community councils, cultural associations, youth, artistic, musical, theater, and religious groups;
- Action in the city: student movements, popular movements, NGOs and other forums;
- Interaction in cyberspace: collective action on the Internet, forums and chats, virtual communities.

Finally, the reflections and proposals that we have discussed seek to emphasize that while the economy of the information society is globalized, individuals continue to be local, and that there is an abyss between the global nature of wealth and power and the local significance of individual experiences. We propose the image of educational mediation from the cultural perspective as a possibility for navigation not in a river—which separates and unites—of which we spoke at the beginning, but in a large digital sea. As in the song *Pela internet*, by Gilberto Gil,[28] this kind of mediation involves discovering "with how many gigabytes one makes a *jangada*, a boat that can sail in this info-sea."

We hope to have provided some leads in this direction and an understanding of digital inclusion as construction of citizenship in which media education assures the real participation of children, young people, and adults in the culture. Even if we clearly did not exhaust all the issues involved, the complexity of which are renovated each day, we sought to contribute to the discussion in a tone which, although critical, is also hopeful.

REFERENCES

Adorno, S. (2002). *As cidades brasileiras do século XXI*. São Paulo: Publicação do Centro de Gestão e Estudos Estratégicos.

Almeida, M.E. (2005). Letramento digital e hipertexto: contribuições à educação. In N. Pellanda, E. Schlünzen & K. Schlünzen (Eds.), *Inclusão digital: Tecendo redes afetivas/cognitivas* (pp. 171-192). Rio de Janeiro: DP&A.

Andrade, O. (1928). Manifesto antropofágico. *Revista de Antropofagia, 1*(1)

AZEVEDO, R. (2006). *Formação de leitores, cultura popular e contexto Brasileiro*. Retrieved November 18, 2006, from www.ricardoazevedo. com.br/artigo10.htm

Bazalgette, C. (2005). Media education in Inghilterra: incontro con Cary Bazalgette nel suo ufficio. In *Boletim InterMED,* anno 10, n.3, Roma.

Belloni, M.L. (2006). Infância, Técnica e Cidadania: Cenário de mudanças. Retrieved October 11, 2007, from www.comunic.ufsc.br

Buckingham, D. (2000). *After the death of childhood: Growing up in the age of electronic media.* Cambridge: Polity Press.

Buckingham, D. (2003). *Media education: Literacy, learning and contemporary culture.* Cambridge: Polity Press.

Cadimo, F. (2004). Miragens digitais. Retrieved October 11, 2007, from http:www.fcsh.unl.pt/cadeiras/httv/artigos/Miragens%Digitais.pdf

Castells, M. (1996/2006). *The rise of the network society [A sociedade em rede, vol. 1].* São Paulo: Paz e Terra.

Castells, M (1996/2002). *End of millennium [Fim de milênio, vol. 3].* São Paulo: Paz e Terra.

Fantin, M. (2006). *Mídia-educação: Conceitos, experiências, diálogos Brasil-Itália.* Florianópolis: Cidade Futura.

Fantin, M (2006a). *As crianças interagindo nos cenários contemporâneos: A "escola estação cultura."* Unpublished paper presented at Universidade Federal de Santa Catarina.

Flusser, V. (1998). *Ensaio sobre a fotografia: para uma filosofia da técnica.* Lisboa: Relógio d'Água.

Freire, P. (2000). *Pedagogia da indignação: Cartas pedagógicas e outros escritos.* São Paulo: Editora Unesp.

García Canclini, N. (1989/1998). *Culturas híbridas: estratégias para entrar e sair da modernidade [Culturas híbridas: Estratégias para entrar y salir de la modernidad].* São Paulo: Editora da USP.

Gil, G. (2004). *Aula Magna* at Universidade de São Paulo. Retrieved October 11, 2007, from http://www.cultura.gov.br/noticias/discursos/index.php?p=833&more=1

Green, B., & Bigum, C. (1995). Alienígenas na sala de aula. In T.T. Silva (Ed.), *Alienígenas na Sala de Aula: Uma introdução aos estudos culturais em educação.* Petrópolis: Vozes.

Jobim e Souza, S., Gamba Jr. (2003). Novos suportes, antigos temores: tecnologia e confronto de gerações nas práticas de leitura e escrita In Jobim e Souza, S. (Ed.) *Educação@pós-modernidade: ficções científicas e ciências do cotidiano.* Rio de Janeiro: 7 Letras.

Lemos, A. (2003). Dogmas da inclusão digital. *Correio Braziliense.* Retrieved October 11, 2007, from http:www.facom.ufba.br/ciberpesquisa/andrelemos

Lemos, A., & Costa, L. (2005). Um modelo de inclusão digital: O caso da cidade de Salvador. In *Revista de Economia Política de las Tecnologias de la Información y Comunicación.* Vol. VIII, n.6. Retrieved October 11, 2007, from http:wwweptic.com.br/português/Revista%20EPTIC%20VIII%20-%20AndreLemos-LeonardoCosta.pdf

Martín-Barbero, J. (2002/2004). Ofício de cartógrafo: travessias latino-americanas da comunicação na cultura [*Ofício de cartógrafo: Travessias lationoamericanas de la comunicación en la cultura].* São Paulo: Loyola.

Martin-Barbero, J.(1998). Herdando el futuro: Pensar la educación desde la comunicación. In *Cultura y Comunicación, 9.* Universidad de Salamanca, Salamanca.

Morcellini, M. (Ed.). (2004). *La Scuola della Modernità: Per un manifesto della media education.* Milano: Franco Angeli.

Neri, M. (2003). *Mapa da exclusão digital.* Rio de Janeiro: FGV/IBRE, CPS.

Pinto, M. (1997). A infância como construção social. In Pinto, M. e Sarmento, M. *As crianças, contextos e identidades.* Minho: Centro de Estudos da Criança.

Rivoltella, P.C. (2002). *Media education: Modelli, esperienze, profilo disciplinare.* Roma: Carocci.

Rivoltella, P. C. (2005). *Media education: Fondamenti didattici e prospettive di ricerca*. Brescia: Editrice La Scuola.

Rivoltella, P. C. (2006). *Screen Generation: Gli adolescenti e le prospettive dell'educazione nell'etá dei media digitalli*. Milano: Vita e Pensiero.

Rogoff, B. (2003/2005. *The culture nature of human development [A natureza cultural do desenvolvimento humano]*. Porto Alegre: Artmed.

Santos, L.G. (2003). A informação após a virada cibernética. In L.G. Santos et al. (Eds.), *Revolução Tecnológica, Internet e Socialismo*. São Paulo: Fundação Perseu Abramo.

Schwartz, G. (2000). Exclusão digital entra na agenda econômica mundial. *Folha de São Paulo*, São Paulo, 18 de junho 2000.

Silveira, S. (2001). A. Exclusão digital: A miséria na era da informação. São Paulo: Editora Fundação Perseu Abramo.

Silveira, S. (2003). Inclusão digital, software livre e globalização contra-hegemônica. In S. Silveira & J. Cassino (Eds.), *Software livre e inclusão digital*. São Paulo: Conrad Editora do Brasil.

Soares, M. (2002). Novas práticas de leitura e escrita: letramento na cibercultura. In Dossiê *Letramento, Revista Educação e Sociedade*, n.81. Campinas: Cedes.

Soares, M. (2005). *Letramento: um tema em três gêneros*. Belo Horizonte: Autêntica.

Sodré, M.(2002*). Antropológica do espelho: uma teoria da comunicação linear em rede*. Petrópolis: Vozes.

Sorj, B. (2003). *brasil@povo.com: a luta contra a desigualdade na Sociedade da Informação*. Rio de Janeiro: Jorge Zahar; Brasília: Unesco.

Souza Santos, B. (2002). *A globalização e as ciências sociais*. São Paulo: Cortez.

Taylor, M., & Saarinen, E. (1994). *Imagologies: Media philosophy*. London: Routledge.

Thompson, J. (1995/1998). *The media and modernity: A social theory of the media [A midia e a modernidade: uma teoria social da mídia]*. Cambridge: Polity Press. Brazilian translation, Petrópolis: Vozes.

Vianna, H. (2004). A disseminação silenciosa do software livre. Caderno Mais, *Folha de São Paulo*, 18/04/2004

SUGGESTED SITES

Comitê para a Democratização da Informática: www.cdi.org.br

Comitê Gestor da Internet Brasil: www.cgi.org.br

Cúpula da Sociedade da informação: www.wsis.org

Digital Divide Networks: www.digitaldividenetwork.org

Free Software Foundation: www.fsf.org

From Acces to Outcomes: Digital Divide Report – Morino Institute: www.morino.org.divides

IBOPE - Instituto Brasileiro de Opinião Pública e Estatística: www.ibope.com.br

Internet World Stats: www.internetworldstats.com

Programas do Governo Federal para Inclusão Digital: www.idbrasil.gov.br

Somos@telecentros: www.tele-centros.org.br

UNESCO–Internet Rights Forum: www.foruminternet.org

ENDNOTES

[1]   Sodré observes that there is often a buying and selling of technologically outdated equipment, making it clear that Brazilian and foreign commercial interests are stronger than the needs of civil society.

[2]   Ministry of Communications and the Internet Management Committee of Brazil, 2006.

[3]   INEP/MEC/Pro Brasil 2005.

[4]   Brazil has 15 million illiterate people 15 years or older (IBGE).

[5]   A dimension related to this issue is that of self-learning, which has an important role in the processes of development of multiliteracies.

[6]   Bazalgette (2005) proposed the "3 Cs," culture, criticism, and creation, as three essential aspects of media education.

[7]   Personal notes from the course "Tecnologia dell'istruzione e del aprendimento," given by Pier Cesare Rivoltella, at UCSC, Milano, 2005.

[8]   Internet World Stats, www.internetwordlstas.com

[9]   IBOPE: www.ibope.com.br

[10]   There has been a significant increase in the purchase and use of cell phones among Brazilians of a variety of classes and age groups. Considering that today a cell phone can be a multimedia center, becoming at the same time a camera and a video, a pocket computer with Internet access, and a television receiver and broadcaster, and that Brazil is a country open to new technological developments, this trend can bring new possibilities for digital inclusion. After all, mobile connections are changing the perception of cyberspace, and we are increasingly more "immersed in a nomadism that articulates the space of flow with the space of place." (Lemos, 2003, p.2). The relationship between the multiplication of cellular telephones and digital inclusion is beyond the scope of this study. We merely note this complexity, from a socio-economic as well as cultural perspective.

[11]   See Lemos and Costa (2005, p. 6).

[12]   Analyzing various projects of digital inclusion, Lemos and Costa (2005) maintain that the majority of them emphasize the technical dimension at the cost of the social, cultural, and intellectual.

[13]   See Canclini (1998) and Thompson (1998).

[14]   See Pinto (1997) and Buckingham (2000).

[15]   See, for example, Pinto and Sarmento (1997).

[16]   Reported by MTV Networks, the study was conducted over six months. Interviews were conducted with 5,200 children (ages 8 to 15) and young people from 16 to 34. The survey was conducted in the following countries: Argentina, Germany, Brazil, China, Denmark, the United States, France, India, Indonesia, Japan, Mexico, England, South Africa, and Sweden. Retrieved October 11, 2007, from http://www.multirio.rj.gov.br/portal/riomidia/rm_materia_conteudo.asp?idioma=1&v_nome_area=Materias&idMenu=3&label=Materias&v_id_conteudo=66749

[17]   Noel Gladstone, research of vice-president MTV Networks.

[18]   When the issue is concern for beauty and aesthetics, Brazilians take first place. Nearly 66% of Brazilian children, 50% of Indonesian, and 41% of Mexicans said they are concerned with their weight. For the children of Brazil (93%), Argentina (87%), and Mexico (84%) to take care of oneself is a sign of status. In relation to sex, Latin American youth from 6 to 34 believe they have better sexual performance. Brazilians come in first place, (66%), then Argentines (48%), and Mexicans (46%). The Japanese were last (5%). Terrorism occupied the eighth

place on the list of the main fears of youth today and in tenth place among the children. In general, children and young people said that they are afraid of losing their parents, of having cancer or AIDS, and of frequent crime in large cities. All of these issues are clearly influenced by the representation of these themes in the media, and are thus directly related to the role of media education.

19   See discussion by Jobim and Souza (2003, p. 38).

20   See Martin-Barbero (2000).

21   Various authors have considered the relationship of children with the media in the realm of "cultural ecology." In their philosophy of media, Taylor and Saarinem (1994) maintain that dealing with children means accepting the responsibility for "creating and sustaining structures and networks to support life." In the culture of the media ("simcult"), they add, "this means that we must act to shape and reshape the telecommunications environment that is the world in which our children are destined to dwell." (Taylor & Saarinem, 1994, p. 37).

22   In the Foucaultian sense, stressing here the reflexive practices around media use and consumption.

23   Telecenters are spaces with computers with broadband Internet connections, which offer free use of equipment, basic computer courses, and special workshops. According to the federal government proposal, "each Telecenter has a Management Council, formed by members of the community elected by the community, who help the staff monitor and manage the space. It is a project for intensive use of information technology to broaden citizenship and combat poverty, seeking to guarantee digital privacy and security for the citizen, his insertion in the information society, and strengthen local development. One of the principal objectives of the project

is to organize a network of units of multiple functions that allow people to acquire basic technological autonomy and privacy based on open source software." Retrieved October 11, 2007, from http://www.idbrasil.gov.br/docs_telecentro/docs_telecentro/o_que_e

24   See Graham (apud Lemos, 2005, p.3).

25   There are various examples and the experiences of projects that support the call for digital inclusion in Brazil. In the field of public policy, the Brazilian government sought the integration of existing digital inclusion programs at the federal state and municipal levels, and created the Brazilian Digital Inclusion Model, which was an attempt to improve the activities and avoid the duplication of projects. From the many projects of NGOs, we can highlight the pioneer work of the Committee for the Democratization of Computing. See http://www.idbrasil.gov.br and http://www.cdi.org.br

26   This is even more relevant considering the social reality of the favelas in Brazilian cities. According to Adorno "the thesis that sustains causal relations between poverty, delinquincy and violence, is now highly questioned by many studies. Nevertheless, relations between the persistance, in Brazilian society, of the concentration of wealth, the concentration of the precarious quality of collective life in so-called peripheral neighborhoods in large cities and the general explosion of violence, must be recognized. Maps of violence, created for some Brazilian cities such as Rio de Janeiro, Salvador, Curitiba, and São Paulo (...) indicate that homicide rates are much higher in these areas than in neighborhoods that compose the urban belt better served by urban infrastructure, a labor market and leisure and cultural services." Adorno (2002). "As cidades brasileiras no século XXI." Retrieved October 11, 2007, from http://www.nevusp.org/conteudo/index.php?conteudo_id=367

[27]   See Rogoff (2005).

[28]   Gilberto Gil is a prominent Brazilian
        singer-songwriter and the current Minister
        of Culture.

This work was previously published in Digital Literacy: Tools and Methodologies for Information Society, edited by P. Rivoltella, pp. 310-340, copyright 2008 by IGI Publishing, formerly known as Idea Group Publishing (an imprint of IGI Global).

Chapter V
Cultural Impact on Global Knowledge Sharing

Timothy Shea
University of Massachusetts Dartmouth, USA

David Lewis
University of Massachusetts Lowell, USA

ABSTRACT

This chapter introduces how culture impacts global knowledge sharing. Effective knowledge sharing (KS), one of the four interdependent dimensions of knowledge management (KM), is particularly important in today's global environment in which national cultural differences are negotiated all the time. Knowledge sharing is described along six dimensions and national culture along four dimensions. A model is presented, which provides guidelines for effectively sharing different types of knowledge within different cultural environments. Several examples are presented to illustrate the model's effectiveness. Using the model as a guide, the authors believe that decision makers will increase the chances that information and knowledge will be shared successfully.

INTRODUCTION

Information and communications technology—in particular, when it is used to gather and utilize knowledge—are key to the growth of today's dynamic and highly competitive world economy (OECD, 1996). Companies are under constant pressure to have the right knowledge at the right time in the hands of the right person in order to help increase productivity, be more innovative, and increase competitiveness. Whether a company is coordinating activities among its various manufacturing and sales operations around the world, managing far-flung outsourcing relationships, or engaging in other value chain activities with geographically dispersed companies, companies of the 21st century operate in environments with insatiable needs for collaborating, sharing, and organizing knowledge. As an indication of the magnitude of the situation, more than one-third of world trade is conducted by multinational companies.

Given how organizations today have an unprecedented ability for information coordination through IT developments in ERP systems, global communications, and the like, effective information resource management (IRM) is paramount. One IRM tenet is that organizations need to be able to share information in ways that improve both efficiency and effectiveness. Today, knowledge management (KM) provides a methodology for defining and measuring knowledge needs and implementing an appropriate technical solution. Within KM's typical processes, effective knowledge sharing is particularly important in order for the various business networks to be effective both within companies and between companies (Moller & Svahn, 2003). A company's competitiveness is influenced more and more by its ability to identify and apply its specialized knowledge resources (Bhagat, Kedia, Harveston, & Triandis, 2002). For example, innovations and new ideas often are born out of having the right people in touch with one another.

So, how does an organization create and manage effective KM systems? Moffett, McAdam, and Parkinson (2003) suggest that there has been an over-emphasis on technology issues. Nemati (2002) reaffirms that technology is just one of five major factors that influence knowledge management from a global management perspective: culture, firm strategy and structure, IT infrastructure, organizational/managerial, and industry specifics.

To date, there has been limited research on how cross-cultural issues relate to knowledge management or to knowledge sharing (Ford & Chan, 2003). Therefore, this chapter will focus on cultural impacts and their role and impact on knowledge sharing; specifically, national culture issues, not organizational culture issues. The chapter will review the evolution of KM and knowledge sharing (KS), provide a background on national culture, and explore the impact of national culture on knowledge sharing. The chapter will end with a discussion of future trends in KM/KS and KM/KS research.

BACKGROUND: LITERATURE REVIEW

Knowledge management/knowledge sharing and national culture are areas of research in which each has a large body of work. This section begins with an overview of knowledge management and knowledge sharing and follows with a discussion of literature related to ethnic or national culture.

KNOWLEDGE MANAGEMENT

Knowledge management (KM) initiatives by companies seek to "achieve knowledge integration and benefit from the collective knowledge of the organization through learning" (Mason, 2003, p. 31). More specifically, KM "facilitates the creation, capturing, organization, accessing, and use of an enterprise's knowledge capital," consisting of human capital (e.g., knowledge and skills), structural capital (e.g., systems, processes, and methods), and relational capital (e.g., relationship with customers, suppliers, and external organizations) (Cloete & Snyman, 2003, p. 237). This section discusses what knowledge is, the components of KM, where knowledge sharing fits in, and the goals of knowledge management systems.

The KM literature is comprised of varying views of what KM entails. Early studies referred to improving the information value chain (Rayport & Sviokla, 1995), organizational memory (Walsh & Ungson, 1991), and organizational learning (Huber, 1991). More recently, Grover and Davenport (2001) discussed the KM processes of creation, codification, transfer, and realization. Others describe knowledge acquisition (KA), knowledge documentation (KD), knowledge sharing (KS), and knowledge application (KP) as the four interdependent basic dimensions of the KM process. Nevertheless, organizations are likely to practice KM differently by adopting various tactical and operational implementations of knowledge-related activities (Bhatt, 2001).

Knowledge takes different forms and types, such as explicit and tacit, objective and experience-based, organizational routines and procedural knowledge, general and domain-specific, individual and organizational knowledge, as well as external and internal knowledge. Perhaps the most familiar distinction in the knowledge management domain has been between explicit and tacit knowledge (Nonaka, 1991). Explicit knowledge refers to knowledge that is easily formalized and documented through different tools such as information technology, rules, and procedures. Tacit knowledge, on the other hand, is personal and remains in the human mind, behavior, and perception. It exists in the form of people skills, competences, experiences, and expertise, know-how, and even organizational and national culture. While tacit knowledge is difficult to describe using words (Karhu, 2002), it is argued that since it is difficult to document or transfer, it may be central to a firm's competitive advantage (Ambrosini & Bowman, 2001).

Knowledge management systems (KMS) are information systems that support knowledge management initiatives within and between companies. Today, especially with the impetus of the Internet (and intranets), there is a wide variety of technology tools that support KM, ranging from low-cost and easy-to-install options to expensive options that require a major system development effort (Fichter, 2005; Moffett, McAdams, & Parkinson, 2004):

- **Collaborative tools:** Groupware, meeting support systems, knowledge directories, blogs, instant messaging, and wikis
- **Content management:** Web portals, company intranets, agents and filters, electronic publishing systems
- **Business intelligence:** Data warehousing, data mining, group decision support systems, decision support systems, executive information systems, expert systems

Knowledge management systems (KMS) usage can be supported or hindered by organizational factors (e.g., the workplace culture, whether it is a knowledge-sharing culture or not), supervisory control (e.g., user expectations and management's need for control), system characteristics (e.g., usefulness and ease of use), and the role of the KMS (Fichter, 2005; King, 2006). These characteristics also impact which tools to use for knowledge sharing and collaboration in an organization.

Today, communities of practice (CoPs) are an increasingly popular and effective means for implementing KM and KS initiatives. Similar in some ways to knowledge networks mentioned previously, CoPs are groups that "share a concern, a set of problems, or a passion about a topic, and ... deepen their knowledge and expertise in this area by interacting on an ongoing basis" (Wenger, McDermott, & Snyder, 2002, p. 4). A community of practice has three main characteristics:

- **Domain:** A CoP is not just a group of friends. Involvement in the community requires some knowledge and some competence in the focus area, or domain. The domain is the definition of the area of shared inquiry and of the key issues.

- **Community:** Members of the community interact and learn together. The community is the relationships among members and the sense of belonging.
- **Practice:** The CoP develops as members interact, especially as they solve problems. The practice is the body of knowledge, methods, stories, cases, tools, and documents.

Technically, CoPs often are implemented as Web portals that provide a single point of access for personalized, easy-to-navigate internal and external information content; numerous means for connectivity among the community members (e.g., e-mail, forums); and increasingly, KM components such as capture-and-store, collaborate, and solve-or-recommend. These portals can serve as a network-based memory for the community (Cloete & Snyman, 2003).

Increasingly, communities of practice (CoPs), specifically virtual CoPs, are becoming the heart of a knowledge management (KM) system (Furlong & Johnson, 2003), especially for multinational corporations (Ardichvili, Page, & Wentling, 2003). A well-designed and managed online CoP can speed up problem solving, encourage innovation, and support creative thinking (Chung, 2004). It also can enhance the trust especially critical to colocated teams—trust that supports participation, development of team identity, and interpersonal confidence (Kimble & Hildreth, 2005).

The implementation of KM strategies and initiatives are expected to lead to major cost reductions and performance increases (Cavaleri, 2004). What the organization comes to know explains its performance (Argote & Ingram, 2000). In order for an organization to remain competitive, it must effectively practice the activities of acquiring, documenting, sharing, and applying knowledge to solve problems and exploit opportunities (Sharkie, 2003). However, like most information systems, KM initiatives by themselves are not the end but rather the means.

Thus, KM initiatives provide organizations with opportunities for organizational learning (Stata, 1989), the development of competencies (Alavi & Leidner, 2001), and knowledge integration (Kogut & Zander, 1996).

KNOWLEDGE SHARING

Whether the term employed is knowledge sharing, knowledge transfer, or knowledge dissemination, it is becoming a more and more important part of an organization's competitive advantage. In a world where every year the amount of knowledge is doubling, while at the same time, vast quantities of knowledge are becoming obsolete, and only 5% of employee knowledge is accessible across the company, effective knowledge sharing—in particular, as part of organizational learning—is becoming a more important part of an organization's competitive advantage (Drucker, 1997; Senge, 1997; Wells, Sheina, & Harris-Jones, 2000). Alternatively, knowledge sharing is only worthwhile if the knowledge is worth sharing (Schulz, 2001).

Knowledge sharing (KS) refers to sharing both explicit information as well as tacit information such as beliefs and experiences (Davenport & Pruzak, 1998; Nonaka, 1991). However, Kimble and Hildreth (2005) argue that when the tacit/explicit model is discussed, the primary goal of traditional KM and KS is typically an externalized representation of knowledge; that is, explicit knowledge, such as a report. In their study on the use of CoPs and KM, they found that effective knowledge sharing is actually a duality where sharing harder knowledge, such as a planning document, needs to be integrated with softer knowledge that is accomplished through motivated social processes such as meetings. The goal is to manage a balance of hard and soft processes. According to this viewpoint, the primary value of the KM or KS system comes when the hard knowledge is used as a catalyst for soft knowledge processes such as participation. This is quite different from a context where the focus is predominately on increasing hard or explicit knowledge.

How to support and encourage knowledge sharing (e.g., getting employees to contribute to digital knowledge repositories [the supply side] or to post a question [the demand side]) is an open question. It is a complicated activity that involves resistance; intrinsic and extrinsic motivation; and technical, social, cultural, and organizational issues (Ardichvili et al., 2003; Ciborra & Patriota, 1998; Holthouse, 1998; Osterioh & Frey, 2000; Wakefield, 2005). For example, for individual workers, KS includes evaluating the search and transfer costs before deciding whether to knowledge share or seek knowledge (Hansen, Mors, & Lovas, 2005). Kimble and Hildreth (2005) suggest that common interest, task focus, and deadlines help. Dixon (2000) suggests that people are more willing to share information informally (tacitly) than to contribute to a database (explicitly). McLure and Faraj (2000) suggest that when employees perceive work-related knowledge as belonging to the organization and not to the individual, then knowledge sharing is far more prevalent.

Knowledge sharing (KS) environments and systems can support mutual understanding and trust among different groups that support cooperation and sharing, be it between individuals and team members, within a company, or between companies (Janz & Prasarnphanich, 2003; Larsson, Bengtsson, Henriksson, & Sparks, 1998). Knowledge-sharing applications include databases that enhance the corporate memory through customer data, a repository of past projects, or best practices; facilitating communication among the organization's members, such as shared data maps of internal expertise; and knowledge networks connecting pools of expertise (Alavi & Leidner, 2001; Mason, 2003; Ruggles, 1998). However, current technology is limited. For example, current workflow technology solutions, although quite popular as process-oriented coordination

tools, are limited and will not adequately support coordination for knowledge-intensive business processes such as new product development (Marjanovic, 2005).

In sum, knowledge sharing within and across organizations, while generally acknowledged to be critical for business success in today's world, is a complicated and not very well-understood process. When one adds cross-cultural differences to the mix, the water gets even muddier. The next section discusses the cultural aspect and its relationship to knowledge sharing in more detail.

CULTURE

Culture can be described as the way a group of people does things. Culture includes the values, norms, and attitudes expressed by this group. We can analyze groups along a number of dimensions; the most studied are organizational culture and ethnic culture. Our focus for this chapter is on ethnic culture. When evaluating ethnic culture, an individual's country of residence often is used as a surrogate measure since it is easily quantified. There has been a number of researchers that have tried to identify cultural characteristics, specifically which values and norms are universal and which are dependent on an individual's specific background. We begin by describing three studies and their research findings.

The first major study was conducted by the Global Leadership and Organizational Behavior Effectiveness Research Project Team (Javidad & House, 2001). They identified nine dimensions that distinguish one culture from another: assertiveness, future orientation, performance orientation, humane orientation, gender differentiation, uncertainty avoidance, power distance, institutional collectiveness vs. individualism, and in-group collectivism. To have value in practice, one must be able to relate these dimensions to individual countries. For example, from the Globe Study, the United States was the most performance-oriented, and Russia was the least performance-oriented.

Geert Hofstede performed a much older study in the 1960s and 1970s (Hofstede, 1980). His work identified four dimensions similar to four of the dimensions described previously. These were power distance, uncertainty avoidance, individualism/collectivism, and masculinity. The descriptors of these dimensions are similar to those in the Globe study. His study was large enough so that countries could be placed into clusters; those that reacted similarly to those from other countries were in the same cluster. The Globe study identified nine clusters. Hofstede identified seven with an outlier cluster. Overall, the clustering was very similar.

The third researcher who often is reported in the literature is Fons Trompenaars (1993). He identified four value dimensions: obligation, emotional orientation in relationships, involvement in relationships, and legitimization of power and status. All of these authors and others who since have added their own cross-cultural studies using the same instruments (questionnaires in all cases) have identified cultural profiles for the countries studied. There are relatively few but subtle differences among the country profiles. For example, Harris and Moran (2000) developed a profile of Americans at a glance, including that they tend to be informal, competitive, and individualistic.

While these studies have been useful, there has been some discussion, including whether or not Hofstede's dimensions are appropriate. Walsham (2001) believes that while there are endless individual nuances and differences, there are enough similarities in shared symbols, norms, and values to make national culture a useful distinction. Others believe that using the nation as the unit of analysis is, at best, of limited use; for example, there are often many different cultural groups within a nation. In addition, work-related actions have proved hard to link to cultural attitudes (Myers & Tan, 2002).

More specific to KM, Mason (2003) described how boundary-spanning activities—syntactic, semantic, and pragmatic—could be used to support effective coordination among diverse groups as they developed KM systems. Repositories support the syntactic level by enabling communication of facts, tasks, and actions (knowledge transfer and knowledge sharing). Standardized forms and procedures help to create common standards between groups, supporting the semantic level—knowledge translation. Finally, objectives, maps, and models help to make embedded knowledge explicit, supporting the pragmatic level—knowledge transformation and learning. Kimble and Hildreth (2005) add how social interaction (in particular, face-to-face interaction) is essential to knowledge creation, especially the cultural context.

One study recommends proactive management for more effective cross-cultural work when outsourcing between multinationals (Krishna, Sahay, & Walsh, 2004):

- Using systems such as coordination and control systems to harmonize between outsourcer and supplier.
- Understanding differences in norms and values between cultures, for example, differences in hierarchy/power and business practices.
- Encouraging compromise and a negotiated work culture for cross-cultural teams through training and exchange mechanisms.

While such activities can help, they warn that there are limits to how much one can affect deeply ingrained attitudes and values.

Specific to knowledge sharing, Lam (1997) looked closely at work systems in which a British and Japanese firm had engineer's collaborating in high-level technical work. She found that knowledge sharing and cross-border collaborative work was impeded by many differences in culture, including educational background, approaches to coordination of work, and the way knowledge (in particular, tacit knowledge) was organized and disseminated. Ford and Chan (2003) studied knowledge sharing between a company and its international subsidiary. They found that knowledge sharing was impacted negatively by several cultural differences: multiple languages, heterogeneity vs. homogeneity of the national cultures, and culturally acceptable advice-seeking behaviors.

There are numerous cultural variables that managers must consider when working overseas or sharing information or knowledge overseas. Some of these include management style (democratic vs. autocratic), communication (verbal, nonverbal, noise in the communication process), negotiation and decision making (negotiation styles, negotiator characteristics, characteristics of the negotiation), and motivation or leadership

Diagram 1.

Knowledge Dimensions			
Exp	Explicit	Tac	Tacit
Org	Organizational	Ind	Individual
Gen	General	Spec	Specific
Ext	External	Int	Internal
Same	Employee Level Same	Diff	Employee Level Different
Rich	Media rich	NotR	Medium not rich

Table 1. Knowledge-sharing guidelines

Knowledge Dimensions

Cultural Dimensions	*Tacit/ Explicit Information*	*Organizational/ Individual*	*General/ Specific*	*External/ Internal*	*Employee Level*	*Media Richness*
Individualistic /Collective						
° *Individualistic*	Tacit	Ind	ND	Ext	ND	NotR
° *Collective*	Explicit	Org		Int		Rich
Power Distance						
° *High*	Explicit	Ind	Spec	Int	Diff	Rich
° *Low*	Tacit	Org	Gen	Ext	Same	NotR
Uncertainty Avoidance						
° *High*	Explicit	Ind	Spec	Int	Same	Rich
° *Low*	Tacit	Org	Gen	Ext	Diff	NotR
Masculine / Feminine						
° *Masculine*	Explicit	Ind	Spec	Int	Diff	ND
° *Feminine*	Tacit	Org	Gen	Ext	Same	

(what motivates, which type of leadership style). The next section explicitly addresses how cultural issues can be addressed when facilitating knowledge sharing.

RELATING CULTURAL VARIABLES TO KNOWLEDGE SHARING

Sharing of information, like most managerial functions, is more difficult when cross-cultural differences exist. To date, there has been little research on the impact of cross-cultural factors on knowledge-sharing activities. However, Ford and Chan (2003) suggest that "knowledge sharing may also be the most susceptible to effects of cross-cultural difference within a company" (p. 12). For example, if we are a manufacturing company that is developing a new product using a global team, including members from culturally diverse countries such as China, Spain, and the United States, the chances of miscommunication, misinterpretation, and using the incorrect methods of motivation can increase substantially. Cross-cultural differences may be more important than technical variables, organizational culture, and others when examining the failure of complex projects.

However, if we know something about the knowledge that managers or individuals are trying to share and something about the cultures between which information sharing takes place, we can develop a set of guidelines to improve the chances that knowledge sharing is successful. Table 1 provides guidelines, given specific cultural characteristics for which knowledge dimensions are shared more easily. Managers must be very careful about how they share information if they don't have control over the characteristics of the knowledge or if there exist major differences between the cultures of the managers involved.

For purposes of this chapter, we will focus on the four dimensions developed by Hofstede, as they are clearly the most widely used by management theorists to differentiate cultures. Based on the knowledge management literature described in an earlier section, we have selected six major characteristics of knowledge to relate to Hofstede's cultural dimensions: tacit vs. explicit, organizational vs. individual, general vs. specific, external vs. internal, sensitivity to the employee level, and media richness. Table 1 provides guidelines on how knowledge should be packaged in order to successfully share that knowledge, depending on how a country falls on Hofstede's dimensions and the type of knowledge being shared. We introduce abbreviations as shown in Diagram 1.

We then will provide two scenarios that illustrate the model's predictions.

Note that the proposed knowledge-sharing strategies are hypothesized by the authors and must be verified in future research.

It is important that the reader understand the information in the table. The entries within a cell indicate the relationship between the knowledge and cultural variables. The cell combinations describe recommended strategies for successfully sharing knowledge. If there is a disconnect between the cultural and information variables, it is highly likely that information will be lost, that it will not be shared in either an efficient or effective manner.

An example might help. Managers from two individualistic countries (e.g., the United States and Great Britain) would be less likely to share knowledge, since knowledge often is seen as a form of power, part of the competitive landscape, and an aid to success. Their individualistic cultural perspective would tend toward an individual perspective on who owns the data. Meanwhile, managers from collectivist countries (e.g., Spain and Argentina) would be more likely to see data as belonging to the organization and be more inclined to share the data, perhaps by entering new best practices information based on a recent project experience into a company knowledge portal. Lack of cooperation by someone from an individualistic national culture would not be a matter of ill-intent but rather differing perceptions. Implementation of a common knowledge-sharing technique, such as a knowledge portal, clearly would need to take different forms in the two different cultural environments.

What does this all mean in practice? Using the preferred knowledge-sharing technique will increase the success that knowledge is shared correctly. If countries score similarly on one or more of the cultural dimensions and have control over how knowledge is presented by using the results in the table, they can increase the chances that knowledge will be shared successfully. The following scenarios will illustrate.

Scenario 1

An American automobile firm decides to outsource a number of its business functions. Specifically, it subcontracts its call center to India to handle customer support issues, and it subcontracts its engine production to Indonesia. There is expected to be minimal knowledge sharing between the subcontractors. Mostly, the knowledge sharing will be between the home office of the firm in the United States and its individual subcontractors. Let's examine the type of knowledge that must be shared, using the dimensions defined previously, and cultural characteristics as defined by Hofstede to examine how difficult

knowledge sharing will be in this situation.

Before looking at the issue of knowledge sharing, let's first look at the level of cross-cultural differences between these countries. Based on Hofstede's four dimensions, our bases for describing culture, the differences among these four countries can be seen in Table 2.

Immediately we can see that there are potential cross-cultural issues, especially between the home office in the United States and its subcontractors in India and Indonesia. The countries are different on all four cultural dimensions, opposite for three of them. Thus, when looking at the results in Table 1, Knowledge-sharing guidelines, we must be especially careful when the knowledge-sharing strategies between countries are different. Taking care requires us to understand the preferences of the representatives of the other cultures and to try to adapt to their needs as much as possible. Since, at least on these general dimensions, India and Indonesia are similar, once we have identified a knowledge-sharing strategy for one, we will be able to use that strategy fairly easily for the other. In Table 3, we replicate the knowledge-sharing guidelines table in order to show the preferred knowledge-sharing techniques applicable to this scenario.

Reviewing the chart above, it can be seen that the types of knowledge sharing are likely to be different between the U.S. and Indonesia as well as between the U.S. and India. One interesting example is the high power distance rating for

Table 2. National cultural differences of three countries (Hofstede, 1980)

Cultural Characteristics	Country	United States	India	Indonesia
Individualism/Collectivism		Individualistic	Collective	Collective
Power Distance		Low	High	High
Uncertainty Avoidance		Low	High	High
Masculinity/Femininity		Middle	Masculine	Masculine

India and Indonesia compared to a low power distance rating for the U.S. A high power distance rating suggests a more hierarchical organizational structure in which decisions are made by superiors without much consultation with subordinates, and subordinates are fearful of disagreeing or contradicting their superiors. Knowledge sharing is more often one direction, top down, more limited, and, as seen in Table 1, more explicit. A low power distance rating often will lead to flatter organizations and a more participatory style of management. Knowledge sharing is more likely to be both directions, and the sharing of ideas and opinions (examples of tacit knowledge sharing) will be more prevalent. However, explicit knowledge sharing up the organization may be easier in the high power distance culture. Its employees will adapt more readily to the extra data input demands of a new CRM or ERP system, even if

the extra time mostly supports new management reports. Low power distance employees may be more likely to grumble and procrastinate in response to such requests.

Since the American firm is the home firm, it should do its best to accommodate the style of India and Indonesia in order to help with the successful sharing of information. In this case, information, if possible, should be shared in an explicit and formal way, respecting the chain of command, targeting the individual level; as further indicated in Table 1, it should be very specific in nature, based on internal facts to the organization, aimed at the specific level of the employee involved; and extra time should be taken to make sure that the media is rich, maybe requiring multiple technologies to increase the successful exchange of information.

Table 3. Knowledge-sharing guidelines between the U.S. and India or Indonesia

	Tacit/ Explicit	Organizational/ Individual	General/ Specific	External/ Internal	Employee Level	Media Richness
U.S.						
Individualistic	° Tacit	° Ind		° Ext	° ND	° NotR
High Power	° Tacit	° Org		° Ext	° Same	° NotR
Distance	° Tacit	° Org	ND	° Ext	° Same	° NotR
Low: Uncertainty						
Avoidance	° ND	° Org		° Ext	° Same	° ND
Middle:						
Masculinity/						
Femininity						
India/Indonesia						
Individualistic	° Explicit	° Org	° ND	° Int	° ND	° NotR
High Power	° Explicit	° Ind	° SK	° Int	° Diff	° NotR
Distance	° Explicit	° Ind	° SK	° Int	° Diff	° NotR
Low: Uncertainty						
Avoidance	° Explicit	° Ind	° SK	° Int	° Diff	° ND
Middle:						
Masculinity/						
Femininity						

(Note: India and Indonesia are considered together since they show similar cultural characteristics on Hofstede's dimensions)

Scenario 2

You are a project manager in a software firm whose headquarters is in Japan. Specifically, you work in new product development. You have been given the leeway to search throughout the world for the most highly skilled programmers, and your current team is made up of three Indians, four Russians, six Chinese, two Japanese who are not directly involved in the technical aspects, and an Australian who is one of the original developers of the language you are using for writing the new software. Again, we will use the previously discussed cultural and knowledge dimensions to analyze the difficulty in sharing information in this situation.

The cross-cultural management situation is more complex here, first because there are more nationalities involved (American, Indian, Russian, Chinese, Japanese, and Australian), and second, because there is likely to be communication and knowledge sharing among all of these individuals.

As a starting point, we reproduce the research results for these nationalities on Hertzberg's four cultural dimensions.

In this case, we potentially will have all team members interacting together. The specific ways in which information should be shared thus become much more complex. The first step would be to be to try to identify clusters; that is, countries that seem to share common characteristics. The first attempt indicates that the U.S. and Australia are very similar, and China and India show some similarities. Japan seems not to follow any specific cluster, and we do not have enough data on cultural tendencies for Russia to make any definitive statement. Thus, the cultural characteristics scenario in Table 4 and the guidelines for knowledge sharing in Table 1 would be a good place to start to sort through the complexities and establish knowledge-sharing strategies.

- **Step 1:** When Americans are sharing with Australians, they should provide opportunities to use tacit information; for example, face-to-face meetings or lunches that promote conversations, brainstorming, and sharing ideas. In addition, they should provide access to external information to illustrate their points, be less concerned with mixing employee level, and not be concerned with the level of media richness.
- **Step 2:** When Indians are talking to Chinese, just the opposite would be recommended: use explicit information; for example, establish

Table 4. Country cultural characteristics, scenario 2

Country Cultural Characteristics	U.S.	Russia	China	Japan	India	Australia
Individualism/ Collectivism	Individualistic	Individualistic	Collective	Middle	Collective	Individualistic
Power Distance	Low	No data	No data	Middle	High	Low
Uncertainty Avoidance	Low	No data	No data	High	Low	Middle
Masculine/Feminine	Middle	No data	High	High	High	Low

a formal, weekly, detailed, progress report; talk at the organizational level; use information external to the firm to illustrate points; target the information being shared to the level of the employee; and use rich media to make sure the point is being made.

- **Step 3:** When Americans are talking to all others (excluding Australians), they should keep in mind the preferred strategies of the other cultures and, as much as possible, try to adapt their preferred strategies to the other cultures in order to increase the chance that knowledge will be shared successfully.

- **Step 4:** The organization should conduct awareness training to all group members. This training would sensitize individual participants about cultural differences and preferred knowledge-sharing strategies. Having been sensitized to differences, participants will be more able to identify where conflicts may exist and to take the time to adjust and understand the preferred knowledge-sharing strategies of the other countries. Understanding and adaptability would be key to understanding.

These two scenarios illustrate that there is no ready-made prescription to effective knowledge sharing across cultures. Based on six dimensions of knowledge and four dimensions of culture, we can hypothesize the best strategy for cultures that exhibit certain cultural characteristics, the best way of presenting knowledge to them. However, in most cases, differences will exist, and where these differences do exist, sharing of knowledge may be compromised. Understanding these differences and being able to adapt our own preferred type of knowledge to that of the other culture will increase the chances of successful communication and sharing of knowledge.

CONCLUSION AND FUTURE TRENDS

KM initiatives throughout the last 15 years have been typical of many information system innovations—the focus initially was technology-centric while many of the bugs were worked out, vendors identified marketplaces, and companies explored how to effectively incorporate KM into their organizations. Through the experience of hundreds of companies (along with the additional technical capabilities provided over the past 10 years by ERP systems and their analytics, data warehouses, collaboration tools, Web portals, and readily available high-speed communications), KM is maturing to a point where the focus can move to the how, the why, and the value of KM systems. Nontechnical success factors such as culture (both organizational and the diversity of employees' cultural backgrounds) now can be given the attention they deserve.

However, there is still a need for good theory to help ground research in a cross-cultural context studying information systems, knowledge management, and knowledge sharing. This chapter utilized Hofstede's cultural dimensions as a means for exploring effective knowledge sharing. It also discussed some limitations in using Hofstede's cultural dimensions. One area that may contribute is learning theory, specifically culture-based learning. "Culture is a source of differences in cognition" (Mason, 2003, p. 24). Learning studies have shown that the culture of the individual's initial schooling experience makes a difference in how that individual learns, frames problems, solves problems, and utilizes information (e.g., tables, ordering, plans and maps) (Kozulin, 1998; Mason, 2003). Western-style education's recent experiments with problem-based learning (PBL), especially in the sciences and medicine, are showing promise that it can better prepare students to continue to learn (in different environments) after school than traditional education methods (Jones, Higgs, de Angelis, & Prideaux, 2001; Tien, Ven, & Chou, 2003). Since one of KM's primary goals is to support both individual and organizational learning, learning theory might prove beneficial.

One compelling discussion concerns the ultimate result of the collision of cultures that we are now experiencing. Some argue that the importance of culture and the lasting nature of cultural norms and values will keep the need to understand the impact of organizational and national cultural impacts on cross-cultural work on the front burner for the foreseeable future (Appadurai, 1997; Walsham, 2001). Others suggest that there will be standardization. A small example of standardization would be if English tightens its grip as the standard language for global business. A far greater example would be if cultural differences between organizations and societies largely disappear. If that is the trend, then it would be appropriate for KM implementations to be designed as culture-free (Mason, 2003).

Perhaps culture will be both strengthened and weakened. Fulmer (2003) describes one example in which explicit attention was paid to the native language of the users of a KM initiative. The KM forums supported multiple languages through the use of translators. Shortly, separate regional forums developed, including both Spanish and English language forums. However, over time, the forums standardized on English as the common language for forum participants. This supports Mason's (2003) premise that KM initiatives often include a strong push to standardize and strengthen a shared organizational culture, sometimes at the cost of national culture and ethnic differences.

For the foreseeable future, knowledge management and knowledge sharing in cross-cultural work settings will only increase in importance as globalization continues its relentless march. Those organizations that effectively knowledge share

are likely to positively impact their productivity, innovativeness, and competitiveness. However, it appears that the immediate challenge will not be making the information and communication technology pieces work together. Much of that work has been done. It may well be that the organization that understands and incorporates its cultural diversity will have the key that makes the difference.

REFERENCES

Alavi, M., & Leidner, D. E. (2001). Review: Knowledge management and knowledge management systems: Conceptual foundations and research issues. *MIS Quarterly, 25*(1), 107-136.

Ambrosini, V., & Bowman, C. (2001). Tacit knowledge: Some suggestions for operationalization. *Journal of Management Studies, 38*(6), 811-829.

Appadurai, A. (1997). *Modernity at large: Cultural dimensions of globalization*. New Delhi: Oxford University Press.

Ardichvili, A, Page, V., & Wentling, T. (2003). Motivation and barriers to participation in virtual knowledge-sharing communities of practice. *Journal of Knowledge Management, 7*(1), 64-77.

Argote, L., & Ingram, P. (2000). Knowledge transfer: A basis for competitive advantage in firms. *Organizational Behavior and Human Decision Processes, 82*(1), 150-169.

Bhagat, R., Kedia, B., Harveston, P., & Triandis, H. (2002). Cultural variations in the cross-border transfer of organizational knowledge: An integrative framework. *Academy of Management Review, 27*(2), 204.

Bhatt, G. (2001). Knowledge management in organizations: Examining the interaction between technologies, techniques and people. *Journal of Knowledge Management, 5*(1), 68-75.

Cavaleri, S. A. (2004). Leveraging organizational learning for knowledge and performance. *The Learning Organization, 2*(11), 159-176.

Chung, H. (2004). Deciphering six sigma, KM, and CoP. *Logistics Management, 26*(2), 3-5.

Ciborra, C. U., & Patriota, G. (1998). Groupware and teamwork in R&D: Limits to learning and innovation. *R&D Management, 28*(1), 1-10.

Cloete, M., & Snyman, R. (2003). The enterprise portal—Is it knowledge management? *Aslib Proceedings: New Information Perspectives, 55*(4), 234-242.

Davenport, T. H., & Prusak, L. (1998). *Working knowledge: How organizations manage what they know.* Boston: Harvard Business School Press.

Dixon, N. (2000). *Common knowledge: How companies thrive by sharing what they know.* Boston: Harvard Business School Press.

Drucker, P. F. (1997). Looking ahead: Implications for the present. *Harvard Business Review, 75*(5), 18-24.

Fichter, D. (2005). The many forms of e-collaboration: Blogs, wikis, portals, groupware, discussion boards, and instant messaging. *Online, 29*(4), 48-50.

Ford, D., & Chan, Y. (2003). Knowledge sharing in a multi-cultural setting: A case study. *Knowledge Management Research & Practice, 1*, 11-27.

Fulmer, W. E. (2003). *Buckman laboratories (A)* (Report No. 9-800-160). Cambridge, MA: Harvard Business School.

Furlong, G. P., & Johnson, L. (2003). Community of practice and metacapabilities. *Knowledge Management Research & Practice, 1*, 102-112.

Grover, V., & Davenport, T. (2001). General perspectives on knowledge management: Foster-

ing a research agenda. *Journal of Management Information Systems, 18*(1), 5-21.

Hansen, M., Mors, M., & Lovas, B. (2005). Knowledge sharing in organizations: Multiple networks, multiple phases. *Academy of Management Journal, 48*(5), 3-7.

Harris, P., & Moran, R. (2000). *Managing cultural differences* (5th ed.). Houston, TX: Gulf Publishing Company.

Hofstede, G. (1980). *Culture's consequences: International differences in work-related values.* Beverly Hills, CA: Sage Publishing.

Holthouse, D. (1998). Knowledge management research issues. *California Management Review, 40*(3), 277-280.

Huber, G. (1991). Organizational learning: The contributing processes and literatures. *Organizational Science, 2*(1), 88-115.

Janz, B. D., & Prasarnphanich, P. (2003). Understanding the antecedents of effective knowledge management: The importance of a knowledge-centered culture. *Decision Sciences, 34*(2), 351-384.

Javidad, M., & House, R. (2001). Cultural acumen for the global manager: Lessons from project GLOBE. *Organizational Dynamics, 29*(4), 289-305.

Jones, R., Higgs, R., de Angelis, C., & Prideaux, D. (2001). Changing face of medical curricula. *The Lancelot, 357*(9257), 699-703.

Karhu, K. (2002). Expertise cycle—An advanced method for sharing expertise. *Journal of Intellectual Capital, 3*(4), 430-446.

Kimble, C., & Hildreth, P. (2005). Dualities, distributed communities of practice and knowledge management. *Journal of Knowledge Management, 9*(4), 102-113.

King, W. (2006). Maybe a "knowledge culture" isn't always so important after all! *Information Systems Management, 23*(1), 88-89.

Kogut, B., & Zander, U. (1996). What firms do? Coordination, identity, and learning. *Organization Science, 7*(5), 502-518.

Kozulin, A. (1998). *Psychological tools: A sociocultural approach to education.* Cambridge, MA: Harvard University Press.

Krishna, S., Sahay, S., & Walsh, G. (2004). Managing cross-cultural issues in global software outsourcing. *Association for Computing Machinery, 47*(4), 62-66.

Lam, A. (1997). Embedded firms, embedded knowledge: Problems of collaboration and knowledge transfer in global cooperative ventures. *Organization Studies, 18*(6), 973-996.

Larsson, R., Bengtsson, L., Henriksson, K., & Sparks, J. (1998). The interorganizational learning dilemma: Collective knowledge development in strategic alliances. *Organizational Science, 9*(5), 285-305.

Marjanovic, O. (2005). Towards IS supported coordination in emergent business processes. *Business Process Management Journal, 11*(5), 476-487.

Mason, R. (2003). Culture-free or culture-bound? A boundary spanning perspective on learning in knowledge management systems. *Journal of Global Information Management, 11*(4), 20-36.

McLure, M., & Faraj, S. (2000). It is what one does: Why people participate and help others in electronic communities of practice. *The Journal of Strategic Information Systems, 9*(2-3), 55-173.

Moffett, S., McAdam, R., & Parkinson, S. (2003). An empirical analysis of knowledge management applications. *Journal of Knowledge Management, 7*(3), 6-26.

Moffett, S., McAdam, R., & Parkinson, S. (2004). Technological utilization for knowledge management. *Knowledge and Process Management, 11*(3), 175-184.

Moller, K., & Svahn, S. (2003). Crossing east-west boundaries: Knowledge sharing in intercultural business networks. *Industrial Marketing Management, 33*(3), 219.

Myers, M. D., & Tan, F. B. (2002). Beyond models of national culture in information systems research. *Journal of Global Information Management, 10*(1), 24-32.

Nemati, H. (2002). Global knowledge management: Exploring a framework for research. *Journal of Global Information Technology Management, 5*(3), 1-11.

Nonaka, I. (1991). The knowledge creating company. *Harvard Business Review, 69*(6), 96-104.

OECD. (1996). *The knowledge based economy.* Retrieved November 20, 2005, from http://www.oecd.org/dataoecd/51/8/1913021.pdf

Osterioh, M., & Frey, B. S. (2000). Motivation, knowledge transfer, and organizational forms. *Organization Science, 11*(5), 538-550.

Rayport, J. F., & Sviokla, J. J. (1995). Exploiting the virtual value chain. *Harvard Business Review, 73*(6), 75-85.

Ruggles, R. (1998). The state of the notion: Knowledge management in practice. *California Management Review, 40*(3), 80-89.

Schulz, M. (2001). The uncertain relevance of newness: Organizational learning and knowledge flows. *Academy of Management Journal, 44*(4), 661-681.

Senge, P. (1997). Communities of leaders and learners. *Harvard Business Review, 75*(5), 30-32.

Sharkie, R. (2003). Knowledge creation and its place in the development of sustainable competitive advantage. *Journal of Knowledge Management, 7*(1), 20-31.

Stata, R. (1989). Organizational learning: The key to management innovation. *Sloan Management Review, 30*(3), 63-74.

Tien, C.-J., Ven, J.-H., & Chou, S. (2003). Using the problem-based learning to enhance student's key competencies. *Journal of the American Academy of Business, 2*(2), 456-458.

Trompenaars, F. (1993). *Riding the waves of culture.* London: Nicholas Brealey Press.

Wakefield, R. (2005). Identifying knowledge agents in a KM strategy: The use of the structural influence index. *Information & Management, 42*(7), 34-38.

Walsh, J. P., & Ungson, G. R. (1991). Organizational memory. *Academy of Management Review, 16*(1), 57-91.

Walsham, G. (2001). *Making a world of difference: IT in a global context.* Chichester, UK: Wiley.

Wells, D., Sheina, M., & Harris-Jones, C. (2000). *Enterprise portals: New strategies for information delivery.* Retrieved November 7, 2005, from www.ovum.com.

Wenger, E., McDermott, R., & Snyder, W. (2002). *Cultivating communities of practice: A guide to managing knowledge.* Cambridge, MA: Harvard Business School Press.

This work was previously published in Information Resources Management: Global Challenges, edited by W. Law, pp. 262-281, copyright 2007 by IGI Publishing, formerly known as Idea Group Publishing (an imprint of IGI Global).

Chapter VI
E-Government, Democratic Governance and Integrative Prospects for Developing Countries:
The Case for a Globally Federated Architecture

Jeffrey P. Roy
University of Ottawa, Canada

ABSTRACT

The objectives of this chapter are threefold: first, to provide a conceptual framework for understanding e-government as a set of four interrelated dimensions of public sector change; second, to consider the relevance and applicability of this framework for both developed and developing nations; and third, to explore the interface between domestic and transnational governance reforms in an increasingly digital era. The world in the twenty-first century needs a globally federated governance architecture, the design of which must include social, economic, political, and technological considerations. This strengthened focus on transnational governance systems must also be joined by the recognition of the dysfunctional nature of the present system of bilateral international assistance programs among countries. With improved governance conditions of transparency and trust transnationally — facilitated in part by a much more politically creative and aggressive use of new technologies, the resources allocated by each country across their various recipients would serve both developing nations and the world as a whole if they were pooled and coordinated through new transnational mechanisms.

INTRODUCTION

The objectives of this chapter are threefold: first, to provide a conceptual framework for understanding e-government as a set of four interrelated dimensions of public sector change; second, to consider the relevance and applicability of this framework for both developed and developing nations; and third, to explore the interface between domestic and transnational governance reforms in an increasingly digital era. As developing countries represent our primary interest in this chapter, efforts to meet this latter objective are sought through the prism of developing countries generally and the African continent specifically.

There is much debate within the literature on e-government as to whether digital technologies and the Internet are new tools to be deployed mainly within current public sector structures and traditions, or whether they are inherently more transformational in driving the need for more holistic changes to our systems of democratic governance. Both views have merit — as futuristic visions shape the actions of governments today that remain nonetheless bound by present processes and structures. As a result, reform is likely to be uneven and contested and it is important to have some appreciation of both levels of change. This interface between the internal and external environments, between current practices and processes and new potentials, represents an increasingly important imperative for all levels of government (as well as transnationally, as will be discussed later).

In order to be more precise on the potential scope of e-government, it is useful to turn to one definition adopted by many governments (such as that of Mexico) as of late, namely: *The continuous innovation in the delivery of services, citizen participation, and governance through the transformation of external and internal relationships by the use of information technology, especially the Internet.*[1] This definition is also a helpful starting point in underscoring the links between government and governance both internally within the public sector and externally across all stakeholders, including the public (as customers and citizens). The application and relevance of this definition, however, differs significantly across developed and developing countries for many reasons, including the characteristics of the broader infrastructure of information and communication technologies (ICTs) across society as a whole, as well as the specific shapes and persistence of varying forms of digital divides.

Within this context the next section of this chapter presents e-government's four main dimensions, considering their relevance across developed and developing countries. Drawing upon this framework, the recent evolution of globalization is then explored in terms of the implications for both e-government and public sector reform nationally as well as for transnational governance systems. The specific case of Africa is then examined — with the aim of underscoring some key directions worthy of exploration in order to build stronger forms of governance both domestically and transnationally through e-government-inspired reforms.

FOUR DIMENSIONS OF PUBLIC SECTOR CHANGE

In order to understand e-governments impacts and potential, a framework of four main dimensions of change includes service, security, transparency, and trust (Roy 2006). All of these dimensions are related — directly or indirectly — to the widening presence and rapidly expanding importance of a digital infrastructure encompassing information and communication technologies and online connectivity.

The first two of these dimensions are primarily focused on changes to the internal decision-making architecture of government, in response to pressures and opportunities associated with the Internet. Indeed, delivering services online became the hallmark of e-government during the 1990s, as more and more citizens conduct their personal and professional affairs online, these "customers" of government look to do the same in dealing with state, whether it is paying their taxes or renewing permits and licenses of one sort or another (Curtin, Sommer, & Vis-Sommer, 2003). Although the initial impetus for utilizing online channels to deliver information and services was often financial savings through improved automation and efficiency, many such forecasts proved excessively optimistic due to investment costs and governance complexities (Allen, Paquet, Juillet, & Roy, 2005; Fountain, 2001). Functionality also remains limited, particularly with respect to the processing of financial payments. This is a limitation due in large measure to the concerns about security.

The ability to interact effectively with customers online requires a safe and reliable architecture, particularly for the handling of personal information — such as credit card numbers — that often underpins financial transactions. Yet fostering government-wide capacities for receiving, storing, and sharing secure information is a complex undertaking (Bryant & Colledge, 2002; Holden, 2004). In areas such as health care, the benefits of more efficient and integrated care through networked information systems are dependent on secure and interconnected governance architectures (Batini, Cappadozzi, Mecella, & Talamo, 2002).

Security issues have clearly risen to the top of political agendas as of late, and governments have become conscious that more citizen-centric manners may not always be consistent with a philosophy of friendly and efficient customer service. Security can mean surveillance as well as service. It may entail extracting and sharing information not only in response to requests by citizens, but also as a way to better forecast potential actions and choices. The trade-offs between privacy, freedom, and convenience have therefore become more politicized, particularly

in a post-911 context which has seen the security dimension of e-government expand from a largely technical precursor to better service to a more overarching paradigm of public sector action (Brown, 2003; Denning 2003; Hart-Teeter, 2003, 2004; O'Harrow, 2004; Roy, 2005b).

In terms of the relevance of service and security to both developed and developing nations, there is much common ground. There are many examples from the latter group — including Singapore, Hong Kong, and India — where the pursuit of online service channels has been both vigorous and innovative. In some limited instances, the case for online channels may actually be stronger in developing nations where traditional channels — notably face to face interaction — present numerous hurdles to the citizen including corruption and a lack of geographic proximity (Bhatnagar, 2001; Heeks, 1999, 2002). Yet at the same time, much of the developing world remains hampered by resource, organizational, and political requirements — not unlike but often more pronounced than those present in the most developed countries (Basu, 2004; Ndou, 2004).

The first two challenges shape the way governments organize internally to address opportunities and threats in the external environment. Transparency and trust speak to changes rooted less in the internal structures of government and more in the evolving democratic environment within which governments operate — as the Internet has facilitated the creation of new channels of political mobilization and interaction between citizens and their governments. A fundamental challenge is a clash of cultures between the expectations of an increasingly open and online society and the traditions of secrecy that permeate governments — in both developed and developing world contexts (Geiselhart, 2004). While this level of secrecy varies considerably across different governing regimes; even in democratic countries representational politics coupled with intensifying levels of media and public scrutiny are reinforcing an insular mindset of information control (Reid, 2004). While the emergence of e-government and online connectivity has created a growing recognition of the need for broader democratic reform, difficulties and resistance persist (Coleman & Norris, 2005; Kossick, 2004). A major issue is the notion of trust as a basis for democratic legitimacy — increasingly viewed as eroding in many developed countries while paradoxically, democratization is promoted by these same countries to the developing world (a theme returned to later).

In short, whereas service and security focus primarily on retooling the public sector to better deliver information and services within existing political structures, transparency and trust reflect widening pressures to rethink the structures themselves — particularly from the perspective of public participation. These four dimensions of e-government change are axed on how the public sector makes use of new technologies to better reform both its internal governance and the set of external relationships with all stakeholders. At the same time, however, it is important to acknowledge the other side of the coin, namely the necessity of not only a digital infrastructure across the jurisdiction in question for these stakeholders (notably the citizenry), but also the socioeconomic capacities for making use of this infrastructure to engage with government in either a customer-service-oriented or political-democratic role. This latter challenge is, of course, the Achilles heal for many developing nations, the source of the digital divide globally between the richest and poorest countries (Chen & Wellman, 2003).

Dissecting the "Developing World": Sectoral Balance and Good Governance

In the previous century, the categorization of nations stemmed mainly from political ideology and industrialization. Fukuyama (2004) and others now underscore that today distinctions between countries have more to do with good governance as a more holistic capacity to both facilitate and shape development within national borders in a manner that manages the challenges and opportunities of a globalizing world. There is also broad agreement that the invocation of governance as a national system reflects the existence and relative "co-evolution" of three distinct spheres of personal, organizational, and institutional activities: the market (private sector), the state (public sector or government), and civil society (or community) (Paquet, 1997).

Across such fluid terminology the usage of the terms *e-government* and *e-governance* can be distinguished—with the former in reference to state mechanisms and the latter denoting the fuller set of sectoral processes and institutional arrangements encompassing the three sectors within a jurisdiction as a whole (even as governance will have other meanings and applications within each sector as well). Much of the preceding discussion has focused on e-government and four dimensions of change that carry at least the potential for a state transformation, but this potential is very much intertwined with how a jurisdiction (most often a country) both views and pursues e-governance as a national strategy and the manner by which the three sectors interact and exert influence on one another.

The most obvious example of this relationship is developed countries with failed states unable or unwilling to provide even a basic level of sustenance for their population: in such circumstances, e-government will be a less pressing matter than other more crisis-driven priorities. The role of the state in facilitating a marketplace generally and specifically for ICT production and adoption is also critical to the emergence of e-governance across all sectors, since developing nations that have effectively deregulated state monopolies in favour of competitive environments have enjoyed faster ICT adoption than others (Waverman, Meschi, & Fuss, 2005).

With respect to the private sector and the existence of a clearly established and well functioning marketplace, such conditions also directly shape e-government's purpose and evolution. First, not only is there more likely to be a strong pool of technology providers from the private sector to facilitate public sector adoption and reformation, but e-government will morel likely be viewed as a national development project designed to both benefit from and underpin economic competitiveness for companies as well as the jurisdiction as a whole (Chou & Hsu, 2004). In the most technologically advanced, newly industrialized countries, governments are pressured by maturing industries adopting new technologies into their own production and customer service strategies, thereby shaping public expectations in the realm of state activity. In contrast, in those least developed nations without strong market actors, e-government may be viewed as a process to facilitate private sector development but there is little evidence to suggest that public sector ICT adoption is instrumental in spurring the creation of domestic market activity and demand.

The existence and relative strength of civil society is an equally important variable. Strong community and civic ties have been shown to be powerful enablers of both economic innovation and democratic development and the capacity to create such ties is a central component of an e-governance system that is strengthened by collective learning and adaptation (Coe, Paquet, & Roy, 2001; Goodman, 2005). The degree to which civil society is aligned with the state — or rather opposing it with the aim of political change — varies considerably across jurisdictions (undoubtedly in both developing and developed world contexts), dependent on, for example, the level of online connectivity and the freedom and ability to use it. Conversely, state efforts to monitor and control such usage and generally deploy technology as a means to social containment and the preservation of power existing structures may reflect the view that digital technology is most likely to be used by those in positions of authority to solidify their

positions, at least until the pressure of change is overwhelming (Kraemer & King, 2003).

This latter point speaks to the manner by which democracy has become simultaneously strengthened and weakened by globalization and this somewhat new governance-driven perspective on national development. The strengthening lies in the fact that democratic governance within the state sector is an ideal shared by a widening segment of countries and cultures: conversely, the weakening of the concept comes in its dilution as many different forms of democracy emerge across different sorts of developing countries (while in many developed countries, questions are also raised about the appropriateness of existing institutions). China and India are illustrative as emerging technological powerhouses with important implications for e-government, while the latter functions as the world's largest democracy and the former largely rejects democratic aspirations in favour of a more state-centric development trajectory that has forced the world's largest Western-based technology companies to curtail freedoms and adapt their practices to a uniquely Chinese context.[2]

In sum, the relative strength of a developing country's governance in terms of its state, market, and societal sectors both situates and shapes e-government purpose and prospects for success. At the same time, however, national variables are insufficient in this regard since the actions of developed nations — both in their own domestic environments and transnationally, are also highly consequential (Brown, 2002; Ferguson & Jones, 2002).

SERVICE, SECURITY, OR DEMOCRACY?

In the developed world, when speaking of e-government's transformative potential from within the public sector, the agenda is most often less about changing the nature of democracy and more about improving the business of government via better customer relations (Norris, 2005; Roy, 2005a). This customer-centric focus has chronologically shaped e-government's first decade in many parts of the world — at the national level in particular, where governments have raced (often with one another) to develop online platforms for service delivery (Langford & Roy, 2005). The following quote is illustrative of the manner by which such changes are often viewed as outside of the purview of the typical citizen:

To make e-Government happen requires a complete re-design of the internal operations of the government and the operating systems of the broader public sector. Our I&IT Strategy guides these efforts. However, much of this re-design work is, and will remain, invisible to the general public. (Government of Ontario, 2005)

The notion of "invisibility" is consistent with the service mentality of more efficient, convenient, and integrated service offerings — a mentality based on a characterization of the public as uninterested and intolerant of jurisdictional boundaries (either within or between governments) and more concerned about outcomes. Invariably, public sector organizations are compared and benchmarked with the practices of private sector reforms operating in the electronic marketplace (Curtin et al., 2003). It is largely because of this service orientation and chronological evolution that the notions of transparency and trust — notions that frame democratic reforms, have not fit easily into the e-government plans of developed nations (Mahrer, 2005). Not only is there no obvious organizational apparatus to address such issues from within the government of the day but in many countries, politicians are often uncertain and resistant of e-democratic reforms as a result (Mahrer, 2005).

In contrast, much of the focus on developing countries has been on leveraging e-government as a lever to overcome traditional governance weaknesses, notably an absence of openness, excessive corruption, and weak accountability to citizenries as a result. The following quote is indicative of such an emphasis:

To the extent that increased transparency, accountability and predictability (of rules and procedures) are made priorities, e-government can be a weapon against corruption. (Pacific Council on International Policy, 2002, p. 10)[3]

The reality here is a schism between developed and developing countries in terms of their views of e-democracy for themselves and for one another. While many developing countries are themselves beginning to take the prospects for domestic reforms seriously, linking e-governance, e-government, and stronger democracy (Kossick, 2004), the primarily service orientation of developed countries with respect to their own e-government agendas may, in turn, influence their international assistance efforts aimed to recipient countries in the developing world. The first major e-government initiative in the Philippines undertaken by the Canadian government's development agency underscores this point.[4] Such a danger is compounded by findings stemming from a wider set of e-government initiatives involving project sponsors and knowledge transfers from developed to developed countries: an absence of sufficient cultural sensitivity in crafting e-government within the contours of a localized setting is a common source of failure (Heeks, 2004).

The point here is not to suggest that countries such as Canada are abandoning democratic aims in the developing world, but rather that e-government may well be defined in a very precise way, perhaps more reflective of the service-driven mindset that predominates domestically. While this service orientation alone is unlikely to displace democratic capacity building as a centerpiece of developmental assistance, a combination of service aims with a much stronger emphasis on security may, at the very least, overshadow democratic ideals and improvements in transparency and trust dimensions of e-government. Such a risk is accentuated in the post-911 security orientation of many Western democratic governments — by which the meaning of security has shifted from largely underpinning service capacities to those emphasizing public safety and antiterrorism (Hart-Teeter, 2004; Henrich & Link, 2003; Roy, 2005b). Moreover, while Canada may not be abandoning democratic ideals in this context, one major review of the country's development assistance strategies argues persuasively that efforts to forge a democratic culture in recipient countries are insufficient (Sundstrom, 2005).

The parameters of information management, democratic freedom and technological deployment have shifted considerably due to the 911 terrorist attacks. Many governments have begun exploring bolstered forms of identity management through more technologically sophisticated devices for authentication, such as national identification cards and biometrically enabled passports.[5] The former approach, for example, has been adopted by the British government which plans to introduce such a card by 2008.[6] Hong Kong is currently implementing a new national "smart card" that would serve as an identity link to all public and private transactions conducted electronically. Many other jurisdictions, including Canada and the United States, are presently exploring modified passports that would make use of biometric devices to improve authentication and identity management capacities (Salter, 2004).

This expanded focus on security shifts the bilateral relationships between developed and developing nations, forged through traditional efforts of international assistance in numerous ways. For many Western countries, the exporting of democracy must now compete with the implications of an expanded and more technologically sophisticated security apparatus and agenda, with both domestic and international dimensions (Nugent & Raisinghani, 2002). Accordingly, how

governments in the developed world reorganize domestically — to better focus on security and terrorism prevention — carries important implications for their ability to reach out and engage developing countries (Fitz-gerald, 2004).

This shifting focus also reshapes global governance realities. Sensing a need to adjust, security has recently been positioned at the heart of the United Nation's encompassing framework for global development. As a basis for both reforming and strengthening existing global institutions, UN Secretary Annan recently framed the issues in this manner:

We cannot have security without development; we cannot have development without security; and we cannot have either without respect for human rights. The challenges we face are truly interconnected. Action on each of these fronts reinforces progress on the others. Inaction on any one of them threatens progress on the others. (United Nations 2005)[7]

However, to act effectively on a transnational plane through a shared system of governance requires both levels of political legitimacy and a degree of technological interoperability that are neither in place nor agreed upon by all countries and cultures as warranted. Such issues are likely to determine the emerging set of linkages between developed and developing nations and the degree to which e-government evolves, primarily as a project for more open and democratic government and governance beyond national borders, or one focused more on service improvement domestically and security arrangements based on national bargaining, relative power (politically, economically, militarily, and technologically), and a much less formalized and more secretive set of governance arrangements.

Here lies a key determinant of e-government's future orientation and the sorts of relationships likely to evolve between developed and developing countries (and through what sort of relational mechanisms). The pursuit of security via new informational, digital, and online capacities has little to do with democracy, and the richest countries of the world are aggressively pursuing military defence and security-oriented alliances where democratic openness is secondary to stability through either cooperative or coercive alliances (Barber, 2003; Denning, 2003; Meyers, 2003; Roy 2005b). Yet, a more open networked and interdependent world requires governance capacities in kind. The prospects for e-governance transnationally—and the implications for e-government—thus merit closer attention.

E-GOVERNANCE TRANSNATIONALLY

With respect to transparency and trust, existing international bodies face widening questions pertaining to their performance and legitimacy in a manner not unlike national governments. These questions and pressures are rooted in the emergence of some basic tenants of a globalizing civil society (Norris, 2000, 2005). Moreover, existing institutions, such as of the developing world, viewed as instruments under the dominant influence of western, industrialized countries.

In one sense, e-government alone may not provide much optimism in progress for two reasons since the overarching domestic e-government agendas of developed countries emphasize service and security aims nationally, lessening the prospects for meaningful political innovation and institutional reform beyond national borders. Moreover, the absence of any form of direct global polity means that national governments essentially possess a veto over any meaningful project reform (the strength of which correlates to a country's power internationally).

Despite such blockages, however, reasons are put forth to justify a more hopeful, countervailing movement toward strengthened forms of governance transnationally. First and foremost, the existence and expansion of a global communications infrastructure creates visibility and coverage that provides at least one foundational element of transnational community formation (Ougaard & Higgott, 2002). More than mere awareness, the activism and associational capacities of globally-minded citizens represent an important new dimension of globalization in this new century (Hayden, 2005; McGrew, 2002). Viewed as more credible than either government or industry—and often acting as an interface between developed and developing world, NGO and other associational and nonprofit movements are key stakeholders in this new environment (Aart Scholte, 2002; Edelman, 2005; Selian, 2004).

There may also be the basis for an important alliance between civil society and the private sector in this regard, as the sustainability and stakeholder movements of corporate action have grown in prominence. Much as natural resource companies and industries have adapted their practices to new sustainability frameworks, technology companies have been an important force in addressing the global digital divide (with an eye on potentially expanding markets to the vast majority of the world's population). The values of global openness, responsiveness, and democratization that drive many (but not all) segments of civil society may also serve as the basis of a partnership with multinational corporations prepared to embrace wider stakeholder commitments to global development (Brown, 2002).

While such stakeholder considerations may include philanthropy among them, there is also an important market imperative for such corporate leadership. The rise of e-commerce has brought about a major step forward toward broader global interconnectedness, at least in terms of market structure, organization, and behaviour (Ronchi, 2003). Given that the scope of online commerce is inherently transnational (open to all with Internet access at least), there is a corresponding need to ensure that common structural rules and cultural standards are in place to facilitate the effective working of this expanded market place. At least until September 2001, this market-led expansion of online activity underpinned the emergence of a decidedly unpublicized set of governance mechanisms in order to facilitate the growth and reliability of the Internet. Here Drake defines ICT global governance as "the collective rules, procedures and related programs intended to shape social actors' expectations, practises and interactions concerning ICT infrastructure and transactions and content" (W. J. Drake, 2004, Memo #3 for the Social Science Research Council's Research Network on IT and Governance).

ICANN is perhaps the most prominent governance body in this regard: "Neither a government nor a for-profit corporation, ICANN is a hybrid that interacts with both and with individuals as well" (Geiselhart, 2004, p. 334). This entity has even experimented with direct and digital forms of democracy in electing members to the board overseeing its operations, although the "ambiguities of legitimacy and lapses of transparency and accountability that have characterized ICANN are typical of other attempts at global governance" (ibid). Others argue that ICANN's selection also reveals an explicit strategy to bypass traditional intergovernmental bodies (such as the International Telecommunications Union) in favour of a new organizational structure and style (Drezner, 2004). There is much that is American about this new structure and style — a point not lost on those skeptical of ICANN's ability to serve as a global agent of the public interest:

The US government maintains policy control over the "hidden server" root server that sits atop the Internet's hierarchical domain name system. The server, which is operated by VeriSign under contract with the US Department of Commerce, contains the authoritative listing of all generic and country code Top Level Domains called the root zone file. ... The US government's control of the master root server translates into ultimate authority over much of the institutional organization of the Internet's infrastructure.
A great many governments around the world
are deeply uncomfortable with this unilateral US control, and some even fear the possibility of politically inspired decisions to manipulate, disrupt or terminate their nation's connections to the Internet. ... For its part, the US government repeatedly has stated that it has no intention of transferring its authority over the master server to any entity, although there is some ambiguity as to whether this will remain the policy. (Drake, 2004, Memo#3 for the Social Science Research Council's Research Network on IT and Governance, p. 18)

Although much new focus on ICANN and other bodies underpinning online connectivity exists, from the perspective of international politics, there is also much that is familiar, in particular the uneven power dynamics between countries of greater wealth and influence and those with less. The U.S.'s most recent pronouncement of its intent to maintain control over the Internet's central infrastructure — in contrast to previous pledges that an eventual transfer of authority to a more neutral, multiparty entity reflects ongoing tensions between unilateralism over multilateralism.[8] Moreover, such a stance is reflective of the security mindset trumping democratic considerations with regard to shaping global governance in the Internet Era.

AFRICA'S PROSPECTS FOR REFORM

It is not difficult to succumb to cynicism or pessimism (or both) when envisioning e-government's prospects in the poorest regions of the world, notably Sub-Saharan Africa. Not only do many countries suffer from an absence or unevenness in the functionality of public, private, and civic institutions, in many areas, more pressing issues than technological connectivity and innovation persist — notably famine, disease, war, and general disorder. As current events in the Sudanese region of Darfur, it is not obvious that the rest of the world is prepared to provide as many resources as rhetoric in addressing such pressing matters.

Conversely, a case for optimism rests in part on the growing presence of e-government and e-governance as key elements of reform agendas. Underpinning this movement is the expansion of a telecommunications infrastructure at impressive, albeit uneven, speeds—most notably the penetration rates of mobile phones to growing segments of the African population. Based on the encouraging experiences of African leaders, such as South Africa and Morocco (the former, leading the world in ICT spending between 1992 and 1999, according to Onyeiwu, 2002), and broader continental awareness and interest in ICT-driven transformation, there is some hope that both the global digital divide may be in decline and that ICT-driven reforms can yield strengthened democracies, improved public sector capacities and more adaptive governance systems (Cunningham, 2004; Gough & Grezo, 2005; Kovacic, 2005).

What is also encouraging for many is the growing awareness and activism of all sectors in recognizing the need for more aggressive global action aimed at the least developed parts of the world. Public sector leaders from G8 countries have begun to champion various African-centric initiatives such as debt relief, the dotcom task force aimed at bridging the digital divide, and trade policy reforms. Industry is increasingly active in addressing Africa's plight, and the Summer 2005 concert initiative, Live 8, reflects the mobilization of at least some elements of civil society in favour of stronger global action (in a manner that sought to reframe developmental assistance away from charity to one of duty and responsibility, an important shift in language that is a precursor to a genuine transnational community). The expansion of digital media coverage both online and through other electronic channels—notably television—suggests that it will become increasingly difficult for citizens of the developed world to not be exposed to the plight of poorer countries, while rising levels of commerce and human mobility mean that this exposure is more than mere imagery, as immigration, security, environmental, and global health systems become more closely intertwined.

Yet, in order to leverage such optimism into concrete progress, three systemic blockages must be recognized and overcome. The first blockage is the now familiar theme of national predominance and interest over transnational governance building. Along with the traditional alignment of the "public sector" to national borders (or jurisdictions within such borders), national economies — and their integration and performance in a broader global marketplace — continue to be viewed as the main prism of wealth creation, and democratic governments are correspondingly accountable to their national citizenries for the results achieved primarily within their own borders.

Secondly and somewhat related to the first point, government actions pertaining to specific international issues such as African development and the digital divide continue to be addressed largely through a set of mechanisms that remain country-centric in terms of their functioning and influence. In other words, the persistence of political sovereignty—despite economic and technological interdependence, continues to dominate transnational political processes generally and international assistance efforts most specifically. This ongoing disconnect is illustrated by the Government of Canada's recent decision to "streamline" its development assistance efforts from an existing set of programs that extends to more than 150 countries to a more "focused" group of 25 (still an unreasonably large number of countries for a country spending just over $3 billion in developmental assistance, an amount encompassing managerial and operational infrastructures as well as actual aid delivered; Canadian developmental assistance in Africa accounts for just 2.2% of total aid flowing into the continent from all donor countries.[9]

The third blockage was dramatically underscored by the July 2005 terrorist bombings in London. The overarching importance of security—domestically and internationally—is clearly intensified by such events, fuelling pressures for international cooperation in ways that do not bode well for more openness and democracy transnationally. The manner by which the London bombings stalled momentum for an Africa agenda (at the G8 summit and even more so in the days and weeks that followed) further underlines the severity of such trends for the developing world.

Continental capacities also matter. In North America, for example, prominent observers have made the point that without sustained and specific commitments by Canada and the U.S., involving financial investments and deeper governance ties, Mexico has little hope of narrowing the development gap between itself and its North American "partners" (Pastor, 2003).[10] Pastor's call for more North American governance—itself partly inspired by the European experience (Jorgensen & Rosamond, 2002)—highlights one important aspects of African governance that is often overlooked, namely, the emergence of a continental dimension to African governance—the African Union.[11] Granted the African Union remains in its infancy, by forging a set of shared governance mechanisms that can leverage the knowledge and leadership of Africa's most successful nations with the struggles of the poorest members, the continent can seek strengthened endogenous capacities for action and a greater voice globally.

Perhaps most importantly, a stronger set of pan-African regional governance capacities can continually facilitate greater transparency within and across countries in terms of how developmental assistance is deployed and the sorts of results that are being achieved. Such openness would help overcome a significant barrier in the developed world, namely, the perception that donor aid does not actually reach the people and communities most in need. Moreover, this openness would also apply to developed countries, often criticized for reannouncing the same funding to multiple projects, placing a variety of conditions on the funding itself, or simply not delivering on public pronouncements. Finally, an agreement by multiple countries to endorse and jointly support a pan-African framework would create some basis for lessening the various national objectives and interests that currently permeate bilateral assistance programs in favour of more collective approaches selected, pursued, and evaluated by agreed-upon mechanisms.

The great leap that is required in terms of governance building involves two interrelated elements transnationally and domestically: first, ensuring greater interoperability between national, regional, and global institutions in order to improve transparency, legitimacy, and trust; and second, abandoning the traditional model of international assistance within Western countries (that at present is more shaped by service and security matters) in favour of larger, more ambitious, and better orchestrated mechanisms to design and deliver aid solutions through such an interoperable governance framework. Whereas scholars such as Sundstrom (2005) argue convincingly for a much stronger emphasis on "democratic partnerships" in bilateral development assistance strategies (an emphasis situated more within the realms of transparency and trust than security and service), what is also required is an elevation of such a mindset to continental, pan-regional, and global dimensions.

In this manner, the nexus between transparency and trust (that at present is discomforting for national governments and transnational institutions) can be leveraged as a basis of a new governance ethos encompassing both developed and developed nations—where openness facilitates an expansion of dialogues and pressures for reform (as well as costs for not doing so) in a manner that creates shared awareness and identities and stronger collective forums and more integrated development processes.

A federated global architecture encompassing an emerging African Union is critical since a more exclusive relationship between a subset of donor countries (i.e., the G8, for instance) and Africa would merely facilitate the expansion of other forms of bilateral ties outside of the purview of what should ideally be a more scrutinized and legitimizing approach to governance the world over (as the case of rising Chinese influence in Africa underscores[12]). Moreover, with respect to support for specific e-government initiatives within countries, this sort of federated architecture would help facilitate more sensitivity in both knowledge transfer and project design, reducing the risk of "contextual collision" between developed and developing world (Heeks, 2004).

As a starting point, what is crucial—and now more feasible than ever with the advent of a global telecommunications infrastructure (including online connectivity in limited parts of the world), is to foster a stronger basis for a globalizing polity based on openness and interdependence (Kamel, 2003). In this respect it is important that an analysis of the multiple digital divides within the African continent, as well as the key explanatory factors, suggests that when a country enjoys a healthy and productive mix of governance conditions its capacity to narrow the digital divide is greatly enhanced: chief among them is openness to globalization (Onyeiwu, 2002).

Such findings suggest that a stronger effort to embrace more segments in the world within a common social, economic, and political framework may be an important precursor to not only reducing the digital divide globally, but leveraging this macroreduction into a set of more country-specific trajectories for accelerated capacities for growth, development, and self-governance.

CONCLUSION

E-government is only now entering its second decade. Quite aside from digital reforms inside and outside of government, the challenges confronting the world are vast and complex, but they are also becoming more interdependent. Governance building, nationally and transnationally, is therefore a gradual process requiring patience and persistence, but also adaptability, as today's structures and solutions fall short of tomorrow's requirements.

The world in the twenty-first century needs a globally federated governance architecture, the design of which must include social, economic, political, and technological considerations. The emergence of a more digital and interconnected world creates new opportunities for building communities at all levels. In particular, an online infrastructure may well be the most uniquely powerful force for individual freedom and democracy if embraced as such. Without overstating the case as a shift away from democracy, many developed countries appear more intent on deploying new technologies to further service and security capacities. The signal sent to the developing world is, in this regard, worrisome in light of democracy's uneven support and prospects across this large group of countries. Transparency and trust—the pillars of democratic legitimacy, public engagement, and adaptive governance—must be viewed as equally important segments of evolving transnational governance processes, with the former central not only to countering the inherent secrecy of security-driven processes but also to building sound governance capacities within and among countries.

Finally, the strengthened focus on transnational governance systems must also be joined by the recognition of the dysfunctional nature of the present system of bilateral international assistance programs among countries. With improved governance conditions of transparency and trust transnationally—facilitated in part by a much more politically creative and aggressive use of new technologies and online connectivity, the resources allocated by each country across various recipients would serve developing nations and the world as a whole if they were pooled and coordinated through new transnational mechanisms designed to facilitate socioeconomic and political development through a truly globalizing prism.

ACKNOWLEDGMENT

This article was written while on sabbatical at the University of Victoria's School of Public Administration. The author is grateful for the support provided by the School — and in particular, the research assistance of In-In Pujiyono. The helpful comments of the blind reviewers are also graciously acknowledged.

REFERENCES

Aart Scholte, A. (2002). Civil society and governance. In M. Ougaard & R. Higgott (Eds.), *Towards a global polity*. London: Routledge.

Allen, B. A., Paquet, G., Juillet, L., & Roy, J. (2005). E-government as collaborative governance: Structural, accountability and cultural reform. In M. Khosrow-Pour (Ed.), *Practising e-government: A global perspective* (pp. 1-15). Hershey, PA: Idea Group.

Barber, B. (2003). *Fear's empire: War, terrorism and democracy*. New York: W.W. Norton and Co.

Basu, S. (2004). E-government and developing countries: An overview. *International Review of Law, Computers and Technology, 18*(1), 109-132.

Batini, C., Cappadozzi, E., Mecella, M., & Talamo, M. (2002). Cooperative architectures. In W. J. McIver & A. K. Elmagarmid (Eds.), *Advances in digital government: Technology, human factors and policy*. Boston: Kluwer Academic Publishers.

Bhatnagar, S. (2001). *Enabling e-government in developing countries: From vision to implementation*. Washington, DC: World Bank.

Brown, C. (2002). G-8 collaborative initiatives and the digital divide: Readiness for e-government. In *Proceedings of the 35th Hawaii International Conference on System Sciences*.

Brown, M. (Ed.). (2003). *Grave new world: Security challenges in the 21st century*. Washington, DC: Georgetown University Press.

Bryant, A., & Colledge, B. (2002). Trust in electronic commerce business relationships. *Journal of Electronic Commerce Research, 3*(2), 32-39.

Chen, W., & Wellman, B. (2003). *Charting and bridging digital divides: Comparing socio-economic, gender, life stage, and rural — Urban Internet access in eight countries*. Retrieved May 11, 2006, from the AMD Global Consumer Advisory Board, http://www.amdgcab.org

Chou, T., & Hsu, L. (2004). Managing industry enabled e-government: Lessons learned from the IT industry in Taiwan. *Electronic Government, 1*(3), 335-348.

Coe, A., Paquet, G., & Roy, J. (2001). E-governance and smart communities: A social learning challenge. *Social Science Computer Review, 19*(1), 80-93.

Coleman, S., & Norris, D. (2005). A new agenda for e-democracy. *International Journal of Electronic Government Research, 1*(3), 69-82.

Cunningham, P. (2004). The digital divide and sustainable development in Africa. *International Journal of Technology, Policy and Management, 4*(1), 18-27.

Curtin, G., Sommer, M.H., & Vis-Sommer, V. (Eds.). (2003). *The world of e-government*. New York: Haworth Press.

Denning, D. (2003). Information technology and security. In M. Brown (Ed.). (2003). *Grave new world: Security challenges in the 21ˢᵗ century.* Washington, DC: Georgetown University Press.

Drezner, D. (2004, fall). The Global Governance of the Internet: Bringing the State Back In. *Political Science Quarterly, 119,* 477-498.

Edelman. (2005). *Sixth Annual Edelman Trust Barometer: A global study of opinion leaders.* Retrieved May 11, 2006, from http://www.edelman.com

Ferguson, Y. H., & Jones, B. R. J. (Eds.). (2002). *Political space: Frontiers of change and governance in a globalizing world.* Albany: State University of New York Press.

Fitz-gerald, A. M. (2004). *Addressing the security-development nexus: Implications for joined-up government.* Montreal: Institute for Research on Public Policy.

Fountain, J. E. (2001). *Building the virtual state: Information technology and institutional change.* Washington, DC: Brookings Institution Press.

Fukuyama, F. (2004). State-*building: Governance and world order in the 21ˢᵗ century.* Ithaca: Cornell University Press.

Geiselhart, K. (2004). Digital government and citizen participation internationally. In A. Pavlichev & G. D. Garson (Eds.), *Digital government: Principles and best practises.* Hershey, PA: Idea Group Publishing.

Goodman, J. (2005, March). Linking mobile phone ownership and use to social capital in rural south Africa and Tanzania. In N. Gough & C. Grezo (Eds.). *Africa: The impact of mobile phones* (The Vodafone Policy Series Paper #2).

Gough, N., & Grezo, C. (Eds.). (2005, March). *Africa: The impact of mobile phones* (The Vodafone Policy Series Paper #2.

Government of Ontario. (2005). *E-government.* Retrieved May 11, 2006, from the Office of the Corporate Chief Information Officer, http://www.cio.giv.on.ca

Hart-Teeter. (2003). *The new e-government equation: Ease, engagement, privacy and protection.* Washington, DC: Council for Excellence in Government.

Hart-Teeter. (2004). *From the home front to the front lines: America speaks out about Home and Security.* Washington, DC: Council for Excellence in Government.

Hayden, P. (2005). *Cosmopolitan global politics.* Burlington: Ashgate.

Heeks, R. (Ed.). (1999). *Reinventing government in the Information Age: International practice in IT-enabled public sector reform.* London: Routledge.

Heeks, R. (2002). E-government in Africa: Promise and practise. *Information Polity, 7,* 97-114.

Heeks, R. (2004). *eGovernment as a carrier of context* (iGovernment Working Paper Series #15). Manchester: Institute for Development Policy and Management, University of Manchester.

Henrich, V. C., & Link, A. N. (2003). Deploying Homeland Security technology. *Journal of Technology Transfer, 28,* 363-368.

Holden, S. (2004). *Understanding electronic signatures: The keys to e-government.* Washington, DC: IBM Center for the Business of Government.

Jesdanun, A. (2005, June 30). US won't cede control of Internet computers. *The Globe and Mail.*

Jorgensen, K. E., & Rosamond, B. (2002). Europe: Regional laboratory for a global polity. In M. Ougaard & R. Higgott (Eds.), *Towards a global polity.* London: Routledge.

Kamel, S. (Ed.). (2003). *Managing globally with information technology.* Hershey, PA: IRM Press.

Kossick, R. (2004). *The role of information and communication technology in strengthening citizen participation and shaping democracy: An analysis of Mexico's initial experience and pending challenges.* New York: United Nations Telecommunications Research Program.

Kovacic, Z. J. (2005). A brave new e-world? An exploratory analysis of worldwide e-government readiness, level of democracy, corruption and globalization. *International Journal of Electronic Government Research, 1*(3), 15-32.

Kraemer, K., & King, J. L. (2003). *Information technology and administrative reform: Will the time after e-government be different?* Irvine: Center for Research on Information Technology and Organizations.

Mahrer, J. (2005). Politicians as patrons for e-democracy? Closing the gap between ideals and realities. *International Journal of Electronic Government Research, 1*(3), 1-14.

McGrew, A. (2002). From global governance to good governance: Theories and prospects of democratising the global polity. In M. Ougaard & R. Higgott (Eds.), *Towards a global polity.* London: Routledge.

Meyers, D. W. (2003). Does "smarter" lead to safer? An assessment of the US border accords with Mexico and Canada. *International Migration, 41*(1), 5-44.

Ndou, V. (2004). E-government for developing countries: Opportunities and challenges. *Electronic Journal of Information Systems in Developing Countries, 18*(1), 1-24.

Norris, P. (2000). Global governance and cosmopolitan citizens. In J. S. Nye & J. D. Donahue (Eds.), *Governance in a globalizing world.* Cambridge: Brookings Institution Press.

Norris, D. (2005). Electronic democracy at the American grassroots. *International Journal of Electronic Government Research, 1*(3), 1-14.

Norris, P. (2005). The impact of the Internet on political activism: Evidence from Europe. *International Journal of Electronic Government Research, 1*(1), 20-39.

Nugent, J. H., & Raisinghani, M. S. (2002). The information technology and telecommunications security imperative: Important issues and drivers. *Journal of Electronic Commerce Research, 3*(1), 1-14.

O'Harrow, R. (2004). *No place to hide.* New York: Free Press.

Onyeiwu. (2002). *Inter-country variations in digital technology in Africa: Evidence, determinants and policy implications* (Discussion paper #2002/72). United Nations University, World Institute for Development Economics Research.

Ougaard, M., & Higgott, R. (Eds.). (2002). *Towards a global polity.* London: Routledge.

Pacific Council on International Policy. (2002). *Road-map for e-government in the developing world.* Retrieved May 11, 2006, from http://www.pacificcouncil.org

Paquet, G. (1997). States, communities and markets: The distributed governance scenario. In T. J. Courchene (Ed.), *The nation-state in a global information era: Policy challenges the Bell Canada Papers in Economics and Public Policy 5* (pp. 25-46). Kingston: John Deutsch Institute for the Study of Economic Policy.

Pastor, R. (2003). *North America's second decade. Foreign affairs.* Retrieved May 11, 2006, from the Council on Foreign Relations, http://www.foreignaffairs.org

Reid, J. (2004). Holding governments accountable by strengthening access to information laws and information management practices. In L. Oliver & L. Sanders (Eds.), *E-government reconsidered: Renewal of governance for the Knowledge Age.* Regina: Canadian Plains Research Center.

Ronchi, S. (2003). *The Internet and the customer-supplier relationship.* Aldershot: Ashgate.

Roy, J. (2005a). Services, security, transparency and trust: Government online or governance renewal in Canada? *International Journal of E-Government Research, 1*(1), 48-58.

Roy, J. (2005b). Security, sovereignty and continental interoperability: Canada's elusive balance. *Social Science Computer Review.*

Roy, J. (2006). *E-government in Canada: Transformation for the Digital Age.* Ottawa: University of Ottawa Press.

Salter, M. (2004). Passports, mobility and security: How smart can the border be? *International Studies Perspective, 5,* 71-91.

Selian, A. (2004). The World Summit on the information society and civil society participation. *The Information Society, 20*(3), 201-215.

Sundstrom, L. M. (2005). Hard choices, good causes: Exploring options for Canada's Overseas Assistance. *IRPP Policy Matters, 6*(4), 1-40. Montreal: IRPP.

United Nations. (2005). *In larger freedom: Towards security, development and human rights for all.* New York: Report of the Secretary General of the United Nations for Decisions by Heads of State and Government.

Waverman, L., Meschi, M., & Fuss, M. (2005, March). The impact of telecoms on economic growth in developing countries. In N. Gough & Grezo (Eds.). *Africa: The impact of mobile phones* (The Vodafone Policy Series Paper #2).

ENDNOTES

[1]   Among others this definition was deployed by the Government of Mexico in recent years, though its' precise origins are unknown. The author adopted it as the basis for a recent article that developed the framework of the four dimensions discussed in this section (Roy 2005a).

[2]   Many large American-based technology companies—notably Microsoft, Google and Yahoo, have agreed to filter online content according to local laws in China (filtering or blocking discussion forums and sources pertaining to democracy and other politically sensitive concepts and topics), sparking debate about free speech and the role of the Internet. Defenders of the companies point out that they are merely abiding by local laws, and in engage in similar practises to monitor online behaviour in the Western world that pertains to illegal activity of one sort or another.

[3]   As an illustration, "Mexico's federal government established Compranet for government procurement as part of its efforts to curb corruption by automating procurement processes. By facilitating a process of bidding and reverse bidding online, it seeks to make government purchasing more efficient and transparent. The system allows the public to see what services and products the government is spending its resource von and what companies are providing them with these services. There are more than 6,000 public sector tenders logged daily, and more than 20,000 service-providing firms are regular users. Other countries in the region are looking to imitate Mexico's successful Compranet" (ibid.).

[4]   The Electronic Governance for Efficiency and Effectiveness (E3) Project in the Philippines is a five year, $10 million (Cdn) project (including monitoring and evaluation) designed to increase the awareness of the Government of the Philippines about the value and use of (ICTs) in the social services sector through a combination of: (a) increasing the knowledge and skills of the government, (in

general), to address the strategic and cross-government issues of e-governance and, (in particular), the capacity for targeted social service agencies to strategically plan and implement e-governance projects; and (b) implementing a number of e-governance ICT pilot projects in selected rural areas of the country, designed to demonstrate the sustainable use of ICTs to support and improve the provision of social services in rural areas (e.g. credit assistance, employment, health, education, etc.).

[5] Because biometrics can be used in such a variety of applications, it is very difficult to establish an all-encompassing definition. The most suitable definition of biometrics is: "The automated use of physiology or behavioural characteristics to determine or verify identity" (http://www.biometric-group.com).

[6] The British Government has introduced legislation to establish a new agency by 2008 that would issue both passports and a national identification card, with the cards being compulsory for all citizens by 2013. The card would feature a biometric chip with an identifier unique for each individual, and its purpose is to facilitate better and more integrated access to government services for citizens, while also enabling authorities to counter identity theft, fraud and domestic security threats. Many European countries already use similar cards and there is general interest and a growing commitment to biometrically enabled forms of identification for both passports and domestic mechanisms in many countries around the world, including the United States and Canada.

[7] http://www.unis.unvienna.org/unis/press-rels/2005/sgsm9833.html

[8] The U.S. government said Thursday (30/06/05) it would indefinitely retain oversight of the Internet's main traffic-controlling computers, ignoring calls by some countries to turn the function over to an international body. The announcement marked a departure from previously stated U.S. policy. Michael D. Gallagher, assistant secretary for communications and information at the U.S. Commerce Department, shied away from terming the declaration a reversal, calling it instead "the foundation of U.S. policy going forward … he said other countries should see the move as positive because "uncertainty is not something that we think is in the United States' interest or the world's interest" (Jesdanun 2005).

[9] The Government of Canada has promised to double aid directed to Africa by 2008-2009 (from 2003-2004 levels), an increase with an overall doubling of international aid spending by 2010 (from 2001 levels). Such increases (that would translate into annual aid spending in Africa of roughly $3 Billion) do nothing to alter the argumentation put forth here, a problem further compounded by the range of programs and initiatives managed by the Canadian overseas development agency across areas such as health services, education, entrepreneurship and most recently e-governance.

[10] Pastor's efforts underpin the trilateral vision endorsed by prominent representatives of Canada, the U.S. and Mexico and released by the Council of Foreign Relations (at a time chosen in part to coincide with the North American Leaders Summit in Waco, Texas in March 2005). The trilateral initiative is bold — albeit incrementally so, in proposing to complement more integrative security measures with a new political dialogue and shared economic investment aimed at the collective prosperity of all parts of the continent.

[11] Formerly created in 1999, the African Union (AU) today comprises 53 member nations. Although its institutional composition reflects many aspects of the European Union,

many AU bodies and functions remain more intention than reality, an intuitive reflection of the many decades of growth and deepening of the European project. Details on the AU can be found on its' main Web-site: www.african-union.org.

[12] Many stories of late have circulated in the U.S. media about China's growing activism and economic presence in Africa. A concern raised by some observers, both inside and outside of Africa, is that a form of competitive advantage for Chinese industries exists due to their willingness to ignore issues such as human rights, government corruption, insufficiently rigorous labour standards and other such issues that are predominant in the western world.

This work was previously published in Global E-Government: Theory, Applications and Benchmarking, edited by L. Al-Hakim, pp. 320-339, copyright 2007 by IGI Publishing, formerly known as Idea Group Publishing (an imprint of IGI Global).

Section II
Development and Design Methodologies

Chapter VII
Capacity Development Initiatives for Marginal Communities:
A Few Case Studies

M. Aminul Islam
United Nations Development Program, Bangladesh

Elena Murelli
Università Cattolica del Sacro Cuore, Italy

Frederick Noronha
Bytesforall, India

Hakikur Rahman
Sustainable Development Networking Program, Bangladesh

ABSTRACT

Capacity development initiatives for marginal communities with information and knowledge under the contemporary global scenario perhaps could be one of the effective instruments to make a meaningful change towards sustainable human development in developing countries. Information networking can play a key role in the initiatives toward enhancing opportunities for improved livelihood, health for all, food security, disaster management, and sustainable development. Best practices are already known in this regard such as e-commerce for better livelihood and employment, telemedicine for health, tele-food for food security, early warning for disaster preparedness, and sustainable development network as a comprehensive treatment for the sustainable development. This chapter focuses on how capacity development initiatives for marginal communities work with reference toward achieving the Millennium Development Goals (MDGs) in developing countries. It approaches the issues and concerns related with the empowerment of the marginal communities, problems, and apprehensions in human and social capacity development in the information and communications technology (ICT) sector. A lot more effort is required from governments, NGOs, and other multilateral agencies in order to bring about a sustainable mechanism of ICT planning, implementations, and development in developing countries. This chapter aims at highlighting the importance of ICT development, and the issues and concerns that are related for its expansion in the developing world for securing sustainable development.

INTRODUCTION

The 21st century predominately constitutes an information- and knowledge-based society, where every country hopes to achieve its goal of social and economic development, including education, food security, health, environment, gender equity, and cultural pluralism. However, the most important problem remains attaining and sustaining these goals. Therefore, every continent should concentrate on building its own information society, until a global village is formed.

In contrast to the developed countries that have been steadily capitalizing the rapid pace of information and communications technology (ICT), a large number of developing countries, particularly low-income countries, have failed in the adaptation of these technologies by contributing to the digital-divide (UNDP, 2001). This is also true for rural villages where modern technologies have yet to reach. The majority of people living in rural areas has neither access nor the means to obtain modern ICT because of their low economic position (Gunatunge & Karunanayake, 2004).

For the past seven years, it has been fashionable to speak of the global village, yet the Human Development Report of 1998, published by the United Nations Development Program (UNDP, 1998), indicates that not everyone is a full member of this village. The benefits of globalization have largely gone to the developed and wealthiest nations (Landes, 1998). In fact, information tech-

nology is scarcely available in parts some areas of the developing world. This is especially true for Africa. According to the UNDP report, the 22 nations with the lowest human development index are in Africa.

ICT brings profound changes to every community. It influences how the community knows and understands the world. It changes working methods and the ways in which people communicate. Similarly, it affects how the community accesses and shares it with others and establishes information as an important source of power (Heeks, 1999). By acquiring the equipment and necessary skills to use information effectively, the poor and marginalized population can gain access to power. The Internet can act as the tool to raise their skills and share knowledge-based information among communities.

Even though there have been increased global initiatives to reduce digital divides, the technology gap is expanding at the periphery. An electronic divide is amplifying between developed and developing countries; between reached and unreached, the haves and have-nots, especially in developing countries (Norrish, 1998, 1999). According to the Global Reach (2001) survey, about 218 million of the world's population use English (45%) as their medium of communications, while 266 million use other languages (55%). However, the first cluster is representing a community of English-spoken countries of about 500 million (44%) and the other cluster is representing the rest of the global population of nearly 5,600 million (5%).

Another survey by NUA (2002) found that the number of users connected to the Net is about 605.60 million: World Total 605.60 million, Africa 6.31 million, Asia/Pacific 187.24 million, Europe 190.91 million, Middle East 5.12 million, Canada and USA 182.67 million, Latin America 33.35 million.

It is an indicative picture that Internet subscribers are rapidly increasing in Asia, Africa, and Pacific regions. Thereby, taking pragmatic steps (discussed in following case studies), marginal communities in these regions can be brought under an ICT-based development umbrella. This chapter discusses three case studies that proved to be successful in raising the capacity of the marginal communities through the use of ICTs.

BACKGROUND

ICT can facilitate economic development by availing information to make the choice of development priorities easier and to plan and manage development activities better (Waema, 1996; Robinson, 1998). Many developing countries have made economic management their prime agenda and use opportunities provided by the ICT to overcome the problems of rural poverty, inequality, and environmental degradation (Bhatnagar, 2000). In these countries, it is believed that management of information systems, such as document management, electronic data exchange, file sharing, electronics groups, groupwares, open source software, and the Internet, can lead to innovative planning, and thereby become a means of empowering the communities through raising their capacity (Bhatnagar, 2000; Kiangi & Tjipangandjara, 1996; Traunmuller & Lank, 1996; Gunatunge & Karunanayake, 2004).

At the same time, knowledge networking and information networking are becoming a basic instrument of development society. To substantiate these, ICT development had sped up at a much higher rate than ever before. During previous years the number of Internet subscribers increased many times in the U.S., Europe, and Asia. ICT is providing a dramatic impact on achieving specific social and economic development goals as well as playing a key role in boarder national development strategies. The real benefit is the creation of the powerful social and economic network by improving communication and the exchange of information (Benjamin, 1999; Duncome, 1999).

In the beginning of the information technology revolution, governments in many of the develop-

ing countries were not only slowly catching up with the new communication technologies, but also in a few cases adopted a negative view on the expansion of electronic networks to the community level. At the same time, networking at the civil society level was found to be increasingly challenging to national governments on many issues (Slim & Thompson, 1993). However, as NGO networking within and among countries of common peripheries, as well as in many outreach programs related to marginal people increased over time—mostly through the use of e-mail, private sector TV, radio, and cell phones — their leverage vis-à-vis national governments has also increased.

ICT offers new opportunities for individuals and communities in two ways: one as information consumers and the other as information generators. Through media convergence, ICTs can also build on and integrate the capacities of other media (e.g., cell phone, radio, and television) to cover people at large. This facilitates low-cost infrastructure development, access, and distribution of information, which requires a distributed approach rather than a centralized one (Stillitoe, 1998). There is a need for people-centered ICT institutions in the public and non-profit sectors to seize these new opportunities. With that objective in mind, this chapter recognizes that the key to the impact of ICTs is not technology itself, but the networking and information exchange, with particular emphasis on the information that marginal people need. This chapter focuses on both ICT strategies and program activities with reference to eight broad areas of intervention of Millennium Development Goals (MDGs), including community mobilization, capacity building, information networking, ICT policy issues, sustainability, and ICT applications and research.

The turn of a new century is often marked by reflection on the past and fresh aspirations for a better future. In one way this has been addressed at the global level through the Millennium Declaration, adopted by 189 Member States of the

United Nations at its 55th General Assembly in September 2000. Through the Declaration, some 147 Heads of State and Government reaffirmed their commitment to working together to uphold the principles of human dignity, equality, and equity at the global level, and to reducing poverty.

The Millennium Declaration expresses some targets that the UN is trying to reach in the near future. Target 18 says that "in cooperation with the private sector, make available the benefits of new technologies, especially information and communications technologies to developing countries." The three indicators expressed above are being used to evaluate the case studies included in this chapter.

ISSUES AND CONCERNS

At the outset, promoting a culture of information management and inclusion of new skills has always been considered as a necessity. Human and social capacity development through ICT, aiming at empowering marginal people, involves establishment of targeted, goal-oriented, horizontal and vertical linkages. First, capacity development should be achieved through development at the individual level, then bringing the individuals under a network, and finally through congenial national, as well as international policy support; the whole initiative can be turned towards a result-based outcome. At the horizontal level, each individual should be brought under a network of multi-faceted information blankets for creating a positive change in the marginal society as a whole.

At the vertical level, adequate awareness-raising programs need to be initiated for decision makers, researchers, academics, and stakeholders on the investment assessment in ICT capacity building through formal and non-formal methods. This may include training of development workers incorporating ICTs in their activities with emphasis on training of rural women, youth, and deprived groups. With respect to content and its

applications, it is observed that currently available and practiced networks have limited scope of empowering marginal communities as well as rural uplift. To make it applicable to the community beyond physical access to information, it has to be made timely, retrievable, and easily applicable by a broad range of users, accessible in their own languages and consistent with their need, and it should be demand driven.

To improvise these processes further, needs assessment for information flow in various network layers should be implemented to enable feedback and widen participation in developing these resources with user-specific, locally sensitive content and applications. This calls for piloting, monitoring, evaluating, and documenting of successful and unsuccessful applications of ICTs for the marginal community. From these applications, models should be developed for identifying strategic future investments and replication programs.

SOLUTIONS AND RECOMMENDATIONS

Overcoming the barriers toward empowering marginal communities through information networking vary over place and time, which need to be addressed horizontally and vertically. Literature so far reviewed with respect to policy formulation (Accascina, 1999; Gurstein, 2003; Keniston & Kumar, 2004; UNDP, 2001; World Bank, 2000; Bridges, 2004; OECD, 2004; G8DOT Force, 2001; DFID, 2001; ITU, 2003) indicate that contemporary trends tend to be biased against marginal populations. There is, therefore, a need for broad-based and equitable access to ICTs in areas consistent with the processes of decentralization, democratization, mobilization of targeted population, and policy revisions with good governance. Adequate ICT education and capacity-building programs should facilitate a coalition of stakeholders and organizational partners, in conjunction with other agencies, to develop policies for supporting the application of ICTs to empower marginal communities. Integration of ICT application in achieving MDGs at the community level through networking with marginal communities would be one of the most effective tools to meet the challenge.

To achieve long-term benefit out of ICT integration, ICT initiatives have to be self-reliant and financially sustainable as well. A recent report (UNICTTF, 2004) reveals the fact that development of open and proactive policies for the rural telecommunication sector is attaining considerable demand for expansion of its services at a grassroots level. However, this type of development process should proceed within a social accountability context and specific demand from deprived populations. A portion of revenue from the telecommunications sector can be used to support the expansion of ICTs for the marginal community as well as in rural areas. In turn, there is a need for integration of policies and extended investments to stimulate initial demand for reducing investment risk for rural ICTs. This could include, for example, enabling the potential of e-commerce for rural producers.

At the national level of ICT design, there is a need to develop strategies and planning for rural areas by taking care of the differences in languages, culture, socio-economic conditions, and infrastructure. This should be reflected in participatory needs assessment and development of the technology itself. The forms of information content, including linkages to more conventional communication media such as rural radio, can be thought of as development media. There is also a need to move away from a centrally managed hub of information towards a distributed repository system, which should not assume ownership of information resources that are generated by a variety of providers.

A few cases have been included in the following sections, portraying success stories on ICT initiations for empowering marginal communities.

Case 1: ICT and the Millenium Development Goals (MDGs)

ICTs can be potentially an important instrument of poverty reduction in poor countries which can directly help improve the welfare of the poor through its many innovative applications in the areas of health, education, dissemination of market information, disaster management, and creation of new employment opportunities. Integration of ICT application in achieving MDGs at the community level through networking with the marginal communities would be one of the most effective tools to meet the challenge.

MDGs represent a fundamentally new way of doing business development. They are both a mobilization and accountability tool; a call for action and a means of keeping track of results (WSSD, 2002). Capacity development initiatives for marginal communities towards achieving the MDGs need to establish horizontal and vertical linkages in: (1) development of ICTD strategies and policies; (2) strengthening citizen participation and promoting entrepreneurship; (3) enhancing government capacity and public services; and (4) coalescing stakeholders on global issues for local responses. This includes assistance and capacity development in formulating and implementing ICTD strategies and programs, mainstreaming ICTs, to achieve poverty reduction, democratic governance, sustainable environment, and HIV/AIDS prevention and mitigation strategies. To bridge the gap between local needs and the level of human rights and equity, in particular by strengthening the role of community-based initiatives toward achieving the target of MDGs including poverty reduction, could be learned from the following case study (see Table 1).

Way Forward

It is important to understand whether and how an information network might further marginalize

Table 1. MDG goals and different ICT projects

MDG	ICT projects and challenges
GOAL 1: ERADICATE EXTREME POVERTY AND HUNGER	Grameen Phone in Bangladesh introduced the first of its kind distribution of cell phones to poor women as a source of gainful income earning. Sangam Krishi Sangam (SKS) is a micro credit project in one of the poorest parts of India — the drought-prone Medak District. SKS has developed a robust backend management information system through the use of a smart card to record details of savings and loans. The use of a smartcard enables data collected at the field level to flow seamlessly to top management. Staff, many with only five to 6 years of schooling, are able to easily record data on the smart card through the use of a handheld computer. Smart cards eliminate the need for manual collection sheets and passbooks. This means that SKS staff can multiply their client load to help the micro finance project achieve financial sustainability more quickly. Additional benefits of the smart card include more flexible financial services and stronger financial controls.
GOAL 2: ACHIEVE UNIVERSAL PRIMARY EDUCATION	The Bangladesh Friendship Education Society (BFES) established a knowledge-based comprehensive village development program, including universal primary education through application of ICTs. Katha's poverty alleviation through IT initiative is a project in India that combines educational programs with IT tools to educate the children of the rural poor in computer-based technologies. Katha's IT project focuses on street children. It helps breaking class and caste barriers by expanding the reach of English into poorer communities. Katha's innovative curriculum combines leadership training, holistic learning, and IT skills with traditional subject learning.
GOAL 3: PROMOTE GENDER EQUALITY AND EMPOWER WOMEN	Dimitra in India and SDNP in Bangladesh are working with the aims of highlighting rural women's contributions to their communities and their countries. Both projects seek to promote information exchange, and update and disseminate information on gender and rural development issues. The Dimitra database is accessible in both French and English. It contains profiles on organizations based in Europe, Africa, and the Near East that have organized projects or programs involving rural women and development. Dimitra values local knowledge and works closely with local partners' participation to exchange information on good practices, ideas, and experiences.
GOAL 4: REDUCE CHILD MORTALITY	The tele-medicine program of SDNP in Bangladesh in collaboration with the professional organizations helping women in remote offshore islands for health care for mother and child. The Naujhil Integrated Rural Development Project for Health and Development in India seeks to emancipate women and children below the poverty line. Computerized health records enable that the due date for vaccination is given to the village health worker so that when he/she reaches the village, he/she does not have to look for the users. Other related data are also computerized and are used for pregnancy detection.

Table 1. MDG goals and different ICT projects (cont.)

MDG	ICT projects and challenges
GOAL 5: IMPROVE MATERNAL HEALTH	Creating local digital health content in Ghana, a project aims to create and distribute local knowledge relevant to maternal and child health in a digital format to help the illiterate and semi-literate. Working with local communities in rural Ghana, this research project is testing ways to help the 'push' for local content by building community capacities to create and distribute local knowledge on mother and child health in digital format (Appleton, 1995).
GOAL 6: COMBAT HIV/AIDS, MALARIA, AND OTHER MAJOR DISEASES	Health & Development Networks (HDN) through its HIV/AIDS E-Forums seeks to promote a more effective response to HIV/AIDS and other health- and development-related issues by improving information, communication, and the quality of debate. The HIV/AIDS E-Forums initiative uses electronic networking to increase the number of voices and perspectives in the preparation and follow-up to major HIV/AIDS conferences. Radio was used to promote AIDS awareness in Africa. The entire program in Mozambique was presented by children with their music. Bangladesh has made substantial advances in prevention of cholera and malaria, and near elimination of polio and leprosy through several NGO-driven programs (ASA, BRAC, etc.) and a few government initiatives from the Health Ministry.
GOAL 7: ENSURE ENVIRONMENTAL SUSTAINABILITY	E-governance in the Ministry of Environment and Forest of Bangladesh has brought the Forest Department and the Environment Department under Wide Area Network and linked to all environmental NGOs as well as development agencies that are working together to achieve the MDGs and ensure environmental sustainability in the country. SDNP programs in many countries are also devoted to facilitating public and private sectors in achieving MDG 7.
GOAL 8: DEVELOP A GLOBAL PARTNERSHIP FOR DEVELOPMENT	The Urban Poor Consortium (UPC) in Indonesia is working with marginalized groups to develop strong community-based organizations and networks. The UPC, in collaboration with local communities, has recently launched three radio stations with a broadcast range of approximately 10 kilometers. The community centers are used as the station bases, and are usually managed by unemployed youths of the community. Current programs broadcast have covered religion, health, politics (land rights and updates on the community's ongoing court battles), education, and entertainment. Future programs plan to address substance abuse and domestic violence.

disadvantaged communities, and determine what could be done to mitigate those adverse effects. The concern is how modern ICTs can be utilized to strengthen and develop the information systems for marginal communities in developing countries and contribute to poverty reduction. However, recent trends of information and communication technologies are rapidly consolidating global communication networks and international trade with implications for communities in developing countries.

Despite this, there is a grey area of empirical evidence or analysis on the actual experiences and effects of ICTs upon poor people's economic and social livelihoods. The implications and constraints of existing information systems on poor marginal communities and their intersection with ICTs are also little understood in relation to their livelihoods. There should be a paradigm shift from technology-driven projects to content-driven ones by considering the wider economic, social, and communication demands of marginal communities with a focus on MDGs.

Case 2:
e-HL Project in Bangladesh

In Bangladesh, as in many other developing counties, medical practitioners often operate in relative isolation, dealing with diverse health care needs, poor health care infrastructure for diagnosis and treatment, and limited specialist doctors. Worldwide there is difficulty in retaining specialists in non-urban areas. Tertiary care hospitals are also concentrated mainly in urban areas, where large segments of the population have no access (Murelli & Arvanitis, 2003). Barriers to accessing continuing medical education (CME)

are raised by the remoteness of major academic centers, especially for rural physicians, limited time owned to practice responsibilities, and cost of the CME training.

Limited CME in Bangladesh, isolation of health operators, and the growing need to acquire skills for accessing and critically appraising Web-based medical literature make the use of information and communication technologies increasingly relevant. The e-Health & Learning Project aims to actively promote the idea of accessing Web-based medical guidelines and medical literature as part of the medical practice in developing countries such as Bangladesh. The E-Health & Learning (e-HL) project was financed by the European Commission under the Asia IT&C Program in January 2003 for 15 months. The coordinator of the project is the Center for Research of Applications of Telematics to Organization and Society (CRATOS) of Catholic University in Italy; the

Figure 1. Index page of e-HL Bangladesh Web site

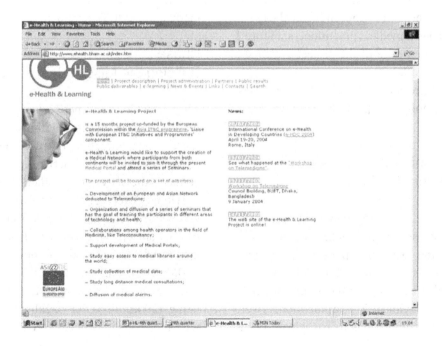

partners are: Birmingham University (UOB), Bangladesh University of Engineering and Technology (BUET), and Sustainable Development Networking Program (SDNP), Bangladesh.

The project aimed to train health operators to keep them informed about new diseases and treatments. The project explored the feasibility of Web-delivered distance learning courses by using the evidence-based medicine (EBM) approach and proposed indicators of educational effectiveness in different types of Web-based seminars. Practicing EBM requires a positive attitude, use of information and communication technologies (ICTs) to access relevant guidelines, reviews and primary literature, and relevant critical appraisal skills (Straus et al., 2000).

The e-HL project activities include the organization and diffusion of a series of seminars on diagnosis, therapy, and prevention of common diseases or other medical conditions relevant to the Bangladeshi population. These seminars attempt to raise awareness about EBM. The seminar themes were accompanied by studying easy access to medical database and improving skills for critically appraising medical literature, and concluded with a discussion room for exchanging information between European medical experts and Bangladeshi medical practitioners. Figure 1 shows the index page of the project's Web site (http://www.ehl-bd.org).

The e-HL project was developed in five phases, described in following paragraphs.

Phase 1:
Collecting Information About
Bangladeshi Clinicians

In this phase 300 medical practitioners were randomly selected from a database maintained by one of the external experts of the project, the Comfort Nursing Home Ltd. in Dhaka. The questionnaire assessed attitudes and practices concerning EBM and ICT. The practitioners were given personal invitations to participate in the survey. Of the 226/300 (75%) who accepted the survey, there were 157 general practitioners, 14 cardiologists, five clinical epidemiologists, eight oncologists, nine orthopedists, 17 respirologists, and 16 gynecologists.

According to the survey, in Bangladesh there is limited access to and use of ICTs. Nevertheless, the practitioners showed a very positive attitude towards EBM and strongly acknowledged the need for further training. However, as noticed in other surveys (Dwarakanath et al., 2000), the respondents' confidence in assessing research evidence did not reflect their ability to critically evaluate medical literature.

This questionnaire survey (Arvanitis et al., 2004) allowed the construction of a database of doctors who were potentially interested in participating in the seminars. A subset of 61 clinicians, out of the total of 226 who replied to questionnaires, was identified according to their limited ICT skills. Those participants more familiar with IT were invited into the third phase of the project — in the Web-based asynchronous interactive seminars. However, a needs analysis phase focusing on Bangladeshi clinicians' views, attitudes, and practice concerning evidence-based medicine and ICTs remained unexplored.

Phase 2:
Building the Missing Infrastructure

The project built two network segments, using a point-to-point radio link with transmitter and a receiver in bi-directional way, with a bandwidth of two Mbps. The first network is in Dhaka and connects the SDNP node with the Comfort Nursing Home, covering a distance about eight km. The second network established is from SDNP node in Mymensingh (120 km away from Dhaka) to a Community Based Medical College and Hospital (CBMCH), about 6 km away from Mymensingh node, creating a length of 134 km (including existing 120 km of SDNP backbone) of radio link with four hops in between (see Figure 2). Figure

Figure 2. Comfort, Dhaka to CBMCH, Mymensingh radio link

2 shows that Comfort in Dhaka reaches CBMCH via SDNP, Dhaka to Bangabandhu Agricultural University, Salna to Rural Electrification Board Mymensingh, Bhaluka to Bangladesh Agricultural University, Mymensingh. India

The total network established by the project was comprised of:

- Janet University Network in the UK connecting UoB to London node;
- HDSL Telecom Network in Italy connecting UCSC to Cilea node in Milan;
- Public network connecting London and Milan nodes to Singapore;
- VSAT connection from Singapore to SDNP node in Dhaka;
- Radio link connection from SDNP Dhaka node to Comfort Nursing Home in Dhaka; and

- Radio link connection from SDNP Mymensingh node to Community Hospital in Mymensingh.

Phase 3:
Making a Comparison Between the Different Technologies Available

In this phase a comparison analysis for delivering content over a public network was done. Particularly, the following technologies were selected and analyzed:

- Specific e-learning platforms,
- Videoconference over ISDN,
- Videoconference over IP,
- Downloading media content,
- Streaming media content, and
- Microsoft Live Meeting.

After various analyses, comparisons, and tests, the streaming technology was selected as the best possible available technology to deliver content under different hypotheses and constraints. Thus, the project choses four streaming solutions to be tested and validated through questionnaire feedback from final users and statistic tests. The seminar typologies (corresponding to different streaming solutions) chosen were:

Real-time streaming, in which a medical expert was filmed while taking a seminar. The captured audio and video are used as input for a Streaming Server. The Streaming Server streams the live audio and video content. A client for each hospital in Bangladesh was connected to the server, and the seminar was displayed with a projector to the doctors in a common room. After the seminar, the doctors could ask questions of the experts using an instant messaging (IM) software.

Recorded media streaming over a public network, where a medical expert was filmed and recorded while taking a seminar, and the audio/video were stored in a file in uncompressed format (e.g., AVI). A media file was produced then made after a post-production phase. The produced file was published on a Streaming Server located in Europe for the streaming experience over a public network. At the time scheduled for the seminar, a computer from each hospital/health center in Bangladesh involved in the project was connected to the Streaming Server with a streaming media player. The seminar was displayed with a projector to the doctors in a common room or watched directly from the doctor's personal computer in his/her office. At the end of the seminar, the doctors and the expert could interact in a synchronous way simply using an IM software.

Recorded media streaming over a local area network is similar to the second method, but in this sequence the produced file was published in a media server located at SDNP node in Dhaka for the streaming experience over a LAN.

Web-embedded streaming content, where the media file from the seminar was published on a streaming server that feeds its content to a Web server containing some specific Web pages written during the post-production phase. The Web pages showed the video link and synchronized with the slides used by the teacher during the seminar. These files were made available on the e-HL medical portal. People from each hospital/health center in Bangladesh involved in the project could connect to the Web portal and access the seminar on their own personal computer whenever they needed. The only requirement in terms of software was having a Web browser installed in their computers. The participants could then ask any questions to the expert by e-mail by starting an asynchronous communication.

Phase 4:
Delivering the Continuing Education Medical Seminars via Videoconference

This was eventually implemented with video-streamed seminars downloadable from the project Web site, in lieu of the planned videoconference seminars, which were technically impossible to deliver.

One of the purposes in this phase was to appreciate the effectiveness and acceptability of interactive video-streamed seminars as a medium for providing continuing medical education in Bangladeshi urban and rural communities. The project linked specialists of the Faculty of Medicine of the Catholic University (UCSC) in Rome, Italy, and of Birmingham University, UK, with a small rural medical hospital (Community Hospital, Mymensingh) and a larger urban private clinic (Comfort Nursing Home, Dhaka) for the provision of continuing medical education.

Eight seminars were delivered to doctors in Dhaka and Mymensingh in Bangladesh. The original plan was to deliver the seminars via videoconference, however a series of technical problems obliged the project to abandon that solution for a less technologically demanding one, video streamed seminars. However, the project delivered the medical seminars on a different selected subset for each group of clinicians using different technologies mentioned before.

The arrangement of video-streamed seminars compromised the interactivity between the lecturer and the participants during the seminar. To moderate this effect, a live interactive question-and-answer (Q&A) session took place after every seminar, using the Windows Messenger platform (a live chat platform). On one side, the questions of the Bangladeshi participants were coordinated by a local seminar assistant and typed into Windows Messenger. On the other side, the lecturer of the seminar responded to the questions online. The chat was projected in the seminar room for all the participants to read.

After the end of the seminar and the Q&A session, the participants were asked to fill in a questionnaire addressing issues related to the delivery, relevance, and resources (e.g., handouts) of the seminar. Their understanding of the seminar content was also informally addressed.

Phase 5:
Data Analysis, Outcomes, and Results

Several indexes were built to show and describe both the level of satisfaction for each seminar/methodology and the quality of the learning experience for the final user. The main outcome from the project showed how the technology used to deliver the seminar can strongly affect the overall level of satisfaction of the end user.

The first two streaming methods (real-time streaming and recorded media streaming over a public network) were evaluated poorly in terms of quality of service by the end users. Hence, the first conclusion was that these technologies are not suitable for medical distance learning in a

context of poor bandwidth and lack of financial resources to adopt more sophisticated technological solutions.

The most significant results came from the comparison between Web-embedded mode and the seminar delivered over a local network. It was noticed that any improvement in favor of the Web-embedded mode was significant when the seminar quality level and seminar available resources were compared. It was producing a notable result when it was considered that in the Web-embedded mode the users were free to access the Web searching for additional resources, whereas in the streaming over a LAN mode they were not given the access to the Internet.

The result could be justified by the lack of skills on ICT of the project target groups. The initial survey showed that 49% of medical practitioners have never accessed the Internet. This data explains how the target group has not understood the Web access as an added value. This demands extensive capacity development of the stakeholders for successful implementation of ICT-driven projects.

Impact of the Project

This project received tremendous dissemination through the medical practitioners and the news media in Bangladesh. It generated a lot of interest among the doctors' community and the general public regarding telemedicine. It will not be an overstatement to affirm that with the implementation of this project, a large portion of the doctors' community and the educated population of Bangladesh have developed considerable awareness about the telemedicine method. Furthermore, as the European commission remained actively associated with this project, it helped to generate a lot of confidence in the minds of the doctors' community and the general public about the success of telemedicine projects in Bangladesh.

Case 3:
Building Low-Cost, Non-Profit Information Bridges: Case Study of a Mailing List in Cyberspace, the Goanet

When a few friends started chatting via the Internet in mid-1994, little did they think their light-hearted banter would lead to a network that linked thousands of expatriates from this former Portuguese colony. Ten years on, it has clearly turned into something larger than anyone dreamt.

Goanet uses old-fashioned technology, that of the mailing list. Like Usenet newsgroups (before it got clogged with all that spam, in particular), mailing lists too can be very useful tools. They are less glamorous than Web sites — at first glance they do not seem as obviously useful as e-mail and definitely not as luring as chat. They are not even buzz words like blogs and wikis currently are. Yet, the simple but priceless tool of mailing lists, which comes from an earlier Internet era, has an important role to play in the developmental debate of the Third World.

Goanet today acts as a link among the Goan diaspora — Goans, who come from the tiny region (3,700 square kilometers and 1.4 million population currently) along western coastal India, which was a Portuguese colony from 1510 to 1961, for over four and half centuries, and has the strongest and most-impactful tradition of migration among most South Asian communities.

Spread across two mailing lists, Goanet (http://www.goanet.org/pipermail/goanet) and Goanet-News (http://www.goanet.org/pipermail/goanet-news), this decade-old venture links an estimated 9,000 readers each day who get their news, meet old friends, discuss and sometimes fight, and even get married via Goanet.

An Academic Perspective

Writing in Social Analysis: Journal of Cultural and Social Practice on the theme of computer-mediated communication, a Goan-expat Alberto G. Gomes takes a detailed look at Goanet. The article was titled "Going Goan on the Goa-Net: Computer-Mediated Communications and Goan Diaspora." (Reflecting its non-hierarchical and loosely knit network, Goanet has been called GoaNet, Goa-Net, and a range of other terms, varying both the case of the alphabet and the use or non-use of the hyphen in the name. As if this confusion was not enough, there are at least three Goanets in Goa today. Besides this mailing list scattered across cyberspace, the Goa government opted to call its own wide area network as Goanet. There is another service offering cable connections to the Internet that also calls itself Goanet, and advertises fairly heavily on local TV channels.)

Currently, the rules of Goanet are simple and few. No foul or abusive language, no personal attacks, and no name calling. Spam is, obviously, not allowed. Attachments are not allowed. Use your real name as the sender of the message, with a meaningful subject line. No posts in HTML or MIME. Post only URL with a brief description from a Web site. No advertisements, and commercial messages have to be paid for. Discussions which go "on endlessly" may be closed. Fundraising on Goanet needs the consent of the Admin team.

Guidelines suggest posting material which is "relevant to Goan communities worldwide" and keeping "your message brief." Private mail is not to be forwarded without permission of the author. Complaints (over dealings with other members) ought to be brought to the Goanet Admin rather than the entire list. Avoid changing subject lines midway through a discussion, or posting admin-related mail to the entire list.

Some of Goanet's archives are located at these sites:

http://www.goanet.org/pipermail/goanet/
http://groups.yahoo.com/group/Goanet2003/
http://groups.yahoo.com/group/Goa-net/

though because of the shifting of servers on which it was based, and poor archiving possibilities on the Internet, specially for mailing lists, earlier on, much of the early archives seem to be unavailable. This is especially true for the 1994-2000 period.

Of a New Generation

As one has argued elsewhere, places like Goanet can be the cyber-kudds of the 21st century. (The kudds were clubs of sorts set up by Goans migrating to bigger cities such as Bombay or Mumbai, where they stayed together, shared experiences and living space, mainly to help newer migrants cope with the harsh realities of the new worlds they were migrating to. Today too, some derelict kudds exist in parts of downtown Bombay.) Just as an earlier generation of Goans set up places for Goans to stay in the hostile environments of a new city (Bombay), networks with Goanet help to build networks that are mutually beneficial, linking people in cyber terms, across the globe, wherever they might have migrated to.

Today, as things stand, Goanet has some plusses and minuses. It lacks sufficient participation from all its membership: like any mailing list, it would have about 5 to 10% of its membership who have ever posted to the list. Women's voices are not much heard. Debates — which sometimes get too personalized or impolite — tend to be dominated by the voices of a few. In such a setting, newcomers tend to be wary of introducing themselves. While Goanet does occasionally talk about building social capital, there is still an overall lack of understanding of what role such networks can play in networking communities, especially those divided by generations of migration and the distance of continents.

But there are other positives: the spirit of sharing still exists. Goanet remains an interesting place through which to keep informed about things Goan. It offers a mix of news and discussion, while the voluntary and not-for-profit nature of this list has its own advantages.

Goanet has also played a role in inspiring other initiatives. It drove home the point that low-cost, simple-tech tools like mailing lists can play an influential and useful role. In its turn, Goanet has influenced the setting up of a number of other mailing lists, within India and beyond. Some of these include this author's network at http://www.indialists.org.

With a minimum budget and loads of volunteer work, an ezine (electronic magazine) was brought out by a retired university librarian in the UK who is maintaining old links and building new ties among the Goan diaspora widely spread out across the globe. Goanet-UK (since converted to GoanVoiceUK, http://www.goanvoice.org.uk) is published weekly by former University-College of London Engineering Librarian Eddie Fernandes, who sends it out to hundreds of readers each week without charge by e-mail. Some months back, the number of subscribers to this list was over 1,400.

Keeping abreast with the latest Net techniques, Fernandes who is in his fifties and who grew up in Kenya though of Goan origin, scours the globe for every small bit of information he can come across relating to Goa. For a community that has been migrating overseas for a hundred years and more, this brings out a variety of news which otherwise most are simply unaware about.

Updates on one recent issue of this list looked at the local Goan community in the east African city of Mombasa celebrating the 100th anniversary of their club there, and the municipal corporation of Lisbon giving a new purpose-built headquarters for an association of Goans settled there.

There were links to the Goans of Arusha (GOA), and a goa_youth network set up on http://www.yahoogroups.com.

Reports meanwhile spoke of how the Goans in Toronto celebrated the feast of 16th-century Catholic Saint Francis Xavier. (Goa has a significant Catholic minority, and most who migrated internationally from this region are of this religious affiliation, meaning they are often mistakenly not recognized as South Asian).

This ezine also manages to keep Goans in touch with community events — whether it is a shopping trip by UK Goans to France, or the Young London Goans Social Salsa Nite organized recently in Middlesex, UK. Treading its unusual path, it breaks new ground in low-cost, community-run media initiatives in a world where the Internet is opening up new possibilities.

What Makes It Different?

Other Goa-related ventures have also come up in cyberspace; a few were formed around the same time or earlier than Goanet. Goa-Web, an Internet site now amalgamated with another site to form Goacom (http://www.goacom.com), was the first elaborate Web site devoted to Goan issues and information. Then there is Goenkar (http://www.goenkar.com), set up by Joseph "Boogie" Viegas and currently run by Mario Alvares.

For those interested in research in Goa, there is a Web site, Goa Research Net (http://www.goenkar.com), which focuses on research themes in Goa. In 1999, there was a proliferation of new Web sites with at least six new sites and a number of mergers. A new site called GOYAN (http://www.goacom.com/goyan), which stands for Goan Young Adult Network, was established for young Goans in North America.

While many of the earlier-generation sites pertaining to Goa were clearly directed to non-resident Goans and travelers who might be lured to this coastal destination, almost all the Web sites provide a range of information from news from Goa to advertisements of real estate, hotels, and travel agents in Goa. On Yahoogroups.com, a search for the word Goa at one point resulted in 511 hits (with some false-positives wholly unconnected to Goa).

What makes Goanet different is its non-commercial nature (though admittedly there are other prominent ventures which are also non-commercial), its ability to run 10 years on volunteer-driven lines, and the fact that it seeks to build itself through a participative network.

Volunteers play the main role in keeping Goanet going. In February 2004, the first advertisement on Goanet was accepted, and this is still an insignificant factor in the network. Appeals have been made to volunteers to help publicize the lists, volunteer their time, encourage "the newer and silent members" to post to the lists, send in e-mail addresses of people who might be interested in signing up, and overall giving feedback.

Goanetters have been involved in organizing some ventures to benefit their home state — including campaigning against pedophilia, lobbying for better Internet access, building a computers-for-schools initiative back home, and networking between the diaspora and the resident population in a way that is often easy to overlook. It has acted as a channel for building links among various specialized interests of Goans and a tool for mobilizing overseas expat populations.

Carneiro estimates that Goanet is read by expat Goans in about 50 countries globally. Subsequent to the formation of Goanet, other mailing lists have also been set up and host discussions by diasporic Goans. Some like Goa-Goans and GoanCauses (both on Yahoogroups) are general purpose discussion lists. Others are being set up to focus on certain villages (like Vasco, Sancoale-Cortalim, or Saligao) and yet others on issues (education, gardens and horticulture issues, etc.).

Case 4:
Capacity Development Initiative at the Grassroots: e-SriLanka

Rationale

Sri Lanka is categorized as a dynamic adopter in ICT (HRD, 2001), and has been ranked 71 among 104 countries in the networked readiness index ranking (Global IT Report, 2004-2005). It is among the developing nations that have made impressive growth in the communication infrastructure (David & Liyanage, 2004). During the period of 1999-2002, the number of Internet users has doubled, and personal computer users have increased by 130% (ITU, 2002).

However, like in many other developing countries, a majority of the progress is being confined to the urban areas. It is estimated that about 90% of the Internet users are in the capital of Colombo and 70% of landline telephones are in the Western province (Gunawardana & Wattegama, 2004). Furthermore, according to the census of 2002, the urban sector scored 1.7 on the poverty gap index, while the rural and plantation sectors scored 5.6 and 6.0 respectively (David & Liyanage, 2004). Hence, by looking at a wider socio-economic environment, an inner-country digital divide seems inevitable.

To improve the ICT perspectives within the country, Sri Lanka has made significant strides in telecommunications liberalization since the inception of sector reforms in 1991. An important step in this context is the enactment of the Sri Lanka Telecommunications Act in 1991, which has separated the policy and business wings of the Ministry of Post and Telecommunications, and carved out Sri Lanka Telecom (SLT) as a separate entity.

In 1996, SunTel and Lanka Bell were issued local loop licenses utilizing Wireless Local Loop (WLL) technology, and in 1997 the government divested 35% of its stake in SLT to the Japanese company NTT (Zita & Kapur, 2004). The vision of the National Information Technology Policy (NITP, 2002) of Sri Lanka envisages providing information on the country to the world at large and as a tool for the acquisition of information as one of its objectives. In order to achieve this objective successfully, they have realized that human resource development must be enacted into the policy decisions. Along this perspective, with several other policy initiations, at the end of 2003, the Sri Lankan Parliament passed an act to create a new implementing agency, namely the Information and Communication Technology Agency (ICTA) of Sri Lanka.

As a way forward, among the key responsibilities, ICTA has started to implement an extensive e-SriLanka program, which has been pledged an estimated $65 million from the World Bank. The program encompasses a range of activities, most of which are development oriented, and many of which will have an impact on the country's rural uplift. Within this program, up to 100 rural telecenters (Vishva Gnana Kendras, or VGKs) will be built to support the demand in rural areas, and a number of e-government initiatives will be undertaken, including connecting thousands of government agencies and offices.

In this context, ICTA has a vision, which is "To harness ICT as a lever for economic a and social advancement by taking the dividends of ICT to every village, to every citizen, to every business and to re-engineer the way government thinks and works" (see Vision under http://www.esrilanka.lk). This statement clearly indicates capacity development of a marginal community for economic development of the country.

The Project

The government, private sector, and other stakeholders in Sri Lanka development arena share a belief that ICT is the bedrock upon which a society can be built through equitable distribution of opportunity and knowledge. This belief has resulted in a shared vision for e-SriLanka — an initiative that uses ICT to develop the economy of Sri Lanka, reduce poverty, and improve the quality of life for her people.

To realize the vision of ICTA through e-SriLanka, a five-pronged strategy program has been initiated which embraces building the implementation capacity and sets out a national ICT Roadmap. They are:

- Building information infrastructure and an enabling environment;
- Developing ICT human resources;
- Modernizing government and delivering citizen services;
- Leveraging ICT for economic and social development through public-private partnerships; and
- Promoting Sri Lanka as an ICT destination.

A key element of the implementation policy for this national ICT Roadmap is a stakeholder-led approach with the creation and use of focus groups in all program areas and implementation through public-private partnerships. In the meantime, e-SriLanka has gained the national momentum to apply ICT at the marginal community level to reduce poverty; it has also increased economic development in Sri Lanka (e-SriLanka, 2001).

However, before launching the main phase, several pilot projects have been initiated under e-SriLanka. The Pilot Project Program plays a key role with regard to the success of the e-SriLanka vision. It was envisaged that, before embarking on a number of larger projects that will impact the citizens of Sri Lanka, the potential success of key areas in the ICT Roadmap need to be tested. The Pilot Project Program aims to do this by testing critical hypotheses in a number of crucial areas.

One aspect of the e-SriLanka initiative is that the ICTA will address the current ICT infrastruc-ture deficiencies in rural areas. A key objective of this program is to establish multi-service community information centers, or Vishva Gnana Kendras (VGKs: meaning global knowledge centers), providing access to Internet, telephones, and other information services, along with training and so forth to the public in rural communities. The main aim of VGKs is the dissemination of positive economic, social, and peace-building impact on a long-term and sustainable basis. In the first phase of the current plan, it is estimated that around 100 VGKs will be created in Northern, Eastern, and Southern regions.

In this phase, VGKs will need managerial, logistical, and technical support from partner institutions, which have professional expertise in the operation of community information centers. Therefore, VGK initiatives initially address the to-build capacity of such institutions, which will be known as VGK Support Institutions (VGK SIs). As part of the planning process for the VGK implementation project, ICTA requested proposals from different organizations that wish to establish themselves as VGK SIs. A mandatory criterion for a Full-Service VGK SI was to submit a sub-proposal on how to set up a pilot VGK.

As the rural telecenter (VGK) concept has not been tested and experienced earlier in Sri Lanka, it was decided to implement up to six pilot VGKs before the beginning of the main project. The selection process is underway from the VGK pilot sub-proposals that were received along with the VGK SI proposals. That selection process was kept independent from the VGK SI selection.

The objectives of the pilots were to obtain information about the services a VGK could provide to the people, to determine the services and content people may demand from VGKs, to gather information on connectivity issues, to formulate ideas on different VGK models, and to gather experience on the process and issues for setting up and running a VGK.

Selection Process

Altogether, 42 proposals were received from different organizations that wished to be considered as VGK Support Institutions. The VGK SI evaluation and selection process was carried out as a separate activity, independent of the VGK pilot selection.

From those 42, 30 submissions were Full-Service VGK SI proposals and also had (as a mandatory requirement) proposals on how to set up pilot VGKs.

Out of the 30 complete submissions, 18 included the relevant financial proposals to set up pilot VGKs. The submissions without financial details were rejected. Those 18 proposals were initially reviewed for implementing pilot VGKs. The evaluation process looked at the completeness (comprehensiveness) of the proposal, the capability and experience of the organization in setting up the VGK, and the realistic ability to have a VGK up and running by the end of the year.

At that stage, 11 proposals were short-listed after initial evaluation. During the second evaluation, cost of implementation, suggested models, financial sustainability, technology requirements, organizational commitment (how much are they investing), locations, and geographical spread were considered.

Finally, six proposals were selected to implement pilot VGKs. The selection was approved by the External Approval Committee and the ICT Agency's Board of Directors. The selected pilot

VGKs are shown in Table 2 with their names and locations.

Pilot Project Programs

Similarly, ICTA invited proposals to participate in different pilot project programs under the following issues:

1. Training
2. Educational content
3. IT promotion/VC
4. Consultancy
5. Infrastructure
6. Telecenters
7. Company automation
8. Portals
9. Media related
10. Government services
11. Market services
12. Digital security
13. Services/Call centers
14. Agriculture and fishing services
15. Distance e-learning services
16. Health
17. Rural or wide area finance
18. E-government main study

In total, 150 proposals were received. They were evaluated and 14 projects were initially chosen as pilots. Table 3 gives the name of pilots with their implementing organizations.

Table 2. Organization's name and location of who will implement VGKs

Organization	Location
Vanik Incorporated Ltd.	Embilipitiya
Sarvodaya	Nuwara-Eliya
David Pieris Information Technologies	Matara
Sewa Lanka Foundation	Dick-oya
Spectrum Training	Jaffna
Ceylon Chamber of Commerce	Kurunegala

Table 3. Pilot projects and their implementing organizations

Name of Pilot Project	Implementing Organization
Sinhala Fonts	ICTA
Public Registry	TBA
Government Printer On-line	ICTA
National Operations Room	PricewaterhouseCoopers
Empowering the Workplace	Informatics Information Systems (Pvt) Ltd.
Distance e-Learning	Arthur C. Clarke Institute of Modern Technology
Govi Gnana System	e-Development L abs/Interblocks Ltd./ Pricewaterhouse Coopers
e-Money Order	University of Colombo, School of Computing
SME Portal N	ational Chamber of Commerce of Sri Lanka
Internally Displaced Persons	Finder2000 (Pvt.) Limited
Legal Draftsman	e -Futures (Pvt) Ltd
e-Cabinet	ICTA
e-Parliament	ICTA
e-Office of the President	ICTA

The Pilot Project Program plays a key role with regard to the success of the e-SriLanka vision. Similar to VGKs, it was thought that, before embarking on a number of larger projects, the potential success of key areas in the ICT Roadmap should be tested. The program aims to do this by testing critical hypotheses in a number of areas. The results from each pilot will provide invaluable input into the main projects' specifications, ensuring greater efficiency during implementation. As a result, each pilot project undertaken has scope for replication and scalability across the country in the future.

The pilot projects comprised top-ranked pilots received in response to the requests for proposals. Certain projects, which were initiated from CINTEC, have been brought into the Pilot Project Program. All proposals received for pilot projects were interesting, demonstrating a high quality of innovation and a variety of ideas across many sectors. However, out of the diverse range of projects received, for the purpose of this particular venture, the chosen pilots had to encompass a variety of sectors and types, satisfying the strict evaluation criteria.

Apart from these initiatives, e-SriLanka has taken a specialized approach to human resource development with the following vision, objectives, and strategies.

Human Resource Development: e-SriLanka

The Vision: Use ICT to enhance education at the school and tertiary level, to increase the number and quality of high-level ICT professionals, and to develop a computer-literate citizenry.

Objectives:

- To establish a multi-layered and multi-skilled pool of ICT-trained staff at workforce, professional, and managerial levels;
- To provide ICT education to students in schools throughout the country;
- To increase the number of undergraduates at university courses in ICT and provide higher-level training to university staff;
- To enhance the opportunities and incentives for improving English and ICT literacy; and

- To increase the supply of ICT professionals to the rest of the world and to encourage foreign ICT professionals to set up training institutes in Sri Lanka.

To achieve these objectives, a three-pronged strategy has been adopted. First, build an ICT skilled workforce and increase the employability of school leavers with the help of the government, the private sector, and academia to:

- Facilitate the establishment of quality, affordable ICT skills enhancement programs and recognized ICT qualifications, both at a foundation and a diploma level;
- Facilitate the upgrading of the skills of trainers at IT training institutes, especially in the outstations; and
- Improve the quality and availability of textbooks and course materials for IT training.

Second, strengthen teaching in primary and secondary schools, tertiary education, and universities, so that:

- All school children would obtain basic ICT training and user-level skills through e-learning programs;
- The management of school IT centers would be strengthened;
- ICT could be introduced into national curricula; and
- Schools could be connected to the Internet.

Third, strengthen management and professional skills in ICT industry by:

- Organizing scholarship programs for postgraduate/specialist qualifications;
- Providing grants for short courses;

- Assisting national conferences, seminars, and study tours; and
- Empowering the ICT industry to attain excellence by strengthening HR and promoting innovation.

Similar Ventures in Sri Lanka

Two other projects—the Telecenter project (an initiative of Sarvodaya, Sarvodaya Shramadana Movement) which has expanded its network into 15,000 villages, and the Kotmale Community Radio project (a community radio-based pilot project), the first of its kind in Sri Lanka (Gunawardana & Wattegama, 2004; Slater, Tachhi, & Luvis, 2002) — can be included here. Both of these successful projects are continuing to date, expanding into many regions by adapting new technologies and building up new partnerships with the latest ICT-based project initiatives in Sri Lanka (David & Liyanage, 2004).

Way Ahead

By following modular expansion of these successful initiations, countries of similar socio-economical, cultural, and geographical context may be highly benefited. It has been found that the Sagarmatha Community Radio project in Nepal is a replication of the Kotmale Community Radio project. e-SriLanka is a follow up of many e-country projects around the globe; e-Korea, e-Singapore, e-Thailand, and so forth are but a few. Telecenter projects attained high interest at the recently concluded WSIS (World Summit on Information Society) in Tunisia in February 2005. Most of the developing countries are adopting these types of projects by accommodating into their communities. To wrap up this chapter on these case studies, a few recommendations can be made in support of capacity development initiatives through utilization of ICT, a stated in the next section.

CONCLUSION

The basic objective of human capacity development is to broaden the range of people's choice and make development more participatory and democratic (UNDP, 1991). ICT can improve the knowledge and awareness of people by providing information about social and economic programs, markets, employment opportunities, medical, agricultural, educational and training, weather, and disaster warning. These can be achieved by establishing integrated knowledge centers/information centers within the communities and integrating them into the nearest communication/local/regional center (Barton & Bear, 1999; Gunatunge & Karunanayake, 2004; Rahman, 2004).

In this cyberspace context of developing countries, a mixture of adoption of innovations and of the national cultural values, as well as the cooperation among all the nations, is creating a positive atmosphere for providing easy access to information and knowledge which can be used for the development of the country and to eliminate the gap between the rich and the poor. This demands integration of available lower-level information networks to form bigger networks covering wider areas and regions opting for updated contents of local demand. It will create not only positive attitude of the participants, but also enhance their knowledge and capacity. Eventually these networks of networks will emerge as knowledge hubs for the entire community, region, and country.

In conclusion it is imperative to recommend a coordinated network of access centers acting as delivery nodes for community empowerment, which in turn could be powerful resources in developing countries' contexts (Fouche, 1999; Robinson, 1998). These access centers should support marginal communities and at the same time have their sustainability by providing accurate information about local needs, and facilitating cooperation and interaction among organizations, institutions, and communities distributed

throughout the country. They may be termed as information centers or knowledge centers or village centers where appropriate. But their rationale lies in shared-access models that allow provision of a wide range of services to more users at lower cost than commercial entities, which are often out of financial reach of poor people (Digital Dividend, 2003). Widespread rollout of these access centers, however, can be achieved only by mobilizing private sector entrepreneurship and investment (Wellenius, 2003).

Finally, looking into causes and effects of these case studies, it can be derived that to address policy issues related to information management and access to needs-based information at the community level, it is essential to improve not only the capacities of the outreach communities, but also capacities of decision makers and professionals for achieving community empowerment, sustainable development, and sustainable livelihood.

REFERENCES

Accascina, G. (1999, March 24-27). Keynote presentation. In *Proceedings of the APDIP Regional Information Technology Conference.* Kuala Lumpur, Malaysia.

Appleton, H. (Ed.). (1995). *Do it herself: Women and technical innovation.* London: Intermediate Technology Publications.

Arvanitis, et al. (2004). South Asian health: What is to be done? Skills of evidence-based medicine need to be taught. *British Medical Journal, 328*(7443), 839-845.

Dwarakanath, A., et al. (2000). Postgraduate obstetrics and gynecology trainees' views and understanding of evidence-based medicine. *Medical Teacher, 22*(1), 27-29.

Bhatnagar, S. (2000). Social implications of information and communication technology in developing countries: Lessons from Asian success stories. *The Electronic Journal on Information Systems in Developing Countries, 1,* 1-9. Retrieved from http://www.unimas.my/fit/roger/EJISDC/EJISDC.htm

Bridges. (2004, November). *The real access/real impact framework for improving the way that ICT is used in development.* Retrieved from http://www.bridges.org

Barton, C., & Bear, M. (1999, March). *Information and communication technologies: Are they the key to viable business development services for micro and small enterprises?* (Report for USAID as part of the Micro Enterprises Best Practices Project). MD: Development Alternatives Inc.

Benjamin, P. (Ed.). (1999, October). *Universal access review.* South Africa: Graduate School of Public and Development Management, University of Witwatersrand.

David, M. J. R., & Liyanage, K. H. (2004). *Second generation problems at bridging digital divide in Sri Lanka: Practitioner's assessment.* Retrieved from http://www.oii.ac.uk/collaboration/seminars/20050304_david_and_liyange_paper.pdf

Duncome, R. (1999). *The role of information and communication technology for SME development in Botswana: Interim report.* A research project sponsored by the Department for International Development (DFID), UK. Retrieved from http://www.man.ac.uk/idpm

DFID. (2001). *Sustainable livelihoods guidance sheets.* Department for Informational Development, UK.

Digital Dividend. (2003). Retrieved June 8, 2003, from http://www.digitaldividend.org

e-SriLanka. (2001). Retrieved from http://www.esrilanka.lk

Fouche, B. (1999, March). *A Web-based agricultural system for South Africa. Feasibility study:*

Part 1. Unpublished document, National Department of Agriculture, South Africa.

G8DOT Force. (2001, May). *Digital opportunities for all: Meeting the challenge* (Report of the Digital Opportunity Task Force [DOT Force], including a proposal for a Genoa Plan of Action).

Global Information Technology Report. (2004-2005). World Economic Forum. Retrieved March 12, 2005, from http://www.weforum.org

Global Reach. (2001). Retrieved from http://www.glreach.com

Gunatunge, R. S., & Karunanayake, M. M. (2004). *Information and communication technologies for enhancing socio-economic development at the local level in Sri Lanka: Issues, challenges and strategies* (Research Report for Sida/SAREC Research Cooperation Project on Overcoming Regional Imbalances and Poverty).

Gunawardana, N., & Wattegama, C. (2004). Sri Lanka. *Digital review of Asia Pacific.* Kuala Lumpur, Malaysia: GKP.

Gurstein, M. (2003). Effective use: A community informatics strategy beyond the digital divide. *First Monday, 8*(12).

Heeks, R. (1999, June). *Information and communication technologies, poverty and development* (Development Informatics: Working Paper Series. Paper No. 5). Institute of Development Policy and Management. Retrieved from http://www.man.ac.uk/idpm

International Telecommunications Union (ITU) Report. (2002). *World Telecommunication Development Report: Reinventing Telecoms.* Retrieved from http://www.itu.int/ITU-D/ict/publications/wtdr_02

International Telecommunication Union (ITU) Report. (2003). *Measures access to the information society: Monitors impact of ICTs on global development goals.* Retrieved from http://www. itu.int/newsarchive/press_releases/2003/31.html

Keniston, K., & Kumar, D. (Eds.). (2004). *Bridging the digital divide: Experience in India.* Thousand Oaks; London; New Delhi: Sage Publications.

Kiangi, G. E., & Tjipangandjara, K. F. (1996). Opportunities for information technology in enhancing socio-economic development of a developing country. In M. Odedra-Straub (Ed.), *Global information technology and socio-economic development* (pp. 73-81). Nashua, NH: Ivy League Publishing.

Landes, D. (1998). *The wealth and poverty of nations: Why some are so rich and some so poor.* New York: W. W. Norton & Company.

Murelli, E., & Arvanitis, T. (2003). *E-health & learning: The Bangladesh experience.* Dhaka: MEDNET.

NITP. (2002). NITP: Sri Lanka. Retrieved June 24, 2002, from http://www.saarcnet.org/saarcnetorg/srilanka/IT/1Vision.htm

Norrish, P. (1998). Foreword. In D. Richardson (Ed.), The first mile of connectivity: Advancing telecommunications for rural development through a participatory communication approach. Rome: FAO.

Norrish, P. (1999). *Best practice guidelines for improved communication strategies for the promotion and dissemination of natural resource research outputs* (Draft Report, Vol. 1, AERDD). UK: The University of Reading.

NUA Internet Surveys. (2004). Retrieved from http://www.nua.ie/surveys/how_many_online

OECD. (2004). Organization for economic cooperation and development. *Annual Report.*

Rahman, H. (2004, July 4-8). Empowering marginal communities with interactive education systems, commonwealth open learning (COL). In *Proceedings of the 3rd Pan-Commonwealth*

Forum on Open Learning (PCF3). Dunedin, New Zealand.

Robinson, S. (1998). Telecenters in Mexico: The first phase. In *Proceedings of UNRISD Conference.*

Straus, S., et al. (2000). *Evidence-based medicine: How to practice and teach EBM.* New York: Churchill-Livingstone.

Slater, D., Tacchi, J., & Luvis, P. (2002). *An ethnographic evaluation of the Kotmale Internet community radio.* UK: London School of Economics.

Slim, H., & Thompson, P. (1993). *Listening for a change: Oral history and development.* London: Panos Publications.

Stillitoe, P. (1998). The development of indigenous knowledge: A new applied anthropology. *Current Anthropology, 49*(2), 223-253.

Traunmuller, R., & Lenk, K. (1996). *New public management and enabling technologies, advanced IT tools.* London: Chapman and Hall.

UNDP. (1991). *Human development report.* Oxford: Oxford University Press.

UNDP. (1998). *Human development report.* United Nations Development Program, New York.

UNDP. (2001). *Human development report 2001: Making new technologies work for human development.* United Nations Development Program, New York.

UNICTTF. (2004, June 28-July 23). *Second annual report of the United Nations ICT Task Force.* New York.

Waema, T. M. (1996). Implementation of IT projects and economic development: Issues, problems and strategies. In M. Odedra-Straub (Ed.), *Global Information technology and socio-economic development* (pp. 8-18). Nashua: Ivy League.

Wellenius, B. (2003, January). *Sustainable telecenters* (Note Number 251). Private Sector and Infrastructure Network, World Bank.

World Bank. (2000). *World development report 1999/2000: Entering the 21ˢᵗ Century.* New York: Oxford University Press.

Zita, K., & Kapur, A. (2004, April 21-23). Sri Lanka telecom brief. In *Proceedings of the USTDA South Asia Communications Infrastructure Conference.* New Delhi, India.

KEY TERMS

Economic Development: A sustainable wealth creation process that works within the framework of community parameters to maximize the efficient and effective utilization of community resources for economic gain of the local population. It is the process of raising the productive capacities of societies, in terms of their technologies (more efficient tools and machines), technical cultures (knowledge of nature, research, and capacity to develop improved technologies), and the physical, technical, and organizational capacities and skills of the elements.

Human Development Index (HDI): A measurement of human progress introduced by the United Nations Development Program (UNDP) in its Human Development Report of 1990. HDI is a composite index based on real GDP per capita (PPP), life expectancy at birth, and educational achievement that measures socio-economic development of a country.

ICT-Based Development Initiatives: A complicated term to define. ICT-based development initiatives are a key resource for identifying creative ways that ICTs are being deployed at the grassroots level and support development activities across a variety of sectors, in helping developing nations move into the information age.

Through information and knowledge transfers, these initiatives have become the network of networks for global sustainable development and improved the lives of societies across the globe. ICT-based development initiatives are based on a participatory model to be effective and sustainable, and resources are most effectively mobilized to help harness the potential of ICT to promote basic human development.

Information-Based Society: A type of society in which economic and social aspect is critically dependent on ICTs and information becomes the main product or essential to other products, with recognition that society's success depends on the ability to exploit information. An information-based society is a society integrated by complex communication networks that rapidly develop and exchange information, and which makes extensive use of information networks and ICT, produces large quantities of information and communications products and services, and has a diversified content.

Knowledge-Based Society: Knowledge is the awareness and understanding of facts and figures, truths, or information gained in the form of experience and/or learning. Knowledge is an appreciation of the possession of interconnected information which, in isolation, is of lesser value. Society is a system, composed of many parts, which may be called members, and which are intelligent systems or societies themselves. A knowledge-based society creates, shares, and uses knowledge for the prosperity and well-being of its community.

Social Development: Encompasses a commitment to individual well-being and volunteerism, and the opportunity for society to determine their own needs and to influence decisions which affect them. Social development incorporates public concerns in developing social policy and economic initiatives.

This work was previously published in Empowering Marginal Communities with Information Networking, edited by H. Rahman, pp. 318-353, copyright 2006 by IGI Publishing, formerly known as Idea Group Publishing (an imprint of IGI Global).

Chapter VIII
How to Globalize Online Course Content

Martin Schell
New York University, USA

ABSTRACT

Considering that 347 languages have over 1 million speakers each and account for 94% of the world's population, localization is unsustainable as a strategy for making online courses globally accessible. Writing Web content in Global English is the best way to ensure that people from all linguistic backgrounds have a reasonable chance of comprehending course materials. This chapter shows how to transform native English text into Global English (simpler syntax, less jargon, fewer idioms, no slang). It also discusses e-learning design issues such as cultural perspective and Internet logistics (speed and cost of connection). Finally, it addresses the future of English as a global language, particularly in reference to its supposed "rivalry" with Mandarin.

INTRODUCTION

Consider the following two approaches to discussing the use of English online.

During the occasion of preparing for the production of teaching materials to be used for e-learning, one should not neglect giving serious thought to reflecting upon the choice of language to be used for writing the e-learning content. Since English has not unequivocally become a global language, it is difficult, if not impossible, to deny its suitability as the source language for such a project. The evidence for it will be presented during the course of this chapter as follows.

Get with the program, dude! Keep it simple, stupid. Word: English is the language of choice. It's what works, but be cool about it.

Clearly, neither of the preceding paragraphs is an example of using English as a global language. The first is too stilted. Its opening sentence torments the reader with a series of phrases that hesitate to state the point: during the occasion, preparing for, production of, to be used. The first paragraph also has double negatives (not neglect and not unequivocally), an ordinary word that is ambiguous regarding its part of speech (since), and a useless phrase that repeats an obvious point (as follows). On the other hand, the second paragraph is too sketchy and overloaded with slang.

Let's start again:

Before producing e-learning materials for a global audience, consider the language in which the content will be written. Among the major languages of the world, English is the closest to being a global language. Writing your text in clear English is the best way to reach a worldwide audience, as I will explain in this chapter.

This situation naturally is an advantage for any e-learning provider who is a native speaker of English, or at least can employ native speakers to write the home page and other key parts of the Web site. However, the English normally spoken by Americans, Canadians, British, Australians, New Zealanders, Singaporeans, Indians, Jamaicans, and others is not itself a global language. Each of these countries speaks and writes its own dialect, full of local idioms and slang: American English, Queen's English, and so forth.

In order to serve a worldwide audience (as in World Wide Web), it is necessary to use Global English—English which is written in such a way that it can easily be understood by non-native speakers, as well as native speakers from diverse parts of the planet. This chapter teaches you how to recognize and write Global English.

THE CASE FOR GLOBAL ENGLISH

Nowadays, most Web sites that aim for multi-national markets will localize their content by translating it into languages spoken by major groups of Internet users: Spanish, Chinese, Russian, and so on. In August 2003, the software developer, Jordi Mas i Hernàndez (2003) tallied the presence of various languages on the Web by inputting keywords specific to each language. He found that English was the dominant language of the text on 1,280 million pages, followed by German (182 million), French (100 million), and then a cluster of four languages in the 65-70 million range: Japanese, Spanish, Chinese, and Korean.

Some people interpret his results as a call for increasing the localization of Web pages into languages other than English. Unfortunately, localization can never succeed in reaching a worldwide audience because, by definition, its purpose is to serve specific groups of users. Adding up a handful of local or regional groups does not equal a global audience.

There are presently 6,912 living languages, including 347 that have over 1 million speakers each (Gordon, 2005). Nobody will localize a Web site into all of them. How often do you see sites that offer the option of viewing pages in Bengali, Gujarati, Marathi, Punjabi, Telugu, Thai, Turkish, or Wu, each of which has over 40 million speakers?

The usual explanation for excluding these languages is that they are spoken in countries which currently have low Internet penetration. This justification reveals that localization is a short-term strategy, one which will become increasingly difficult to implement as time goes on. The number of Internet users more than doubled worldwide from 361 million in 2000 to 958 million in 2005, with doubling or tripling on every continent and in nearly all countries that began the 21st century with low percentages of users (Internet World Stats, 2005).

In poor countries, many people (especially youths) who lack a computer at home access the Internet via cyber cafes. This sharing of hardware is analogous to the pass-around readership of a newspaper, or people reading a book in a library instead of buying it. Statistics about total Internet users in such countries are often based on multiplying the number of Internet service provider

(ISP) accounts by a sharing factor.1 Because the multiplier is a rough estimate, one should view these statistics (as well as most other statistics related to the Internet) with some skepticism.

Nevertheless, the shortage of Web pages in many languages is quite obvious to people who are native speakers of those languages. If a Web site does not consider their language important enough to merit localization, these users are likely to access the English version of the site. At cyber cafes in Indonesia, for example, a few people will gather around a single user whose English is fluent enough to provide impromptu translation while they surf as a group.

There is also evidence that people who know English as a second language sometimes choose the English Web pages even when a site offers pages in their native language. A survey conducted by Research & Research found that only 8% of Hispanic American Internet users prefer Spanish-language Web sites and 41% prefer English-language Web sites. The remaining 51% said they were bilingual and would visit and purchase from sites in either English or Spanish. In other words, 92% of Hispanic American Internet users feel comfortable with English-language Web sites, despite the fact that 63% of this market segment were born outside the United States (Romney, 2000).

The high percentage who use English on the Web is supported by a comScore survey of language preferences in Hispanic American households: 21% of this ethnic group prefer to speak Spanish at home, 51% prefer English there, and 27% speak both languages (Greenspan, 2003); thus, 78% use English conversationally in the home. Similarly, 57% of Hispanic American students in kindergarten through 12th grade spoke mostly English at home in 1999, 25% spoke mostly Spanish, and 17% spoke English and Spanish equally (National Center for Education Statistics, 2003), resulting in a total of 74% who felt comfortable speaking English at home.

TRANSCENDING ONE'S NATIVE ENGLISH

Broadening our outlook means more than becoming aware of prospective students whose native language is not English; it means thinking globally. The global language is often used between two people who are both non-native speakers. For example, a Japanese person might use English to write to a Russian or Brazilian person, who would probably be less skillful with idioms than a native speaker of English.

If your e-learning course has an online facility for students to discuss what they are learning, it is essential to establish a chat environment that discourages idioms and slang. This may seem counterintuitive because chatting is a way to open up and express oneself with few restrictions. Instant messaging can be so fast and fluid that it seems like speech instead of writing, but it lacks the nonverbal clues of face-to-face chatting (or even phone conversations). Consequently, online chat content is prone to misinterpretation, especially when participants are from diverse cultural backgrounds.

The instructor or moderator should strive to remind discussion group members that clarity is important. Pointing out incomplete sentences and gently discouraging the use of the latest slang may slow the action, but it will surely make the class discussion more inclusive. Casual Internet English is great for communicating with friends, but it is too parochial for a Web site that aims to be worldwide in outlook.

Slang should also be minimized in online course content that is intended for a global audience. A report by Stanford University's Persuasive Technology Lab (Fogg, Soohoo, Danielson, Marable, Stanford, & Tauber, 2002) listed "writing tone" among the top 10 factors that users mentioned when describing the trustworthiness of a Web site. "People generally said that sensationalism or slang hurt a site's credibility, while a straight-forward, friendly writing style boosted credibility" (p. 43).

In addition to the absence of slang, Global English is characterized by smoother sentence structure, fewer idioms, and less jargon. In "Standards for Online Content Authors," Rachel McAlpine (2005) emphasizes conciseness as a key to clarity. She recommends that writers aim to limit sentences to a maximum of 21 words and paragraphs to 65 words. Indeed, it is usually less tiring to read sentences that have fewer words, and paragraphs that have fewer sentences, because reader comprehension improves when the "bites" of information are smaller. These types of streamlining will not restrict your writing style much, but they will greatly expand your potential audience by making your online content easier to understand.

WRITING IN GLOBAL ENGLISH

Consider the following sentence that ends a paragraph promoting an online clothing store:

Which is just the right feature for users who want what works.

This type of colloquial usage is easy for a domestic audience to understand. However, the incomplete sentence can confuse non-native speakers of English, many of whom would expect the sentence to end in a question mark.

Changing the initial *which* to *this* might decrease the sentence's trendiness in the American market, but it would greatly increase the number of people who could understand the sentence in the global market. In addition, the word *just* and the idiom *what works* should be modified, resulting in

This is exactly the right feature for users who want efficient online shopping.

The "coolness" of Web content in American eyes often depends on using the latest buzzwords and slang. However, many people in other countries became fluent in English while studying or working in the United States 20 or more years ago. After they returned to their native countries, they retained their fluency but their slang eventually became outdated. For example, they might not know that an expression like "it sucks" is now inoffensive enough to appear in mainstream print media and TV ads.

Slang and idioms are not the only tendencies that hinder successful global communication. Many of the words that we consider ordinary in Standard English have multiple meanings (and even different parts of speech) that can create ambiguity in the reader's mind, particularly if he or she is less than fully fluent in English. Ambiguity also makes a translator's work harder, slower, and less accurate (N. Hoft, personal communication, September 6, 2005; G. Fletcher, personal communication, September 9, 2005). Therefore, writing your original text in Global English will bring the added benefit of saving time and money when your course content is translated from English to another language, which is a likely scenario if it attracts a lot of students.

Here are two examples of ambiguity that most native speakers of English would read without hesitation. However, a non-native speaker might become confused. And even a good translator might render the word into a phrase that is ambiguous or incorrect in the target language.

The word *once* can be confusing as a conjunction, because some readers might misinterpret it as an adverb meaning "one time." For example:

Once the prompt appears, enter the course title.

Some people might think the prompt appears only once, regardless of the number of course titles. It would be better to write:

After the prompt appears, enter the course title.

A similar type of confusion can occur if you use since as a conjunction, because it can be misinterpreted as an adverb or preposition meaning "after."

Keep a log, since the use of this device produces momentary fluctuations in the supply of power to other electrical equipment in the room.

Someone might think that the log does not need to be started until a fluctuation occurs. To remove the ambiguity, use because as the conjunction:

Keep a log, because the use of this device produces momentary fluctuations in the supply of power to other electrical equipment in the room.

After you finish your final draft, read through your text again and look for points of ambiguity. If you find any words or phrases that could hinder comprehension or translation, try to replace them. However, you cannot anticipate everything that might seem unclear to a reader or translator.

A more comprehensive approach to removing ambiguity is to put some redundancy into your writing. This does not mean reiterating each sentence with a subsequent one that starts with "In other words...." You do not need to be that blunt. Simply write in a way that provides some overlap between your sentences, so they support each other and create a clear context for all of the paragraph's ideas.

For example:

We recommend the purchase of this factory because it is a good medium-term investment. If our company buys the manufacturing facility this year, we will be able to upgrade it by the middle of next year. After we modernize the equipment, the factory will provide additional production capacity to help us meet the increase in demand for our products that is expected two years from now.

Note the redundancy of key concepts in this example: purchase...buy, factory...facility, upgrade...modernize. In addition, the references to time are in chronological order and support the use of medium-term.

To appreciate the effectiveness of Global English, remember that the Web is still primarily a written medium despite the use of animation and music. People who are not completely fluent in English usually can read our language more easily than they can speak it. They can go over written words several times at their own pace with a dictionary, a process that is awkward during a conversation or a performance.

GLOBALIZING ONE'S PERSPECTIVE

Globalization of our thinking involves broadening our minds to accommodate other worldviews. I recall editing a speech by a Japanese businessman who asked, "Why is it that the term classical always refers to Europe? If we want to refer to the traditional arts and culture of other regions, we must insert another adjective: classical Japanese music, classical Indian dance, classical Chinese calligraphy."

In this global era, it is respectful as well as strategically important to avoid alienating entire cultures (i.e., markets). You can never anticipate all of the possible types of touchiness that might exist, but you can do a little research, particularly if your course material focuses on a specific region or culture.

People often say, "History is written by the victors," but there are exceptions to this cliché; Genghis Khan, for example, never lost a battle. If a country wins a war of independence, its people generally date their sovereignty from the year of declaration, not the year of the subsequent peace treaty; for the United States, it is 1776 rather than 1783. However, most Western history books ignore the August 17, 1945 declaration of independence in Indonesia and refer to The Hague Conference late in 1949 instead.

The national languages of Indonesia and Malaysia are often combined into Malay in discussions of the number of native speakers of various languages. For example, the online marketing company Global Reach (2004) states, "Malay is the same language that is spoken in Indonesia" (footnote 26) when tallying the number of speakers online, but indicates that most of them live in Indonesia. So, an Indonesian might wonder why the combined language is not called Indonesian instead of Malay. The confusion is primarily due to the conflation of modern Bahasa Malaysia with the older language that gave birth to it and its sister Bahasa Indonesia (Labor Law Talk, 2005), a situation analogous to combining Romanian and French into Romance language speakers and then saying, "Romance is the same language that is spoken in France."

Other cultural assumptions are unrelated to political favoritism. They merely lead to embarrassment or confusion, without arousing national pride. One example is shown by Jakob Nielsen (1999) in his seminal book Designing Web Usability. A banner ad for Apple Computer asked users to turn on a virtual light switch by clicking it. However, the switch was in the down position, which is the "on" position in many countries. Nielsen says this type of variation among countries is rarely mentioned in guidebooks that tell how to internationalize software or Web sites, but it can be discovered by testing the image on a sample of users overseas before uploading to the World Wide Web (p. 315).

LOGISTICAL CONSIDERATIONS

Although digital subscriber line (DSL), cable, satellite, and other fast connections are now well established in industrialized economies, a significant fraction2 of users rely on older ways to access the Internet. Many of your prospective students are likely to use an integrated digital services network (ISDN), or even 56 kilobits-per-second (Kbps) modems. Connection rates and speeds can be low, particularly during business hours when Internet traffic is heavy in their countries, overloading the local ISPs. Therefore, it would be a mistake to design a Web site that only works smoothly if it is accessed via a broadband connection.

In addition, it is important to consider that Internet time is often charged by the minute, as is telephone time. Thus, your students might be paying their ISP and telecom company a dollar or more per hour to access your course's Web site. These additional costs can severely impact online course enrollment.

Therefore, streamlining your content is a key to retaining students. It is wise to reduce the loading time of every page on your site, in order to make each student's participation smoother and cheaper. Also, talk to your Webmaster about how to make pages easy to re-access if a student's connection unexpectedly fails.

Citing a presentation by Robert Miller at a computer conference in 1968, Jakob Nielsen (1999) summarizes three thresholds of attention span (pp. 42-44):

1. A delay equal to 0.1 second is the limit for most users to feel that the system is reacting "instantly."
2. A delay of 1 second is the limit for feeling that one's flow of thought is uninterrupted (for example, after clicking on a link to read another page of text).
3. A delay of 10 seconds is the maximum for keeping a user's attention on the site.

Allowing for a half-second of latency in system responsiveness, Nielsen (1999) cautions that the 10-second limit for maintaining a person's attention on the task is reached with only 34 kilobytes (KB) for modem connections and 150 KB for ISDN connections (p. 48). Any Web page over these limits is likely to seem slow when loading, thereby provoking impatience.

Connection speed does not matter much for text-rich Web pages because they rarely exceed 10 KB. However, be careful about delays in loading time due to the inclusion of photos, music, or animation on your Web site. A digital photo in .jpg format is likely to exceed 34 KB, and a .wav file of instrumental or vocal music is typically 5-10 KB per second of playing time.

When you plan a Web page, check the size of every multimedia file that will be part of it. Minimize or eliminate the use of moving images and carefully consider the visual quality of each photo in relation to its file size. Even with an ISDN connection, a page that totals 500 KB is likely to take more than half a minute to appear on screen.

Try to make explanatory text as independent of the images as possible. Work with your Webmaster and include the ALT attribute in the HyperText Markup Language (HTML) code for each page. This attribute lets you insert descriptive text that displays in the box which outlines the photo while its image is loading on a user's screen.

Plan your tables and graphs to accommodate translation of the text into other languages. German, for example, typically expands the length of the equivalent English text by about 30% (Nielsen, 1999, p. 318). This can lead to problems in a table if your Web designer does not make the column widths flexible enough.

THE FUTURE OF GLOBAL ENGLISH

Is another language likely to replace English as the global language? After the British Council published The Future of English? by David Graddol in 1997, the mass media began sounding an alarm that English was being surpassed by "Chinese" (Lovgren, 2004). The excitement arose because Graddol (2000) divided English speakers into three categories (p. 10): those who speak it as a first language (native speakers, or L1), those who speak it fluently as a second language that has some official status in their country (L2), and those who are learning English as a foreign language (EFL).

Graddol (2000) estimated that there are 375 million L1, 375 million L2, and 750 million EFL speakers of English (p. 10, Figure 4). Although the L1 figure is well above those for Hindi and Spanish, it is far below the 1,100 million that he estimated for "Chinese" (p. 8, Table 1). The popular press echoed his estimates without asking him why his three-way analysis of L1, L2, and "foreign language" applies to English but not to "Chinese."

Most linguists do not recognize a monolithic language called "Chinese" that is spoken as a first language by nearly everyone in the People's Republic of China (PRC). "Chinese" consists of several large languages that are unified by a common system of writing but are mutually unintelligible when spoken (Columbia University, 2001).

Mandarin is the official language of the PRC and the standard language of instruction in its public schools. This situation is analogous to the use of national languages to unify diverse populations in Indonesia (Bahasa Indonesia) and the Philippines (Filipino). In its Ethnologue encyclopedia of world languages, SIL International (formerly the Summer Institute of Linguistics) claims that two thirds of the 1,300 million people in China speak Mandarin as their native language, yielding an L1 of 867 million (Gordon, 2005).

However, in May 2005, the PRC's Xinhua news agency reported a survey by the National Language Commission which found that only 53% of the population can speak Mandarin, and many of them "are not frequent Mandarin users, preferring their local dialect" ("Half of all Chinese people can't speak Mandarin," 2005). This yields a combined L1+L2 of 689 million; and if all of the L1+L2 Mandarin speakers among the 23 million

Taiwanese and "51 million overseas Chinese" (Graddol, 2000, p. 37) are included, Mandarin might exceed the estimated 750 million L1+L2 total for English.

Regardless of the numbers, there are two solid reasons why Mandarin is not a strong candidate to be a global language: It is hard to speak and hard to write. Tones in speech and ideograms in writing make it virtually inaccessible as a second language to the majority of the world's people. Adults whose native language is a tonal one such as Thai or Vietnamese sometimes learn Mandarin by overhearing conversations or watching movies, but speakers of non-tonal languages have a lot more difficulty doing so and need twice as much time in an immersion setting such as Automatic Language Growth (J. M. Brown, personal communication, 1990). Learning enough ideograms to read a newspaper requires a long-term diligent effort.

Graddol's (2000) report contains much more than a tally of speakers at various levels of fluency. He predicts that English will remain globally dominant but it will be influenced by non-native speakers. "New hybrid language varieties" (p. 36) will arise as millions of people "migrate" from EFL to L2 (e.g., using English to speak to fellow countrymen when no foreigners are present); for example, an "Asian standard English" might emerge in that region (p. 56).

It is widely recognized that the globalization of American movies, music, and fast food make English trendy among millions, even billions, of people who are not fluent in it. This cultural "wave" is supported by a socioeconomic "wave" in many developing countries, where governments have decreed in recent years that English should be taught as a foreign language in elementary schools. It is unclear, however, whether these two waves will be sufficient to create a critical mass of L2 speakers in dozens of countries, each of which will develop its own form of English.

Consider the case of Singapore, which has four official languages: English, Mandarin, Malay,

and Tamil. English is the default language when two Singaporeans from different ethnic groups make each other's acquaintance, earning it an L2 in the typology of Graddol (2000, p. 11, Table 5). This L2 "Singlish" is flavored with words and structures from other languages (including non-Mandarin forms of Chinese) and thus appears to be a harbinger of the hybridization that he predicts will occur during the next few decades. However, few if any "Singlish" words have entered the vocabulary of L2 English speakers in Thailand or the Philippines, let alone more distant areas.

A Japanese acquaintance of mine recounted an incident that occurred when she was teaching her native language to Indonesians in North Sumatra. One day, her students invited her to go hiking, pronouncing the word in Japanese fashion (haikingu) as part of a Japanese sentence. Etsuko was confused when they told her everyone would gather in the evening—she understood haikingu to be a day trip on level ground or in low hills. Instead, the students trekked up a small mountain, arriving at the peak in time for sunrise. In Indonesian, the borrowed word hiking refers to an activity that Japanese consider to be mountain climbing.

It therefore seems to me that the proliferation of "hybrid languages" predicted by Graddol will make Global English even more essential in the future, as a way for speakers of diverse forms of English to communicate with each other. To be truly effective, information and communication technology (ICT) must be accompanied by the development of human infrastructure, specifically the ability to express ourselves clearly to audiences who do not share our cultural background. In addition to transcending our native English when we produce online courses, we should promote the use of Global English in physical schools and other organizations.

Graddol (2000) presents a pyramid diagram (p. 12, Figure 6) to explain how the expansion of viewpoint beyond a person's village is accompanied by changes in the choice of language in India. At the base of the pyramid are local languages used within families and learned by infants as L1. A step higher are languages of wider geographical scope, which are used in media broadcasts and primary schools. Another step higher are state languages (e.g., Malayalam in Kerala), which are used in government offices and secondary schools. At the top are Hindi and Indian English, which are used nationally and in universities. I propose that Global English is a step beyond the top of his pyramid, serving as a lingua franca for international communication and e-learning.

CONCLUSION

Localization is essential in marketing, but it is incomplete as a global strategy for online course design because it can never accommodate everyone. The limits of localization are becoming more apparent in the 21st century, with Internet access increasing dramatically in virtually every country. It is likely that the total number of Internet users will surpass 1 billion in early 2006, but it is very unlikely that any Web site will localize its content into all of the 347 languages that each claim at least 1 million speakers.

To make the Web truly a worldwide medium, it is essential to write English text in a way that can be easily understood by non-native speakers: simpler syntax, less jargon, fewer idioms, no slang. Writing online course materials in Global English is the best way to ensure that people from all linguistic backgrounds have a reasonable chance of comprehending your content. Global English will become more important in the near future as e-learning expands its scope and market. It will also become essential for maintaining English as a lingua franca if the expansion of L2 speakers leads to a proliferation of new varieties of the language in diverse cultures throughout our world.

Suggested URLs

http://www.algworld.com/history.htm (Automatic Language Growth and the work of Dr. J. Marvin Brown at AUA Language Center in Bangkok)

http://www.anglistik.tu-bs.de/global-english/GE_Was_ist_GE.html (A list of links to online articles that use the term Global English)

http://www.davidcrystal.com (The work of Prof. David Crystal, editor of The Cambridge Encyclopedia of the English Language)

http://www.globalenglish.info/globallyspeaking/index.htm (Tips on intercultural communication in the Internet age)

http://www.globelanguage.com (Translation company co-owned by George Fletcher)

http://hotwired.wired.com/hardwired/wiredstyle/index.html (Wired Style: a trendy set of guidelines that are basically not Global English)

http://www.netratings.com (Nielsen-Net Ratings)

http://www.oecd.org/document/60/0,2340,en_2649_34225_2496764_1_1_1_1,00.html (OECD broadband statistics, based on ITU data)

http://www.research-research.com (Research & Research)

http://www.world-ready.com/academic.htm (A list of links offered by Nancy Hoft, a consultant in "world-readiness")

REFERENCES

Columbia University. (2001). *Chinese language*. In *The Columbia Electronic Encyclopedia* (6th ed.) New York: Columbia University Press. Retrieved December 6, 2005, from http://www.bartleby.com/65/ch/Chinese.html

Federal Communications Commission (2005, June 10). *Frequently asked questions (FAQs) about FCC Form 477 (local telephone competition and broadband reporting)*. Retrieved October 2, 2005, from http://www.fcc.gov/broadband/broadband_data_faq.html

Fogg, B. J., Soohoo, C., Danielson, D., Marable, L., Stanford, J., & Tauber, E. R. (2002, November 11). *How do people evaluate a Web site's credibility?* Stanford, CA: Persuasive Technology Lab, Stanford University.

Global Reach. (2004, September 30). *Global Internet statistics (by language)*. Retrieved May 24, 2005, from http://global-reach.biz/globstats/index.php3 (the table's footnotes appear in full at http://www.global-reach.biz/globstats/refs.php3)

Gordon, R. G., Jr. (Ed.). (2005, May). Statistical summaries. In *Ethnologue* (15th ed.). Retrieved May 23, 2005, from http://www.ethnologue.com/ethno_docs/distribution.asp?by=size

Graddol, D. (2000). *The future of English?* (2nd ed.). London: British Council.

Greenspan, R. (2003, April 9). *Hispanics driven to auto sites*. ClickZ Network. Retrieved May 23, 2005, from http://www.clickz.com/news/article.php/2178711

Half of all Chinese people can't speak Mandarin: Report. (2005, May 23). *Taipei Times,* 5. AFP Beijing. Retrieved May 24, 2005, from http://www.taipeitimes.com

International Telecommunication Union (2003). *Technical notes*. Retrieved May 24, 2005, from http://www.itu.int/ITU-D/ict/statistics/WTI_2003.pdf

International Telecommunication Union. (2005, April 26). *Economies by broadband penetration, 2004*. Retrieved May 24, 2005, from http://www.itu.int/ITU-D/ict/statistics/at_glance/top20_broad_2004.html

Internet World Stats. (2005, September 30). *World Internet users and population statistics*. Retrieved October 2, 2005, from http://www.internetworld-stats.com/stats.htm

Ipsos. (2005, March 2). *The majority of global Internet users using a high-speed connection*. Retrieved May 26, 2005, from http://www.ipsos-na.com/news/pressrelease.cfm?id=2583

Labor Law Talk. (2005). *Indonesian language*. Retrieved November 6, 2005, from http://encyclopedia.laborlawtalk.com/Indonesian_language

Lovgren, S. (2004, February 26). *English in decline as a first language, study says*. National Geographic News. Retrieved May 23, 2005, from http://news.nationalgeographic.com/news/2004/02/0226_040226_language.html

Mas i Hernàndez, J. (2003, September 2). *La salut del català a Internet*. Retrieved May 25, 2005, from http://www.softcatala.org/articles/article26.htm

McAlpine, R. (2005). *Standards for online content authors*. Quality Web Content. Retrieved September 5, 2005, from http://www.webpagecontent.com/arc_archive/177/5/

National Center for Education Statistics (2003). *Status and trends in the education of Hispanics: Language spoken at home*. Retrieved November 4, 2005, from http://nces.ed.gov/pubs2003/hispanics/Section11.asp

Nielsen, J. (1999). *Designing Web usability: The practice of simplicity*. Indianapolis, IN: New Riders.

NUA (2001). *Methodology*. Retrieved May 24, 2005, from http://www.nua.ie/surveys/how_many_online/methodology.html

Romney, L. (2000, January 6). The cutting edge: Survey looks at online habits of U.S. Latinos. *Los Angeles Times*. Retrieved May 29, 2005, from http://www.latimes.com

Web Site Optimization (2005, January). *January 2005 bandwidth report*. Retrieved May 26, 2005, from http://www.websiteoptimization.com/bw/0501/

ENDNOTES

[1] According to NUA (2001), "An Internet User represents a person with access to the Internet and is not specific to Internet Account holders. When the figure for Internet Account holders is the only information available, this figure is multiplied by a factor of 3 to give the number of Internet users" (para. 2).

However, in its Technical Notes for "Internet indicators," the International Telecommunication Union (ITU) implies that the factor can vary from country to country: "Countries that do not have surveys generally base their estimates on derivations from reported Internet Service Provider subscriber counts, calculated by multiplying the number of subscribers by a multiplier" (2003, p. 4).

[2] For most of this century, South Korea has had the world's highest proportion of Internet users who subscribe to broadband. According to ITU figures for the country, 11.9 million of 31.6 million Internet users subscribed, resulting in a penetration of less than 38% at the end of 2004 (W. Yasandikusuma, personal communication, May 27, 2005). However, "broadband penetration" figures are calculated in different ways, showing perhaps the greatest variance of all Internet statistics. The term broadband is sometimes applied to speeds less than the ITU minimum of 256 Kbps (V. Gray, personal communication, May 26, 2005). For example, the Federal Communications Commission (FCC) of the United States defines broadband as a connection that "enables the end user to receive information from and/or send information to the Internet at information transfer rates exceeding 200 kilobits per second (kbps) in at least one direction" (2005, question 5).

In addition, the term penetration is defined in several ways. Some surveys divide a country's total number of broadband subscribers by the total number of inhabitants. Although the U.S. had the most broadband subscribers as of December 2004, the ITU (2005) ranked it only 16th globally on the basis of 11.4% penetration of its general population, compared to 24.9% for South Korea.

Other surveys divide the total number of households or users who have broadband capability installed (but might not actually subscribe) by the total number of "active Internet users." For example, over 69 million U.S. households had the capability as of December, 2004, yielding a penetration of 54.7% for home users according to Web Site Optimization (2005). This figure is bloated even more in the "Face of the Web 2004" study by Ipsos-Insight, which claims that 62% of the entire world "accessed" the Internet via broadband in October, 2004 (Ipsos, 2005).

Chapter IX
The Diffusion of New Technologies:
Community Online Access Centres in Indigenous Communities in Australia

Anne Daly
University of Canberra, Australia

ABSTRACT

This chapter presents data from the 2001 Census of Population and Housing to highlight the low levels of computer and Internet usage by indigenous Australians. This result is not surprising, given the well-documented connection between education, income, location of residence and use of these technologies. One possible way of addressing the digital divide between capital city dwellers and other Australians is through the development of community online access centres. Using evidence from the literature and from fieldwork in New South Wales, the chapter considers some factors that are likely to make these centres more successful. These include a strong commitment by the community to the development of a centre and a close integration of the centre with community activities. It is important that significant funds be budgeted to training for all involved including centre staff and community members.

INTRODUCTION

There has been a general concern that particular groups have been left behind in the diffusion of new information and communications technology (ICT) and the related skill development, and that this may have long term implications for the ability of these people to participate in society. indigenous Australians, both aboriginal and Torres

Strait Islanders, are among those at risk. Earlier research by Lloyd and Hellwig (2000) looked at the determinants of the take-up of the Internet. They found that educational qualifications and income were the major determinants of access to the Internet at home. Living outside a major urban area was also associated with lower levels of computer and Internet usage. On the basis of all these indicators, indigenous Australians were expected to fall on the wrong side of the digital divide. Education levels and income are lower for this group than for non-indigenous Australians (Altman, Biddle, & Hunter, 2004). In addition, a larger proportion of indigenous compared to other Australians live outside the capital cities. Access to the Internet has been less reliable and more costly in these areas than in the cities (Besley, 2000; Regional Telecommunications Inquiry [RTI], 2002).

The 2001 Population Census was the first census to ask Australians about their access to computers and the Internet. The results show that while 30% of non-indigenous Australians had access to the Internet at home, less than 10% of indigenous Australians did. Other research has also documented low levels of computer access at home for school-aged indigenous Australians (Dyson, 2003). The purpose of this chapter is to examine the census evidence on computer and Internet usage for indigenous Australians and to consider whether the development of community online access centres can help to bridge the digital divide between indigenous and other Australians. It highlights the indicators of success and the limitations these centres have faced using evidence from the literature and fieldwork conducted in New South Wales (NSW).

Computer and Internet Access for Indigenous Australians

The 2001 Census provides a useful aggregate picture of home access to computers and the Internet and includes information on indigenous

Australians for the first time. Several studies have used these data to investigate the use of new technologies by indigenous Australians. Lloyd and Bill (2004) developed a model for explaining the determinants of home computer and Internet usage. They found that Australians with higher levels of educational attainment and incomes were more likely to access the Internet at home than those less qualified and with lower incomes. Their results show that people with poor English language skills, indigenous Australians and those living in remote areas were less likely to use a home computer or access the Internet than a non-indigenous urban married man working in a white-collar job with no children and no tertiary qualifications. While the probability of the latter person using a computer at home was 43.8%, a person with identical characteristics, except that they were indigenous, only had a probability of home computer usage of 20.3% — a gap of 23.5 percentage points. There was also a substantial gap of 22.5 percentage points in the predicted probability of using the Internet for the non-indigenous male compared with an indigenous person with otherwise identical characteristics. According to Lloyd and Bill's results, being indigenous was one of the most important negative determinants of computer and Internet usage.

Biddle, Hunter, and Schwab (2004) have used the census data on Internet access to analyse indigenous participation in education. Based on a detailed geographical analysis of those data, they found that access to the Internet at home raised the probability of educational attendance. They interpreted this variable as an indicator of educational attainment in a household and support for educational participation. Their analysis shows substantial differences between indigenous and other Australians in their access to the Internet, particularly in remote areas.

The census data are used here to present a broad picture of computer and Internet access; for more detailed tables see Daly (2005). Table 1 summarises the census evidence on access to

Table 1. Proportion of indigenous and non-indigenous populations that used a computer at home, by state, 2001 (Source: 2001 Census of Population and Housing)

	Indigenous (1)	Non-Indigenous (2)	Ratio (1)/(2)
New South Wales	0.22	0.43	0.51
Victoria	0.28	0.45	0.62
Queensland	0.18	0.44	0.41
South Australia	0.17	0.42	0.40
Western Australia	0.13	0.46	0.28
Tasmania	0.31	0.39	0.79
Northern Territory	0.06	0.43	0.14
Australian Capital Territory	0.41	0.59	0.69

Table 2. Proportion of indigenous and non-indigenous populations that had access to the Internet at home, by state, 2001(Source: 2001 Census of Population and Housing)

	Indigenous (1)	Non-Indigenous (2)	Ratio (1)/(2)
New South Wales	0.11	0.29	0.38
Victoria	0.16	0.33	0.48
Queensland	0.08	0.29	0.28
South Australia	0.07	0.27	0.26
Western Australia	0.06	0.31	0.19
Tasmania	0.15	0.23	0.65
Northern Territory	0.03	0.29	0.10
Australian Capital Territory	0.24	0.41	0.59

a computer at home for indigenous and non-indigenous Australians for each of the Australian States and Territories (hereafter referred to as "States"). It shows that the proportion of the total indigenous population that used a computer at home was well below that for the non-indigenous population in each State. The Australian Capital Territory (ACT) had the highest proportion of computer users among both the indigenous and non-indigenous populations. The two States that stand out as having the lowest ratio of indigenous to non-indigenous computer users in the population were Western Australia and the Northern Territory, where the ratio of indigenous to non-indigenous users was less than one-third. When State data are divided between the capital city

Table 3. Proportion of indigenous and non-indigenous populations that used the Internet, by state, 2001 (Source: 2001 Census of Population and Housing)

	Indigenous (1)	Non-Indigenous (2)	Ratio (1)/(2)
New South Wales	0.18	0.38	0.47
Victoria	0.26	0.40	0.65
Queensland	0.15	0.38	0.39
South Australia	0.17	0.37	0.46
Western Australia	0.12	0.41	0.29
Tasmania	0.28	0.35	0.80
Northern Territory	0.07	0.42	0.17
Australian Capital Territory	0.40	0.57	0.70

and the rest of the state, they show that only 8% of the indigenous population of Western Australia and 3% of the indigenous population of the Northern Territory living outside the respective capital cities had access to a computer at home (Daly, 2005).

While about two-thirds of non-indigenous Australians who used a computer at home also had access to the Internet, the figure was closer to a half for indigenous Australians. Table 2 focuses on access to the Internet at home for both indigenous and non-indigenous Australians. The data show that less than 10 per cent of the indigenous population of Queensland, South Australia, Western Australia and the Northern Territory had Internet access at home. The ratio for Internet access at home was particularly low for indigenous people in Western Australia and the Northern Territory compared with the non-indigenous population.

Table 3 includes all sources of access to the Internet. This is comprised of the census categories home (the focus of Table 2), work and elsewhere (for example schools, libraries, friends' homes and community online access centres). A comparison of Tables 2 and 3 highlights some interesting results.

While indigenous Australians were less likely to use the Internet than other Australians, the gap was smaller if all usage of the Internet was the focus rather than Internet usage at home. A shift of focus from home usage to usage from all sources doubled the proportion of indigenous people accessing the Internet in South Australia, Western Australia and the Northern Territory but from a very low base (see Tables 2 and 3). The inclusion of other access points was particularly important outside the capital cities in Queensland, Western Australia, South Australia and the Northern Territory (Daly, 2005).

The census data are now three years old and, in this area of rapid change, there has probably been substantial growth in computer and Internet usage in the Australian population. Given certain characteristics of the indigenous population—relatively low levels of educational attainment, low incomes and location outside the capital cities—it seems likely that they continue to exhibit levels of computer and Internet access well below the national average.

THE ROLE OF COMMUNITY ONLINE ACCESS CENTRES

Policymakers have been concerned about the development of a digital divide based on location for some time. There have been two recent Commonwealth government enquiries into the state of communications systems outside the capital cities (Besley, 2000; RTI, 2002) and a report focusing directly on remote indigenous communities, the Telecommunications Action Plan for Remote Indigenous Communities (TAPRIC) (Department of Communications, Information Technology and the Arts [DCITA], 2002). One recommendation of these reports has been the need to further encourage the use of community facilities to promote access to ICT in situations where private households are unlikely to pay for these services themselves. Remote indigenous communities fall within this category. Residents have low incomes and low levels of education and technical expertise. The physical environment is harsh, making maintenance of the equipment difficult.

There are potentially many benefits for remote communities from access to ICT. These technologies have the ability to increase access to goods and services, for example, Internet banking and health and education services, and to facilitate access to information and the preservation of local history and culture. There is also a negative side where opening a community to the Internet may increase the availability to residents of socially undesirable influences such as pornography and gambling. However, there are many examples of new technologies providing positive outcomes for remote communities (Daly, 2002; Farr, 2004). Government-funded centres are one way of bringing these services to remote communities and bridging the digital divide.

The Commonwealth government has used revenue from the partial privatisation of Telstra (the main telecommunications carrier in Australia) to fund almost 700 communications projects costing a total of $325 million in remote and regional Australia through Networking the Nation (NTN). It has included 60 projects worth $35.1 million of "exclusive or significant benefit to indigenous communities" (DCITA, 2002, p. 26). State governments also have programs designed to improve public access to the Internet outside the capital cities. These include the Community Technology Centres (CTCs) in NSW (CTC@ NSW), the West Australian telecentre program and Tasmanian Communities Online. These programs are jointly funded by NTN and their respective State governments. They provide public access to computers, photocopiers, fax machines, the Internet and videoconferencing in small rural and remote towns. Public libraries and schools in all states also offer public access to the Internet in numerous locations (DCITA, 2003).

There are some important factors in creating successful community online access centres discussed in the literature and highlighted during fieldwork undertaken by the author in 2003 in NSW. In the fieldwork, visits were made to CTCs in Dubbo, Menindee and Wilcannia. Extensive discussions were held with the managers of these centres, members of the indigenous communities, employees of Commonwealth and State government departments, the Outback Telecentre Network and other service providers to indigenous communities. While indigenous communities in NSW may not face the same issues of geographical isolation as those in other Australian States, they often face major problems of social and economic isolation. In Australia, most of the centres have only been running for a short time, so an evaluation of their impact in their communities can only be partial.

The Role of Community Support

For these centres to be successful, it is important that community members are involved in their development from the initial stages of the project through to the ongoing operation of the centre. Several studies discussed by Farr (2004) emphasise the importance of local champions in establishing and maintaining centres. Further examples include the CTC in Dubbo that was run from a community centre providing a range of facilities for the local indigenous population, including health and education services; a management committee of community leaders oversaw the operations of the community centre and the CTC. On Cape York Peninsula, the Cape York Digital Network (CYDN) has been established through detailed partnership agreements with the Community Councils in each location.

One method of fostering community support is by using the centres for the preservation of local culture and history. For example, pictures, stories and artefacts of the Bawgutti people have been digitally recorded and archived at the Bowraville CTC. The information has been made generally available on CD-ROM. Where literacy levels are low, special strategies may be required to engage the community in ICT activities.

The Development Role of the Centres

Related to the previous point is the need to recognise the role of online access centres in the development of communities. If they are to be successful, they need to be integrated into other activities in the community. It is important that centres engage in outreach activities to show how they can contribute to community life and development. For example, the development of radio and Internet access has been used in the Torres Strait to disseminate more accurate and detailed weather forecasts that are critical for fishing activity. In the CTCs visited in NSW, facilities were used for local meetings, educational purposes and for organising community transport. The Wilcannia CTC planned to establish a small local museum in the same building and a driver reviver centre to encourage passing tourists into the building.

There are currently very few Australian examples of a community online access centre that has been used as a base for a successful business enterprise. One example was the CTC at White Cliffs in NSW that was successfully used as a call centre but was later closed down. Overseas examples show the importance of a skilled workforce to make these ventures successful (Farr, 2004).

Schwab and Sutherland (2003) have proposed a similar role for schools as part of indigenous learning communities at the centre of community activities. It is only by integrating these institutions with community life that they can offer real opportunities for people to enhance their skills and foster development in the communities.

Local Employment and Training in the Centres

There are considerable difficulties in finding local people with the relevant skills to work in an online access centre. It is important that ongoing training of community members is available in an attempt to build the skill base, and that centre managers are also given the opportunity to upgrade their skills. While there are some funds for training, in general the budgets of these centres are very small and there is not much scope for training expenditure. The CTCs visited in NSW had not been very successful in their attempts to employ local indigenous people in the centres. A major constraint was the limited budget under which these centres were operating. In addition, many of the people who were available through the Community Development Employment Projects (CDEP) scheme or Work for the Dole were not suitably skilled, and some of them were not acceptable for working with children for other reasons.

Community online access centres offer the opportunity to provide online training to people in remote areas who might otherwise not have access. Many centres offer basic training in computer skills for community members (for example the NSW CTCs, CYDN and PY Media in South Australia). Technical and Further Education (TAFE) Colleges are now developing a range of online courses and are able to provide interactive education sessions to dispersed groups of students. One example from the Northern Territory is a pilot of virtual business education where participants establish virtual businesses and interact online to learn how to run them. However, it is important that the courses recognise the existing levels of skills and the requirements of those they are planning to teach in order to be successful.

What Can the Centres Do for Youth?

Young people are very keen computer and Internet users and have been a primary focus of efforts to integrate online access centres into communities. While they may be interested in using the Internet chiefly for entertainment rather than conventional education purposes, access to Internet facilities can provide young people with reading and communication skills that they would otherwise not be acquiring.

An innovative example of the use of Web technology for young indigenous people is the dEadly mOb Web site run from the Gap Youth Centre in Alice Springs (http://www.deadlymob.org). The site displays artwork and information about youth activities in Alice Springs and surrounding communities. It also provides a mentoring service for young indigenous people interested in gaining work experience.

The New South Wales CTCs have also focused on the needs of this group, for example, by establishing homework clubs for students after school, holding a photo competition run throughout NSW and a videoconferencing session on healthy lifestyles that enabled interaction between participants in communities and some professional football players. A significant issue with respect to youth is the importance of supervision. Several community leaders expressed concern

that young people should only be able to access suitable Web sites. This has also been a concern for CYDN (2004). Another important issue from the viewpoint of the financial sustainability of the online centres is that these young people are unlikely to have the income to pay for their use of the centres' facilities. There needs to be some way of cross-subsidising their access, and one potential solution, access to large government contracts, is discussed in the next section.

Use of Community Online Access Centres for Government Service Delivery

Several authors have argued that a way of making these centres financially viable is for them to establish contracts with government departments for the supply of services to remote communities. This idea is currently being explored in some detail and is beginning to be put into operation. For example, the Australian Tax Office has provided training to CTC@NSW managers in using their Web site and pays a retainer to CTC@NSW to provide ongoing support for individuals accessing the Web site through the CTCs. However there are significant problems that must be overcome before community online access centres could be used to deliver many services. For example, to use a centre for a legal or health consultation via videoconferencing would require a secure network connection and the privacy of a separate room to ensure the confidentiality of the consultation. Most of the centres do not have these facilities. The CTC@NSW policy has been to undertake negotiations on behalf of all the CTCs in NSW with Commonwealth and State government departments. The agencies have been supportive of the proposals but are concerned about possible customer resistance to videoconferencing and the need to protect the privacy and security of the service. The ability to use income from these sources to cross-subsidise community activities remains a long-term objective.

Technical Support

The experience in NSW, Western Australia and the CYDN shows that it is very important that there is a strong centralised technical support network for the centres. This support is necessary for dealing with technical problems, brokerage with government agencies and as a source of new ideas. If the centres are going to be successful in remote communities, support information must be timely and available in a form that is accessible to people in the communities.

Use of Appropriate Technology

The technology available in these centres must be appropriate for the conditions and requirements of the communities. This includes social, cultural and economic constraints as well as physical ones. Supplying the most up-to-date technology may not lead to the best outcomes. For example, in each of the CTCs visited in NSW, there were videoconferencing facilities available at very reasonable rates by commercial standards. They were, however, still too expensive for members of the local community and were under-utilised. Managers argued that most of the limited use that was made of this equipment resulted from its implementation being "Sydney-driven" rather than initiated in the communities. Any equipment that is provided to these centres needs to come with a budget for use and maintenance training. If the skills are not available in the community to keep the equipment operating successfully, then there is limited advantage in its being there.

Long-Term Sustainability

Under many of these government-sponsored programs there is a goal of long-term financial independence for each centre. All the evidence of developments in Australia and in remote communities overseas suggests that this is unlikely to happen for a long time in indigenous communities (Caspary & O'Connor, 2003; DCITA, 2003). The communities do not have the resources to make these centres financially self-supporting. In this context, the only way that the centres can be made self-supporting is if they can generate income from government or business sources to cross-subsidise community activities, for example youth support programs. Current movement in this direction has been slow.

In order to be sustainable in the long run, community online access centres must offer a range of services. One example from Canada is K-Net Services (http://www.services.knet.ca), a regional broadband network for First Nations which offers Web site and e-mail hosting, network services, videoconferencing and Web site and graphic design. On a less sophisticated level, this may involve running a café as well as a set of computer terminals. Centres seem to perform better where they are integrated with other key organisations in a community, for example, the health centre, the library and the school. While long-term experience with online access centres in Australia is limited, there is a much longer history in radio communications in remote communities, and the Broadcasting for Remote Aboriginal Communities Scheme (BRACS) has been reviewed on several occasions (Aboriginal and Torres Strait Islander Commission [ATSIC], 1999). One of the important lessons of the BRACS reviews has been the need for continuing technical support and a budget for ongoing skill development in the communities.

CONCLUSION

This chapter has presented the evidence from the 2001 Census on computer and Internet access for indigenous Australians. It shows that access to computers is well below that for other Australians, particularly in Western Australia and the

Northern Territory. Home Internet access is even more limited for indigenous Australians with less than 10% of the population having access to the Internet at home. The census evidence confirms a digital divide between indigenous and other Australians.

One way of trying to bridge this divide is by the development of community online access centres. While the development of these centres is in its early stages in Australia, there are some factors that appear to be associated with likely success. It is important that the community actively supports the introduction of a centre and is closely involved with its development and management. Centres should take a developmental role in their community and focus on ways in which they can contribute to its future. The centre management must be actively involved in outreach activities to show residents how they can benefit from using the facilities. They can have a special role in developing the skills of young people in the community and expanding opportunities.

A lack of appropriate skills among the local population is likely to be a significant issue in developing these centres in remote indigenous communities. It is imperative that there is a budget available for training and upgrading skills and that the management has ready access to support from outside the community.

There are many important underlying reasons for the economic disadvantage apparent in remote indigenous communities. These include the lack of employment opportunities, high levels of welfare dependence and low levels of income and education. These underlying factors are of paramount significance in addressing the long-term disadvantage of indigenous Australians. The development of a successful network of community online access centres could contribute to a reduction in these underlying determinants of economic disadvantage.

ACKNOWLEDGMENTS

I would like to thank all the people who gave me their time during the fieldwork in NSW that is used as a basis for this chapter, particularly Kerry Fraser and Susan Locke. I would also like to thank Boyd Hunter and Diane Smith for useful comments on an earlier draft.

REFERENCES

Aboriginal and Torres Strait Islander Commission (ATSIC). (1999). *Digital dreaming, a national review of indigenous media and communications.* Canberra, Australia: ATSIC.

Altman, J. C., Biddle, N., & Hunter, B. (2004). *Indigenous socioeconomic change 1971–2001: A historical perspective* (CAEPR Discussion Paper No. 266). Canberra, Australia: Centre for Aboriginal Economic Policy Research, Australian National University.

Besley, T. (Chair). (2000). *Connecting Australia, report of the telecommunications service inquiry*, Retrieved September 19, 2005, from http://www.telinquiry.gov.au/final_report.html

Biddle, N., Hunter, B. H., & Schwab, R. (2004). *Mapping indigenous educational participation* (CAEPR Discussion Paper No. 267). Canberra, Australia: Centre for Aboriginal Economic Policy Research, Australian National University.

Cape York Digital Network (CYDN). (2004). *Clean IT for Cape York*, media release January 28th. Retrieved September 19, 2005, from http://www.cydn.com.au/359.html

Caspary, G., & O'Connor, D. (2003). *Providing low-cost Information Technology access to rural communities in developing countries: What works? What pays* (OECD Development Centre, Working Paper no. 229). Paris: OECD. Retrieved September 19, 2005, from http://www.oecd.org

Daly, A. (2002). Telecommunications services in rural and remote indigenous communities in Australia. *Economic Papers, 21*(1), 18-31.

Daly, A. (2005). *Bridging the digital divide: The role of community online access centres in indigenous communities* (CAEPR Discussion Paper 273). Canberra: Centre for Aboriginal Economic Policy Research, Australian National University.

Department of Communications, Information Technology and the Arts (DCITA). (2002). *Telecommunications action plan for remote indigenous communities.* Retrieved September 19, 2005, from http://www.dcita.gov.au

Department of Communications, Information Technology and the Arts (DCITA). (2003). *Maintaining the viability of online access centres in regional, rural and remote Australia* (discussion paper). Canberra: DCITA. Retrieved September 19, 2005, from http://www.dcita.gov.au.

Dyson, L. (2003, June 19-21). Indigenous Australians in the information age: Exploring issues of neutrality in Information Technology. In C. Ciborra, R. Mercurio, M. De Marco, M. Martinez, & A. Carignani (Eds.), *New paradigms in organizations, markets and society: Proceedings of the 11th European Conference on Information Systems (ECIS),* Naples, Italy. Retrieved September 19, 2005, from http://www-staff.it.uts.edu.au/~laurel

Farr, P. (2004, September 5-7). *Achieving sustainability and "triple bottom line": Outcomes for community online access centres.* Paper presented to the International Telecommunications Society 15th Biennial Conference, Berlin.

Lloyd, R., & Bill, A. (2004). *Australia online: How Australians are using computers and the Internet* (Australian Census Analytic Program, cat. No. 2056.0). Canberra: Australian Bureau of Statistics.

Lloyd, R., & Hellwig, O. (2000). The digital divide. *Agenda, 17*(4), 345-58.

Regional Telecommunications Inquiry (RTI). (2002). *Connecting regional Australia: The report of the Regional Telecommunications Inquiry.* Retrieved September 19, 2005, from http://www.telinquiry.gov.au/rti-report.html

Schwab, R. G., & Sutherland, D. (2003). Indigenous learning communities: A vehicle for community empowerment and capacity development. *Learning Communities: International Journal of Learning in Social Contexts, 1*(1), 53-70.

Chapter X
Global Knowledge Management Technology Strategies and Competitive Functionality from Global IT in the International Construction Industry

William Schulte
Shenandoah University, USA

Kevin J. O'Sullivan
New York Institute of Technology, USA

ABSTRACT

Information and knowledge management technologies and globalization have changed how firms in service industries formulate, implement, and sustain competitive advantage. This research project contributes to our understanding of the relationships between global knowledge management technology strategies and competitive functionality from global IT. Based on field research, this study found that global knowledge management technology strategies have a positive impact on competitive advantage from information technology applications functionality from global IT. This study provides recommendations to international engineering, procurement, and construction industry executives regarding the impact of knowledge management strategies and global information technology on competitive advantage of firms in their industry.

RESEARCH ISSUE

Global knowledge management technologies have changed how firms in service industries formulate, implement, and sustain competitive advantage (Schulte, 2004). Moreover, information technology and telecommunications have been driving forces behind the globalization of many industries (Roche & Blaine, 2000). In addition, global information technology has ushered in the knowledge economy and enabled knowledge management to enhance competitive advantage (Stankosky, 2005; Schulte, 1999; Giraldo & Schulte, 2005). Knowledge creating factors managed by governments have also enhanced the innovation of many firms and patent production in industries around the world (Revilak, 2006).

Moreover, the strategic importance of information technology is an established proposition in the information systems and strategic management literature (Roche & Blaine, 2000). In addition, scholars have argued that multinational corporations (MNCs) have improved performance by ensuring that their information technology and knowledge management strategies are congruent with their business and corporate strategies (Giraldo & Schulte, 2004; Stankosky, 2004). In general, knowledge management is a widely accepted factor in creating efficiency, effectiveness, and sustainable competitive advantage (Stankosky, 2004; Schulte & Sample, 2005; Davenport & Prusak, 1997; Drucker, Garvin, Leonard, Straus, & Brown, 1998; Edvinsson & Malone, 1997; Dixon, 2000; Nonaka & Takeuchi, 1995; O'Dell & Grayson, 1998; Schwartz, 2005; Sveiby, 1997; Stewart, 1997; Choo & Bontis, 2002; Liebowitz & Wilcox, 1997; Revilak, 2006).

RESEARCH QUESTION

This research project will attempt to contribute to our understanding of the relationships between global information technologies, knowledge management, and competitive advantage. Competitive advantage is the most important common denominator in the global information technology, knowledge management, and international corporate strategy literature. This study is an exploration of the factors that contribute to the competitive performance of firms competing in international engineering, procurement, and construction industry. The purpose of this study is to explore the following research question:

To what extent do global information and knowledge management technologies affect the competitive advantage of global organizations in the international engineering, procurement, and construction industry?

This study provides recommendations, based on the results of the research, to international engineering, procurement, and construction industry executives about how knowledge management technology strategies can impact functionality competitiveness from information technology applications including knowledge management systems.

THE INTERNATIONAL ENGINEERING, PROCUREMENT, AND CONSTRUCTION (IEPC) INDUSTRY

Construction is one of the most influential industries in the world (Schulte, 1997, 2004). This position is based on the following nine arguments. First, it is the world's largest industry, representing a significant percentage of the world's total Gross Domestic Product. Because construction is labor intensive, it creates a significant share of global employment, especially in developing countries.

Second, changes in the construction services industry have an exponential impact on the world economy. Construction's impact extends far into the value chain, both upstream and downstream in many industries. Construction projects increase sales in related industries such as heavy equipment, transportation, cement, steel, and financial and other services. Furthermore, the spin-off effect of the industry influences all major industries in the economy, particularly those requiring industrial plant, commercial facilities, or infrastructure construction.

Third, despite recent increases in privatization, regional economic integration, and market liberalization in emerging markets, construction continues to have some degree of government protection worldwide. Many governments on all levels provide local content rules or erect barriers to entry from foreign competitors to ensure the viability of domestic firms.

Fourth, the long-term consequences of the IEPC industry affect many stakeholders in society. Projects promote higher standards of living and economic development. This fosters an increase in the number and variety of goods and services available to consumers. The spillover creates not only economic, but also social benefits.

Fifth, the IEPC industry is inextricably linked to government. Government is both a major client and a major supplier to contractors. While they are sometimes used as an instrument of a government's domestic and foreign policies, contractors also exert a significant influence on government policy.

Sixth, while its impact on the world economy and government policies is considerable, as discussed above, the IEPC industry is extremely sensitive to macroeconomic adjustments, political changes, and advancements or setbacks in related and even unrelated industries.

Seventh, the industry is also highly concentrated. A relatively small group of very large firms control a significant amount of billings awarded to foreign contractors in the worldwide market.

Eighth, another unique trait is that, unlike most exports, the exported product is constructed almost entirely in the host country.

Finally, construction projects in the IEPC industry typically extend over a long time period. Therefore, success in the industry is affected by a contractor's ability to manage overlapping projects at different stages at different job sites over time, and by building sustainable competitive advantage (Schulte, 1997).

LITERATURE REVIEW

The new globally competitive information economy increases complexity for information execu-

tives to more than they have had to manage in the past. For example, traditional national and regional boundaries are being redrawn by information and Web technologies. Also, regulations, standards, trade policies, tax policies, and other economic and political forces are responding to the needs of the knowledge economy. Social and other external pressures are evolving to keep pace with the global changes. Infrastructure investment priorities are also adapting. Telecommunications infrastructures in many nations are privatizing and moving toward more advanced technologies, leapfrogging ahead of many more economically advanced countries. As global competition increases, the integration of strategic management and information technology will become a more significant factor in the competitive advantage, innovation, and financial performance of firms around the world (Schulte, 1999; Revilak, 2006).

Also, scholars have recently begun to integrate research from different disciplines including international strategic management, global information technology, and knowledge management to explore answers to questions about the management of global information and knowledge management technology. In recent years, studies have been conducted providing support for the strategic impact of global information and knowledge management technology, and competitive advantage in global organizations (Giraldo & Schulte, 2005; Schulte, 2004).

Knowledge Management and Competitive Advantage

Leaders in global organizations need to develop adaptive knowledge management skills to achieve competitive advantage. They usually formulate strategic plans based on models that do not address complexity and dynamic knowledge workplaces. They also focus on precise metrics instead of patterns generated by the flow of global knowledge. Traditional approaches to gain sustainable competitive advantage are limited. Recent research answered the following research question: Are there any correlations between knowledge management technologies, knowledge flows, communities of practice, and actions conducted to adapt an organization to its external and internal environments? Strong correlations were found using an organizational learning and action framework (Giraldo & Schulte, 2005).

Moreover, scholars have identified the need for an organizational transformation that emphasizes collective knowledge and team development. It is clear in their literature that survival depends on converting the organization into a knowledge-based organization (Drucker, 2001). Knowledge is becoming a critical resource for global success and is a source of competitive advantage (Nonaka & Takeuchi, 1995; Grant & Spender, 1997: Grant, 1997; Spender, 1997). Consequently, efforts in developing collaboration and knowledge management are essential to the survival of the firm that attempts to compete in the global knowledge economy (Doz, Santos, & Williamson, 2001).

Both external and internal knowledge are sources of competitive advantage (Stankosky, 2005). Frameworks have been posited that attempt to understand the flow of knowledge and

the knowledge creation process within an organization as a source of competitive advantage (Nonaka & Takeuchi, 1995). Others suggest that a relationship between organizational knowledge and competitive advantage be moderated by the firm's ability to integrate and apply knowledge. Many scholars have explored the impact of accumulating knowledge, creating value, and establishing competitive advantage (Choo & Bontis, 2002; Liebowitz & Wilcox, 1997).

Global Knowledge Integration and Local Responsiveness Framework

Simon and Grover (1993) explored the strategic use of information technology in international business and developed a framework for information technology applications. The authors explored the use of information technology by applying the global integration and local responsiveness (I/R) framework as proposed by Prahalad and Doz (1987). Their study also explored the dimensions of competitive advantage that theoretically emerges from an overall fit between information technology strategy and business strategy. Simon and Grover (1993) conclude:

Figure 1. Global knowledge integration/local knowledge responsiveness: International corporate strategy categories (Adapted from Bartlett et al., 2003; Prahalad & Doz, 1987; Schulte, 2004)

...the link between IT and international business strategy can define the boundaries of the firm and facilitate its success or failure. The ability to coordinate and control the dispersed activities of these global firms is essential to the attainment of competitive advantage in the global marketplace. The [I/R] framework demonstrates how the fit between a firm's strategic decisions and IT applications can be used to attain competitive advantage in the international environment. (p. 40)

The transnational solution provides new structures and new leadership requirements to compete globally (Bartlett, Ghoshal, & Birkinshaw, 2003; Johnson, Lenn, & O' Neill). Interestingly, some scholars who discuss global information and knowledge management technology management also applied the global integration/local responsiveness model to help explain the impact of information technology decisions on a firm's competitive advantage (Schulte, 2004; Deans & Ricks, 1993; Palvia, Palvia, & Zigli, 1992). Figure 1 provides a modification of the global integration and local responsiveness framework introducing the knowledge dimension (Schulte, 2004).

Global Information and Knowledge Management Technology

The management of global information and technology is a rapidly growing area of interest to researchers in information systems, international management, and strategic management (Roche & Blaine, 2000; Schulte, 1999; Banker, Kauffman, & Mahmood, 1993). Consequently, they argue that the strategic information technology capabilities of management have a positive and significant impact on firm competitiveness (Palvia et al., 1992).

In summary, important conclusions can be derived from the literature on the management of global information and knowledge management technology:

1. Firms competing in the global marketplace that align their information and knowledge management technology capabilities with their overall corporate and business strategies will benefit from increased sustainable competitive advantage.

2. Information and knowledge management technology capabilities are not the primary contributors to this competitive advantage. Technology is an enabler of management capabilities (Schulte & Sample, 2005; Deans & Ricks, 1993; Ives & Jarvenpaa, 1991).

Given the strategic importance of information technology, how can it be measured? The next section of this document addresses the issue of strategic information technology measurement. In the search for reliable tools to measure information technology impacts on competitive advantage, one framework has endured. Not only has it been developed from a foundation in strategic management theory, but it also has been empirically validated and tested for reliability (Schulte, 1999). That framework is the Competitive Advantage Provided by an Information Technology Application (CAPITA) developed by Sethi and King (1994). The next section of this chapter discusses this useful framework.

Competitive Advantage Provided by Information Technology Applications

Sethi and King (1994) developed a replicable model and framework to understand the relationships between information technology applications and competitive advantage. They identified attributes that characterize the competitive advantage of the firm. The advantage of this approach is that it provides information about how and why information technology affects competitive advantage.

The CAPITA framework was empirically tested to assess the measurement properties to ensure the framework's usefulness as a research tool by evaluating unidimensionality, convergent validity, discriminant validity, predictive validity, and reliability. According to Sethi and King (1994), "the CAPITA dimensions are positively correlated with each other and...all coefficients are significant. This implies that the CAPITA dimensions accrue multiple benefits to the organization" (p. 1616).

This study borrows from the CAPITA construct to identify and measure the global strategic information technology capabilities and knowledge management strategies of the firm. The CAPITA dimensions used in this study include resource management functionality and resource acquisition functionality. "Resource acquisition functionality measures the impact of the firm's ability to order, acquire and accept a resource. Resource management functionality consists of the impact of IT on the utilization, upgrade, transfer, disposition, accounting and post-acquisition leverage of the firm's resources" (Sethi & King, 1994, p. 1613).

These strategic information technology capabilities are grounded in both the industrial organization economics and the resource-based views of the firm. Functionality competitive advantage theoretical constructs and relevance to firm performance are summarized in Table 1.

RESEARCH HYPOTHESIS

Global knowledge management technologies (GKMTs) have become important determinants for international expansion and competitiveness in the IEPC industry. This section of the chapter will discuss the framework hypotheses, revised conclusions, implications, and recommendations for extension and replication of this research.

Based on the literature review, it is logical to ask: What impact does global knowledge management technology strategy have on CAPITA functionality from global information technology? This exploration brings us closer to an approximation of the real relationships between global information and knowledge management technology and competitive advantage in the IEPC industry. The following is the hypothesis generated from the literature review and field interviews:

H1:   As global knowledge management technology strategies increase, CAPITA functionality from global IT increases.

To test the hypothesis in this study, the independent and dependent variables were calculated and transformed by creating indexes of the means of

Table 1. CAPITA dimensions supporting theoretical concepts, authors, and relevance to firm performance (Adapted from Sethi & King, 1994, p. 1605; Schulte, 1999)

CAPITA Dimension	Theoretical Constructs	Relevance to Firm Performance
	Differentiation	Uniqueness
	Customer service	Build and maintain customer loyalty
Functionality	Add value for customers	Increase innovator's market share
	New products and services	Change the nature of the industry
	Unique product features	Increase market power

the items used to measure each construct. The key constructs of interest were CAPITA functionality from global information technologies (GITs) and global knowledge management technology strategies. CAPITA functionality from global IT index was calculated from the responses to the surveys by the CIOs of the firms. The global knowledge management strategy index was calculated from responses from the firm's CEOs.

Table 2. Survey items used to calculate CAPITA functionality from global IT

	Survey Measure Items Respondents were asked to respond on a scale from 1 to 7 on statements based on the following effect of global IT on the item.
CAPITA Functionality from Global IT Variables	• Impact on primary users to monitor the use of the resource • Impact on primary users to upgrade the resource if necessary • Impact on primary users to transfer or dispose of the resource • Impact on primary users to evaluate the overall effectiveness or usefulness of the resource • Impact on primary users to order or put in a request for the resource • Impact on primary users to acquire the resource • Impact on primary users to verify that the resource meets specifications

Table 3. Survey items used to calculate global knowledge management technology strategies

• The main role of foreign operations should be to implement parent company strategies. • New knowledge should be developed at the parent company and then transferred to foreign units. • A firm should provide coordination and control necessary for efficient operations throughout the firm. • A firm's systems should be simultaneously globally efficient, provide local responsiveness, and quickly diffuse organizational innovation. • Solutions should use international standards and a planned common architecture that meets the needs of various-sized foreign operations in diverse environments. • Solutions and applications should be shared across the worldwide organization. • A firm should use universal dictionaries for understanding solutions and applications. • Innovation should be a cooperative activity sharing knowledge between home office and foreign operations. • A firm should build information and communication cost advantages through centralized knowledge management. • A firm's strategy should be focused on worldwide efficiencies from a global information and communications system. • Organization learning should emerge from contacts between home office and foreign operations personnel. • A firm should have strong linkages between the home office and foreign operations based on cooperation and mutual assistance. • A firm should rapidly disseminate innovations while continuing to provide flexibility required to be responsive to local needs of foreign operations. • Foreign operations receive and adapt products and services offered by the parent company to the best advantage in the countries in which they operate. • A firm should centralize its systems to achieve global economies of scale.

Table 4. Internal reliability of the constructs in the study using Cronbach's alpha

Construct	Cronbach's Alpha
CAPITA Functionality from Global IT	.9323
GKMT Score	.9110

DATA COLLECTION AND TARGET SAMPLE

Questionnaires were mailed to the CEO and CIO of the top 225 firms in the international engineering, procurement, and construction industry as defined by the *Engineering News Record,* a top-tier professional journal for the GCS industry. This choice was considered the most appropriate single source. Sethi and King (1998) acknowledged that "the use of multiple respondents, including senior business executives and IT users, would have enriched the data further and eliminated some biases and inaccuracies" (p. 1608).

The population for this study was the Top 225 global contractors as described by the *Engineering News Record.* The response rate was about 20% (46 out of 225) respondent firms, and the population's global market share growth and other measures were compared to ensure representative nature of the sample. This is a typical operation procedure in strategic management research and was used in previous studies (Schulte, 1999).

Given that this study does not attempt to explain firm behavior beyond the population of the top 225 firms, this sample can be used for purposes of statistical inference. This study only generalizes to the industry segment represented by the top 225 firms described by *ENR.* Statistical significance, therefore, is relevant in this case and was used to make statements from the specific sample to the whole industry segment. Moreover, this study does not attempt to claim casualty.

In addition, this study enriched the data collection process and reduced potential limitations by gaining support of *ENR*'s publisher and editor, and other international engineering, procurement, and construction industry opinion leaders. In his study, Schulte (1999) found the items to measure CAPITA functionality from global IT and global knowledge management technology to have a high degree of reliability and construct validity. Survey measures for CAPITA functionality from global IT are listed in Table 2. The items used to measure global knowledge management technology strategies are summarized in Table 3.

RELIABILITY OF MEASURES

A key concern in this type of research is ensuring reliable measures—that is, variables that constantly measure the same phenomenon. Strategies to enhance reliability of measures included the following: consistently recording data, using continuous rather than discrete data for performance measures, and using multiple items to measure concepts so that the relationships can be empirically analyzed using multiple statistical techniques including cluster analysis and discriminant analysis. As summarized in Table 4, Cronbach's alpha was calculated for the constructs derived from the items in the survey instruments that yielded high reliability.

CONCLUSION

This study explored the relationships of CAPITA functionality from global IT and GKMT strategy.

To that end, correlations and regressions were conducted between GKMT and CAPITA functionality from global IT to test the hypothesis. CAPITA functionality from global IT served as the dependent variable in each case. The independent predictor variable was the global knowledge management technology index. As can be seen in Table 5, CAPITA functionality from global IT is significantly correlated to global knowledge management technology at the $p < .01$ level. Multicollinearity was not an issue.

Based on the data collected, it appears that increases in knowledge management technology strategies will increase the functionality competitive advantage provided by global information technology applications. In this sample of IEPC firms, as GKMT scores increased, CAPITA functionality from global IT also increased as illustrated in Figure 2.

MANAGERIAL IMPLICATIONS

These findings support a strategy that global information and knowledge management technology should have more recognition and resources in IEPC firms. In addition, GKMT managers in IEPC firms could use these results to negotiate for an influential role in the strategic formulation discussions of the firm. Specific global knowledge management technology strategies are strongly correlated with CAPITA functionality from global IT. This study provides a heuristic guide for IEPC executives to make decisions and formulate global knowledge management technology strategies to achieve competitive advantage from IT applications. The following list provides a summary of strategic guidelines to achieve competitive functionality using global knowledge management technologies.

- The main role of foreign operations should be to implement parent company strategies.

- New knowledge should be developed at the parent company and then transferred to foreign units.

- A firm's KMT should provide coordination and control necessary for efficient operations throughout the firm.

- A firm's KMT systems should be simultaneously globally efficient, provide local responsiveness, and quickly diffuse organizational innovation.

- KMT solutions should use international standards and a planned common architecture that meets the needs of various-sized foreign operations in diverse environments.

- KMT solutions and applications should be shared across the worldwide organization.

- A firm should use universal KMT dictionaries for understanding solutions and applications.

- Innovation should be a cooperative activity sharing knowledge between home office and foreign operations.

- A firm should build information and communication cost advantages through centralized knowledge management.

- A firm's KMT strategy should be focused on worldwide efficiencies from a global information and communications system.

- Organization learning should emerge from contacts between home office and foreign operations KMT personnel.

- A firm should have strong KMT linkages between the home office and foreign operations based on cooperation and mutual assistance.

- A firm should rapidly disseminate KMT innovations while continuing to provide flexibility to respond to local KMT needs of foreign operations.

- Foreign operations should receive and adapt KMT products and services offered by the parent company to the best advantage in the countries in which they operate.

- A firm should centralize its KMT systems to achieve global economies of scale.

Table 5. Correlations of CAPITA by GIKMT scores

	GKMT SCORE
CAPITA Functionality from Global IT	.586**

*** Correlation is significant at the 0.01 level (2-tailed).*

Figure 2. Plot of CAPITA functionality and GKMT score

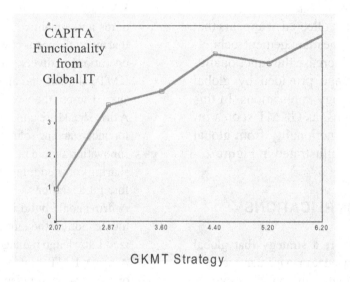

Implications for IEPC executives from these strategies include several changes to the management of their firms including the construction value chain. For example, some IEPC firms work 24 hours a day on design projects and proposals as teams share knowledge and engineering drawings on a global intranet. At the end of the workday, the design team in the United States hands off their work and tacit knowledge to the team in Europe, who then passes along their work to the team in Asia. Eight hours later the team in the United States resumes work on the plans with the added knowledge and insight by the entire global design team.

SUGGESTIONS FOR FUTURE RESEARCH

This was an exploratory study in a single segment of the world's largest service industry. Obviously, much more research, replications, and interpretation must be done. In general, this study calls for more global and interdisciplinary research combining insight from practitioners and theorists from strategic knowledge management, international strategic management, and global information technology. This type of multidisciplinary research is needed to better understand the complex dynamics of a globalizing knowledge economy.

Several areas of research could include the following:

1. The RBV school plays an important role in understanding Global Information and Knowledge Management Technology.
2. The knowledge-based view may provide additional insight into the strategic management of global information and knowledge management technology.
3. Other dimensions of competitive advantage from knowledge and information technologies should be analyzed including efficiencies, innovation, and sustainable competitive advantage.

Clearly, more research must be done to develop a comprehensive understanding of global information and knowledge management technologies and their impact on competitive advantage. Knowledge can be seen as part of the resource-based view of the firm, where global IT knowledge and knowledge creation, application, and storage are strategic capabilities of the firm.

REFERENCES

Banker, R.D., Kauffman, R.J., & Mahmood, M.A. (Eds.). (1993). *Strategic information technology management: Perspectives on organizational growth and competitive advantage.* Hershey, PA: Idea Group.

Bartlett, C.A., & Ghoshal, S. (1991). Global strategic management: Impact on the new frontiers of strategy research. *Strategic Management Journal, 12,* 5-16.

Bartlett, C.A., Ghoshal, S., & Birkinshaw, J. (2003). *Transnational management: Text and cases* (4th ed.). New York: McGraw-Hill/Irwin.

Choo, C., & Bontis, N. (2002). *The strategic management of intellectual capital and organizational knowledge.* New York: Oxford University Press.

Davenport, T., & Prusak, L. (1998). *Working knowledge.* Boston: Harvard Business School Press.

Deans, P.C., & Karwan, K.R. (Eds.). (1994). *Global information systems and technology: Focus on the organization and its functional areas.* Hershey, PA: Idea Group.

Deans, P.C., & Ricks, D.A. (1993). An agenda for research linking information systems and international business: Theory, methodology and application. *Journal of Global Information Management,* (1), 6-19.

Dixon, N.M. (2000). *Common knowledge: How companies thrive by sharing what they know.* Boston: Harvard Business School Press.

Doz, Y.L., Santos, J., & Williamson, P. (2001). *From global to metanational: How companies win in the knowledge economy.* Boston: Harvard Business School Press.

Drucker, P. (2001). *Management challenges for the 21st century* (1st ed.). New York: Collins.

Drucker P.F., Garvin, D., Leonard, D., Straus, S., & Brown, J.S. (1998). *Harvard business review on knowledge management.* Boston: Harvard Business School Press.

Edvinsson, L., & Malone, M. (1997). *Intellectual capital: Realizing your company's true value by finding its hidden brainpower.* New York: HarperCollins.

Giraldo, J.P., & Schulte, W.D. (2005). An exploration of the effects of knowledge management on global leadership. *Proceedings of the Academy of International Business Southeastern United States Annual Meeting* (pp. 206-217).

Grant, R.M. (1997). The knowledge-based view of the firm: Implications for management practice. *Long Range Planning, 30*(3), 450-454.

Grant, R., & Spender, J.C. (Eds.). (1997). Knowledge and the firm: An overview. *Journal of International Business, 17,* 5-9.

Ives, B., & Jarvenpaa, S.L. (1991). Application of global information technology: Key issues for management. *MIS Quarterly,* 33-49.

Johnson, J.H. Jr., Lenn, D.J., & O'Neill, H.M. (1997). Patterns of competition among American firms in a global industry: Evidence from the U.S. construction equipment industry. *Journal of International Management, 3*(3), 207-239.

Liebowitz, J., & Wilcox, L.C. (1997). *Knowledge elements and its integrative elements.* New York: CRC Press.

Nonaka, I., & Takeushi, H. (1995). *The knowledge-creating company.* New York: Oxford University Press.

Palvia, S., Palvia, P., & Zigli, R. (Eds.). (1992). *The global issues of information technology management.* Hershey, PA: Idea Group.

Prahalad, C.K., & Doz, Y.L. (1987). *The multinational mission: Balancing local demands and global vision.* Boston: The Free Press.

O'Dell, C., & Grayson Jr., C.J. (1998). *If only we knew what we know: The transfer of internal knowledge and best practice.* New York: The Free Press.

Revilak, A. (2006). *Knowledge management and innovation: An analysis of knowledge factors controlled by governments and their impact on patent creation.* Unpublished Doctoral Dissertation, George Washington University, USA.

Ribiere, V., Park, H., & Schulte, W.D. (2004). Critical attributes of organizational culture that promote knowledge management technology success. *Journal of Knowledge Management, 8*(3), 106-117.

Roche, E., & Blaine, M. (Eds.). (1993). *Information technology in multinational enterprises.* Northampton (USA): Edward Elgar.

Schulte, W.D. (2000). The strategic management of global information technology: Theoretical foundations. In E. Roche & M. Blaine (Eds.), *Information technology in multinational enterprises.* Northampton (USA): Edward Elgar.

Schulte, W.D. (2004). Information and knowledge management technologies and competitive advantage in global organizations. *Proceedings of the Academy of International Business Southeastern United States Annual Meeting* (pp. 25-36).

Schulte, W.D. (1997). Is globalocalization the most effective strategic response for international contractors? *Proceedings of the Academy of International Business UK Chapter Annual Meeting* (pp. 455-473).

Schulte, W.D., & Sample, T.L. (2006). Efficiencies from knowledge management technologies in a military enterprise. *Journal of Knowledge Management, 10*(6).

Schwartz, D. (Ed.). (2005). *Encyclopedia of knowledge management.* Hershey, PA: Idea Group.

Sethi, V., & King, W.R. (1994). Development of measures to assess the extent to which an information technology application provides competitive advantage. *Management Science, 40*(2), 1601-1621.

Simon, S.J., & Grover, V. (1993). Strategic use of information technology in international business: A framework for information technology application. *Journal of Global Information Technology, 1*(2), 33-44.

Spender, J.C. (1996). Organizational knowledge, learning and memory: Three concepts in search of a theory. *Journal of Organizational Change Management, 9*(1), 63-78.

Stankosky, M. (Ed.). (2005). *Creating the discipline of knowledge management: The latest in university research.* Oxford: Elsevier Butterworth-Heinemann.

Stewart, T. (1997). *Intellectual capital: The new wealth of organizations.* New York: Doubleday.

Sveiby, K.E. (1997). *The new organizational wealth: Managing & measuring knowledge-based assets.* San Francisco: Berrett-Koehler.

Section III
Tools and Technologies

Chapter XI
Cross Cultural Adaptation in E–Learning

Emmanuel Blanchard
University of Montréal, Canada

Claude Frasson
University of Montréal, Canada

ABSTRACT

This chapter introduces the concepts of culturally aware systems (CAWAS), a new family of adaptive systems that try to adapt learning contents and pedagogical strategies according to learners' cultural background. CAWAS is based on the notion of cultural intelligence and on the representation of a culture as both a static system, that is, a "relatively stable system of shared meanings, a repository of meaningful symbols…" and a dynamic one, that is, "a process of production of meanings." A methodology for cultural evaluation and selection of appropriate resources is described. A system implementing this methodology is finally introduced. The aim of this work is to develop systems that will be better accepted by learners and de facto will work more efficiently by showing a cultural proximity with learners during a learning session.

INTRODUCTION

E-learning, the way of teaching people through the Internet, is a growing practice in educational systems. High-speed Internet, lower costs of computers, and the increase of the computer science understanding in the population make this methodology accessible to more people over the years. This "democratization" is undoubtedly positive news, but it also implies new objectives for this study. While information is globally accessible and networking technologies have greatly evolved, we can now think of e-learning applications accessible and available, where thousands of learners coming from all six continents could coexist synchronously and learn together.

Current literature (Hofstede, 2001) suggests that culture can have a great impact on the way people and learners behave in particular situations. This impact concerns the way the learner or student interacts with his/her environment, with his/her peers, and on the meaning he/she gives to specific concepts or symbols. In this respect, within the cross-cultural studies framework, the relationship between cultural membership and concept/symbols interpretation is obvious.

If the content of a global e-learning activity is not adapted according to culture, there are risks that learners with different cultural backgrounds will interpret the same concept in a different manner. The representation that an author (within the framework of a particular country) makes of the domain to be learned could also be disturbing for learners with different cultural values. Following this same idea, we have noticed that the positive impact of pedagogical strategies used in intelligent tutoring systems (ITS) (i.e., software systems that use artificial intelligence techniques to adapt the teaching to the profile of the learner) may differ depending on the cultural background of the learner. How to adapt content displayed to a learner and how to choose the most suitable pedagogical strategy for this learner depending on his/her cultural specificities. This is the question we try to deal with in this work.

BACKGROUND

According to Kashima (2000), there are two schools of thought when defining culture. Some researchers see a culture as "a process of production and reproduction of meanings in particular actors' concrete practices or actions or activities in particular contexts in time and space." For others, it is a "relatively stable system of shared meanings, a repository of meaningful symbols, which provides structure to experience." From our perspective, a major distinction between the two definitions is the way culture is seen as a static or dynamic system. Both definitions agree on the fact that culture and concept/symbol interpretation are closely linked. In fact, many studies have shown that, depending on one's cultural background, the learner can give drastically different meanings to concepts, symbols, and practices (Hofstede, 2001).

But concept representation is just one among others' examples of elements that are important in the e-learning and ITS research fields and can be influenced by the cultural background of a learner. The following are examples that illustrate the aforementioned points:

- **Emotions:** Emotions have a growing importance in the e-learning and ITS research field (Chaffar & Frasson, 2004; Conati, 2002). It appears that there are strong links between culture and emotional behaviors. According to Scollon, Diener, Oishi, and Biswas-Diener (2004), the frequency to which someone feels positive or negative emotions is culturally dependant, and the categorization itself of an emotion as positive or negative can in some cases depend on the cultural background (Kim-Prieto, Fujita, & Diener, 2004). There is also the belief that, depending on the culture, emotions of the learners can be expressed in a very different manner (Shaver and Schwartz, 1992).

- **Preference for a pedagogical strategy:** Learners from some cultures tend to prefer collaborative works, whereas in other cultures, the preference is given to individualistic works (Blanchard & Frasson, 2005).

- **Reward allocation:** Depending on the culture, the way teachers reward their students and the ways these students react to these rewards have been found to be different from culture to culture (Fischer & Smith, 2003).

- **Test anxiety:** Some students find it more or less stressful to take a test or an assessment, depending on their cultural background (Cassady, Mohammed, & Mathieu, 2004).
- **Motivation and autonomy support:** According to the self-determination theory (Ryan & Deci, 2000), autonomy support, that is, the need for someone to see their behaviors as self-endorsed, has been proven to be a cross-cultural way of enhancing motivation. But methods used to fulfill this psychological need can change from a culture to another (Chirkov, Ryan, Kim, & Kaplan, 2003; Chirkov, Ryan, & Willness, 2005; Levesque, Zuehlke, Stanek, & Ryan, 2004).

The next section presents the architecture of our main work called CAWAS: a culturally aware system for e-learning activities (Blanchard & Frasson, 2005). Following this, there will be a discussion on the implementation process of the authoring tool to create *cultural templates* of documents.

A CAWAS uses the so-called cultural templates in a process we have proposed in order to adapt displayed multimedia contents to a learner's cultural specificities. This process also depends on the methodology we have chosen to represent cultural groups and cultural specificities of learners and resources. Currently, research is underway to adapt this methodology to help selecting the most suitable behaviors that a pedagogical agent (i.e., an autonomous software module that has pedagogical abilities for teaching learning contents) will exhibit in an ITS.

Finally, we introduce the system in which we implemented our methodology and that is being enhanced to allow the management of culturally sensitive elements, such as autonomy support, management of learner's emotions, or selection of the most suitable pedagogical strategy.

CULTURALLY AWARE SYSTEMS

There are two main ideas behind the CAWAS design for e-learning: a notion of cultural intelligence and a dual representation of cultural rules.

Cultural Intelligence

The objective of this system is to adapt to learners' cultural specificities. This means that our system must be culturally intelligent, which is described by Earley and Mosakowski (2004) as a "seemingly natural ability to interpret someone's unfamiliar and ambiguous gestures the way that person's compatriots would." Two different aspects of the concept of cultural intelligence are needed in a CAWAS:

- **Understanding:** Understanding is the ability for the system to translate a learner's behavior/feeling/result depending on the learner's cultural specificities. This translation must allow the system to judge learners on the same basis.
- **Adaptation:** Adaptation is the ability for the system to display different interfaces and/or to start different learning strategies depending on the learner's cultural specificities. This translation must allow the system to give a better answer to the needs of a learner.

To resolve this constraint, we have designed CAWAS with a *culturally intelligent agent* (CIA) as a central module. A CIA is composed of two inner agents: (1) a *cultural transcriptor agent* (CTA) for the understanding aspect and (2) a *cultural action agent* (CAA) for the adaptation aspect.

Dual Representation of Cultural Rules

As mentioned earlier, there are two ways of defining a culture. We think that both of these

Figure 1. An architecture for a Culturally AWAre System CAWAS

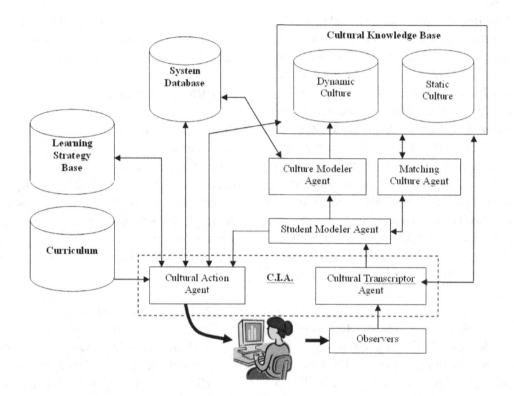

definitions can present advantages for e-learning activities. For instance:

- The first definition, culture as "a process of production of meanings…" (i.e., a dynamic system), could be used conjointly with cognitive assessments of emotional state in order to better understand learner's reaction in a specific emotional context.
- The second definition, culture as a "relatively stable system of shared meanings, a repository of meaningful symbols…" (i.e., a static system), could be used to explain variations in learning results, practices, and behaviors across cultural clusters.

In a CAWAS, in order to fit with this dual definition, the cultural knowledge base contains two kinds of cultural data:

- **Static culture data:** Static rules obtained from readings in the cross-cultural domain; for instance, *pride can be considered as a positive emotion for a learner of a western country.*
- **Dynamic culture data:** Rules that are dynamically obtained by analysis of the use of the system; for instance, *French learners in the system prefer to work collaboratively.*

Architecture of a Culturally Aware System for E-Learning

In this part, we describe the general architecture of a CAWAS as shown in Figure 1.

The learner is first observed according to a variety of parameters able to distinguish specific behaviors.

These data are culturally interpreted by the CTA using cultural knowledge obtained from the culture knowledge base (for instance, "*pride can be considered as a positive emotion for a learner coming from this country*"). As we have seen before, cultural data express more a tendency than the exact attitude for every member of a cultural group.

The *student modeler agent* (SMA) receives both data from the observer and the CTA. The SMA asks the *matching culture agent* in order to obtain the learner's cultural types. It also transmits the learner profile to the *culture modeler agent* (CMA). This one generates new cultural clusters that are stored in the dynamic culture module. Those clusters are composed of a set of empirical rules deducted from the use of the system. The static culture module, on the other side, contains theoretical rules and assumptions on the cultural behaviors. For instance, we can

use assumptions deduced from Hofstede's (2001) values and cross-cultural studies. An example of such an assumption can be: "*if Hofstede's IDV is high, people will have a tendency to work individually.*" (Marcus and Gould [2000] have also proposed a set of rules inspired by Hofstede's work and concerning the cultural adaptation of user interface. However, all these suppositions have to be validated empirically.) A factor of certainty is also allowed to each of the cultural rules. These factors evolve given outcomes produced by the learner while he uses CAWAS.

The SMA provides a complete status of the learner profile to the CAA. This profile includes the level of knowledge of the learner, information on his/her personality traits, on his/her cognitive state (emotion and motivation), and on his/her membership to specific cultural groups obtained from the matching culture agent. The CAA asks the cultural knowledge base to obtain the certainty

Figure 2. Interface of an authoring tool for cultural templates and two possible resulting documents

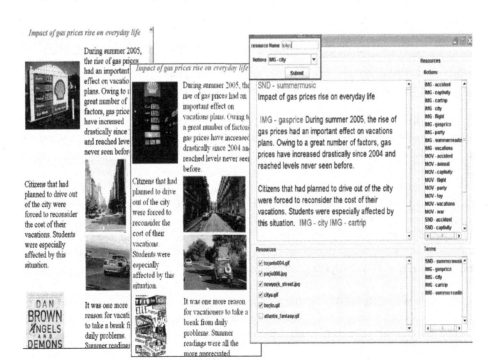

values associated with the rules of the cultural profile of the learner. Given all the information provided by the SMA, the CAA is then in charge of planning the learning session, determining learning strategies to use, and selecting information and resources in the curriculum and in the system database in order to present the course.

IMPLEMENTATION OF AN AUTHORING TOOL TO PRODUCE CULTURAL TEMPLATES

In this section, we present the implementation of an authoring tool for cultural templates. A cultural template has some similarities with an HTML document. The difference is that there are no multimedia tags. Instead, specific tags represent multimedia contents that will be culturally adapted according to the learner's cultural specificities.

Figure 2 presents the interface of our authoring tool and two documents generated.

In order to create a course, the author can write the text on the text area, in the center of the interface. If he/she wants to add multimedia contents, he/she can browse a list of pairs of values describing the multimedia type of content and the concept he/she wants to illustrate on the right of the interface. Thus he/she is able to select the multimedia content that is needed, that is, a resource of a *type T* representing a *concept C*.

All of the resources linked with the selected pair are listed at the bottom of the interface, and the author has the opportunity to unselect resources that are irrelevant. For instance, in Figure 2, the text concerns a course on the importance of global economy in daily life. "*Atlantis_fantasy.gif,*" an image showing the mythological city of Atlantis is irrelevant for such a course. So this resource is unselected. When a multimedia content is inserted, a text in color representing the pair of values appears in the main text area.

Figure 3. An example of a cultural template

```
(SND - SUMMERMUSIC: socaParty.mp3;sambaDoBrasil.mp3; macarena.mp3;
onTheBeach.mp3) Impact of gas prices rise on everyday life

(IMG - GASPRICE: europompe.jpg; gas.jpg; gasPrice.jpg) During summer
2005, the rise of gas prices had an important effect on vacations
plans. Owing to a great number of factors, gas prices have increased
drastically since 2004 and reached levels never seen before.

Citizens that had planned to drive out of the city were forced to
reconsider the cost of their vacations. Students were especially af-
fected by this situation. (IMG - CITY: toronto094.gif; paris008.jpg;
newyork _ street.jpg; cityA.gif; berlin.gif)(IMG -CARTRIP: deuche.gif;
ontheroad.jpg; car04.gif; maTutureAMoi.jpg)

(IMG - SUMMERREADING: revuepresse.gif; danbrown.gif; vsd.jpg; pelt-
zer.gif) It was one more reason for vacationers to take a break from
daily problems. Summer readings were all the more appreciated.
```

The author has the opportunity to add new resources to the resource base by selecting a pair in the list of available pairs and clicking on a "*add resource*" button. A menu (on the top left corner of the interface in Figure 2) will then be displayed.

Figure 3 presents the cultural template obtained for the example shown in our interface.

In the next part, we present the process of cultural adaptation of multimedia contents.

A PROCESS FOR THE CULTURAL ADAPTATION OF MULTIMEDIA CONTENT

The objective is to obtain a multimedia document adapted to learner's cultural specificities. First, an author has to generate a cultural template. When the author finishes his/her work, the cultural template file is created by the authoring tool.

Figure 4. Process of cultural adaptation of multimedia content

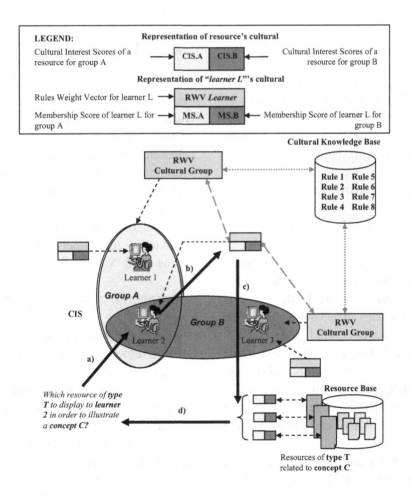

Later, a learner connects to the CAWAS and the system detects that he/she needs to learn some specific knowledge. The system will thus load the cultural template corresponding to the knowledge to be learned. Before displaying the course to the learner, the system will launch a process that will choose which multimedia resources to show to this specific learner.

Many resources can represent the same concept. For instance, if we have to represent the concept "*party,*" we can have pictures of people dancing, eating, discussing, clubbing, laughing, and so forth. The difficulty is to choose the appropriate resource to represent the concept depending on the learner's cultural characteristics. For instance, if we display a picture showing people discussing and drinking alcohol to represent the concept "*party,*" it could have a negative impact on some Muslim learners.

Figure 4 presents this process of choosing a resource to illustrate a concept.

In the next subsections, we will explain how we represent cultural groups, cultural specificities of learners, and the cultural interest score (CIS) of a resource. Then we will describe the process of selecting the correct resource.

Cultural Representations

Representing Cultural Groups

Figure 4 shows two different cultural groups A and B. As mentioned earlier, a CAWAS contains a cultural knowledge base that holds static and dynamic cultural rules. A *rules weights vector* (RWV) is linked to each cultural group. A RWV is a set of weights that are associated to each rule existing in the cultural knowledge base. In Figure 4, the fact that height cultural rules are currently defined in the cultural knowledge base means that each RWV in this CAWAS is currently composed of height weights.

Each weight has a value between 0 and 1. If, in a RWV, the weight of a rule is close to 0, then the people belonging to this cultural group do not refer so much to this rule. The closer the weight is to 1, the stronger the relationship between the rule and people belonging to this cultural group.

Representing Learners' Cultural Specificities

The legend of Figure 4 shows the elements that are present in a learner's model to represent his/her cultural specificities.

As for cultural groups, learners have a personal RWV to represent the extent to which they endorse each of the cultural rules. They also have a membership score for each existing cultural group (MS.A and MS.B in Figure 4). The membership score for a group X (MS.X) is obtained with the following formula:

$$MS.X = \sum_{i=1}^{n} \frac{1 - |L.RWV_i - X.RWV_i|}{n}$$

In this formula, n is the number of existing cultural rules, $L.RWV_i$ is the weight associated to the *rule number i* for the *learner L* and $X.RWV_i$ is the weight associated to the *rule number i* for the cultural group X. One should notice that, given this formula, an MS.X has a float value between 0 and 1. If an MS.X of a learner is high (around 1), the learner belongs to the group X. If an MS.X is around 0, the learner does not belong so much to the group X.

Representing the CIS of a Resource

As stated earlier, in a cultural template of a document, a resource is designated by a pair of values representing the type of the resource and the name of the concept the resource relates to. The CIS represents the suitability of this resource for illustrating the concept to a given cultural group. Each resource has a CIS for each existing cultural group in the system (see the legend of Figure 4). This score is a float number going from 0 (not suitable to use this resource with this cultural group) to 1 (very suitable to use this resource with this cultural group). The evolution of the CIS depends on the learner's results. If a learner belonging to a cultural group X uses this resource and succeeds in an activity, this resource s' CIS increases for the cultural group X; if the learner fails, the CIS for the group X is lowered.

Evolution of the RWV

Weights' evolution in the learner RWV depends on the learner's results. If a rule is used by the CAWAS in order to adapt its response to the learner and the learner succeeds in an activity, the weight associated to this rule will grow; if the learner fails, the weight is lowered.

Weights' evolution in the cultural group RWV depends on the RWV of the member of this group. Frequently, the CAWAS requests RWV of all the learners that belong to a cultural group. The new RWV for the group is obtained by calculating the average value for each weight of the RWV.

Frequently, the CAWAS run learners' RWV through an unsupervised neural network: the self-organizing map (Kohonen, 1990). Clusters thus obtained are composed of learners with similar RWV. If there are a sufficient number of learners in this group, the mean RWV is calculated and becomes the RWV for a new dynamic cultural group. By default, if needed, resources' CIS related to a newly discovered cultural group are initialized to 0.5.

Selecting the Resource

As shown in Figure 4, the process of selecting a resource is as follows:

1. The request for finding a resource of *type T* for a *concept C* for a *learner L* is initialized.
2. The system obtains all of *learner L*'s membership scores.

3. Then, for each of the resources of *type T* related to *concept C,* the system looks for CISs for all the groups to which *learner L* belongs. For each of those resources, a CIS for the learner L (**CIS.L**) is determined, given the following formula:

$$CIS.L = \sum_{i=1}^{n} (MS.X_i \times CIS.X_i)$$

In this formula, **n** is the number of currently existing cultural groups, **MS.Xi** is the membership score of *learner L* for the cultural group Xi and **CIS.Xi** is the CIS of the resource for the cultural group Xi.

4. The chosen resource, that is, the one with the biggest **CIS.L** value is inserted in the document deduced from the cultural template, for example, an HTML file).

FUTURE TRENDS: CROSS CULTURAL ADAPTATION OF BEHAVIORS OF PEDAGOGICAL AGENTS IN A VIRTUAL E-LEARNING ENVIRONMENT

We implemented our approach in a game-like e-learning environment that we call MOtivational and Culturally Aware System (MOCAS). MOCAS is aimed at enhancing the motivation of e-learners by providing teaching in an autonomy-supportive way as suggested by the self-determination theory (Ryan & Deci, 2000). It also integrates the different modules that are present in CAWAS in order to be culturally aware and sensitive. Being culturally aware is important for MOCAS, particularly because methods to support autonomy can differ depending on cultures (Chirkov et al., 2003; Chirkov et al., 2005; Levesque et al., 2004).

In MOCAS, learners and pedagogical agents coexist: both pedagogical agents and learners are represented by 3-D avatars in a game-like 3-D environment. Similar embodied pedagogical agents are already used in ITSs and according to Lester et al. (1997) , embodied pedagogical agents can "play a critical motivational role as they interact with students" and have "an exceptionally positive impact on students" this is called the *persona effect* (Lester et al., 1997).

There are three different parts in the MOCAS interface: (1) the interface for the game-like, 3-D learning environment (where the avatar of the learner can navigate and interact with avatars of pedagogical agents), (2) the communication interface (to allow the learner to communicate with other online learners), and (3) the learning content interface.

At the time we are writing this chapter, our pedagogical agents have one main behavior: when the learner interacts with a pedagogical agent (by selecting it with the mouse for example), the pedagogical agent can react by provoking a display of learning contents in the *learning content interface*. The learning content displayed corresponds to information needed by the learner to progress in the course and resources to illustrate the course are

chosen following the culturally adaptive method that we described before.

However, as we said in the previous parts of this chapter, concept representation is not the only element that is culturally sensitive in e-learning. The suitability of emotional management behaviors, pedagogical strategies, and autonomy supportive methods also differs depending on the culture. All those elements can be taken into account by pedagogical agents' behaviors. Thus we are currently broadening our methodology. We want our pedagogical agents to dispose of different versions of behaviors for each of these goals. These versions will be culturally rated following a process similar to the one we previously presented in this chapter, and our agent will be able to exhibit behaviors that are the most suitable for a learner with a given culture.

Figure 5 presents the learner's interface of our system. The course here is concerning Greek mythology. One of the possible cultural adaptations in this course is to decide whether or not to show

Figure 5. The learner's interface in MOCAS

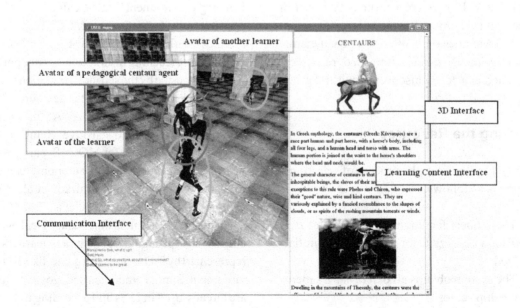

pictures of nude Greek statues because it appears that some cultures are more sensitive than others to the display of images of nudity, even if it is in art or historical domain.

CONCLUSION

With the constant evolution of information technologies, opportunities of cross-cultural interactions throughout communication networks increase. It is the source of many promises but it also raises new issues.

This chapter describes one of the first attempts to create an e-learning system where the cultural background of the learner is fully integrated in the learning process. It emphasizes some elements of e-learning systems that are culturally sensitive such as the concept representation and understanding. A new family of systems named CAWAS (i.e., culturally aware systems) is introduced. The aim of CAWAS is to be able to culturally understand a learner and to provide a culturally adapted answer to his/her needs. To this extent, we have proposed a methodology to culturally adapt the learning content. This methodology is currently enhanced in order to help select the most culturally suitable behaviors for a pedagogical agent that interacts with a learner of a given culture within our system.

We think the domain of automatic cultural management is promising for the e-learning research field, and there are still many remaining questions. For instance, one of our next objectives will be to find ways of upgrading the collaboration of learners with different cultural backgrounds, whereas they have sensibly different values.

ACKNOWLEDGMENT

We acknowledge the support for this work from Valorisation Recherche Québec (VRQ). This research is part of the DIVA project: 2200-106. We also acknowledge the support for this work from the Fond Québecois pour la Recherche sur la Société et la Culture (FQRSC). We also thank the help of Ryad Razaki for the development of the authoring tool for cultural templates.

REFERENCES

Blanchard, E., & Frasson, C. (2005). Making intelligent tutoring systems culturally aware: The use of Hofstede's cultural dimensions. In H. R Arabnia & R. Joshua (Eds.), *International Conference on Artificial Intelligence, ICAI 2005* (pp. 644-649). Las Vegas: CSREA Press.

Cassady, J. C., Mohammed, A., & Mathieu, L. (2004). Cross-cultural differences in test perceptions: Women in Kuwait and the United States. *Journal of Cross-cultural Psychology, 35*(6), 713-718.

Chaffar, S., & Frasson, C. (2004). Inducing optimal emotional state for learning in intelligent tutoring systems. In J. C. Lester, R. M. Vicari, & F. Paraguaçu (Eds.), *LNCS 3220, International Conference on Intelligent Tutoring Systems, ITS 2006* (pp. 45-54). Berlin: Springer-Verlag.

Chirkov, V. I., Ryan, R. M., Kim, Y., & Kaplan, U. (2003). Differentiating autonomy from individualism and independence: A self-determination theory perspective on internalization of cultural orientations and well-being. *Journal of Personality and Social Psychology, 8*(1), 97-110.

Chirkov, V. I., Ryan, R. M., & Willness, C. (2005). Cultural context and psychological needs in Canada and Brazil: Testing a self-determination approach to the internalization of cultural practices, identity and well-being. *Journal of Cross-Cultural Psychology, 36*(4), 423-443.

Conati, C. (2002). Probabilistic assessment of user's emotions in educational games. *Journal of Applied Artificial Intelligence, 16*(7-8), 555-575.

Earley, C., & Mosakowski, E. (2004). Cultural intelligence. *Harvard Business Review, 82,* 139-146.

Fischer, R., & Smith, P. (2003). Reward allocation and culture: A meta-analysis. *Journal of Cross-cultural Psychology, 34*(3), 251-268.

Hofstede, G. (2001). *Culture's consequences: Comparing values, behaviors, institutions, and organizations across nations* (2ⁿᵈ ed.). London: Sage.

Kashima, Y. (2000). Conceptions of culture and person for psychology. *Journal of Cross-cultural Psychology, 31*(1), 14-32.

Kim-Prieto, C., Fujita, F., & Diener, E. (2004). *Culture and structure of emotional experience.* Unpublished Manuscript, University of Illinois, Urbana-Champaign.

Kohonen, T. (1990). The self-organizing map. In *Proceedings of IEEE, 78*(9), 1464-1480.

Lester, J. C., Converse, S. A., Kahler, S. E., Barlow, S. T., Stone, B. A., & Boghal, R. S. (1997). The persona effect: Affective impact of animated pedagogical agents. In S. Pemberton (Ed.), *International Conference of Human Factors in Computer Systems, CHI'97* (pp 359-366). ACM/Addison-Wesley.

Levesque, C., Zuehlke, A. N., Stanek, L. R., & Ryan, R. M. (2004). Autonomy and competence in German and American university students: A comparative study based on self-determination theory. *Journal of Educational Psychology, 96*(1), 68-84.

Marcus, A., & Gould, E. W. (2000). *Cultural dimensions and global Web user-interface design: What? So what? Now what?* Retrieved July 13, 2006, from http://www.amanda.com/resources/hfweb2000/hfweb00.marcus.html

Ryan, R. M., & Deci, E. L. (2000). Self determination theory and the facilitation of intrinsic motivation, social development and well-being. *American Psychologist, 55,* 68-78.

Scollon, C. N., Diener, E., Oishi, S., & Biswas-Diener, R. (2004). Emotions across cultures and methods. *Journal of Cross-cultural Psychology, 35*(3), 304-326.

Shaver, P. R., & Schwartz, J. C. (1992). Cross-cultural similarities and differences in emotion and its representation. In C. Z. Malatesta & C. Izard (Eds), *Emotions in adult development* (pp. 319- 338). Beverly Hills, CA: Sage.

KEY TERMS

Culturally Aware System (CAWAS): CAWAS is a software system that tries to be culturally intelligent. To this end, a CAWAS must have the ability for *cultural understanding,* the ability to culturally interpret a user's behavior/feeling/result, and *cultural adaptation*, the ability to display different interfaces and/or starting different strategies depending on the users' culture.

Intelligent Agent: An intelligent agent is generally described as autonomous software that has different capabilities such as *reactivity,* the ability to perceive its environment and to adapt to its changes; *proactiveness*, the ability to take the initiative to have a specific behavior; and *social ability*, the ability to communicate/interact with other agents in order to achieve a specific goal.

Intelligent Tutoring System (ITS): ITS is a computer-supported learning system which uses artificial intelligence techniques in order to adapt to the learner. An ITS is composed of four inter operating modules: the *curriculum* or expert model, which contains the domain to be taught among other things; the *student model* that is the representation of the learner; the *planner* that organizes the learning session; and the *tutor* that gives the course.

Multi Agents System (MAS): MAS is a software system composed of several agents that can be more or less complex and "intelligent." These agents act together in order to reach a common goal. In fact, a MAS can be seen as a methodology for distributed problem solving.

Pedagogical Agent: A pedagogical agent is an intelligent agent that provides interactive teaching on a subject matter according to pedagogical strategies. In some cases (for example in virtual learning simulations), it can be associated with a 3-D body.

Self-Determination Theory (SDT): SDT is a modern theory of motivation proposed by Ryan and Deci (2000). Among other things, SDT stipulates that fulfilling psychological needs (i.e. *autonomy, relatedness,* and *competence*) during a task is necessary in order to be motivated.

This work was previously published in Handbook of Research on Instructional Systems and Technology, edited by T. T. Kidd and H. Song, pp. 829-841, copyright 2008 by Information Science Reference, formerly known as Idea Group Reference (an imprint of IGI Global).

Chapter XII
Globalisation and New Technology[1]:
The Challenge for Teachers to Become "Translators" and Children, Knowledge Seekers

André H. Caron
Université de Montréal, Canada

ABSTRACT

Whether globalisation results in a "métissage" of cultures or the hegemony of one culture will depend on the analytical and social skills of those who make up our communities. The introduction of new technologies in education such as laptops, MP3s, and Ipods and the new concept of mobile learning require an examination of the teacher's role in facilitating innovation, conveying culture, and acting as a conceptual translator. By modeling and teaching students critical and social skills, teachers can help tomorrow's citizens to use the new flow of information to meet the challenges of globalisation.

INTRODUCTION

Is new technology the magic bullet for education? In many places, policy makers have embraced new technologies as the answer to most of education's ills. They have persuaded the public that spending money on computers and high-speed Internet connections is a concrete, easy-to-understand, quantifiable way to improve education. New technology has been said to reduce dropout rates, increase innovation, and spark student enthusiasm. However, examination of discourse on these issues reveals that new information and communication technologies (NICT) might not be the whole solution.

As we get caught up in the mythical information society ideology, NICT's real usefulness and potential for education often gets overlooked. As its short history shows, NICT's role in education has to be analyzed in accordance with the dynamics of learning and teaching, as well as the aims of education.

The issues that arise in using new technologies in education are much the same as those raised by globalisation. New technologies give us rapid access to incredible quantities of information and vast new markets, but we should ask ourselves: do they always provide us with the tools for assessing and analyzing the information and how reliable is that information? Having the data is useless if we do not have the skills to make links and draw justifiable conclusions. Likewise, globalisation, which could indeed be facilitated by the use of new technologies, presupposes getting different cultures and subcultures to work together, not merely in parallel. Whether globalisation results in a *métissage* of cultures or the hegemony of one culture will depend on the analytical and social skills of those who make up our communities.

In this chapter,[2] we will look at the discourse in specific cases where educators have used new technologies in their classes, or government and administrators have implemented programs to promote the use of new technologies in education. The experiences in these cases may shed some light on the challenges we face in education with respect to new technologies as globalisation increasingly becomes a reality.

ATTITUDES TO GLOBALISATION, NEW TECHNOLOGIES, AND EDUCATION

Some depict globalisation as a kind of crusade, an *épopée*, a grand tale of actors. It is linked with the technological evolution of history, in which archaic resistance to opening up markets, states, and cultures has been overcome, and the right way of doing things has been revealed (Lessard, 1998). Others adopt a more critical discourse, and denounce the cult of adapting to the dominant trend (Petrella, 1997). They take a somber view of capitalism, seeing it as a source of social confrontation. For them, the discussion on globalisation requires that we reconsider old questions of equality, links between local and global forces, and frontiers between nations.

In *Le Bien commun*, Petrella (1997) argues that the past few decades have produced six new commandments. The new commandments are (1) globalisation, (2) technological innovation, (3) liberalization, (4) deregulation, (5) privatization, and (6) competitiveness. These terms are very familiar to us. They are increasingly present in governmental and educational discourse today. Indeed, the second commandment, technological innovation, is at the heart of many newly announced social changes. On this view, new information and communication technologies are to be integrated and resistance is not only futile but wrong, for they are the keys to achieving an information society.

According to Petrella (1997), obeying the commandments means seeing the world as a series of new markets to conquer, with education obviously one of them. He draws a parallel between the conquests 500 years ago and a renewed culture of conquest of the global village. We speak of new areas to be exploited, new electronic highways to be built, and so forth. However, while the main actors in the 15th Century were political, such as the Kingdoms of Portugal and Spain and the Republic of Venice, today they are multinationals, private financial groups, and private industries. This vision could appear somewhat radical to some, but should not appear more so than the opposite view, which celebrates the mythical virtues of new technologies. Also we should remember that the anticipated role of new technologies in a global village is not new. Some 35 years ago, a certain

Marshall McLuhan (1965), and even before him his mentor, Harold Innis (1951), described the coming of a new society and era of communication in which universal networks of information transmission would bring humankind closer together. McLuhan wrote, "Time has ceased, space has vanished, we now live in a global village, a simultaneous happening" (McLuhan, 1967). In his poetic way, he was proposing that if the networks and channels exist, then people will connect as intensely and quickly with people across the planet as with people in their own community.

In a review of McLuhan's work, Benjamin Symes notes:

It is easy to see why McLuhan was popular in the counter culture of the 60s, and is again today, with the computer revolution, for his ideas encompass an ideal that has perhaps in some ways always been with us...Is there not a possibility that if we place too much importance in achieving an idealistic, unified global village, we perhaps risk losing a sense of our physical humanity and our identity and thus forgetting why we are communicating at all. (Symes, 1995)

This brings us back to a basic question about what communication is in education, that of what education's role should be in this brave new world.

In his report to UNESCO, Jacques Delors (1998) says that education has to be viewed first and foremost as an ongoing process for both the individual and society and as something that extends beyond the classical physical and geographical boundaries of school and university. It is an ongoing process of enrichment of knowledge. In particular, it is the process of construction of the person and his or her relationship with other individuals, groups, and nations. Delors warns, "often we want quick answers and instantaneous solutions when the problems encountered require strategic patience, co-operation and negotiation" (Delors, 1998, p. 15). Strangely, these last three

concepts are seldom associated with new technologies in government discourses.

Today, some children come into class with more information than their teachers. However, this does not mean that they have more knowledge. As Delors (1998) points out, "education has to enable each individual to access, gather, select, order, manage and use information." New technologies might improve access, but they cannot do the rest. They do not teach us judgment.

How will students learn in the 21st Century? Surprisingly today, they will learn in much the same way that they learned when formal schooling was first introduced. This might seem impossible, with all the changes in society, all the information available, and the technologies today, but the basics remain the same. Children learn by interacting with each other and teachers on a personal basis. They learn ways of coping in society, critical skills, problem-solving strategies, and so on.

CHILDREN AS SEEKERS OF KNOWLEDGE

If they are taught properly, children become seekers of knowledge. This is where new technologies, such as the Internet, can be really useful. However, we must first invest in people, discovery, and innovation so that they can use the technologies properly. We need to think less in terms of information-rich societies and more in terms of knowledge-rich societies.

Our children have much the same stance with respect to NICT as we adults now have with respect to television. As a sociotechnological object, the television set is somewhat of a black box for us. In other words, we do not have to know anything about its internal components or even wonder about how it works or how the actors and technologies bring us our favorite evening program in the comfort of our homes. Immersed in an ultratechnological universe since their birth, our children are much more at ease with the new black boxes than are their parents and teachers. The new technology is not, however, merely various objects that unexpectedly emerge in our world as tools or instruments for work. As some have noted (Tardif & Mukamurera, 1999), they are much more than that. The technical objects are built and "boxed" by human beings, and they embody tangible mediations and practices and, especially, represent symbolic systems. They carry *praxis*.

Each piece of technology is a cultural artifact, created for specific purposes. Moreover, it is used by people in well-defined social contexts for their own aims and brings about new forms of "moving cultures" (Caron & Caronia, 2005, 2007). Inserted into a school setting, new technology conveys certain aspects of the culture of its creators. However, it is also used by teachers and students for their own purposes and in accordance with their own culture or cultures. The technology becomes adjunct to the social interaction in the classroom.

Central to the interaction is communication between the teacher and pupils, which has to go far beyond the linear transmitter-message-receiver model to become instead a model of intersubjectivity. A teacher is neither an educating machine programmed to simply process data nor a means of filling a brain with information as if it were a hard disk. In the classroom, the teacher is present with the students and interacts with them, which often leads to unexpected and innovative situations. A classroom is a place where there is sharing of meanings and symbols, mutual understanding and cooperation. If the number of instances of communication is multiplied by the number of years that a child spends in school, we soon see that communication is an enduring and powerful force. School strongly socializes students, integrating them into a specific culture. At school, students learn to live and survive in society.

FROM GLOBAL TO LOCAL: A FEW OBSERVATIONS FROM CANADA

As the interconnections become more tangible and globalisation is felt at various levels in Canadian social institutions, we have had no option but to adapt those institutions, particularly in education. Moreover, in the early 1990s, many Canadian children began demonstrating information acquisition and mastery of new technologies resulting from contact with new information and communications technologies (NICT) elsewhere than at school (at home or their parents' workplaces). They therefore often came to class with skills and knowledge that their teachers did not have. In order to adapt to such new social changes, school had to reassess its way of doing things, particularly with respect to school use of NICT.

In Canada, education is under provincial jurisdiction. Each province is therefore responsible for developing an educational system that meets the needs of its population. In Québec, the Ministry of Education is responsible for creating educational programs. However, another independent government organisation assesses the Ministry's programs in view of the current situation in Québec: the *Conseil supérieur de l'éducation*. Its mandate is to reflect on major needs in education and it publishes an annual report on its findings.

In 1994, the *Conseil supérieur de l'éducation* issued its first report on action to be taken to ensure that school adapts to the knowledge society into which we were being swept by major developments in NICT (Conseil supérieur de l'éducation, 1994). The Council members recommended that Québec schools pursue three main objectives with respect to use of NICT: (1) Schools needed to enable students to develop the cognitive and social abilities required to participate fully as citizens and workers in a society where NICT play a major role; (2) Students also had to develop critical thinking skills with respect to the role of NICT in society and media; (3) Teaching practices had to be changed to integrate NICT, which was considered to have a net positive effect, particularly with respect to student interest and motivation. These broad principles could probably be seen in one form or another at the time, and even today, in most institutional discourse on education in many countries.

In 2000, the results of this action were assessed. The amounts promised had been invested, and the objectives seemed to have been met. Within 5 years, the number of children per computer had gone from 21:1 to 7:1, and Internet connection from 56:1 to 10:1 (Ministère de l'Éducation du Québec, 2001). Young people now had access to the Internet at school, thanks to investments from the Ministry of Education, and also in other public institutions, such as libraries, through a high-speed telecommunications network. The Connecting Families to the Internet Program also made it easier for families in Québec with modest incomes to buy a computer and get access to the Internet at home. In short, a few years after the wave of computerisation in schools, democratisation of access was relatively advanced. However, the need for effort of another order was becoming increasingly clear.

The *Conseil supérieur de l'éducation* issued another report in 2000 on the integration of NICT in schools (Conseil supérieur de l'éducation, 2000). While it recognized the importance of having adequate equipment in sufficient quantity, it noted that a key component seemed to have been left out of the Ministry's action plans: pedagogical use of NICT and the results of such use. The Council expressed its disappointment in the lack of assessment of how classroom use of NICT affected school results. At the same time, there seemed to be less enthusiasm for NICT than before. Whereas the previous report had sung the praises of NICT's effects on student motivation and interest, the 2000 report was more realistic. It said that NICT had to be used in all areas of learning in order to acquire, produce, and transmit knowledge in line with the program of studies. NICT had to be a catalyst for the development of new skills and knowledge and it was no longer seen as a miracle solution.

School officials seemed to have come to this conclusion when they saw that, despite several years of use of NICT, there had been little progress in student motivation and success. Use of NICT had not significantly reduced school dropout rates, which were 20% among those aged 19 in the year 2000 (Ministère de l'Éducation du Québec, 2002). The real solution seemed to lie in deep changes to how things are done in school. It had become clear that new technologies, that is, hardware, alone would not bring about innovation. Instead, a way had to be found to improve school culture and student motivation as the real engines of success.

Thus, whereas the second half of the 1990s was marked by the integration of NICT into the Québec school system, the early 2000s focused on success in school for all students, as set out in the Québec Ministry of Education's 2000-2003 strategic plan. Various measures were planned, but in particular the Ministry hoped to increase school success by promoting the value of education to all of Québec's population through major media campaigns (Ministère de l'Éducation du Québec, 2000).

The first campaign, *L'éducation: pour qu'éclatent les passions*, was launched in fall 2000. It lasted 3 years and was intended to promote education and success using traditional media such as television, film, radio and print. Another campaign was pursuing the same objectives with respect to students from underprivileged communities. The New Approaches, New Solutions strategy specifically targeted 200 secondary schools in underprivileged areas where the drop out rate was abnormally high. The strategy primarily involved local action and therefore did not involve the media.

Also, the Ministry of Education contributed to a campaign launched by the Québec Department of Health and Social Services in 2000. Its purpose was to prevent depression among young people aged 13 to 17. *Parler... c'est grandir* encouraged communication on various topics. In this case, a broad media campaign on television, film, and radio was accompanied by a competition. Interestingly enough, after these first initiatives, the ministry published research in 2004 that reported how teachers were using new technologies in their classroom. A little more than half (58%) said they often or very often used new technologies in their formal teaching and approximately the same number of teachers (56%) mentioned also using them for seeking information on the Web (Bertrand, 2003, p. 87). This did indicate, however, that close to half the teachers did very little use of ICTs. Profuse to say that the overall strategy of the Ministère de l'Éducation in these times of new technological mutations still require important new initiatives.

A few recent observations in the field, at this point, should be made. The first observation concerns a policy adopted by a major business school in Montreal. A few years ago, the administrators decided that all students should be wired to the information highway, so they required every student to purchase a laptop. All students were required to buy the same model so that, hopefully, all information in the school could flow electronically, with no boundaries. A few years later, it was discovered informally that many of the idealistic illusions had disappeared, at least from the students' perspective. Substantial numbers of teachers did not want to provide information on their courses electronically, or did not have the time to do so. When students began coming to class with their laptops on, many teachers found it distracting to see the fronts of 150 laptops instead of their students' faces. The noise of incessant

typing sometimes made it difficult to hear. Then it became clear that students were not necessarily taking notes, but sending each other jokes, chatting, and so forth. Attempts were made to use filters and to adopt certain codes of conduct, but to little avail. The end result is that today PC use is even discouraged in some classes. There are still thousands of students walking around the school with laptop cases over their shoulders, but actual classroom use is much more limited than anticipated. Yet this year the school is offering students an even more expensive model with a high-speed connection. The question is whether this decision is technology-driven, pedagogically well-thought through, or simply an advantageous business deal, not perhaps for the students but for the school.

In the last few years, there has been some interesting explorations in new pedagogical uses of technologies in the classroom such as the use of Weblogs for more interaction between students and teachers and the new concept of mobile learning (Corbeil & Valdes-Corbeil, 2007; Naismith, 2004; Quinn, 2000). This latter concept has most recently focused on "podcasting": the new word of the year appearing in the New Oxford American Dictionary, as the newest form of e-learning.

As in the past, this has created, in the educational world, an infatuation by universities and school administration for the technology itself and not necessarily for its content, its optimum pedagogical use or the way it should be introduced in the educational system. This, of course, raises many questions. Beyond access and interest, students need to acquire their skills through a dialogical approach with their teachers; a clear-cut differentiation must be made between information obtained and knowledge acquisition.

The introduction of MP3 and Ipod technologies in universities is a good example. Indeed, some universities have rushed into "Ipoding" their classes, which could seem at the onset as a good idea, allowing students to complete their curriculum with mobile learning. Although one can find a number of recent articles making useful observations on this technology (Corbeil & Valdes-Corbeil, 2007; Whindham, 2007), few if any have invested in systematically sound research in defining what would be the best possible conditions before introducing such technologies. One study that is now being completed at the University of Montréal, in Canada, attempted to look at this question more rigorously. Some 125 students were provided for a full semester with Zen Creative and Ipod technologies. Teachers in English and Italian languages, Communication, Pharmacy, and Urban Design volunteered to include podcasts in their curriculum. It ranged from some teachers providing full length two and a half hour podcasts of their course to others offering short "meet the authors" capsules or simple interview podcasts. Students filled in diaries, Weblogs, questionnaires, and participated in interviews. Although it is still at the preliminary stage of analysis, first indications are that we often overestimate student's facility to appropriate the technology. In fact, only half the students owned a MP3 or Ipod technology before this trial and few knew what podcasts were. Their real mobile use most often went towards music, radio reception (Zen Creative), using it as a USB stick, and recording classes. Rarely did it include the podcasts provided by their teachers. Why? Lack of common cultural references and mostly expectations of a much more down to basic approach to educational content (such as summaries, exam drills, etc.) partially explained their low interest. As for the teachers, they found they needed a whole new way of preparing and finding content for their courses. Interestingly, although one of the participating teachers had been honored as the best teacher in his faculty the previous year when it came to his podcast material, they were rarely consulted.

It could be thought that this is another example of a technological fiasco, given that among other MP3 technologies, Ipods remain a one way media (Corbeil & Valdes-Corbeil, 2007). But on the contrary, what it raises is the possibility that we are on the verge of a cultural transformation where teachers could solicit their students for finding relevant contents that can be shared as podcasts, and that this material could become an integral part of the curriculum if properly validated. This would lead to a mutual construction of credible knowledge for a given course and the students would truly become active knowledge seekers. The technology then becomes a facilitator and the teacher the "translator" of knowledge and provider of cultural skills.

INNOVATION, INFORMATION, AND THE ROLE OF CULTURE IN EDUCATION

Some major universities are rethinking their approaches to the use of new technologies. For example, the importance of the teacher's role is illustrated and affirmed by MIT (Massachusetts Institute of Technology in USA)'s Open Courseware project, as is the difference between having access to information and getting an education. MIT has been publishing the lecture notes, reading lists, exams, and answers of some of its professors' courses online, with the goal of eventually making the content of all of its courses available free of charge. However, MIT will not be actually offering any courses online. In order to get a degree from MIT, people will still have to attend classes in person. As quoted on the MSNBC Web site, the MIT spokeperson argued, "We are fighting the commercialization of knowledge, much in the same way that open-source people are fighting the commercialization of software." (Festa, 2002)

New technologies, however, are still seen by many politicians and school administrators as a way to achieve a more profitable educational system. But the MIT initiative is forcing some to re-evaluate their objectives. Tony Masi, Vice Dean, Information Systems and Technology, at McGill University says:

All the major universities—Stanford, Colombia, Harvard and, alas, McGill—are trying to make money with the Internet, to commercialize teaching. At MIT, they are going back to a university's primary role: educating people, in a universal way. In universities, we are starting to lose sight of the fact that students are not consumer products. (Leduc, 2002, p. A1)

Financial investment and the electronic highway linking all schools and homes to an ever-abundant flow of information are therefore for many still considered the key to innovation. In Canada and many other countries, this has been the official political position for a decade. Yet should we maybe reassess what really is innovation?

In a series of articles published in the *Harvard Business Review* (2002), a number of very successful business entrepreneurs were asked about how they encourage innovation in their companies. Surprisingly, when describing how they brought about innovation, Dells (of Dell Computer), Bushnell (the creator of Atari), and Wynett (of Proctor and Gamble) failed to mention the two concepts we have just been discussing above: new technologies and money. The top people in a wide range of businesses instead mentioned people and the organisational culture they fostered. For many of these people, being innovative is a question of culture or, in a sense, to solve problems.

Michael Dell, CEO, Dell Computer reported that:

At Dell, innovation is about taking risks and learning from failure. To tap into this kind of innovation, we do our best to make sure the people aren't afraid of the possibility of failure. And we do a lot of experiments. (Harvard Business Review, 2002, p. 41)

Nolan Bushnell, the creator of Atari, said, "I think it's essential to build a culture where there's no such thing as a bad idea" (Harvard Business

Review, 2002, p. 46). Finally, according to Esther Dyson, chairman of EDventure Holdings:

So how do you encourage useful innovations? By doing two things. One, you have to promote risk taking, be open to experimentation, and philosophical about things that go wrong. My motto is "Always make new mistakes." There's no shame in making a mistake, but then learn from it and don't make the same one again. Everything I've learned, I've learned by making mistakes. (Harvard Business Review, 2002, p. 49)

What we see in these remarks is that the most fruitful activities are those in which people explore ideas together. In other words, the attitudes of the captains of innovation mentioned above are inspired by an underlying constructivist approach according to which learners build knowledge themselves. As they try to integrate their experiences, they classify or structure new material in accordance with past knowledge so as to make sense of it.

Applied to new technologies, the constructivist approach redefines our views about the pedagogical styles to be used in classrooms in the future. However, we must be careful to avoid thinking of information technologies purely as information providers. They are, in fact, tools that can be used flexibly while offering learners opportunities to construct their own models of learning. Technology should not be seen as the way to change the teaching environment in a class; instead, teachers should know how to use the technology in innovative ways.

We often believe that the most significant aspect of technology is its speed and effectiveness, which is rooted directly in the cybernetic paradigm. However, communication is a transaction between active participants, not an operation in which information is transferred from one hard disk to another.

The key to using communications networks to their full potential is culture. A struggle over any issue is possible only if those involved have judgment, knowledge, control of the language, and a clear purpose. Without these components, we immediately find ourselves in a primitive, instinctive situation that can be resolved only through inarticulate brute force. Just as it is useless to give NICT to someone who is technologically illiterate, it is useless to give it to a cultural illiterate. Education with NICT therefore has to be carried out on two fronts: cultural and technical.

TEACHERS AS "TRANSLATORS"

On the cultural front, we need teachers to help pupils find ways of understanding new information in their own terms. Just as a translator ideally bridges the gap between cultures and languages, a teacher restates new concepts in various ways so that they become notions that students can use in their own contexts. In translation terms, this is known as "localisation," which is a growing business with globalisation, and involves adapting text to a specific culture or subculture so that it has the same impact as in the original or source culture. In the classroom, this involves negotiation, as the teacher and students ask each other questions and test each others' meaning. Not only does this allow students to broaden their horizons, but the teacher serves as a model so that students can learn similar skills and ways of conveying information to others.

One of the major problems now arising with respect to NICT and culture is the risk of losing certain essential experiences and knowledge. People are increasingly called upon to research information in various databases in different formats. This can create beings who are informed, but completely ignorant of the whole social, political, and economic world in which they live. This means the death of communication in the intersubjective sense. In other words, learning online without a teacher could make people look knowledgeable,

but they would not really be so because they would not have developed their critical skills.

As previously mentioned, teachers have to become translators for students because content delivered by NICT cannot become stable without real interaction. Does this mean that only interpersonal teaching will succeed and that the media and new technologies are of no use? Not necessarily. However, we have to be careful when they are promoted as solutions to economic and political problems, and proposed and packaged in political discourse, to look good.

Undeniably, the role of teachers is important in a world of increased circulation of information allowed by ICTs. It is even more imperative nowadays because of the impact of the global market on the education sector that follows the trend toward neo-liberalism, deregulation, privatization of services, and withdrawal of state intervention. For these reasons, the Québec *Conseil Supérieur de l'éducation* did look at this question in its Annual Report titled *The Governance of Education: Market Logic or Political Process?* The Council saw the problem in terms of equity and justice pitted against efficiency and competitiveness. Obviously, the former do not exclude the latter, and vice versa, but the Council recommended state intervention as a means of promoting these values. The Council warned against returning to an educational system not governed by a democratic political process because equitable educational infrastructure is so expensive that it can be delivered only by society as a whole. Similarly, the way that education is provided and the tools that are used will have to be negotiated with a view to the community's basic values.

There is no doubt that globalisation will continue to transform education, but what remains undetermined is the capacity of education to keep a critical distance, its capacity to be something other than the echo of an economic imperialism. If some distance cannot be maintained, public educational services will inevitably be seen as a form of merchandise and not as something that is for the common good.

As Hargreaves (1994) points out, we must reflect on the following questions: Will there be a culture of uncertainty, with knowledge developing at an ever quicker pace, but also becoming more and more temporary? Will universal, scientific certainties be replaced by contextualised certainties constructed by stakeholders in a community of meaning?

Educational institutions no longer hold or control a monopoly over information. A significant portion is now produced outside such institutions. Their role is now not so much to produce more information, but to analyze the implications and uses of information, thereby selecting and converting it into knowledge. The history of our efforts to bring electronic technology into schools has, in many instances up until now, been one of missed opportunities. This is not because innovations did not work, but because we did not understand that successful technological change in education is always linked to events, attitudes, and values in the society at large.

ACKNOWLEDGMENT

I would like to express my gratitude to a number of people who played an active role in the research and the preparation of this presentation. These people are Marie-France Vermette, Laurent Lux, Mary Baker, and Nicoletta Dolce. I would also want to express my appreciation to the Ministère de l'Éducation du Québec.

REFERENCES

Bertrand, D. (2003). *Diversité, continuité et transformation du travail professoral dans les universités québécoises (1991-2003)*. Québec: Conseil supérieur de l'éducation. Retrieved October 11, 2007, from http://www.cse.gouv. qc.ca/fichiers/documents/publications/Etudes-Recherches/Renou2.pdf

Caron, A.H., & Caronia, L. (2005). *Culture mobile: Les nouvelles pratiques de communication*. Montréal, Canada: Les Presses de l'Université de Montréal.

Caron, A.H., & Caronia, L. (2007a). *Moving cultures: Mobile communication in everyday life*. Montreal, Canada: McGill-Queen's University Press.

Caron, A.H., & Caronia, L. (2007b). *MP3, zen et Ipod: La culture mobile dans le monde de l'éducation*. Rapport de recherche. Montréal, Canada: CITÉ, département de communication.

Charland, J.-P. (2002). *Le rapport à l'histoire et à la citoyenneté des élèves des régions métropolitaines de Montréal et de Toronto*. Ph.D. Québec, Canada: Université Laval.

Conseil supérieur de l'éducation du Québec. (1994). *Les nouvelles technologies de l'information et de la communication: Des engagements pressants. Rapport annuel 1993-1994 sur l'état et les besoins de l'éducation*. Québec, Canada: Les publications du Québec.

Conseil supérieur de l'éducation du Québec. (2001). *La gouvernance de l'éducation. Logique marchande ou processus politique. Rapport annuel 2000-2001 sur l'état et les besoins de l'éducation*. Québec, Canada: Conseil supérieur de l'éducation.

Conseil supérieur de l'éducation du Québec. (2000). *Éducation et nouvelles technologies. Pour une intégration réussie dans l'enseignement et l'apprentissage. Rapport annuel 1999-2000 sur l'état et les besoins de l'éducation*. Québec, Canada: Conseil supérieur de l'éducation.

Corbeil, J.R., & Valdes-Corbeil, M.E. (2007). Are you ready for mobile learning? *Educause Quarterly, 2*. Retrieved October 11, 2007, from http://

www.educause.edu/apps/eq/eqm07/eqm0726.
asp?bhcp=1

Delors, J. (1998). *Education: The treasure within.* Paris, France: Task Force on Education for the Twenty-First Century, UNESCO.

Festa, P. (2002). *MIT offers all its courses free online.* Retrieved October 11, 2007, from http://www.msnbc.com/news/819892.asp?0si=-&cp1=1

Hargreaves, A. (1994). *Changing teachers, changing times: Teachers' work and culture in the postmodern age.* New York: Teachers College Press.

Harvard Business Review. (2002, August). Inspiring Innovation. *Harvard Business Review, The Innovative Entreprise.*

Innis, H.A. (1951). *The bias of communication.* Toronto, Canada: University of Toronto Press.

Julien, M. (2005). *La mobilité internationale des étudiants au sein des universités québécoises.* Québec, Canada: Conseil supérieur de l'éducation. Retrieved October 11, 2007, from http://www.cse.gouv.qc.ca/fichiers/documents/publications/EtudesRecherches/50-2098.pdf

Leduc, L. (2002, September 30). Le MIT virtuellement gratuit. *La Presse*, p. A1.

Lessard, C. (1998, March 26-27). *Globalisation et éducation.* Conférence d'ouverture du forum Éducation et Développement, ayant pour thème: éducation, développement, coopération et recherche dans le contexte de la mondialisation. Faculté des sciences de l'Éducation, Université de Montréal. Retrieved October 11, 2007, from http://www.unige.ch/fapse/SSE/groups/life/textes/Lessard_A1998_01.html

McLuhan, M. (1965). *Understanding media: The extension of man.* Toronto, Canada: McGraw-Hill.

McLuhan, M., & Fiore, Q. (1967). *The medium is the massage.* New York, Toronto: Bantam Books.

Ministère de l'Éducation. (1996). *Les technologies de l'information et de la communication en éducation.Plan d'intervention.* Québec, Canada: Ministère de l'Éducation. Retrieved October 11, 2007, from http://www.mels.gouv.qc.ca/nti_plan/plan_nti.htm

Ministère de l'Éducation. (2000). *Plan Stratégique 2000-2003 du Ministère de l'Éducation. Mise à jour 2001.* Québec, Canada: Ministère de l'Éducation. Retrieved October 11, 2007, from http://www.meq.gouv.qc.ca/ADMINIST/plan_strategique/PlanStrat0003/abrege_f_miseajour.pdf

Ministère de l'Éducation du Québec. (2001). *L'introduction des technologies de l'information et des communications (TIC) à la formation des jeunes et des adultes. Bilan de l'an IV du plan ministériel d'intervention. Année scolaire 1999-2000.* Québec, Canada: Ministère de l'Éducation, du Loisir et du Sport, direction des ressources didactiques. Retrieved October 11, 2007, from http://www.meq.gouv.qc.ca/drd/tic/pim.html

Ministère de l'Éducation du Québec. (2002). *Indicateurs de l'éducation.* Québec, Canada: Ministère de l'Éducation, direction générale des ressources informationnelles.

Petrella, R. (1997). *Le bien commun: éloge de la solidarité.* Lausanne: Éditions Page deux.

Symes, B. (1995). *Marshall McLuhan's global village.* Retrieved October 11, 2007, from http://www.aber.ac.uk/media/Students/bas9401.html

Tardif, M., & Mukamurera, J. (1999). La pédagogie scolaire et les TIC: l'enseignement comme interactions, communication et pouvoirs. *Éducation et francophonie, 27*(2). Retrieved October 11, 2007, from http://www.acelf.ca/c/revue/revuehtml/27-2/Tardif.html

Whyndam, C. (2007). Confessions: Podcast junkie. *Educause Review, 42*(3). Retrieved October 11, 2007, from http://www.educause.edu/apps/er/erm07/erm0732.asp

ENDNOTE

[1] The present chapter is a revised and updated version of a text that was originally published in Italian under the title *Le nuove tecnologie è la riposta...Ma a quale domanda?* in "Senso della politica e fatica di pensare" (pp.260-274) a cura di Antonio Erbetta con la collaborazione di Piero Bertolini Clueb 2003

Chapter XIII
Modern Technology and Mass Education:
A Case Study of a Global Virtual Learning System

Ahmed Ali
University of Wisconsin – LaCrosse, USA

ABSTRACT

This case study examined the effectiveness and significance of the Internet and interactive video broadcasting as instructional and communication media in a global virtual learning system. The study explored how differences in students' technology experiences, curriculum, cultures, and access to technology influence learning and student attitude in a technology-based distance education environment. The research also investigated whether the use of online references and materials is adequate and appropriate for successful distance learning. The setting was a virtual campus that linked universities in the U.S., Australia, and Canada with learning centers in different African countries. E-mail and face-to-face interviews, observations, and Web-based surveys were utilized to collect the data. The study reveals that students had mixed perceptions about the effectiveness of technology, with positive attitudes exhibited towards interactive video and some anxiety and dissatisfaction with the use of the Internet.

BREAKING CAMPUS BARRIERS

Distance learning has been touted as a viable alternative to classroom learning because it allows students to obtain relevant knowledge in their preferred style and time. The existence of various technologies such as interactive video and the Internet facilitate and promote distance education. The Internet, in particular, has become an increasingly important medium for providing instruction in distance education (Simonson, Smaldino, Albright, & Zvacek, 2003). Studies report that traditional teaching and learning may not effectively respond to the learning styles of 21st century students (U.S. Department of Education, 2000). Schools and universities are adopting the Internet as an instructional delivery medium that can complement, and in some circumstances change, traditional classroom instruction.

This change has already begun, propelled by diverse programs ranging from Web-enhanced learning to full-fledged online learning. Virtual schools and colleges have sprung up, and the Web has become an important medium for distance learning. One program with the pseudonym, the Pioneer Global Campus, has created a global virtual learning system that connects universities in developed countries to learning centers in Africa. As a consortium of several universities worldwide, the Pioneer Global Campus is unique in its global focus unlike other major distance education programs that are regional in scope.

Rising educational costs, limited opportunities for qualified students in local universities, and a desire to utilize technology led to the development of the Pioneer Global Campus. This virtual university was created to provide African students with access to education in diverse fields such as science, technology, journalism, languages, and accounting. The university has graduated several thousand students since it was founded during the second half of the nineties.

The university operates by creating partnerships with institutions of higher learning in the United States, Canada, and Australia. The external university partner accredits the programs. Individuals who participate in the program include students pursuing degrees in the receiving country as well as individuals interested in short-term, non-credit courses that do not have entry require-

ments. This makes the Pioneer Global Campus a mass education institution that caters and appeals to diverse individuals and groups.

Various communication technologies are utilized to deliver content at a distance and to facilitate communication between students and instructors. The Internet and interactive video broadcasting are two common instructional channels. Over 50 learning centers in more than 20 African countries are equipped with satellite and Internet technologies. Students attend the learning centers to receive instruction via video broadcasting and the Internet.

DISTANCE LEARNING: USE OF THE INTERNET

Use of the Internet for education is common in the developed world, though there is increasing need for online education in the developing world (Zembylas & Vrasidas, 2005). In the developed world, educators and students use the Internet to supplement classroom learning. The Internet is also increasingly utilized as a distance education medium.

Whichever way the Internet is used, the potential of the Internet as an instructional tool and instructional medium has been recognized globally. To integrate technology in distance learning, learning experiences should not based on traditional classroom concepts of teacher-directed instruction, but rather should include interactive learning principles that apply student-centered learning styles. Further, it is important to consider the audience for which online education is developed because, "in a global context, online course designers and teachers may face many questions concerning how to design and teach across geographical, social, linguistic, and cultural distances..." (Zembylas & Vrasidas, p. 62)

Scholars and practitioners have talked and written about the application of online learning. Miller, Rainer, and Corley (2003) posit that although Web-based learning has tremendous potential, poor application can be detrimental to effective learning. Poor pedagogical and course management practices can negatively affect learning as traditional classroom techniques do not necessarily work in an online environment. For example, factors such as lack of structure and organization, poor time management on the part of instructors, and lack of interaction can hinder the effectiveness of the online medium as an ideal instructional tool.

Online communication may supplement traditional classroom meetings and discussions. Discussion and dialogue are extended beyond the classroom meeting times through online discussion forums. However, in a study of online discussion boards, Warner (2003) found that online and traditional students were concerned about slow Internet connections, limited computer experience, anxiety about computer skills, and limited Web experience. Warner further reported that course-related concerns raised by the students include: lack of motivation for online discussions and participation, teachers not requiring students to use discussion boards, and lack of interesting discussion topics. Personal concerns raised by the students include time and inconvenience, though Warner stated that both online and traditional students had these similar concerns.

Considerable emphasis has been placed on developing best practices for online teaching. However, in an age when the constructivism mantra is common, considering student learning preferences and technology abilities is crucial. As a student-centered instructional theory, constructivism allows students to construct their own knowledge and meaning.

METHODOLOGY

This case study (Stake, 1995) is about the use of technology, particularly the Internet and interactive video broadcasting, for instruction, communication, and interaction in a global virtual learning system. While prior studies about technology and distance education have addressed similar questions, this case is unique because the setting is an inter-continental, cross-cultural system, and the study is meant to shed the spotlight on Africa. Levy (1988) and Tellis (1997) suggest that the single-case, exploratory case study is a preferred and reliable method for examining the use of information technology in higher education.

This study examined the effectiveness and significance of various distance education technologies that are used for content delivery and for communication and interaction across continents. The study explored how differences in students' technology experiences, cultures, and curriculum influence learning and attitude in a technology-based distance education environment. The research also investigated whether the use and content quality of online references and materials is adequate and appropriate for successful learning.

Multiple data collection techniques in case studies contribute to adequate information collection and the validity and reliability of findings (Tellis, 1997). In this study, interviews, observations, and surveys were used for data collection. Over 60 students, instructors, learning facilitators, and administrators participated in the study. All students were of different undergraduate levels and fields of study such as business administration and computer science.

Individual, focus group, and open-ended e-mail interviews were used to collect data about technology and pedagogy in distance education across continents. A learning center in Kenya was observed during different visits over a one-month period. During the visits, some of the activities observed included classroom learning, use of computers (particularly online course management system), use of online libraries, and the role of facilitators.

Conducting a study that spans several countries requires time and resources. In order to obtain adequate data with minimal costs, a Web-based survey was utilized to explore the influence of technology on learning, communication, and interaction. The survey collected information on students' technology skills, attitude towards technology, Internet use in distance education, perceptions regarding the use and quality of on-line libraries, and use of communication media. Though many of the students who participated in the survey came from Kenya and Ghana, the possibility of other individuals masquerading as students to complete the survey cannot be ruled out, as the Website was not password-protected. However, random follow-up e-mails and triangulation of the data prevented any considerable cause for concern. Further, the survey data was collected over a two-month period during which the administrators and teachers announced to the students the existence of the survey and encouraged participation.

Qualitative data were analyzed by grouping and categorizing the data, and by reducing the information to manageable size (Miles & Hubermann, 1994). Information was coded using common keywords found in the data. A computer software program was used in the analysis of the survey data. Information sources such as interviews, observations, and surveys were triangulated, and member-checking was conducted to improve reliability and trustworthiness of the study.

INSTRUCTIONAL SETTING AND RESOURCES

The Pioneer Global Campus combined face-to-face structure with distance learning. Although this was a distance education program, students collaborated on campus while the course instructor taught from thousands of miles away. This helped students obtain easy access to technology

and support from course facilitators. While the distance instructor provided the course content, the local facilitator explained the content. The instructor and the facilitator had complimentary roles, and the facilitator provided students with the support and confidence to enroll in a distance education program as noted in the following observational record:

It is 10:00 am and all students are listening to the facilitator explaining the content of a lesson unit. One would be forgiven for assuming that this is a traditional classroom as the facilitator is using the chalk and board to teach, and room arrangements depict a regular classroom, only that there are computers in this room. Students seem attentive and ask questions which attest to the important role that facilitators play in this distance education program.

...Students are downloading materials placed on WebCT by a distant instructor that they did not meet. Considering the subject the students were learning and lack of prior experience in the course content, it is possible that some of the students in the room would not be present if a facilitator was not here.

The impact of limited interaction between students and the distant course instructor of record was reduced by the presence of course facilitators. Every course had a qualified facilitator that assisted the instructor. This added support was helpful and appropriate, as Dodds (1994) also found out, considering that many of the students were young learners who did not yet have the self-directed and independent-learning attitude and experience of adult learners. In one of the classrooms observed, almost all of the students appeared to be recent high school graduates. From interviews done with the students in the classroom, the facilitator had an indispensable role in guiding students who might otherwise not have had the experience and self-discipline which a distance education course requires. To address concerns about the lack of real-time classroom contacts with the instructor, interactive video conferencing and Web-based communications technologies were used.

To improve learning and facilitate access to learning materials, the Pioneer Global Campus created an online library that students could access at anytime. The library contained academic journals, e-books, and other materials. Although the students appreciated the quality of materials, they expressed concerns about accessibility. They particularly disliked the length of time required to download materials and the fact that the online library materials were text-based only. While their desire for audio and video is understandable, providing materials in these complex formats is not practical considering that students encountered problems with downloading simple text. Scholars outside the African continent produced most of the learning materials available through the online library, though this is not unique to the online library only.

In the online survey, diverse students stated that they visited local libraries because of the limited availability of materials in the online library and the slowness of the Internet. Many of the students reported that they used the local library as their primary source of research because of the variety of materials and easy accessibility.

In interviews, several students complained that sluggish and poor access to the Internet hindered the effective use of the online materials, and this forced them to seek alternative sources for research:

Chris: *... I use it (online library) sometimes. But I use the (local) library more because I can go there anytime without paying and I have many books and materials (to select from).*

Irene: *I only use it when I am at work because I have a good (fast) computer. Also, at work, I can print. It is expensive to print at the (Internet) cafés.*

I am a poor student who has part time job.

Michael: *Yes, it (Internet) is good but it needs some improvement. When I click (download) a paper I have to wait for a long time.*

Mary: *Oh my (the rest of the students in the focus group laughing) ... it is as slow as tortoise ... It would have been better if they build a library for our students. It will make it easy for us.*

INSTRUCTIONAL MEDIA

The Pioneer Global Campus used different media and methods to deliver content to students, including a combination of satellite video broadcasting, Web-based instruction, VHS tapes, CD-ROM, and print. When the program began, interactive one-way and two-way video broadcasting and print materials were mostly used. Because of increased access and development of digital technology and the rising costs of interactive video conferencing, use of the Internet and CD-ROMs gradually increased, eventually surpassing application of satellite video broadcasting. The use of VHS tapes also increased due to their low costs and the students' familiarity with this medium.

The administrators made great efforts to utilize the various media concurrently. However, there is lately more asynchronous learning compared to the beginning years of the program, when real-time communication and interaction was common. Prohibitive costs necessitated a switch from live satellite broadcasting to Web-based learning. Administrators and staff also reported that dwindling donor funding and reduced student enrollment led to a reassessment of the instructional medium.

According to one of the administrators, students and the public had an overwhelming positive reaction when this virtual distance education program started. The administrator stated that one of the reasons for this reaction was that major donors such as the World Bank were supporting the project. A more compelling reason is that many traditional institutions and students were attracted by the use of information and communication technology (ICT). Many people in Africa, particularly Kenya, had not yet used satellite video conferencing and computers and were intrigued by the technology. A combination of all the aforementioned and other factors played a strong role in the initial robust implementation of the program, and this has worked to the advantage of the Pioneer Global Campus.

The Pioneer Global Campus later implemented use of cost-effective and modern instructional media, such as online course management systems. WebCT ™ was selected and utilized to replace the satellite broadcast. The digital technology infrastructure in many African countries is not sufficiently developed to take advantage of the interactivity that WebCT™ allowed. Problems such as slow internet, limited access to Internet facilities and services, and limited technology skills and experience hindered effective use of WebCT ™. As the course management system of choice, WebCT™ was limited to instructors posting lecture notes and students submitting assignments. Most of the valuable interactive technology features of WebCT™ such as chat rooms and discussion forums were rarely utilized.

An advantage of the Web-based learning is the ubiquitous nature of the Internet. Unlike the video broadcasting that confined students to specific centers, the Web allowed students to access learning materials anytime, anywhere. Unfortunately, however, many of the students had no access to a computer at home, and the few students who had computers mostly used them for productivity applications such as word processing to complete assignments. For many, home Internet services were non-existent due to high costs. Several students revealed that they used Internet cafés as they were easily available and less costly:

Peter: *I do not have a computer at a home. I only survive because I used the Internet cafés ... And nowadays, they are so cheap I only pay a shilling (Kenyan currency) for each minute. I can use it for hours and pay peanuts ... I like using it in the morning when there are not many people ... I don't like going to the cafés in the evenings and weekends because I see all this kids playing on the Internet.*

Rose: *... You know what! My father bought a computer for us. We use it to play (video) games. When we tell him we need the Internet, he tells us go to the (Internet) cafés ... I don't like it. But it is very close to our home. I just walk there.*

VHS tapes containing lectures were mailed as an alternative and occasionally to supplement Web-based learning. Students and faculty were overwhelmingly positive about the VHS-taped lectures because the video and audio quality was good and downloading time was not an issue. A limitation was the lack of interactivity; students appeared to be passive learners in the learning process. Students watched the tapes with no inquiry or questioning, discussion, and interaction with instructors and peers.

This study revealed that the level of technological development, accessibility, and cost are important determinants of the instructional medium. More effective technologies such as video conferencing could not be widely adopted because of cost. The Internet was not an appealing alternative because of poor technology infrastructure in the local countries. Recognizing the poor state of the technological development and resources of many African countries such as Kenya and Ghana, one of the brochures of the program stated:

Cognizant of the underdeveloped ICT infrastructure in Africa, the program will use a variety of modes of delivery to include VHS videotaped lectures, CD- ROMs, DVDs, WebCT™ platform with its variety of e-mail, online chat, both synchronous and asynchronous lectures, lecture notes, electronic quizzes, in addition to occasional video conferences. Most materials and different delivery media allows for flexible, mixed-mode of delivery.

CURRICULUM

The curriculum of the Pioneer Global Campus is strongly influenced by external universities. Instructors and administrators at the external universities played a major role in planning and designing course content and materials, assessment, and teaching styles and schedules. However, the Pioneer Global Campus collaborated with the external universities in implementing the curriculum.

In designing the curriculum and selecting course instructors, it is crucial to consider student learning styles and preferences. Unlike the traditional, face-to-face learning programs where locally-developed curriculum is widely used, several students, though a minority, were of the view that course content and the curriculum were designed for students in developed countries. Some administrators also shared this view. At a presentation at one of the donor conferences, the administrators of the Pioneer Global Campus recognized that one of the challenges they faced was the need to have content developed and delivered by local universities. Locally-developed content has the potential to more effectively relate to student needs and circumstances. For example, students enrolled in business and technology courses revealed that the business portfolios and the software programs that were utilized were widespread in the developed countries, but not common in the local countries. The content appeared to consist of prepackaged materials given to an audience whose needs and preferences had not been taken into consideration. Helen, a second-year student,

was occasionally intrigued that some of the notes and programs did not correlate with what she has been learning in high school. She attributed her puzzlement to the way some of the courses were designed, the terminologies used, the examples given, and the general structure of some of the course content that did not naturally flow with what she had become familiar.

On the other hand, several students stated they liked the course content and materials developed by faculty in developed countries because they were getting a "first class" education that their peers in traditional universities were not. Two students, Mary and Michael, underscored such students' sentiments as they used words like "developed," "ahead," "21st century," "leading," "motivated," and "connected (to developed world)."

To illustrate and describe the disparity between educational systems in many African countries and some of the developed world, an American education system comparison may be helpful. In general, American curriculum and pedagogy focuses on student-centered learning. Many courses, instructional strategies, and educational philosophies demonstrate the need to facilitate active student participation in learning. In contrast, curriculum and pedagogical practices in many African countries have the hallmark of a traditional and structured education system within which teachers transmit knowledge to the students. For the most part, in many African countries, education is centralized and curriculum is standardized. Conversely, in America, education is decentralized, and the curriculum is approved at the local level.

Even though considerable efforts have been made to change the curriculum in several African countries such as Kenya, the traditional curriculum and educational system is still dominant. Meanwhile, advocating for curriculum and pedagogical change is not to negate the time-tested, valuable instructional practices traditionally used in classrooms. Nevertheless, as the Pioneer Global Campus is implementing a modern concept of educational delivery, it is appropriate to adopt suitable curriculum and instructional styles that promote and enhance successful learning.

TRADITIONAL DIFFERENCES

Culture and attitude play an important role in distance education. While distance education is increasing in Africa, many people perceive it as an alternative educational program for people who have failed academically and do not qualify for admission to local traditional universities. Use of the Internet for learning is has been suspect to criticism because the Internet is considered by many to be more of a communication and entertainment tool rather than an educational tool. Several students reported that they had initial hesitation when informed that they would use the Internet for learning. Such students held more positive views about video broadcasting because it looked similar to a classroom as a teacher "stood" in front of them while in class. Because of longstanding cultural and educational traditions, some students thought they were missing out on knowledge that came with direct face-to-face instruction. Yolanda, Rose, and Catherine stated that many of their peers in the traditional colleges have a negative attitude towards distance education. Their peers and other members of the community believed that the virtual university (Pioneer Global Campus) was for students who were from wealthy families or those who had no other option for obtaining a college degree. Displaying displeasure with the attitude of some of the cynics, Rose retorted:

I wish they could understand how much we are far ahead of them (traditional students). We have the best education, we know technology more than them, we will graduate faster than them and our

degrees will be from better and world recognized universities...

Some of the criticism stem from the limited technology use in education in Africa because colleges and schools cannot afford them. The technology is new, is generally limited to business and office use, and is used as a communication and entertainment tool by the public. When the Pioneer Global Campus introduced Internet use for education, the concept was alien to many students who, as a result, initially doubted and resented the Internet.

Though not a major issue, two students cited language as an issue that needed to be addressed. A legacy of the British colonial presence in African countries such as Ghana and Kenya is the present-day educational curriculum and the widespread use of the English language. American instructors delivered their lectures in American English, but the students used British English. Two students called attention to the possibility that students could lose points for using British spelling and grammar when being graded by an American instructor. However, these same students added that when watching the VHS tapes, they had no problems understanding the instructor.

Time differences between the external universities and the local countries interfered with real-time learning. Instructors were stationed in the U.S., Canada, and Australia, and this meant that time adjustments had to be made by students to make it easier for the instructors to synchronously interact with their students. According to a member of the teaching staff, the time difference was resolved by scheduling courses during times that were convenient for both students and instructors, such as having classes in the late afternoon in Kenya and morning in the U.S. Some administrators and teaching staff stated that variety and increased access to technology reduced the time difference constraint.

USE OF TECHNOLOGY

Experience, skills, access, and attitude played a significant role in Internet use. Students who had more technology skills preferred using the Internet while those with limited technology skills were less inclined to use the Internet for learning. The Web survey revealed that students who had computer experience were more likely to use the Internet and demonstrated greater comfort with it, compared to their counterparts with limited computer technology experience. According to the data, more computer experience translated to increased positive attitude towards computers. With time, the students who initially were not enthusiastic about Internet use changed their perceptions about computers. Meanwhile, several students noted that though they were comfortable with using the Internet for communication and learning, they had reservations abaout using it as the primary learning tool. These students declared preference for the interactive video broadcasting, for it was the closest they could get to a face-to-face classroom learning setting style. They cited the support they obtained from an instructor when using video broadcasting, compared to the Internet lessons where they were literally left on their own.

While appreciating the use and the potential of the Internet, students exhibited negative attitudes toward the use of the Internet as the sole medium of instruction. The problems that plagued the use of the Internet, such as poor accessibility, poor reliability, and limited interactivity, led to some resentment regarding Internet use. In one of the computer-equipped classrooms that was observed, students appeared frustrated in accessing and downloading the course content. In one of the lessons, an Australian university offered the course, and the instructional medium was WebCT. The students had difficulty using the materials because the computers were slow.

However, many students and all administrators and facilitators were optimistic and confident that the quality learning eclipsed the technological setbacks which students faced.

Access was another key issue. Students with limited access to the Internet preferred the video broadcasting, and information supplied in VHS tapes and CDs. Difficulty accessing reliable Internet was a recurring issue. A combination of two-way satellite video broadcasting and phone conferencing produced instant and interactive communication between students and the instructor, but the expected increase in interaction and communication through the use of the Internet did not happen.

Students reported in the Web-based survey that they spent an average of twelve hours per week on the Internet, which was not enough time for students taking online classes. The limited Internet use demonstrates the preference the students had for other learning tools and media. While many of the students stated they used Internet cafés for online leaning, they indicated concerns such as noise and lack of privacy which made Internet cafés inconvenient.

Glaring differences in the available Internet services existed. Internet services in South Africa were faster and more reliable than in Ghana and Kenya. An interview with one administrator revealed Internet problems were not caused by the Pioneer Global Campus' failure to provide reliable technology, but by the generally underdeveloped Information Technology of the local countries. The interviewee highlighted the relative success and popularity of the Internet in South Africa with its better infrastructure compared to Kenya. Despite the concerns raised about the use of Internet as a learning tool, there was an encouraging perception that the Internet is an important medium for distance education and a useful learning tool.

CONCLUSION

This case study reports that distance education programs provide educational opportunities to people who otherwise would not be able to obtain educational or career advancement prospects. A distance education program such as the Pioneer Global Campus is playing an important role in increasing access to education. A significant contribution of the Pioneer Global Campus is the mass education that it provides despite some problems associated with the delivery medium. Although the students were receiving quality education, great strides need to be made towards localizing the curriculum to adapt to student needs and existing educational practices.

The choice of delivery mechanism and instructional medium is critical. As revealed in this case study, cost greatly determines the choice of instructional medium; however, the selection of the instructional medium should prioritize student learning preference and needs. The appropriateness and reliability of the medium is equally worthy of great consideration. The Pioneer Global Campus' combination of interactive video broadcasting, Web, VHS/CD, and print is commendable and appropriate. However, the use of the various instructional media should be complementary and not replace one another. A variety of media would facilitate accessibility and interaction, and would provide students with choices and alternatives.

A thorough needs assessment should be conducted before making major decisions about content delivery media. Access, reliability, and usability of media are important considerations that should not be overlooked. For example, many students could access VHS tapes as they were able to watch the tapes using home video playback machines. In contrast, use of CD-ROMS was found to be inappropriate because many students did not have home computers. Internet cafés, widely used by students, were found to be cumbersome because of noise from other patrons,

cost, and lack of privacy. Inadequate and poor technological development leading to slow and unreliable Internet made the use of the Internet as a learning tool less appealing.

Students can learn effectively via distance education if learning structures promote individualized and independent learning. Individualized learning has the added advantage of making students learn at their own pace and styles and according to their abilities. Making students learn in a classroom cohort using traditional teaching and learning strategies undermines the independence and individualized learning that accompanies distance education. If classroom learning becomes necessary, as is the case with the Pioneer Global Campus where facilitators provided tutoring, classroom learning should be supplementary to the distance learning.

Considering some of the issues raised in the study, the selection of the instructional medium should be done carefully when designing courses to ensure successful distance education. Designing a course for distance delivery, particularly one that involves use of technology, should accommodate the flexibility that is traditionally associated with distance education.

Although correspondence study dominated the field of distance education in Africa for decades (Dodds, 1994), the information society of the 21st century calls for an overhaul of the approach, management style, and mode of distance education delivery. Distance education was not initially widely-adopted in Africa because of limited well- organized and independent programs and institutions that focused on distance learning, and the perceptions people held about distance education as a nondescript alternative education. With the inception of the Pioneer Global Campus, the first continent-wide virtual distance education program, a new ground has been broken that will forever alter the distance education landscape in Africa. The use of information technology, as demonstrated by the Pioneer Global Campus, will play a significant role in making distance education a strong competitor to traditional classroom learning in the near future.

REFERENCES

Dodds, A. (1994). Distance learning for pre-tertiary education in Africa. In M. Thorpe & D. Grugeon (Eds.), *Open learning in the mainstream* (pp. 321-327). Harlow, UK: Longman Group.

Levy, S. (1988). *Information technologies in universities: An institutional case study.* Unpublished doctoral dissertation, Northern Arizona University, Flagstaff.

Miles, M. B., & Huberman, A. M. (1994). *Qualitative data analysis.* Thousand Oaks, CA: Sage Publications.

Miller, M. D., Rainer, R. K., & Corley, J. K. (2003). Predictors of engagement and participation in an online course. *Online Journal of Distance Learning Administration, 6*(1). Retrieved April 15, 2004, from http://www.westga.edu/%7Edistance/ojdla/spring61/miller61.htm

Simonson, M., Smaldino, S., Albright, M., & Zvacek, S. (2003). *Teaching and learning at a distance.* Upper Saddle, NJ: Pearson Education, Inc.

Stake, R. (1995). *The art of case research.* Newbury Park, CA: Sage Publications.

Tellis, W. (1997). Application of a case study methodology. *The Qualitative Report, 3*(3). Retrieved February 10, 2004, from http://www.nova.edu/ssss/QR/QR3-3/tellis2.html

U.S. Department of Education. (2000). E-learning: Putting a world-class education at the fingertips of all children. *The National Educational Technology Plan.* Washington, DC: U.S. Department of Education.

Warner, D. (2003, March 30-April 1). Student recommendations for discussion boards: Conclusions of student problems. *Eighth Annual Mid-South Instructional Technology Conference, Teaching, learning & technology: The Challenge Continues.* Murfreesboro, TN: Middle Tennessee State University.

Zembylas, M., & Vrasidas, C. (2005). Levinas and the "inter-face": The ethical challenges of online education. *Educational Theory, 55*(1), 60-78.

This work was previously published in Globalizing E-Learning Cultural Challenges, edited by A. Edmundson, pp. 327-340, copyright 2007 by Information Science Publishing (an imprint of IGI Global).

Chapter XIV
GlobalMind:
Automated Analysis of Cultural Contexts with Multicultural Common–Sense Computing

Hyemin Chung
The Media Laboratory, MIT, USA

Henry Lieberman
The Media Laboratory, MIT, USA

ABSTRACT

The need for more effective communication between people of different countries has increased as travel and communications bring more of the world's people together. Communication is often difficult because of both language differences and cultural differences. Attempts to bridge these differences include many attempts to perform machine translation or provide language resources such as dictionaries or phrase books; however, many problems related to cultural and conceptual differences still remain. Automated mechanisms to analyze cultural similarities and differences might be used to improve traditional machine translators and as aids to cross-cultural communication. This article presents an approach to automatically compute cultural differences by comparing databases of common-sense knowledge in different languages and cultures. Global-Mind provides an interface for acquiring databases of common-sense knowledge from users who speak different languages. It implements inference modules to compute the cultural similarities and differences between these databases. In this article, the design of the GlobalMind databases, the implementation of its inference modules, as well as an evaluation of GlobalMind are described.

INTRODUCTION

The number and scale of multinational organizations are increasing and the interactions among countries are more frequent. While these changes have increased the need for effective cross-cultural communication, it remains difficult because of cultural and language differences.

GlobalMind is an attempt to automate the analysis of cultural differences. We describe how the multicultural common-sense database can improve cross-cultural communication and how the automated inference modules can analyze the cultural differences based on the database.

Difficulties in Cross-Cultural Communication

In cross-cultural interactions, people should consider and understand each other's cultural background in order to have successful interactions (Adler & Graham 1989, Herring, 1990). Expected behaviors, signals, and contexts of communication differ by the cultural backgrounds of the speakers. Even small misunderstandings that arise from cultural differences can cause the failure of entire negotiations (Sawyer & Guetzkow, 1965). Condon (1974) emphasized the importance of understanding cultural differences in cross-cultural communication because misunderstandings from cultural differences could not easily be deciphered and corrected. Consideration of cultural contexts in cross-cultural communication is essential to successful interactions.

Many linguistic problems also have their roots in cross-cultural problems. Language differences have been researched and studied by many people, from linguistic researchers to elementary-school students. Efforts to solve language difference problems with automated mechanisms have resulted in many different approaches to machine translation (Jurasky & Martin, 2000). While the research community has solved many aspects of the linguistic problem, many non-literal transla-

tions cannot be properly made without consideration of cultural differences.

There is discussion as to whether an accurate translation between two different cultures is even possible (Scheff, 1987). It remains difficult to make an accurate translation between two cultures; in many cases, a vocabulary or an idiom in one culture is not found in another culture. Even when a similar vocabulary exists, it may not reflect the same experience when the cultural backgrounds are different (Sechrest, Fay, & Zaidi, 1972). Munter (1993) observed that English does not have a word for the Korean word "KI BUN," which has a similar but different meaning to the English phrase, "inner feelings of a person" or "mood." The existence or absence of a word in languages is also closely related to the existence or absence of the concept itself in the culture. Although the problem of translation is grounded in language differences, it cannot be solved without cross-cultural understanding.

Some expressions with the same meanings can be used totally differently between cultures. Other expressions with different meanings can be used in the same way in different cultures. For example, Americans often say "sure" in response to "thank you" or "I'm sorry," while Korean people often say "A NI E YO(no)" in response to thanks or apologies. "Sure" and "no" have almost opposite meanings, but in this situation, they are used for the same speech act.

Thus, consideration of cultural contexts in cross-cultural communication is essential to successful interactions both in behavioral and verbal communication. However, to our knowledge, no previous work has seriously considered a systematic method to automate analysis of cultural differences.

GlobalMind Design Points

As previously discussed, cross-cultural communication needs much consideration of cultural backgrounds. Although people have recognized the importance of consideration of cultures, it has been difficult to use the cultural contexts in automated cross-cultural communication tools such as machine translators.

GlobalMind is designed to provide culture analysis tools for other automated applications aiding cross-cultural communication. Global-Mind provides large-scale databases of several different cultures and analysis modules of the databases.

Automated Mechanisms for Cultural Context Analysis

To develop cross-cultural communication assistant tools, it is essential to have an automated mechanism to analyze cultures that the tools use. Anacleto et al. (2006) showed the possibility of an assistant program to improve the understanding of cultural differences. However, it has limitation in both depth and breadth of data because the database of the differences between two cultures are analyzed and entered manually by a human, not automatically computed. With manual input, it is difficult to extend and generalize the work. ThoughtTreasure (Mueller, 1998) has a database with bilingual knowledge in English and French, but this knowledge has been handcrafted by the (bilingual) author, and it does not have an automatic method for establishing new cultural correspondences and cultural analogies.

One of the goals of GlobalMind is the automated analysis of cultural contexts. For this goal, GlobalMind provides two inference modules: the similar-concept inference module and the differences inference module. These inference modules compute the similarities and the differences between two cultures automatically. With this automated mechanism, the comparison and analysis of cultural contexts can be easily extended to any other cultures and various kinds of applications.

Flexible and Extensible Multilingual/ Multicultural Database

To analyze cultural contexts, it is necessary to know about the cultures. In other words, we need to have data about the cultures. As the cultures continue to change over time, the data about the cultures also needs to be updated continuously. Thus, GlobalMind should build and keep a flexible and extensible database system with the knowledge of cultures, the sets of common senses of various cultures.

The appearance of very large common-sense knowledge bases is quite recent. The three most developed resources are OpenMind Common Sense (Singh, 2002), Cyc (Lenat, 1998), and ThoughtTreasure (Mueller, 1998). Although their projects showed how common-sense knowledge databases can be successfully used to analyze people's language and thoughts, they were limited to one or two languages and did not consider the cultural background of each common-sense knowledge.

The GlobalMind database is designed for multicultural/multilingual common-sense knowledge. All the knowledge in the database is tagged with its cultural origin and is written in its original language. The database is designed to be flexible with dynamic culture network structure described later in this article because not only are the common-sense knowledge in culture groups changing, but also the definition and border of culture groups themselves are continuously changing.

Context-Based Analysis

A concept can be described with other concepts related to the original concept. When an adult person who already has a sufficient store of common concepts faces a new concept, mostly he or she tries to understand the new concept by relating it to other concepts he or she already has. For example, if a person meets a new concept "apple" for the first time in his or her life, he or she will understand the concept "apple" by relating this new concept to other concepts such as "it's color is red," "it is a kind of fruit," "it looks circular," "it tastes sweet," "it is to eat," and "it is smaller than melons." Later if he or she sees a red, sweet, circular fruit to eat, he or she determines the fruit as a kind of "apple." In this article, we call these related concepts "context."

These contexts are not limited to verbal expressions, but are expanded to something, which cannot be described by languages such as its own tastes and touches. However, as the language is the primary tool of human communication, people try to explain the contexts in verbal forms. Thus, a verbal database of concepts and relations among them are still useful. ConceptNet used a networked database of concepts linked to other concepts via relationships, and showed how it can assist people's activities by analyzing people's intention with the verbal database of concepts (Liu & Singh, 2004).

The cultural differences can be represented with the differences in contexts. "Spoon" in America has the contexts of "soup" and "tea," whereas "spoon" in Korea has different contexts such as "steamed rice," and Japanese "spoon" has the contexts of "ceramics" and "noodle soup." American "restaurant" may have the context "give waiters tips" but Korean "restaurant" may not because the tips are not common in Korea. To use the context-based approach, GlobalMind adopts the ConceptNet system and uses a networked database of common sense taken from various cultures, where the context is represented by common-sense knowledge.

Relation-to-Relation Mapping

Many concepts do not have exactly the same matching concepts or the same contexts in other cultures (Munter, 1993; Sechrest et al., 1972). Thus, one concept in one culture cannot be directly matched with another concept in another culture because it ignores the differences in their contexts and, moreover, once a connection is established it is hard to change even if the contexts of the concept change significantly. Gentner suggested a structure mapping theory in which the topologies of relations are mapped with other topologies rather than single words or concepts (Gentner, 1983). GlobalMind uses a similar method, relation-to-relation mapping, to fully support the context-based approach.

The term relation-to-relation mapping is used here in contrast to the concept-to-concept mapping or, as the concepts are represented by words or phrases in our databases, word-to-word mapping. Relation-to-relation mapping does not match a phrase with another phrase, but it matches a relation between two concepts with another relation between another two concepts. For example, mapping between an American/English relationship "tree-KindOf-plant" and a Korean/Korea relationship "NA MU(tree)-KindOf-SIK MUL(plant)" is used in GlobalMind over mapping between "plant" and "SIK MUL(plant as living organisms)."

DATA-STRUCTURE DESIGN

GlobalMind data are a network of networks of common-sense dataset in different culture groups. Common-sense knowledge is connected with other common-sense knowledge. Thus, common-sense data of each culture group form a complicated network. Liu et al. (2004) established a common-sense network, ConceptNet, and showed useful results with this network form. GlobalMind uses a similar common-sense network for the network of each culture group. The common-sense knowledge of one culture group is connected with common-sense knowledge of another culture group, establishing connections between networks.

This section describes the design of the GlobalMind data structure from the smallest to the largest unit.

Node

A node is the smallest unit in the GlobalMind database. One node represents one concept. One node may consist of one or more words. For example, "student" or "school," as well as "wake up in morning," or "drive fast" can be nodes. A node is combined with another node through a link and becomes an assertion.

Link

A link is the relationship between two nodes. A link has direction, which shows the origin and designation nodes, and the relationship, which shows the kind and strength of the relation be-

Table 1. Relationships used in GlobalMind links

Relationship	"A-->relation-->B" means	Example of A	Example of B
CapableOf	A can do the activity of B	anteater	eat ant
DefinedAs	A is defined as B	prince	son of king
DesireOf	A desires B	people	live
DesirousEffectOf	A makes someone wants B	hunger	eat food
EffectOf	A makes effects like B	stay up late	wake up late
FirstSubeventOf	B happens first while A	take shower	turn on water
InstanceOf	A is an instance of B	MIT	university
IsA	A is a kind of B	apple	food
LastSubeventOf	B happens last while A	do homework	hand in
LocationOf	A is in/at B	MIT	USA
LocationOfAction	A is done in/at B	study	school
MadeOf	A is made of/from B	spoon	metal
MotivationOf	B is the motivation of A	eat	hunger
NotDesireOf	A does not desire B	people	die
OnEvent	On the event A, B happens	funeral	mourn
PartOf	A is a part of B	wheel	car
PrerequisiteEventOf	B should be done before A	eat	wash hand
PropertyOf	A has characteristics like B	snow	white
SubeventOf	B happens while A	eat	chew food
SymbolOf	A is a symbol of B	dove	peace
ThematicKLine	A reminds B	keyboard	mouse
UsedFor	A is used for B	computer	surf the Internet

tween two nodes. The link "-->LocatedAt -->" means the left node is located at the right node and the link "<--IsA<--" means the right node is a kind of left node. GlobalMind adopted 22 different types of relationships from links from ConceptNet (ConceptNet, 2005). Table 1 shows the 22 relationships used in GlobalMind.

It is arguable if the current 22 relationships used in the GlobalMind system are the perfect set to describe the common-sense knowledge of all the different cultures and languages. People from different cultures have different points of view in observing the world and use different logic systems to analyze what they observed. Thus, some relationships that provide adequate cover of common senses in one culture may not be suitable to cover common sense in other cultures. This issue should be discussed and researched further.

Assertion

An assertion is a combination of two nodes and the link between the two nodes, which represents how two concepts are related to, and become a "context" of, each other. One assertion contains one common-sense datum and thus it is the basic unit of the GlobalMind database for processing and analyzing common sense. In this article, the size of database or the number of common-sense items means the number of assertions.

For example, a node "student" and a node "school" combined with a link "-->LocatedAt-->" form an assertion "student-->LocatedAt-->school," which validates the common-sense statement "a student is usually found at a school."

Culture Network

A culture network is a set of assertions in one culture group. One network represents the common sense within one culture group.

Because nodes in one assertion can be shared with other assertions as the number of assertions is increased, more links and connections are established among nodes. Thus, when we gather the assertions of one culture, the assertions form a complicated graph, where an assertion's nodes are used as nodes in the graph and links as used as edge in the graph. The graph of assertions of each culture group is called a culture network in GlobalMind. Thus, each culture group has one culture network with numerous assertions. Figure 1 shows a snapshot of a network around the node "shampoo."

How to divide one culture group from other culture groups or how to define a border among them is arguable. Thus, GlobalMind does not use the definition of culture groups or fixed structure of culture networks. Rather, it structures a culture network dynamically by a user's definition of culture groups. The GlobalMind database keeps various information about the author of each assertion such as nationality, age, and occupation. This information, or combinations of this information, can be used to define the culture groups. The only exception is the language in which the assertion is written. A basic assumption of GlobalMind is that culture and language are inseparable; all the assertions in one culture network should be written in one language. Thus, each culture group should be defined with one language and/or other information.

For the convenience of describing examples in this article, culture groups are defined by nationality and referred to as the nation/language network. For example, a culture network with the assertions written in English and written by American people will be represented as the American/English network.

Bicultural Connections

Because GlobalMind is more interested in interactions between or among culture groups rather

Figure 1. Snapshot of GlobalMind network about shampoo

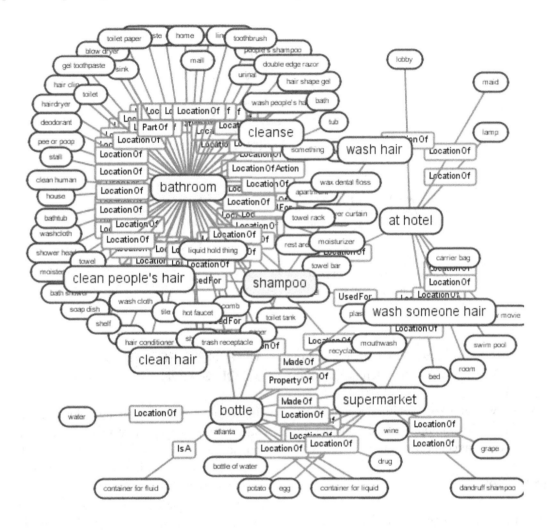

than the interactions within one culture group, GlobalMind provides the connections between/ among culture networks.

One assertion in one culture network can be connected with another assertion in another culture network. For example, an assertion "tree- ->KindOf-->plant" in American/English culture network can be connected with a Korean/Ko- rean assertion "NA MU(tree)-->KindOf-->SIK MUL(plant)." These types of connections can serve as links between different culture networks, and called as bicultural connections.

In GlobalMind, there are two types of bicul- tural connections. The first one is an explicit bi- cultural connection, which is manually entered by volunteers or collected from bilingual manuscripts such as dictionaries. The number of established bi- cultural connections is relatively small compared to the number of the GlobalMind common-sense data. The other type of the bicultural connection is the inferred connection, which is automatically computed by the GlobalMind inference modules. Based on explicit connections, GlobalMind auto- matically computes the relationship between any

Figure 2. Conceptual image of GlobalMind global network

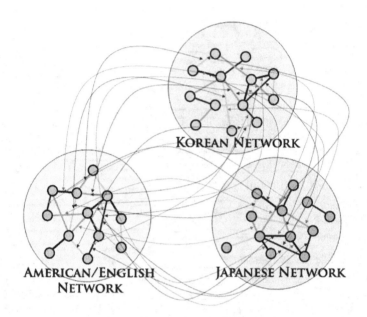

KOREAN NETWORK

AMERICAN/ENGLISH
NETWORK

JAPANESE NETWORK

node in one culture network and other nodes in another culture network. The inference module is described next.

(When we refer the bicultural connections without more description, it usually means the explicit bicultural connections.)

Global Network

With all the culture networks and bicultural connections among them, one large network can be integrated. This large network is called a global network and represents the relationships among culture networks.

The global network contains the connections between assertions in different culture groups in addition to all the assertions in GlobalMind. Figure 2 shows the concept of a global network, the final form of the GlobalMind data structure.

WEB SITE FOR DATA ACQUISITION

In order to make use of the GlobalMind data structure, it is important to gather a sufficient quantity and quality of common-sense knowledge. To achieve this goal in relatively short time, we used two methods to gather the data.

The first method was importing the Open-Mind common-sense data to the GlobalMind database. OpenMind is the project to collect human common-sense knowledge and to use them for artificial intelligence systems (Singh, 2002). The OpenMind database already had more than 700,000 common-sense knowledge data collected from all over the world. The data was imported into and re-used as the base of the GlobalMind database. However, in addition to this database, we needed more data tagged with cultural background information.

The other method was accumulating common-sense knowledge through a public Web site by volunteers. This method of utilizing the Web site to accumulate numerous but common data was used successfully by other project such as Wordnet (Fellbaum, 1998), Wikipedia (Wikipedia, 2006), and OpenMind (Singh, 2002). For example, the OpenMind Web site was designed to gather a large amount of common-sense knowledge in the form of sentences. The users of OpenMind could type in their common-sense assertions, and the typed sentences were parsed and stored in the OpenMind database. To help users, the Web site had several different kinds of activities and templates; for example, users could fill in the blanks in templates like "[ ] can be found at [ ]," describe a picture with sentences, or write a story in collaboration with other users. The OpenMind Web site was launched in 1999 and gathered more than 700,000 common-sense sentences as of March of 2006.

We built and launched the GlobalMind Web site to leverage OpenMind Web site's success. The GlobalMind Web site (2006) was designed to gather common-sense knowledge from various cultures and languages as well as relationships and connections between common sense of different culture groups. The basic structure of the Web site is almost the same as the structure of the OpenMind Web site. Users can type in their common-sense knowledge by filling in blanks in templates. By using a similar data form input method, we avoided conflicts between the OpenMind imported data and the newly collected ones. Users can choose their own languages among the various languages the Web site supports; the background information of users such as nationality, age, or occupation is tagged to the common-sense sentences they enter. Additionally, the GlobalMind Web site supports bilingual/bicultural activities to gather connections between different culture groups. Users can read sentences written by other users in different culture groups, evaluate the validity of the common-sense knowledge in their

own culture groups, or translate the sentence to their own languages if the sentence is common sense in their culture groups. Figure 3 shows the GlobalMind Web site.

The GlobalMind Web site was launched on December 12, 2005 with four open languages, including English, Korean, Japanese, and both simplified and traditional Chinese, and expanded to include two more languages, Spanish and Finnish. As of June 14, 2006, the Web site has gathered 32,254 new common-sense sentences with cultural contexts and 11,023 bicultural connections. Table 2 shows how many items and data have been accumulated by the GlobalMind Web site as the date of June 14, 2006. The table excludes the data from the original OpenMind database.

INFERENCE MODULES

While the GlobalMind Web site provides the data to be processed, the inference modules are used to compute the cultural differences and to provide meaningful results to help users. Here GlobalMind presents two different kinds of inference algorithms to find similarities and differences between two cultures/countries.

Similar-Concept Inference Module

In cross-cultural communication, it often happens that one person uses a concept but the other person misunderstands it because the concept is used differently in two cultures. To avoid this kind of misunderstandings, it is helpful to know which concept is similar to and different from another concept of another culture.

GlobalMind provides the inference module to find the most similar concepts between two cultures/languages. It determines the concept of "forks and knives" in the American culture is similar to the concept of "chopsticks" rather than that of "forks and knives" in the Korean culture.

Table 2. Statistics of data accumulated through the GlobalMind Web site

Languages	Korean	15140
	Japanese	9010
	English	7787
	Chinese	317
	total	32254

Cultural Backgrounds	Korea	19031
	Japan	9129
	Germany	1657
	USA	1360
	Finland	212
	Taiwan	208
	Unknown	190
	Etc	467
	Total	32254

Bilingual Connections between	English and Korean	5556
	English and Japanese	4444
	Japanese and Korean	733
	Chinese and Korean	218
	Chinese and Japanese	58
	Chinese and English	9
	Chineses	2
	total	11023

The GlobalMind similar-concept inference module (SIM) is novel in that it enables a context-based approach rather than a word-meaning-based approach to the problem of word matching.

Figure 3. GlobalMind Web site

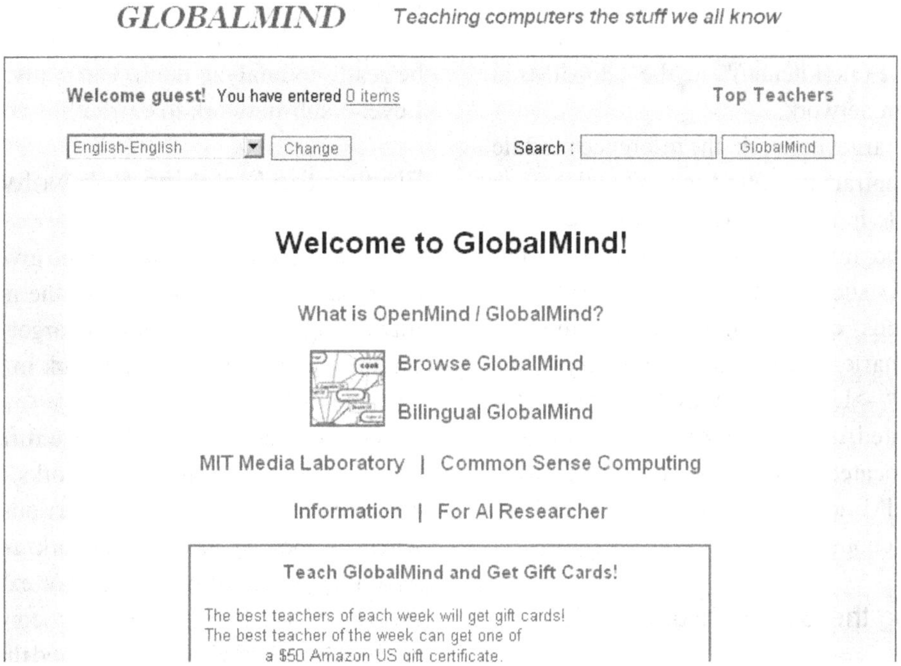

GLOBALMIND
Teaching computers the stuff we all know
Welcome guest! You have entered 0 items
Top Teachers
English-English
Change
Search :
GlobalMind
Welcome to GlobalMind!
What is OpenMind / GlobalMind?
Browse GlobalMind
Bilingual GlobalMind
MIT Media Laboratory | Common Sense Computing
Information | For AI Researcher
Teach GlobalMind and Get Gift Cards!
The best teachers of each week will get gift cards!
The best teacher of the week can get one of
a $50 Amazon US gift certificate.

Figure 4. Expand and contract method

English Network
Expand
Compare
Korean Network
Contract

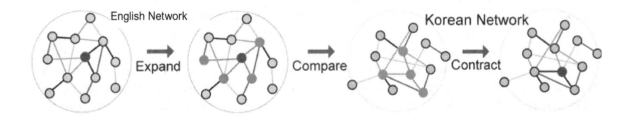

GlobalMind uses an expand-and-contract method to find the matching link or node for a particular link or node. Figure 4 shows the concept of the expand-and-contract method.

1. The context of the given concept is extracted by expanding the GlobalMind network from the node for the given concept to its neighboring nodes. In the case of "fork and knife," the expanded context is "-->UsedFor-->eat," "-->LocatedAt-->dinner table," and "-->LocatedAt-->kitchen."
2. The context found in (1) is compared and matched with another group of context in

the target culture/language network. The inference module finds "-->UsedFor-->MEOK DA(eat)," "-->LocatedAt-->SIK TAK(dinner table)," and "-->LocatedAt-->BU EOK(kitchen)" in the GlobalMind Korean network.

3. In the target network, the inference module will contract the found context with a node suitable in the context. The given concept and the inferred concept have a similar context such as their uses, properties, or locations, even though their meanings in dictionaries could differ. For example, the node "-->UsedFor-->MEOK DA(eat)," "-->LocatedAt-->SIK TAK(dinner table)," and "-->LocatedAt-->BU EOK(kitchen)" in the GlobalMind Korean network is "JEOT GA RAK(chopsticks)."

Expanding the Sub-Network

The input to the SIM is a concept of which a user wants to find a matching concept, a culture network of the given concept, and a target culture network. The first task SIM does from the input data is extracting contexts of the given concept by expanding the sub-network in the given culture network.

When there is a concept in a culture network, there is a node, which represents the given concept. We refer to the node as a root node, and its neighboring nodes and neighboring links are referred to as children nodes and children links. For a root node "fork and knife," a child node "eat" is connected to the root node through a child link "-->UsedFor-->." The sub-network consisting of a root node and its children is a Level-0 network. In the same way, a sub-network can be expanded to Level 2 with grandchildren nodes and links such as "kitchen-->UsedFor-->cook," and to Level 3 with great-grandchildren nodes and links such as "cook<--CapableOf<--mother."

Children nodes and links provide the context of the root node (i.e., how the given concept is related with other concepts), such as what it is used for, where it is located, and what it looks like. By expanding a sub-network of a root node, we can extract the contexts of the given concept and be ready to analyze them. Currently, SIM uses Level-3 sub-network to extract the context.

Finding the Matching Sub-Network

After extracting the context of the given concept by expanding the sub-network, the next task is translating the context into the target culture by finding the matching sub-network in the target-culture network.

This process utilizes the bicultural connections between two culture networks. Bicultural connections refer to two assertions, each of which is located in each network and both of which have similar meanings. For example, the assertion "kitchen-->UsedFor-->cook" in the GlobalMind American network and the assertion "BU EOK(kitchen)-->UsedFor-->YO RI(cook)" in the GlobalMind Korean network might be biculturally connected to each other, which is manually inputted for a small fraction of the entire network. SIM searches for bicultural connections between the given sub-network and the target culture network.

The biculturally connected assertions in the target networks will be members of the translated context sub-network in the target networks. As the distances between the root node and any assertions in the given sub-network are less than three levels, the distances between the biculturally connected assertions in the target network and the future target node are also expected to be less than three levels. Thus, SIM expects the future target node to be within the Level-3 sub-network from the biculturally connected assertions in the target network. SIM extracts each Level-3 sub-network from each connected assertions in the target network, and the final target sub-network is the union of all the target sub-networks.

Contracting the Sub-Network

At this stage, SIM has the translated context in the target culture network. By analyzing the translated context, SIM finds nodes with the most similar concept to the given concept. This process is named contracting because it is done by contracting the target sub-network into one or a few nodes.

To contract the target sub-network, SIM compares the given sub-network and the target sub-network, and then scores each node in the target sub-network.

We can assume that in the ideal culture network, if node GA and node GB have similar concepts, then both nodes GA and GB are similarly related to node GC, and they have similar routes, a series of links between two nodes, to the node GB. For example, if node GA "fork" is related with node GC "cook" via "-->LocatedAt-->kitchen-->UsedFor-->," a similar node GB "knife" is related with node GC "cook" via the same route "-->LocatedAt-->kitchen-->UsedFor-->" while another node GD "car" does not have the same route to the node B.

With the previous assumption, SIM compares the routes; if a node in a target network has the same routes as the given root node has, SIM adds a score to the node. If a given node "fork" has a route to a node "cook" via "fork-->-->LocatedAt-->kitchen-->UsedFor-->cook," and "kitchen-->UsedFor-->cook" has a bicultural connection "BU EOK(kitchen)-->UsedFor-->YO RI(cook)" in a target network, then a node which has a route "-->LocatedAt-->BU EOK(kitchen)-->UsedFor-->YO RI(cook)" has higher possibility of having the same/similar concept to a node "fork" than other nodes without the same routes.

Let's define an equation (A, B) ~ R, which represents node A and node B are connected through Route R. Also, let's say A = C if node A and node C are confirmed as similar/same, and A ≈ C if node A and node C are guessed as similar/same.

In the ideal culture network, which has all the common-sense assertions possible in the culture,

if (GA, GC) ~ R, and GA = GB, then (GB, GC) ~ R.

Also, if GC = TC, and (GA, GC) ~ R, then (GA, TC) ~ R.

In reverse, we can assume that if (GA, GC) ~ R, and (GB, GC) ~ R, then GA ≈ GB.

With all the above SIM assumes that if (GA, GC) ~ R, (TA, TC) ~ R, and GC=TC, then GA ≈ TA. Let's say GA and GC are nodes in the given culture network, and TA and TC are nodes in the target culture network, and GC and TC are biculturally connected. In this case, for the given concept GA, the node TA can be a candidate for the target concept and thus SIM adds a score to TA.

Even if nodes have routes between biculturally connected assertions and itself, the impact of the routes can all be different. If a node "fork" has a route "-->MadeOf-->metal" and another route "-->IsA-->tool for eat," the latter route has more impact than the former route because a node with the latter route has more possibility of having the similar concept to the given node "fork" than another node with the former route. This impact is represented as the weight of routes, and the weight of routes is calculated by the weight of the links on the routes.

Several factors can determine the impact of a route. The first factor considered in this research is a number of children nodes of each node. In Liu's ConceptNet system, the strength of link is affected by the number of children nodes (Liu et al., 2004). According to Liu, connection between two nodes becomes weakened as the nodes have more children. For example, a node "heat" and one of its 12 children nodes "CapableOf-cause fire" has a stronger connection than a node "person" and one of its 3000 children nodes "CapableOf-build."

The second factor is the distance from the root node. It is obvious that a neighboring node is more related with a root node than a not-neighboring node. As distance between a node and a root node becomes greater, the strength of the relationship between those two nodes becomes weakened.

Another factor, which can be considered but has not been implemented in GlobalMind yet is the kind of relationships. Among 22 different types of relationships, some of them make stronger connections than others. Two nodes, "apple" and "fruit," which are connected with the "IsA" relationship, might have a stronger connection than other two nodes "dog" and "steak," which are connected with the "DesireOf" relationship.

The weight of each link is decided by the number of children and the type of relationship. The weight is between 0 and 1, where 1 means the highest impact and 0 means the lowest impact. The weight of the route is calculated by multiplying all the weights of the links on it. Because the weights of links are not larger than 1.0, as the distance between two nodes becomes greater, the weight of the route between those two nodes becomes smaller. For example, if the link "fork-->UsedFor-->eat" has a weight of 0.8 and the link "eat-->LocationOfAction-->kitchen" has a weight of 0.9, the weight of the route "fork-->UsedFor-->eat" is 0.8 while the weight of the route "fork-->UsedFor-->eat-->LocationOfAction-->kitchen" is 0.72, which is 0.8 * 0.9.

After scoring all the nodes in the target subnetwork, SIM considers the node with the highest score as the target node, which most probably has the same or similar concept to the given concept. Currently SIM provides two target nodes with the highest and the second highest scores.

Difference Inference Module (DIM)

A nice and gentle businessman from Korea visited the USA. He went into a restaurant ignoring a hostess at a small front desk by the door and grabbed an empty table near the windows. He raised his hand and shouted "here" to call any waiter around him. After finishing his meal, he paid the price of the food and left no tips.

He made several rude mistakes in the restaurant. He should have waited for the hostess to escort him to his table, waited for his own waiter/waitress to address him, and paid tips in addition to the cost of his food for his waiter/waitress. However, these mistakes are not caused from his rudeness but from his ignorance of cultural differences. To resolve his situation and to avoid misunderstanding others intentions and making rude mistakes in cross-cultural communication, it is essential to know the difference of common sense between two cultures.

The GlobalMind difference inference module is designed to find the cultural differences between two culture networks in a given situation. For example, if a user gives "restaurant" to DIM, it returns "in America you should give waiters tips / in Korea you don't" or "in America there is one fixed waiter for your table / in Korea any waiter in the restaurant serves any table."

There were several attempts to approach the cultural difference problems. For example, Anacleto's work (Anacleto et al., 2006) also used a common-sense based approach in this problem. However, GlobalMind DIM is different from previous work in that DIM automatically extracts the difference by comparing the common-sense databases of each culture while other approaches used manually built databases about cultural differences. Thus, GlobalMind DIM can be easily extended to any pair of two different cultures.

DIM uses the compare-and-remove method to find the differences between two cultures:

1. DIM extracts the common-sense knowledge related with the given situation in both culture networks by expanding the subnetworks from the given situation node;

2. It compares two sub-networks with each other. If there is shared or duplicated com-

mon-sense knowledge in two sub-networks, the shared common-sense is removed;

3. The remaining sub-networks are provided as cultural differences between two cultures about the given situation.

In this compare-and-remove process, the most difficult obstacle is comparing the common-sense assertions written in different languages and determining if they have the same meaning or not. Currently, DIM uses machine translators to compare assertions written in different languages.

Extracting Sub-Networks

The first step of DIM processing is analyzing the given situation and extracting the contexts of the situation.

Because the situation is given in one language while DIM uses two culture networks that may be written in different languages, the given situation should be translated into the other language (in our case, by using the Google machine translator (2005)). For example, if a user wants to compare the American culture and Korean culture about "restaurant," DIM translates "restaurant" into Korean, "SIK DANG(restaurant)."

If the given situation includes several concepts in it such as "restaurant at evening on birthday," DIM analyzes and divides the given situation into several pieces, "restaurant," "evening," and "birthday," and each of them is translated separately. In this case, although all the situation concepts will be used for the inference, the first concept has the most impact while the last concept node has the least impact on the inference.

To extract the common sense related to the given situation, the situation nodes are searched in both culture networks, and the sub-networks are expanded from all the situation nodes. For the "restaurant" and "SIK DANG(restaurant)," "restaurant<--LocatedAt<--waiter" or "SIK DANG(restaurant)-->UsedFor-->MUK DA(eat)"

will be extracted as a part of the sub-network. Unlike SIM, which contracts the sub-networks into one or a few nodes before returning the result, DIM, which does not contract its result, should restrict the sub-networks only to the common sense strongly and directly related to the given situation from the beginning. Thus, DIM extracts only the Level-1 sub-networks.

The final sub-networks are the union of the sub-networks of each culture network.

Comparing and Removing

Now we have two sub-networks, one for each culture network. DIM compares the sub-networks with each other, removes the same or similar common sense, and returns the remaining sub-networks which means the differences between two networks.

How can we find the shared common sense?

At first, we can use bicultural connections between two sub-networks. The two assertions connected by bicultural connections are the same or similar. However, considering that the bicultural connections are a kind of translation, and the translated assertions are not regarded as original common sense in the culture network, it is meaningless to remove the biculturally connected assertions themselves—it is nothing but removing the connections. The assertions, which should be removed, are the culture group's original assertions, which are similar to the translated assertions. Thus, DIM removes the original assertions, which share the same nodes and the same relationships with the translated assertions.

Additionally, DIM compares the sub-networks with machine translators to find the shared common sense. If two assertions have similar nodes and the same relationship between those two nodes, they can be regarded as the shared common sense. Because nodes are represented by phrases, it is easy to compare nodes and determine if they are the same or not if they are written in the same language. Thus, DIM translates nodes in one culture network into the language used in the other culture network, and then compares the nodes, which are now written in the same language. For example, "SIK DANG(restaurant)-->UsedFor-->MUK DA(eat)" will be translated to "restaurant-->UsedFor-->eat." For this translation, the Google Machine Translator (2005) is used.

The machine-translated assertions in one sub-network are compared to the other assertions in the other sub-network, and if DIM finds matching assertions in both sub-network, the assertions are removed.

Because of the limited performance of the machine translator, we cannot expect the texts of two nodes to be exactly matched even when they have the same meanings. Thus, DIM regards two nodes sharing the same words in them as the same nodes. Stop words such as "the" and "of" are not included in this comparison. If two assertions have the same two nodes and the same relationship between those two nodes, the assertions are regarded as shared. For an assertion "restaurant-->UsedFor-->eat food," a translated

assertion "public restaurant-->UsedFor-->eat" is the shared assertion, but other translated assertions "restaurant-->UsedFor-->meal" or "restaurant<--LocatedAt<--food" are not the shared assertions.

After removing all the shared common sense, the remaining sub-networks are returned as the cultural differences between two cultures. The quality of the remaining sub-networks as the cultural differences is critically dependent on the quantity and quality of data of both of culture networks.

EVALUATION

The performance of inference modules is mostly dependent on the quality and quantity of databases. At this point, the size of the GlobalMind databases is not large relative to the typical knowledge of a human user, so inference in necessarily imperfect. However, still we can do a preliminary evaluation to test the potential and to inform future directions

Table 3. Human answers for SIM evaluation

Relationship		Count		Rate	
Same	Matched	325	364	76.47%	85.65%
Similar		39		9.18%	
Related	Unmatched	35	61	8.24%	14.35%
Not related		26		6.12%	
Total		425		100%	
Inter-raters reliability (Fleiss' Kappa)					
0.437	0.668				

for the improvement of GlobalMind. This section describes the preliminary test for the GlobalMind system and its results.

Because the American/English database and the Korean/Korean database are the top two largest databases in GlobalMind, this evaluation is done with those two databases.

Similar-Concept Inference Module

When there is a given concept in one culture group, the GlobalMind similar-concept inference module finds matching concepts in another culture group. The found matching concepts can be dictionary words, or they can be different from dictionary words but have similar concepts to the given concept.

This evaluation is designed to test if SIM can extract similar concepts with relatively high probability, and if SIM can extract the concepts that are similar to a given concept but that cannot be found in a dictionary. Because of the limited size of databases, we cannot expect human-level results. However, this evaluation can determine whether GlobalMind is making some plausible inferences.

Design

SIM is given some English concepts and extracts the most similar Korean concepts for the given concepts. The similarity of a given English word and an extracted Korean word is measured.

Korean human raters evaluate whether the words in each pair have the similar concepts or not. Each pair will be divided into four categories: if the English word and the Korean word share the same dictionary meaning, "same"; if they do not have the same meaning but are conceptually similar based on contexts, "similar"; if they are neither same nor similar but if the subject automatically reminds the other word when he or she sees/hears one word in the pair, "related"; and in other cases, "not related at all." For example "fork" in American/English, "PO K(fork)" is "same," "JEOT GA RAK(chopsticks)" is "similar," "SIK SA(eating meal)" is "related," and "NAM JA(man)" is "not related at all."

In "same" and "similar" pairs, the American/English word and the Korean/Korean word can substitute for each other, while in "related" and "not related at all" they cannot. Thus, for a simple comparison, "same" and "similar" can be grouped

Table 4. Human answers for the unconfirmed pairs

		Total Answers		Rate	
Matched	Same	10	24	12.05%	28.92%
	Similar	14		16.87%	
Unmatched	Related	33	59	39.76%	71.08%
	Not at all	26		31.33%	
Total		63		100%	

as "matched," and "related" and "not related at all" can form another group, "unmatched." In the best case, all the pairs will be evaluated as "matched," and in the worst case, all the pairs will be evaluated as "unmatched."

Test Concept Sets

The given concepts were chosen from the 300 most-frequently used English words (ESL Desk, 2006). Among the 300 words, the words whose primary meanings are nouns were chosen, and the stop words such as "a," "and," "to," and "also" were removed. After the removal, the remaining 72 English nouns were given to SIM as American/English concepts. SIM extracted the most similar Korean/Korean concepts for 61 English words among 72 words, while 11 words could not be processed with the current database.

Human Raters

Human raters must be very familiar with Korean culture and language, and be able to read and write in English. Korean people who have lived in Korea more than 20 years and lived outside of Korea for less than two years during the last two years of their life are chosen as human raters. Seven Korean people including five males and two females participated; ages are between 24 and 29 where the average is 26.5, and the durations of living in Korea are between 20 and 28, where the average is 24.

Evaluation Form

The human raters are asked to fill out an online evaluation form. The form shows pairs of an English word and a Korean word. The subjects choose the relationship between the two words among "same," "similar," "related," and "not related at all."

Results

Table 3 shows the answers of our raters. Count means how many times each answer is selected by human subjects. Because there are 61 pairs and seven human raters, the maximum count of answers for the word pairs is 427. In this evaluation, one of the raters missed two pairs, thus these two pairs were not counted.

For the two groups, "matched" and "unmatched," the rate of each group is 50% for random selection. Because the goal of SIM is searching the words with the same/similar concepts, if it is working, the rates of "matched" become high and that of "unmatched" become low. Thus, if the result of SIM test shows the rate higher than 50% in "matched" and the rate lower than 50% in "unmatched," it indicates a positive result for SIM.

Here we used statistical hypothesis testing with the null hypothesis that the rate of the "matched" word pairs will be lower than "unmatched" word pairs and the alternative hypothesis of that the rate of "matched" word pairs will be higher than that of "unmatched" word pairs. With the rates of 85.65% for the matched pairs and 14.35% for the unmatched pairs, the p-value is less than 0.001, which means there is high likelihood that the alternative hypothesis is true. It shows the word pairs are not perfect but well inferred and meaningful.

Considering the small size of the databases, which limits the performance of SIM, it shows the strong potential of our inference algorithms. In the most common case of "unmatched" word pairs, the GlobalMind Korean/Korean database itself does not have the matching word for the given American/English words at all. Thus, we can guess that the main reason for SIM's failure, the unmatched pairs, is the limited size of the database rather than the failure of the inference algorithm, and the performance of SIM can be

Table 5. Human decisions on each set

	Count			Rate			Inter-raters Reliability (Fleiss' Kappa)	
	Similarities	Differences	Total	Similarities	Differences	Total	Korean	American
Initial Set	51	6	57	89.47%	10.53%	100%	0.270	0.566
Remaining Set	32	5	37	86.50%	13.50%	100%	0.249	0.476
Subtracted Set	19	1	20	95.00%	5.00%	100%	0.476	0.609

improved by adding more common-sense knowledge into the databases.

The word pairs generated by SIM were also compared to the Yahoo English-Korean dictionary (Yahoo Korea English Dictionary, 2006). If the Korean word in a pair can be found when the English word in the pair is looked up in the dictionary, the pair is marked as "confirmed," and if not, "unconfirmed." The 49 pairs out of the 61 word pairs are "confirmed" by the dictionary. Twelve "unconfirmed" pairs include incorrect inferences and indirect inferences.

Here our hypothesis is that SIM can find similar concepts even when they are different from dictionary words, but have the same uses based on the contexts. If SIM can only find the words in a dictionary and cannot make inference based on the contexts, "matched" pairs and "confirmed" pairs will be the same. If the hypothesis is correct, some of "unconfirmed" pairs will be "matched" pairs, mostly "similar" pairs.

Table 4 shows the result of the human rater's answers to the "unconfirmed" pairs. Of the "unconfirmed" pairs, 28.92% are "matched" and it shows that SIM can find matching words that are missed in a dictionary.

Cultural Differences Inference Module

The performance of DIM is sensitive to the size of the database, which will be described next. With the limited size of the current database, this evaluation of DIM is only designed as the preliminary test to see if the inference module works as we intended and which parts we should improve.

To review, GlobalMind differences inference module extracts cultural differences. First DIM extracts all commonsense knowledge related to a given topic, and subtracts common-sense knowledge that is shared by both cultures. The remaining common-sense facts after subtraction are the cultural differences suggested by DIM.

The performance of DIM is largely influenced by the subtraction. Two factors are important in the quality of subtraction: the quality of subtracted common sense and the number of subtracted common sense statements. First, DIM should subtract only shared commonsense knowledge; if DIM subtracts unshared common sense by mistake, performance will be lowered. Second, DIM should subtract shared common-sense knowledge as much as possible; if DIM cannot subtract much of shared common-sense knowledge, the suggested cultural differences will include knowledge that are not "differences."

Figure 5 shows the idea of this process. Each circle represents a common-sense statement in one culture network, where black circles are shared common sense and white circles are different common sense. Figure 5(a) shows the initial knowledge set that has not yet been processed. In the ideal case, subtracting the set temporarily looks like Figure 5(b) and winds up looking like Figure 5(c). In the worst case, it can subtract unshared common sense by mistake and it will look like Figure 5(d).

DIM determines shared knowledge by data accumulated in the databases; if knowledge is located in both the American and Korean databases, it is shared knowledge. Thus, the amount of shared knowledge is mostly dependent on the size and overlap of databases while the quality of subtracted knowledge is mostly dependent on the inference module. With the current limited

databases, this evaluation will not measure the amount of subtracted shared knowledge but only the quality of subtracted shared knowledge. In Figure 5, this evaluation will measure which DIM is closer between Figure 5(b) or Figure 5(d) rather than between Figure 5(b) and 4(c).

Design

During the inference process, DIM generates the initial set, the subtracted set, and the remaining set. The initial set is the collection of all common-sense knowledge related to the given situations, the subtracted set is the collection of all shared common-sense knowledge determined by DIM, and the remaining set is the cultural differences provided by DIM.

In this evaluation, the proportion of "differences" and "similarities" of each set is rated. If the inference algorithm works as it is intended to, the proportion of "differences" of the initial set will be higher than that of the subtracted set and lower than that of the remaining set. In the

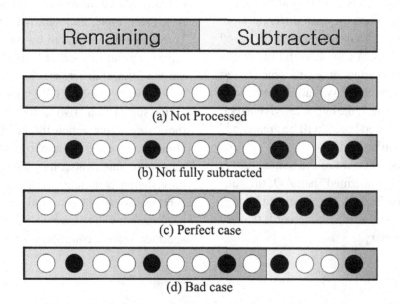

Figure 5. GlobalMind DIM processes and performance

best case, the proportion of "differences" of the subtracted set is 0%, that of the remaining set is close to 100%, and that of the initial set is between them. In the worst case, the proportions of all sets will be the same.

The "differences" and "similarities" are evaluated by the human raters. American human raters and Korean human raters evaluate each knowledge sentence if it is common sense in their own cultures or not. If both Korean and American raters agree

Figure 6. GlobalMind Intercultural Dictionary shows the result of "fork"

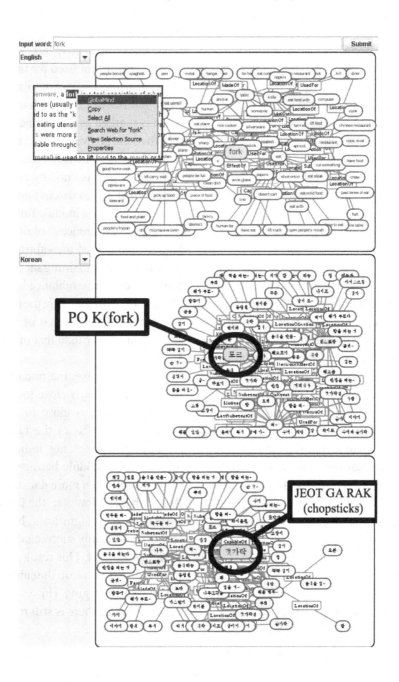

the sentence is common sense in their cultures, the sentences is one of "similarities," and if not, "differences."

Test Common-Sense Sets

For the ideal evaluation, the test topics should be chosen randomly. However, as the size of the databases is limited, we chose the test topics inside of the databases. "Funeral" and "restaurant" are chosen for this evaluation because both topics are familiar with people and both topics have some knowledge in the database.

The American/English common-sense knowledge related to the topics is 63 sentences including 13 sentences about "funeral" and 50 sentences about "restaurant." DIM processed the initial set, the 63 sentences, and produced the remaining set with 37 sentences and the subtracted set with 20 sentences.

Human Raters

Korean human raters are people who have lived in Korea for more than 20 years, have not lived outside of Korea for more than recent 3 years, and can read and write in English. Five Korean people participated in the evaluation including one female and four males. Ages are between 24 and 35 where the average is 28.4. The participants have lived in Korea for from 20 years to 28 years and the average duration is 24.2.

Five American people participated in the evaluation as American human raters including two females and three males. The ages are between 19 and 33, where the average is 25.8. None of them have ever lived for a significant time outside America.

Survey Forms

The raters are asked to fill the survey forms out online. The survey forms show the sentences and check boxes with "yes" or "no." If participants think the sentence is common sense in their own culture, they mark "yes," and if not, "no."

Result

Among five raters in each group of Korean and American's, if more than half of the raters agreed that a sentence is "yes," then the sentence is regarded as "yes"; if more than half of the participants agreed a sentence is "no," then the sentence is regarded as "no." In the case of 50:50, the sentence is not used for the evaluation.

For a sentence, if American raters answered "yes" but Korean raters answered "no," the sentence is marked as "differences by human," and if both raters answered "yes" then the sentence is marked as "similarities by human." The sentences that are judged as "no" by American raters are disregarded in this discussion.

If the inference module functions as intended, the rate of "differences" of the initial set will be higher than that of the subtracted set and lower than that of the remaining set. The results in Table 5 show a close resemblance to our expectations. The rate of "difference" in the initial set is 10.53%, which is higher than that of the subtracted set, 5.00%, and lower than that of the remaining set, 13.50%.

In the best case, the rate of "differences" of the remaining set is close to 100% and the rate of "similarities" is close to 0%. However, the large rate, 86.50%, of the false positive in the remaining set does not indicate the failure of the inference module because they can be subtracted later when more data are accumulated in the databases. However, the false negative in the subtracted set is significant, because once a sentence is mistakenly subtracted, it never returns to the remaining set. This result shows the very low rate of false negative in the subtracted set, 5.00%, which is encouraging. However, the fact that it is not 0% implies there is still room to improve the inference module.

APPLICATIONS

The core of GlobalMind is the database of multi-cultural common sense and the inference modules to analyze the data. To present how the system can be used in real applications, we developed two applications, one for each inference module: intercultural dictionary with similar-concept inference module and personal intercultural assistant with differences inference module.

Intercultural Dictionary

Intercultural dictionary is a FireFox extension to look up the most similar concept between two culture groups. The dictionary works between any

Figure 7. Personal intercultural assistant

two culture groups in GlobalMind and shows the matching concept of a given word. For example, while surfing the American Web sites, if a user finds a word "fork" and wants look up the most similar concept of "fork" in Korea, he or she clicks the right button on the Web site and the dictionary shows "JEOT GA RAK(chopsticks)."

A user can configure the given culture group and the target culture group. When the user clicks the right button on a selected word or phrase, the dictionary window pops up and shows the candidates a list of the most similar concept of the selected phrase in the target culture group and the related networks used for the inference. Once popped up, the user can use the dictionary program to browse the networks and find more concepts by double-clicking the nodes in the program.

Figure 6 shows the intercultural dictionary serviced in the GlobalMind Web site. It shows "PO K(fork)" as the first candidate for the most similar concepts of "fork" and "JEOT GA RAK(chopsticks)" as the second candidate. It also shows the contexts of each word.

Personal Intercultural Assistant

Another application for GlobalMind is personal intercultural assistant (PIA). PIA is a cell phone application intended to help foreign visitors to adapt themselves easier to the visiting countries. PIA helps users by providing the information of cultural differences between the users' original culture and the visiting culture.

PIA is developed on a cellular phone, Motorola i870 (Figure 7). A user can hold the cellular phone with PIA anywhere he or she wants and get help from PIA anytime he or she needs. When the user runs PIA on his or her cellular phone, PIA will ask him or her their current situation. After entering their current situation, PIA will prompt the cultural difference on the current situation between two cultures. For example, if the user enters "restaurant" as the current situation, and

PIA knows the he or she is from Korea and he or she is now in the USA, PIA will show the information such as "please leave tips for your waiter," which is common sense in the USA but not in Korea.

Because a cellular phone can provide contexts information of users such as time, contact lists, and location through the GPS system, we can think about improving PIA to more context-based services. For example, if the cellular phone is located at a restaurant in the evening, PIA can assume that the user enters a restaurant to have a dinner, and then it can provide services before the user asks.

CONCLUSION

Communication without misunderstanding is important in human interactions. However, it is difficult to avoid misunderstanding in the interactions between people from different countries because they experience different cultures and behave and analyze other's behaviors based on different contexts.

This article described how large-scale common-sense knowledge databases and their inference modules can enrich the communication and the interactions among people from different cultures. Although this research has not fully matured and still has many issues to be discussed more, it shows the potential of automated mechanisms to analyze cultural differences and similarities though the GlobalMind project, and provides the basic steps toward further research on enriched intercultural communication.

The quality of GlobalMind depends on the quantity of common-sense knowledge entered. Thus, it may take a few more years for Global-Mind to gather enough data to enable accurate analysis of cultures. However, we believe that this research represents an important and innovative step in approaching the problem of how to automate the search for cultural comparison. By doing so, we hope to provide the foundation for improving communication and understanding between various cultures and countries.

ACKNOWLEDGMENT

We'd like to thank the late Push Singh for his great ideas, Wonsik Kim for his contribution to programming, and the Samsung Lee Kun Hee Scholarship Foundation for their financial support.

REFERENCES

Adler, N. J., & Graham, J. L. (1989). Cross-cultural interaction: The international comparison fallacy? *Journal of International Business Studies*, *20*(3), 515-537.

Anacleto, J., Lieberman, H., Tsutsumi, M., Neris, V., Carvalho, A., Espinosa, J., & Zem-Mascarehnhas, S. (2006). Can common sense uncover cultural differences in computer applications? World Computer Congress.

ConceptNet. Retrieved November 09, 2005, from http://www.conceptnet.org/

Condon, J. C. (1974). Perspective for the conference. In J. C. Condon & M. Saito (Ed.), *Intercultural encounters with Japan*. Tokyo: Simul Press.

ESL Desk - Learn English as a Second Language. Retrieved August 1, 2006, from http://www.esldesk.com/esl-quizzes/mostused-english-words/words.htm

Fellbaum, F. C. (1998). *WordNet: An electronic lexical database*. Cambridge, MA: The MIT Press.

Gentner, D. (1983). Structure-mapping: A theoretical framework for analogy. *Cognitive Science*, *7*(2), 155-170.

GlobalMind. Retrieved June 26, 2006, from http://globalmind.media.mit.edu

Google Translate. Retrieved November 09, 2005, from http://translate.google.com/translate t

Herring, R. D. (1990). Nonverbal communication: A necessary component of cross-cultural counseling. *Journal of Multicultural Counseling and Development, 18*(4), 172-179.

Jurafsky, D., & Martin, H. (2000). *Speech and language processing: An introduction to natural language processing, computational linguistics and speech recognition.* Cambridge, MA: The MIT Press

Lenat, D. B. (1998). *The dimensios of context space.* Austin, TX: Cycorp.

Liu, H., & Singh, P. (2004). ConceptNet: A practical commonsense reasoning toolkit. *BT Technology Journal, 22*(4), 211-226

Mueller, E. T. (1998). *Natural language processing with ThoughtTreasure.* New York: Signiform.

Munter, M. (1993). Cross-cultural communication for managers. *Business Horizons, 36*(3).

OpenMind Common Sense. Retrieved November 09, 2005, from http://commonsense.media.mit.edu/

Sawyer, J., & Guetzkow, H. (1965). Bargaining and negotiation in international relations. In H. C. Kelman (Ed.), *InternationalBehavior: A social-psychological analysis* (pp. 464-520).

Scheff, T. J. (1987). Is accurate cross-cultural translation possible? *Current Anthropology, 28*(3), 365.

Sechrest, L., Fay, T. L., & Zaidi, S. M. H. (1972). Problems of translation in cross-cultural research. *Journal of Cross-Cultural Psychology, 3*(1), 41-56.

Singh, P. (2002). The public acquisition of commonsense knowledge. In *Proceedings of AAAI Spring Symposium on Acquiring (and Using) Linguistic (and World) Knowledge for Information Access.*

Wikipedia. Retrieved July 28, 2006, from http://www.wikipedia.org/

Yahoo Korea English Dictionary. Retrieved July 28, 2006, from http://dic.yahoo.com/

This work was previously published in International Journal on Semantic Web & Information Systems, Vol. 3, Issue 1, edited by A. P. Sheth and M. D. Lytras, pp. 65-95, copyright 2007 by IGI Publishing, formerly known as Idea Group Publishing (an imprint of IGI Global).

Chapter XV
Challenges in Building a Culture–Centric Web Site

Tom S. Chan
Southern NH University, USA

ABSTRACT

This chapter discusses the challenges in constructing a culture-centric Web site. The Internet has expanded business opportunities into global marketplaces that were virtually unreachable in the past. With business Web sites reaching international audiences, cultural differences are an important issue in interface design. Global Web sites must be culture-centric, taking into account the attitude, technology, language, communication, sensibility, symbolism, and interface usability of targeted communities. Site design and development also should follow the Unicode standard for multilingual support with implementation done on UTF-8-enabled operating systems and applications. Globalization has led many people to become more sensitive to cultural diversity. The author hopes that understanding and awareness of international user needs, limitations, and expectations will lead to global Web sites with improved usability and sensitivity.

INTRODUCTION

The Internet has revolutionized international business and global marketing. Roughly speaking, the Internet is a network of computers interconnected throughout the world and operating on a standard protocol that allows data to be transmitted. Until the early 1990s, the Internet was primarily the domain of the military and academia. The development of new software and technologies turned the Internet (Net) into a commercial medium that has transformed businesses worldwide. There is a strong international market, and businesses are taking note. From 106.4 million online buyers worldwide in 2000, the number is expected to hit 464.1 million by 2006 (Campanelli, 2004). Along with incorporating user-centric design, a business Web site must be culture-centric. A U.S. Web site designer must understand that international users' needs and expectations may be different than U.S. users. Differences in cultural attitudes, technological limitations, linguistics, communication, aesthetic sensibility, symbolism, and interface usability all must be well thought out. Furthermore, the computer platforms also must have multilingual supports.

BACKGROUND

Constructing successful global Web sites involves three knowledge domains: business operation, technical standard, and interface design. Business issues facing global e-commerce operations are abundant. Chun, Honda, and Schwane (2005) show that these issues include logistics and distribution, financial and technological infrastructures, legal frameworks, and strategic business alliances. The technical standard domain deals with issues such as HTML, Unicode, character set, operating system, application, and browser supports; these are prerequisites for proper multilingual content implementation. This article focuses on both technical standard and interface design issues for global Web sites.

Research in user interface design has been centered on layout, navigation, and performance issues (Lynch & Horton, 1999, Spool, Scanlon, Schroeder, Snyder, & DeAngelo, 1999). While the research provides good guidance for page design, it does not address global site design issues. Scheiderman (1998) proposed a universal

accessibility concept that addresses user diversity. Marcus and Gould (2000) studied interface design in terms of cultural perception of information content, images, icons, and symbolism. Huang and Tilley (2001) examined content and structure challenges associated with multilingual Web sites. These research efforts provided a glimpse at both the complexity and opportunity associated with Web usability design in a global economy. The research is still in its early stages, and more investigations are needed on usability, cultural, and linguistic issues.

THE DIGITAL AND CULTURAL DIVIDES

The term *digital divide* traditionally has described inequalities in access to technology among social or cultural groups. Although there has been a huge increase in Net speed in the industrialized world, the trend is not global. A recent survey revealed about 36 million broadband lines in the U.S. compared to 295,000 in India (Point Topic, 2005), and India is a high-tech powerhouse with a population 30 times that of the US. Many international users also use older technologies (including older computers and browsers) or lack items such as video and sound cards. Net access is only one aspect of the digital divide. The quality of connections and auxiliary services, the processing speed and the capabilities of the computer used, along with many other technical factors are also important issues (Davison & Cotton, 2003). Designers who ignore users' technological capabilities by creating sites that must be viewed with the latest technologies or with the fast connections are dooming their projects from the outset.

Culture is the collective programming of the mind that distinguishes members of one group from another group. It is also the set of values and attributes of a given group (Hofstede, 1997). The Internet is a new medium, and in a survey as recent as five years ago (Walsh, McQuivey, & Wakeman, 1999), it was reported as the least trusted medium. The situation is improving, and 25% of consumers now express a great degree of trust in online purchases (*Business Journal*, 2003). Yet, cultural differences exist in the degree of trust. For example, U.S. users trust information from the Net more than their UK cousins. However, both groups are unlikely to use Web advertisements in making purchasing decisions (Rettie, Robinson, Mojsa, & Parissi, 2003). Ethnocentricity is the tendency to look at the world primarily from the perspective of one's own culture. While the Net both facilitates and limits interaction by its virtual representation, ethnocentrism survives in cyberspace (Halavais, 2000). It is crucial to understand this cultural divide when designing Web sites for users in another region.

North American users are more likely than the rest of the world to access the Net from home. In many developing countries, access is limited by resource constraints. Cybercafés are popular in these countries. Not surprisingly, public terminal users use the Net for recreational or social purposes more than for instrumental or business purposes. Users from developing countries also have the strongest sense of online community, followed by users from other industrialized countries, with North America last (Boase, Chen, Wellman, & Prijatelj, 2003). People visit cybercafés to be with their friends, to learn languages, and to socialize with others from different cultures. For these users, the Net is more a socializing point than a venue for commerce and transactions. Even within industrialized nations, cultural divides exist: Americans are more home-oriented than Europeans; Europeans and Japanese have a more mobile life; and Japanese like gaming more than Americans.

A Web site is not the business itself. The business runs the Web site. It is important to understand that a site supports a business; and in order for a business to prosper, it must serve its users well. The first task in site design is defining its objectives. One sometimes assumes that a technically elegant system is a successful system, but this is far from the truth. Many technically sound systems fail because the people side of the system is ignored. Ultimately, the system is only a success if it meets the users' requirements, fits comfortably within their capabilities and sensibilities, and above all, makes the users happy with it.

CONTENT TRANSLATION, HUMAN VS. MACHINE

Although many non-English users can read English, they do not always appreciate it. They are more apt to enjoy the site if it is in their native language. A survey indicated that 80% of Net users have a preference for their native language and are four times more likely to purchase from sites that communicate in their own language (McClure, 2001). To seize this opportunity, a business must localize its documents, Web content, and, in some cases, product interfaces. For an English-only site, this means translation. The easiest approach to translating a site is to hire a professional translating service, but this option is expensive. Computerized translation is available. With a large number of Web pages today generated on the fly using scripting languages from contents stored in a database, a middle-tier translation engine would appear to easily solve the multilingual problem for global Web sites. Yet, computerized translation is not always accurate and should be used with great caution.

Research in machine translation began in the late 1950s. Early systems used pattern matching, semantic and syntactic approaches. Programmers wrote lists of rules that described all possible relationships between verbs, nouns, and prepositions for each language (Arnold, Balkan, Humphreys, Meijer, & Sadler, 1994). These systems were little more than word-for-word translations, not addressing the problems of word sense disambiguation and syntactic rearrangement. The results were often unpredictable and unintelligible.

For example, in the sentence, "Fruit flies like a baseball," not all fruit, when thrown, would fly through the air like a baseball, except, perhaps, an apple, orange, or peach. But if one substitutes "peach" for "baseball," there is a new meaning. Then fruit flies are pesky insects crawling on a peach having a feast (Melby, 1995).

With the increase in processing speed and the decrease in storage price of computers, modern example-based systems are devoting more time to source analysis and translation synthesis. The system selects the most likely translation using statistical and mathematical models. The system can learn continuously from past translations (Rupley, 2004). Such systems will have enough intelligence to resolve earlier dilemmas. Another current approach is a computer-aided translation system in which human translators work with a computer, allowing for rapid, efficient, and high-quality translations. As translators type, the system provides them with suggestions to complete a sentence. The suggestions are created based on statistical models of machine translation engines that predict words that will come next (Esteban, 2005). Remember, translation can get complicated with regional and cultural differences within specific languages. For example, Spanish is not quite the same in Mexico as it is in Spain or Argentina, nor is Quebecois the same as Parisian French.

NONVERBAL AND CONTEXTUAL COMMUNICATION

Content is only half of the challenge in translation. Perception is not a passive, objective, and neutral process. It is a subjective experience, deeply rooted in one's personality structure and cultural environment (Maletzke, 1996). A number of nonverbal cues, such as body movements, space organization, eye movement, and touching behavior, plays a crucial role in communication (Dahl, 2004). As the Net incorporates more mul-

timedia, nonverbal cues will play an increasing role in communication.

Translation consists of providing the closest equivalence in terms of both meaning and style. It is always a challenge dealing with a language that has a different feel and nuance embedded more in culture than in literal meaning. Accommodations in translation are often necessary in such instances (Shi, 2004). For example, Asians favor implicature in talking to people as opposed to the direct way favored by Westerners. Adjustments often are needed so that the translation does not irate the readers. Thus, proper copy tone is often critical. In the U.S., it would be fine to say, "Welcome back, Tom." In Japan, public language is much more formal, and a proper translation would be, "We are honored by your return visit, Mr. Chan." Apart from cultural attitudes, another topic deserving no less attention is politics. One must be careful with statements that can be construed to be offensive to local governments. In some regions, such neglect could carry costly consequences.

In low-context societies, communication relies more heavily on the literal meaning of words. Meanings of communication are more explicit. To people from high-context cultures, the bluntness of low-context communication styles seems insulting or aggressive. In high-context cultures, much more of the surrounding context is involved in conveying a message. Meaning in high-context communication has to be interpreted within the context of the social relationship between the individuals (DeVito, 2004). Special care must be taken when translating between these two different types of languages to ensure the preservation of the original text's intended meaning.

With the advent of globalization, the language barrier is a major obstacle to the creation of global communities. Efficient and effective translation can create linguistic transparency within these communities. Remember to translate the site fully, including all messages, labels, icons, prompts, supports, search keywords, and results.

Furthermore, different cultures react to layouts differently, such as left-to-right or right-to-left. Site design must take into account text flow and object layout. Apart from semantic and contextual correctness, the text must not be culturally offensive, archaic, or nonsensical. To achieve this objective, the translated site should be validated by a focus group from the targeted local community. A site is not usable if it is merely translated into another language without any thought given to user experience.

DESIGNING COLOR AND HIDDEN MEANINGS

The Net has come a long way from being a collection of black and white text pages to a portal of color, image, sound, and animation. Color and images are vital tools that a Web designer must master, as it is impossible to create a site without them. However, they sometimes can have hidden meanings. When designing for international users, be aware that color and images could have symbolic meanings in different cultural settings.

Color helps a site to catch and hold attention. As the primary aesthetic tool, it helps to sustain, reinforce, and enhance a positive experience (Morton, 2001). Colors are also an element of design that people react to viscerally, though often subconsciously. Colors can solicit a universal physical reaction; for example, red has been shown to raise blood pressure. Reaction to color also can be culture-bound; white is for weddings in the U.S., but it is the color for funerals in China (Morton, 2004). Many colors, especially black, white, red, and blue, have strong and varying symbolic or religious meanings in many cultures.

Black is the absence of color. It makes objects appear to shrink in size and makes other colors appear to be brighter. The ancient Egyptians and Romans used black for mourning, as do most Europeans and Americans today. Black often stands for evil or the unknown. Among young people, black is seen as a color of rebellion and as racy and trendy. Of course, in the Wild West, good guys wore white, while bad guys wore black. The color black conveys a sense of elegance, sophistication, and mystery.

White is the presence of all colors. White is a brilliant color that can be blinding. In the West, white is the color for brides. In the East, it is the color for funerals. White is often associated with hospitals, doctors, and nurses. White signifies goodness and purity, and in many cultures, it is the color of royalty or deity (Fact Monster, 2005). The color white conveys a sense of wholesomeness, cleanliness, and softness. Colors such as beige, ivory, and cream have the same attributes but are more subdued and less blinding than pure white.

Red is a stimulant, the hottest of all colors. Studies show that red can increase the rate of respiration and blood pressure. For most cultures, red signifies power; hence, the red carpet for VIPs. But red also signals danger. In some cultures, it denotes celebration and prosperity. The Bolsheviks used a red flag when overthrowing the Tsar; thus, red became the color of communism. The color red grabs attentions, making an object stand out. A little bit of red goes a long way, and smaller dosages are more effective.

Blue is a calming color but too much blue can be depressing. In many cultures, blue is significant in religious beliefs, bringing peace and keeping bad spirits away. Blue conveys importance and confidence without the somber and sinister feeling of the color black; hence, a blue suit for the corporate world. Dark blue is associated with intelligence, stability, and truthfulness, but sometimes it is seen as stale and old fashioned. Blue is often considered the safest global color.

Colors obtain symbolism through cultural references in the society. Colors can have very different meanings depending on the culture. Thus, some colors can be risky because of their cultural significance. Yet, like all things in design, colors go in and out of fashion. Apart from cultural factors, age, gender, and even social class also can affect color preferences. By understanding the audience makeup, one can create a very effective color scheme. Remember that basic design principles still hold. Too much red or blue overwhelms a site, and black fonts on red or blue backgrounds are hardly readable.

IMAGE, MOVEMENT, AND SYMBOLISM

A symbol is an image that stands for something, and it does not need to be explained or accompanied by words. Symbols often invoke strong feelings. While not necessarily engrained in one's subconscious, some symbols nevertheless will bring on emotional responses. The responses could be from one's upbringing, religious beliefs, or even misconceptions (Liungman, 1994). The same symbols can have different cultural interpretations. For example, in Chinese culture, dogs represent faithfulness; in Islamic culture, they represent impurity.

The Nazi swastika, for obvious reasons, evokes very powerful negative feelings. Yet, the swastika is just one of many versions of a symbol that goes back thousands of years. Apart from the history and meaning given to it by the Nazis, it is also a religious symbol that signifies health, life, and good luck in cultures from Tibet, India, Japan, and China (Badlani, 1997). To avoid problems, one should pick logos and icons from internationally accepted symbols when possible (Smith & Siringo, 1997). One also should look to current research whenever in doubt (Symbol.com, 2005).

Hofstede (1997) distinguishes between cultures in terms of their masculinity. For example, men are supposed to be assertive, tough, and focused on material success, whereas women are supposed to be modest and tender. The masculine-feminine cultural orientation, as described by Hofstede, is also applicable in cyberspace (Dormann & Chisalita, 2002). Masculine societies favor clear and distinct social gender roles, but these roles tend to overlap in feminine societies. Masculine cultures like Middle Eastern favor traditional family and gender distinctions. Thus, male-only or father-and-son images are deemed more appropriate in Web sites. Feminine cultures such as the European show less such distinction, and mixing gender images are totally acceptable.

Human sexuality is always a sensitive subject. Regions vary greatly on the degree of body exposure acceptable on the Net. Some cultures expect human images to have much of their body covered, whereas exposing most of the body is acceptable in others. For example, the same nude image may be perfectly okay in France, deemed inappropriate in North America and Asian Pacific, and downright illegal in the Middle East. Cultural sensitivity associated with female and male images must be taken into account when developing a culture-centric site. Designers are well advised to emphasize the preferred social values when designing sites in different cultural communities.

Research shows that up to 90% of the meaning in a message is transmitted nonverbally (Fromkin & Rodman, 1983). This makes communicating across cultures very difficult. For example, body movements convey specific meanings, and the interpretations are culture-bound. Many gestures have several meanings. Some gestures extend across linguistic boundaries, while others are truly national (Desmond, Collett, Marsh, & O'Shaughnessy, 1979). Many people in the U.S. use the OK gesture, symbolized by the letter O, without even thinking. In South America, the gesture carries sexual connotations, symbolizing female genitalia, and is understood to be obscene (Axtell, 1991). Imagine a Web site that has a photo of happy engineers at a major project celebration giving a classic OK gesture with their hands. Such an image would be highly offensive to Brazilian viewers. Avoid using finger gestures or feet in images because they are high-risk elements (Nieilsen, 1999).

A poor choice of colors and images can send the wrong message to users. Bear in mind that cultural constructs are dynamic and that there always will be exceptions. No two people behave in precisely the same way, nor do people from the same culture all interpret symbols uniformly. Often, some clearly understandable images in one culture are nonsense in another. Sometimes an ordinary gesture or image in one culture can be highly offensive in another.

PAGE DESIGN AND GLOBAL USABILITY

A good Web site must be visually appealing, clear, easy to navigate, and forgiving. For international users, a simple layout is the best, as it makes scanning and translating text into other languages easier. Navigation text should be concise and brief. Confusion irritates users who already may be having difficulty with the language. For multinationals, sites in different countries should be linked. This typically is achieved by using a text-based navigation bar at the bottom of the home page. A site map showing hierarchically structured areas and subareas can facilitate navigation. It can be the most helpful design element for international users.

A standardized template can greatly facilitate communication, reduce efforts, and maintain consistency across sites. It also reinforces the unique corporate branding in a global environment. The template defines all Web elements such as logo, color, navigation, icons, font size, and style, and their positioning on the page layout. It also must be in agreement with corporate branding and be in accordance with site construction best practices.

A font is a complete set of characters of one size, in one style, and of one typeface. A typeface is a set of letters, numbers, and symbols with a common weight, width, and design. A type style is a variation of the typeface, such as regular,

bold, or italic. Common fonts such as Arial and Times Roman can be used for Western European languages, but they do not contain characters for languages such as Japanese, Chinese, or Russian. Since each language has its own sets of scripts with various font types, the selection process for global sites is far from trivial. As a general guideline, the selected font should go well with other design elements and with the fonts selected for other languages, and most importantly, it should be readily available in the local browsers.

In order to maintain consistency and to simplify the implementation process, logos and icons should be identical image files for all multilingual sites. Thus, text should not be embedded in a graphic object. Instead, the image should be in the background, and the text should be positioned on top of it. If text elements are part of a Web graphic, save them in separate layers, and save the graphic file in its native format before exporting to GIF or JPEG formats. Most graphic tools support layers allowing the localizable text to go into a separate layer, leaving the image layer unchanged.

The greatest challenge in multilingual site design is screen space that either expands or contracts, depending on the language used. When an interface design allows space for a particular set of words and the text length expands in translation, truncation occurs. Designers often want to get the most information into a limited space. It is common to see translated words truncated in the interface. When designing the interface, one should be mindful that the text could expand or contract. The variance could be as little as 30% for large sections of text or as much as 300% for a single word. Take precautions in form, and label designs, as they certainly will run into truncation problems. Finally, when a browser views a page with multiple languages, the default font size may cause one script to be readable and others to be illegibly small or anesthetically large. Thus, one also should set explicit font size attributes for the text for each language.

FORMAT AND INPUT VALIDATION

Notations and formats are another challenge for multilingual site designers. For example, the metric system is the norm for global measurements, but the US does not use it. The following is a short list of areas to which designers should pay attention:

- **Currency:** The currency symbol and its abbreviation.
- **Text sorting sequence:** Is it alphabetical or by stroke?
- **Number format:** For example, Chinese count in units of ten thousands instead of thousands.
- **Salutation:** Mister, Herr, Señor, or Monsieur?
- **Person's name:** First name first or last name first, and what about middle name?
- **Postal address:** Street first or state first, zip code or no zip code?
- **Date format:** Month/date/year or year/month/date?
- **Time format:** 24-hour or 12-hour clock, how many time zones, daylight savings or not?

The HTML form is perhaps the most important tool in e-commerce. Since no one enjoys filling out forms, it is very important to make the usability of the form easy. Over-zealous and culturally insensitive input splitting and validation are major annoyances to international users. As already noted, formats and notations differ in many countries (Starling, 2001). The number-one complaint in form design is address verification. For example, an Australian living in South Australia has a postal code of 5000. This user should not receive a prompt stating that "SA is not a valid state" or be forced to enter "05000" as a postal code. Further, some countries such as Singapore do not have state notation, and Canada's postal codes are alphanumeric and six characters long (Cruz,

2005). Other validation insensitivities include limiting phone numbers to numeric; not accepting e-mail addresses other than .com, .net, or .org; and month/date vs. date/month formatting.

Over-splitting input fields also can be annoying to international users. For example, breaking an address into apartment, flat, street number, and street name requires four separate inputs instead of one. Likewise, using state or province to label state input expands its understanding across national boundaries. Consider using a single-name field, and let users enter what they feel comfortable with, whether that is a full name, first name first, last name first, or even a nickname.

Determine if the priority is to correctly fill up the database or to provide a positive use experience. The gospel according to Customer Relationship Management would say both! Over-restricted requirements often lead to user frustration, and often, users needing to pass through form validation will just enter junk. As with all design, simplicity works best for international users. If possible, encourage users to input the correct data rather than implementing overly strict validation.

UNICODE AND MULTILINGUAL STANDARDS

As the Net grows ever more internationalized with an increasing multicultural audience, the standards and protocols supporting the Web are showing limitations in terms of multilingual supports. The original Web was designed around the ISO/IEC 8859-1, or Latin-1 character set that supports only Western European languages. This system of character encoding, ANSI, used a 256-characters set. The first 128 characters will be identical to the ANSI standard, but the second set of 128 will be taken by a different character set, which is lingual-dependent. The same number can represent a different character in different alphabet systems. Unlike reading hard copy, reading electronic documents from another country, particularly one with a different alphabet, poses a very serious challenge for Web site design and supporting technology.

An early approach to handling multilingual Web pages was to use the <FONT FACE> attribute of the HTML tag to denote non-Latin scripts. This approach has several serious drawbacks. First, an HTML document is transferred on the Net as a sequence of coded characters with each value corresponding to a standard character that the application can interpret and display. By using <FONT FACE> to specify a different text, the browser is being lied to about the identity of the characters that supposedly are identified by the standard codes in the client's computer, perhaps causing logic errors. Second, as a matter of good style and practice, just as one should use <Hn> instead of the <FONT SIZE> tag to denote hierarchy levels of the text, language is a logical and not a physical markup. For example, Chinese is logically a different type of language script and not a Latin script within a different physical layout. However, the most serious consequence is that the document now totally depends upon the availability of the particular font. Users will have to download the particular font if it is not on their machine. Asking a user to download a unique font prior to visiting the Web site is like asking a guest to bring his or her own plate and utensils for dinner. This additional viewing requirement is likely to be ignored along with the site.

The Unicode Consortium was incorporated in January 1991 to promote the Unicode Standard as an international encoding system for information interchange, to aid in its implementation, and to maintain quality control over future revisions. Unicode assigns a unique number to each character in each of the major languages of the world. It is intended to be used with a large set of special characters in all computer systems, not just Windows, and all languages, not just English. Unicode is designed to allow a single document to contain text from multilingual scripts and char-

acters and to allow those documents to remain intelligible in electronic form, regardless of the operating system. It is an ideal language for the World Wide Web. By assigning a unique identifier to each character from the value of 0 to 65535 or x'FFFF' in hexadecimal notation, different language scripts can coexist in the same document without conflicts. The current version (4.1) of the Unicode Standard defines 97,720 characters covering the scripts of the world's principal written languages and many mathematical and other symbols (Unicode, 2005).

There are different techniques to represent a unique Unicode character in binary using either UTF-8, 16, or 32 encoding schema. To meet the requirements of byte-oriented and ASCII-based systems, UTF-8 is the most popular standard in the Net today. The variable-width encoding schema minimizes the number of bytes required to store Unicode characters and allow for efficient string parsing commonly used to encode Web contents. Each character is represented in UTF-8 as a sequence of up to 4 bytes, where the first byte indicates the number of bytes to follow in a multibyte sequence. Since plain ASCII files are already Unicode compliance, these legacy files do not need to be changed when viewing under the UTF-8 standard. The UTF-16 standard uses a 16-bit representation. The first 63,486 characters are represented in 16 bits, while the remaining 2,048 combine with a second 16-bit value to represent another 1,048,544 characters as a pair of 16-bit values. Finally, the UTF-32 standard stores Unicode characters as 32-bit integers, allowing a simple one-to-one correspondence of Unicode character to an integer.

The large number of characters in Unicode naturally poses a severe problem for font vendors and on storage requirements for systems that use the standard. Yet, Web standards are built to ensure interoperability. While standards are still evolving, the design of an internationalized Web site should respect existing standards interpreted within a multi-linguistic framework. Proper implementation of Unicode is a very important task. Even when building a U.S.-only site, the advice is to look at these issues up front in order to make the globalization process at a later date much easier.

HTML SUPPORT FOR UNICODE

The HTML 4.0 uses Unicode as its base character set. It adopted the Universal Multiple-Octet Coded Character Set (UCS), equivalent to Unicode standard 3.0 (W3C, 1999). It also has provision for language direction, such as Arabic and Hebrew that are written right-to-left, for appropriate punctuation, and for combining of letters and diacritics (RFC 2070 - Internationalization of the HyperText Markup Language). In 2002, W3C reformulated HTML 4 as XHTML 1.0, an XML application. XHTML 1 is backward compatible with full UTF supports (W3C, 2002). Naturally, the interest here is not in teaching readers to use HTML. The focus will be on the tags and attributes relevant to the creation of internationalized multilingual HTML documents instead.

It is not necessary to have to write all Web documents in Unicode. However, the browser must be able to recognize and interpret the encoding standard used. Therefore, the encoding standard should be declared at the beginning of a document. For an HTML or XHTML file that contains Unicode data, the character encoding is specified in the *char set* parameter of a meta tag in the <head> of an HTML document; for example:

```
<meta http-equiv="content-type" content="text-html;
char set=utf-8">
```

The HTTP specification mandates the use of ISO-8859-1 standard as the default character code over the Internet. The HTML specification also is formulated in terms of ISO-8859-1, and an HTML document that is transmitted using the HTTP protocol is by default ISO-8859-1 prior to

HTML 4.0. UTF-8 is the current character-encoding standard for any HTML file. It allows any of the characters in the document character set to be included, while others such as ISO-8859-1, Latin-1 Western European standard, only allow for subsets.

While *char set* defines the base language of a document, HTML 4 also allows the use of the *lang* attribute to specify language and the *dir* attribute to specify direction of text flow. These attributes can be used in any HTML tag. Naturally, whether it is relevant for a given attribute depends on the syntax and semantics of the attribute and the operation involved. The following example consists of text in three languages: Greek, Chinese, and Japanese.

```
<HTML lang="el">
<HEAD></HEAD>
<BODY>
...Interpreted as Greek...
<P lang="zh">...Interpreted as Chinese... </P>
<P>...Interpreted as Greek again... </P>
<P>...Greek text interrupted by <EM
lang="ja">some
    Japanese</EM> Greek begins here again... </P>
</BODY>
</HTML>
```

Language tags can be used to indicate the language of text in HTML and XML documents. An element uses the language attribute based on what is set for the element itself, or the closest parent element's language setting. Information is inherited along the document hierarchy when inner attributes overwrite outer attributes.

A language tag is composed of a primary tag, followed by zero or more optional tags, separated by hyphens. The primary tag represents a language, and any following tags serve to qualify the dialect of the language. In the example, the primary language of the document is Greek ("el"). One paragraph is declared to be in Chinese ("zh"), after which the primary language returns to Greek.

The following paragraph includes an embedded Japanese ("ja") phrase, after which the primary language returns to Greek. The list of valid language codes for the primary tag is controlled and maintained by the ISO 639-2 Registration Authority (Library of Congress, 2005).

Optional tags can be added to indicate geographic, dialectal, script, or other refinements to language defined in the primary tag. The 2-letter optional tag must be valid ISO 3166 country codes (ISO, 2005). Any number of optional tags can follow the primary tag, although it is unusual to see more than one. Currently, there are no rules for any third and subsequent optional tags that are being used. For example, one can use an optional tag to specify English "en" on the web page as either the U.S. version of English "en-US" or the Great Britain version of English "en-GB."

```
<P lang="en-US">...In United States, my car needs
gasoline to run ... </P>
    <P lang="en-GB">...In Britain, I need to find some
petrol instead ... </P>
```

It is also possible to register both primary and optional language tags with IANA, and the IANA tags can have three- to eight-letter optional tags (IANA, 2005). Using IANA-registered tags can be beneficial in some instances. For example, under the ISO standards, Simplified Chinese is defined using "zh-CN" for Mainland China as compare to Traditional Chinese using "zh-TW" for Taiwan. Apart from the possibility of mislabeling or misleading, one could not guarantee that others would recognize these conventions or even follow them. For example, some people would use "zh-HK" (Hong Kong) to represent Traditional Chinese. IANA defines the "zh-Hans" tag for Simplified and the "zh-Hant" tag for Traditional Chinese, which definitely would eliminate confusion and increase interoperability. On the other hand, IANA tags may be deprecated as new codes are added to the ISO standard. For this reason, there may be some risk to long-term interoperability when using IANA-registered tags.

FUTURE TRENDS

With continuing deployment and improvements in technology, more people than ever are interconnected. As the global village shrinks and cultures collide, we must become more sensitive to the myriad cultures surrounding us. Constructing an effective culture-centric Web site requires both technical and design understandings. The technical aspect is becoming more transparent as the multilingual frameworks are well-standardized; and XML/UTF-enabled platforms and applications are widely available. The design aspect remains a challenging and learning process that requires designers keeping current with researches on the subject. In recent years, however, Western and contemporary ideas have become more globally popular. These ideas either have influenced or even replaced some traditional values. Understanding human behavior is getting even trickier nowadays.

CONCLUSION

Web sites are usually an international user's first glimpse of a company. A good first impression is important to a company, as business is about capturing attention. Globalization has led many people to become more sensitive to cultural diversity. Most know that different things have different meanings to people in different places. This is especially important to businesses that market products and services across geographical boundaries. A Web site designer must be aware of international user needs, limitations, and expectations, and must be culture-centric. Globally, Net usage is growing enormously. Because of the competitive nature of business, cultural usability and sensitivity are critical components for any global business site. The success or failure of the site, and consequentially the business, ultimately is determined by evaluations of real users from the targeted communities.

REFERENCES

Arnold, D., Balkan, L., Humphreys, L., Meijer, S., & Sadler, L. (1994). *Machine translation: An introductory guide*. London: Blackwell Publishing.

Axtell, R. (1991). *Gestures: The do's and taboos of body language around the world*. New York: John Wiley & Sons.

Badlani, C. (1997). Nazi swastika or ancient symbol? Time to learn the difference. *An End to Intolerance, 5*. Retrieved August 17, 2005, from http://www.iearn.org/hgp/aeti/aeti-1997/swastika.html

Boase, J., Chen, W., Wellman, B., & Prijatelj, M. (2003). Is there a place in cyberspace: The uses and users of public Internet terminals? *Proceedings of the Association of Internet Researchers Conference,* Toronto, Canada.

The Business Journal. (2003, January 7). Survey: Consumer trust of Internet grows. *The Business Journal.* Retrieved August 4, 2005, from http://southforida.bizjournals.com/southflorida/stories/2003/01/06/daily54.html

Campanelli, M. (2004). A world of goods. *The Digital M, 3*(2). Retrieved August 3, 2005, from http://www.digitalm.biz/Issues/April04/WorldOfGoods.html.

Chun, M., Honda, G., & Schwane, C. (2005). An uphill battle. *Graziadio Business Report, 8*(2). Retrieved August 22, 2005, from http://gbr.pepperdine.edu/053/china.html

da Cruz, F. (2005). Frank's compulsive guide to postal address. *The Kermit Project*. New York: Columbia University. Retrieved August 21, 2005, from http://www.columbia.edu/kermit/postal.html

Dahl, S. (2004). Intercultural research: The current state of knowledge. *Middlesex University Discussion Paper No. 26*. Retrieved August 16, 2005, from http://ssrn.com/abstract=658202

Davison, E., & Cotton, S. (2003). Connection discrepancies: Unmasking further layers of the digital divide. *First Monday, 8*(3). Retrieved August 5, 2005, from http://firstmonday.org/issues/issue8_3/davison/index.html

DeVito, J. (2004). *The interpersonal communication book*. Boston: Allyn & Bacon.

Dormann, C., & Chisalita, C. (2002). Cultural values in Web site design. *Proceedings of the ECCI1 & SAFECOMP 2002 Usability Forum Conference,* Catania, Italy.

Dsmond, M., Collett, P., Marsh, P., & O'Shaughnessy, M. (1979). *Gestures: Their origins and distribution*. New York: Stein and Day.

Esteban, J. (2005). Computer aid ensures speedy, high-quality translations. *Information Society Technologies*. Retrieved August 15, 2005, from http://istresults.cordis.lu/index.cfm/section/news/tpl/article/BrowsingType/Features/ID/73666.

Fact Monster. (2005). What colors mean. *Fact Monster from Information Please*. Retrieved August 17, 2005, from http://www.factmonster.com/ipka/A0769383.html

Fromkin, V., & Rodman, J. (1983). *An introduction to language*. New York: CBS College Publishing.

Halavais, A. (2000). National borders on the World Wide Web. *New Media and Society, 2*(1), 7-28.

Hofstede, G. (1997). *Cultures and organizations: Software of the mind.* New York: McGraw Hill.

Huang, S., & Tilley, S. (2001). Issues of content and structure for multilingual site. *Proceedings of the Annual ACM Conferences on Systems Documentation,* Santa Fe, New Mexico.

IANA. (2005). *Tags for the identification of languages. Internet assigned numbers authority.* Retrieved September 20, 2005, from http://www.iana.org/assignments/language-tags.

ISO. (2005). English country names and code elements. *International Organization for Standardization.* Retrieved September 20, 2005, from http://www.iso.org/iso/en/prods-services/iso3166ma/02iso-3166-code-lists/list-en1.html

Library of Congress. (2005). Codes for the representation of names of languages. *Library of Congress.* Retrieved September 20, 2005, from http://www.loc.gov/standards/iso639-2/langcodes.html

Liungman, C. (1994). *Thought signs: The semiotics of symbols—Western non-pictorial ideograms.* London: IOS Press.

Lynch, P. J., & Horton, S. (1999). *Web style guide: Basic design principles for creating Web sites.* Boston: Yale University Press.

Maletzke, G. (1996). *Interkulturelle kommunikation.* Opladen: Westdeutscher Verlag.

Marcus, A., & Gould, E. (2000). Cultural dimensions and global user interface design. *Proceedings of the 6th Conference on Human Factors and the Web,* Austin, Texas.

McClure, S. (2001). Language matters. *IDC Viewpoint.* Retrieved August, 5, 2005, from http://www.idc.com/getdoc.jsp?containerId=VWP000061

Melby, A. (1995). *Why can't a computer translate more like a person?* Retrieved August 15, 2005, from http://www.ttt.org/theory/barker.html

Morton, J. (2001). *Color voodoo for e-commerce.* Color Voodoo Publications. Retrieved September 20, 2005, from http://www.colorvoodoo.com/cvoodoo7.html

Morton, J. (2004). *Global color: Clues & taboos.* Color Voodoo Publications. Retrieved September 20, 2005, from http://www.colorvoodoo.com/cvoodoo2_globalcolor.html

Neilsen, J. (1999). *Designing Web usability.* Indianapolis: New Riders Publishing.

Point Topic. (2005). World broadband statistic. *Point Topic.* Retrieved August 5, 2005, from http://www.point-topic.com.

Rettie, R., Robinson, H., Mojsa, M., & Parissi, E. (2003). Attitudes to Internet advertising: A cross cultural comparison. *Proceedings of the Academy of Marketing Conference,* Aston, UK.

Rupley, S. (2004, July). Scaling the language barrier. *PC Magazine.* Retrieved August 15, 2005, from http://www.pcmag.com/article2/0,1759,1612204,00.asp

Scheiderman, B. (1998). *Designing the user interface: Strategies for effective human-computer interaction.* Boston: Addison Wesley.

Shi, A. (2004). Accommodation in translation. *Translation Journal, 8*(3). Retrieved August 15, 2005, from http://www.accurapid.com/journal/29accom.htm

Smith, A., & Siringo, M. P. (1997). The acceptability of icons across countries. *Proceedings of the 7th International Conference on Human Computer Interaction,* San Francisco, California.

Spool, J., Scanlon, T., Schroeder, W., Synder, C., & DeAngelo, T. (1999). *Web site usability: A designer guide.* San Francisco: Morgan Kaufman.

Starling, A. (2001). Usability and HTML forms. *Web Developer's Virtual Library.* Retrieved August 21, 2005, from http://wdvl.internet.com/Authoring/Design/Basics/form1.html

Symbol.com. (2005). *Online encyclopedia of graphic symbols.* Stockholm, Sweden: HME Media. Retrieved August 21, 2005, from http://www.symbols.com/index.html

Unicode. (2005). *Unicode 4.1.0.* Retrieved September 20, 2005, from http://www.unicode.org/versions/Unicode4.1.0

W3C. (1999). The HTML 4.01 Specification. *W3C Recommendation.* Retrieved September 20, 2005, from http://www.w3.org/TR/html401

W3C. (2002). XHTML 1.0 The Extensible HyperText Markup Language (2nd ed.). *W3C Recommendation.* Retrieved December 20, 2005, from http://www.w3.org/TR/xhtml1

Walsh, E., Mcquivey, J., & Wakeman, M. (1999, November). Consumers barely trust Net advertising. *Forrester Research.*

This work was previously published in Information Resources Management: Global Challenges, edited by W. Law, pp. 192-209, copyright 2007 by IGI Publishing, formerly known as Idea Group Publishing (an imprint of IGI Global).

Section IV
Utilization and Application

Chapter XVI
Cultural Effects on Technology Performance and Utilization:
A Comparison of U.S. and Canadian Users

Susan K. Lippert
Drexel University, USA

John A. Volkmar
Otterbein College, USA

ABSTRACT

Research to date on information technology (IT) adoption has focused primarily on homogeneous single country samples. This study integrates the Theory of Reasoned Action (TRA) and the Technology Acceptance Model (TAM) with Hofstede's (1980, 1983) Masculinity/Femininity (MAS-FEM) work value dimension to focus instead on post adoption attitudes and behaviors among a mixed gender sample of 366 United States and Canadian users of a specialized supply chain IT. We test 11 hypotheses about attitudes towards IT within and between subgroups of users classified by nationality and gender. Consistent with the national MAS-FEM scores and contrary to the conventional consideration of the U.S. and Canada as a unitary homogenous cultural unit, we found significant differences between U.S. men and women, but not between Canadian men and women. These results support the importance of the MAS-FEM dimension—independent of gender—on user attitudes and help to clarify the relationship between culture and gender effects. Implications for managers responsible for technology implementation and management are discussed and directions for future research are offered.

INTRODUCTION

In today's world of information technology (IT), there are many paths to growth and development through new system design and the generalizability of applications. The concept of globalization in business practice has infiltrated the use and management of technologies. Nominally stated, globalization of IT involves the use of technologies across cultural boundaries, including country, region, industry, geography, and social demography. Many business operations today have segmented their activities across wide geographic domains, including operations that require coordination between units located in different countries or regions. The goal behind the implementation of new IT is the integration of operations and the use of common elements, such as language, functions and scales, across social group (e.g., nationality and gender) boundaries. The degree to which this integration is successful can have a profound effect on the functional utilization of systems to support operations. Of these elements, the need to develop and apply a common metric of technology performance provides a substantial challenge, both within and between groups. This challenge is magnified by the differences in value and attitudinal orientations among technology users who apply different judgments, assessments, and evaluations in their daily utilization of information systems.

Global competitive pressures are compelling firms in supply chains to continually evaluate and re-assess their network designs. In doing so, many are finding that cross-border organizational linkages are becoming essential for developing and maintaining effective strategic partnerships. Maintaining these cross-border relationships requires not only developing, implementing, and maintaining a consistent technology across partnering organizations, but also the capability to effectively manage cultural differences across groups of technology users.

With the increasing globalization of manufacturing and service businesses around the world, the adoption and utilization of new technology in the workplace constitutes a vital aspect of creating and maintaining organizational productivity

and competitiveness (Hicks & Nivin, 2000). Such technologies are recognized as drivers of globalization because of the coordination and control capabilities they provide (Deresky, 2006; Hill, 1997). On a micro level, the integration of supply chain management networks across borders highlights the importance of both software and hardware technologies in facilitating the visibility, inter-organizational coordination, and higher levels of performance necessary to make these diverse systems work effectively (Hannon, 2003; Trebilcock, 2001).

The reliance on cross-border integration of value-producing activities results in the offshore sourcing of intermediate manufactured goods and services (e.g., software engineering, customer service, and reservation services) to both developed and developing countries (Esterl, 2004; Gumpert, 2004). This means that the particular information technologies that have been designed to facilitate and manage such integration must be implemented and used simultaneously by organizations and workers of different nations and cultures, who bring different value sets and attitudinal orientations to the work tasks. For managers charged with responsibility for the performance of distributed supply chain activities, the potential difficulties associated with implementing new IT in cross-national settings add an important dimension of complexity to their task.

The performance of a technology is a function both of its capabilities and the extent to which these capabilities are used by the individual technology operators within the workplace. Thus, a better understanding of factors associated with technology performance is useful for organizations and provides an important tool to help managers more effectively introduce and manage new systems.

The importance of cultural factors in shaping the context of technology utilization and performance has long been recognized. A recent comprehensive review by Leidner and Kayworth (2006) identified and classified cultural values that impact information systems applications, and presented findings on differences by subgroup in the information systems research domain. Using cultural conflict to reflect cultural difference, Leidner and Kayworth (2006) applied the Hofstede (1980, 1983) dimensions of national culture—power distance, uncertainty avoidance, individualism-collectivism, and masculinity-femininity—to frame their examination of differences in IT values. The present paper links to Leidner and Kayworth (2006) in addressing more specifically the implications of Hofstede's masculinity-femininity (MAS-FEM) dimension—arguably the most problematic of the four to address, both conceptually and empirically.

The research question addressed by this study emerged over the course of collecting and analyzing data for a larger study of supply chain management technology implementation in U.S and Canadian firms and centers on the implications of empirically established cultural value differences between the U.S. and Canada for IT implementation. Specifically, *how are country differences on Hofstede's (1980, 1983) MAS-FEM value dimension related to user attitudes towards, and utilization of, a new information technology?*

It should be noted here that we will be addressing the implications of differences on Hofstede's (1980, 1983) MAS-FEM cultural value dimension on users' attitudes and behaviors, not the implications of gender per se. While the two constructs are clearly interrelated, MAS-FEM reflects collective patterns in attitudinal and value orientations aggregated at the level of 'national culture,' not the individual level attribute of gender (Hofstede, 1980; 2003). To the extent that gender is socially constructed, it reflects, in part, the underlying cultural (social) dimension MAS-FEM. As such, the nature and impact of the distinction between genders can be seen as culturally bound, and therefore will vary across cultures.

The globalization of supply chain activities does not have to be 'global' in scope, as evidenced by the extensive trade and organizational relation-ships that span the U.S.-Canadian border. In this case, where obvious and real commonalities in history, language, and level of development exist between the two countries, it is common to assume a high degree of cultural homogeneity as well. However, the assumption carried forth in the research reported in this article is that there are attitudinal and behavioral differences between the U.S. and Canada that significantly affect user perceptions of the same technology.

This study has two primary objectives. The first is to explore the cross-cultural dimension of technology use. In a cross-national setting, country and cultural effects on the relationships between user attitudes and the utilization and performance of technology are investigated. Identifying and understanding the nature of any such effects can better prepare managers charged with the implementation and performance of a new IT. The second objective is to investigate post adoption utilization and performance of an IT by identifying specific attitudinal characteristics of users associated with differing levels of technology performance. To address the objectives, technology performance is studied in the context of a cross-national (Canada and U.S.) implementation of a specific IT—a supply chain management system used within the automotive industry to provide part-level visibility for scheduling and transportation requirements. This research addresses the influence of national cultural differences attributable to differences on Hofstede's (1980, 1983) MAS-FEM value dimension on the implementation of a technology as the basis for the development of hypotheses.

ORGANIZATION OF THE MANUSCRIPT

The remainder of this article is organized into six sections. The first provides the theoretical grounding for this study in the literatures addressing national cultural differences and the post adoption use of new information technologies. The second discusses the proposed relationships among attitudes, utilization and technology performance, and develops the specific hypotheses to be tested. In the third section the overall research methodology, including the research design, sample, and measures, is introduced before presenting the results of the analysis in section four. A discussion of the results is presented in section five. The last section contains the contributions, implications, and limitations of the study together with recommendations for further research.

THEORETICAL GROUNDING

Comparing Cultures: Canada and the United States

Canada is an important partner in both manufacturing and service sector jobs for the U.S., particularly within the automotive industry. Canada's importance in this respect is highlighted by NAFTA, geographic proximity, a common language (with the notable exception of Quebec Province), and similar socio-economic status. For these same reasons, international management research has often clustered Canada and the U.S. together as representing a unitary (Anglo) 'North American' culture with minimal significant differences between the two (Ronen & Shenkar, 1985; Root, 1994). However, differences at the national level, along individual value dimensions, have been demonstrated in various surveys of worldwide cultural values (e.g. Hofstede, 2001; House, Hanges, Javidan, Dorfman, & Gupta, 2004; Trompenaars & Hampden-Turner, 1998). The present study seeks to identify and assess the influence of such differences among Canadian and U.S. users of a specialized technology and to clarify their association with differing levels of technology utilization and performance.

Substantial research has been devoted to producing cultural maps that offer meaningful and useful ways to differentiate one culture from another. While treating culture as a national phenomenon tends to dismiss what can be significant regional differences within a country (Myers & Tan, 2002), the international management literature has, for both empirical and practical reasons, tended to view culture at a national level (Clark, 1990; Hofstede, 2001; House et al., 2004; Trompenaars & Hampden-Turner, 1998). Various frameworks for distinguishing cultural values have been developed with the practical aim of enabling managers and businesses operating in cross-cultural environments to better understand, communicate, and manage their operations (Hall & Hall, 1990; Hofstede, 2001, 1984; Hofstede & Bond, 1988; Javidan & House, 2001; Lane, Maznevski, & DiStefano 2006). While these frameworks differ in the number of value dimensions, they are consistent in identifying underlying cultural values—e.g., individualism, emotionality, masculinity, and time orientation—that collectively distinguish the attitudes, beliefs, and behaviors of one culture from another.

Because of the fundamental importance of cultural values in shaping attitudes, beliefs and behavior (Adler, 1997), research in this area has addressed linkages between particular elements of national culture and a range of specific international managerial activities. Examples include the role of cultural values in foreign entry decisions (Kogut & Singh, 1988), strategic decision making (Schneider, 1989), new product development (Nakata & Sivakumar, 1996), budget control practices (Ueno & Sekaran, 1992), and the exercise of supervisory influence (Rao & Hashimoto, 1996).

In the context of information technology, Evaristo (2003), using Hofstede's values framework, examined and supported the notion of investigating differences in culture. Choi and Choi (2003) examined cross-cultural differences between the U.S. and Korea with a focus on managerial performance. Singh et al., (2003) examined culturally based differences in web usage practices between

Table 1. A taxonomy of cultural values*

Value Dimension	Description of Value
Power Distance (PDI): Hofstede (1980, 1983)	The extent to which members of a society accept that power in institutions and organizations is distributed unequally; status differences among workers may either be very pronounced (high power distance) in contrast to workers in low distance countries that follow a more egalitarian philosophy when making decisions (Tan et al. 1995)
Uncertainty Avoidance (UAI): Hofstede (1980, 1983)	The degree to which members of a society feel comfortable with uncertainty and ambiguity. Members in high uncertainty avoidance countries prefer less ambiguity than do those in low uncertainty avoidance countries.
Individualism (IND) vs Collectivism: Hofstede (1980, 1983)	The preference for a social framework where individuals take care of themselves (individualism) as opposed to collectivism where individuals expect the group to take care of them in exchange for their loyalty.
Masculinity-Femininity (MAS): Hofstede (1980, 1983)	High preference for achievement, assertiveness and material success (masculinity) vs. low preference (femininity).
* Adapted from Leidner and Kayworth (2006)	

the U.S. and China. Mao, Srite, Thatcher, and Yaprak (2005) reinforced the research structure of cross-cultural investigations by examining cultural differences in technology acceptance between the U.S. and Turkey. In a cross-cultural study between the U.S. and Uruguay, McCoy, Everard, and Jones (2005) examined information systems adoption using the technology acceptance model (TAM) (Davis, 1989) as theoretical grounding.

To simplify the task of the international manager, researchers have sought to organize countries into cultural clusters where within-group similarities outweigh the differences and between-group differences are meaningful. Such clusters are empirically established (Hofstede, 2001; Ronen & Shenkar, 1985; Sullivan, 1994), and allow the manager to consider a smaller number of cultural entities in the exercise of her managerial responsibilities. Canada and the U.S. are commonly considered to be members of the

same (Anglo) 'North America' (Nath & Sadhu, 1988) or 'Anglo' (Hofstede, 2001; House et al., 2004; Ronen & Shenkar, 1985) cluster or psychic zone (Sullivan, 1994).

However, a significant potential danger of grouping national cultures is the underlying assumption of similarity, which can result in a tendency to ignore important differences between the cultures comprising the group. Differences that may warrant a differential approach to the actual management of people and business operations across countries should not be neglected.

As an example, research has also identified significant differences between Canada and the U.S. that suggest caution in applying such a unitary perspective to the two countries. In a thorough literature review, O'Grady (1991) presented research supporting the notion that while Canada and the U.S. share substantial cultural similarities, they also exhibit important differences in such areas as self orientation (greater in the U.S.), achievement

Table 2. Canada-U.S. comparison on the Hofstede (2001) value dimension index scores

	Canada	US
Power Distance (PDI)	39	40
Uncertainty Avoidance (UAI)	48	46
Individualism (IND)	80	91
Masculinity (MAS)	52	62
Note: Sample size, mean, and standard deviation data provided in the appendices to Hofstede (2001) indicate that the difference between Canada on the U.S. on both IND and MAS is significant at p < .001.		

orientation (greater in the U.S.), and collective orientation (greater in Canada). In their study of Canadian retailers' experiences in the U.S. market, Evans, Lane, and O'Grady (1992), while acknowledging a 'North American' culture comprising both Canada and the U.S. (but not Mexico), also found significant differences in Canadian and U.S. social and business values, behaviors, and institutions. Similarly, Abramson, Keating, and Lane (1996) found significant differences in the cognitive process preferences of Canadian and U.S. managers. In particular, Abramson et al., found evidence that Canadians were more theoretical and imaginative but slower decision makers than Americans and warned against the clustering and combined use of Canadians and Americans in research samples.

A key issue in research that undertakes to examine cultural differences and similarities is the choice of value framework on which to base the research model (Pauleen, 2003), since each has inherent strengths and weaknesses due to the sample composition and size, and age of the data. Hunter (2006), employing the Hofstede (1980) cultural framework, reinforced the Pauleen (2003) findings by extending the examination of the difficulties to cross-cultural research in applied settings. The current study follows the widely accepted and validated Hofstede framework, with

the four primary value dimensions summarized in Table 1.

The national scores for Canada and the U.S. on Hofstede's (1980, 1983) four primary value dimensions are presented as Table 2. As can be seen, Canada and the U.S. are very similar in their scores on the Power Distance (PDI) and Uncertainty Avoidance (UAI) indices. The differences in the two country scores on the Individualism (IND) and Masculinity (MAS) indices also appear to be relatively small numerically, supporting the conventional presumption of cultural homogeneity across the U.S. and Canada. However, the differences on IND and MAS are statistically significant. This article focuses on the MAS dimension and has as a key premise that this difference can have an important effect on workplace attitudes and behavior with respect to technology acceptance and utilization.

As previously mentioned, it is important to distinguish between the effects of MAS-FEM and those of gender per se. Since the former helps to shape the latter, national differences in MAS-FEM should result in different 'gender effects' for the U.S. and Canada. Hofstede (2001) associates a lower MAS score, as seen in Canada, with less gender role stereotyping, a greater concern with quality of life over money and material things, a greater importance attached to relationships, and, a smaller difference between the values of women and men. Conversely, the higher U.S. MAS score would suggest that U.S. men and women differ more in the values and roles they hold in the workplace than do their Canadian counterparts. Higher MAS would also lead to greater expectations that men be assertive, tough, and focused on material success, while women should be more distinctively modest, tender, and concerned with the quality of life (Hofstede, 2001). That MAS-FEM related differences can be important related to IT issues was demonstrated by Stafford et al. (2004) in their examination of differences in online shopping behavior in the U.S., Finland and Turkey.

The arguments in this article are grounded in Hofstede's Masculinity (MAS) dimension. The MAS dimension is particularly useful as an exploratory value, due to the nominal bipolar nature of the measure, leading to its usefulness in a wide variety of analytical applications. The MAS-FEM dimension is frequently employed in the exploration of cultural difference in a variety of disciplines including marketing (Dwyer, Mesak, & Hsu, 2005; Garrett, Buisson & Yap, 2006), accounting (Su, 2006), and information systems (McCoy, Galletta, & King, 2005).

Germane to the present study is the observation that the raw data from which the U.S. MAS score was calculated reflects only male respondents (Hofstede, 2001). However, the overall validity and usefulness of the MAS index in management research is supported by other studies (e.g., Caligiuri & Tung, 1999; Zeira, Newburry, & Yeheskel, 1997). Additionally, the Canadian—U.S. differences along the MAS dimension that underpin the arguments of this article are consistent with other research, most notably the recent GLOBE study (House et al., 2004). The two GLOBE dimensions of humane orientation and gender egalitarianism are those most closely related to Hofstede's (1984, 2001) MAS index. These two GLOBE dimensions, like Hofstede's, provide evidence of significant differences between English-speaking Canada and practices in the U.S. (House et al., 2004).

It is recognized that there continues to be important discussion and some controversy about the meaning and limitations of this scale. Recognizing the need for more clarifying research in this area, Hofstede (1998) compiled a collection of individual studies on the MAS-FEM dimension. Lonner and Berry (1998) suggest that the MAS-FEM dimension is perhaps the most controversial and misunderstood of Hofstede's four dimensions. In a review of Hofstede's book, Rich (2000) highlighted the difficulties caused both by considerations of 'political correctness' in researching a cultural value dimension labeled 'masculinity-femininity,' and by misperceptions of its nature.

Both the differences related to the values inherent in Hofstede's MAS-FEM dimension and those attributable to gender have been found to be significant cultural variables. In particular, gender is frequently included within information systems studies that investigate technology acceptance (e.g., Gefen & Straub, 1997; Hess, Fuller, & Mathew, 2005; 2006; Lorigo, Pan, Hembrooke, Joachims, Granka, & Gay, 2006; Moores & Chang, 2006) and has repeatedly been shown to be a significant predictor of differences in perceptions of technology utilization. Therefore, the present study addresses both as important interrelated determinants of technology acceptance and use.

Alternative Explanatory Theory

A number of theories and models have been used to explain individual-level and organizational-level technology adoption in diverse business settings. The Theory of Reasoned Action (TRA) (Ajzen & Fishbein, 1980; Fishbein & Ajzen, 1975) suggests that individuals' behavioral intentions are based on the perceived consequences of their behavior as well as the subjective norms and influences from credible sources. The Theory of Planned Behavior (TPB) (Ajzen, 1991) extends TRA by suggesting that adoption behavior is also influenced by the amount of perceived control individuals have over their environment. Similarly, Triandis (1971, 1980) suggests that affect, in addition to social norms, influences adoption behavior. The Technology Acceptance Model (TAM) (Davis, 1989), based on TRA, does not consider influences of subjective norms, but rather suggests that technology acceptance results from an individual's perceptions of how easy a system is to use (perceived ease of use) and that the IT is useful (perceived usefulness). Innovation Diffusion Theory (IDT) (Rogers, 1995) is often used as the theoretical grounding for examining individual-level acceptance of systems within social structures.

While alternative models and theories of adoption have been proposed and employed to understand usage behaviors, TRA and its linkage to TAM represent the most often used grounding theory. TRA provides a broad potential of independent variables for examination of technology adoption within a variety of contexts using different technologies. The integration of TRA with TAM as the theoretical grounding for this study is employed because the use of these theories provides the most comprehensive structure to understand technology adoption. Additionally, TRA has consistently been found to be an effective baseline theory for addressing technology acceptance.

Technology Acceptance

The Theory of Reasoned Action (TRA) (Ajzen & Fishbein, 1980; Fishbein & Ajzen, 1975) originated in the field of social psychology and explains how and why attitudes affect behavior. TRA asserts that an individual's behavior is determined by his attitude toward the outcome of that behavior and by the opinions of others within his social environment. Ajzen and Fishbein (1980) proposed that an individual's intention to perform leads to a specific behavior. Behavior is the transition of intention into action. Intention to behave is a

function of an individual's attitude toward the behavior and his subjective norms. TRA is designed to enable generalizations regarding behavior, since individuals make conscious choices based on: (1) How strongly they perceive the benefits leading to a positive outcome; and, (2) the social norms, risks, and rewards they associate with that choice.

Attitudes comprise the beliefs an individual develops through direct experience, outside information, and self-generated inferences. An attitude is an individual's belief about whether the outcome of his action will be positive or negative. If the person has affirming beliefs about the outcome of his behavior, then he is said to have a positive attitude toward the behavior.

Normative expectations are beliefs regarding what peers will think about the behavior and include perceptions of how influential others will perceive the outcome of the behavior (normative belief). The degree to which normative beliefs affect behavior is a proxy for motivation. Subjective norms are an individual's beliefs regarding social pressures to behave and are shaped by the opinions of others considered to be significant.

TRA has been employed in a number of IT studies (e.g., Ahuja & Thatcher, 2005; Bock, Zmud, Kim & Lee, 2005; Lee & Kim, 2005; Shih, 2004; Wu, 2003). Ahuja and Thatcher (2005) employed TRA to examine the effects of work environment and gender on post adoption IT use and argue that work environment impediments render intentions inadequate for examining post adoption technology use. Rather, Ahuja and Thatcher (2005) include the construct of 'trying to innovate' as a measure of post adoption IT utilization. Investigating post adoption behavior is used in lieu of the traditional measure of 'intention to adopt' for several reasons. First, intention to adopt reflects the individual's probability of how he may behave in the future. As a predictor of future behavior, intentions are subject to change based on intervening factors such as time, unforeseen environmental events, stability of intentions, and new information (Peter & Olson, 1999). As such, the resulting behavior is likely to be different than the intention.

Second, post adoption behavior addresses the actual behavior of individuals which makes the construct more practical for managers who are interested in learning how to increase technology performance. Third, investigation into the antecedents of post adoption provides a stronger mechanism for researchers and managers interested in manipulating these factors as a means to improve the likelihood of actual utilization of the technology.

For more than a decade, the cornerstone of research on the acceptance and utilization of information technology in the workplace has been the Technology Acceptance Model (TAM) (Davis, 1989; Davis, Bagozzi, & Warshaw, 1989; Venkatesh & Davis, 2000). TAM models the behavioral intention to use a new technology as a function of two attitudinal dimensions of individual users—the perceived usefulness and the perceived ease of use of the new technology. According to TAM, a new technology is more likely to be adopted if individuals believe the technology to be useful and easy to use. TAM has been a robust model for predicting *intention to use* innovative technologies and has provided an anchor for rich and varied subsequent research on related topics. Examples include the role of gender and social influence on individual technology acceptance (Lai & Li, 2005; Venkatesh & Morris, 2000), technology use in less developed countries (Rose & Straub, 1998), and individual user differences in technology acceptance (Agarwal & Prasad, 1999; Taylor, 2004).

The objective of TAM is to predict usage intent and TAM-based research often stops short of addressing the actual utilization of a technology. Perhaps more interesting from a business standpoint is the question of how well the technology actually performs its intended functions. Technology performance comprises both a technical (designed capabilities) and a behavioral (actual utilization patterns by employees) component. For example, are the various designed capabilities fully exploited or do users operate only within some subset of more basic functionalities in order to accomplish daily tasks? By examining the association of users' attitudinal characteristics with reported levels of technology performance, this study provides insight into this important but under-researched issue.

Legris, Ingham and Collerette (2003) compiled a detailed review and meta-analysis of the TAM literature. In their review of 28 TAM-based measurements in 22 different studies, they identified several limitations of this research stream, including an emphasis on student samples and the use of personal productivity-oriented software technologies (e.g., word processing and spreadsheet applications) instead of business process applications. The present study specifically addresses these two limitations by analyzing a sample frame of actual technology users in a working environment, and by using the Collaborative Visibility Network (CVN), a business process application, as the technology context. Additionally, this article addresses two other limitations of the TAM/TRA research stream on IT acceptance: (1) the relative scarcity of cross-cultural research that juxtaposes cross-national samples drawn from actual work settings; and, (2) the limited investigation of gender differences in technology utilization from an international perspective.

HYPOTHESIS DEVELOPMENT

Mason (2003) offered a theoretical argument for a culture-bound approach to research on knowledge management systems. Additionally, research on the importance of national culture to global information management issues has provided evidence of a cultural effect (Lim, 2004; Sagi, Carayannis, Dasgupta, & Thomas, 2004). For example, Sagi et al., (2004) found a significant effect for culture among U.S., Greek, and UK students in their attitudes toward e-commerce. Lim (2004) reported a significant moderating effect for Hofstede's (2001) power distance measure on the relationship between the availability of an explanation facility within a knowledge-based system and trust placed in online bargaining agents, but did not find a power distance effect on bargaining performance. In another study incorporating Hofstede's (2001) value dimensions, Bagchi, Hart, and Peterson (2004) affirmed the importance of national cultural differences in predicting IT product adoptions (e.g., fax, cell phone, Internet) in 31 countries, after controlling for GNP and other societal indicators. However, Liu, Marchewka, and Ku (2004) found no evidence of a national or cultural effect between U.S. and Taiwanese students in their investigation of a privacy-trust-behavioral intentions model to study attitudes, perceptions, and use of various information technologies.

The potential for cultural differences to affect how and to what degree a new technology is implemented has been the subject of a growing body of research. While TAM has been tested with positive results for cross-cultural validity in a marketing context (Lee & Green, 1991), the model has been shown to have limited application in cross-national settings. Rose and Straub (1998) tested the applicability of TAM in an Arabic setting and Al-Gahtani (2001) investigated the use of TAM in a British environment. The findings of both studies affirm the robustness of TAM *intra-culturally* rather than examining cross-cultural implementation differences. However, in a separate study of technology adoption in Japan, the U.S., and Switzerland, Straub, Keil, and Brenner (1997) found that while TAM provided a good model for adoption in the U.S. and Switzerland, it did not fit the Japanese adoption patterns. In the present study, we add to the existing literature by incorporating a cross-national sample involved in the simultaneous implementation of the same business process technology.

While TAM has proven useful in predicting intention to use and the adoption of an IT, it is less useful in situations where acceptance is assumed—i.e., where a particular technology has already been adopted and implemented by management. In this case, the managerial focus shifts to how and to what degree the technology is actually being utilized in the workplace and TRA provides an appropriate model for analysis. TRA emphasizes the importance of user attitudes and subjective norms on behavioral intentions and actual behavior. In the context of a particular technology, we would expect that actual utilization would be closely associated with the individual's attitudes about the technology itself, the context in which it is used, and how well it performs. Linking the importance of these attitudinal characteristics to technology utilization, as suggested by TRA, with the differences of Hofstede's (2001) MAS dimension between Canada and the U.S., provides the basis for the hypotheses to be examined in this study.

One key aspect of Hofstede's (2001) MAS dimension is the degree to which women and men in a given culture tend to have similar values. This similarity of values is greater in lower masculinity cultures than in higher masculinity cultures. Specifically, in higher MAS cultures, the difference in values is greater between men and women and therefore one should expect a more differentiated attitudinal perception, by gender, in response to the same stimuli. In the context of this study, the attributes or characteristics of a particular new technology are examined. The strength of the gender effect is therefore culture-bound and can be expected to vary between cultures. The importance of a gender effect on technology perceptions and use has been demonstrated by Gefen and Straub (1997). For the present study, the significant difference in masculinity scores between Canada and the U.S. suggests that we should expect a wider range of values for U.S. men and women than between Canadian men and women. In terms of the specific attitudinal responses suggested by TRA to be important in the utilization of a particular technology, several hypotheses are proposed.

Hypotheses 1 through 6 are introduced to test this underlying prediction of the MAS-FEM dimension that the significantly lower score for Canada will result in Canadian women and men being more similar in relevant work value related attitudes and behaviors than are U.S. women and men—in other words, that the gender effect differs by country as a function of differing MAS-FEM scores. Specifically, these hypotheses are offered to investigate whether users within these countries are indeed different in their perceptions of the supply chain management technology. This leads to our expectations that:

H1:   Canadians (both genders) will respond with less difference in their overall evaluation (multivariate) toward a new technology than U.S. men and women.

H2:   Canadians (both genders) will respond with less difference on normative expectations for a new technology than U.S. men and women.

H3:   Canadians (both genders) will respond with less difference on awareness of supply chain functions of a new technology than U.S. men and women.

H4:   Canadian men and women have less difference in attitudes toward technology than U.S. men and women.

H5:   Canadian men and women have less difference in perceptions of technology performance than U.S. men and women.

TRA suggests that behavior is a function of relevant attitudes. To the extent that attitudes toward a particular technology differ between groups of users, we would expect that the utilization behavior would also differ across those groups. Therefore,

H6:   Canadian men and women have less difference in the degree of technology utilization than U.S. men and women.

The above hypotheses reflect predictions of greater homogeneity across Canadian men and women than across U.S. men and women based on the difference in Hofstede's (2001) MAS dimension between the two countries. An implicit assumption of the expected heterogeneity between U.S. men and women is that U.S. women, as a group, are lower MAS than U.S. men. In Hofstede's (2001) terms, U.S. women should express greater concern with quality of life over money and material things and a greater importance attached to relationships than U.S. men. These expected gender differences in perceptions and attitudes are also discussed in detail by Gefen and Straub (1997). Because we know that Canada has a lower masculinity index than the U.S. (Table 2.), we can also have expectations concerning the nature of the attitudinal differences between various groups of technology users.

More specifically, one important characteristic of lower masculinity cultures is a greater importance attached to relationships than in higher masculinity cultures. Because relationships are more salient, we would expect Canadians to be more aware of and sensitive to the opinions and expectations of other members of the groups with which they identify. In a logistics context, having supply chain awareness representing knowledge of how supply chain activities affect one another should be positively associated with both lower masculinity and lower individualism scores. Hypotheses seven through eleven were crafted as a function of the existing literature indicating that U.S. men have a significantly higher MAS-score than the grouping of Canadians and U.S. women. This suggests that:

H7:   Canadians, as a group, along with U.S. women will demonstrate greater awareness of normative expectations associated with a new technology than will U.S. men.

H8: Canadians, as a group, along with U.S. women will demonstrate greater supply chain awareness than will U.S. men.

Since lower masculinity cultures place greater emphasis on quality of life and the working environment (Hofstede, 2001), some attributes of a new technology that may not be directly related to task performance should be more salient in a lower MAS setting. In other words, lower MAS cultures should be more inclined than higher MAS cultures to notice, non-task attributes of a technology such as the fun and enjoyment from use. Therefore,

H9: Canadians, as a group, along with U.S. women are more likely to express positive attitudinal sentiments about technology than will U.S. men.

Lower MAS cultures create a context within which a new information technology is more instrumental in accomplishing the task for which it is designed, and also in addressing relationships, group identification, and quality of life issues. In a higher masculinity environment, the utility of the technology is more narrowly defined in terms of task and functionality. Since utility in the former is substantially broader, we would expect that this increased utility will engender a greater degree of utilization. Specifically,

H10: Canadians, as a group, along with U.S. women will make greater use of a new technology than will U.S. men.

Finally, because the new technology addresses a wider range of values in a lower masculinity, lower individualism setting such as relationships, group identification, quality of life, and task-related aspects, it is expected that users will rate the overall performance of the technology higher in a higher MAS/higher IND context. Even if the strictly task-related aspects might not perform exactly as expected, relationship issues are still being positively addressed simply by using the technology. As such, this reinforces values that are more important in a lower-MAS context. Therefore,

H11: Canadians, as a group, along with U.S. women will perceive a higher level of technology performance for the new IT than will U.S. men.

It could be argued that the essential nature of a supply chain management technology—as a means to centralize and integrate disparate activities and supply chain organizations—would also appeal to and reinforce the higher achievement and mastery orientation associated with a higher MAS culture (particularly for the men in that culture). Arguing from this perspective would confound the predicted relationships in hypotheses 9 through 11 and possibly justify opposite predictions. This would be especially true if the technology users surveyed were primarily concerned with, and responsible for, visibility and performance of the supply chain as a whole (i.e., a headquarters perspective). In the present research setting, however, the individual technology users that constitute the sample represent individual links in the supply chain (i.e., a particular supplier or transporter). As such, they are more likely to be concerned with their role in the collective supply chain network than with the overall system performance, a situation that should resonate more strongly with the 'feminine' characteristics addressed in hypotheses 9 through 11 than with achievement and mastery.

METHODOLOGY

Research Design

This research uses a self report perception survey to capture individual supply chain users' responses to five constructs: Normative expectations (NE), supply chain awareness (SCA), attitude toward technology (ATT), utilization (UTL), and technology performance (TPF). Data were collected through a mail survey to all authorized CVN users, representing a population census. A mail survey was used rather than a Web-based survey due to Institutional Review Board (IRB) limitations and concerns about excluding less technologically proficient users, whose limited technology experience only enabled the completion of specific task-directed activities. Data were analyzed using multivariate and univariate analyses to test the eleven hypotheses. This research recognizes the inherent limitations of survey research and self-report perception data.

Technology Studied

The technology investigated in this research is the Collaborative Visibility Network (CVN), a web-based technology designed to facilitate a number of logistics functions. CVN is designed to reduce operating costs by providing part-level visibility to different users throughout the supply chain. Shippers use the technology to schedule and confirm shipments when they are ready to be delivered to the distribution centers. Once entered into CVN, parts can be tracked across the entire route to the receiving facility via the Internet. The use of CVN requires suppliers to undertake a new task of entering cubic dimensions and weights into the system. This information is then extracted to optimize the usage of trailer cubic space and to select the optimal routes to increase trailer utilization and reduce congestion at the distribution centers.

The use of CVN carried a "mandatory" disclaimer label as indicated by several memos sent out to suppliers by the automotive manufacturer and the fourth-party logistics (4PL) firm. This label, however, was a "soft" label in that suppliers were not—at the time of the data collection—penalized for failing to use the IT. While some of the suppliers complied because they believed its use was required, others made the choice not to use the technology because they did not find it useful or because they did not have the technological capability to do so.

Research Sample

The hypotheses were tested on a cross-national sample of (English-speaking) Canadian and U.S. technology users in firms supplying parts to a major automotive manufacturer. To ensure comparability of the response data, the sample represented only users of the technology.

The U.S. and Canada were selected for a cross-cultural comparison because they were the two countries using the supply chain management technology within the same supply chain that was the specific focus of a broader study of supply chain management issues. Within the particular automotive supply chain investigated, supplier organizations were only located in the United States and Canada. The research design began with the identification of the supply chains that used the CVN technology. Next, the application of that technology for this supply chain was used because the supply chain has affiliates in only those two countries.

The final survey instrument was synthesized from four sources: (a) existing scales within the literature; (b) subject matter experts within the supply chain; (c) prior experiences of the primary researchers; and, (d) guidelines derived from the Council of Logistics Management. The sample and survey data were those collected for the larger study of supply chain management technology,

Table 3. Key sample descriptors—number of respondents

	Canada	U.S.	Overall
Respondents			
Women	24	194	218
Men	23	125	148
Overall	47	319	366
Days CVN in Use			
Mean	565.8	578.1	576.5
Standard deviation	192.6	195.6	195.0

applied to the emergent research question that underlies the present study. In this sense, the sample used in this study was one of convenience, used to explore in the context of grounded theory an important and complementary aspect of supply chain management —whether and how cultural differences manifest themselves as predictors of post-adoption perceptions.

Surveys were mailed to a contact identified at every site using CVN, comprising 3,348 contacts at different production sites in the Canadian province of Ontario and the U.S. One hundred twenty-three were returned for incorrect addresses. Of the 701 surveys returned by respondents, 366 were complete and usable in all respects for this study, for a net response rate of approximately 10.9%. Of the usable responses, 47 (12.8%) were Canadian and 319 (87.2%) were from the U.S. This compares favorably with the proportion of Canadian to U.S. respondents in the overall population (14.2% vs. 85.8%). The participants were asked to answer the survey questions based on their own experience with the technology. For all respondents, the average time since CVN had been placed in use was greater than eighteen months. A summary of descriptive information for the study sample is provided in Table 3.

Usable response data from U.S. respondents was received from sites located in various U.S. states including the North-Central, Mid-Atlantic, Northeast, South, and Mid-South regions. The majority of the respondent data were concentrated in the states of Michigan, Tennessee, Kentucky, and Indiana.

Because all Canadian sites using CVN were located in the province of Ontario, only data from Ontario site users was available for analysis. While an all-Ontario sample cannot be assumed to be statistically representative of the Canadian nation as whole, there are several factors that argue for its usefulness in the present study. First, as shown in Table 4., the provincial population is quite similar to that of the nation as a whole in median age, population by sex, education level, labor force composition by occupational skill group, and frequency of English as the language of work (after controlling for Quebec Province).

Similarly, Abramson et al., (1996) found no evidence in their study of cognitive process differences between MBA students from an Ontario university and MBA students from a university located in British Columbia. Third, while the within-Canada geographic distribution of the respondents to the original IBM study from which Hofstede developed his value dimension framework is not known, we do know that the Canadian questionnaire was administered in English (Hofstede, 2001), which provides at least the commonality of language between the context in which the original data were collected and the current study's respondents from English-speaking Ontario. Taken together, the above suggest that while a degree of caution may be warranted in generalizing from the Ontario-based sample analyzed in this study to Canada as a whole (and particularly to French-speaking Canada), there are also indications that such generalizations are appropriate.

The role of culture with respect to cognitive processes is more likely to surface as these processes are actively operationalized. For example, as an individual advances through the management hierarchy from operational to tactical to strategic decision-maker, cultural differences manifest to a greater degree. However, consistent with the literature on the role of culture in job motivation (e.g., Deresky, 2006; Francesco & Gold, 2005; McFarlin & Sweeney, 2006), we also believe that culture plays an important role 'below the surface' in shaping underlying attitudes and beliefs about what is important. These issues may include a sensitivity to relationships, how one's behavior affects others, and the expectations of significant others that influence any technology user, regardless of hierarchical position. A basic premise of this study is that a cultural effect can have an impact on technology utilization and performance even when the system is used to accomplish structured tasks.

Administrative Procedures

Survey recipients were encouraged to complete and return the questionnaires using three distinct methods: (1) a message posted to the CVN login page; (2) a scripted reminder offered by a logistics technician whenever users bypassed CVN and directly contacted the technician; and, (3) an e-mail reminder distributed three weeks after the initial mailing. To assess the likelihood of a non-response bias, the respondents were divided into quartiles based on the order in which their responses were received. We then compared key characteristics of the earliest and latest quartiles. There were no significant differences ($p \leq 0.05$) between the two groups in the length of time that CVN had been in use, nor in the country or gender mix. This suggests that there is no significant response bias as a function of when participants responded.

Measurement Scales

The measures used for this study reflect the attitude and normative belief constructs of TRA. Four of the five variables included in this study (attitude toward technology, normative expectations, utilization and technology performance) were measured by scales developed and validated in prior research on technology adoption and acceptance. One variable (supply chain awareness) was measured by a scale developed as part of this research project. Table 5 includes the construct and definition, the number of items and reliability alpha of the original scale and the original scale source.

Each variable is discussed briefly below and the specific wording for all items is provided in the Appendix. All items were framed on 7-point Likert scales, with possible responses ranging from "1 - strongly disagree" to "7 - strongly agree." The measurement used in the analysis is the composite mean of the responses to the individual scale items. Where appropriate, the wording of individual items was modified to reflect the specific technology (CVN) involved.

Normative expectations measures the extent to which an individual believes that specific individuals with whom he has ongoing relationships through work (e.g., peers, supervisor, and customers) think or expect that he should use CVN. The individual items comprising normative expectations are adapted from the Karahanna, Straub, and Chervany (1999) study of the adoption of the Windows operating system and are compiled in this study into a single six-item scale.

Table 4. Population comparison of Ontario and Canada (selected variables)

	Ontario	Canada
Total population (2001)	11,410,046	30,007,094
Median age (2001)	37.2	37.6
% Female (2004)	50.6	50.5
% Male (2004)	49.4	49.5
Education level (≥ 15 years of age (2001)		
Less than high school	31.6 %	33.2 %
Completed high school	23.8 %	23.0 %
Bachelor's degree	11.1 %	10.1 %
Labor force composition (≥ 15 years of age) (2001)		
Less than high school	43.1 %	43.4 %
Completed college or university	37.5 %	37.9 %
Apprenticeship	8.0 %	8.3 %
Managers	11.4 %	10.4 %
Frequency of English as work language (2001)	94.4 %	76.3 %
Controlling for Quebec Province	94.4 %	95.2 %
Source: www.statcan.ca		

Supply chain awareness measures the extent to which users believe that an understanding of the players, relationships, and processes in the user's supply chain firm is important in the effective use of CVN. The positive influence of an understanding of the bigger picture on performance in general has long been asserted in the production quality literature (Deming, 1986) and more recently by Holweg and Bicheno (2002) in their finding that supply chain decision-making can be enhanced by an informed awareness of one's own role in the supply chain. SCA is a seven-item scale identified as an antecedent to supply chain technology internalization in the Supply Chain Internalization Model (Forman & Lippert, 2005).

Attitude toward technology was measured by users' responses to four questions concerning the extent to which they found CVN to be fun and enjoyable. The scale used in this study was first developed by Agarwal and Prasad (1999) to measure user attitudes towards a specific target technology.

Utilization employs a five-item scale asking the user to rate the extent to which he uses CVN to perform various specific logistics functions for which the technology was designed. The scale used in this study was first introduced by Lippert and Forman (2005) to measure the use of specialized logistics operations.

Technology performance comprises a six-item scale adapted from the Dahlstrom, McNeilly, and Speh (1996) scale to measure vendor performance in logistical supply relationships. In this study, the six-item Dahlstrom et al., (1996) scale was used

Table 5. Research constructs

Construct	Construct Definition	Number of Items	Reliability Alpha	Scale Source
Normative Expectations	The extent to which an individual believes that specific individuals with whom he has ongoing relationships through work (e.g., peers, supervisor, and customers) think or expect that he should use the technology	6	Not Reported	Karahanna, Straub, & Chervany (1999)
Supply Chain Awareness	The degree to which an individual understands the supply chain management context	5	Not Reported	Forman & Lippert, 2005
Attitude Toward Technology	The degree to which an individual likes various attributes of the technology	4	0.83	Agarwal & Prasad, 1999
Utilization	The extent to which users take advantage of the most important operational features of the technology	5	0.64	Lippert & Forman, 2005
Technology Performance	The technology's (CVN) performance across multiple logistics functions	6	0.83	Dahlstrom et al., 1996

with the 'percentage of orders' question reframed into a 'provides visibility' item to contextualize the scale. Technology performance is a measure of the technology on several performance criteria related to order processing, meeting productivity standards, providing part-level visibility in transit, and providing order status information to address key issues. Order processing accuracy was included since many users felt that the data contained in CVN were incorrect and believed that the inaccuracy was related to the technology and not due to user error.

ANALYSIS AND RESULTS

Descriptive statistics, Pearson correlation coefficients, and inter-item reliabilities for the five variables included in the analysis are presented as Table 6. All bi-variate correlation coefficients are significant at $p < 0.01$. While collinearity may be an issue when high correlations exist among the included variables, even the greatest correlation in Table 6. (attitude toward technology and technology performance, $r = 0.66$) is well below the threshold of 0.90 suggested by Hair, Anderson, Tatham, and Black (1992). Thus, there is no indication of a collinearity problem in the data used in this study.

According to Nunnally and Bernstein (1994) and Hair et al., (1992), values for Cronbach's α greater than 0.70 indicate a satisfactory level of item reliability. Alpha values for four of the five variables were substantially above this threshold, ranging from 0.88 to 0.97. For the remaining variable, utilization, Cronbach's α was 0.64. This lower value is likely attributable in large part to the nature of the five items comprising the utilization scale since each item addresses utilization of a specific CVN function. Based on an individual's job responsibilities, he may use selected functions to a greater degree, others to a lesser degree, and still others not at all. This produced limited variance in the inter-item responses and reduced the

Table 6. Descriptive statistics, Pearson correlation coefficients, and inter-item reliabilities (Cronbach's α on diagonal) for included variables (N = 366)

	Mean	Standard Deviation	1	2	3	4	5
1. Normative Expectations	4.28	1.54	(.88)				
2. Supply Chain Awareness	4.54	1.50	0.40	(.97)			
3. Attitude Toward Technology	3.96	1.77	0.48	0.41	(.97)		
4. Utilization	1.66	0.79	0.27	0.21	0.19	(.64)	
5. Technology Performance	4.50	1.50	0.49	0.38	0.66	0.25	(.90)
All correlations are significant at the 0.01 level (2-tailed)							

strength of the correlations among the separate responses. However, the α of 0.64 for utilization does exceed the minimum standard of 0.50 suggested by Nunnally and Bernstein (1994) for exploratory research and Hinkin (1998) contends that values of 0.40 or greater are acceptable.

Results by Hypothesis

Hypothesis 1 was evaluated with the multivariate analysis of variance (MANOVA) procedure in SPSS, testing whether the responses across the five variables differ, as a whole, based on the nationality and/or gender of the respondent. By simultaneously comparing the mean response vectors of two (or more) groups, MANOVA provides a more robust assessment than performing multiple t-tests on the equality of a series of mean responses and helps to control Type 1 errors (Hair et al., 1992). H2 through H6 were evaluated by uni-variate tests on each of the five variables that individually were analyzed by ANOVAs.

Results of the MANOVA procedure are presented in Table 7., together with the results of the individual univariate tests on each of the five

variables. F-values for the MANOVA test statistic are reported along with their significance levels. Individual test statistics (Pillai's trace, Wilk's lambda, Hotelling's trace, and Roy's greatest root) were not included in the table because while the values of these four statistics may be different, the F-values, and therefore the resulting significance for all four are identical.

Hypothesis 1 predicted that the higher-MAS score attributed to the U.S. can be expected to be manifest in a greater degree of differentiation between the attitudes, priorities, and behaviors of U.S. men and women than between Canadian men and women. The U.S. MANOVA results show a significant difference between the overall means of responses for men and women (F = 3.46, p < 0.01). For Canadians, there was no significant overall difference in the responses of Canadian men and Canadian women (F = 1.608, p = 0.180). Therefore, H1 is supported.

Hypotheses 2 through 6 predicted that there would be greater similarity between Canadian men and women for each of the five variables than between U.S. men and women because of the lower-MAS score for Canada. Table 7 shows that

Table 7. Results of MANOVA tests for hypotheses 1 though 6

	Gender (U.S.)		Gender (CAN)	
	F	Sig.	F	Sig.
Multivariate (overall) (H1)	3.46	**	1.61	0.180
ES (η_p^2)	0.05		0.16	
Univariate				
Normative Expectations (H2)	14.43	***	3.09	0.086
Supply Chain Awareness (H3)	5.40	*	0.31	0.579
Attitude Toward Technology (H4)	10.32	**	0.42	0.522
Technology Performance (H5)	6.32	*	4.45	*
Utilization (H6)	2.03	0.155	0.693	0.409

* $p < 0.05$; ** $p < 0.01$; *** $p < 0.001$

ES = Effect Size, reported as partial eta-squared (η_p^2)

Note 1.   Individual multivariate test statistics (Pillai's trace, Wilk's lambda, Hotelling's trace, and Roy's largest root) are not included in the table. They are available upon request from the authors. The F-values and significance levels shown are identical for each of the four test statistics.

Note 2.   Intercept statistics for multivariate and the univariate tests are not shown. F-values for all cases are significant at $p < .000$. The statistics are available, upon request, from the authors.

for U.S. respondents, men and women differed significantly ($p < 0.05$) for all measures except utilization and that for Canadian respondents, there was no difference except on technology performance. Therefore, H2 through H4 are supported, while H5 and H6 are not supported.

The remaining five hypotheses (H7 though H11) address the differential effects of the three groups—U.S. men, U.S. women, and Canadians as an aggregate —for each of the five variables. Levene's test for homogeneity of variance was performed for each group across the variables of interest. Variances for all the variables except utilization (U.S. men versus U.S. women) were

found to be equal across the three groups, with the unequal variance for utilization significant at $p < 0.01$. Means and standard deviations for the three groups, as well as results of the t-tests, are provided in Table 8.

Based upon the cultural attributes associated with lower MAS and lower IND cultures (Hofstede, 2001), hypotheses 7-11 predicted between-group differences in the responses on the key TRA-based attitudinal and behavioral factors relating to the adoption of the new IT. The results in Table 8 strongly support the predictions of H8, H9, and H11. Hypothesis 7 (normative expectations) is partially supported, with U.S.

Table 8. Results of t-tests for hypotheses 7 through 11

	Mean (Standard Deviation) (U.S. Men) N = 125	Mean (Standard Deviation) (U.S. Women) N = 194	t-Statistic (U.S. Women v. U.S. Men)	Mean (Standard Deviation) (Canadians) N = 47	t-Statistic (Canadians v. U.S. Men)
Normative Expectations (H7)	3.86 (1.44)	4.53 (1.60)	3.79***	4.33 (1.29)	1.95
Supply Chain Awareness (H8)	4.27 (1.58)	4.66 (1.42)	2.58**	4.80 (1.50)	1.99*
Attitude Toward Technology (H9)	3.53 (1.67)	4.17 (1.79)	3.38**	4.20 (1.75)	2.32*
Utilization (H10)	1.29 (0.56)	1.42 (0.86)	-1.56	1.37 (0.59)	0.82
Technology Performance (H11)	4.20 (1.56)	4.64 (1.47)	2.77**	4.74 (1.39)	2.07*
* $p < 0.05$; ** $p < 0.01$; *** $p < 0.001$					

women significantly more aware than U.S. men ($p < 0.001$), and Canadians marginally more aware than U.S. men ($p = 0.053$). Hypothesis 10 (utilization) is not supported since no difference is noted among the three groups.

Of particular note were the data from the 24 Canadian women sub-sample which showed less within group variance than the other three sub-groups. This internal consistency suggests that Canadian women appreciated the new technology's performance capabilities ($\sum = 5.15$) to a high degree. Canadian women as a sub-group indicated a greater overall awareness of supply chain operations ($\sum = 4.92$) than any of the other sub-groups. Additionally, there was less within group variance for Canadian women regarding their reported use of the technology.

To summarize, the results of the analysis broadly support the expected effects of the difference in MAS scores between the U.S. and Canada on the homogeneity of attitudinal responses across men and women using a new technology, except for utilization and perceived technology performance. Additionally, sensitivity to normative expectations was found to be only marginally higher among Canadians than among U.S. men.

This study found both differences and similarities between Canadian and U.S. men and women. Greater differences are noted by gender and greater similarity by nationality. In the following section, the results and implications are discussed, before concluding with the limitations of the present study and suggestions for future research.

DISCUSSION

Overall Findings

Overall, our results suggest that it is important to consider combined elements of national culture and gender effects in evaluating similarities and differences across technology users in Canada and the U.S. While substantial similarities in cultural values exist between Canada and the U.S., they should not be allowed to mask the differences that exist between these two cultures. The results of the analyses for H1 through H6 provide evidence of real attitudinal and behavioral distinctions between Canadian and U.S. technology users, manifest most prominently in the finding of a clear gender effect in the responses of U.S. technology users, but not in those of Canadian users. This suggests that gender plays a larger role in the U.S. than it does in Canada with respect to utilizing new technologies. This result reinforces the importance of value differences related to MAS-FEM in shaping gender expectations and attitudes.

This differential effect was not found for the measures of utilization and technology performance. Interestingly, there was no gender effect in either country for utilization, but a clear and significant gender effect in both for technology performance. This result reinforces the finding by Gefen and Straub (1997) that women and men differ in their perceptions but not use of a particular technology (in their case, e-mail). Overall, the results suggest differences attributable to MAS that can impact both managerial (implementation planning) and operational (technology performance) aspects of new technology adoptions.

The greater similarity between Canadian men and women than between U.S. men and women with respect to their normative expectations is consistent with the lower-MAS score for Canada. Additionally, U.S. women were found to be significantly more aware of the normative pressures than U.S. men, a result consistent with the higher MAS score for the U.S. This suggests that the perceived social pressure to perform a particular behavior is of greater consequence to U.S. women than U.S. men. Optimally, U.S. managers can capitalize on this finding by employing the social networks in organizations to transmit positive insights regarding the new technology to U.S. women as part of the implementation process.

Together, there is strong evidence of attitudinal differences between U.S. men and U.S. women

and between Canadians and U.S. men. This has broad implications for the management of technology in the workplace. The traditional focus on a national culture effect alone is inadequate. Rather, consideration of the presence and implications of a gender effect within a particular cultural context is prescribed to increase the internal validity of the research results. In finding that the extent of the gender effect is a cultural artifact that varies between cultures, the present study lies at the intersection of two distinct conventional research domains: national culture and gender. Specifically, this finding suggests that what may be important to a predominantly Canadian workforce may be more important to U.S. women than to U.S. men. This supports the contention of Myers and Tan (2002) that the concept of 'national culture' may be too simplistic, and that researchers (and managers) should be cautious not to allow the presence or absence of national borders to unduly influence how they perceive and manage their workers and work processes.

Hypotheses 7 through 11 address the implementation of a new technology that considers specific factors that differ between higher MAS or lower MAS groups. The hypotheses considered the expected influence of the lower MAS and lower IND index scores (Hofstede, 2001) on Canadian technology users. The positive results for supply chain awareness (H8), attitude toward technology (H9), and technology performance (H11), together with the slightly significant results for normative expectations (H7), are associated with characteristics of lower MAS scores. These characteristics include: (1) Maintaining social relationships; (2) experiencing greater sensitivity to group member expectations; (3) acknowledging the importance of quality of life; and, (4) an increased consciousness of non task-related aspects of the work environment.

No difference was found in actual utilization (a dependent behavior in TRA) of the new CVN technology. It should be noted that while TRA provided the basis for selecting which variables to include in the analysis, this study did not replicate or test TRA as a causal model. Rather, we considered TRA-based predictors (normative expectations, supply chain awareness, and attitude toward technology) as independent variables in evaluating country and/or gender effects. Therefore, our findings that higher means for these variables did not coincide with greater utilization should not be viewed as either supporting or not supporting TRA or TAM as a model.

A possible explanation for the lack of difference in utilization between the groups may lie in the context within which this study was conducted. The target technology had been in place at all user organizations for many months (Table 3) and had been designed as a mandated solution for the accomplishment of daily tasks. Therefore, it is likely that some comparable level of utilization would be evident across all users, a likelihood consistent with the results of H10. This suggests that utilization per se, as a sole dependent measure, may not provide enough data for management to properly assess the effectiveness of a new IT implementation and is the rationale for including a measure of the technology's actual performance in this and future studies.

While there was no difference between the groups in their utilization of CVN, both U.S. women and Canadians rated the performance of CVN significantly higher than did U.S. men (H11). When considered together with the between-group differences found for normative expectations (H7), supply chain awareness (H8), and attitude toward technology (H9), this suggests some important implications for the management of technology implementations.

For this sample, the groups (U.S. women and Canadians, as an aggregate) exhibited greater awareness of the normative expectations of supervisors, customers, and suppliers. Additionally, this group displayed a greater sense of supply chain awareness representing an understanding of the interrelations among supply chain activities. U.S. women and Canadians, as an aggregate, expressed greater positive attitudes toward technology and experienced a greater perception of the technology's performance. The converse is true for U.S. men. However, the fact that our analysis identifies associations, not causal relationships, among the variables calls for a degree of caution in interpreting these results.

The strong association found among the variables suggests that managerial emphasis on the importance of normative expectations, supply chain awareness, and a positive attitude toward technology can assist in making the implementation of a new technology more effective for U.S. women and Canadians, as an aggregate. For example, training sessions that highlight the inter-linkages and dependencies among supply chain members both inside and outside the user's own organization might be particularly effective for enhancing successful implementation. Additionally, frequent reinforcement of the normative expectations of important members of the users' referent groups is another managerial strategy for effective technology implementation. These strategies could be approached via joint information and training sessions that include various stakeholders (suppliers, customers, and users) of the technology as active participants. Recurring feedback or status mechanisms that reinforce the effects of the users' actions on other stakeholders would also be helpful.

The implications for managing technology implementation for U.S. men are less clear. The results of this study suggest that technology performance can be expected to increase if normative expectations, supply chain awareness, and attitudes toward technology increase. This expectation is based in the higher MAS and higher IND scores for U.S. men who are less sensitive to the effects of these factors. To achieve the desired attitudinal changes, a stronger emphasis on such measures is recommended.

Significant Differences

Of the findings from this study, the most dramatic difference seems to be the alignment of U.S. men being different than the aggregate of Canadian women, Canadian men and U.S. women. This group alignment might be interpreted as support for cultural similarities related to gender more than to nationality. Alternatively, this finding of difference might suggest that Canadian men are the key difference between the groups since they aligned with women from both countries. Furthermore, the non-gender cultural values of Canada and the United States may be so sensitive as to be latent in this study. This phenomenon is likely explained by the strong cultural similarities between Canada and the U.S. However, the differences, as a function of gender, are more robust and interesting for the study's findings.

CONCLUSION

Contributions and Implications

This study makes several significant contributions addressing both the theory and practice of cross-cultural management of technology. First, the interrelationships among national culture, gender, and user attitudes towards a new technology are reinforced. Our findings are consistent with other research that focuses on the effects of gender (e.g., Sagi et al., 2004; Stedham & Yamamura, 2004), but emphasizes that gender is most constructively examined together with nationality. Perhaps the most significant implication for both theory and practice is the recognition that greater attention should be paid to how the effects of gender can differ even across cultures that are nominally similar.

Second, the findings improve our understanding of the cultural similarities and differences between Canada and the U.S. in the context of implementing a new technology. The results indicate that the common tendency to consider the two countries as members of the same cultural cluster can reduce awareness of important differences in attitudes and behaviors for which a more adaptive approach to management may be appropriate. Testing hypotheses grounded in Hofstede's (2001) MAS dimension, it was found that grouping by country was inadequate and that a consideration of both country and gender may be more meaningful.

A third contribution is in providing a better understanding of how the culturally-based differences that distinguish the two groups impact attitudinal and behavioral factors key to the implementation of new information technologies. Prior research on the acceptance of IT has examined single-country samples; this is the first study, to our knowledge, to explicitly incorporate a cross-national sample implementing a single technology. Our findings of significant differential effects of culture on the factors underlying both the TRA and TAM models can inform future research in this area.

The fourth contribution is in addressing technology performance as a dependent variable of interest. Prior research on technology adoption tended to focus on the intent to use as the dependent variable. While certainly important, especially in the early stages of adoption or implementation of a new technology, utilization per se becomes less important over time than how well the technology is actually performing its designed tasks. The incorporation of a measure of technology performance in the present study helps to address this limitation.

A fifth contribution lies in the implications of the study's results for practicing managers. The findings underscore the importance of making an informed assessment of the underlying values that characterize a particular set of technology users and suggest specific insights relevant to normative expectations, supply chain understanding, and attitudes toward technology that can be important in facilitating the implementation of new systems.

This is not simply a *cross-cultural* management issue; indeed, a direct comparison of Canadian with U.S. technology users showed no significant difference. The finding that U.S. women appeared to have more in common with Canadian women and men than they did with their national counterparts, U.S. men, reinforces the need for managers even within intra-domestic settings to be aware of and sensitive to value differences among their individual technology users.

Limitations

This study has several limitations. While the size of the Canadian sample substantially exceeds minimum guidelines for the multivariate and univariate procedures employed and the number of variables included in the analysis (Hair et al., 1992), a more balanced Canadian-U.S. mix would increase the power of the tests applied and give greater confidence in interpreting the results. Although the Canadian/U.S. ratio in this study closely mirrors the actual population of suppliers, a subsequent study with a more balanced Canadian-U.S. mix would be useful, as would a sample drawing from other Canadian provinces and territories in addition to Ontario.

Second, in this study, the grounding theory for examination of effect is based on TRA and TAM. Therefore, the outputs of TRA are recognized as main effects. In order to provide interpretive and contextual understanding of the interaction (secondary) effects in this study, the main effects (H1-H6) are required. An alternative to this procedure might have been the exploration of secondary effects (H7-H11) without consideration of the main effects.

Third, the internal reliability coefficient for the utilization scale employed ($\alpha = 0.64$) is below the 'rule-of-thumb' standard of 0.70 (Nunnally & Bernstein, 1994) commonly applied. While Hinkin (1998) suggests that an $\alpha = 0.40$ is acceptable, further refinement of the utilization scale can benefit future research.

Fourth, the technology performance scale employed reflects the user's subjective self-evaluation of how well CVN accomplishes various functions, rather than an external assessment or comparison with an objective standard. It might be useful to apply alternative measures such as individual user's productivity or other objective indicators of technology performance to validate users' self-reported perceptions.

Fifth, with respect to external validity, this study addressed the implementation of a single information technology across multiple components of a single automotive manufacturing supply chain network in the U.S. and Ontario, Canada. Care should be exercised in generalizing the findings to non-manufacturing contexts, across entities that are not interlinked as members of a common supply chain, or even to French-speaking Canada.

Sixth, while much of the prior research on technology acceptance and implementation has focused on general, personal productivity applications such as e-mail, word processing, or spreadsheets, the CVN system used in this study is a proprietary and highly customized technology, specifically tailored to the functions of the organizations using it. This suggests the use of caution in extending these findings to dissimilar technologies.

Recommendations for Future Research

The present study does not test for causal relationships among the variables addressed. Even though the factors tested here for cultural effects are taken from the TRA model, this analysis does not directly test or extend TRA. While the culturally-based distinctions identified in the test results are important, causality should not be inferred from these results, and caution should be applied to their interpretation. Designing future studies that specifically model and test causality among the variables can be a useful area of future research.

Other opportunities for further research include increasing the range of industries, countries, cultures, and technologies to validate and extend the findings of the present study. While the characteristics of the MAS dimension grounding much of this study are consistent with empirical results of other studies (e.g., House et al., 2004), additional manifestations of cultural differences should be systematically explored. Some examples of empirical structures include Project GLOBE (Javidan & House, 2001; Trompenaars & Hampden-Turner, 1998) and the Value-Orientation (V-O) framework (Lane et al., 2001). Lastly, future research designs can specifically address causal relationships among the various factors relating to technology adoption, utilization, and performance, and examine the influence of these factors on the overall performance of the organization.

Since the ultimate use of applied research is the application to real-world settings, this research can be extended to link perceptions of technology utilization and performance to corporate financial performance. Firm performance constitutes the effect on the overall organizational outcomes of improved operational process through technology. Future investigations into the summative effects of technology adoption on firm performance are warranted.

ACKNOWLEDGMENT

The authors are grateful to Dr. Howard Forman for his substantial contributions to the development of this article, to Mark Peterson, and to the anonymous reviewers and editorial staff of the Journal of Global Information Management for their insightful and constructive comments and suggestions.

REFERENCES

Abramson, N., Keating, R.J., & Lane, H.W. (1996). Cross-national cognitive process differences: A comparison of Canadian, American and Japanese managers. *Management International Review, 36*(2), 123-147.

Adler, N.J. (1997). *International dimensions of organizational behavior,* (3rd ed.). Cincinnati, OH: South-Western.

Agarwal, R., & Prasad, J. (1999). Are individual differences germane to the acceptance of new information technologies? *Decision Sciences, 30*(2), 361-391.

Ahuja, M.K., & Thatcher, J.B. (2005). Moving beyond intentions and toward a theory of trying: Effects of work environment and gender on post-adoption information technology use. *MIS Quarterly, 29*(3), 427-459.

Ajzen, I. (1991). The theory of planned behavior. *Organizational, Behavior and Human Decision Processes, 50*, 179-211.

Ajzen, I., & Fishbein, M. (1980). *Understanding Attitudes and Predicting Social Behavior.* Englewood Cliffs: Prentice-Hall.

Al-Gahtani, S. (2001). The applicability of TAM outside North America: An empirical test in the United Kingdom. *Information Resources Management Journal, 14*(3), 37-46.

Bagchi, K., Hart, P., & Peterson, M. (2004). National culture and information technology product adoption. *Journal of Global Information Technology Management, 7*(4), 29-46.

Bock, G.W., Zmud, R.W., Kim, Y.G., & Lee, J.N. (2005). Behavioral intention formation in knowledge sharing: Examining the roles of extrinsic motivators, social-psychological forces, and organizational climate. *MIS Quarterly, 29*(1), 87-111.

Caligiuri, P., & Tung, R.L. (1999). Comparing the success of male and female expatriates from a US-based multinational company. *International Journal of Human Resource Management, 10*(5), 763-782.

Choi, H.Y. & Choi, H. (2003). An exploratory study and design of cross-cultural impact of information systems managers' performance, job satisfaction and managerial value. *Journal of Global Information Management, 11*(2), 1-30.

Clark, T. (1990). International marketing and national character: A review and proposal for an integrative theory. *Journal of Marketing, 54*(4), 66-79.

Dahlstrom, R., McNeilly, K.M., & Speh, T.W. (1996). Buyer-seller relationships in the procurement of logistical services. *Journal of the Academy of Marketing Science, 2*(42), 110-124.

Davis, F.D. (1989). Perceived usefulness, perceived ease of use, and user acceptance of technology. *MIS Quarterly, 13*(3), 319-340.

Davis, F.D., Bagozzi, R.P., & Warshaw, P.R. (1989). User acceptance of computer technology: A comparison of two theoretical models. *Management Science, 35*(8), 982-1003.

Deming, W.E. (1986). *Out of the crisis.* Cambridge, MA: MIT Center for Advanced Engineering Study.

Deresky, H. (2006). *International management: Managing across borders and cultures*, (5th ed.). Upper Saddle River, NJ: Pearson Prentice Hall.

Dwyer, S. Mesak, H. & Hsu, M. (2005). An exploratory examination of the influence of national culture on cross-national product diffusion. *Journal of International Marketing, 13*(2), 1-27.

Esterl, M. (2004) New offshoring study puts India, China at top of heap, *Wall Street Journal Online*, 3/30/2004. Retrieved April 23, 2003, from http://online.wsj.com.

Evans, W., Lane, H., & O'Grady, S. (1992). *Border crossings: Doing business in the US*. Scarborough, ONT: Prentice Hall Canada.

Evaristo, R. (2003). The management of distributed projects across cultures. *Journal of Global Information Management, 11*(4), 58-70.

Fishbein, M., & Ajzen, I. (1975). *Belief, attitude, intention, and behavior: An introduction to theory and research*. Reading, PA: Addison-Wesley.

Forman, H., & Lippert, S.K. (2005). Toward an integrated model of technology internalization with the supply chain context. *International Journal of Logistics Management, 16*(1), 4-26.

Francesco, A.M., & Gold, B.A. (2005). *International organizational behavior: Text, cases, and exercises*, (2nd ed.). Upper Saddle River, NJ: Pearson Prentice Hall.

Garrett, T.C., Buisson, D.H., & Yap, C.M. (2006). National culture and R&D and marketing integration mechanisms in new product development: A cross-cultural study between Singapore and New Zealand. *Industrial Marketing Management, 35*(3), 293-307.

Gefen, D., & Straub, D.W. (1997). Gender differences in the perception and use of e-mail: An extension to the technology acceptance model. *MIS Quarterly, 21*(4), 389-400.

Gumpert, D.E. (2004). An atlas of offshore outsourcing, *BusinessWeek Online*. Retrieved April 23, 2003, from http://businessweek.com.

Hair, J.F., Anderson, R.E., Tatham, R.L., & Black, W.C. (1992). *Multivariate data analysis with readings*, (3rd ed.). New York: Macmillan Publishing Company.

Hall, E.T., & Hall, M.R. (1990). *Understanding cultural differences*. Yarmouth, ME: Intercultural Press.

Hannon, D. (2003). Transportation technology: The unhappy marriage between process and technology. *Purchasing, 132*(9), 61-62.

Hess, T.J., Fuller, M.A., & Mathew, J. (2005-2006). Involvement and decision-making performance with a decision aid: The influence of social multimedia, gender, and playfulness. *Journal of Management Information Systems, 22*(3), 15-54.

Hicks, D.A., & Nivin, S.R. (2000). Beyond globalization: Localized returns to IT infrastructure investments. *Regional Studies, 34*(2), 115-127.

Hill, C.W.L. (1997). *International Business: Competing in the Global Marketplace*, (2nd ed.). Boston, MA: Irwin McGraw-Hill.

Hinkin, T.R. (1998). A brief tutorial on the development of measures for use in survey questionnaires. *Organizational Research Methods, 1*(1), 104-121.

Hofstede, G. (1980). *Culture's Consequences: International Differences in Work-Related Values.* Beverly Hills, CA: Sage Publications.

Hofstede, G. (1983). The cultural relativity of organizational practices and theories. *Journal of International Business Studies, 14*(2), 75-89.

Hofstede, G. (1984). *Culture's Consequences: International Differences in Work-related Values.* (Abridged ed.). Newbury Park, CA: Sage Publications.

Hofstede, G. (Ed.). (1998). *Masculinity and Femininity: The Taboo Dimension of National Cultures.* Thousand Oaks, CA: Sage Publications.

Hofstede, G. (2001). *Culture's Consequences: Comparing Values, Behaviors, Institutions, and Organizations across Nations*, (2nd ed.). Thousand Oaks, CA: Sage Publications.

Hofstede, G., & Bond, M.H. (1988). The Confucius connection: from cultural roots to economic growth. *Organizational Dynamics, 16*(4), 4-21.

Holweg, M., & Bicheno, J. (2002). Supply chain simulation: A tool for education, enhancement, and endeavor. *International Journal of Production Economics, 78*(2), 163-175.

House, R.J., Hanges, P., Javidan, M., Dorfman, P., & Gupta, V. (Eds.). (2004). *Culture, Leadership, and Organizations.* Thousand Oaks, CA: Sage Publications.

Hunter, M.G. (2006). Experiences conducting cross-cultural research. *Journal of Global Information Management, 14*(2), 75-89.

Javidan, M., & House, R.J. (2001). Cultural acumen for the global manager: Lessons from project GLOBE. *Organizational Dynamics, 29*(4), 289-305.

Karahanna, E., Straub, D.W., & Chervany, N.L. (1999). Information technology adoption across time: A cross-sectional comparison of pre-adoption and post-adoption beliefs. *MIS Quarterly, 23*(2), 183-213.

Kogut, B., & Singh, H. (1988). The effect of national culture on the choice of entry mode. *Journal of International Business Studies, 19*(3), 411-432.

Lane, H.W., Maznevski, M.L., & DiStefano, J.J., (2006). *International Management Behavior,* (5th ed.). Malden, MA: Blackwell Publishers.

Lee, C., & Green, R.T. (1991). Cross-cultural examination of the Fishbein behavioral intentions model. *Journal of International Business Studies, 22*(2), 289-305.

Lee, J.N., & Kim, Y.G. (2005). Understanding outsourcing partnership: A comparison of three theoretical perspectives. *IEEE Transactions on Engineering Management, 52*(1), 43-58.

Legris, P., Ingham, J., & Collerette, P. (2003). Why do people use information technology? A critical review of the technology acceptance model. *Information & Management, 40*(3), 191-204.

Leidner, D.E., & Kayworth, T. (2006). A review of culture in information systems research: Toward a theory of information technology culture conflict. *MIS Quarterly, 30*(2), 357-399.

Lim, J. (2004). The role of power distance and explanation facility in online bargaining utilizing software agents. *Journal of Global Information Management, 12*(2), 27-43.

Lippert, S.K., & Forman, H. (2005). Utilization of information technology: Examining cognitive and experiential factors of post-adoption behavior. *IEEE Transactions on Engineering Management, 52*(3), 363-381.

Liu, C., Marchewka, J.T., & Ku, C. (2004). American and Taiwanese perceptions concerning privacy, trust, and behavioral intentions in electronic commerce. *Journal of Global Information Management, 12*(1), 18-40.

Lonner, J.L., & Berry, J.W. (1998). Series Editors' Introduction. In G. Hofstede (Ed.), *Masculinity and femininity: The taboo dimension of national cultures.* Thousand Oaks, CA: Sage Publications.

Lorigo, L., Pan, B., Hembrooke, H., Joachims, T., Granka, L., & Gay, G. (2006). The influence of task and gender on search and evaluation behavior using Google. *Information Processing and Management, 42*(4), 1123-1131.

Mao, E., Srite, M., Thatcher, J.B., & Yaprak, O. (2005). A research model for mobile phone service behaviors: Empirical validation in the U.S. and Turkey. *Journal of Global Information Management, 8*(4), 7-28.

Mason, R.M. (2003). Culture-free or culture-bound? A boundary spanning perspective on learning in knowledge management systems. *Journal of Global Information Management, 11*(4), 20-36.

McCoy, S., Everard, A., & Jones, B.M. (2005). An examination of the technology acceptance model in Uruguay and the US: A focus on culture. *Journal of Global Information Management, 8*(2), 27-45.

McCoy, S., Galletta, D.F. & King, W.R. (2005). Integrating national culture into IS research: The need for current individual level measures. *Communications of the Association for Information Systems, 15*(12), 1-22.

McFarlin, D.B., & Sweeney, P.D. (2006). *International management: Strategic opportunities and cultural challenges,* (3rd ed.). Boston, MA: Houghton Mifflin.

Moores, T.T., & Chang, J.C.J. (2006). Ethical decision making in software piracy: Initial development and test of a four-component model. *MIS Quarterly, 30*(1), 167-180.

Myers, M.D., & Tan, F.B. (2002). Beyond models of national culture in information systems research. *Journal of Global Information Management, 10*(1), 24-32.

Nakata, C., & Sivakumar, K. (1996). National culture and new product development: An integrative review. *Journal of Marketing, 60*(1), 61-72.

Nath, R., & Sadhu, K.K. (1988). Comparative analysis. Conclusions, and future directions. In N. Raghu (Ed.), *Comparative management-A regional view* (pp. 273). Cambridge, MA: Ballinger Publishing Company.

Nunnally, J.C., & Bernstein, I.H. (1994). *Psychometric theory.* New York: McGraw-Hill.

O'Grady, S. (1991). *Canadian retail companies doing business in the U.S. market: A cultural perspective.* [Unpublished Dissertation]. London, Ontario: The University of Western Ontario.

Pauleen, D.J. (2003). Lessons learned crossing boundaries in an ICT-supported distributed team.

Journal of Global Information Management, 11(4), 1-19.

Peter, P.C., & Olson, J.C. (1999). *Consumer behavior and marketing strategy*, (5th ed.). Boston: McGraw-Hill.

Rao, A., & Hashimoto, K. (1996). Intercultural influence: A study of Japanese expatriate managers in Canada. *Journal of International Business Studies, 27*(3), 443-466.

Rich, G.J. (2000). To be a man, to be a woman: Gender in global context. *Journal of Sex Research, 37*(1), 96-98.

Rogers, E.M. (1995). *Diffusion of innovations*, (5th ed.). New York: Free Press

Ronen, S., & Shenkar, O. (1985). Clustering countries on attitudinal dimensions: A review and synthesis. *Academy of Management Review, 10*(3), 435-454.

Root, F.R. (1994). *Entry strategies for international markets*. San Francisco: Lexington Books.

Rose, G., & Straub, D.W. (1998). Predicting general IT use: Applying TAM to the Arabic world. *Journal of Global Information Management, 6*(3), 39-46.

Sagi, J., Carayannis, E., Dasgupta, S., & Thomas, G. (2004). ICT and business in the New economy: Globalization and attitudes towards eCommerce. *Journal of Global Information Management, 12*(3), 44-64.

Schneider, S.C. (1989). Strategy formulation: The impact of national culture. *Organization Science, 10*(2), 149-168.

Shih, H.P. (2004) An empirical study on predicting user acceptance of e-shopping on the Web. *Information & Management, 41*(3), 351-368.

Singh, N., Xhao, H., & Hu, X. (2003). Cultural adaptation on the web: A study of American companies' domestic and Chinese websites. *Journal of Global Information Management, 11*(3), 63-80.

Stafford, T.F., Turan, A., & Raisinghani, M.S. (2004). International and cross-cultural influences on online shopping behavior. *Journal of Global Information Management, 7*(2), 70-87.

Stedham, Y.E. & Yamamura, J.H. (2004). Measuring national culture: Does gender matter? *Women in Management Review, 19*(5), 233-243.

Straub, D., Keil, M., & Brenner, W. (1997). Testing the technology acceptance model across cultures: A three country study. *Information & Management, 33*(1), 1-11.

Su, S.H. (2006). Cultural differences in determining the ethical perception and decision-making of future accounting professionals: A comparison between accounting students in Taiwan and the United States. *Journal of American Academy of Business, 9*(1), 147-158.

Sullivan, D. (1994). Measuring the degree of internationalization of a firm. *Journal of International Business Studies, 25*(2), 325-342.

Tan, B.C.Y., Watson, R.T., & Wei, K. (1995). National culture and group support systems: Filtering communication to dampen power differentials, *European Journal of Information Systems, 4*(2), 82-92.

Taylor, W.A. (2004). Computer-mediated knowledge sharing and individual user differences: An exploratory study. *European Journal of Information Systems, 13*(1), 52-64.

Trebilcock, B. (2001). Careful! They may be watching! *Modern Materials Handling, 56*(6), 21-25.

Triandis, H.C. (1971). *Attitude and Attitude Change*. New York: Wiley.

Triandis, H.C. (1980). Values, attitudes, and interpersonal behavior. In *Nebraska Symposium on*

Motivation, 1979: Beliefs, Attitudes, and Values. Lincoln: University of Nebraska Press, 195-259.

Trompenaars, F., & Hampden-Turner, C. (1998). *Riding the Waves of Culture: Understanding Diversity in Global Business*, (2nd ed.). New York: McGraw-Hill.

Ueno, S., & Sekaran, U. (1992). The influence of culture on budget control practices in the USA and Japan: An empirical study. *Journal of International Business Studies, 23*(4), 659-674.

Venkatesh, V., & Davis, F.D. (2000). A theoretical extension of the technology acceptance model: Four longitudinal field studies. *Management Science, 46*(2), 186-204.

Venkatesh, V., & Morris, M.G. (2000). Why don't men ever stop to ask for directions? Gender, social influence, and their role in technology acceptance and usage behavior. *MIS Quarterly, 24*(1), 115-139.

Welcome to Canada Statistics(2001). Retrieved August 9, 2005 from www.statcan.ca.

Wu, I.L. (2003). Understanding senior management's behavior in promoting the strategic role of IT in process reengineering. *Information & Management, 41*(1), 1-11.

Zeira, Y., Newburry, W., & Yeheskel, O. (1997). Factors affecting the effectiveness of equity international joint ventures (EIJVs) in Hungary. *Management International Review, 37*(3), 259-279.

APPENDIX.
SCALE ITEM AND DESCRIPTIVE STATISTICS BY CONSTRUCT

Var	Mean	S.D.	Item Wording
NE1	4.14	2.00	Top management thinks I should use CVN
NE2	4.02	1.97	The CVN champion thinks I should use CVN
NE3	4.25	2.00	My supervisor thinks I should use CVN
NE4	3.69	1.94	My peers thinks I should use CVN
NE5	5.72	1.66	Our customers thinks I should use CVN
NE6	3.85	2.14	Our suppliers thinks I should use CVN

Supply Chain Awareness (SCA)

Var	Mean	S.D.	Item Wording
SCA1	4.70	1.60	It is important to understand the actual end user demand that drives our supply chain in order to use CVN effectively
SCA2	4.54	1.63	It is important to understand how production processes in the supply chain are linked with each other in order to use CVN effectively
SCA3	4.44	1.60	It is important to understand how inventory levels are managed along the supply chain order to use CVN effectively
SCA4	4.46	1.63	It is important to understand the role of integration of supply chain members in order to use CVN effectively
SCA5	4.69	1.65	It is important to understand the role of transportation services along the supply chain in order to use CVN effectively
SCA6	4.47	1.64	It is important to understand why my company shares information with other members of the supply chain in order to use CVN effectively
SCA7	4.51	1.64	It is important to understand why my company work as a team with other members of the supply chain in order to use CVN effectively

Attitude toward Technology (ATT)

Var	Mean	S.D.	Item Wording
ATT1	4.30	1.92	I like using CVN
ATT2	3.70	1.81	CVN is fun to use
ATT3	3.90	1.86	I enjoy using CVN
ATT4	3.93	1.80	CVN provides an attractive working environment

Utilization (UTL): To what extent do you use CVN to:

Var	Mean	S.D.	Item Wording
UTL3	1.43	1.13	Use the Exception Management Feature
UTL4	1.64	1.56	Use the Search function to manage workload planning
UTL5	1.22	0.84	Use the Search function to prioritize the unloading process
UTL6	1.25	0.91	Use the Supplier scorecard to manage logistical performance
UTL7	1.33	1.12	Manage Just-In-Time corrugated to mirror inbound arrivals

Technology Performance (TPF): How would you rate CVN on these performance issues?

Var	Mean	S.D.	Item Wording
TPF1	4.80	1.73	Order processing accuracy
TPF2	3.84	1.97	Provides product visibility in transit
TPF3	4.08	1.87	Meets productivity standards
TPF4	4.71	1.81	Meets on-time delivery standards
TPF5	4.87	1.79	Responds to our customers' requests
TPF6	4.72	1.89	Provides order status information

This work was previously published in Journal of Global Information Management, Vol. 15, Issue 2, edited by F. B. Tan, pp. 56-90, copyright 2007 by IGI Publishing, formerly known as Idea Group Publishing (an imprint of IGI Global).

Chapter XVII
Balancing Local Knowledge within Global Organisations through Computer–Based Systems:
An Activity Theory Approach

Somya Joshi
National Technical University of Athens, Greece

Michael Barrett
University of Cambridge, UK

Geoff Walsham
University of Cambridge, UK

Sam Cappleman
Hewlett-Packard Ltd, UK

ABSTRACT

This article investigates how, and with what success, global organisations design computer-based systems for knowledge sharing which aim to balance centralised and standardised approaches against more diverse local needs. The empirical basis for the article is provided by an analysis of two different global organisations, each with its own knowledge-sharing infrastructure in place. We use third-generation activity theory as the theoretical basis for our analysis. The contributions from this article are twofold. The first is our theoretical lens, where activity theory is applied to the domain of global information systems and their organisational context. This analysis provides a new approach in addressing both the mediation of and motivations behind knowledge-sharing activity. The second contribution concerns the theoretical and practical insights this gives on the problems and challenges of achieving a balance between global and local priorities within highly distributed work contexts, and the role of computer-based systems in this arena.

INTRODUCTION

Global organisations today face an inherent dilemma between maintaining closeness to their customers and stakeholders whilst the geographic reach of their operations and markets expands. There is a justified desire to retain the traditional economy of scale based on extensive routinisation and standardisation, in order to present a reasonably coherent and uniform face or identity (Ger, 1999; Leidner, 1993), but there is also pressure from local partners to pay closer attention to contextual details and to support different and often conflicting needs. The challenge that emerges from this is one of balancing the diversity presented by the increasing number of local stakeholders and partners, and at the same time working towards a degree of consistency and coherence in operations. Global information systems and infrastructures are aimed to address this complexity, but they remain limited in terms of the extent of contextual diversity they end up capturing (Pan & Leidner, 2003).

There is a significant body of literature concerned with the need for adaptation of information systems to local contextual demands. Typically this is discussed with reference to the heterogeneity of information systems and the subsequent need to adapt to local needs (Ciborra, 1994; Davenport, 1998; Kyng & Mathiassen, 1997); the inscription of interests into artefacts (Bloomfield, Coombs, Knights, & Littler, 1997; Sahay, 1998); and local resistance to top-down initiatives (Ciborra, 1994, 2000). Our intention in this article is to go beyond this acknowledgement of the situated nature of information systems and the dichotomy of global-local narratives by asking how firms attempt to achieve a 'pragmatic balance' (Rolland & Monteiro, 2002) between the uniqueness of local context and the implied uniformity of globally applicable 'solutions'. More specifically the research question that we address in this article is: *How, and with what success, do global organisations design computer-based tools for knowledge shar-ing aimed to balance standardised approaches against local needs?*

In order to carry out this research enquiry, we draw upon empirical material from two case studies of global organisations, each with its own distinct computer-based knowledge sharing system in place. The first case is that of a leading pharmaceutical company working within the private sector, which we refer to as GP. We focus in this case on the integrated information system that provided GP's communicators worldwide with the opportunity to share knowledge through a standardised interface. The second case study we examine is that of a not-for-profit organisation working within the context of open source software certification, in particular that based on Linux, which we will refer to in this article as LC. We focus here on the electronic mailing lists used by LC for both internal communications and product development.

The analytical lens of activity theory is used to analyse findings from the above case studies. This theory is described in the next section of the article. Following this, we provide a detailed description of our methodology and research design, before moving on to the analysis of the case studies. We then use results from our case analyses to draw some implications and conclusions for theory and practice.

ACTIVITY THEORY

Cultural-Historical Activity Theory

The cultural-historical theory of activity has its roots in Russian psychology of the 1920s and 1930s. The fundamental concept of this approach was formulated by Lev Vygotsky (1978), who spoke of artefact-mediated and object (motivation)-oriented action. In the early work of the cultural-historical school, however, mediation by other individuals and social relations were not theoretically integrated into the model. Such

Figure 1. The activity model (Engeström, 1987, p. 78)

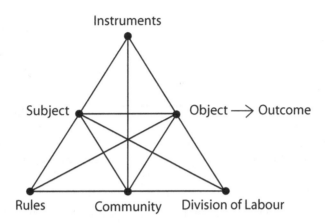

integration required distinguishing between collective activity and individual action. The second generation of activity theory attempted to interlink these two frames, and in doing so it derived its inspiration largely from Leont'ev's (1978) work. With subsequent developments and applications in different educational, cultural, technological and organisational contexts, it was Engeström (1987) who presented a model of the collective activity system (see Figure 1).

At the apex of this model lies the mediating tools (instruments) which are situated between the group undertaking the activity (subject) and their desired goals and motivations (object). Whilst the constraints and access points (rules) determine the interactions between the subject group and the stakeholders (community), the hierarchies of power and expertise within an organisation (division of labour) mediate between the stakeholder communities and the overarching objectives and outcomes of the activity. It is important to note that an activity system is never static. Tasks are reassigned and re-evaluated; rules are bent and re-interpreted. There is constant movement between the nodes of the activity system. What initially appears as an object may soon be transformed into an outcome, subsequently turned into an instrument, and perhaps later into a rule (Engeström,

1996). This dynamic nature of the activity system makes it a highly relevant lens with which to analyse organisations undergoing transformation, with evolving roles and motivations.

Third-Generation Activity Theory

Having moved from its original application context (i.e., cognitive psychology), to the highly distributed work context of present day organisations, activity theory faces the task of responding to increasing heterogeneity. Engeström (2001) argues the need for third-generation activity theory focused on networks of activity systems. These networks have at least two interacting activity systems (see Figure 2).

In the third-generation model, we find the concept of a potentially shared object that emerges through a collaboratively constructed understanding between two or more interacting activity systems. The object of activity in this model is described by Engeström (2001, p. 136) as 'a moving target, not reducible to conscious short-term goals'. He is implying that no one subject group can determine the object, but rather that it is jointly constructed between different interacting groups, with different sets of stakeholders, rules of behaviour and divisions of labour.

Figure 2. Minimal model of third-generation activity theory

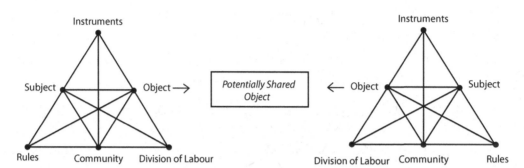

In recent studies (Engeström, Engeström, & Kärkkäinen, 1995; Engeström, Engeström, & Vähäaho, 1999; Hasu & Engeström, 1999), special attention has been given to organisational settings in which collaborative work between the partners is allotted high priority, without however strong predetermined rules or central authority. Engeström (1999) refers to such forms of collaborative work as 'knotworking'. The knot here suggests the distributed and dynamic nature of collaborative relationships between otherwise loosely connected actors and organisational units. As suggested by Figure 2, collaboration between such actors may be problematic since, for example, objects may not be shared, and rules and divisions of labour between different activity systems may at times be in conflict.

Engeström (2001) illustrates his third-generation activity theory with an interesting case study of contradictions between different activity systems (health centre, children's hospital, patient's family) in the health care of sick children in Helsinki. Other writers have also analysed the conflict between different activity systems. A good example is the paper by Oshri, Pan, and Newell (2006). Although the authors do not use activity theory explicitly, they explore the tension between an expertise development activity system and a knowledge management activity system in the context of product development processes in a particular company. However, as far as we

are aware, there is no existing literature which uses third-generation activity theory explicitly to explore the issues in this article, namely the use of computer-based knowledge sharing systems across global organisations.

The case analyses later in this article will use the theory for this purpose. In particular, we will organise the case analyses around the five principles developed by Engestrom (2001) for an application of third-generation activity theory:

- **Unit of Analysis:** The first principle involves taking the entire tool-mediated and object-oriented network of interconnected activity systems as a cohesive unit of analysis.
- **Historicity:** Activity systems take shape and get transformed over lengthy periods of time. It is thus necessary to pay close attention to the history of how the activity systems evolved.
- **Multivoicedness of Activity:** A network of activity systems always involves subjects and communities with multiple viewpoints. As illustrated in Figure 2, the activity systems interact around potentially diverse perceptions of shared goals.
- **Contradictions:** As a driving force for change–both within and between activity systems. This refers to the differing perceptions and 'voices' regarding the potentially shared object, and the contradictions and

possible conflicts that may subsequently arise.

- **Expansive Cycles:** As processes of transformation in objects and activities—the problems and contradictions referred to above open up new possibilities for expansive questioning and debate, and the search for innovative solutions. Engeström (2001, p. 137) defines this principle as 'when the object and motive of the activity are reconceptualised to embrace a radically wider horizon of possibilities than in the previous mode of activity'.

A brief summary of the five principles of third-generation activity theory is to say that expansive cycles are action-oriented approaches to help resolve contradictions and conflicts in networks of activity systems, the latter emerging from multivoicedness in the context of historical relationships.

RESEARCH METHODOLOGY

The work reported in this article formed part of a larger research project concerned with 'ICTs and knowledge communities in global organisations'. The broad objectives of the project were to study knowledge practices in organisations with a global reach, to theorise these empirical observations, and to draw conclusions for both academic and practitioner communities. In this article, we report on two of our in-depth case studies, namely GP and LC, as introduced earlier. GP had its headquarters in a European country, whilst LC had its headquarters in North America. Both organisations had an impressive global reach in terms of affiliates, partners and customers.

An interpretive approach in our research was adopted, as the aim was to produce 'an understanding of the context of the information system, and the process whereby the information system influences and is influenced by the context'

(Walsham, 1993, p. 4-5). We were interested in accessing the diverse interpretations of people in the field situations through in-depth qualitative interviews. The field research for the two cases was longitudinal in style and took place over a period of a year and a half, from April 2004 to September 2005. During this time, we interviewed people at all levels of the organisational hierarchy, including senior management at the headquarters, executives at the region and country level, down to lower level staff officers in the various affiliate locations. We visited country offices in Japan, India, China, Brazil, Jamaica, and the UK, as well as the organisational headquarters in Europe and North America. This ensured a broad spectrum of input from individuals and communities with diverse business and cultural backgrounds. In addition to on-site face-to-face interactions, we also conducted interviews via telephone and e-mail. Most of the interviews were tape-recorded and transcribed, whilst others were recorded by taking extensive field notes, when it was felt that some respondents would be more likely to be open in their opinions if the interviews were not taped. In Table 1, we provide a summary of the formal interviews conducted.

In addition to the above interviews, we had a wide range of additional contacts with staff of the two organisations. In the case of GP, we met team members involved in the design and execution of the information system outside of a formal office setting on a number of occasions. This enabled us to have broader discussions which covered areas such as the organisation's internal power struggles, as well as the role played by information systems within the context of the pharmaceutical industry. In the case of LC, in order to have a broader understanding of the IT certification field, we attended Linux conferences where LC participated. We also attended three meetings between LC, their affiliates, and a wider set of Linux certification providers in the field. We took part in audio conferences with our primary contacts and colleagues at GP and

Table 1. Summary of formal interviews conducted

Level/Case	GP	LC	Job Role of Contacts
Headquarters	12	10	Heads of departments, senior officials, staff officers, IT staff
Region	2	2	Heads of section, project managers, staff officers

LC headquarters over the course of the research project. The flow of communication in these audio conferences was two-way. Hence we would report our findings and recommendations from our visits to country affiliate offices, whilst we would receive updates and relevant information keeping us abreast of the organisation's development and strategic intent.

Our analysis took place in an iterative way throughout the research. We generated sets of themes from each of our field visits, and discussed these amongst members of our research team and, as noted above, at times with staff from the case studies as well. We selected the theoretical framework of activity theory to analyse our empirical findings, as we felt it offered a unique lens through which organisations that were evolving and undergoing transformation could be studied. The attention paid to history and object-oriented activity enabled us to undertake a deeper, more comprehensive analysis of organisational change. Second, a key theoretical construct we pick up on in our analysis is that activity systems are mediated by cultural artefacts (Cole, 1996; Wertsch, 1991). These mediating artefacts include material tools and technologies, but they also include aspects such as language and cultural modes of working (D'Andrade & Strauss, 1992). In examining global organisations, this is of critical significance, since it allows us to focus both on the strengths and constraints of the technical information system, as well as the local contextual factors that influence the use of information systems, and subsequent flows of knowledge within an organisation.

ANALYSIS OF THE GP CASE

As outlined in the earlier theoretical section, we will now analyse the GP case study from the perspective of the five principles of third-generation activity theory. The entire network of activity systems is taken as the unit of analysis and we then describe the case from the perspective of the remaining four principles: historical analysis, multivoicedness of activity systems, contradictions as potential driving forces for change, and expansive cycles.

History of GP and Computer-Based Knowledge Sharing Tools

GP was a world leader in the discovery, development, manufacture and marketing of prescription medicine, and pharmaceuticals generally. GP also contributed as an organisation to the areas of corporate responsibility and investor relationships. With such a large mandate, it faced the challenge of maintaining uniformity in how its product line was represented by the media, across diverse local sites. Thus, not surprisingly, the global communications team within GP had a critical role in ensuring that a certain standard of information delivery was met in terms of consistent media relations across the globe. Within the larger organisational structure of GP, the communicators group was divided into three subgroupings, namely global, regional and divisional media (the latter referring to the divisions relating to specific health areas, such as vision, infant care, neuroscience and so on).

The rationale behind our selecting the communicators group within GP as the focus of our case study was that it offered an excellent opportunity to examine the balancing of standards-setting on the one hand, and local work priorities on the other. From GP's initial intention to provide its communicator group with a standardised information system across geographic and professional boundaries, as well as its articulated need to harness existing knowledge resources, emerged the call for an integrated information system that would provide the crucial link between its various units. The information system that finally took shape out of this context, which we call ISX, was designed with an interface that supported multiple screens offering parallel information feeds. The services built into it ranged from media enquiries (i.e., local media queries and responses) and news portals, to contacts databases, e-mail and calendar functions.

As an information system, ISX emerged in response to a preceding initiative called Infotool, which was introduced into the organisation without any user consultation. The agency to which this task was outsourced went on to be the design team for ISX. We were informed by them that the design of Infotool was largely concerned with monitoring information flows. This command and control method of operation did not succeed in procuring any buy-in with the local communicators in GP, since its conception, roll-out and implementation lacked context or relevance for the stakeholders concerned. A new challenge emerged from this historical context, and GP's mandate now became to engage all communicators across global sites in a decentralised manner to facilitate a two-way information flow between headquarters and country sites.

To meet this challenge, ISX offered a new collaborative information sharing environment within which all stakeholders could engage. Many of the respondents we spoke to within headquarters were enthusiastic about the potential success of ISX, as they felt that it had direct support from top management and had champions within the organisation who could take it forward, unlike the case with Infotool. A key consideration for ISX then was how to not replicate the mistakes of its precursor, by being more responsive to the contextual demands of its stakeholders, and by focusing on information content rather than just the technology. As a system, it was designed to offer its target group of communicators the ability to channel their work flow through this system (be it personal functions such as e-mail or calendar, or group-related activity such as coordinating media enquiries and news feeds). ISX was rolled out to users both within the setting of their headquarters, as well as a broad range of local sites, with the overall target being to reach 300 users by June 2004. This rolling out process involved installation and training over the phone and/or in person, which was then followed up through feedback sessions, and via the ISX system itself.

Multivoicedness of the Activity System Around ISX

ISX as an *instrument* thus emerged in direct response to a historically accumulated dynamic tension (Il'enkov, 1977). Before it was even designed as a system, ISX contained within it the *object* of the system designers in the GP communicators group, that is, to address the perceived shortcomings of the previous system, but it was not clear to what extent this goal was shared, stable or well-articulated. In other words, there were many voices present in the activity systems around ISX, and this multivoicedness increased as ISX was rolled out across the organisation:

When an activity system adopts a new element from the outside (for example, a new technology or a new object), it often leads to an aggravated secondary contradiction where some old element (for example, the rules or the division of labour) collides with the new one. (Engeström, 2001, p. 137)

The GP case demonstrated precisely this effect with regard to central management's call for more fluid knowledge flows on the one hand, whilst retaining a traditional, structured and hierarchical *division of labour*. When the additional element of a new information system (ISX) was thrown into the mix, the resulting contradictions became clearly evident. A senior project manager articulated the motivations for using the ISX system when she said:

ISX is not merely a tool to track workflows but to more fundamentally "change" workflows...Top management exposure worked more effectively in terms of making people use the system, than any strategy explanations.

So, one element of the multivoicedness surrounding ISX was that the designers and their management backers saw its *object* as both supporting free and lateral knowledge flows as well as central monitoring by top management through gentle coercion to enforce use. These goals are often contradictory, since monitoring and coercion tend to inhibit the freedom of lateral knowledge sharing.

A second element of the multiple voices surrounding the ISX-based activity system came from the local communicators groups around the world. They often saw the *object* of the system as providing them with useful information from head office, but they did not want to take time to communicate the other way, contradicting central management's desire for monitoring and two-way knowledge flows. One member of the communicators group in GP Brazil expressed this frustration:

We need to think globally but I won't have time to do my local job if it is imposed that we feed back everything (to head office). Global (HQ) should help us to act locally. "You have to do that" would not be the best way.'

Interestingly, in activity theory terms, what we see here is a classic example of the tool replacing the original object of activity, and becoming a *substitute object* (Engeström & Escalante, 1996; Hasu & Engeström, 1999). The original object (knowledge sharing) is completely excluded from the discourse, and what occupies the speaker's attention is the tool (ISX) and her mandatory use of it. Thinking in terms of third-generation activity theory (see Figure 2), the object of the ISX-based activity system for its central designers (two-way lateral flows) was not shared by the GP Brazil communicators group activity system, where ISX was viewed as a central management imposition.

Contradictions as a Potential Driving Force for Change

We have seen some of the contradictions that arose after the introduction of the ISX system in GP, for example, in terms of the object of the system from the viewpoint of its designers and local users. Now, activity theorists argue that such contradictions are often the stimulus to change, and we will discuss aspects of this change process a little later in the article. However, first, a further example of contradiction between two activity systems will be given below, with a particular focus on cross-cultural issues arising in a global organisation like GP.

The communicators group (*community*) in GP Japan told us that they were using two mediating information tools in their day-to-day work activity. For communicating with headquarters and within the organisation (globally), they engaged with the

ISX information system, as they had directives from top management to do so. However, for their interactions with local media, they engaged with an internal database, which predated ISX and was in the Japanese language. The justifications offered for this dual use were captured in the following statement by one of the communicators in the Japan office:

Because local journalists only use the Japanese language, to translate material constantly is a slow process. It is additional work. So for us, the Japanese database is consistent and relevant to our local needs as hardly anyone here communicates in English.

The use of two tools emerged as a compromise in this case, where global directives were balanced with local media preferences. A potentially *shared object* that could have emerged here would have been if ISX could have been integrated with the pre-existing Japanese system, making the everyday work of its communicators in the Japan office that much more effective. Whilst the contradiction between the needs of the Japan office and the ISX system was a potential driving force for such a change, as suggested by activity theory, this did not occur during the research period at least.

In addition to language issues in cross-cultural use of ISX, there were matters of technical speed of the ISX system, which further hampered ease of adoption. These concerns were often not articulated or communicated back to HQ, due to the pressure (real or perceived) to appear to be enthusiastic about the global community around ISX, despite serious reservations about it. Furthermore, a member of the GP communicators group, based at headquarters, reflected on the broader reasons why global knowledge-sharing goals in GP were proving problematic:

I am sceptical about technology features enhancing transparency and knowledge-sharing, when the people involved don't want to share. We first

need to build environments within the organisation in which people can trust one another and feel secure.

Building an environment of trust, and changing established hierarchical flows of knowledge and decision making would have involved a much deeper level of change than the designers and project managers of ISX had previously envisioned. In activity theory terms, this would have meant a shift in the *rules* and *division of labour* in the organisation as a whole, something which is much harder to achieve than the mere introduction of a technical tool such as ISX.

Expansive Cycles

A final principle from third-generation activity theory, which was introduced earlier in the theoretical section, is that of *expansive cycles* as possible approaches to the transformation of activity. Engeström describes this in the Helsinki case as involving repeated attempts to resolve contradictions between different activity systems through collaborative attempts, by all the stakeholder groups involved, to rethink the object and motive of the activity to embrace a radically wider horizon of possibilities than in the previous mode of the activity.

How could this concept of expansive cycles have been used in the GP case? It would have involved bringing together representatives from the headquarters and local groups to discuss the contradictions between the activity systems around ISX, as analysed above, and thus to try to arrive at a new definition of what the global-local knowledge sharing activity should involve, and what the role of tools such as ISX should be. Although some interaction did take place between the designers and users of the ISX system, no concerted effort was made along these lines. It is worth noting that Engeström was dealing with a case of *knotworking* between relatively autonomous health care groups, with no central direction. In contrast, GP was a strongly hierarchical organisation, and its top management was unlikely to want to participate in a collaborative discussion of strategy with local stakeholder groups at lower hierarchical levels. We will discuss the issue of expansive cycles further, and possible reasons for their lack of use, in the implications section of the article.

ANALYSIS OF THE LC CASE

We turn now to our second case study, that of LC, and its key mediating tool, namely the electronic mailing list (EML) system. As in the previous section, we will analyse the case through the third-generation activity theory principles of historical analysis, multivoicedness, contradictions as driving forces for change, and expansive cycles. One key point to note before we begin the analysis is that LC, by virtue of being a grassroots open source technology organisation, had a greater reliance on computer-mediated communications to communicate with both internal and external stakeholders than would normally be the case in more traditional organisational contexts.

Historical Evolution of LC Within the Broader Open Source Community

As a not-for-profit organisation, LC served the community of Linux software users, vendors and developers. Its core product was to design and deliver exams which provided individuals with certifications of competence in Linux-based software development. LC was set up in 1999, and was built around three core ideals:

1. **A community defined standard:** Through participatory design and development processes, LC held as a binding goal (*object*) the creation of a standard for Linux certification that would be accepted by its broad *community* of stakeholders;

2. **Peer-reviewed sensibility:** professional status was sought for the LC exams and certifications through a rigorous system of testing and expert review;

3. **Separation of training and testing:** LC did not provide any training; its mandate was solely to provide the testing, thereby aiming to avoid potential conflicts of interest and maintain high standards of quality.

The LC activity system thus emerged in response to a need felt by the wider open source software community for quality standards and globally accepted markers for professionalism. Its EML system in turn emerged to facilitate this goal by providing a collaborative knowledge-sharing environment for the entire LC community, both for internal communications and product (exam) development. More specifically, three lists were designed to meet this need. The first was the LC Exam Development EML, which was the most subscribed to and active with approximately 600 members. It involved the day-to-day work of exam content creation and development. The discussions on this list were frequently raucous and lively. The second list was for LC Staff, thus making it an internal community list of volunteers, contractors, staff (present and past) and Board members. Debates within this list were mainly concerned with organisational and strategic issues. The third list was devoted to public exam development, which again served as a collaborative work space for all who wished to participate in LC work activity. As is evident, there was a significant overlap in membership and participation within the three EMLs.

Arriving on the certification scene as a grassroots organisation with its headquarters in North America, LC grew globally by finding itself affiliates in a very wide range of countries in Europe, Asia, Latin America and Africa. With LC's increasing reach in operations, the EML *instrument* took on a far-reaching mediatory role within the overall activity system. The potential of this tool to bridge geographic boundaries, as well as the merits of low cost, transparency and efficiency, made this the communication medium of choice within the LC community.

Multivoicedness within LC and the EML-Mediated Activity Systems

The LC certification process could at one level be seen as a collective, tool-mediated, object-oriented activity system. However, at another level, third-generation activity theory focuses on networks of activity systems where there are different *subjects* and *communities*, operating through different *rules* and *divisions of labour*, and where *objects* and even *instruments* are not necessarily shared. We begin our analysis of this by noting multiple voices within the EML-mediated activity systems, arising from the diverse histories and positioning of the various participants within the broader LC community. A senior board member and executive of LC used the Staff EML to express his motivations with respect to increasing LC visibility:

My goal is to not just to get LC exposure in the Linux press and the conventional IT media... My target is to get into internationally-read mainstream media ...

Whilst the *object* of increasing LC visibility was widely shared amongst the whole LC community, the suggested *instrument* of using mainstream media was disputed. On the Exam Development EML, there was a strong push for using existing collaborative technical platforms such as wikis, jabber (OS instant messenger), blogs and so on. In the words of one exam developer on the list, these platforms were, '*... where the open source community converged to share knowledge*'.

Apart from the *instrument* through which LC's visibility was to be increased, there were also multiple voices on what staff *community* should

be emphasised in future LC activity. A senior LC executive said on the Staff EML:

Thus far, our volunteers have been entirely driven out of idealism and community spirit, and we have not applied the traditional rules of ... recruitment, retention, recognition, reward. The problem is, as Linux becomes more accepted, the volunteer base is starting to dwindle away.'

One approach to this problem, articulated vigorously within the LC volunteer community, was to develop and strengthen the volunteer base. In contrast, a senior member of the Japanese affiliate, who was also an LC board member, expressed the view that LC's key staff priority should lie elsewhere, that is, not in developing the volunteer base, but in developing management skills and experience:

LC is being run at headquarter level by people who have no management marketing/sales experience. They run the organization on ideological grounds, rather than as a service business .... I feel the biggest challenge we're facing is that there isn't any proper infrastructure. By this I don't mean financial support. I'm talking more about ... the management skill set—which desperately needs to be developed here.

Third-generation activity theory suggests that the multiple voices within the network of activity systems, of which we have given two brief illustrations above, may result in contradictions and conflict. We turn now to examples of this and how they can provide a stimulus to change.

Contradictions as a Source of Change in LC

Engeström (2001, p. 5) refers to contradictions as 'historically accumulating structural tensions within and between activity systems'. This is illustrated quite effectively in the first contradiction we analyse, which refers to the tensions between adhering to an open source ideology that operated at a community level, and maintaining a competitive advantage within the global certification market.

LC's global community was initially bound together by an over-arching ideological affiliation to open source knowledge networks. The 'buy-in' and 'perceived credibility' from the Linux community was a key rallying point for the group in its early days. However, as the organisation matured and widened its reach in the global market, it began to feel a strain on its existing infrastructure. The core LC *object* of staying distribution neutral (being relevant to all Linux systems providers) became a significantly contested point when a senior board member suggested on the EML system that a new family of exams would be developed that were distribution-specific in nature (linked to a particular Linux supplier). This caused a division of two camps within the LC community. On the one side were the purists who felt this would mean drifting away from the core ideology and entering a domain where LC didn't have the resources to compete effectively, nor the inclination (that it might be spreading itself too thin and not providing expertise in any one domain). On the other side, were those more receptive to market pressures, who felt that LC's insistence on sticking to what they described as *'outdated ideological stances'* were against its long-term interest.

Given that LC's exam development still largely remained a product of volunteer work, there was an inherent *contradiction* here, in activity theory terminology, between the LC management group as *subject* and the broader LC stakeholder *community*. The shifting *object*, from the perspective of the former, was from providing a community based standard to competing effectively in a global market. The contradiction with the primarily volunteer workforce then acted as a source for change by identifying the need for a new

management strategy and shift in organisational culture within LC. A reconfiguration was called for, of the organisation's old community-based paradigm, towards a more professional and competitive one.

A second area of contradiction appeared in the tension between LC's need to establish a 'global face', and the competing need for context sensitivity and diversity with regard to its local affiliates. For example, language emerged as a critical factor for the Chinese affiliate, especially within the context of EML-mediated activity. The LC Chinese staff complained about their exclusion from key decision-making processes and exam development sessions on the EML, which were conducted only in English, thereby adding to their feeling of alienation from the organisational 'community'. Both the Chinese and Japanese affiliates mentioned that often the tone, style or content of electronic communication on LC's mailing lists was misunderstood by them, resulting in awkward and tense relations. The style of communication in practice on the EMLs (i.e., language, expression, form) was of an informal nature and the membership was predominantly North American. However, the confusion in sharing knowledge using EMLs was felt even by the European partners, such as the affiliate in the U.K., who said:

The way I see it, communication in particular (is) very frustrating. There is no clear definition of roles. They say they'll e-mail and they don't, and you have to chase people up all over the place.

Thus, moving away from language, we find another global-local source of tension and contradiction on the EML-mediated activity systems, namely the lack of clearly defined roles. Sharing knowledge and sustaining relationships with affiliate partners across far flung sites proved challenging for LC, which relied heavily on electronically-mediated communication. Misunderstandings and frustration emerged when the social and organisational cultures were not effectively mediated on the EML system. Subsequently, from these contradictions, arose the need for change, which was articulated as a call for greater resource allocation for translation, and a more effective facilitation of discussion between global partners on the EML system.

Expansive Cycles

Contradictions such as those discussed above can, according to third-generation activity theory, be a stimulus to an expansive cycle in which all stakeholder groups are involved in rethinking the object and motive of the activity in order to embrace a radically wider horizon of possibilities. In contrast to the GP case, we would argue that elements of this did occur in the LC case, particularly towards the later part of our research period. Indeed, the electronic mailing lists provided a good and well-used forum for debate about some of the important issues described above, such as volunteer labour vs. increasing professionalisation, open source ideology vs. global competitiveness, and global face vs. local sensitivity.

There is an important qualification to this positive message with respect to the potential for open debate in networks of activity systems though electronic media. The forums were particularly effective for the core group of exam developers and headquarters staff who used the resource extensively. Affiliate groups were less well represented on the lists and, as noted earlier, the lists were in English, which acted to largely exclude some stakeholders. In addition, even within common language zones, issues of cultural style and differing roles were sometimes problematic in the LC case. One of the ironies of information systems with a global technological reach is that their cultural reach is often narrower.

In cases where good debate took place, did the 'expansive cycles' result in radically new approaches as suggested by the theory? We have argued above that new approaches were certainly

adopted in some instances, for example, in shifting goals towards professionalisation, although whether they were 'radical' in many instances is debatable. One relatively dramatic change which occurred was the replacement of a key senior executive of the organisation towards the end of the research period. The reasons for this were complex, but it represented an interesting shift, since he was highly vocal on the importance of community-based standards but rather less enthusiastic about issues such as local customisation and professionalisation. His departure could thus be seen as symbolic of a subtle but important change in organisational direction.

IMPLICATIONS FOR THEORY AND PRACTICE

We have applied third-generation activity theory to two cases of knowledge-sharing in global organisations supported by computer-based tools. This is a novel domain for application of the theory, and we believe that we have demonstrated that the sophisticated conceptual tools of the theory are highly relevant to analysing such cases. The cases were rather different in terms of the nature of the organisations studied, one being a traditional hierarchical private sector company, and the other a not-for-profit community-based organisation. However, in both cases, activity theory concepts such as networks of activity systems, multivoicedness, contradictions and expansive cycles could be used to offer insights into the dynamics of the organisations and their use of computer-based systems to support global knowledge-sharing. Thus, our study offers activity theory as a form of theoretical generalisation appropriate to an interpretive study (Walsham, 1995). We hope that other researchers will wish to build on this conceptual basis in future papers.

A specific theoretical area for further investigation was mentioned earlier in the article, namely 'the tool becoming an object'. An intriguing illustration of this was given in the GP case description, where the ISX tool and its use became the focus of attention rather than the original object of knowledge sharing. We can see a similar effect in the LC case, where the EML system for sharing knowledge amongst LC volunteers and staff could be considered to have become something of an object in itself, perhaps at odds with the broader object of increasing LC visibility in the wider global arena. It seems that computer-based systems start as tools or instruments, but may become ends in themselves, not necessarily to the advantage of the organisations they serve. This hypothesis, however, needs further research investigation.

We would argue that third-generation activity theory is not of interest for academic analysis only, but also for supporting practice. It is interesting to note that Engeström's (2001) paper which introduced this version of the theory was related to the project on children's health care in Helsinki, and this was an action-research project which helped to design new approaches to health care in practice. Although we did not adopt a similar hands-on approach in our case studies, we did feed back and discuss our research results with practitioners in both cases, and thus our work undoubtedly influenced aspects of the ongoing activity in our case organisations.

The focus of our article has been on organisations attempting the difficult task of finding a balance between global approaches and standards whilst remaining responsive to local needs. We hope that our analytical approach offers a new way of looking at the issues involved in such a balancing act. However, we are aware that organisations such as GP and LC are not ignorant of the issues and problems involved in using knowledge-sharing approaches and tools which are effective in achieving this balance. They may not express these in activity theory terms, but multivoicedness and contradictions in objectives and motivations are well-recognised issues by those with experience in the area. Why, then, is more effort not directed

to approaches such as expansive cycles which make a major and serious effort to bring diverse stakeholders together to agree policy?

We do not have a simple answer to this question, but we discuss some possible reasons now. As noted above, many organisations such as GP are strongly hierarchical in nature, and have not yet fully tackled the paradox that lateral knowledge sharing requires trust and openness, but this is often deterred by the organisational structure, rules and division of labour of the existing hierarchy. In contrast, the LC case concerned a not-for-profit organisation with a community emphasis and a flatter hierarchy than GP, which had certainly made some progress in developing expansive cycles to achieve a balance of local knowledge within global organisations through widespread EML-mediated participation. However, even here, the voices of some stakeholder groups were muted, for example, through the use of the English language in the electronic mailing lists, and more subtly through the style and form of communication being North American in nature. Organisations such as GP and LC are still struggling to find ways of fully involving stakeholder groups who are more remote from the headquarters organisation. What is clear is that it is much easier to manage and measure 'hard' parameters of an enterprise, such as technology or processes, rather than 'softer' components such as personal interaction, community and culture.

Information and communication technologies offer ways to involve remote stakeholder groups, but global initiatives based around computer-based systems involve significant time and resources. Management is often willing to spend the money on the hardware and software technology, but is less willing to devote significant resources to the 'softer' human issues of involving stakeholder groups, particularly if these groups are in far-flung places such as Brazil and Japan. Mechanisms are needed to encourage dialogue and mediation, supported by senior management backing and substantial resources. Many organisations still seem to subscribe to a form of technological determinism where the technology, in this case, computer-based knowledge-sharing systems, is thought to produce the result of better collaboration by itself. Whilst technology undoubtedly has a key role in global knowledge-sharing initiatives, it is necessary to manage both technology *and* context to be effective (Barrett, Cappleman, Shoib & Walsham, 2004), the latter including aspects such as appropriate incentives to share, and perceived freedom to express views and learn from others.

CONCLUSION

Our initial research question asked how, and with what success, do global organisations design computer-based tools for knowledge sharing aimed to balance standardised approaches against local needs. We have answered the 'how' question in the case descriptions, but the 'success' issue is more problematic. With respect to the GP case, there is no doubt that the ISX system was less successful than its head office designers and implementers intended, since its use was less widespread than they had hoped, and its global reach was limited by factors such as local relevance and cultural fit. However, we would certainly not argue that the ISX tool was a failure. It was used by many communicators across the organisation and provided some degree of global integration amongst the widely-separated groups.

In the LC case, the EML system could be considered to be a success in broad terms, since the mailing lists were the primary medium for core areas such as exam development and also, to a lesser extent, for debate and knowledge sharing between members of the open source community engaged in Linux certification activities. However, global knowledge sharing was less successful in LC when dealing with radically different cultural contexts than its North American headquarters. In both cases, therefore, the emphasis of the use of

instruments tended to be more on global standards and less on local needs. The balance still seemed to be biased towards the centre and less towards the periphery. We have discussed some possible reasons for this in the previous section.

We believe that a key contribution of our article is to show how third-generation activity theory can be used as an analytical approach to increase understanding of these issues of global/local balance. An examination of multivoicedness of activity systems, and contradictions as a potential driving force for change, offer novel ways of viewing the history of events and issues in particular organisations. We also believe that the concept of expansive cycles has much to offer as a way of thinking about approaches to transforming activity through the involvement of all stakeholder groups in the reconceptualisation of the object and motives of the activity. We would add that such reconceptualisations also need to look carefully at the instruments being used in the activity systems, which has been a key focus of this article.

REFERENCES

Barrett, M., Cappleman, S., Shoib, G., & Walsham, G. (2004). Learning in knowledge communities: Managing technology and context. *European Management Journal, 22*(1), 1-11.

Bloomfield, B.P., Coombs, R., Knights, D., & Littler, D. (Eds.). (1997). *Information technology and organisation: Strategies, networks, and integration.* Oxford: Oxford University Press.

Ciborra, C.U. (1994). The grassroots of IT and strategy. In C. Ciborra, & T. Jelassi, (Eds.), *Strategic information systems—European perspective.* Chichester: Wiley.

Ciborra, C.U. (Ed.). (2000). *From control to drift. The dynamics of corporate information infrastructures.* Oxford: Oxford University Press.

Cole, M. (1996). *Cultural psychology: A once and future discipline*. Cambridge, MA: Harvard University Press.

D'Andrade, R.G., & Strauss, C. (Eds.). (1992). *Human motives and cultural models*. Cambridge: Cambridge University Press.

Davenport, T.H. (1998, July-August). Putting the enterprise into the enterprise system. *Harvard Business Review*, 121-131.

Engeström, Y. (1987). *Learning by expanding: An activity-theoretical approach to developmental research*. Helsinki: Orienta-Konsultit.

Engeström, Y. (1996). Interobjectivity, ideality, and dialectics. *Mind, Culture, and Activity, 3*(4), 259-265.

Engeström, Y. (1999). Activity theory and individual and social transformation. In Y. Engeström, R. Miettinen, & R.-L. Punamäki (Eds.), *Perspectives on activity theory*. New York: Cambridge University Press.

Engeström, Y. (2001). Expansive learning at work: Toward an activity theoretical reconceptualization. *Journal of Education and Work, 14*(1), 133-156.

Engeström, Y., Engeström, R., & Kärkkäinen, M. (1995). Polycontextuality and boundary crossing in expert cognition: Learning and problem solving in complex work activities. *Learning and Instruction, 5*(4), 319–336.

Engeström, Y., Engeström, R., & Vähäaho, T. (1999). When the center does not hold: The importance of knotworking. In S. Chaiklin, M. Hedegaard, & U.J. Jensen (Eds.), *Activity theory and social practice*. Aarhus, Denmark: Aarhus University Press.

Engeström, Y., & Escalante, V. (1996). Mundane tool or object of affection? The rise and fall of the postal buddy. In B.A. Nardi (Ed.), *Context and consciousness: Activity theory and human-computer interaction*. Cambridge: The MIT Press.

Ger, G. (1999). Localizing in the global village: Local firms competing in global markets. *California Management Review, 41*(4), 64–83.

Hasu, M., & Engeström, R. (1999). *Measurement in action: An activity-theoretical perspective on producer-user interaction* (Working Paper). Helsinki: University of Helsinki.

Il'enkov, E.V. (1977). *Dialectical logic: Essays in its history and theory*. Moscow: Progress.

Kyng, M., & Mathiassen, L. (Eds.). (1997). *Computers and design in context*. Cambridge, MA: MIT Press.

Leidner, R. (1993). *Fast food, fast talk: Service work and the routinization of everyday life*. Berkeley: University of California Press.

Leont'ev, A.N. (1978). *Activity, consciousness, and personality*. Englewood Cliffs, NJ: Prentice Hall.

Oshri, I., Pan, S.L., & Newell, S. (2006). Managing trade-offs and tensions between knowledge management initiatives and expertise development practices. *Management Learning, 37*(1), 63-82.

Pan, S.L., & Leidner, D.E. (2003). Bridging communities of practice with information technology in pursuit of global knowledge sharing. *Journal of Strategic Information Systems, 12*(1), 71–88.

Rolland, K.H., & Monteiro, E. (2002). Balancing the local and the global in infrastructural information systems. *The Information Society, 18*(2), 87-100.

Sahay, S. (1998). Implementing GIS technology in India: Some issues of time and space. *Accounting, Management and Information Technologies, 8*(2-3), 147-188.

Vygotsky, L.S. (1978). *Mind in society: The development of higher psychological processes.* Cambridge: Harvard University Press.

Walsham, G. (1993). *Interpreting information systems in organisation.* Chichester, UK: Wiley.

Walsham, G. (1995). Interpretive case studies in IS research: Nature and method. *European Journal of Information Systems, 4*(2), 74-81.

Wertsch, J.V. (1991). *Voices of the mind: A socio-cultural approach to mediated action.* Cambridge: Harvard University Press.

This work was previously published in Journal of Global Information Management, Vol. 15, Issue 3, edited by F. B. Tan, pp. 1-19, copyright 2007 by IGI Publishing, formerly known as Idea Group Publishing (an imprint of IGI Global).

Chapter XVIII
Global Information Ethics:
The Importance of Being Environmentally Earnest

Luciano Floridi
Università degli Studi di Bari, Italy & Oxford University, UK

ABSTRACT

The article argues that Information Ethics (IE) can provide a successful approach for coping with the challenges posed by our increasingly globalized reality. After a brief review of some of the most fundamental transformations brought about by the phenomenon of globalization, the article distinguishes between two ways of understanding Global Information Ethics, as an ethics of global communication or as a global-information ethics. It is then argued that cross-cultural, successful interactions among micro and macro agents call for a high level of successful communication, that the latter requires a shared ontology friendly towards the implementation of moral actions, and that this is provided by IE. There follows a brief account of IE and of the ontic trust, the hypothetical pact between all agents and patients presupposed by IE.

INTRODUCTION: FROM GLOBALIZATION TO INFORMATION ETHICS

Globalization is a phenomenon too complex even to sketch in this brief introduction.[1] So I hope that I shall be forgiven if I am rather casual about many features that would deserve full attention in another context. Here, I wish to highlight just six key transformations characterising the processes of globalization. I shall label them *contraction, expansion, porosity, hybridization, synchronization,* and *correlation*. They provide the essential background for making sense of the thesis developed in the rest of the article, which is that Information Ethics (IE) can provide a successful approach for coping with the challenges posed by our increasingly globalized reality.

Contraction

The world has gone through alternating stages of globalization, growing and shrinking, for as long as humanity can remember. Here is a reminder:

In some respects the world economy was more integrated in the late 19th century than it is today. ... Capital markets, too, were well integrated. Only in the past few years, indeed, have international capital flows, relative to the size of the world economy, recovered to the levels of the few decades before the first world war. (The Economist, 1997)

The truth is that, after each "globalization backlash" (think of the end of the Roman or British Empires), the world never really went back to its previous state. Rather, by moving two steps forward and one step back, sometime towards the end of the last century the process of globalization reached a point of no return. Today, revolutions or the collapse of empires can never shrink the world again, short of the complete unravelling of human life as we know it. Globalization is here to stay.

Globalization has become irreversible mainly thanks to radical changes in worldwide transport and communications (Brandt & Henning, 2002). Atoms and bytes have been moving increasingly rapidly, frequently, cheaply, reliably, and widely for the past 50 years or so. This dramatic acceleration has shortened the time required for any interactions: economic exchanges, financial transactions, social relations, information flows, movements of people, and so forth (Hodel, Holderegger & Lüthi, 1998). And this acceleration has meant a more condensed life and a contracted physical space. Ours is a smaller world, in which one may multitask fast enough to give and have the impression of leading parallel lives. We may regain a nineteenth-century sense of distance (space) and duration (time) only if one day we travel to Mars.

Expansion

Human space in the twenty-first century has not merely shrunk, though. ICTs have also created a new digital environment, which is constantly expanding and becoming progressively more diverse. Again, the origins of this global, transnational common space are old. They are to be found in the invention of recording and communication technologies that range from the alphabet to printing, from photography to television. But it is only in the last few decades that we have witnessed a vast and steady migration of human life to the other side of the screen. When you ask, "Where were you?," it is now normal and common to receive the answer "Online". More than 6 million people throughout the world play *World of Warcraft*, currently the leading subscription-based MMORPG (massively multiplayer online role-playing game, http://www.blizzard.com/press/060119.shtml). Globalization also means the emergence of this sort of single virtual space, sharable in principle by anyone, any time, anywhere.

Porosity

An important relation between our contracting physical space and our expanding, virtual environment is that of *porosity*. Imagine living as a flat figure on the surface of an endless cylinder. You could travel on the surface of the cylinder as a two-dimensional space, but not through it. So in order to reach any other point on the cylinder, the best you could do would be to follow the shortest path (geodesic) on the cylindrical surface. The empty space inside the cylinder would be inconceivable, as a third dimension would. Imagine now that the surface became porous and hence that a third dimension were added. The geodesics would be revolutionized, for you could travel through the vacuum encircled by the cylinder and reach the other side, thus significantly shortening your journeys. To use the rather apt vocabulary of surfing, you would be *tubing*: space would be curling over you, forming a "tube", with you inside the cylindrical space. From a 2D perspective, you would literally come in and out of space. This sort of porosity characterizes the relation now between physical and virtual space. It is difficult to say where one is when one is "tubing", but we know that we can travel through cyberspace to interact with other physical places in a way that would have been inconceivable only a few decades ago. Telepresence (Floridi, 2005) in our porous environment is an ordinary experience and this is also what globalization means.

Hybridization

During the last decade or so, we have become accustomed to conceptualize our life online as a mixture between an evolutionary adaptation of analogue/carbon-based agents to a digital/silicon-based environment, and a form of postmodern, neocolonization of the latter by the former. This is probably a mistake. The threshold between *analogue-carbon-offline-here* and *digital-silicon-online-there* is fast becoming blurred, but this is as much to the advantage of the latter as it is of the former. Adapting Horace's famous phrase[2], "captive cyberspace is conquering its victor". ICTs are as much re-ontologising (that is, modifying the essential nature of) our world as they are creating new realities. The digital is spilling over into the analogue and merging with it. This recent phenomenon is variously known as "ubiquitous computing", "ambient intelligence", or "the Internet of things" (ITU report, November 2005, http://www.itu.int/internetofthings), and it

is, or will soon be, the next stage in the digital revolution. In the (fast approaching) future, objects will be *ITentities* able to learn, advise, and communicate with each other. "RoboticCookware" is already available (http://www.vitacraft.com.nyud.net:8090/rfiq/home.html); MP3 players will soon be able to recommend new music to their users by learning from the tunes they (the users, we had better be clear) enjoyed (http://www.semanticaudio.com/). Your next fridge (http://www.lginternetfamily.co.uk/homenetwork.asp) will inherit from the previous one your tastes and wishes, just as your new laptop can import your favourite settings from the old one; and it will interact with your new way of cooking and with the supermarket Web site, just as your laptop can talk to a printer or to another computer. We have all known this in theory for some time; the difference is that it is now actually happening in our kitchen.

Globalization also means the emergence of this common, fully interactive, and responsive environment of wireless, pervasive, distributed, *a2a* (anything to anything) information processes, that works *a4a* (anywhere for any time), in real time. We are probably the last generation to experience a clear difference between *onlife* and *online*.

Synchronization

In a world in which information and material flows are becoming so tightly integrated and enmeshed, it is not surprising to see global patterns emerging not only from well-orchestrated operations (consider the tedious experience of any launch of a major blockbuster, with interviews in magazines, discussions on TV programs, advertisements of merchandise, and by-products throughout the world, special food products in supermarkets and fast-food, etc.), but also inadvertently, as the result of the accidental synchronization of otherwise chaotic trends.

All of a sudden, the world reads the same novel, or wears the same kind of trousers, or listens to the same music, or eats the same sort of food, or is concerned about the same problems, or cherishes the same news, or is convinced that it has the same disease. Some of this need not be the effect of any plan by some Big Brother, a secret agency, a powerful multinational or any other *deus ex machina* that is scheming behind the curtains. After all, worldwide attention span is very limited and flimsy, and it is very hard to compete for it. The truth is that at least some global trends may merely arise from the constructive interference of waves of information that accidentally come into phase, and hence reinforce each other to the point of becoming global, through the casual and entirely contingent interaction of chaotic forces. It may happen with the stock markets or the fashion industry or dietary trends. The recurrent emergence of temporarily synchronized patterns of human behaviour, both transculturally and transnationally, is a clear sign of globalization, but not necessarily of masterminded organization. There is no intelligent plan, evil intention, autonomy, or purposeful organization in the billion snowflakes that become an avalanche. Social group behaviour is acquiring a global meaning. The distributed power that generates Wikipedia is the other side of the dark, mindless stupidity of millions of slaves of fashions and trends.

Correlation

Imagine a safety net, like the one used in a circus. If it is sufficiently tight and robust, the heavier the object that falls into it, the larger the area of the net that will be stretched, sending waves of vibration throughout the net. Globalization also refers to the emergence of a comparable net of correlations among agents all over the world, which is becoming so tight and sensitive that the time lag in the transmission of the effects of an event "dropping" on it is fast shortening, to the point that sometimes there is almost no distinction between what counts as local or remote. Global often means not everywhere but actually delocalized, and in a delocalized environment social friction is inevitable, as there is no more room for agents that allows for absorption of the effects of their decisions and actions. If anyone moves, the global boat rocks.

GLOBALISING ETHICS

If we consider now the profound transformations just sketched, it would be rather surprising if they did not have serious implications for our moral lives (see Ess, 2002; Weckert, 2001). In a reality that is more and more physically contracted, virtually expanded, porous, hybridized, synchronized, and correlated, the very nature of moral interactions, and hence of their ethical analysis, is significantly altered. Innovative forms of agenthood are becoming possible; new values are developing and old ones are being reshaped; cultural and moral assumptions are ever more likely to come into contact when not into conflict; the very concepts of what constitutes our "natural" environment and our enhanced features as a biological species are changing; and unprecedented ethical challenges have arisen (a reference to the notorious problem of privacy is *de rigueur* here), just to mention some macroscopic transformations in which globalization factors, as sketched above, play an important role.

What sort of ethical reflection can help us to cope successfully with a world that is undergoing such dramatic changes? Local approaches are as satisfactory as burying one's head in home values and traditions. The ethical discourse appears to be in need of an upgrade to cope with a globalized world. Each ethical theory is called upon to justify its worldwide and cross-cultural suitability. This seems even more so if the theory in question seeks to address explicitly the new moral issues that arise from the digital revolution, as it is the case with IE.

I shall say more about IE in the next two sections. The specific question that I wish to address is whether, in a world that is fast becoming more and more globalized, information ethics can provide a successful approach for dealing with its new challenges. I shall argue in favour of a positive answer. But to make my case, let me first clarify what *global information ethics* may mean.

GLOBAL-COMMUNICATION ETHICS VS. GLOBAL-INFORMATION ETHICS

There are at least two ways of understanding Global Information Ethics: as an *ethics of global communication* (Smith, 2002) or as a *global-information ethics* (Bynum & Rogerson, 1996). Since I shall concentrate only on the latter, let me briefly comment on the former first.

Global-information ethics, understood as an ethics of worldwide communication, may be seen as a commendable effort to foster all those informational conditions that facilitate participation, dialogue, negotiation, and consensus-building practices among people, across cultures and through generations. It is an approach concerned with new and old problems, caused or exacerbated by global communications or affecting the flow of information. Global-communication ethics is therefore a continuation of policy by other means, and it does not have to be reduced to a mere gesture towards the importance of mutual respect and understanding (meeting people and talking to each other can hardly do any harm and often helps). It is, however, faced by the serious problem of providing its own justification. What sort of ethical principles of communication and information are to be privileged and why? Is there any macroethics (e.g., some form of consequentialism or deontologism or contractualism) that can rationally buttress a global-communication ethics? And is not any attempt at providing such a macroethics just another instance of "globalization" of some values and principles to the disadvantage of others? Without decent theorization, the

risk is that we will reduce goodness to goodiness and transform the ethical discourse into some generic, well-meant sermon. At the same time, a robust foundation for a global-communication ethics may easily incur the problem of failing to respect and appreciate a plurality of diverse positions. The dilemma often seems to be left untouched, even when it is not overlooked. The good news is that it may be possible to overcome it by grounding a global-communication ethics on a global-information ethics.

GLOBAL-INFORMATION ETHICS AND THE PROBLEM OF THE LION

If we look at the roots of the problem, it seems that:

1. In an increasingly globalized world, successful interactions among micro and macro agents belonging to different cultures call for a high level of successful communication; but

2. Successful, cross-cultural communications among agents require, in their turn, not only the classic three "e"s—*embodiment, embeddedness* and hence *experience* (a sense of "us-here-now")—but also a shared *ontology* (more on this presently); and yet

3. Imposing a uniform ontology on all agents only seems to aggravate the problem, globalization becoming synonymous with ontological imperialism.

By "ontology" I do not mean to refer here to any metaphysical theory of being, of what there is or there is not, of why there is what there is, or of the ultimate nature of reality in itself. All this would require a form of epistemological realism (some confidence in some privileged access to the essential nature of things) that I do not hold, and that, fortunately, is not necessary to make my case. Rather, I am using "ontology" to cover the outcome of a variety of processes that allow an agent to appropriate (be successfully embedded in), semanticize (give meaning to and make sense of), and conceptualize (order, understand, and explain) the agent's environment. In simplified terms, one's ontology is one's world; that is, the world as it appears to, is experienced and interacted with, by the agent in question.[3]

Agents can talk to each others only if they can partake to some degree in a shared ontology anchored to a common reality to which they can all refer.[4]

Imagine two solipsistic minds, α and β, disembodied, unembedded, and devoid of any experience. Suppose them living in two entirely different universes. Even if α and β could telepathically exchange their data, they could still not *communicate* with each other, for there would be absolutely nothing that would allow the receiver to interpret the sender. In fact, it would not even be clear whether any message was being exchanged at all.

The impossibility of communication between α and β is what Wittgenstein (2001) had in mind, I take it, when he wrote that "if a lion could talk, we could not understand him." The statement is obviously false (because we share with lions a similar form of embeddedness and embodiment, and hence experiences like hunger or pain) if one fails to realize that the lion is only a placeholder to indicate an agent utterly and radically different from us, like our α and β. The lion is a Martian, someone you simply cannot talk to because it is "from another ontology".[5]

From this perspective, the famous phrase *hic sunt leones* (here there are lions) acquires a new meaning. The phrase occurred on Roman maps to indicate unknown and unexplored regions beyond the southern African borders of the empire.[6] In a Wittgensteinian sense, the Romans were mapping the threshold beyond which no further communication was possible at all. They were drawing the limits of their ontology. What was beyond the border, the *locus* inhabited by the lions, was nothing, a nonplace. Globalization has often meant that what is not inglobate simply is not, that is, fails to exist.

We can now formulate the difficulty confronting a global-information ethics as *the problem of the lion*: cross-cultural communication, which is the necessary condition for any further moral interaction, is possible only if the interlocutors partake in a common ontology. When Crusoe and Friday meet, after 25 years of Crusoe's solitude, they can begin to communicate with each other only because they share the most basic ontology of life and death, food and shelter, fear and safety. Agents may be strangers to each other ("stranger" being an indexical qualification[7]). They do not have to speak the same language, empathize, or sympathize. But they do need to share at least some basic appropriation, semanticization, and conceptualization of their common environment, as a minimal condition for the possibility of any further moral interaction.

Can information ethics provide a solution to the problem of the lion? The short answer is yes; the long one is more complicated and requires a brief diversion, since it is now necessary to be more explicit about what I mean by information ethics.

GLOBAL INFORMATION-ETHICS AND ITS ADVANTAGES

Information ethics[8] is an *ontocentric, patient-oriented, ecological* macroethics. An intuitive way to unpack this definition is by comparing IE to other environmental approaches.

Biocentric ethics usually grounds its analysis of the moral standing of bio-entities and eco-systems on the intrinsic worthiness of *life* and the intrinsically negative value of *suffering*. It seeks to develop a patient-oriented ethics in which the "patient" may be not only a human being, but also any form of life. Indeed, land ethics extends the concept of patient to any component of the environment, thus coming close to the approach defended by information ethics. Any form of life is deemed to enjoy some essential proprieties or moral interests that deserve and demand to be respected, at least minimally if not absolutely, that is, in a possibly overridable sense, when contrasted to other interests. So biocentric ethics argues that the nature and well-being of the patient of any action constitute (at least partly) its moral standing and that the latter makes important claims on the interacting agent, claims that in principle ought to contribute to guiding the agent's ethical decisions and constraining the agent's moral behaviour. The "receiver" of the action is placed at the core of the ethical discourse, as a centre of moral concern, while the "transmitter" of any moral action is moved to its periphery.

Now substitute "existence" for "life" and it should become clear what IE amounts to. IE is an ecological ethics that replaces *biocentrism* with *ontocentrism*. It suggests that there is something even more elemental than life, namely *being*—that is, the existence and flourishing of all entities and their global environment—and something more fundamental than suffering, namely *entropy*. The latter is most emphatically *not* the physicists' concept of thermodynamic entropy. Entropy here refers to any kind of *destruction* or *corruption* of entities understood as informational objects (not as semantic information, take note), that is, any form of impoverishment of *being*, including *nothingness*, to phrase it more metaphysically.[9]

We are now ready to appreciate some of the main advantages offered by information ethics when it comes to the new challenges posed by globalization.

1. Embracing the New Informational Ontology

Not only do we live in a world that is moving towards a common informational ontology, we also experience our environment and talk and make sense of our experiences in increasingly informational ways. *Information is the medium.* This calls for an ethics, like IE, that, by prioritising an informational ontology, may provide a valuable approach to decoding current moral phenomena and orienting our choices.

2. Sharing a Minimal, Horizontal, Lite Ontology

There is a risk, by adopting an ontocentric perspective, as IE suggests, that one may be merely exchanging one form of "centrism" (American, Athenian, Bio, European, Greek, Male, Western, you-name-it) with just another, perhaps inadvertently, thus failing to acknowledge the ultimate complexity, diversity, and fragility of the multicultural, ethical landscape with which one is interacting. We saw how the problem of the lion may become a dilemma. This justified concern, however, does not apply here because IE advocates a *minimal* informational ontology, which is not only timely, as we have just seen, but also tolerant of, and interfaceable with, other local ontologies. Thick cultures with robust, vertical ontologies—that is, deeply-seated, often irreconcilable, fundamental conceptions about human nature, the value and meaning of life, the nature of the universe and our place in it, society and its fair organization, religious beliefs, and so forth—can more easily interact with each other if they can share a lite, horizontal ontology as little committed to any particular *Weltanshaung* as possible. The identification of an absolute, ultimate, monistic ontology, capable of making all other ontologies merge, is just a myth, and a violent one at that. There is no such thing as a commitment-free position with respect to the way in which a variety of continuously changing agents appropriate, conceptualize, and semanticize their environment. Yet the alternative cannot be some form of relativism. This is no longer sustainable in a globalized world in which choices, actions, and events are delocalized. There simply is not enough room for "minding one's own business" in a network in which the behaviour of each node may affect the behaviour of all nodes. The approach to be pursued seems rather to be along the lines of what IE proposes: respect for and tolerance towards diversity and pluralism and identification of a minimal common ontology, which does not try to be platform independent (i.e., absolute), but cross-platform (i.e., portable).

As in Queneau's *Exercises in Style*, we need to be able to appreciate both the ninety-nine variations of the same story[10] and the fact that it is after all the same story that is being recounted again and again. This plurality of narratives need not turn into a Babel of fragmented voices. It may well be a source of pluralism that enriches one's ontology. More eyes simply see better and appreciate more angles, and a thousand languages can express semantic nuances that no global Esperanto may ever hope to grasp.

3.   Informational Environmentalism

The ontocentrism supported by IE means that at least some of the weight of the ethical interpretations may be carried by (outsourced to) the informational ontology shared by the agents, not only by the different cultural or intellectual traditions (vertical ontologies) to which they may belong. Two further advantages are that all agents, whether human, artificial, social or hybrid, may be able to share the same minimal ontology and conceptual vocabulary; and then that any agent may take into account ecological concerns that are not limited to the biosphere.

4.   Identifying the Sources and Targets of Moral Interactions

One of the serious obstacles in sharing an ontology is often how the sources and targets of moral interactions (including communication) are identified. The concept of person or human individual, and the corresponding features that are considered essential to his or her definition, might be central in some ontologies, marginal in others, and different in most. IE may help foster communication and fruitful interactions among different, thick, vertical ontologies by approaching the problem with conceptual tools that are less precommitted. For when IE speaks of agents and

patients, these are neutral elements in the ethical analysis that different cultures or macro-ethics may be able to appropriate, enrich, and make more complex, depending on their conceptual requirements and orientations. It is like having an ontology of agency that is open source, and that anyone can adapt to its own proprietary *Weltanshaung*.

THE COST OF A GLOBAL-INFORMATION ETHICS: POSTULATING THE ONTIC TRUST

It would be silly to conclude at this point that a global-information ethics may provide an answer to any challenge posed by the various phenomena of globalization. This would be impossible. Of course, there will be many issues and difficulties that will require substantial extensions and adaptations of IE, of its methodology and of its principles. All I have tried to do is to convince the reader that such a great effort to apply IE as a global ethics would be fruitful and hence worth making.

It would be equally wrong to assume that the adoption of IE as a fruitful approach to global challenges may come at no conceptual cost. Every ethical approach requires some concession on the part of those who decide to share it and IE is no exception.

The cost imposed by IE is summarizable in terms of the postulation of what I shall define as the *ontic trust* binding agents and patients. A straightforward way of clarifying the concept of ontic trust is by drawing an analogy with the concept of "social contract".

Various forms of contractualism (in ethics) and contractarianism (in political philosophy) argue that moral obligation, the duty of political obedience, or the justice of social institutions, have their roots in, and gain their support from a so-called "social contract". This may be a real, implicit, or *merely hypothetical* agreement between the parties constituting a society (e.g., the people and the sovereign, the members of a community, or the individual and the state). The parties accept to agree to the terms of the contract and thus obtain some rights in exchange for some freedoms that, allegedly, they would enjoy in a hypothetical state of nature. The rights and responsibilities of the parties subscribing to the agreement are the terms of the social contract, whereas the society, state, group, an so forth, are the entity created for the purpose of enforcing the agreement. Both rights and freedoms are not fixed and may vary, depending on the interpretation of the social contract.

Interpretations of the theory of the social contract tend to be highly (and often unknowingly) anthropocentric (the focus is only on human rational agents) and stress the coercive nature of the agreement. These two aspects are not characteristic of the concept of ontic trust, but the basic idea of a fundamental agreement between parties as a foundation of moral interactions is sensible. In the case of the ontic trust, it is transformed into a primeval, entirely hypothetical *pact*, logically predating the social contract, which all agents cannot but sign when they come into existence, and that is constantly renewed in successive generations.[11] The sort of pact in question can be understood more precisely in terms of an actual trust.

Generally speaking, a trust in the English legal system is an entity in which someone (the trustee) holds and manages the former assets of a person (the trustor, or donor) for the benefit of certain persons or entities (the beneficiaries). Strictly speaking, nobody owns the assets. Since the trustor has donated them, the trustee has only legal ownership and the beneficiary has only equitable ownership. Now, the logical form of this sort of agreement can be used to model the ontic trust, in the following way:

- The assets or "corpus" is represented by the world, including all existing agents and patients;

- The donors are all past and current *generations* of agents;
- the trustees are all current *individual* agents;
- The beneficiaries are all current and future *individual* agents and patients.

By coming into being, an agent is made possible thanks to the existence of other entities. It *is* therefore bound to all that already is both *unwillingly* and *inescapably*. It *should be* so also *caringly*. Unwillingly, because no agent wills itself into existence, though every agent can, in theory, will itself out of it. Inescapably, because the ontic bond may be broken by an agent only at the cost of ceasing to exist as an agent. Moral life does not begin with an act of freedom but it may end with one. *Caringly* because participation in reality by any entity, including an agent—that is, the fact that any entity is an expression of what exists—provides a right to existence and an invitation (not a duty) to respect and take care of other entities. The pact then involves no coercion, but a mutual relation of appreciation, gratitude, and care, which is fostered by the recognition of the dependence of all entities on each other. A simple example may help to clarify further the meaning of the ontic trust.

Existence begins with a gift, even if possibly an unwanted one. A foetus will be initially only a beneficiary of the world. Once it is born and has become a full moral agent, it will be, as an individual, both a beneficiary and a trustee of the world. It will be in charge of taking care of the world, and, insofar as it is a member of the generation of living agents, it will also be a donor of the world. Once dead, it will leave the world to other agents after it and thus becomes a member of the generation of donors. In short, the life of an agent becomes a journey from being only a beneficiary to being only a donor, passing through the stage of being a responsible trustee of the world. We begin our career of moral agents as strangers to the world; we should end it as friends of the world.

The obligations and responsibilities imposed by the ontic trust will vary depending on circumstances but, fundamentally, the expectation is that actions will be taken or avoided in view of the welfare of the whole world.

The ontic trust is what is postulated by the approach supported by IE. According to IE, the ethical discourse concerns any entity, understood informationally, that is, not only all persons, their cultivation, well-being, and social interactions, not only animals, plants, and their proper natural life, but also anything that exists, from buildings and other artefacts to rivers and sand. Indeed, according to IE, nothing is too humble to deserve no respect at all. In this way, IE brings to ultimate completion the process of enlargement of the concept of what may count as a centre of a (no matter how minimal) moral claim, which now includes every instance of *being* understood informationally, no matter whether physically implemented or not. IE holds that every entity, as an expression of *being*, has a dignity, constituted by its mode of existence and essence (the collection of all the elementary proprieties that constitute it for what it is), which deserve to be respected (at least in a minimal and overridable sense) and hence place moral claims on the interacting agent and ought to contribute to guiding and constraining the agent's ethical decisions and behaviour. The ontic trust (and the corresponding ontological equality principle among entities) means that any form of reality (any instance of information/*being*), simply by the fact of *being* what it is, enjoys a minimal, initial, overridable, equal right to exist and develop in a way which is appropriate to its nature.[12]

The acceptance of the ontic trust requires a disinterested judgement of the moral situation from an objective perspective, that is, a perspective which is as non-anthropocentric as possible. Moral behaviour is less likely without this epistemic virtue. The ontic trust is respected whenever actions are impartial, universal and "caring" towards the world.

CONCLUSION

One of the objections that is sometimes made against IE is that of being too abstract or theoretical to be of much use when human agents are confronted by very concrete and applied challenges (Siponen, 2004). Unfortunately, this is an obvious misunderstanding. Imagine someone who, being presented with the declaration of human rights, were to complain that it is too general and inapplicable to solve the ethical problems the person is facing in a specific situation, say in dealing with a particular case of cyberstalking in the company that employs the person. This would be rather out of place. The suspicion is that some impatience with conceptual explorations may betray a lack of understanding of how profound the revolution we are undergoing is, and hence how radical the rethinking of our ethical approaches and principles may need to be in order to cope with it. IE is certainly not the declaration of human rights, but it seeks to obtain a level of generality purporting to provide a foundation for more applied and case-oriented analyses. So the question is not whether IE is too abstract—good foundations for the structure one may wish to see being built inevitably lie well below the surface—but whether it will succeed in providing the robust framework within which practical issues of moral concern may be more easily identified, clarified, and solved. I agree that it is in its actual applications that IE, as a global ethics for our information society, will or will not qualify as a useful approach; yet the need to build on the foundation provided by IE is an opportunity, not an objection.

REFERENCES

Brandt, D., & Henning, K. (2002). Information and communication technologies: Perspectives and their impact on society. *AI & Society, 16*(3), 210-223.

Bynum, T. W., & Rogerson, S. (1996). Global information ethics: Introduction and overview. *Science and Engineering Ethics, 2*(2), 131-136.

The Economist. (1997, December 18). 1897 and 1997: The century the earth stood still.

Ess, C. (2002). Computer-mediated colonization, the renaissance, and educational imperatives for an intercultural global village. *Ethics and Information Technology, 4*(1), 11-22.

Floridi, L. (2005). Presence: From epistemic failure to successful observability. *Presence: Teleoperators and virtual environments, 14*(6), 656-667.

Floridi, L. (in press). Information ethics. In J. van den Hoven & J. Weckert (Eds.), *Moral philosophy and information technology.* Cambridge: Cambridge University Press.

Floridi, L., & Sanders, J. W. (2004). The method of abstraction. In M. Negrotti (Ed.), *Yearbook of the artificial. Nature, culture and technology. Models in contemporary sciences* (pp. 177-220). Bern: Peter Lang.

Floridi, L., & Sanders, J. W. (in press). *Levelism and the method of abstraction.* Manuscript submitted for publication.

Held, D., & McGrew, A. (2001). Globalization. In J. Krieger (Ed.), *Oxford companion to politics of the world.* Oxford/New York: Oxford University Press. Retrieved January 25, 2007, from http://www.polity.co.uk/global/globocp.htm

Held, D., McGrew, A., Goldblatt, D., & Perraton, J. (1999). *Global transformations: Politics, economics and culture.* Cambridge: Polity Press.

Hodel, T. B., Holderegger, A., & Lüthi, A. (1998). Ethical guidelines for a networked world under construction. *Journal of Business Ethics, 17*(9-10), 1057-1071.

Siponen, M. (2004). A pragmatic evaluation of the theory of information ethics. *Ethics and Information Technology, 6*(4), 279-290.

Smith, M. M. (2002). Global information ethics: A mandate for professional education. In *Proceedings of the 68th IFLA Council and General Conference,* Glasgow. Retrieved January 25, 2007, from http://www.ifla.org/IV/ifla68/papers/056-093e.pdf.

Weckert, J. (2001). Computer ethics: Future directions. *Ethics and Information Technology, 3*(2), 93-96.

Wittgenstein, L. (2001). *Philosophical investigations: The German text with a revised English translation* (3rd ed.). Oxford: Blackwell.

ENDNOTES

[1] For a very synthetic but well-balanced and informed overview, I would recommend Held and McGrew (2001). In their terminology, I am a subscriber to the transformationalist approach, according to which "globalization does not simply denote a shift in the extensity or scale of social relations and activity. Much more significantly, argue the transformationalists, it also involves the spatial re-organization and re-articulation of economic, political, military and cultural power" (see Held et al., 1999).

[2] *Graecia capta ferum victorem cepit-* Epistles.

[3] How an ontology is achieved and what sort of philosophical analysis is required to make sense of its formation is not a relevant matter in this context, but the interested reader may wish to see Floridi and Sanders (in press).

[4] More technically, this means that two agents can communicate only if they share at least some possible level of abstraction.

On the method of abstraction see Floridi and Sanders (2004) and Floridi and Sanders (in press).

5   If it took endless time and efforts to decipher the hieroglyphics, imagine what sense an extraterrestrial being could make of a message in a bottle like the plaque carried by the Pioneer spacecraft (http://spaceprojects.arc.nasa.gov/Space_Projects/pioneer/PN10&11.html)

6   Unfortunately, we do not have African maps drawn from the "lions' perspective". The Da Ming Hun Yi Tu, or Amalgamated Map of the Great Ming Empire, the oldest map of Africa known so far, dates back "only" to 1389.

7   Indexical expressions, such as "here", "yesterday", or "I", acquire their meaning or reference depending on who utters them and in which circumstances. Thus, "stranger" is indexical (people are strangers to each others), whereas the original meaning of "barbarian" is not, if we believe its Greek etymology to be "to babble confusedly", that is, someone who is unable to speak Greek properly.

8   The IEG, a research group in Oxford, has developed a general interpretation of Information Ethics in a series of papers. Here I provide a summary based on Floridi [in press]. The interested reader is invited to check the Web site of the group at http://web.comlab.ox.ac.uk/oucl/research/areas/ieg/.

9   Destruction is to be understood as the complete annihilation of the object in question, which ceases to exist; compare this to the process of "erasing" an entity irrevocably.

Corruption is to be understood as a form of pollution or depletion of some of the properties of the object, which ceases to exist as that object and begins to exist as a different object minus the properties that have been corrupted or eliminated. This may be compared to a process degrading the integrity of the object in question.

10   On a crowded bus, a narrator observes a young man with a long neck in a strange hat yell at another man whom he claims is deliberately jostling him whenever anyone gets on or off the bus. The young man then sits down in a vacant seat. Two hours later the same narrator sees that same young man with another friend, who is suggesting that the young man have another button put on his overcoat.

11   There are important and profound ways of understanding this *Ur-pact* religiously, especially but not only in the Judeo-Christian tradition, where the parties involved are God and Israel or humanity, and their old or new *covenant* (διαθήχη) makes it easier to include environmental concerns and values otherwise overlooked from the strongly anthropocentric perspective *prima facie* endorsed by contemporary contractualism. However, it is not my intention to endorse or even draw on such sources. I am mentioning the point here in order to shed some light both on the origins of contractualism and on a possible way of understanding the onto-centric approach advocated by IE.

12   In the history of philosophy, a similar view can be found advocated by Stoic and Neo-platonic philosophers, and by Spinoza.

This work was previously published in Int. Journal of Technology and Human Interactionm, Vol. 3, Issue 3, edited by B. C. Stahl, pp. 1-11, copyright 2007 by IGI Publishing, formerly known as Idea Group Publishing (an imprint of IGI Global).

Chapter XIX
Envisioning a National E–Medicine Network Architecture in a Developing Country:
A Case Study

Fikreyohannes Lemma
Addis Ababa University, Ethiopia

Mieso K. Denko
University of Guelph, Canada

Joseph K. Tan
Wayne State University, USA

Samuel Kinde Kassegne
San Diego State University, USA

ABSTRACT

Poor infrastructures in developing countries such as Ethiopia and much of Sub-Saharan Africa have caused these nations to suffer from lack of efficient and effective delivery of basic and extended medical and healthcare services. Often, such limitation is further accompanied by low patient-doctor ratios, resulting in unwarranted rationing of services. Apparently, e-medicine awareness among both governmental policy makers and private health professionals is motivating the gradual adoption of technological innovations in these countries. It is argued, however, that there still is a gap between current e-medicine efforts in developing countries and the existing connectivity infrastructure leading to faulty, inefficient and expensive designs. The particular case of Ethiopia, one such developing country where e-medicine continues to carry significant promises, is investigated and reported in this article.

INTRODUCTION

Healthcare consumers in general tend to seek access to affordable health services that will meet their needs. From an ethical standpoint, healthcare has to be available when and where consumers need it; physical separation between consumers and healthcare facilities must not pose severe limitations on the delivery of efficient healthcare, even if patients are located in remote areas. In this sense, information and communications technology (ICT) has been demonstrated to offer a competitive choice for accessing affordable and effective health services, especially when access is difficult and limited (Horsch & Balbach, 1999; Kirigia, Seddoh, Gatwiri, Muthuri, & Seddoh, 2005; Tan, Kifle, Mbarika, & Okoli, 2005). More recently, with the continued maturity of network such as Integrated Services Digital Network (ISDN) and Asynchronous Transfer Mode (ATM) networks and related technologies (Perednia & Allen, 1995; Tan, 2001), e-medicine implementation has entered a stage where both the health providers and consumers can now benefit significantly.

IT-based horizontal and vertical communications among the healthcare facilities within the organizational structure of the healthcare system are essential. Such communications facilitate efficient information exchange and help the delivery of essential health services to underserved rural areas. These communications can be supported through a nationwide e-medicine network that is based on affordable telecommunications infrastructure. The network should connect all regional clinics to urban area hospitals. The benefits of such a network include: (a) establishing reliable horizontal-vertical communications and information sharing among facilities, thereby driving up quality, improving efficiency, and enhancing cost-effectiveness of services; (b) achieving e-health commitments and bringing healthcare closer to underserved and un-served rural areas; (c) strengthening collaboration among hospitals within a multi-provider care management context; (d) minimizing long distance travels among rural people in need of proper medical care to urban areas or the capital city; and (e) providing medi-

cal information to clinical practitioners that will help them keep abreast of clinical breakthroughs as well as new technological advances.

For Ethiopia, a lesser developing country with significant challenges in meeting basic healthcare needs, it is argued that e-medicine development is emerging and can be fruitfully cultivated over the coming years if a vision and long-term strategy for this technology can be used to help increase the number of citizens receiving care and decrease the subsequent healthcare costs. This article lays out such a vision and strategy for a nationwide e-medicine infrastructure to be designed. It is organized as follows. First, the background and various design considerations for a nationwide e-medicine network is presented. Next is an overview of the requirements for the network design followed by a more in-depth description of the local and wide area network (LAN/WAN) architecture envisioned. The focus of the discussion will then shift to the existing Broadband Multimedia Network (BMN) and Very Small Aperture Terminal (VSAT) infrastructures and how these networks may be integrated into the nationwide e-medicine infrastructure. Finally, the article concludes with insights into potential future work in e-medicine for developing countries.

E-MEDICINE NETWORK DESIGN CONSIDERATIONS

E-medicine refers to the electronic delivery of healthcare and sharing of medical knowledge over a distance employing ICT. A national e-medicine network allows sharing and exchanging of clinical data among physicians, administrators, even patients or other participating health professionals regardless of physical distance separation or geographical terrain of the whereabouts of these network participants within the national boundaries. The network also facilitates communications among physicians and academics across diverse cultures, affiliated healthcare organizations, and publicly or privately funded research institutions. Since there is lack of transportation and communication infrastructure in developing countries, medical and clinical data exchanges can be further secured and facilitated through an existing e-medicine network.

In developed nations, e-medicine services (Wright, 1998) can benefit remote locations that may not be easily accessed due to unpredictable or harsh weather conditions found during certain times of the year, for example, parts of North America and Scandinavian countries are often heavily affected by snow and other natural hazards such as avalanches, falling boulders and closure of highways due to multi-vehicle accidents or other calamities. Mountainous terrain in certain parts of North American regions such as Alaska, British Columbia, Alberta and New Territories implies the need for viable distance healthcare delivery solutions. E-medicine allows health professionals around the world to establish faster communication and exchange information with clients and regional authorities irrespective of geographical locations. It may also support rural dwellers to get healthcare services delivery similar to their urban counterparts. A mobile e-medicine system, for instance, provides a convenient platform for acquisition, transmission and delivery of health-related data to healthcare providers through 2G/3G-based wireless networks (Wootton, 2001). Recognizing these benefits, the International Telecommunications Union (ITU) has set a global agenda to promote e-medicine applications in developing countries. Ethiopia, one of the beneficiaries of such an initiative, has commissioned some ICT projects such as School-Net, WoredaNet and BMN to enable fully-fledged connectivity to make better use of the ICT in the health and education sectors.

Network Architecture

The design of suitable national e-medicine network architecture in a lesser developing country such as Ethiopia requires several key components to be integrated into a dynamic and enterprising communication infrastructure. Major architectural components include: (1) LAN architecture for local networking and sharing of health-related information; here, communications may be established using wireless cellular or ordinary fixed telephone lines; (2) WAN architecture for national networking and sharing of health-related data; this will allow communications among local and national physicians, healthcare workers and clients covering urban and rural communities; and (3) designing a suitable back-end database and front-end user interface applications that integrate seamlessly with the (prototype) implementation of the proposed architecture. The overall goal of the nationwide e-medicine network architecture is then to provide an affordable and a low-cost system that facilitates uninterrupted communications among physicians and health professionals across the country. The system bolsters connectivity among rural clinics and urban area hospitals to support primarily clinical e-consultation and maintenance of stored patient records.

This network should also be cost-effective, expandable, and secure. It must support a state-of-the-art ICT access schema and connectivity to rural area clinics. Existing ICT infrastructure will be given priority to minimize the cost of implementing the nationwide network. In the Ethiopia design, expandability is a concern. First, few hospitals are built in the country while more clinics are being added every year. Moreover, there is a chance to incorporate private hospitals in the nationwide e-medicine network as and when necessary, which will further increases the number of future connected sites. As well, the area of e-medicine applications will not be limited to just some specific diseases, but will be expected to increase in type and number over the long haul. In fact, the network should also support advanced applications, which require real-time connectivity such as videoconferencing capabilities for future use.

During e-consultation or patient referral, most of the data exchanged over the network are sensitive patient information. Confidentiality of patient information must therefore be respected. For secure communications, protocols such as Secure Socket Layer (SSL) could be used. SSL ensures secured communications over web-based applications and provides the ability to safely exchange patient information across the network (Elmasri, 2000). When doctors exchange patient information, they could adhere to medical protocol that defines the rules to be followed during this process. In addition, the network and accompanying servers could be protected by firewall against hacking from external parties. Firewalls are software or hardware for the sole purpose of keeping digital pests such as viruses, worms, and hackers out of the network (http://www.cisco.com, Tanenbaum, 2004).

NETWORK DESIGN REQUIREMENTS

As cost must be one of the driving factors for choosing among existing or emerging ICT infrastructures in the country, implementing nationwide e-medicine network infrastructure may seem at first to be more expensive than building clinics or supplying existing regional clinics with medical personnel and equipment. Yet, a cost-benefit analysis comparing various IT investment approaches will provide best directions to achieving a lower cost solution to the problem of delivering adequate and proper healthcare and disseminating confidential health information to

and from various connecting points throughout the country. With today's oil prices at a premium, network connectivity among the healthcare facilities, both in the urban and rural areas over an existing ICT infrastructure is now considered a cost-effective solution. Of course, set-up costs depend on the type of WAN to be used—to ensure low installation cost, it is proposed that the network design will incorporate an existing WAN provided by the Ethiopia Telecommunication Corporation (ETC).

In Ethiopia, most of the inter-hospital communications are traditionally dependent on telephone and hand-delivered referral messages. During referrals patients have to travel afar to one of the urban referral hospitals, carrying the written messages of the referring physician. Clinics located in the telephone coverage areas communicate using telephone to exchange information about availability of specialist(s) or bed in another hospital. Yet, the communication needs of hospitals have grown over the years ahead of its technological capabilities. Geographically dispersed clinics lack modern telecommunication technology access. Among them are instantaneous access to patient information, access to electronic medical records, and access to the Internet. These and other communication needs of health providers also require the development of e-medicine application software backed by electronic patient record systems. Design of such communication networks will also require the understanding of organizational structure of the clinics involved in the network.

Since the government/public clinics are owned and organized under their respective regions, the WAN design should follow the organizational structure of the administrative regions in the country. A detailed study about the inclusion of various clinics, their locations relative to the nearest access point to existing ICT infrastructure, traffic load and its characteristics, security, LAN/WAN protocol, topology and bandwidth requirements and utilization, and allocation of bandwidth, among other issues, have to be considered while trying to design a nationwide e-medicine network architecture. For example, issues of communicating patient information electronically may further raise question on medical ethics, the need for developing standard medical protocols, and detailing policies for use in routine activity via the e-medicine network.

LAN Architecture

To design the LAN for each hospital, we consider the central site, *Tikur Anbassa Specialized Hospital* located in the capital Addis Ababa, as a model. The hospital is organized into 16 departments with each department further divided into smaller units as necessary. For instance, the Internal Medicine department has several units such as the Renal Unit, the Cardiology Unit, the Neurology Unit, and other units. Physicians in these departments and units need to communicate whenever a patient visits more than one of the units. It is proposed that the LAN follows the hierarchical structure of the hospital.

The decision to make the selection between various LAN technologies was based on: (a) expected application to run on the network and their traffic patterns; (b) physical locations of the offices and users to be connected in campus; (c) the rate of network growth; (d) the abundance of the network technology in the market; and (e) simplicity of installation and maintenance. Each of these criteria will now be explored in more depth.

Expected Application to Run on the Network and their Traffic Patterns

Currently we expect a Web-based e-medicine application to run on the network. The application will use a central database server where all the user and patient information will be stored. The type of data to be transmitted on the network should accommodate both text and image formats.

Since all communications are to be channeled through the server, the traffic pattern around the center is expected to be heavy. Higher speed devices should be installed at the center of the LAN where servers will be located.

Physical Locations of Offices and Users to be Connected on Campus

The sample hospital (*Tikur Anbassa Specialized Hospital*) is housed in a series of five buildings (Blocks A-E). These blocks are not physically separated. Even though precise figures were unavailable, these five buildings are built on roughly 8,000 to 10,000 square meters. While the main offices and departments in the hospital are located in one of the respective blocks, most of these offices are in either of the first two stories of the block they belong. Having routers switches in each of the departments is ideal to design a high-speed and expandable LAN, but it will also make the design expensive to install, support and maintain. A more cost-effective approach is to put switches per building and then get the departments to be connected into various groups by using Virtual LAN technology.

The Rate of Network Growth

The rate of the hospital LAN growth depends on the level of computerization in the hospital. Currently in this central hospital site, there is a LAN that connects a few offices and a computer room. The network employs star topology, using a centrally located hub and Unshielded Twisted Pair (UTP) cables forming a peer-to-peer LAN. The purpose of this LAN was to enable offices to share printer and students to get access to research documents. In this design, it is anticipated that as the use of Web-based applications becomes commonplace, there will be opportunities to add more applications and connect more computers and offices to the LAN. The switches-routers selected in this design should therefore have many free ports to help cascade the growing number of anticipated future connections.

The Abundance of Network Technology in the Market

Capitalizing on the abundance of emerging network technology in the Ethiopia market, we gathered data from existing network technology vendors and organizations that implement computer networks in the capital city, Addis Ababa. Ethernet technology is common in organizations that implement computer networks, such as Addis Ababa University (AAU Net). AAU Net is a network backed by triangular shape fiber optic

cable connecting the three main campuses. The topology is an extended star topology that fastens together fiber optic cables for vertical cabling (backbone cabling) between buildings that house various faculties and departments. These backbone cabling provide interconnection between wiring closets and Point of Present (POP). The zones that fall within a departmental area are served by internetworking devices such as hubs and UTP cables.

Interestingly, what is described so far appears to be the dominant design of the small number of networks existing in the capital Addis Ababa. As such, it is not surprising to find that suppliers of network technology devices and support in

Figure 1. Hospital LAN design

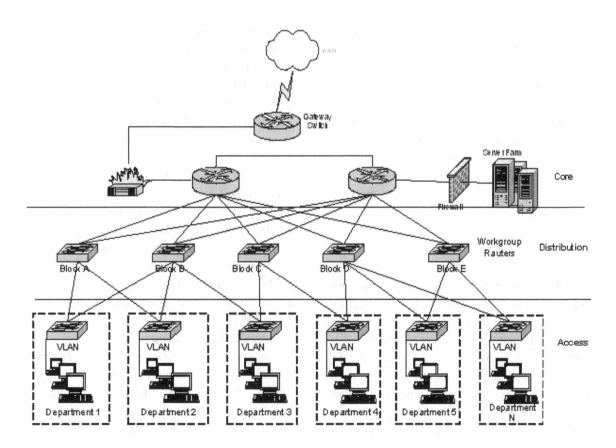

Ethiopia are restricted to only a limited number of vendors.

Simplicity of Installation and Maintenance

To design the LAN architecture we have therefore selected the hierarchical model. This enables us to design and arrange the inter-network devices in layers. Figure 1 depicts the hospital-based LAN architecture.

It is a model preferred by most of network design experts for its ease of understanding, expandability and improved fault isolation characteristics (http://www.cisco.com). The model encompasses the following three layers: (a) first layer (core layer); (b) second layer (distribution layer); and (c) third layer (access layer).

Core Layer

Core layer high performance switches, capable of switching packets as quickly as possible, are to be deployed. Essentially, this layer connects the LAN backbone media as well as connects to the outside world via a firewall through WAN. In this design, the devices in the core layer will be placed at a central location in the hospital. The devices will then be connected with high-speed cables such as fiber optics, or fast Ethernet cables. The servers will also be connected to switches, shielded by a firewall.

Distribution Layer

Distribution layer will contain switches and routers capable of Virtual LAN (VLAN) switching and allow defining departmental workgroups and multicast domains. The devices should also support connectivity of different LAN technologies since they also serve as the demarcation point between the backbone connections in the core layer and the access layer. In this hospital-based LAN design, the distribution layer represents switches/routers at each building connected to the core layer on the one end and to the access layer on the other. Redundant links will be used for maximum availability and the departments could be grouped forming their own Virtual LAN.

Access Layer

Access Layer is where the end-users are allowed into the network. This layer contains switches/hubs from which PCs in each department gain access to the hospital-based LAN. Each department will have at least one switch/hub, which will in turn have redundant links to more than two of the switches in the distribution layer.

WAN Architecture

Designing the WAN architecture for a nationwide e-medicine network raises the issue of WAN service provider. Unlike LAN, WAN connectivity depends on the availability of WAN infrastructure in the country. The sole WAN service provider is the Ethiopian Telecommunications Corporation (ETC).

ETC provides a number of services (http://www.telecom.net.et) from which the WAN infrastructure suitable for the e-medicine network may be derived. Existing WAN services include: (a) Internet Services, or, providing basic Internet services over dial-up or leased lines; (b) Digital Data Network (DDN), supporting dedicated Internet, ISDN and frame relay services; (c) SchoolNet VSAT, covering services for secondary schools and institutes of higher learning; (d) WoredaNet VSAT, covering services for districts (Woreda) administrations; and (e) Broadband Multimedia Network (BMN), offering high-speed optical communications to major cities.

To choose among these possible infrastructures for nationwide e-medicine network, the parameters to be considered include the geographical coverage, bandwidth, mode of communication, rental cost of WAN connection and capacity to

Table 1. Summarized comparison of existing ICT infrastructure

	Internet	DDN	SchoolNet	WoredaNet	BMN
Coverage	Telephone coverage areas only	The capital and regional Urban areas only	About 500 schools covered. There are Woredas that do not have schools	571 Woredas out of 594 are covered	The Capital city and 13 regional towns.
Bandwidth	Maximum of 56k dialup and 1Mbps in Leased line	Maximum of 1Mbps	Can be upgraded to 384k upstream	Downstream/ upstream 45Mbps/ 256k downlink	ADSL Services: Variable bandwidth Downstream/ up-stream 512k/128k and 1024k/256k
Interactivity	Two-way	Two-way	One-way broad-casting	Two-way	Two-way
Cost	0.11 birr/min dialup 1000 birr/ month leased line		Free for schools	Free For Wore-das	Not yet determined, under development
Capacity to scale	Not scalable	Not scalable enough		Will have more than 10 ports free at each Woreda	Can be expanded

add more LANs. Table 1 summarizes the data comparing among the available ICT infrastructures in Ethiopia.

Based on the data, it appears that WoredaNet is best suited to the national e-medicine network, as long as the existing infrastructures are functioning efficiently and effectively. However, as noted in Table 1, there may be a tradeoff between coverage and capacity, that is, when the coverage is acceptable the capacity may be somewhat limited. For example, BMN coverage is ideal as it represents state-of-the-art service and higher bandwidth. However, it is centered primarily in the urban areas. It is also under development and we have thus considered it as a potential option to be used when integrated with the VSAT-based networks to enhance nationwide e-medicine network. Finally, the SchoolNet needs to be upgraded to support two-way interactivity.

Thus, one alternative approach is using a combination of VSAT networks and terrestrial BMN. VSAT-based connectivity is believed to be cost-effective and in the case of WoredaNet and SchoolNet, it enables connectivity to the public, even in the rural areas. In addition to serving the rural areas, it also covers urban areas. Together, this will provide modern, convenient as well as economical connectivity to hospitals. For improving state-of-the-art applications such as videoconferencing, connectivity via the emerging

Figure 2a. Logical WAN design based on BMN and VSAT networks (1st Alternative)

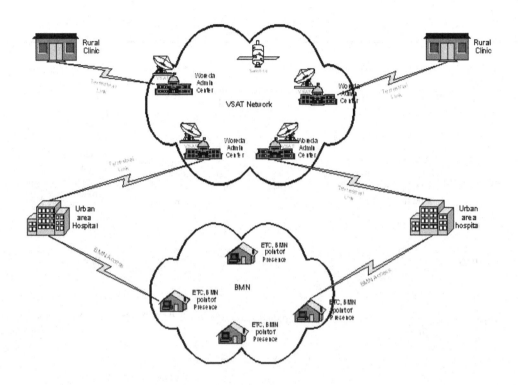

BMN is proposed to connect urban area hospitals in the capital city and in the regions where the network can be easily accessible.

Figure 2a shows the e-medicine network as a first alternative. Note that this approach requires that urban hospitals maintain two WAN connections. Having more than one WAN connection, however, may become expensive in the long run. If the two WAN infrastructures could be integrated, an improved WAN design will result with only one WAN connection to the urban hospitals through which the hospitals will be connected to BMN and the rural area clinics through the WoredaNet. Figure 2b depicts the second alternative solution of the WAN design.

CURRENT ETC INITIATIVES

The recent development in the ETC in providing multimedia network infrastructure is the integration of the VSAT-based networks (SchoolNet and WoredaNet) with the BMN (Tiruneh, 2006). In other words, these VSAT-based networks can now be used as a point of access to the BMN.

As part of a longer term vision and mission of broadband initiatives for socioeconomic development in Ethiopia, ETC has also planned an e-health setting that tries to cover rural areas, schools, clinics, hospitals, prisons, and nursing homes, including assisted living with several requirements: (a) high quality patient data, video

Figure 2b. Logical WAN design based on BMN and VSAT networks (2ⁿᵈ Alternative)

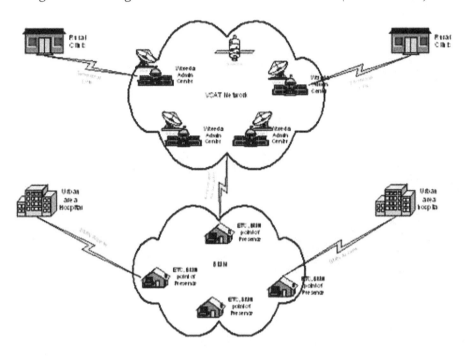

and images to be exchanged between different medical institutions; (b) ICT infrastructure to connect geographically dispersed institutions, nationwide or worldwide; (c) infrastructure that supports data, video and voice/audio (multimedia) services; (d) high quality, secured and fast delivery of medical information; and (e) high speed (BW) connectivity or the deployment of broadband infrastructure.

Key challenges faced are the need to encompass multiple locations, to use multiple access technologies, to deliver multiple services and to address multiple user markets.

Current BMN Development

ETC has already completed building the Core Terrestrial Broadband Infrastructure, which is ca-

pable of providing data, video, and voice services with 24 Points of Presence. This infrastructure services key business sites (urban areas) and supports Multiple Broadband Access via ADSL, FWA, WIFI, and fiber networks.

Current VSAT Development

In Ethiopia, a Broadband VSAT Network platform, which supports integrated services such as video, data, Internet, and voice on a single infrastructure, is currently in place. It has countrywide coverage (450+ schools and 550+ woredas) as part of SchoolNet and WoredaNet deployments. It is integrated with the core multimedia network, also serving as broadband access means. Figure 3 shows the two recent developments.

Figure 3. ETC's broadband-integrated infrastructure for e-health applications

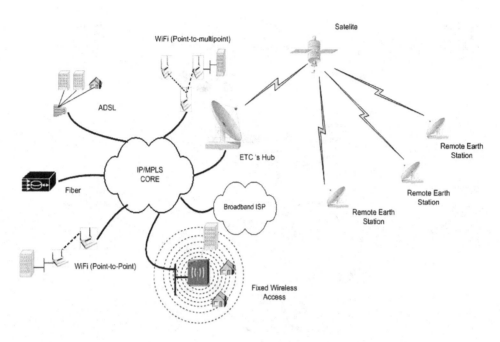

Apparently, the new developments in WAN infrastructure support the 2nd alternative e-medicine WAN architecture discussed here as depicted in Figure 3.

THE PROTOTYPE

Based on the specified network requirements and architecture, a working prototype for the national e-medicine network is now presented and its operations highlighted.

The prototype is a basic e-Medicine service (BEMS), which provides a Web-based graphical user interface (GUI) for health providers. BEMS facilitates the information exchange between remotely located health providers for the purpose of e-consultation, as well as for maintaining electronic patient information. The traditional paper-based forms and patient cards used in

the hospitals will be digitized and reproduced electronically. Web-based technology is chosen for its ubiquity. Using Web-based technology constitutes not only a network that can be used universally, but the technology also supports system-independent platforms, thus providing access to many different computer systems at client sites (http://java.sun.com/products/jsp). Key requirements in these client sites are simply the availability of Web browser software and network connectivity.

For a secured network, password protected system ensures that user login is needed to access capabilities of the system. In addition, user types are defined so that there will be a role-based access to database and system functions in BEMS. To ensure compatibility with most legacy systems, a relational database is advocated for storing user and patient information. Beyond e-mails, this approach allows the users to mobilize structured information exchange among the communicating health providers.

Major Features of BEMS

Basically the BEMS prototype may be conceptualized as a database-driven Web site with the following main features and functions: (a) providing user management services where administrator can register users, assigning username and password, and defining user type, as well as searching and editing user information; (b) providing patient management services where health providers can register patients, search patients and view patient information on a Rolodex-like interface, as and when necessary; (c) providing, on the one hand, referral systems where physicians can write referral messages to a particular department and hospital, and, on the other, a system whereby a physician can retrieve and study the list of referrals forwarded to the department s/he is working in and allowing the physician to write feedback instantaneously after examining the referral message and patient information; (d) providing a system by which physicians can request and schedule lab test at any hospital laboratories so that patients can get tested in the clinic/hospital they are being treated; and (e) providing a list of lab test requests to laboratory technicians and allowing them to input lab test results.

BEMS Architecture

The BEMS architecture is built on three-tiered, client-server architecture. The first layer is where the client machines run Web-browser software. This layer is used to display the user interface (Web pages) of the system and send secure HTTP request to the Web server in the second layer. Along with the Web server, application server resides in the second layer. This application server manages the clinical business logic. The bottom layer contains the persistent data of the system. All data of patients, physicians and other communicated messages will be stored and maintained in this third layer. This layer runs the database management system (DBMS) software. Put simply, BEMS functions as a Web-based application connected to a Web server to provide all the interfaces of the system and that of a database server to manage all the knowledge and information elements stored in the system. Figure 4 charts the BEMS system architecture.

The BEMS prototype is constructed with a combination of open source products and freely available software components. The Web server

Figure 4. BEMS prototype architecture

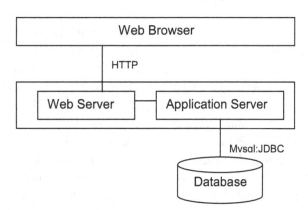

suggested is the Apache Jakarta's Tomcat Web server (http://jakarta.apache.org) with the functionalities as well as the mandated business rules programmed in Java (Haile-Mariam, 2002). Java Server Pages (JSP) is used to capture the user interface and the text of Web pages (http://java. sun.com/products/jsp; http://www.coreservlets. com). Some scripting is included on the Web pages in JavaScript. JSP has a capability to import java classes and run them from the Web pages when the pages are downloaded to the client machine (http://www.coreservlets.com). Unlike other server side languages such as Active Server Pages (ASP), JSP makes the system platform independent. It also allows users to take advantage of the full power of java programming language which overcome some of the limitation of other scripting languages such as PHP (http://www. coreservlets.com).

The database conceptualized is the open source MySql to back up the database driven application. MySql works on many different operating system platforms and is known for its speed of data retrieval (http://www.mysql. com). It provides Application Program Interfaces (API) for many programming languages including Java. Passwords are secure because all password traffic is encrypted when connecting to the MySql server. For database connectivity, we use mm.mysql driver, which is a Java Database Connectivity (JDBC) driver, from MySQL AB, implemented in 100% native Java (http://www. mysql.com/products/connector-j).

Database Design Issues

BEMS needs to keep track of information about patient and related medical records, user's information, and messages for both medical referral requests and feedbacks. A well-designed minimal database is needed to manage this information. A relational database model is selected to store the persistent data of the system, as it could be easier to manage, and provides better management for complex query of such data (Amenssisa & Dabi, 2003). This database is expected to maintain and manipulate basic entities such as users, patients, and medical records.

Each component of the medical record of a patient is an aggregation of different types of data, which are stored in the database. In the traditional paper-based system, the medical record of a patient is identified by an Out Patient Card (OPCard) Number, which is usually called patient record number. OPCard is a four-page hard-paper card, which contains patient's generic information, such as name, sex, age, address on the first page and a table of two columns for date and clinical note so as to record chronologically the compilation of health providers' notes. All other components such as laboratory test results and x-ray reports, among other pieces of information, are stored inside the hard-paper card referenced by the card number or name of the patient. The lab test results may contain zero or more test request forms along with the results for Urine, Parasitology, Blood Chemistry, Hematology, Serology, Bacteriology, Fine Needle Aspiration Cytology and Biopsy.

When a patient is admitted to the hospital, admission and social services information is stored. The admission data include identification information and name and address of next-of-kin, marital status, and number of siblings (children) information, besides occupational information and other demographics, as and when provided by the patient. Subsequently, follow-up data such as vital sign measurements, fluid balance information and other measures will be collected and recorded. Order sheet, which contains a list of treatments to be ordered following admission, is also part of the inpatient medical record. In addition to these, information about the hospitals, departments and laboratories are also stored and captured in respective entities.

To minimize connectivity cost and increase system performance, a distributed database is recommended. Horizontal partitioning that splits tables along rows, based on the location of patient and healthcare facility, is seen to be an ideal choice in the e-medicine application that tries to create nationwide connectivity. Finally, to use the database, transparent data access schemes must be defined for applications that run over the network.

BEMS Interfaces

In this part of the discussion, the design of various BEMS interfaces is presented. BEMS is accessed when opening the initial Web page where user authentication is first performed. The initial page contains a typical login screen for specifying username with authenticated password. There is no need of menu or different buttons to be submitted based on the user types. Since the user types are defined in the database when the user registered, the page corresponding to the specific user type will automatically be opened upon successful login. Currently, administrators, physicians, and lab technician user types are defined and all of these user types will have their own main pages as described below.

Administrator's Main Page

The administrator's main page is used for managing users. The functionalities accessible from this page include: *register new user* and *search user* by a combination of name, father's name, and user name. Figure 5a shows the administrator's main page whereas Figure 5b depicts the user registration page.

The other function provided to administrators is the *search user* function. It is possible to search users by keying in any combinations of name, including father's name and/or user name. Note that username is treated as "unique" in the user table with the search result being quickly displayed. Although not shown here, the full name of the search result is captured as a link. This link then leads to a page containing the relevant user information from which the administrator can edit a particular user.

Physician's Main Page

The physician's main page contains a button to open the patient manager page and has the capability of retrieving a list of referrals forwarded to the department where the physician is located. To open a new page, the physician is free to click on the *manage patients* button or link to one of the referrals. Figure 6a illustrates that the patient, Ato Andualem Lemma, is one of Dr. Aman's referrals. If Dr. Aman chooses to treat this patient in the hospital where he is privileged, he can simply open the patient manager page by clicking on the *manage patients* button.

Figure 6b shows that the patient manager page has two options, that is, physicians can "register new patient" or "search patient" for those who were previously registered. When selecting "register new patient," a patient registration form, similar to the user registration page, will be opened. In contrast, if the physician wants to look for a patient, s/he can input one of the search criteria such as *name* or *record number* of the patient, resulting in the display of a matching record number or name and the hospital where the patient was first registered. The patient full name is a link that leads to the patient information page similar to the traditional patient card used in the hospitals. An example of the patient card, which opens up when the full name link in the previous interface is selected, can be seen in Figure 6c.

The patient card contains patient's general information, address information and clinical notes that are ordered in descending order. In addition to the information displayed on the patient card, laboratory test results and medical images related to the patient are accessible by clicking corresponding buttons from the patient card interface. The physician can add clinical notes, refer, and/or admit the patient. From the

Figure 5a. Administrator's main page within BEMS

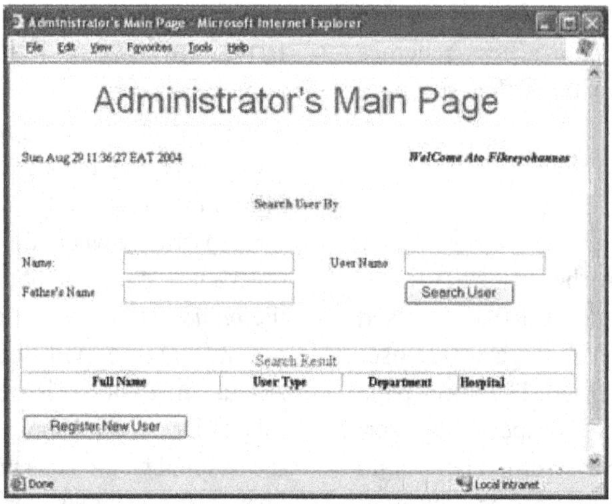

Figure 5b. User registration page

physician's main page, the other option available to the physician is to see referrals forwarded to his or her department. This is possible by clicking the link that opens a referral page corresponding to the patient. The patient referral page contains the referral messages and buttons that will lead the user to patient information as well as a button that can lead to the feedback input page.

If the physician user wants to view the patient information, the *view patient card* button will support such a function. Otherwise, if the physician would like to give feedback to the referral using the feedback slip, the *open feedback slip* button will serve this purpose. Basically, the feedback slip is represented as an input form similar to a traditional form for capturing feedback informa-

Figure 6a. Physician's main page within BEMS

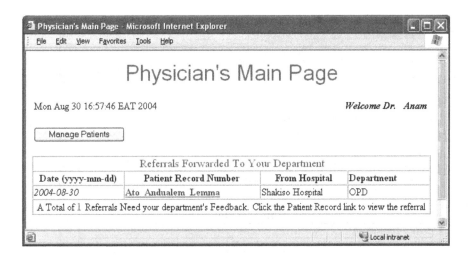

Figure 6b. Patient manager page within BEMS

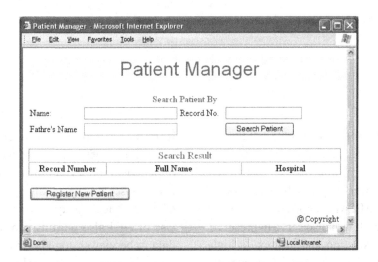

tion related to the current referral. Put simply, the idea here is to mimic within a virtual environment what the physicians have already become accustomed to routinely when working within a paper-based environment, which will only hasten the processing and matching of the stored computerized information for them.

Graphical User Interface

Apparently, human computer interface (HCI) design issues are critical in determining the successful deployment and continuing use of the BEMS prototype. As indicated, the current approach attempts to optimize the interface design

Figure 6c. Patient card page within BEMS

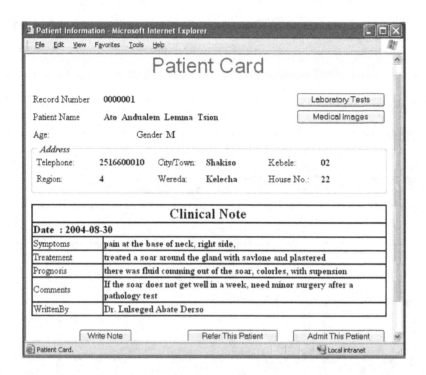

in mimicking more or less the traditional forms, documentation formats and paper-based patient record system that the physicians have grown accustomed to using over the years. In other words, this ensures that the BEMS supports the habits of the physician users. It will also serve to preserve physician user satisfaction and promote a high rate of acceptance among physician users with the new system implementation on the one hand while reducing disruption to the care processes on the other.

Nonetheless, new system development such as the BEMS typically provides new opportunities for revisiting the care processes that have been put in place over the years. Elimination of redundant processes as well as the need to streamline certain administrative and clinical processes may be

warranted to improve quality, cost, efficiency and effectiveness of the care provided. Online requests of patient and referral information and querying of databases are expectedly translatable into more efficient, effective, appropriate and quality care. Use of GUI also permits substantial amount of data to be viewed together, improving the communication, exchange and sharing of patient data. Feedback from physician users should ultimately be channeled to an even more enhanced user interface design. In this environment, clinical test results and specialist reports can also be captured quickly and shared collaboratively among all relevant health providers.

As an example, the physician can be empowered to request laboratory test results in BEMS by viewing the patient laboratory information page, which is accessible from the patient card page by a button called "Laboratory Tests." Figure 7 provides illustrative screenshots for the laboratory information page and a parasitological test request pages. When a physician wants to request lab tests, instead of writing a prescription to the patient and having the patient wait for further scheduling information from the nursing clerk, all that is needed now is a mere click of the button corresponding to the type of "test" required from the laboratory information page. The specific lab test request page can be designed such as to provide the physician user with a dropdown list from which the appropriate lab test can be immediately selected and performed as scheduled. This was found to be important in order to forward the lab test request on a real-time basis to the other user types called, the Lab technicians.

Lab Technician's Main Page

The third type of user, laboratory technician, sees a list of laboratory requests to the department s/he is practicing, on the lab technician's main page. The list contains a link to open lab test result input form where the lab technician can enter his or her report following the test as shown in Figure 8.

CONCLUSION

The key contribution of this effort lies in envisioning the planning and detailing of a Web-interface for a hierarchical model-based LAN architecture that enables the integration of the inter-network devices in layers and a WAN architecture, both fine-tuned for a developing country such as Ethiopia.

The hierarchical model adopted for the LAN is a preferred model due to its ease of expandability and improved fault isolation characteristics. The WAN design considers the existing VSAT-based WAN infrastructure in the country, the WoredaNet. Even if urban areas are relatively better equipped with adequate ICT technologies such as Internet access and digital telephone networks, the communication infrastructure is not well developed in many rural areas. These regions have to be equipped with an access to urban areas. In this context, the newly emerging state-owned, low-cost VSAT networks such as SchoolNet and WoredaNet provide the rural areas with suitable means of communication with urban areas and beyond.

VSAT, an earthbound station used in satellite communications of data, voice and video signals,

Figure 7. Laboratory information and parasitological test request page of BEMS

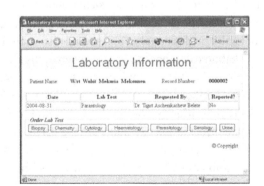
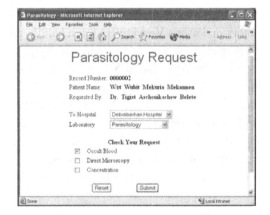

Figure 8. Lab technician's main page of BEMS

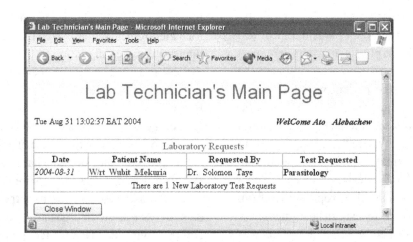

excluding broadcast television, comprises two parts: (a) a transceiver that is placed outdoors in direct line of sight to the satellite; and (b) a device that is placed indoors to interface the transceiver with the end user's communications device, such as a PC. The transceiver receives or sends a signal to a satellite transponder in the sky. The satellite sends and receives signals from a ground station computer that acts as a hub for the system. Each end user is interconnected with the hub station via the satellite, forming a star topology. The hub controls the entire network operation. For one end user to communicate with another, each transmission has to first go to the hub station that then gets retransmitted via the satellite to the other end user's VSAT. VSAT can handle up to 56 Kbps.

More importantly, the BEMS architecture discussed here is designed to integrate with a large part of the existing LAN and WAN infrastructure designs. The system can then be used to facilitate both intra- and inter-hospital communications and for all forms of information exchange. The alternative design selected will not only improve quality of healthcare services while protecting the privacy, confidentiality and integrity of sensitive patient information, but its interfaces have been set up to mimic the physician routines working in a paper-based environment. Moreover, this will also yield opportunities for further review of the paper flow and work processes to cut down on redundancies and errors while simultaneously boosting both administrative and clinical efficiencies and effectiveness of care.

As future work in the area of developing nationwide e-medicine networks, we recommend the following considerations: (a) the intended network should support real-time e-consultations via video and audio conferencing, advocate doctor-to-patient interactions, and facilitate remote training for health professionals; (b) it should also support a distributed database structure, where individual hospitals should keep their own databases, which can be further treated as one "huge" database; (c) the definition of standards is essential to facilitate information exchange among private and government hospitals as well as overseas; (d) the integration of expert systems such as case-based system where doctors can query the database to get experience from previously stored similar cases should also be considered—such a system will aid future physicians and residents working anywhere in the country to learn from past successes and/or failures of the attending specialist(s), especially for non-trivial and complex patient cases; and (e) the infrastructure should be independent of chosen platform and operating systems (e.g., Windows vs. Apple) and be able to support physicians needing to remotely monitor their patients over heterogeneous networks, including handheld devices in 2G/3G mobile networks and wirelessly.

Beyond the design of a nationwide e-medicine infrastructure, there will be a host of potential e-medicine applications that may be supported, including, but not limited to a series of healthy lifestyle promotion programs such as e-consultation and tracking of participation in smoking cessation, weight reduction, dental health, stress reduction, exercise and nutritional programs and many more. In this regard, one of the contributing authors is actively and precisely engaged with a growing network of researchers in generating such a series of educational modules intended for seniors and other population groups that will eventually be serviced on a network such as BEMS discussed in this article (Tan, 2005).

REFERENCES

Amenssisa, J. & Dabi, S. (2003). District-based telemedicine project in Ethiopia. *Ministry of Health*. Addis Ababa, Ethiopia.

Apache Jakarta Project. (2007). Retrieved from http://jakarta.apache.org

Cisco Documentation. (2007). Retrieved from www.cisco.com

Elmasri, R. (2000). *Fundamentals of database systems,* 3rd edition. Addison Wesley.

Ethiopian Telecommunications Corporation. (2007). www.telecom.net.et

Haile-Mariam, A. (2002). Renaissance: Strategies for ICT Development in Ethiopia. M.Sc Thesis, School of Engineering Postgraduate Engineering Program.

Hall, M. (2007). Core servlet and Java server pages. *Sun Microsystems Press,* Retrieved from http://www.coreservlets.com.

Horsch, A. & Balbach, T. (1999). Telemedicine information systems. *IEEE Trans. Inform., Technol. Biomed., 3*, 166-175.

Java Server Pages Documentation. (2007). Retrieved from http://java.sun.com/products/jsp

Kirigia, J., Seddoh, A., Gatwiri, D., Muthuri, L., & Seddoh, J. (2005). E-health: Determinants, opportunities, challenges and the way forward for countries in the WHO African region. *BMC Public Health, 5*, 137.

MySQL. (2007). http://www.mysql.com.

MySQL Connector/J. (2007). Retrieved from http://www.mysql.com/products/connector-j/.

Perednia, D. & Allen, A. (1995). E-medicine technology and clinical applications. *Journal of the American Medical Association, 273*(6), 483-488.

Tan, J. (2001). *Health management information systems: Methods and practical applications*, 2nd edition. Gaithersburg, MD: Aspen Publishers, Inc.

Tan, J., Kifle, M., Mbarika, V., Okoli, C. (2005). E-Medicine in developed and developing countries. In J. Tan (Ed.), *E-healthcare information systems*. Jossey-Bass (A Wiley Imprint).

Tanenbaum, A. (2004). *Computer networks*, 4th edition. Prentice Hall, Inc.

Tiruneh, M. (2006). ETC, broadband network infrastructure for e-health. *ICT-H-2006 Workshop*, Addis Ababa, Ethiopia.

Wootton, R. (2001). Recent Advances: Telemedicine. *British Medical Journal, 323*, 557-560

Wright, D. (1998). Telemedicine and developing countries. A report of study group 2 of the ITU development sector. *J Telemedicine Telecare.*

Chapter XX
E–Government Strategies in Developed and Developing Countries:
An Implementation Framework and Case Study

Y. N. Chen
Western Kentucky University, USA

H. M. Chen
Shanghai Jiaotong University, China

W. Huang
College of Business, Ohio University, USA

R. K. H. Ching
California State University, USA

ABSTRACT

Given the fact that more and more governments invest heavily in e-government design and implementation, e-government has become an evolving and important research area in the IS field. Most, if not all, currently published e-government strategies are based on successful experiences from developed countries, which may not be directly applicable to developing countries. Based on a literature review, this study summarizes differences between developed/developing countries. It identifies key factors for a successful e-government implementation and proposes an implementation framework. As a demonstration, we follow the guidance of the proposed framework in conducting a case study to analyze the implementation strategies of e-government in developed and developing countries.

INTRODUCTION

With the Internet surging, governments at all levels are utilizing it to reinvent their structure and efficiency, coining the term "e-government" to describe this initiative. Bill Gates of Microsoft claims that e-government is one of the most exciting fields in electronic commerce in the near future. E-government is a cost-effective solution that improves communication between government agencies and their constituents by providing access to information and services online. *The Economist* magazine estimates that the potential savings of implementing e-government could be as much as $110 billion and 144 billion English Pounds in the U.S. and Europe, respectively (Symonds, 2000). Though a new subject, e-government has attracted more and more research interest and focus from industries, national governments, and universities (Carter & Belanger, 2005; Chircu & Lee, 2003; Huang, Siau, & Wei, 2004; Jain & Patnayakuni, 2003; Moon & Norris, 2005; Navarra & Cornford, 2003), such as IBM's Institute for Electronic Government and various "E-Government Task Forces" in different countries (Huang, D'Ambra, & Bhalla, 2002).

E-Government is a permanent commitment made by government to improve the relationship between the private citizen and the public sector through enhanced, cost-effective, and efficient delivery of services, information, and knowledge. Broadly defined, e-government includes the use of all information and communication technologies, from fax machines to wireless palm pilots, to facilitate the daily administration of government, exclusively as an Internet-driven activity that improves citizen's access to government information, services, and expertise to ensure citizen's participation in, and satisfaction with government process (UN & ASPA, 2001). Narrowly defined, e-government is the production and delivery of government services through IT applications, used to simplify and improve transactions between governments and constituents, businesses, and other government agencies (Sprecher, 2000).

The development and implementation of e-government brings about impacts and changes to the structure and functioning of the public administration (Snellen, 2000). Unlike the traditional bureaucratic model where information flows only vertically and rarely between departments, e-government links new technology with legacy systems internally and, in turn, links government information infrastructures externally with everything digital (Tapscott, 1995). Moreover, e-government will help breaking down agency and jurisdictional barriers to allow more integrated whole-of-government services across the three tiers of government (federal, state, and local). Government in the offline environment can be difficult to access, which is especially problematic for people in regional and remote locations. E-Government offers a potential to dramatically increase access to information and services. E-Government makes it easier for citizens to participate in and contribute to governmental issues.

Various stages of e-government reflect the degree of technical sophistication and interaction with users (Hiller & Belanger, 2001). A broad model with a three-phase and dual-pronged strategy for implementing electronic democracy is proposed by Watson and Mundy (2000) (see Figure 1). The three phases draw on the principles of skill development (Quinn, Anderson, & Finkelstein, 1996), and the prongs echo the dual foundations of democratic government — effectiveness and efficiency. Note that we identify e-government and e-politics as elements of e-democracy. E-Government informs citizens about their representatives and how they may be contacted and it improves government efficiency by enabling citizens to pay transactions online; whereas e-politics is the use of Internet technology to improve the effectiveness of political decisions by making citizens aware of the how and why of political decision making and facilitating their participation in this process.

Figure 1. Three phases model

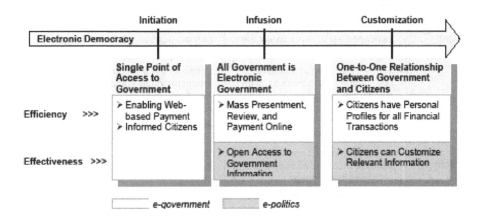

The *initiation phase* focuses on providing citizens with a single point of access to government information and Web-enabling government payments are the critical initial goals. For a minimum level of political involvement, citizens need to know who represents them and what is happening in the political scene.

When the e-democracy proceeds to the *infusion phase*, nearly all governments adopt the principles of e-government. Online review and payment applications are widely installed. Citizens can make most government payments via the Web and electronic bill presentment is the standard. Government becomes more efficient via two major approaches. Small governments opt for an application service provider (ASP) solution, while large governments implement in-house systems. An initiation stage is necessary because governments need to create the infrastructure (e.g., software firms, methodologies, consulting skills), acquaint governments and citizens with the concept of e-government, and learn how to scale from a handful to tens of thousands of online government services. Once the foundation of skills and knowledge has been built and the idea has gained currency, large-scale adoption is feasible.

With the further development of e-government, citizens will not be satisfied with a one-size-fits-all solution, and customization will be demanded. During the *customization phase*, electronic democracy implements a one-to-one relationship between citizen and government. To further improve their personal efficiency, all citizens have an electronically maintained, personal profile of their financial interactions with government. An address change, for example, is a single transaction that automatically notifies all government systems. In addition, citizens can get a detailed breakdown of their particular government payments so that they are more directly connected with how their taxes and fees are spent (e.g., amount contributed to education).

DEVELOPED VS. DEVELOPING COUNTRIES

Every year, the United Nations releases a report on the least developed countries (LDC) and compares their economic conditions in several different categories. For 2002, 49 countries were designated as the least developed. These countries were decided based on their low GDP per capita,

Table 1. Main differences between developed and developing countries

	Developed Countries	Developing Countries
History and Culture	• Government and economy developed early, immediately after independence • Economy growing at a constant rate, productivity increasing, high standard of living • Relatively long history of democracy and more transparent government policy and rule	• Government usually not specifically defined; economy not increasing in productivity • Economy not growing or increasing productivity; low standard of living • Relatively short history of democracy and less transparent government policy and rule
Technical Staff	• Has a current staff, needs to increase technical abilities and hire younger professionals • Has outsourcing abilities and financial resources to outsource; current staff would be able to define requirements for development	• Does not have a staff, or has very limited in-house staff • Does not have local outsourcing abilities and rarely has the financial ability to outsource; current staff may be unable to define specific requirements
Infrastructure	• Good current infrastructure • High internet access for employees and citizens	• Bad current infrastructure • Low internet access for employees and citizens
Citizens	• High internet access and computer literacy; still has digital divide and privacy issues • Relatively more experienced in democratic system and more actively participate in governmental policy-making process	• Low internet access and citizens are reluctant to trust online services; few citizens know how to operate computers • Relatively less experienced in democratic system and less actively participate in governmental policy-making process
Government Officers	• Decent computer literacy and dedication of resources; many do not place eGovernment at a high priority	• Low computer literacy and dedication of resources; many do not place eGovernment a high priority due to lack of knowledge on the issue

their weak human assets, and their high degree of economic vulnerability (UNCTAD, 2002). E-Government implementation and development is a high-priority issue on various countries' agenda. Some countries have surpassed others in online services that they offer to their citizens. Indicators on education and literacy show that, in Mozambique, only 7% of the total population was enrolled in secondary school. Indicators on communications and media show that, in Bangladesh, only 3.4% of the population has a telephone, while 9.3% are in the circulation of daily newspapers (UNCTAD, 2002).

Although e-government technologies have a potential to improve the lives of 80% of the world's population that lives in developing countries, the developed countries such as the U.S., Canada, UK, and Australia are so far leaders in e-government (Annual Global Accenture Study, 2002), reaping the vast majority of initial gains of e-government implementation. Actually, the gap between developed and developing countries in Internet technological infrastructures, practices, and usage has been wider rather than narrower over recent years. Besides the lack of sufficient capital to build up expensive national information infrastructure (NII) on which e-government is based, developing countries also lack the sufficient knowledge and skill to develop suitable and effective strategies for establishing and promoting e-government.

An estimated 500 e-government programs were launched in the year 2001 by governments worldwide (Palmer, 2002). E-Government strategies have had a tremendous impact on the way governments interact with their citizens. More than 75% of Australians file income taxes online, while the mayor of Minnesota receives about 13,000 e-mails from the public each week (Palmer, 2002). According to the 2002 Annual Global Accenture (former Anderson Consulting: AC) Study, Canada is the leader in e-government implementation. The remaining top 10 countries are (in order): Singapore, the United States, Australia, Denmark, the United Kingdom, Finland, Hong Kong, Germany, and Ireland. A survey by the United Nations found that of its 190 member states, only 36 out of the 169 available Web sites had one-stop portals and less than 20 offered online transactions (Jackson, 2002). This clearly shows a big gap in current e-government implementation status in different countries. A more recent study using the United Nations data empirically proves that e-government development and implementation differ in three areas: income level, development status, and region (Siau & Long, 2005).

In comparison with other countries, the United States along with Australia, Singapore, and Canada are the early leaders in the march toward e-government. Governments in the United Kingdom, France, Germany, Spain, Norway, Hong Kong, and New Zealand have vowed to change their policies toward the implementation of e-government in order to take the full advantage of the digital information age. Other cautious implementers include Italy, Japan, Netherlands, and South Africa. Though there has been significant progress made in developed countries in e-government implementation, many developing

countries have been left behind with a long way to catch up. Table 1 summarizes differences between developed and developing countries in various aspects of government.

History and Culture

The history and culture between developed and developing countries are different in many aspects. Developed countries are known more for their early economic and governmental growth, with many governments forming in the 1500s. Several of the developing countries have just recently gained their independence and still do not have a specific government structure. Culture is also a major difference between developed and developing countries. Religious and other backgrounds among citizens of developing countries prevent them from doing certain activities that are commonplace among developed countries. War is also notorious among some developing countries in the Middle East and Asia (e.g., Afghanistan), which depletes their economy and their government structure.

Technology Staff

The in-house staff for most developed countries has been in existence and well-established. Although many of them are old, with half of the existing United States government information technology (IT) workers eligible to retire within the next three years (Ledford, 2002), the existing department is up and working. In contrast, many developing countries do not have an IT department in place or have an IT department that is low-skilled and insufficiently equipped. Education in these countries is a major problem as well as lack of financial resources to pay skilled workers. This brings up major issues with the development and maintenance of systems.

Governments in many developed countries choose to outsource e-government projects. Developed countries often house companies specialized in e-government development within their borders, which makes outsourcing an affordable and convenient alternative. Though companies specialized in e-government development may be available in developing countries, the competitive systems development rates they charge may not be affordable for many developing countries. Even if outsourcing is affordable, without appropriate understanding of IT, many government officials of developing countries will find it difficult to specify requirements and resources to devote for the projects to be outsourced.

Infrastructure

The size and abilities of infrastructures between developed and developing countries differ dramatically. For example, India's capacity for international telecom traffic reached just 780 Mbps by the end of 2000, which is a mere 1.4% of the capacity available in the neighboring country, China (Dooley, 2002). Developed countries have the infrastructure size and abilities to make Internet and telephone access available to almost all of their residents, with some populations over 300 million. The insufficient infrastructure of developing countries is due to economic conditions, war or destruction, which may have recently occurred, and governmental regulations of the telecommunications industry. A dilemma of government regulations also exists in India, where the sector has been a monopoly since its independence from Great Britain in 1947 (Dooley, 2002). All of these factors, unfortunately, hinder the progress of e-government in developing countries.

Citizens

The difference of Internet accessibility between developed and developing countries is a reflection of the countries' infrastructure and telecommunication abilities. As mentioned previously, developing countries lack financial resources and government stability and structure to contain a sizable infrastructure. This results in low access to the Internet and telephone. One third of the world's population has never made a phone call, and 63 countries have less than 1% access to the Internet (ICeGD, 2002). In developed countries, almost every citizen has access to the Internet, and the rate of computer literacy surpasses that of developing countries.

Government Officers

It is imperative that government officials understand and value e-government. The level of resources they are willing to allocate is dependent on their understanding of technology and the benefits that will ensue. In developed countries, most government officials use the Internet or computers on a daily basis. Therefore, government officials in developed countries are familiar with technology and realize how efficient it is. This increases their dedication to allocating additional resources for further implementation. In developing countries, IT is a vague concept, and government officials are somewhat unwilling to allocate already scarce resources toward something they are not familiar with.

A CONCEPTUAL FRAMEWORK OF E-GOVERNMENT IMPLEMENTATION

Most, if not all, e-government strategies and implementation plans in developing countries have been based on theories and experiences of developed countries (Huang, D'Ambra, & Bhalla, 2002). Feeling the pressure and demand from citizens to provide e-government services online, many developing countries have no choice but to hastily jump into the e-government implementation wagon by following e-government development strategies proposed and carried out by developed countries. However, due to substantial differences in many key aspects of e-government related technological and social conditions between developed and developing countries, e-government development strategies and experiences from developed countries may not be directly applicable to developing countries. Even in developed countries, about 20-25% of e-government projects are either never implemented or abandoned immediately after implementation, and a further 33% fail partially in terms of falling short of major goals, causing significant undesirable outcomes or both (Heeks, 2000).

The Center for International Development at Harvard University, USA, supported by IBM, identified four key factors describing differences between developing and developed countries in terms of implementing e-commerce (Kirkman, Osorio, & Sachs, 2002). These four factors are adapted to study e-government in this research, which are termed as National E-Government Infrastructure (NeI) factors.

NeI Factor 1: Network Access

Network access is measured by the availability, cost, and quality of information and communication technology (ICTs) networks, services, and equipment. More specifically, it includes the following key elements:

- **Infrastructure Development.**
  Infrastructure development is a necessity before countries can consider any large projects dedicated to e-government. Citizens must have access to services before any of the cost saving benefits will apply. Also, with a lack of back-end infrastructure, governments and their employees will be unable to move into a transactional process and further stages of e-government implementation.
- **Resources and IT Support.** Outsourcing can be an option for countries to implement e-government. The private sector has an obligation to support governments throughout the world in their dedication to e-government. Developing countries need

financial discounts and support from the private sector to successfully develop applications due to their lack of resources and staff.

- **Utilization.**
  The citizen utilization of the Internet is based on the access to the Internet and the Web site. Technical support must provide 24/7 access in addition to providing a better infrastructure so that more citizens can utilize the Internet. Much like in developed countries, citizen utilization is an important part of the cost savings for countries.

NeI Factor 2: Network Learning

Network learning concerns two key issues: (1) Does an educational system integrate ICTs into its processes to improve learning? and (2) Are there technical training programs in the community that can train and prepare an ICT workforce? Technical staffing and training is a major issue in e-government implementation. In developing countries, the problems lie in the lack of financial resources to hire full–time, in-house support and in the inability to find such support due to the lack of education in these countries. Outsourcing is an alternative; however, affordable and competent companies may not be available. Even if a country can find the finances to support an outsourcing project, stability and maintenance of the application are often difficult.

NeI Factor 3: Network Economy

Network economy concerns how businesses and governments use information and communication technologies to interact with the public and with each other. Key issues involved include collaboration, partnership, public-private sector partnership, e-community creation, and so forth. Boundary removal between different agencies in a government is a major issue in e-government. In many developing countries, government structure is undefined and destabilized by corruption and communism. Consequently, boundary removal and department collaboration is a difficult and slow process. In many countries, war and terrorism is a constant issue that disrupts government operations on a daily basis. Government departments must collaborate with each other, with private sectors, and with related communities in order for e-government to be implemented in an efficient way. Due to the low computer literacy and high cost of online access, long and unnecessary transactions need to be cut down in processes to allow users to quickly access documents and print them or fill them out online.

Nel Factor 4: Network Policy

Network policy concerns the extent that the policy environment promotes or hinders the growth of ICT adoption and use. Some related key issues include legislations, laws, strategies (visions and missions), accountability, and so forth. Government agencies and departments must be accountable for their information and processes they

support. It is essential for processes and duties to be segregated and responsibilities to be assigned to appropriate agencies and departments. These agencies and departments then need to work together to design their Web pages and IT flows. After implementation, they must have the abilities and be held accountable to support the Web pages and troubleshoot them. Governments must also be accountable for their financial and accounting systems. Many developing countries have issues and economic problems due to their lack of reliable accounting systems.

Culture and Society Factors

E-commerce largely deals with business transactions in private sector whereas e-government deals with services in the public sector. Due to key differences between private and public sectors (e.g., Bozeman & Bretschneider, 1986; Caudle, Gorr, & Newcomer, 1991; Rainey, Backoff, & Levine, 1976), factors other than the ones identified by the previously-mentioned Harvard University e-commerce research project may also be important

Figure 2. A conceptual research framework

to e-government strategies and implementations. Prior relevant research suggested some key factors for e-government strategies and implementations, which can be used to identify differences in e-government between developed and developing countries. Those suggested factors include society factors like *history, citizens* (Huang, D'Ambra, & Bhalla, 2002), *government staff and governance* (Wimmer, Traunmuller, & Lenk, 2001), *organizational structure* (Baligh, 1994); and cultural factors like *national culture* (Hoftstede, 1980, 1991), *organizational culture* (Hoftstede, 1980; Schein, 1993), and *social norms* (Ajzen, 1988). Other than those suggested by literature, society factors like *politics* and *information availability* should also be considered. Developing countries are often less democratized with underdeveloped press communication resulting in unbalanced and deficient information availability. These politics and information factors have significant impact on the speed of infrastructure establishment in developing countries, thus should be considered in creating e-government strategies.

Based upon the earlier literature review and discussion, a research framework incorporating critical success factors (CSFs) which influence e-government strategies and implementations is proposed and shown in Figure 2. Some CSFs identified in the proposed framework could be more important to developed countries than to developing countries, or vice versa. The framework can also be used to assess and guide the strategic development of e-government implementation in developed and developing countries.

CASE STUDY

The following case study is used to demonstrate how the proposed e-government implementation framework can be used to analyze different e-government strategies adopted in developed and developing countries. It presents a snapshot of current e-government implementation in the

U.S. (the largest developed country) and China (the biggest developing country in the world, with a focus on Shanghai - the biggest city and economic center of China) in comparing their e-government implementation strategy.

E-Government Implementation Strategy in the U.S.

The U.S., as the largest developed country, has one of the most advanced National E-Government Infrastructures (NeIs) in the world, and it also has a long history and culture of democratic government structure and capitalist economic system. As a result, the U.S. government adopted the following three strategic principles in the implementation of e-government: (1) citizen-centered, not bureaucracy-centered; (2) results-oriented; and (3) market-based, actively promoting innovation (source: www.firstgov.gov). In short, e-government implementation strategy of the U.S. is market-based with the aim of serving and supporting citizens' specific requirements, which is assessed by clear and specific results.

The policy environment in the United States is an important consideration in understanding the strategy for e-government implementation. A complete set of laws relating to the development of e-government has been in the place already, including the Privacy Act, the Computer Matching and Privacy Protection Act, the Electronic Freedom of Information Amendments, the Computer Security Act, the Critical Infrastructure Protection, the Government Paperwork Elimination Act, and the Electronic Government Act (Relyea, 2002).

According to the white paper of the U.S. federal government's e-government strategy (2002 and 2003), more than 60% of all Internet users interact with government Web sites. Moreover, by leveraging information technology (IT) spending across federal agencies, the U.S. federal government will make available over $1 billion in savings from aligning redundant investments. Federal IT spending in the United States exceeded $48 billion in 2002 and $52 billion in 2003. That level of IT spending provides enormous opportunities for making the transformation government into a citizen-centered e-government. Indeed, a good portion of current federal IT spending is devoted to Internet initiatives, yielding over 35 million Web pages online at over 22,000 Web sites. However, past agency-centered IT approaches have limited the government's productivity gains and ability to serve citizens. As a result, the federal government is determined to transform the way it does business with citizens through the use of e-government.

A September 2002 report from the Pew Foundation found that 71 million Americans have used government Web sites – up from 40 million in March 2000. A June 2002 United Nations report, *Benchmarking eGovernment: A Global Perspective,* rated the United States as the world leader in e-government on the basis of achievements over the last year. The United States Web portal, FirstGov. gov, is currently in stage 4 of its implementation (Hiller & Belanger, 2001), which integrates various government services internally and externally for the enhancement of efficiency, usability, and effectiveness. The FirstGov.gov attracts almost 6 million visitors a month, which is America's Gateway to more than 180 million Web pages from federal and state governments, the District of Columbia, and the U.S. territories. Named one of the *"50 Most Incredibly Useful Web Sites"* by Yahoo, July 2002, and to *PC Magazine*'s *Top 100 Classic Site*s, March 2003, FirstGov.gov was most recently awarded the prestigious *Innovations in American Government Award* for transcending traditional government boundaries.

In January 2003, the current e-government project managers met with the members of the 2001 e-government task force. This group of more than 100 government managers shared a number of insights about unresolved e-government challenges that the 2003 strategy should address. None of the identified challenges were involved techno-logical barriers (as discussed earlier, the U.S. has one of the best NeIs in the world so that its main strategic issues for successfully implementing e-government are largely non-technical issues). The challenges were centered around behavioral or policy changes needed, such as leadership support, parochialism, funding, and communication. Another challenge in 2003 is to physically migrate agency-unique solutions to each cross-agency e-government solution, reducing costs, and generating more citizen-centered results. The suggested solutions to these challenges include: establishing single sources of information, accessible by citizens in no more than three clicks (one-stop portals such as Recreation.gov and Regulations. gov); developing tools that provide a simple one-stop method to access government programs; and establishing common sets of standards for data collection and reporting.

In 2003 and 2004, the overall e-government strategy addressed the following areas:

- **Driving results and productivity growth:** IT and management reform investments that create an order of magnitude improvement in value to the citizen, especially in the areas of homeland security information sharing and knowledge flow;
- **Controlling IT costs:** Consolidating redundant and overlapping investments, enterprise licensing, fixing cost overruns, and competing away excess IT services charges;
- **Implementing the E-Government Act of 2002:** Including government-wide architecture governance and Web-based strategies for improving access to high quality information and services; and
- **Improving cyber security:** Desktop, data, applications, networks, threat and vulnerability-focused, business continuity, and privacy protection.

In summary, due to the relatively long history of democratic system, the main goals of the U.S.

e-government focus on increasing effectiveness and efficiency of government work and, at the same time, reducing cost.

Differences between the U.S. and China

The first e-government implementation project in China began in 1994. According to the 11th Report of the Statistic of China National Network Development (RSCNND) by China National Network Information Centre (CNNIC), up to the end of 2002, the Internet users had achieved 59.1 million. It added up to 9% of the Internet users in the world (655 million). There were 371,600 Web sites, among which 291,323 were in com.cn, 6,148 in gov.cn, 54,156 in net.cn, and 1,783 in org.cn. The number of computers linked to the Internet was more than 20.83 million.

Though China has maintained its position as the fastest growing economy in the world in recent years, there still exists a big gap in terms of National E-Government Infrastructure (NeI) between China and other developed countries like the U.S. Even though its economy has developed fast in the last decade, China is still in the process of transitioning from a centrally–controlled, planned economy to a market-based, capitalist economy. Using the proposed framework, we assess the e-government implementation status in China with a focus in Shanghai, the economic centre of China. Shanghai is one of the most developed regions/cities in China. If there exist differences between the U.S. and Shanghai in terms of NeIs and e-government implementation based on the proposed theoretical framework, the differences between the U.S. and China can be even bigger.

1. **Network Access.**
    The information infrastructures in Shanghai have undergone mega changes and made some big progresses in recent years. Up to the beginning of year 2002, the bandwidth of Shanghai's Internet connection to the outside

world was expended to 2.5G; the network cable lines were stretched out for more than 550 kilometers that covered more than 99% of the whole city. The number of broadband Internet users in Shanghai reached 125 thousand that year; the number of fixed phone users exceeded 6 million while mobile phone users exceeded fixed phone users. More than 3.1 million families had access to the Internet, which almost doubled the number of the previous year. However, even in Shanghai, one of the most advanced cities in China, subscribing to Internet service is still more costly in China than in developed countries such as the United States. In China, the charge of ISP (Internet Service Provider) is bi-directional; users pay for not only sending but also receiving information.

2. **Networked Learning.**
    The development of the network learning is speeding up in Shanghai. The broadband of the main network of the Shanghai Science & Education Network (SSEN) was expanded to 1.25G from the 64k in its budding stage. The fibro-cable connecting the educational institutions in Shanghai was longer than 200 kilometers in the year 2001. More than 19 universities in Shanghai made their effects to launch a common-shared database of the book information in these 19 universities' libraries. In this system, people could also search for the key academic periodicals and borrow through the Remote Borrow-ing/Lending Service. Up to the year 2001, the SSEN had a sea-sized collection of materials including: 12 thousand periodical databases, 200 thousand e-book resources, business sub-databases, science and technology sub-databases, digital periodical system database, and so forth. More than 100 multi-functional databases provided a wide range of selections to the students' content. Furthermore, several universities in Shanghai got permission from the govern-

ment to develop their "net-school" projects, which made the e-learning in Shanghai more professional and orderly. According to the *Human Development Report in 2001* by the United Nations Development Program (UNDP), which publiherd the first Technical Achievements Index (TAI) in the world, China is listed as the 45th among the 72 countries whereas the U.S. is ranked 2nd in the list.

3. **Networked Economy.**
The information industry in Shanghai is keeping a fast developing momentum in recent years. The turnover of the information industry in Shanghai was 130.225 billion Yuan by its growth rate of 24.4%, which maintained its strategic position as Shanghai's first pillar industry. The proportion of the added value in this industry in the GDP amounted to 8.1% that was 0.7% more than the previous year. Among the information industry in Shanghai, the turnover of the information product manufacturing industry reached 101.3 billion Yuan, and its growth rate even hit 37.4%. The product sales percentage was also increased by 1.8% and summed up to 97.5%. Meanwhile the information services and software in Shanghai also achieved an output of 28.8 billion Yuan, a 52.2% increase from the previous year. The information industry in Shanghai has remained in the top three throughout the whole country in terms of its scale, so much that it also draws worldwide attention. The network economy is thus greatly enhanced by the strategy Shanghai adopted — "To promote the Industrialization by Informationization." Among the 1,500 industry companies, 80% of them have set up IT departments; 97% of them have popularized the use of computer; 89% of them have become familiar with common software; 12% of them have conducted ERP; and 8% of them have implanted CRM.

More than 500 marketplaces have adopted their MIS; most convenient chain stores and supermarkets have launched POS and also have them linked with each other to form a value-added network system. As a whole, China's e-commerce turnover is relatively small in size, accounting for only 0.23% of the U.S.'s annual e-commerce turnover.

4. **Network Policy.**
Network policy might be the weakest part of the four NeI factors for China. China has been transforming its economic system from the old Soviet Union's "planned economy" model to the capitalist's "market economy". The transition period, though seemingly to be on a right track, is painful and far from completion. The legal systems, laws, and regulations have been gradually established, yet they are far from maturing in managing the big developing economy, not to mention the completeness of its network economy policy and related laws.

Due to its relatively short history of modernized society and long history of feudal governmental system, China's democratic system and policy still have a long way to go even though they have achieved much more progress in the last decade. For example, to the year 2002, 12 policies, statutes, and regulations were taken into consideration by Shanghai municipal government. The major ones are listed as follows:

- Regulations on Shanghai's Informationization Projects Management;
- Detailed Rules of the Regulations on the IC Industry and Software Promotions in Shanghai;
- Decision on the Overall Informationization Construction in Shanghai;
- Suggestions on the Information Security in Shanghai;
- Management Measures on the Social Insurance Card System; and

- Management Measures on the Public Mobile System.

Besides these policies, statutes, and regulations, the implementations are also of the same importance. Shanghai's municipal government is dedicated in the administrations, supervisions, and mutual discussions of the confusions in order to achieve a better legal environmental situation.

5. **Culture and Society Factors.**

Developed countries have a long history and culture of democratic governmental structure and capitalist economic system, with many governments forming in the 1500's. Many developing countries have not completed its process of establishing an effective and transparent governmental structure as well as an efficient capitalist economic system. China has only started its "open door" policy in the late 1970s and "market-driven economy" in 1990s. The differences in history and culture, citizens, government officers, and technical staff between China and other developed countries like the U.S. are also noticeably large.

For example, China was under the feudal government system for nearly 5,000 years, where the dictator of the country, the emperor, has absolute power and possesses absolute wealth in the country. Only until the early 1910s, such a governmental structure was overturned. However, the very long history of ruling by an absolute powerful emperor would have an impact on modern governmental structure and system. Even now, national and provincial governments still have certain privileges to access and use valuable resources, such as financial, human, and production resources. Governmental agencies and organizations are generally more effective/powerful than private sectors in carrying out e-government implementations. The level of transparency

of governmental management mechanism and decision-making process is relatively low. Because of those historical reasons and practically some advantages existing in governments, many university graduates and talents favor to work for governments. As a result, governmental officers and/or technical staff in governments are generally more knowledgeable than those in the private sector using information technologies and systems in their daily work.

In summary, due to the differences discussed earlier in NeIs and other social issues, it may not be feasible for private sector to play a leading role in e-government implementation; instead it may be governments to drive the progress of e-government implementation. Therefore, the e-government implementation strategy between the U.S. and China are largely different, which will be discussed next.

E-Government Implementation Strategy in China

As analyzed earlier, due to the substantial differences in all four key aspects/factors of NeI and other CSFs between China and developed countries like the U.S., instead of adopting the e-government implementation strategies developed in the U.S. directly, China should adopt a strategy that fits well with its current position in terms of the four aspects of NeI and other CSFs as specified in the proposed assessment framework. For example, as the center of China's economy development, Shanghai's e-government implementation can function as a role model for other cities and provinces in China to follow up. Three specific e-government implementation strategies of Shanghai are specified. They are: (1) to increase the transparency of government work, (2) to provide the convenience and better services to citizens and enterprises, and (3) to improve the efficiency of the government administration.

Compared with the U.S.'s e-government strategic principles — "citizen-centered", "results-oriented" and "market-based" (eGovernment Strategy, 2002, 2003), Shanghai has largely different strategic goals. The ultimate goal of e-government implementation could be quite similar, which is to improve the performance and efficiency of the government work and lead to better interactions/cooperation between government and the public and between the government and private enterprises. The unique feature of Shanghai's e-government strategy is to "increase the transparency of the government work". Other than achieving its usual goals, e-government in Shanghai is used as an instrument in expediting government transformation and conformity. Via the implementation of e-government, civil rights are concretized, bribability is minimized, and governance by law and democracy are enhanced.

In general, the e-government implementation in China as a whole is aiming to serve its overall economic development goal, which is to completely transform China's former Soviet Union style "planning economy" to "market economy". Such changes in the overall mechanism of the country will definitely have profound effects on e-government implementation strategy and practice. On the other hand, the U.S. has a long history of a market-economy and democratic system. The government work is relatively much more transparent than that in China. Therefore, "increasing the transparency of government work" may not seem to be important as it is to China.

In fact, based upon the successful experience of e-government implementation strategies in developed countries, China adopted a different e-government implementation strategy, which could be characterized as "government-driven and partnership with the private sector". In this strategy, governmental departments consolidate all forces and resources available in a society (a city or a province) to lead the implementation of e-government while establishing partnership with

private sector for the implementation purpose. So far, China's e-government implementation is still at the stage 1 with some features in stages 2, 3, and 4 in some economically more developed cities and provinces, whereas the U.S. may already be at the stage 3, according to the five-stage model (Hiller & Belanger, 2001), and it has achieved some initial results. Chinese government perceived that the rapid development of the Internet in the U.S. resulted from effective and significant direct support and sponsorship from the government through the military, education, and government procurement policies, which has been regarded as a good example and effective means for driving the development of e-government in China by Chinese government.

The dominant role played by Chinese government generally fits well with the historical and cultural characteristics as well as the NeI of China. In fact, the Chinese government could be the only possible entity in the society that has enough power and capability to coordinate all related government agencies, organizations, and private sectors as well as consolidate all available resources to effectively implement e-government. The government has also had successful experience in playing the leading role in modernizing its previous outdated telecommunication industry, which is perhaps the most successful contemporary example of China's interventionist economic strategy. By mid-2001, China's public switching capacity was 300 million circuits, which is the world's largest. This was largely due to the supply-driven program of network rollout by the government with the growth rate of double digits through the 1990s (Lovelock & Ure, 2001).

The fund for e-government implementation is being mainly covered by governments both at central and provincial levels. For example, the investment by the central national government alone is reportedly standing at least over USD$120 million (Lovelock & Ure, 2001). By 1998, China has set up 145 gov.cn domain names in China.

According to the China Internet Network Center (CNNIC) annual report, the number of current gov.cn domain names is more than 5,864.

The Chinese government is speeding up the construction of network infrastructure in preparing for its completion of e-government implementation in 2005. Since the initiation of first e-government program "Digital Beijing", which the Beijing Municipal Government used on computerization of administration procedure and e-education in 1994, the Chinese government has made much progress on e-government. The purpose of e-government construction falls into three categories: building the internal network to handle government affairs at all levels and the external Web to handle business in connection with enterprises; public services and affairs between government; promoting 12 key services involving customs, taxation, finance, public security, social security, and agriculture and water resource; and accelerating the establishment of important databanks such as population and agricultural information. Services currently offered by government Web sites mainly include function/vocation introduction, government announcement/laws and regulations, government news, trade/regional information, work guide, and so forth (Source: Semi-annual Survey Report on the Development of China's Internet in January 2002, China Internet Network Center).

The Government Online Project (GOP) provides good evidence indicating the government's dominant role and support for e-government development in China, and it has three stages. Stage one focuses upon connecting 800-1,000 government offices and agencies to the Internet; stage two focuses on having government offices and agencies move their information systems into compatible electronic form; and stage three will occur sometime late in the decade when government offices and agencies become paperless.

The purpose of the GOP is to create a centrally accessible administrative system that collects and transports data to and from users, users be-

ing the public and the enterprise system as well as government departments. In other words, the government's strategy for driving the "information economy" is to first launch the GOP by setting up formal government Web sites so that the public can acquire information and procure specific government services via the Internet. The focus then shifts to promoting office automation via government Web sites in order to cut down on excessive bureaucracy and, hence, expenses.

By the end of 2000, 80% of all government agencies, both local and national, had established Web sites. Some examples of the implemented e-government Web sites include:

- State Economic and Trade Commission State Administration of Internal Trade;
- Central Committee of the League Commission of Science, Tech & Industry for National Defense;
- State Administration of Foreign Exchange Control General Office of CPPCC;
- Supreme People's Court Supreme People's Procurator;
- Ministry of Agriculture Ministry of Civil Affairs;
- Ministry of Foreign Affairs Ministry of Foreign Trade and Economic Cooperation;
- Ministry of Information Industry Ministry of Justice;
- Ministry of Labor and Social Security Ministry of Land and Natural Resources;
- National Bureau of Oceanography National Intellectual Property Right Office;
- China Council for Promotion of International Trade China National Space Administration;
- CNNIC General Administration of Civil Aviation of China; and
- General Administration of Customs.
  (Source: Ministry of Information Industry (MII) http://www.mii.gov.cn/mii/index.html)

They are only a few examples of Chinese e-government implementation projects. However, currently most Chinese people cannot pay their taxes, obtain their driver licenses, IDs, residence certificates, and so forth, from the government Web site, and the paperless government still has a long way to go.

The Chinese government, like all governments, is stricken with turf battles between ministries, commissions, and other organizations which all view the Internet as touching on their domain of authority or interest. As noted earlier, the Government Online Project was initiated in early 1999. The following two strategic projects were also planned and will be fully implemented in the near future. *Enterprise Online* is to encourage industries to aggressively adopt the full use of available Internet technologies, and to provide a greater degree of transparency. *Family Online* is to encourage increased use of network resources by families across China, including those in rural areas, and to bring the populace at large onto the government's new communications platform.

In summary, while China has achieved its fast economic development in the late decade, it has also started to move to a more democratic and transparent government system and mechanism. E-Government has become one key implementation mechanism for the government to achieve its goal of a more transparent government. China adopted an e-government implementation strategy different from the U.S. Based on its own economic, historic and social factors, China's e-government implementation is so far largely driven by government, rather than by market forces. In a relatively short time period, it has achieved some noticeable results although there is still a long way to go.

DISCUSSIONS AND CONCLUSION

Although there are some prior studies published on e-government strategies and implementation (e.g., Carter & Belanger, 2005; Chircu & Lee, 2003; Glassey, 2001; Greunz, Schopp, & Haes, 2001; Huang, D'Ambra, & Bhalla, 2002; Wimmer, Traunmuller, & Lenk, 2001), to our knowledge, most if not all published e-government strategies are from the perspective of developed countries, not from the perspective of developing countries. Due to the considerable differences between developed and developing countries, the latter cannot directly adopt e-government strategies used in developed countries. For that reason, the current study intends to do some initial work to bridge this gap. It compares strategic issues and implementations of e-government between developed and developing countries. More specifically, the following issues are addressed:

- Proposing a conceptual framework that includes the critical success factors influencing e-government strategies and implementations for developed and developing countries.
- Using a case study to illustrate how the proposed framework can be used to analyze different e-government strategies in a developed country (the U.S.) and a developing country (China).

Due to the substantial differences in four aspects of NeI and other CSFs as specified in the proposed framework, developing countries cannot and should not directly adopt developed countries' successful e-government implementation strategies. The proposed framework provides a clear structure and guideline for developing suitable e-government implementation strategy. Developing countries should consider their own positions in terms of CSFs as specified in the proposed e-government strategy framework and learn from other countries' successful e-government implementation strategies, and then work out their e-government implementation strategies that fit with their countries' characteristics and conditions.

Future studies can be conducted to collect national data in both developed and developing countries to empirically and statistically verify the proposed framework and study the relationships among the specified CSFs. More specifically, the importance of those CSFs to e-government strategies and implementation can be ranked through using survey research methodology. More complicated relationships existing between CSFs can be determined using Structure Equation Modeling technique. In this way, CSFs for implementing e-government strategies can be specifically identified and validated. With the guidance of the proposed framework, e-government strategies and implementations in developing countries can be more effective and efficient.

REFERENCES

Ajzen, I. (1988). *Attitudes, personality and behavior*. Milton Keynes: Open University Press.

Annual Global Accenture (former Anderson Consulting: AC) Study Report. (2002).

Baligh, H. H. (1994). Components of culture: Nature, interconnections, and relevance to the decisions on the organization structure. *Management Science, 40*(1), 14-28.

Bozeman, B., & Bretschneider, S. (1986). Public management information systems: Theory and prescription. *Public Administration Review*, Special Issue, 47-487.

Carter, L., & Belanger, F. (2005, January). The utilization of e-government services: Citizen trust, innovation and acceptance factors. *Information Systems Journal, 15*(1), 5-25.

Caudle, S. L., Gorr, W. L., & Newcomer, K. E. (1991, June). Key information systems management issues for the public sector. *MIS Quarterly, 15*(2), 171-188.

Chircu, A. M., & Lee, H. D. (2003, August). Understanding IT investments in the public sector: The case of e-government. In the *Proceedings of the American Conference on Information Systems (AMCIS)*, FL.

Dooley, B. L. (2002). Telecommunications in India: State of the marketplace. *Faulkner Information Services* (February), Docid 00016872.

eGovernment Strategy. (2002, 2003). U.S. Federal Government. Retrieved from www.firstgov.gov.

Garretson, C. (2002). Senate passes e-government bill. *InfoWorld Daily News*, June 28.

Glassey, O. (2001, June 27-29). Model and architecture for a virtual one-stop public administration. *The 9th European Conferences on Information Systems* (pp. 969-976).

Government and the Internet Survey. (2000). *The Economist, 355*(8176), 33-34.

Greunz, M., Schopp, B., & Haes, J. (2001). Integrating e-government infrastructures through secure XML document containers. In *Proceedings of the 34th Hawaii International Conference on System Sciences*.

Heeks, R. (2000). *Reinventing government in the information age*. London: Routledge Press.

Hiller, J., & Belanger, F. (2001). Privacy strategies for electronic government. *E-Government Series*. Arlington, VA: PricewaterhouseCoopers Endowment for the Business of Government.

Hofstede, G. (1980). *Culture's consequences: International differences in work-related values*. Newbury Park, CA: Sage Press.

Hofstede, G. (1991). *Cultures and organizations: Software of the mind*. London: McGraw Hill.

Huang, W., D'Ambra, J., & Bhalla, V. (2002). An empirical investigation of the adoption of egovernment in Australian citizens: Some unexpected research findings. *Journal of Computer Information Systems, 43*(1), 15-22.

Huang, W., Siau, K., & Wei, K.K. (Eds.). (2004). *Electronic government: Strategic and implementations.* Hershey, PA: Idea Group Publishing.

International Conference on e-Government for Development (IceGD). (2002). Retrieved September 25, 2002, from http://www.palermoconference 2002.org/en/home_a.htm.

Jackson, N. (2002). State of the marketplace: e-Government gateways. *Faulkner Information Services* (February), Docid 00018296.

Jain, A., & Patnayakuni, R. (2003, August). Public expectations and public scrutiny: An agenda for research in the context of e-government. In the *Proceeding of American Conference on Information Systems (AMCIS),* FL.

Keston, G. (2002). U.S. self-service government initiatives. *Faulkner Information Services* (February), Docid 00018287.

Kirkman, G. S., Osorio, C. A., & Sachs, J. D. (2002). The networked readiness index: Measuring the preparedness of nations for the networked world. In *The global information technology report: Readiness for the networked world* (pp. 10-30). Oxford University Press.

Ledford, J. L. (2002). Establishing best practices for e-government within the U.S. *Faulkner Information Services* (February), DocId: 00018275.

Lovelock, & Ure. (2001). *E-government in China.* Retrieved from http://www.trp.hku.hk/publications/e_gov_china.pdf

Moon, J. M. (2002, July/August). The evolution of e-government among municipalities: Rhetoric or reality? *Public Administration Review, 62*(4), 424-433.

Moon, M. J., & Norris, D.F. (2005, January). Does managerial orientation matter? The adoption of

reinventing government and e-government at the municipal level. *Information Systems Journal, 15*(1), 43-60.

Navarra, D. D., & Cornford, R. (2003, August). A policy making view of e-government innovations in public governance. In the *Proceedings of the American Conference on Information Systems (AMCIS),* FL.

Palmer, I. (2002). State of the world: e-Government implementation. *Faulkner Information Services* (January), Docid 00018297.

Quinn, J. B., Anderson, P., & Finkelstein, S. (1996). Leveraging intellect. *Academy of Management Executive, 10*(3), 7-27.

Perlman, E. (2002). E-government special report: The people connection. *Congressional Quarterly DBA Governing Magazine, 32*(September).

Rainey, H. G., Backoff, R. W., & Levine, C. H., (1976). Comparing public and private organizations. *Public Administration Review,* March/April, 233-243.

Relyea, H. C. (2002). E-gov: Introduction and overview. *Government Information Quarterly,* 19, 9-35.

Schein, E. H. (1993). On dialogue, culture, and organizational learning. *Organizational Dynamics,* Autumn, 40-51.

Siau, K., & Long, Y. (2005). Using social development lenses to understand e-government development. *Journal of Global Information Management* (in press).

Snellen, I. (2000). Electronic commerce and bureaucracies. In the *Proceedings of the 11th International Workshops on Database and Expert System Application* (pp. 285-288).

Sprecher, M. (2000). Racing to e-government: Using the Internet for citizen service delivery. *Government Finance Review,* 16, 21-22.

Symonds, M. (2000). The next revolution: After ecommerce, get ready for egovernment.

The Economist (n.d., June 24). Retrieved from http://www.economist.com/l.cgi ?f=20000624/index_survey

Tapscott, D. (1995). *Digital economy: Promise and peril in the age of networked intelligence.* New York: McGraw-Hill.

UN (United Nations) & ASPA (American Society for Public Administration). (2001). *Global survey of e-government.*

UNCTAD (2002). *Least developed countries at a glance.* United Nation Information Communication Technology Task Force.

U.S. Census Bureau. (1999). *Government Organization: 1997 Census of Governments*, Washington, D.C. Retrieved from http://www.census.gov/prod/www/abs/gc97org.html

Watson & Mundy. (2000). Electronic democracy: A strategic perspective. *Communications of ACM.*

Wimmer, M., Traunmuller, R., & Lenk, K. (2001). Electronic business invading the public sector: Considerations on change and design. In the *Proceedings of the 34th Hawaii International Conference on System Sciences.*

This work was previously published in Journal of Global Information Management, Vol. 14, Issue 1, edited by F. Tan, pp. 23-46, copyright 2006 by IGI Publishing, formerly known as Idea Group Publishing (an imprint of IGI Global).

Section V
Critical Issues

Chapter XXI
Social Institutional Explanations of Global Internet Diffusion:
A Cross–Country Analysis

Hongxin Zhao
Saint Louis University, USA

Seung Kim
Saint Louis University, USA

Taewon Suh
Texas State University – San Marcos, USA

Jianjun Du
University of Houston – Victoria, USA

ABSTRACT

This study attempts to examine empirically how social institutional factors relate to Internet diffusion in 39 countries. Based on nine-year cross-country data, the analytical results show that the rule of law, educational systems, and industrialization significantly influenced the global Internet diffusion, while the economic system did not exert significant impact. Uncertainty avoidance as a national cultural phenomenon significantly inhibited the Internet diffusion. This significant and negative effect is particularly true with less developed countries (LDCs).

INTRODUCTION

One of the most significant technological developments in the last century is the emergence of the Internet. According to the World Bank, between 1995 and 1998, worldwide communication markets connected 200 million telephone lines, 263 million mobile subscribers, and 10 million leased lines. Internet connections increased nearly 65 fold, exploding from 15 million in 1994 to 972.5 million by November, 2005. The adoption of the Internet also grew at a fast rate. It took the World Wide Web (WWW) only four years to reach 50 million users, while it took the telephone close

Table 1. A summary list of related literature

Panel 1				
Author	**Research Focus**	**Study Setting**	**Significant Variables**	**Insignificant Variables**
1 Dutta & Roy, 2005	Application of system dynamics model to the mechanics of diffusion	India	The significant influences of feedback loops	
2 Forma, 2005	Examine inter-firm variation of internet adoption decisions	Finance and serves sector in US	LAN intensity, system communication; NetWare applications, internet clients; pc's per employee; geographic dispersion	
3 Shih, Dedrick, and Kraemer, 2005	Country level determinants of e-commerce activity	30 countries	Number of secure servers; total IT investment; rule of law; internet access cost	Financial resources; direct marketing, revenues; credit card penetration
4 Clarke, 2004	Effects of Ownership and foreign competition	21 East European and Central Asian countries	Positive effects	
5 Dholakia and Kshetri, 2004	Explore factors impacting adoption of internet among SMEs	New England region of the US	Prior technology use, perceived competitive pressure	Past media use
6 Xu, Zhu, and Gibbs, 2004	Explore internet adoption by US and Chinese firms.	262 US firms and 175 Chinese firms.	Technology competence, enterprise integration, competition intensity, and regulatory environment	

continued on following page

Table 1. continued

7	Brown and Licker 2003	Explore differences in internet adoption between advantaged / disadvantaged groups in South Africa.	South Africa	Perceived usefulness, perceived enjoyment, long-term consequences,	
8	Huang, Keser, Leland, and Shachat, 2003	Examine how differences in willingness and trust affect internet adoption rates across countries.	28 countries	Trust, lines, pc's, income	
9	Kula and Tatoglu, 2003	Examine role of firm- and industry-specific factors affecting internet adoption by SMEs in emerging economies	Turkey	Amount of resources allocated for export development, and international experience	Usage frequency of internet applications, competitive intensity of sector
10	Teo and Pian, 2003	Examines contingency factors that affect levels of internet adoption.	Firms from the 'Singapore 1000' and 'SME 500'	Business technology strategy	Technology compatibility, top management support
11	Kiiski and Pohjola 2002	Cross country diffusion of internet	OECD	GNP per capita; internet access cost; telecom investment	Competitive telecom market; average schooling
12	Volken, 2002	Trust effect	47 countries	Positive effects of trust on internet diffusion	
13	Zhu & He, 2002	Effects of perceived features, needs and popularity	China	All positive effects	
14	Hargittai 1999	Internet connectivity	OECD	GDP per capital; phone density;	

continued on following page

Table 1. continued

Panel 2				
	Author	**Research Focus**	**Study Setting**	**Significant Variables**	**Insignificant Variables**
1	Dinlersoz & Hernadez-Murillo, 2005	Describe internet diffusion in manufacturing, retail and service sectors	U.S.	The observed rate of diffusion varies by sectors	
2	Dutta and Roy, 2005	Describe internet diffusion in manufacturing, retail and service sectors	U.S.		
3	Guo and Chen, 2005	Internet diffusion in Chinese companies	Chinese companies	Descriptive	
4	Peng, Trappey, and Liu, 2005	Determine status of internet and e-commerce adoption	Taiwan semiconductor industry	Descriptive	
5	Suraya, 2005	Investigate factors influencing the slow adoption rate of internet usage	Malaysian travel agencies	Descriptive	
6	Wallsten, 2005	Effects of regulated entry	44 developing countries	Negative effect of regulated entry	
7	Brown, Hoppe, Mugera, Newman, and Stander, 2004	Impact of national environment on adoption of internet banking.	Comparison between Singapore and South Africa	Attitudinal and perceived behavioral control factors. Specifically: compatibility, trialability, and self-efficacy.	Relative advantage, banking needs, internet experience, risk, and government support.
8	Warren 2004	Explore internet adoption among farmers	UK farmers	Descriptive, not empirical.	
9	Fornerino 2003	Internet adoption rates in France.	France	Descriptive.	

continued on following page

Table 1. continued

10	Hannemyr 2003	Compare adoption rate of internet with Phone, TV and radio	Worldwide with a focus on US	The adoption rate of internet is faster than others.		
11	Jones, Hecker, and Holland, 2003	Examine strategic acquisition and exploitation of knowledge relating to web-based commerce	5 Tasmanian firms	Descriptive / case study		
12	Zhao 2003	Description of facilitating factors for internet	China	Descriptive		
13	La Ferle, Edwards, and Mizung, 2002	Cultural variables are used to explore differences found in internet diffusion between US and Japan	US and Japan	Individualism, power distance, uncertainty avoidance,	Masculinity/ femininity	
14	Mbarika, Jensen, and Meso, 2002	Factors influencing Internet diffusion in Sub-Saharan Africa	Sub-Saharan Africa	Descriptive.		
15	Mills and Whitacre, 2002	Understanding the non-metropolitan to metropolitan digital divide for consumers	US	Age, family structure, race, use at work, region of US		
16	Mutula and Ahmadi, 2002	Examine contradictions of government policy on internet adoption	Dar es Salaam city, Tanzania	Descriptive		
17	Riquelme, 2002	Comparing internet benefits experienced by Chinese firms, small v medium v large	Shanghai, China	Descriptive,		
18	Robinson & Crenshaw, 2002					

continued on following page

Table 1. continued

19	Takada, Sussan, Ueda, Saito, and Chen, 2002	Dynamic interactive effect between internet diffusion and new generation cellular phones.	Japan	Descriptive.
20	Vlosky, Westbrook, and Poku, 2002	Exploratory study of internet adoption by US wood product mfgs.	US wood product mfgs.	Descriptive, not empirical.
21	Lincoln 2001	Investigate how use of internet by marketing educators changed from 1998 – 2000	Members of Marketing Educators Association	Descriptive, not empirical.
22	Wolcott, et al. 2001	Establish a framework	General	Descriptive
23	Lin and Huarng 2000	Factors affecting internet adoption in pharmaceutical industry	Pharmaceutical industry	Descriptive, not empirical.
24	Sultan and Henrichs, 2000	Examines consumer preferences for adoption of internet based services	US	
25	Montealegre, 1999	Explore the role of institutions in the adoption of information technology in developing countries	4 Latin American countries	Descriptive
26	Pisanias and Willcocks, 1999	Explore reasons for slow internet adoption in ship-broking markets	Greece and UK	Descriptive, not empirical.
27	Burkhart &Goodman 1998	Internet acceptance: Concerns on national security, religion and cultural values influence acceptance	Persian Gulf	Descriptive

continued on following page

Table 1. continued

28	Burkhart, et al. 1998	Government policy	India	Government policy is suggested to play an important role.
29	Press et al. 1998	Establish a framework	General	pervasiveness, geographic dispersion, sectoral absorption, connectivity infrastructure, organizational infrastructure, and sophistication of use.
30	Rai et al. 1998	Assess alternative model for internet diffusion	General	Internal models do not provide valid projection. and alternative models including external factors should be developed
31	Press et al 1997	Tracking internet diffusion pattern	General	Descriptive
32	Quelch and Klein 1996	Internet and marketing in international area	General	Descriptive

to 45 years, radio 38 years, and TV 13 years to reach the same number of users (Hannemyr, 1998). The development of the Internet provides unprecedented opportunities and challenges to the private as well as the public sectors in both developed and less developed countries. The Internet provides a platform for a global marketplace, supporting electronic commerce. In this setting, as more suppliers and buyers enter the arena at low cost but with fast immediate outcomes, the benefits of participation grow exponentially.

Understanding diffusion of the Internet is important because it creates new venues for social interactions and new business opportunities. Total retail e-commerce in the United States (U.S.) alone exceeded $45 billion in 2002 (Bajari & Hortacsu, 2004) and achieved an estimated growth of 25% (eMarketer, 2006). E-commerce outside of the U.S. reached $1,584 billion in 2004 (www.idc. com). According to the company's latest research, Internet traffic will rise from 180 petabits per day in 2002 to 5,175 petabits per day by the end of 2007. By 2007, the International Data Corporation (IDC) expects Internet users will access, download and share the information equivalent of the entire Library of Congress more than 64,000 times over, every day.

There is an increasing amount of research that studies the factors contributing to the rapid diffusion of the Internet. However, the empirical analyses appear only infrequently in the literature (Dutta & Roy, 2003) and need a broad-spectrum interdisciplinary approach (Lu, 2005). An explication of many studies show that they still primarily rely on descriptive and correlation studies (Dutta & Roy, 2004) based on the assumption that later adopters of innovation are increasingly likely to imitate early adopters over time (Rogers, 1995). Rai et al., (1998) were able to show that the contagion models, like logistic and Gompertz models, that ignore external factors, such as government involvement and technological development had poor predictability.

To expand this under-investigated and narrowly-focused research stream that lacks a coherent explanatory framework, the current study attempts first to contribute to the current body of literature by offering a social institutional explanation of Internet diffusion. The fundamental proposition is that the phenomenon of Internet diffusion is far from being the outcome of the operation of technological advances only. Instead, its occurrence is also embedded in social institutional systems that prescribe the acceptance and rejection of it and determine rate of diffusion. The application of social institutional theory to explain Internet diffusion adds new perspectives to the research domain and our understanding of rapid Internet diffusion as a fairly recent global phenomenon. An understanding of the social institutional influences is important because of the nature and profound impact of the Internet on the possibilities of economic leapfrogging (Steinmueller, 2001), on firm and industry competitive dynamics (Dinlersoz & Yorukoglu, 2004), on the welfare gains to consumers (Brynjolfsson et al., 2003), and on export orientations (Clarke, 2002). As a result, researchers examining Internet diffusion should be aware of social institutional factors. The present study assists with this goal and also provides a significant contribution to future research dealing with the broad issues associated with Internet technology. In addition, our social institutional approach to the study of Internet diffusion, to a certain extent, echoes the call for examining the broader context in which innovation takes place in order to overcome the "most serious shortcoming" or the so-called "pro-innovation bias" in diffusion research (Rogers, 1995). Thus, this study not only adds new empirical evidence to this quantitatively under-researched area (Dutta & Roy, 2003; 2004), but also offers a broader social institutional perspective for understanding Internet diffusion.

This article is organized as follows. The next section presents the review of literature and the hypotheses derived from it. The third section explains the data and methods used in the empirical tests. Findings are reported in the fourth section. The fifth section draws the conclusion based on the findings.

REVIEW OF RELATED LITERATURE AND HYPOTHESES

The search of literature through ABI/INFORM using the key words of "Internet diffusion" or "Internet adoption" in academic and peer-reviewed journals since 1995 yielded 46 studies. We used 1995 as a cut-off point because it was the year that a commercially available graphical user interface for the Web became commercially available (Netscape Communications, 1994). Table 1 presents these studies in chronological order. Panel 1 lists quantitative studies and panel 2 the descriptive studies. There are a total of 14 quantitative studies (panel 1, Table 1.). Most of those studies examined the determinants of Internet and Internet-related diffusion (e.g., e-commerce). Two features of this review stand out. First, out of 14 identified quantitative studies, only five studies examined "cross-country" Internet diffusion. Two of them are in the contexts of the Organization for Economic Co-operation and Development

(OECD). The rest of the quantitative studies are in a one- or two- country context and most of these country-specific studies are limited to LDCs. The findings of Hargittai's analysis of Internet connectivity was focused on 18 OECD countries (Hargittai, 1999). This study, based on ordinary least square (OLS) regression of the growth of Internet usage on economic wealth (measured in Gross Domestic Product—GDP), education, English language proficiency, telecommunication policy (monopoly vs. competition) and phone density, showed that economic wealth and telecommunication policy were significant predictors of a nation's Internet connectivity. Consistent with Hargittai's study, Norris (2001) found that the GDP significantly influenced Internet connectivity in a larger group of 179 countries, in addition to R&D spending. However, other social and political factors (adult literacy, secondary education, and the level of democratization) showed no significant effect. An interesting finding of this study is the significant differences between regional dummies used in the model, suggesting that there are social or cultural factors to be included in future research. The study by Kiiski and Pohjola (2002) also focused on OECD countries, but used a cross-section and panel data. In addition, they extended the analysis to non-OECD countries with populations exceeding 1 million and the number of Internet hosts exceeding 50. The findings for both OECD and non-OECD countries consistently indicate that GDP and Internet access costs were significant factors. Again, the regional dummy for OECD countries showed significant relationships with Internet diffusion, suggesting "that there are cultural or technology policy-related differences between the countries in the adoption of the Internet which are hard to capture in the model" (Kiiski & Pohjola, 2002). However, the effect of the average years of schooling on Internet diffusion was only significant for non-OECD countries in a cross-section panel and for three-stage least square models. The study by Shih et al., (2005) examined the rule of law as a moderator in the diffusion of e-commerce in 30 countries and found that the rule of law also positively exerted significant impact on the diffusion of e-commerce measured by the volume of online transactions.

The literature review identified another feature: The majority of the existing studies are descriptive. This is consistent with the claim by Dutta and Roy (2004). Out of 32 of these descriptive studies, half focus on Internet diffusion and the remainder on related areas. Wolcott et al., (2001) offered a 6-dimensional framework (pervasiveness, sophistication of use, geographic dispersion, organizational infrastructure, connectivity infrastructure and sector absorption) for assessing global Internet diffusion. Relying on technological innovation theory, the proposed model focuses typically on the infrastructures. This group of studies tends to be haphazard in their theorizing and the application of the theoretical framework to Internet diffusion. They also are short of providing strong evidence for theoretical development.

Overall, the current literature has advanced our knowledge of Internet diffusion, given that it is a relatively new worldwide phenomenon. However, because of the exploratory nature of many of the existing empirical studies, the disjointed groups of evidence provided in the existing studies suggest the need for more theory-driven research.

THE SOCIAL INSTITUTIONAL EXPLANATION OF INTERNET DIFFUSION

Giddens (1984) describes institutions as "the most enduring features of social life" (Giddens, 1984). Social institutional scholars (e.g., DiMaggio & Powell, 1983; Giddens, 1984; Scott & Meyer, 1991) emphasize the role of institutions and social context in influencing organizational action. Social institutions affect the choice of which industry to enter (Biggart & Guillen, 1999) and entrepreneurship decisions (Busenitz et al., 2000). At a national level, social institutions consist of both formal institutional and informal cultural systems (Schooler, 1996). Institutions are social, economic and political bodies that articulate and maintain widely observed norms and rules (North, 1990; Scott, 1995). Olsen (1991) claims that a social institution is a system of beliefs (i.e.,, concerning wealth and property), activities (i.e., production and distribution), organizations (i.e.,, business firms and regulatory agencies). In so far as "the Internet is not monolithic 'cyberspace,' rather it is numerous new technologies, used by diverse people, in diverse real world locations" (Miller & Slater, 2000, p. 1), its acceptance and adoption is inevitably affected by the social institutional arrangements that establish the framework in which Internet diffusion takes place. Therefore, social institutions have an important impact on a society's capacity to adapt functionally to changing circumstance such as Internet technology. The impetus to adopt arises from well-functioned regulatory institutions, economic capacity, an industrial base, and educational systems. It can be argued that social institutions arise and persist to satisfy societal needs to the extent that they help societies survive in a competitive and changing world, and only in those societies whose institutions render them capable of growth and adaptation. In the following, we advance general arguments of a social-institutional explanation for Internet diffusion by developing a number of hypotheses. These arguments are essentially different from the pure economic and technological explanations already reviewed. Our basic argument is that Internet diffusion is associated with the nature and context of social institutions that favor or discourage the diffusion of Internet.

Regulatory Institutions

Regulatory institutions are clusters of rules and resources that are sustained across time and space within and among social systems (Giddens, 1984).

The influence of the institutional environment has been explicitly linked with private investment studies examining general characteristics of nation-states (Lenway & Murtha, 1994) and specific aspects of the legal or regulatory environment (Oxley & Yeung, 2001). Early studies emphasized the influence of institutional regulation on the development and adoption of information systems (King et al., 1994). To the extent that the adoption of the Internet represents a technological and investment phenomenon, it is expected that regulatory institutions would affect the diffusion of the Internet as well. A favorable regulatory institution triggers mimetic isomorphism (DiMaggio & Powell, 1983). The isomorphism effect works when regulatory institutions legitimize and justify the adoption of new technology such as the Internet. When the Internet is a new and poorly understood technology, its direction and impact are ambiguous, the perceived uncertainty of adoption is high, since regulatory institutions involved in Internet technology may either legitimize or ban the Internet by requiring specific forms and content for Internet services. However, if the policy and rules are favorable and safeguard proprietary knowledge of Internet, regulatory institutions encourage the imitative adoption of the Internet. Early studies suggested that regulated entry negatively impacts the Internet diffusion (Wallsten, 2005) whereas favorable policies can significantly affect the diffusion of the Internet (Greenberg & Goodman, 1996; Petrazzini and Geurrero, 2000; Tan et al., 1999; Zhao, 2002). Therefore, we hypothesize:

H1. The existence of strong regulatory institutions is significantly associated with Internet diffusion: The greater the extent to which the rule of law prevails in a country, the higher the rate of Internet diffusion.

Economic Institution

The economy is one of the major social institutions (Turner, 1997). Economic institutions are those elements that contribute to the constitution of social systems through the allocation of resources and the generation of wealth (Giddens, 1984). It is the system that provides the goods and services consumed by the members of a society (Olsen, 1991). One key important aspect of the economic system is the role played by the state in economic activities. The state has considerable influence on the forms of organizations (Whitley, 1994), firm strategy, economic policies and decisions (Lenway & Murtha, 1994), and individuals (Ingram & Clay 2000). We argue that an economic system affects Internet diffusion depending on the varying degree of state intervention. Under a given economic system, the state can influence the rate of diffusion through the appropriation and redistribution of national economic wealth with different economic and licensing policies. However, the degree of state intervention is commensurate with the economic system. A more active intervention in coordinating and appropriating resources may represent a socialist-oriented economy (Turner, 1997). In a more capitalist economic system where major resources are delegated to private owners and their agents (Whitley, 1994), the Internet is more likely to diffuse rapidly, since Internet growth is basically driven by entrepreneurs and private sectors. In the socialist system where value is placed on social security and equality (Tsoukas, 1994), Internet technology that creates at least initially differentiates rewards and social inequality is unlikely to be adopted at a fast rate. The capitalist economic system is a "self-serving" system where individuals seek their own interests through private ownership (Ralston et al., 1997). The logic of this system is that the market provides differential rewards to stimulate individual and private sectors. Therefore, the Internet as a new technology is likely to flourish in a more market-oriented environment where relatively low state intervention allows individuals and private sectors to choose the technology considered rewarding. Previous related studies also showed that technology adoption can be hindered by the lack of a strong private sector and by limited capital.

H2. The socialist-oriented economic institution is negatively associated with the rate of Internet diffusion.

Education

Education is a powerful institution that not only helps preserve cultural heritage (Olsen, 1991) but also provides expectations for personal development and occupational achievement (Van Deth, 1995). We propose two arguments for the positive effects of education on Internet diffusion. First, educational institutions supply human capital fundamental to technological development and utilization. Accessible educational systems provide individuals with the necessary skills to deal with complicated procedures and issues (Van Deth, 1995). It provides people with knowledge and the means to learn and use Internet technology. It is conducive to the adoption of the Internet since a better-educated workforce is more able to comprehend the technology and appreciate its potential. Thus, it is likely that countries with more accessible education systems are more likely to accept and use the Internet. Second, the educational institution is an important part of normative isomorphism. Learning is legitimized in a cognitive base cultivated by formal training (DiMaggio & Powell, 1983) and is a powerful source that can diffuse knowledge. The root of the early diffusion and subsequent endurance of Internet technology is closely coupled with academic institutions. As countries vary in their educational institutions, they also differ in the ability of educational systems to support the fast-moving Internet technology. While prior studies showed that human capital substantially influenced innovation capacity (Fecker, 2001; Romer,

1990), the lack of technical expertise and training programs for both system administrators and end users in LDCs was found to be an inhibitor to the Internet diffusion process (Press, 1992).

H3. National education accessibility has a positive relationship with the rate of Internet diffusion.

Industrialization

Industrialization has a critical impact on many aspects of societies and economic activities (Kerr et al., 1996). Shifts from agriculture to manufacturing and from manufacturing to information and service bring out challenges and opportunities in society. Recent studies have indicated that more advanced industrialization resulted in a shift from a materialist value system to a postmaterialist value system that emphasizes self-actualization and quality of life (Inglehart & Baker, 2000). A high level of industrialization that is often accompanied by innovations gives rise to a demand for technological sophistication and the fast adoption of technological innovation to maintain the momentum of industrialization. Thus, industrialization not only creates the need for technological innovation, but also offers opportunities for adopting the Internet. As countries evolve into more industrialized societies, information and services increasingly become the backbone of their economy. This, in turn, generates the need for Internet technology to provide information and services; hence the fast adoption of the Internet.

H4. A high level of industrialization of nations is positively associated with a high rate of Internet diffusion.

National Culture

"Institutions are the crystallizations of culture, and culture is the substratum of institutional arrangements" (Hofstede, et al., 2002, p. 800). Culture exerts 'informal constraints' equally as institutions according to North (1990). Culture connotes a "broad tendency to prefer certain states of affairs over others" (Hofstede, 1980, p. 18). Cultural factors also influence how people perceive, process and interpret information (Kale, 1991). To the extent that Internet use and content encounter diverse cultural expectations, human volition also plays a part in Internet diffusion. Cultural traits of countries may affect the growth of Internet usage if the permeation of the Internet is perceived by a culture either as a challenge or as an accompaniment to mainstream social values. For instance, limited studies have shown that country-specific and culturally congruent Web content enhances reach and interactivity, leading to increased Internet use (Fock, 2000; Simon, 1999). Internet use in a social context of high trust was also found to diffuse quickly (Volken, 2002). Since there are very limited literatures about cultural effects on Internet diffusion, and prior descriptive studies suggested no relationship between masculinity and Internet diffusion, we developed hypotheses for three of the four of Hofstede's cultural dimensions.

Individualism

Individualism refers to a culture that places importance on individual empowerment and aspiration over collective gains. Societies of high individualism prize individualism, democracy, individual initiative, and achievement. Herbig and Miller (1991) suggest that the individual-oriented nature of American society explain the ability of Americans to excel in entrepreneurship and innovations that "require the establishment of new behavioral patterns with no established precedence: computers, photocopying ..." Ferle et al., (2002, 70) argued that "being independent and having a desire to be unique are qualities conducive to entrepreneurial behavior and embracing new technology." Following this reasoning, we hypothesize:

H5a. A national culture with a high level of individualism tends to exhibit a high rate of Internet diffusion.

Power Distance

Power distance is the level of acceptance by a society of the unequal distribution of power in institutions. In countries with low power distance, individuals in different positions are apt to regard one another as equal in power. According to Herbig and Miller (1991) cultures with large power distance will be less innovative. This suggests that new innovations such that Internet will be less likely to be accepted in a culture of large power distance where individuals tend to follow directions and avoid standing out through new and original thinking. Thus:

H5b. A national culture with small power distance tends to exhibit a high rate of Internet diffusion.

Uncertainty Avoidance

Uncertainty avoidance refers to the extent to which people in a society feel threatened by ambiguous situations. For countries characterized by a high level of uncertainty, the introduction and use of new technology such as the Internet naturally creates ambiguity, and hence, perceived risks. It follows naturally that societies with a high level of uncertainty avoidance are more reluctant to adopt Internet technology. Previous studies on technological innovation argued that cultures with high uncertainty avoidance are less likely to be early adopters of new technology (De Mooji, 1998; Samiee, 1998). It has also been evidenced that new product sales are slower in societies with a high level of uncertainty avoidance (Tellefsen & Takada, 1999. Hence, we hypothesize:

H5c. A national culture with a high level of uncertainty avoidance tends to exhibit a low rate of Internet diffusion

METHOD

Data

To empirically test the previously derived hypotheses, we gathered data on Internet user growth and social institutional variables from a cross section of countries (n = 39) over a time span of 9 years (from 1995 to 2003). The data before 1995 were excluded because of the extremely primitive conditions of Internet development in some LDCs in the data set and the many missing values. This yields a sample size of 351 observations (Appendix 1 lists countries included in the study).

The data on the rate of Internet diffusion (*INTERNET*), the dependent variable, were collected from the publications *International Telecommunication Union* and *World Development Indicator*. We used Internet users per 1,000 to calculate the annual growth rate of Internet usage. We used the rule of law measurement (*RULE*) by Kaufmann et al (2005) to represent the regulatory institution. Rule of law measures the "extent to which agents have confidence in and abide by the rules of society." For the economic institution, we followed Parboteeah and Cullen (2003) and used government expenditure as a percentage of the GDP (*ECONSYS*). The data were drawn from *World Development Indicators*. Data for education (*EDU*) and industrialization (*INDUSTRY*) were also from *World Development Indicators*. *EDU* is measured by the literacy rate defined as percentage of population (aged 15 and above) "who can read and write simple statement on their everyday life." Some missing data are replaced by data about the labor force with tertiary education. We used labor force with tertiary education because it is highly correlated with the data about literacy rate (correlation coefficient =.892). *INDUSTRY*

Table 2. Means, deviations, and correlations between independent variables

Variable	Mean	S.D.	1	2	3	4	5	6	7	8	9	10	11	12
1. INTERNET	.672	.741	1.00											
2. RULE OF	.936	.963	.58*											
LAW	30.4	11.29	.49*	1.00	1.00									
3. ECONSYS	58.2	28.06	.27	.21	.04									
4. EDU	.314	.156	.40	.19	.08	1.00	1.00							
5. INDUSTRY	49.41	22.71	.39*	.22	.03	.09	-.12	1.00						
6. INDIVIDUAL	53.13	21.52	.24	.12	.05	-.19	.14	.36	1.00					
7. PD	62.56	22.34	-.35*	.15	.08	.15	.18	-.71*	.67*	1.00				
8. UA	21.93	15.33	.20	-.17	.22	-.13	.30	.24	.35	-33*	1.00			
9. NETWORK	30.51	15.25	-.32	.25	.20	.26	-.18	.18	.18	.19	.09	1.00		
10 NETCOST	3.22	3.34	.62*	-.21	.27	-.12	.24	.45*	.30*	.26	.26	-.27	1.00	
11 GDPGROW	.231	.137	.23	.27	.22	.25	.08	.08	.11	.13	.17	.07	.26	1.00
12. OPEN				.12			.10							

Table 3. Regression estimates of explanatory variables on Internet diffusion

Variables	(1)	(2)	(3)
RULE OF LAW 2	.016**	2.113**	2009***
(	.177)	.207)	(.187)
E CONSYS	-1.771	1.573	-1.726*
(	.084)	.068)	(.132)
E DUCATION	2.522** 2	.662***	2.867**
(	.132)	.132)	(.159)
INDUSTRY	1.985** 2	.206**	2.746***
(	.101)	.031)	(.204)
INDIVIDUAL	1.021 1	.344 1	.403
(	.290)	.064)	(.067)
PD –	.581	.530	.452
(	.038)	.023)	(.075)
UA –	1.928**	1.895*	1.914*
(	.172)	.118)	(.111)
NETWORK			2.049**
			(.181)
NETCOST			-6.902***
			(.329)
GDPGROW			1.756*
			(.121)
O PEN			2.686***
			(.169)
R^2	. 571	441	.470
Adjusted R^2	.555	429	454

a. Standardized coefficients are in parentheses. * $p < .10$; ** $p < .05$; *** $p < .01$
b. Column 2: It is a weighted least square estimation. The variables are transformed by dividing the variables by the residuals obtained from column 1 OLS estimation. Column 3: A lagged first-difference model where Y (INTERNET-) = Yi ,t - Y i t-1 and X (ECONSYS, EDUCATION, INDUSTRY, and other controls) = Xi ,t - X i t-1 .

is measured by energy consumption per GDP adjusted by purchasing power parity following the measures used by previous studies (Sacks et al., 2001). The definitions and sources of data are given in Appendix 2.

Analytical Procedures. The previous review of theoretical and empirical literature and the methodological consideration suggests the estimation of multivariate determinants of social institutional variables. We conducted three estimations. First, pooled OLS regression was employed to estimate these effects. Second, because of the cross section and panel data used for this study, there are potential problems of serial correlation and heteroskedasticity that could result in biased or insufficient estimations by OLS, and unobserved effects that violate the exogeneity assumption of the explanatory variables over time. To examine the presence of serial correlation and heteroskedasticity, we performed a diagnostic test by plotting the residuals from OLS estimation against independent variables, following the recommendations by Wooldridge (2001). The test revealed the minor presence of both serial correlation and heteroskedasticity. To correct these problems, we applied the weighted least square procedure suggested by Hsiao (1986). In this transformation we divided all the variables by the estimates of error terms from the original model and re-ran this transformed model by weighted least square procedure. Third, to maintain the exogeniety assumption of the explanatory variables, we adopted the first difference method as suggested by Hausman and Taylor (1981). The first difference approach eliminates the unobserved effect and is the most efficient in meeting the strict exogeneity assumption Wooldridge (2001).

RESULTS

Table 2 presents the mean and standard deviation along with correlations of the variables in the study. As indicated, some variables are indeed correlated, but are only marginally significant. To evaluate the severity of multicollinearity, the diagnostic statistic of variance inflation factor (VIF) was applied. The tolerance value ranged from .41 to .86 and VIF from 1.02 to 2.41. This test showed no VIF values of the variables exceeding the cutoff value of 10 indicating no serious problems of multicollinearity as suggested by Neter et al., (1985) and Gujarati (1995).

Table 3 reports the estimation results of the Internet diffusion model in three (3) sets of regression results. Column 1 presents the estimates of OLS specification that include the hypothesized explanatory variables only. As indicated, hypotheses 1, 3, and 4 are supported. Countries with strong rule of law, accessible education and high level of industrialization tended to experience rapid Internet diffusion. However, the economic system and two cultural variables (individualism and power distance) turned out to be insignificant. The hypotheses 5a and 5b are not confirmed. Uncertainty avoidance (*UA*) has a marginal effect on Internet diffusion as predicted, supporting hypothesis 5c. Column 2 shows the estimation results based on weighted least square using the transformed variables as explained in the above section. The results are consistent with the results in column 1. After correcting the issues of heteroskedasticity and serial correlation, the model produces consistent results, again confirming most of the hypotheses. It should be noted that the negative and significant signs of *UA* indeed evidence that a cultural orientation of high uncertainty avoidance tends to dampen the diffusion of the Internet, whereas social institutions consisting of strong rule of law, high level of education and industrialization all facilitate the diffusion of the Internet. Column 3 presents the results of the first difference model. In this analysis we also include four control variables: *NETWORK, NETCOST, GDPGROW* and *OPEN*. We selected these variables because the previous related studies suggested the associations between Internet diffusion and *NETWORK* (Hargittai,

Table 4. Summary of hypotheses testing

Research Variables	Hypotheses	Findings
Regulatory Institution **(H1)**	Positive relationship	Supported
Economic Institution **(H2)**	Positive relationship	Weakly supported
Education Accessibility **(H3)**	Positive relationship	Supported
Industrialization **(H4)**	Positive relationship	Supported
Individualism **(H5a)**	Positive relationship	Not supported
Power Distance **(H5b)**	Low power distance positively related to Internet diffusion	Not supported
Uncertainty Avoidance **(H5c)**	High level of uncertainty avoidance negative related to Internet diffusion	Weakly supported

1999;Wallstein, 2005), *GDP* (Shih et al., 2005), *NETCOST* (Hargittai, 1999; Mbarika et al., 2002; Volken, 2002;), *OPEN* (Wallstein, 2005). Adding these variables in as controls thus helps us isolate the effects of research variables and reduce the bias of omitted variables. *NETWORK* measured by a composite variable of the standardized scores of personal computers, mobile phones, and telephone mainlines per 10,000 people; *NET-COST* measured by Internet total monthly access price (per 20 hours use); *GDPGROW* measured by annual GDP per capita growth rate, and *OPEN* measured by the total import and export share of GDP. Therefore, the result in column 3 presents a kind of sensitivity test since the inclusion of these variables in the estimation model not only allows us to isolate their effects, but also permits us to test the robustness of the social institutional explanations. As indicated in column 3, inclusion of these control variables does not substantially alter the estimates of social institutional variables. *RULE, EDU, INDUSTRY* and *UC* remain statistically significant with the expected signs when additional variables are added to the model. However, it is interesting to note that *ECONSYS* became significant at a marginal level carrying an expected negative sign. This marginal significance of *ECONSYS* in explaining the Internet diffusion

to some degree provided a weak support to our hypothesis 2.

While the effects of most hypothesized social institutional factors are significant and carry the expected signs (with the exception of PD), the effects of 4 control variables are worth mentioning. *NETWORK* positively contributed significantly to Internet diffusion. Given all other factors, apparently the presence of an adequate networking infrastructure is a necessary condition for the Internet to disseminate. The highly significant and negative impact of *NETCOST* suggests that the high costs of Internet access can significantly hinder the use and hence the diffusion of the Internet. Interestingly *GDPGROW* turned out to be only a marginal factor. This result may suggest that the impact of *GDPGROW* on Internet diffusion can be indirect, passing on through to other explanatory variables. To check the sensitivity of this macroeconomic factor, we replaced it with GDP growth in the model. The result showed an insignificant effect of GDP (t = 1.641; p > .10). *OPEN* also significantly and positively influenced Internet diffusion. This suggests that an externally open trade system is conducive to national Internet adoption.

Table 4 summarizes the results of hypotheses testing. Overall, the results reported in Table 3 supported the majority of the hypotheses. The estimation across three different approaches consistently confirmed the hypothesized effects of **RULE, EDU, INDUSTRY**, and **UA** as social institutional forces driving Internet diffusion. These results confirm the findings of previous studies about the effect of rule of law (Shih et al., 2005; Xu at al., 2004) and offer new evidence on the effects of education and industrialization on Internet diffusion. **ECONSYS** invariably had no significant effects. This unexpected result can be due to the measurement, suggesting other measures need to

be developed and tested in future study. It should be also noted that the national culture characterized with high individualism and low power distance do not exert significant impacts on the Internet diffusion. However, national culture with a high uncertainty avoidance orientation significantly slowed down the Internet diffusion. The results of control variables are also in line with the previous findings on technology infrastructure (Hargittai, 1999; Shih et al., 2005). Whereas **NETCOST** confirmed the finding (Hargittai, 1999; Shih et al., 2005), the insignificant effect of **GDPGROW**

Table 5. Regression estimates of explanatory variables on Internet diffusion

	Variables		DC		LDC
	RULE OF LAW		2.559***		2.506**
	(		.309)		(.271)
E	CONSYS		-.56		1.679
	(		.034)		(.124)
E	DUCATION		3.119***		1.726*
	(		.316)		(.132)
	INDUSTRY		2.995***		2.794***
(			.304)		(.268)
	INDIVIDUAL		.203		-.995
(			.036)		(.086)
	PD	-	.543	-	2.812**
(			.059)		(.277)
	UA	-	.648	-	1.800*
(			.089)		(.201)
	NETWORK	3	.430***	9	.943***
(			.160)		(.345)
	NETCOST	-	3.768***	-	5.673***
(			.136)		(.396)
	GDPGROW	1	.883	1	.036
	(		.150)		(.107)
O	PEN	2	.065**	3	.018***
(			.208)		(.276)
	R^2	.	283		.312
	Adjusted R^2	.	232		.268

a. Standardized coefficients are in parentheses in parentheses. * p < .10; ** p < .05; *** p < .01

b. For both DC and LDC a lagged first-difference model is applied where Y (Internet diffusion) = $Y_{i,t}$ - $Y_{i,t-1}$ and X (ECONSYS, EDUCATION, INDUSTRY, and other controls) = $X_{i,t}$ - $X_{i,t-1}$.

is not in line with the previous finding that it is a significant predictor as reported in the previous study of Hargittai (1999) and Kiiski and Pohjola (2002). This may suggest that the influences of *GDPGROW* could be weakened by the presence of other social institutional factors, indicating the adequacy of the social institutional framework for Internet diffusion analysis.

However, the analytical results presented in Table 3 did not take into account the phenomenon of the "digital divide" as observed and evidenced by existing studies. Though Internet diffusion may be subject to the influences of a similar set of factors across all countries, the reality of 'digital divide' is also important due to the obvious disparities between LDCs and DCs. Because different Internet diffusion models are identified in different countries as some researchers predicted (Goodman et al., 1998) and the global adoption of technological innovation comprises implementation and confirmation stages (Dekimpe, Parker, & Sarvary, 2000), we are interested in further investigating whether the identified social institutional factors have differential impacts on DC and LDCs, as obviously the general social institutions are different between DCs and LDCs. Before we applied the same model as in column 3 Table 3, we ran a simple t-test of the Internet user growth rate between DCs and LDCs. This result shows significant differences between the two groups (t=11.085; p <.000; F =129.58, p <.000). We then estimated the effects of social institutional factors along with control variables respectively for DCs and LDCs. Table 5 presents these results. For social institutional influences, while the effects of *RULE, EDU* and *INDUSTRY* remained the same in terms of the level of significance and coefficient signs, the different effects of cultural variables, *PD and UA*, emerged. The *PD* and *UA* effects are insignificant for DCs but both turned out to be negative significant factors on Internet diffusion in LDCs. Reflecting the fact that most of the LDCs in our sample have large *PD* and *UA* scores, it suggests that the socially

large power distance factor among individuals and high values on uncertainty avoidance in LDC are potentially barriers to Internet diffusion. *INDIVIDUAL* is consistently an insignificant variable. The differential effects are also found in *NETWORK*, *NETCOST* and *OPEN* between DCs and LDCs. Judged by the *t* values *NETWORK*, *NETCOST* and *OPEN* effects are stronger for LDCs than for DCs, suggesting the importance of the development of the information technology infrastructure, the cost of Internet access, and the open economic system in facilitating the Internet diffusion in LDCs.

IMPLICATIONS AND CONCLUSION

The Internet could be considered a commodity service, its growth accelerated by the widespread adoption of browsers and Web technology. Much of the latest attention on the Internet has been on the use of this global information infrastructure as a support for other commercial services (Barua, Whinston, & Yin, 2000; Leiner et al., 1997). We believe that the major contribution of this study is the demonstration that the broad theory of social institutions furthers our understanding of how the social institutional components as part of a national context can influence the diffusion of the Internet. That is, we show the efficacy of a new comprehensive approach to understanding cross-national differences in global Internet diffusion. Our model is not meant to exhaustively capture all the possible determinants of Internet diffusion, but to identify some of the important determinants by applying a social institutional theoretical framework. Based on the findings of this study, we are able to conclude that social institutions theory provides a valuable framework to further our understanding of the phenomenon of Internet diffusion. The results show that the identified key social institutional factors (*RULE, EDU, INDUSTRY, UA*) invariably influenced

Internet diffusion in both developed and less developed countries, though the impact of cultural dimensions varied between these two groups of national economies. In general, our findings are consistent with the propositions that social institution constitutes a major driving force for Internet diffusion (Norris, 2001). Specifically with regard to the social institutional variables, the significant effects of rule of law are consistent with previous findings (Shih et al., 2005). However, our significant effects of education confirmed the similar findings by Kiiski and Pohjola (2002) but, contrary to Hargittai's results, showing no significant influences of education. Our mixed findings of cultural factors did not lend full support to the propositions by Ferle et al., (2002). Based on the findings of our study we can conclude that countries that have a strong rule of law, accessible educational systems and high levels of industrialization are more likely to attain rapid Internet diffusion. However, the economic system failed to exert significant effects on Internet diffusion.

Our findings show that slow Internet diffusion is likely to occur in less developed nations that place high value on uncertainty avoidance and power distance while individualism had no significant impact on Internet diffusion in both DCs and LDCs. This may imply that in the context of LDCs, the diffusion of the Internet is likely to run into more obstacles in societies with high power distances because extensive access to the Internet implies the reduction of existential inequality and represents a challenge to the extant authority that may monopolize information as a means of control.

The findings of this study have important implications for both government policy and business management. For business management, our results suggest that social institutional factors such as the adequacy of the regulatory environment, accessible education and the level of industrialization are all important criteria for deciding in which national markets companies should initiate Internet based business activities. In addition, the availability of a network infrastructure and the expenses of Internet access in a national market are also important factors to be assessed in the choice of a national market. High Internet access costs can significantly slow down the diffusion as our results indicate. Our findings also have implications for firms in emerging market economies. While the use of the Internet in DCs to date has been to link value-adding commercial supply chains into seamless, logistical communication networks that are vastly more efficient [8], the firms intending to invest in Internet-related sectors in LDCs should make the effort to evaluate the social institutional environment of their nations before heavily committing resources in this new sector. To take advantage of fast Internet diffusion in foreign markets, foreign investments in Internet-based technologies and businesses have to be synchronized with national trade and economic policies. A promising strategic decision always abides by a proper environmental scanning. If a national social institutional environment becomes more favorable to business investments, naturally it will induce fast Internet diffusion and its related transactions.

For government policy, our research points to the need for an adequate effective regulatory system to ensure that relevant rules and policies about the Internet and its related online activities be effectively enforced. However, this does not suggest a high degree of government intervention in the Internet sector as our findings do not provide strong evidence that economic systems with high government intervention tend to dampen the growth of the Internet. Our findings also indicate that the thrust of government policies in developing countries should be focused not only on infrastructure building, but also on creating a national social institutional environment that facilitates Internet diffusion. The obstacles comprising cultural values high on uncertainty avoidance and the high costs of providing Internet services to end users need to be removed [29].

This implies that the 'digital divide' between DCs and LDCs could not simply be narrowed without first cultivating competence in the private sectors within LDCs regarding a digital economy. At the government level, it would be conducive to Internet diffusion, if tax and credit policies were formulated favorably for companies that are adopting the Internet and related technology.

Limitations and Future Research

There are several limitations of this study, and these limitations call for future research. Though an examination of the social institutional environment produced stable results, the cultural dimensions generated different findings. Using national cultural variables may not really capture the diverse sub-cultural influences within a country. This could be attributed to many fallacious assumptions underlying Hofstede's cultural dimensions (McSweeney, 2002). This suggests that in future research, instead of repeating the use of Hofstede's cultural dimensions, more refined measures of culture should be developed taking into account national heterogeneity and within-country cultural diversity. Second, the explanatory power of the study is limited since the study primarily relied on national level data. Given that Internet diffusion occurs primarily at firm and individual levels, the dynamic nature of diffusion at the micro level is lost in the analysis, and that could limit the predictability of the model. Therefore, future studies can extend the social institutional framework by making efforts to combine the national level data with firm and even individual data to unravel the dynamic interactions of Internet diffusion. Future studies that can focus more on the cultural sub-groups within a country with respect to the heterogeneous social institutional factors would provide valuable supplementary insights to the theorizing of global Internet diffusion. Combining data information at global, regional, national and individuals in respect to the application diversity factors would

further enhance our ability to predict the future growth of Internets.

REFERENCES

Bajari, P., & Hortacsu, A. (2004). Economic insights from internet auctions. *Journal of Economic Literature*, June, 457-486.

Barua, A., Whinston A.W., & Yin, F. (2000). Value and productivity in the Internet economy. *Computer*, May, 2-5.

Berkhart, G.E., Goodman, S.E., Mehta, A., & Press, L. (1998). The internet in India: Better times ahead? *Communications of the ACM*, *41*(11), 21-26.

Biggart, N. W., & Guillen, M. F. (1999). Developing difference: Social organization and the rise of the automobile industries of South Korea., Taiwan, Spain and Argentina. *American Sociological Review*, *64*, 722-747

Boudreaux, G., & Sloboda, B. (1999). The fast changing world of the internet. *Management Quarterly*, Summer, 2-19.

Brown, I., & Licker, P. (2003). Exploring differences in internet adoption and usage between historically advantaged and disadvantaged groups in South Africa. *Journal of Global Information Technology Management*, *6*(4), 6-26.

Brown, I., Hoppe, R., Mugera, P. Newman, P., & Stander, A. (2004). The impact of national environment on the adoption of internet banking: Comparing Singapore and south Africa. *Journal of Global Information Management*, *12*(2), 1-26.

Brynjolfsson, E., Smith, M.D., & Hu, Y. (2003). Consumer surplus in the digital economy: Estimating the value of increased product variety at online booksellers. *Management Science*, *49*(11), 1580-1596.

Busenitz, L.W., Gomez, C., & Spencer, J.W. (2000).Country institutional profiles: Unlocing entrepreneurial phenomena. *Academy of Management Review, 43*, 994-1003.

Clarke, G. (2002). Does internet connectivity affect export performance? Evidence from transition countries. *Discussion Paper no. 2002/74, World Institute for Development Economics Research*, Helsinki.

De Mooij, M. (1998). *Global marketing and advertising: Understanding cultural paradigms.* Thousand Oaks, CA: Sage Publications.

Dekimpe, M.G., Parker, P.M., & Sarvary, M. (2000). Global diffusion of technological innovations: A coupled-hazard approach. *Journal of Marketing Research, 37*(February), 47-59.

Dholakia, R., & Kshetri, N. (2004). Factors impacting the adoption of the internet among SMEs. *Small Business Economics, 23*(4), 311-322.

DiMaggio, P., & Powell, W. (1983). The iron cage revisited: Institutional isomorphism and collective rationality in organizational fields. *American Sociological Review, 48*, 147-160.

Dinlersoz, E. M., & Yorukoglu, M. (2004). The information and industry dynamics. *Working paper*, University of Houston.

Dutta, A., & Roy, R. (2003). Anticipating internet diffusion. *Communication of the ACM, 42*(2), 66-71.

Dutta, A., & Roy, R. (2004). The mechanics of internet growth: A developing-country perspective. *International Journal of Electronic Commerce, 9*(2), 143-165.

EMarketer. http://www.emarketer.com/

Fecker, L. (2001). *The innovative firm—a cybernetic approach.* Bern: Peter Lang.

Ferle, C. L., Edwards, S. M., & Mizuno, Y. (2002). Internet diffusion in Japan: Cultural considerations. *Journal of Advertising Research, 2*(1), 55-79.

Fock, H. (2000). Cultural influences on marketing communication on the World Wide Web. In *Proceedings of the Multicultural Marketing Conference*, Hong Kong.

Forman, C. (2005). The corporate digital divide: Determinants of internet adoption. *Management Science, 51*(4), 641-654.

Fornerino, M. (2003). Internet adoption in France. *The Service Industrial Journal, 23*(1), 119-135.

Giddens, A. (1984). *The constitution of society: outline of the theory of structuration.* Berkeley, CA: University of California Berkeley.

Goodman, S.E., Burkhart, G., Foster, W., Press, L., Tan, Z., & Woodard, J. (1998). *The global diffusion of the Internet project: An initial inductive study*, Fairfax, VA: The MOSAIC Group.

Goodman, S.E., Press, L., Luth, S., Rutkowski, A. (1994). The global diffusion of the Internet: Patterns and problems. *Communications of the ACM, 37*(8), 27-31.

Greenberg, L.T., & Goodman, S. E. (1996). Is big brother hanging by his bootstraps? *Communications of the ACM, 39*(7), 11-15.

Gujarati, Damoda N. (1995). *Basic econometrics.* McGraw-Hill International Edition

Hannemyr, G. (1998). The internet as hyperbole: A critical examination of adoption rates. *The Information Society, 19*, 111-121.

Hargittai, E. (1999). Weaving the western web: explaining difference in internet connectivity among OECD countries. *Telecommunication Policy, 23*, 701-718.

Hausman, J. A., & Taylor, W. E. (1981). Panel data and unobservable individual effects. *Econometrica, 49*, 1377-1398.

Herbig, P. A., & Miller, J. C. (1991). The effect of culture upon innovativeness: A comparion of United States and Japan sourcing capabilities. *Journal of International Consumer Marketing*, *3*(3), 7-35.

Hofstede, G. (1980). *Culture's consequences: International differences in work-related values.* Beverly Hills, CA: Sage.

Hofstede, G. (2001). *Culture's consequences: Comparing values, behaviors, institutions, and organizations across Nations.* Beverly Hills, CA: Sage.

Hofstede, G., Van Deusen, C. A., Mueller, C. B., & Charles, T. A. (2002). What goals do business leaders pursue? A study in fifteen countries. *Journal of International Business Studies*, 33, 785-803.

Hsiao, Cheng (1986). *Analysis of panel data.* Cambridge, England: Cambridge University Press.

Huang, H., Keser, C., Leland, J., & Shachat, J. (2003). Trust, the internet and the digital divide. *IBM systems Journal*, *42*(3), 507-518.

Inglehart, R., & Baker, W. (2000). Modernization, cultural change, and the persistence of traditional values, *American Sociological Review*, 65, 19-51

Ingram, P., & Baker, W. E. (2000). Modernization, cultural change, and the persistence of traditional values. *American Sociological Review*, *65*, 19-51.

Ingram, P., & Clay, K. (2000). The choice-within-constraints new institutionalism implications for sociology. *Annual Review of Sociology, 26*, 525-546.

International Telecommunication Union. (2005). World Telecommunication Yearbook, Geneva: ITU.

Jones, C., Hecker, R., & Holland, P. (2003). Small firm internet adoption: Opportunities forgone, a journey not begun. *Journal of Small Business and Enterprise Development*, *10*(3), 287-297.

Kale, S. H. (1991). Culture-specific marketing communication: An analytical approach. *International Marketing Review*, *8*(2), 18-30.

Kaufmann, D, Kraay, A., & Mastruzzi,M. (2005). *Governance Matters IV: Governance Indicators for 1996-2004.* World Bank Policy Research Department Working Paper.

Kerr, C., Harbison, F.H., Dunlop, J. T., & Myers, C. A. (1996). Industrialism and industrial man. *International Labor Review, 135*, 383-392.

Kiiski, S., & Pohjola, M. (2002). Cross-country diffusion of the internet. *Information Economics and Policy, 12,* 297-310.

King, J.L., Gurbaxani, V., Kraemer, K.L., McFarlan, F.W., Raman, K.S., & Yap, C.S. (1994). Institutional factors in information technology innovation. *Information System Research*, *5*(2), 139-169.

Kula, V., & Tatoglu, K. (2003). An exploratory study of internet adoption by SMEs in an emerging market economy. *European Business Review*, *15*(5), 324-333.

Leiner, B.M., Cerf, V.G., Clark, D.D., Kahn, R.E., Kleinrock, L., Lynch, D.C., et al. (1997). The past and future history of the Internet. *Communications of the ACM*, *40*(2), 102-108.

Lenway, S.A., & Murtha, T. P. (1994). The state as strategiest in international business research. *Journal of International Business Studies*, *25*(3), 513-535.

Lin, B., & Huarng, F. (2000). Internet in the pharmaceutical industry: infrastructure issues. *American Business Review*, *18*(1), 101-106.

Lincoln D. J. (2001). Marketing educator internet adoption in 1998 versus 2000: Significant progress and remaining obstacles. *Journal of Marketing Education*, *23*(2), 103-116.

Lu, M. (2005). Digital divide in developing countries. *Journal of Global Information Technology Management, 4*(3), 1-4.

Mbarika, V. Mike, J., & Meso, P. (2002). Cyberspace across sub-saharan Africa. *Communication of the ACM, 45*(12), 17-21.

McSweeny, B. (2002). Hofstede's model of national cultural differences and their consequences: A triumph of faith—a failure of analysis. *Human Relations, 55*(1), 89-118.

Miller, D., & Slater, D. (2000). *The internet: an ethnographic approach*. New York: New York University Press.

Mills, B. F., & Whitacre, B. E. (2003). Understanding the non-metropolitan-metropolitan digital divide. *Growth and Change, 34*(2), 219-243.

Montealegre, R. (1999). A temporal model of institutional interventions for information technology adoption in less-developed countries. *Journal of Management Information Systems, 16*(1), 207-232.

Mutula, S. M., & Ahmadi, M. (2002). Contradictions of Tanzania government policies on internet service provision: case study of Dar Es Salaam city. *Library Hi Tech., 20*(3), 359-369.

Neter, J., Wasserman, W., & Kutner, M. (1985). *Applied Linear Statistical Models*, Homewood, Il: Irwin.

Netscape Communications. (1994). University of Illinois and Netscape Communication Agreement. Retreived from http://www.mediamtrix.com/press/release

Norris, P. (2001). *Digital divide: Civic engagement, information poverty, and the internet worldwide*. Cambridge: Cambridge University Press.

North, D. (1990). *Institutions, institutional change, and economic performance*. Cambridge, MA: Harvard University Press.

Olsen, M.E. (1991). *Societal dynamics: Exploring macrosociology*. Englewood Cliffs, NJ: Prentice-Hall.

Oxley, J.E., & Yeung, B. (2001). E-commerce readiness: Institutional environment and international competitiveness. *Journal of International Business Studies, 32*(4), 705-723.

Parboteeah, K. P., & Cullen, J. B. (2003). Social institution and work centrality: Explorations beyond national culture. *Organization Science, 14*(2), 137-148.

Peng, Y., & Trappey, C. V. (2005). Internet and e-commerce adoption by the Taiwan semiconductor industry. *Industrial Management & Data systems, 105*(4), 476-490.

Petrazzini, B.A., & Guerrero, A. (2000). Promoting internet development: The case of Argentina. *Telecommunication Policy, 24*(2), 89-112.

Petrazzini, B.A., & Kibati, A. (1999). The internet infrastructure in developing countries. *Communications of the ACM, 42*(6), 31-36.

Pisanias, N., & Willcocks, L. (1999). Understanding slow internet adoption: 'infomediation' in ship-broking markets. *Journal of Information Technology, 14*, 399-413.

Press, L. (1992). The Net: Progress and opportunity. *Communications of the ACM, 35*(12), 21-25.

Press, L. (1997). Tracking the global diffusion of the internet. *Communications of the ACM, 40*(11), 11-17.

Press, L., Burkhart, G., Foster, W., Goodman, S.E., Wolcott, P., & Woodard, J. (1998). An Internet diffusion framework. *Communications of the ACM, 41*(10), 22-26.

Quelch, J.A., & Klein, L.R. (1996). The Internet and international marketing. *Sloan Management Review, 37*(3), 60-75.

Rai, A., Ravichandran, T., & Samaddar, S. (1998). How to anticipate the internet's global diffusion. *Communication of the ACM, 41*(10), 97-104.

Ralston, D.A., Holt, D. H., Terpstra, R.H., & Kai-Chen, Y. (1997). The impact of national culture and economic ideology on managerial work values: A study of the United States, Russia, Japan, and China. *Journal of International Business Studies, 28,* 177-207.

Riquelme, H. (2002). Commercial internet adoption in china: Comparing the experience of small medium and large business. *Internet Research, 12*(3), 276-286.

Rogers, E. (1995). *Diffusion of innovations.* New York: Free Press.

Romer, P. (1990). Endogenous technological change. *Journal of Political Economy, 86*(2), 71-102.

Sacks, M. A., Ventresca, M. J., & Uzzi, B. (2001). Global institutions and networks. *The American Behavioral Scientist, 44*(10), 1579-1601.

Samiee, S. (1998). The internet and international marketing: is there a fit? *Journal of International Marketing, 12*(4), 5-21.

Schooler, C. (1996). Cultural and social-structural explanations of cross-national psychological differences. *Annual Review of Sociology, 22,* 323-349.

Scott, W., & Meyer, J. (1991). The organization of societal sectors: propositions and early evidence. In W. Powell and P. DiMaggio (Eds.), *The New Institutionalism in Organizational Analysis* (pp. 108-142). Chicago: University of Chicago Press.

Scott, W. R. (1995). *Institutions and organizations.* Thousand Oaks, CA: Sage Publications.

Shih, C.F., Dedrick, J., & Kraemer, K. (2005). Rule of law and the international diffusion of e-commerce. *Communications of the ACM, 48*(11), 57-62.

Simon, S. J. (1999). A cross cultural analysis of Web site design: An empirical study of global Web users. In *Proceedings of the Seventh Cross-Cultural Consumer Business Studies Research Conference,* Cancun, Mexico.

Steinmueller, W. E. (2001). ICTs and the possibilities for leapfrogging by developing countries. *International Labor Review, 140*(2), 193-210.

Sultan, F., & Henrichs, R. B. (2000). Consumer preferences for internet services over time: Initial explorations. *The Journal of Consumer Marketing, 17*(5), 386.

Suraya, R.M.R. (2005). Internet diffusion and E-business opportunities amongst Malaysian travel agencies. *Journal of American Academy of Business, 6*(1), 78-84.

Takada, K. T., Fiona, C., Ueda, T., Saito, K., & Chen, Y. (2002). Analysis of dynamic interactive diffusion processes of the internet and new generation of cellular phones. *Journal of American Academy of Business, 2*(1), 269-271.

Tan, Z., Foster, W., & Goodman, S.E. (1999). China's state-coordinated internet infrastructure, *Communications of the ACM, 42*(6), 44-52.

Tellefsen, P., Gentry, J. W., John, J., Manzer, J.J., & Cho, B. J. (1991). A cross-national examination of innovation resistance. *International Marketing Review, 8*(3), 7-20.

Tellefsen, T., & Takada, H. (1999). The relationship between mass mmedia availability and the multicountry diffusion of consumer products. *Journal of International Marketing, 7*(1), 77-96.

Teo, T. S., & Pain Y. (2003). A contingency perspective on internet adoption and competitive advantage. *European Journal of Information Systems, 12,* 78-92.

Tsoukas, H. (1994). *Riding the Waves of Culture.,* Chicago, IL: Irwin Professional Pubishing.

Tuomela, R. (2003). Collective acceptance, social institutions, and social reality. *American Journal of Economics and Sociology*, *62*(1), 123-165.

Turner, J. H. (1997). *The institutional order.* New York: Addison-Wesley Educational Publishers.

Van Deth, J. W. (1995). A macro setting for micro politics. J. W. Van Deth, E. Scarbrough, (Eds.). *The Impact of Values.* (pp.48-75). New York: Oxford University Press.

Vlosky, R. P., Westbrook, T., & Poku, K. (2002). An exploratory study of internet adoption by primary wood products manufacturers in the western United States. *Forest Product Journal*, *52*(6), 35-42.

Volken, T. (2002). Elements of trust: The cultural dimension of internet diffusion revisited. *Electronic Journal of Sociology*, ISSN: 1198 3655.

Wallsten, S. (2005). Regulation and internet use in developing countries. *Economic Development and Cultural Change*, *53*(2), 501-522.

Warren, M. (2004). Farmers online: Drivers and impediments in adoption of internet in UK agricultural business. *Journal of Small Business and Enterprise Development*, *11*(3), 371-381.

Whitley, R. (1994). Dominant forms of economic organization in market economies. *Organization Studies*, *15*, 153-182.

Wolcott, P., Press, L., McHenry, W., Goodman, S., & Foster, W. (2001). A framework for assessing the global diffusion of the internet. *Journal of the Association for Information Systems*, *2*, November.

Wooldridge, J. M. (2001). *Econometric Analysis of Cross Section and Panel Data.* Cambridge, MA:The MIT Press.

World Bank. *World Development Indicators 1996 - 2005*, Washington, D.C.: The World Bank.

Xu, S., Zhu, K., & Gibbs, J. (2004). Global technology, local adoption: A cross-country investigation of internet adoption by companies in the United States and China. *Electronic Markets*, *14*(1), 13-24.

Zhao, H. (2002). The internet development in china: Identifying facilitating and limiting factors. *Thunderbird International Business Review*, *44*(1), 119-138.

APPENDIX A. COUNTRIES INCLUDED IN THE DATA

	Country Name
LDCs (n = 19)	Brazil, Chile, China, Columbia, Czech, Hungary, India, Indonesia, South Korea, Malaysia, Mexico, Philippine, Poland, Russia, Singapore, South Africa, Thailand, Turkey, Venezuela
DCs (n = 20)	Austria, Canada, Denmark, Finland, France, Germany, Greece, Ireland, Israel, Italy, Japan, Netherlands, New Zealand, Norway, Portugal, Spain, Sweden, Switzerland, United Kingdom, United States

APPENDIX B. DEFINITIONS AND SOURCES OF VARIABLES

Variable Name	Definition
INTERNET	*Growth of Internet users*: The annual growth of Internet users per 1,000 (Source: *World Telecommunication Report and the World Development Indicators*).
RULE	The extent to which agents have confidence in and abide by the rules of society. (*Source: Daniel, Kraay, and Mastruzzi, 2005*)
ECONSYS	*Government's Expenditure*: Central government's total expenditure including nonrepayable current and capital expenditure, percent of GDP. (*Source: World Development Indicators*)
EDU	*Education*: percentage of people aged 15 and above "who can read and write simple statement on their everyday life" multiplied by labor force with tertiary education as percentage of total population (*Source: World Development Indicators*)
INDUSTRY	*Industrialization*: Energy consumption per PPP GDP (kilograms of oil equivalent per capita). (*Source: World Development Indicators*)
INDIVIDUAL	The index of individualism (*Source: Hofstede (2001)*.
UA	The index of uncertainty avoidance (*Source: Hofstede (2001)*.
PD	The index of power distance (*Source: Hofstede (2001)*.
NETWORK	*Network Infrastructure*: Composite variable of the standardized scores of personal computers, mobile phones, and telephone mainlines per 10,000 people. (Source: *World Development Indicators; International Telecommunication Union*).

Variable Name	Definition
NETCOST	Internet total monthly price (per 20 hours of use) (*Source: World Development Indicators*).
GDPGROW	Annual GDP per capital growth *(Source: World Development Indicators)*.
OPEN	Total national import and export divided by GDP *(Source: World Development Indicators; International Financial Statistics)*

This work was previously published in Journal of Global Information Management, Vol. 15, Issue 2, edited by F. B. Tan, pp. 28-55, copyright 2007 by IGI Publishing, formerly known as Idea Group Publishing (an imprint of IGI Global).

Chapter XXII
A Time Series Analysis of International ICT Spillover

Juan Juan Zhang
National University of Singapore, Singapore

Sang-Yong Tom Lee
Hanyang University, Korea

ABSTRACT

This article studies the role of international spillover of information and communication technology (ICT) in economic growth. We examine the performance of ten countries from 1982 to 1999. By empirically analyzing the relationship between total factor productivity (TFP) and domestic and foreign ICT investment with time series analysis tools, we find limited evidence that there exist international ICT spillovers for a group of countries. Further, we discuss the possible ICT policies to improve productivity and balance out a win-win situation for both ICT spillover sending and receiving countries.

INTRODUCTION

Nowadays, ICT is considered an extremely important factor that contributes to the accelerated rate of productivity of a nation, especially in many newly industrialized economies (NIEs) and developing countries. ICT is the combined utilization of electronics, telecommunications, software, networks, and decentralized computer workstations, and the integration of information media (Granville, Leonard, & Manning, 2000), all of which impact firms, industries, and the economy as a whole. ICT is comprised of a variety of "communication equipment" which includes radio, TV, and communication equipment and software. Therefore, ICT investment includes "investments in both computer and telecommunications, as well as related hardware, software and services" (Dedrick et al., 2003, p. 4).

In recent years, the combination of computer and telecommunication equipment helps and enables businesses and organizations to share and exchange huge amounts of information. It also eliminates vast amounts of paperwork and speeds up transaction processes by the Internet, Intranets and other networks. In addition, technology and computer production has been a high growth sector in many countries. The ICT industry itself can be a source of economic growth and jobs (Kraemer & Dedrick, 2001). Consequently, it is widely believed that ICT investment helps to enhance productivity and economic growth.

ICT capital exhibits both traditional and non-traditional effects (Dedrick, et al., 2003). As traditional capital, ICT's returns accrue primarily to the firms, industries, or countries that make the investment, and diminish with continuing investment. Contrarily, due to its informational and transformational roles, ICT capital is similar to knowledge capital (Dedrick et al., 2003). ICT capital, if used properly, facilitates knowledge creation. We define knowledge capital as the data, information, knowledge, and wisdom necessary to support and grow an organization or economy. ICT enhances the productivity of employees, and therefore contributes positively to the generation of knowledge capital. Since knowledge capital is not rivalrous and has public goods properties, it leads to potential "spillovers.".

Grossman and Helpman (1991) define spillovers as follows: "By spillovers, we mean that (a) firms can acquire information created by others without paying for that information in a market transaction, and (b) the creators (or current owners) of the information have no effective recourse, under prevailing laws, if other firms utilize (the) information so acquired." From this definition of spillover, one may derive that ICT spillover is an increase in social benefits without compensat-

ing the ICT investors. If we regard investors as a national economy as a whole, then we have the concept of "international ICT spillover." In other words, international ICT spillover is an increase in national productivity due to ICT investments in foreign countries.

ICT spillover emerges when social returns on investment exceed their private returns, creating situations in which investment in ICT becomes an innovator or investor, thereby, also benefiting other parties (Leeuwen & Wiel, 2003). "The Information Technology Boom" has given rise to many discussions about the potential of ICT to yield production externalities. Production spillovers or externalities can show up in the form of rent (pecuniary) spillovers or in the form of so-called technology/knowledge spillovers. These arise from the fact that knowledge and technology have some public good characteristics—knowledge capital can be owned and used by many parties simultaneously, leading to potential spillovers (Leeuwen & Wiel, 2003).

Globalization and rapid communications among innovators in different locations facilitate the process of invention and the spread of new ideas across different countries. Scholars have concluded that R&D is transferred from the innovating country to other countries mainly through trade, which helps to stimulate the receiving countries' economic growth. Many researchers have also tried to prove ICT spillovers among firms or industries within a country. However, to our knowledge, studies on international ICT spillovers are rare. Therefore, our main research question is whether foreign ICT investments, just like R&D expenditures, will have spillover effects on domestic productivity growth.

In this article, we would like to examine the relationship between international ICT spillovers and national productivity growth. This article would fill the literature gap on ICT spillovers at the country level. A sample of 10 countries was chosen based on data availability. We deployed time series analysis. If the existence of ICT spillovers at country level is empirically proven, it may have strong policy implications especially for developing countries.

The organization of the article is as follows: The next chapter is a review of relevant studies in productivity and technology spillovers. Section 3 presents the methodological framework. Section 4 shows a brief discussion of the data sources. The following Section 5 discusses the empirical findings, and comments on the possible limitations. Finally, Section 6 concludes the article with a few thought-provoking issues on policy implications.

LITERATURE REVIEW

TFP as a Measure of Productivity Growth

Total factor productivity (TFP) is not a new concept in the studies on economic growth. Most authors track its origin back to Solow's (1957) empirical work, the so-called "Solow's Residual." TFP is believed to be a residual of production growth, which cannot be explained by increases in factors of input. The unexplained output growth should contain the contribution of new technology (such as R&D, IT, etc.), improved management, and more efficient markets and institutions (Evenson, 1997). TFP as a measurement of technological change is vital because technological change is believed to be the ultimate cause of long-term economic growth (Carlaw & Lipsey, 2002).

The implementation of TFP, or Solow's Residual, offers a better measurement of actual productivity attributed to technology. The majority of earlier research used tangible outputs such as GDP, national wealth, revenue, and other perceptible values in their analysis. These output measures might not have captured ICT's entire contribution to an economy's productivity. Since it had been widely acknowledged that ICT usage provides a wide range of intangible impacts,

such as better processes, improved products, and enhanced services, Solow's Residual better appraises the efficiency of IT, providing better data than using GDP directly.

Technology Spillovers

Technology has become a ubiquitous topic in economic growth theory. Even before technology became so prominent in the mainstream theory, pioneers in the empirical field, like Griliches (1979) and Scherer (1982), were aware of the influence an industry's technology generation can exert on the productivity of other industries, through so-called technology spillovers. In the 1980s and 1990s, many studies confirmed their main findings that technology spillovers have significant productivity effects (Los, 1997).

Technology spillovers are said to exist if market partners receive productivity benefits from technologies developed by others, although there is no monetary compensation for the technology transfer (Meijl & Tongeren, 1999). ICT and R&D can be treated as important technological knowledge. To a large extent, technological knowledge generates public good. The use of a unit of knowledge by one research employee does not prevent other researchers from using it (knowledge is non-rival); however, technological knowledge such as R&D can be appropriated only to a certain extent (knowledge is partly non-excludable) (Mankiw, 2001). Danny Qual defines knowledge-products as "computer software, new media, electronic databases and libraries, and Internet delivery of goods and services" (Granville, Leonard, & Manning, 2000). Hence, both ICT and R&D have the common characteristics of knowledge capital.

Endogenous Growth Model to Estimate Technology Spillovers

An *endogenous growth model* assumes that technology investment is like knowledge capital investment. Recent developments of endogenous growth models have stressed the role of knowledge spillovers in generating growth (Lucas, 1988; Romer, 1986). The endogenous theory of growth suggests that technological innovations are becoming increasing important contributions to economic growth (Evenson & Singh, 1997).

Coe and Helpman (1995) argued that endogenous growth models emphasize innovation and trade as vehicles for technological spillovers, thus permitting developing countries to catch up to industrialized ones. The role knowledge plays in technological progress has been the subject of much recent attention in the economic growth literature. Several studies find that the returns from investment in knowledge are positive; they are greater than returns from investment in equipment, infrastructure, and machinery (Madden & Savage 2000; Griliches, 1994; Nadiri, 1993).

In 1995, Coe and Helpman extended Grossman and Helpman's (1991) "Product variety" model of innovation to show that national productivity increases with the accumulation of both domestic and foreign knowledge (Bayoumi, Coe, & Helpman, 1996). The new knowledge, which prevents diminishing return on capital stock, is produced by investment in technology (Evenson & Singh, 1997). Hence, an endogenous growth model is a very suitable means to measure knowledge capital and technology spillover on economic growth.

If the study result does conclude that ICT spillover exists and is positive and significant, this finding would have important implications for national trade liberalization and economic integration policy. For example, Madden, et al. (2000) argue that ICT is an important source of international knowledge transfer in an emerging global information economy. International trade in ICT equipment and services generates direct productivity benefits through lower transaction costs and improved marketing information, as well as other indirect benefits due to accelerated information and knowledge diffusion across borders (Jussawalla & Lamberton, 1982; Antonelli, 1991). As such, ICT and trade policy are becoming

priorities for many governments and international agencies endeavoring to improve national productivity and economic growth (European Bank for Reconstruction and Development, 1995; Spiller & Cardilli, 1997).

R&D Spillovers

R&D is technological knowledge (Mankiw, 2001), sharing the same characteristic of knowledge capital with IT. As a generator of new technology, the effect of R&D spillover is significant in terms of productivity. Grossman and Helpman (1991) suggested that spillovers from R&D might be one possible engine of endogenous growth in recent years. Much research has been done regarding R&D spillovers both at disaggregate and aggregate levels.

Luukkainen and Niininen (2000) stated that researchers have demonstrated that R&D performed by the original innovating company generates widespread value in the economy through spillovers. Braconier & Sjoholm (1997) suggested that spillovers from R&D exist within industries, both nationally and internationally. The empirical evidence further suggests that intra-industry spillovers are confined to industries that are relatively R&D intensive.

Coe and Helpman (1995) and Engelbrecht (1997) demonstrate an empirical relationship between accumulated R&D expenditures and TFP, and show that the benefits of R&D can spill across countries through trade. These findings have implications for countries considering trade liberalization and economic integration policies. Evenson & Singh (1997) examined the contribution of international technological spillovers using panel data from eleven Asian countries over the period 1970 to 1997. By deploying the new endogenous economic growth models, they offered new insights into the growth process. A country's productivity growth not only depends on its domestic R&D investment but also on the R&D investment from its trading partners. Countries benefit from purchasing and imitating technology created in other countries as well.

ICT Spillovers at Firm and Industry Level

IT investment, with its informational and transformational roles, is similar to knowledge capital and may generate considerable economic externalities from both network externalities and knowledge spillovers (Dedrick et al., 2003; Mun & Nadiri, 2002). Romer (1986) argued that the knowledge that enables a firm or an industry to adopt advanced technology successfully would naturally spill over to other firms or industries. Knowledge from ICT capital is often diffused by entities such as technology user groups, academic institutions, management consultant firms, and, especially, labor mobility. It is often the case that competing firms rapidly copy ICT investments made by innovative firms (Dedrick et al.,2003).

Leeuwen & Wiel (2003) have argued that ICT spillovers predominantly materialized at the firm level via production efficiency gains arising from the streamlining or upgrade of internal business processes or improved communications. The emergence and rapid development of the Internet is a good example. The Internet increased the ability of firms to transfer information among themselves. Luukkainen and Niininen (2000) also concluded that technology spillovers among firms would increase both customer and competitor benefits.

The empirical results of Mun and Nadiri's study (2002 of US private industries over the period 1984-2000 showed that computerization of an industry's customers and suppliers reduces both labor and material costs for the whole industry. They also found that industries in the services sector enjoy more benefits from ICT spillovers than industries in other sectors because of their high ICT capital intensity and composition of inter-industry transaction.

Results might be substantially different in different industry sectors. An important question is whether there are spillovers from IT-producing industries to IT-using industries. As stated by Ganley, Kraemer, and Wong (2002), the correlation between production of ICT and use of ICT is confined to specific scenarios. There is evidence of a positive spillover effect from ICT production to ICT spending among most developed countries, and a negative spillover effect in East Asian producer countries. They argued that it is because East Asian countries are trapped in low margin ICT manufacturing sectors, that their ability to build their resources in design, ICT services and software development is stifled. Contrarily, the US and other developed countries, where their ICT production has a variety of scope, enjoy a positive effect from IT-producing to IT-using industries.

HYPOTHESES, METHODOLOGY, MODEL, AND FRAMEWORK

Hypotheses

The objective of this study is to determine if ICT investment from foreign countries does, indeed, contribute to domestic economic growth. To investigate the long term relationship among variables, we first deploy the Cobb-Douglas production function. The Cobb-Douglas functional form can be viewed as a linear approximation of the actual underlying production function. It has been shown to be a good approximation in the ICT and productivity contexts by Dewan and Min (1997). It is pervasive in the productivity research literature. The production function approach has been widely used in previous studies of ICT impact on firm performance (Loveman, 1994; Brynjolfsson & Hitt, 1995). Typical production requires labor (L) and capital (K). Hence, we have the following production function:

$$Y = A(E, S) f(K, L) = A(E, S) K^{\alpha} L^{1-\alpha}, \quad (1)$$

where Y is GDP or output, K is the aggregate capital stock, and L is the labor force. $0 < \alpha < 1$ is the share parameter, representing the share of production contribution elasticity. A is a technology shift parameter, which is a function of the national specific (knowledge) capital, E, and the spillover effects, S. A is also known as the Total Factor Productivity, or Solow's Residual. It is what economists used to refer to when discussing that part of a country's economic productivity which remains "unexplained," but suspected to be a result of technology. Using the Cobb-Douglas production function in Equation (1), Solow's Residual A, can be derived as:

$$A = Y/ K^{\alpha} L^{1-\alpha} = A(E, S). \quad (2)$$

Since data on output (GDP), capital stock, and labor input are acquired, and α is approximated by the share of profit in total output, Solow's Residual can be determined from Equation (2). Economists tend to place the value of α between 0.3 and 0.4. In this article, the value of this share parameter is set to $\alpha = 0.3$ because it is more commonly used.

Now, since the national knowledge capital is a function of domestic ICT investment, and the spillover effect is a function of foreign ICT investment, Equation (2) can be rewritten as follows:[1]

$$\ln TFP_t = \beta_0 + \beta_1 \ln DICT_t + \beta_2 \ln FICT_t + \varepsilon_t \quad (3)$$

where t denotes years, DICT is domestic ICT investment, and FICT is foreign ICT investment.

In Equation 3 we may see the impact of domestic and foreign ICT investment on total factor productivity. Hence, we posit our main hypotheses as follows:

Hypothesis 1: Domestic ICT investments would cause an increase in total factor productivity

(TFP). In other words, domestic ICT investments would contribute to national economic growth.

Hypothesis 2: Foreign ICT investments would cause an increase in total factor productivity (TFP). In other words, there exists a spillover effect.

Causality Test

Although hypotheses look simple to test, due to the nature of time series data, we cannot perform the test by estimating Equation (3) with the ordinary least squares (OLS) method. Statisticians and econometricians know that if time series variables are non-stationary and not co-integrated, the OLS results are spurious. In other words, one can never trust the OLS results unless time series variables are either non-stationary or co-integrated.

Accordingly, the implementation of time series analysis tools in this research is aimed to eliminate the spurious regression problems. Before the co-integration tests between ICT investments and TFP, we implement the Augmented Dickey-Fuller (ADF) test to determine whether the variables are stationary (Dickey, 1979). For example, if the order of integration is 2, that is, I(2), the series becomes stationary after the second differences.

If the variables ($\ln A$, $\ln DICT$, and $\ln FICT$) are integrated in different orders, we conclude easily that the variables are not co-integrated. If the variables are non-stationary, but integrated in the same order, then we need to determine whether they are co-integrated. In this case, we perform the Johansen Co-integration test. [2]

Depending on whether they are co-integrated, different tests would be necessary to determine the causal relationship between the two variables. If the variables are co-integrated, we deploy the vector error correction model (VECM) and the regular Granger Causality test is conducted for non-cointegrated variables. Also, another benefit of adopting causality tests is that we don't need to worry about intermediating variables from ICT investment to TFP.

When variables are co-integrated, there still can be disequilibrium in the short run. Hence, the vector error correction model (VECM) has to be applied before implementing the causality test. Applying VECM, which is a VAR in first difference with the addition of a vector of co-integrating residuals, results in the so-called Pairwise VEC Granger Causality Test, in contrast to the Standard Granger Causality.

$$\ln A_t = \gamma_1 ECT_{t-1} + \sum_{i=1}^{n} \alpha_i \ln A_{t-i} + \sum_{i=1}^{m} \beta_i \ln ICT_{t-i} + u_t, (4)$$

$$\ln IT_t = \gamma_2 ECT_{t-1} + \sum_{i=1}^{p} \lambda_i \ln ICT_{t-i} + \sum_{i=1}^{q} \mu_i \ln A_{t-i} + v_t, (5)$$

where $\ln ICT$ is either $\ln FICT$ or $\ln DICT$, and ECT is the error-correction term, which is the residual of the co-integration equation and explains short-term disequilibrium among the variables. Also it is assumed that the disturbances u_t and v_t are uncorrelated.

When variables are not co-integrated, then we perform the standard Granger Causality test that does not include the error-correction term. If the variables are non-stationary, we need to difference the series to make it stationary (Granger, 1969). Corresponding to the stationary time series data of $\ln A$, $\ln DICT$, and $\ln FICT$, the causality test involves estimating the following VAR (Vector Auto-regression) models:

$$\ln A_t = \sum_{i=1}^{n} \alpha_i \ln A_{t-i} + \sum_{i=1}^{m} \beta_i \ln ICT_{t-i} + u_t, \quad (6)$$

$$\ln IT_t = \sum_{i=1}^{p} \lambda_i \ln ICT_{t-i} + \sum_{i=1}^{q} \mu_i \ln A_{t-i} + v_t, \quad (7)$$

We select the lag structure of the model based on Akaike Information Criteria (AIC), as reported by the EVIEWS software package. Using the models (4) and (5), or (6) and (7), we perform the Granger Causality test that $\beta_1 = \beta_2 = ... = \beta_m = 0$. It follows that, if the computed F statistic exceeds the critical value at the chosen level of significance,

the null hypothesis is rejected, thus there exists the causal relationship of FICT→A (Hypothesis 2) or DICT→A (Hypothesis 1).

DATA AND VARIABLES

We selected 10 countries based on the data availability. Each country consists of annual time series data for 4 main variables—GDP(Y), Capital (K), Labor (L), and Information Technology Investment (IT):

- *Developing Countries:* China, India, and Malaysia
- *Newly Industrialized Economics (NIEs):* Korea, Hong Kong, and Singapore
- *Developed countries:* Finland, Ireland, Japan, and the US

The time series data are selected from 1982 to 1999, a total of 18 years. GDP (Constant 1995 US dollars), capital stock, and labor data were obtained from World Development Indicators (WDI). However, WDI only provides value for Gross Fixed Capital Formation (Constant 1995 US dollars), which is actually gross domestic fixed investment (denoted by I), not really the capital stock we need to calculate for TFP. Thus, an adjustment to data of the capital variable is essential. Non high-tech capitals are commonly depreciated with a 10% rate annually. The individual annual values are derived as $K_t = I(t) + (1-\delta) \times K_{t-1}$, where $\delta = 0.1$ the depreciation rate.

Relative difficulty and complexity occurs in collection of ICT data, a long time sequence is necessary in order to implement time series analysis tools. Apparently, data unavailability for ICT investment is quite common in the 1980s, especially for developing countries. Hence, we use telecommunication investment (1981-1999) from the International Telecommunication Union (ITU) as a proxy for ICT investment. The For-

Table 1. Basic statistics of A, DICT, and FICT

Country	lnA		lnDICT		lnFICT	
	Mean	Std. Dev.	Mean	Std. Dev.	Mean	Std. Dev.
China	4.408481	0.273329	21.28123	1.772508	24.55728	0.337422
India	4.536943	0.119301	21.04040	0.572088	24.60669	0.409038
Korea	6.649668	0.156121	21.75028	0.592708	24.57595	0.402875
Hong Kong	7.143254	0.155160	19.83525	0.989156	24.62541	0.406478
Singapore	7.080996	0.218419	19.35520	0.648559	24.62970	0.411739
Malaysia	6.116630	0.155212	20.27137	0.783519	24.62069	0.409316
Finland	7.339356	0.098926	20.07135	0.454712	24.62446	0.412509
Ireland	7.278669	0.198050	19.43815	0.390441	24.62951	0.412832
Japan	7.602688	0.072753	23.54201	0.588513	24.21258	0.340114
United States	7.534318	0.046924	23.79587	0.109261	23.99497	0.681412

Table 2. ADF unit root test summary

Economies	lnA	lnDICT	lnFICT	Co-integration Test Implemented Next
China	I(2)	I(2)	I(2)	Yes
India	I(2)	I(2)	I(2)	Yes
Korea	I(2)	I(2)	I(2)	Yes
Hong Kong	I(2)	I(2)	I(2)	Yes
Singapore	I(2)	I(2)	I(2)	Yes
Malaysia	I(2)	I(2)	I(2)	Yes
Finland	I(2)	I(2)	I(2)	Yes
Ireland	I(2)	I(2)	I(2)	Yes
Japan	I(2)	I(2)	I(1)	No
US	I(2)	I(2)	I(2)	Yes

* The significant level of the ADF unit root test is 1%.

Table 3. Summary of the principal findings

Country	Causality Test Results	Test Model
China	FICT→A*	VECM
India	DICT→A***	VECM
Korea	DICT→ A* FICT→ A*	VECM
Hong Kong	No	VECM
Singapore	DICT→A*** FICT→A**	VECM
Malaysia	No	VECM
Finland	DICT→ A***	VECM
Ireland	FICT→ A***	VECM
Japan	DICT→ A**	Standard Model
US	DICT→ A** FICT→ A**	VECM

* significant at 10% level

** significant at 5% level

*** significant at 1% level

eign ICT investment variable (FIT) is calculated by summing up all the ICT investments except the domestic one. Table 1 summarizes the basic statistics for *A, DICT,* and *FICT.*

EMPIRICAL RESULTS

Discussion and Analysis of Statistical Findings

Table 2 shows the basic results of the unit root test on the time series of DICT, FICT, and TFP (or *A*).

Table 3 illustrates the principal findings from the co-integration and causality tests for the sample countries. The variables are co-integrated in most of countries except Japan. Therefore, we apply the vector error correction model for them. For Japan, we use the standard Granger Causality test. The results for causality test vary across countries.

If the causal relationship of a certain country from DICT to TFP (Hypothesis 1) or FICT to TFP (Hypothesis 2) is significant, it is indicated in the second column of Table 3. As one can see in that column, Hypothesis 2 is supported, i.e., there exist positive and significant international spillover effects for Ireland, Korea, Singapore, the United States, and China.

Except for China, the other four countries are notable for governmental efforts to boost ICT industries. The governments provide adequate funding for education and universities and technology institutions contribute major advances in technology innovations and inventions in all four countries. In the meantime, each country has well-trained ICT specialists and workers in

ICT-sectors have built up their knowledge base. From the hardware point of view, the telecommunication infrastructure and networks are well established.

These four countries all promote trade liberalization and globalization. Therefore, knowledge and advanced information technologies can be comparatively easier to transfer to these countries. At the same time, because of their already established telecommunication infrastructures and human capital, such as education, the ICT investment in foreign countries is not only being transferred, but is also more promptly digested and absorbed (transformed) by the local workforce. Hence, foreign ICT spillovers occurred and the effects are positive and significant.

It is a bit surprising to see that China belongs to this group, because the openness of its economy is limited and telecommunications infrastructure is still restricted compared to other countries. However, China also thinks highly of education. Its human capital is already well established, so that China's local labor forces follow relatively easily what other countries are doing. This may explain why foreign ICT investment has positive impact on China's productivity.

Finland does not have international spillover in our empirical result while its domestic ICT investment causes TFP growth. Finland's government invests a large amount of capital in knowledge and information technology and achieves a huge payback for the investment in economic performance. Thirty years ago, 70% of Finland's exports were wood and paper products. Now, more than 50% of the country's exports are knowledge-intensive products. For instance, Nokia, a telecommunication giant, contributes 4% of Finland total GDP, 35% of total business sector R&D and 25% of the total exports. Compared to Finland's strong contribution of domestic ICT investment, the effect of foreign ICT investments seems less significant.

Japan, the second largest economy in the world and the largest exporter of technology products,

did not have the co-integrated relationship between ICT and TFP. Also, only domestic ICT investment causes national productivity growth while foreign ICT investment does not. This may be due to Japan's special situation of ICT industry. For example, NTT DoCoMo is using its unique standard Personal Digital Cellular (PDC) for 2G mobile phone, which was developed and used only in Japan. Now, as Japan is using WCDMA for 3G mobile phone standard following worldwide trend, we may see international spillover for Japan in the future.

Moral of the Story: ICT Maturity and Network/Path of Infrastructures

The creation of new ICT knowledge by one firm/industry/country is assumed to have a positive external effect on the production of opportunities for other parties because it is possible to create a large pool of ICT knowledge when the technologies are being used by many parties. With more trade of ICT products and higher mobility of international labor forces, ICT knowledge can be transferred faster and more easily. After being absorbed by local labor forces, ICT spillover effects will take place.

Shapiro and Varian (1999) argued that ICT value does not simply mean implementation of hardware or software, but ICT usage that needs a certain period of time for users to train themselves until they find ICT useful. Put simply, ICT investment generally requires a learning period for users before gains occur. In general, creating an ICT knowledge base requires a longer time period than ICT implementation. ICT-matured countries benefit more from information technology because of the ICT knowledge base. For instance, Singapore and Korea enjoy foreign ICT spillovers much more than Malaysia.

Furthermore, the contribution of ICT investment is a product of individual efforts taking place in a network context where the infrastructure and communication technology, together with changing externalities in the use of ICT, affect the historical paths taken in shaping the growth of ICT contributions (Shapiro & Varian, 1999). David (1990) also argues that ICT may require substantial changes in complementary infrastructure (e.g., human and knowledge capital, global communications infrastructure, etc.) before the generation of output. In other words, the networks and paths must be built up before benefits of spillover from other countries occur. Therefore, the two main conditions for the existence of ICT spillovers are ICT maturity and networking, which create paths of infrastructures and telecommunications.

Limitations

We have had difficulties in finding a good time series dataset of ICT investments. Relatively better samples were telecommunications investments. Still, we have 19 years, which is just acceptable for time series analysis. In the future, we need to collect longer series of data and will see whether the findings are still robust. Also, telecommunications investments may not be sufficient to reflect the full effect of foreign ICT spillovers towards domestic economic growth.

Another limitation is the number of countries for the analysis. The sample set only contains 10 economies because of data availability. Foreign ICT spillover is limited among the 10 countries, but not in a worldwide aspect. In future study, more countries should be included to generalize the results.

CONCLUSION AND IMPLICATIONS

Productivity is the amount of goods and services produced from each hour of a worker's time. The key role of productivity is to determine a nation's living standards. Policymakers who want to encourage growth in standards of living must aim to increase their nations' productivity by encouraging rapid accumulation of the factors of production and ensuring that these factors are employed as effectively as possible. From time series analysis, we found the limited evidence of international ICT spillovers which would contribute to economic growth. This article lets the policy makers and scholars look at another dimension of productivity growth, i.e., spillovers.

The ICT spillovers would create a mutually beneficial situation across countries. With productivity growth, the total wealth and welfare of the receiving countries will be higher, which may result in stronger purchasing power in those countries. With stronger purchasing power, these countries would likely purchase more goods, services, and advanced technology from sending countries to further improve their living standards and productivity. Hence, both parties benefit from the spillover effects and it is a win-win situation. ICT spillovers would have very important implications in economic development plans. Thus, international organizations, such as United Nations and World Bank, could formulate possible ICT policies to enhance ICT spillovers by promoting free trade, globalization, and so on.

At the same time, policymakers of each country would consider foreign ICT spillover as a key factor of economic growth. For countries with limited ICT investment, foreign ICT investments may be a good source of productivity growth. They should open up the domestic market, encourage imports and exports, remove trade obstacles, support trade liberalization and globalization, build up ICT infrastructures, and promote education and train their labor force to let foreign ICT investment more easily spill over into domestic industry.

REFERENCES

Antonelli, C. (1991). *The diffusion of advanced technologies in developing countries.* OECD, Paris.

Bayoumi, T., Coe, D., & Helpman, E. (1996). *R&D spillovers and global growth.* Center for Economic Policy Research Discussion Paper, No. 1467, CEPR, London, UK.

Braconier, H., & Sjoholm, F. (1997). *National and international spillovers from R&D: Comparing a neoclassical and an endogenous growth approach.* Working Paper Series in Economic and Finance No. 211, December 1997.

Brynjolfsson, E., & Hitt, L.M. (1995). Information technology as a factor of production: The role of differences among firms. *Economic Innovation New Technology3*(3), 183-199.

Carlaw, K. I., & Lipsey, R.G. (2002). Productivity, technology and economic growth: What is the relationship? *Journal of Economic Surveys17*(3), 457-495.

Carr, N.G. (2003). IT doesn't matter. *Harvard Business Review81*(5), 41-49.

Coe, D., & Helpman, E. (1995). International R&D spillover. *European Economic Review 39*, 859-887.

David, P.A. (1990). The dynamo and the computer: An historical perspective on the modern productivity paradox. *The American Economic Review80*(2), 355-361.

Dedrick, J., Gurbaxani, V., & Kraemer, K.L. (2003). Information technology and economic performance: A critical review of the empirical evidence. *ACM Computing Surveys35*(1), 1-28.

Dewan, S, & Min, C. (1997). The substitution of information technology for other factors of production: A firm level analysis. *Management Science43*(12), 1660-1675.

Dickey, D.A., & Fuller, W.A. (1979). Distribution of the estimation for auto-regressive time series with a unit root. *Journal of the American Statistical Association74*, 427-431.

Engelbrecht, H. (1997). International R&D spillovers, human capital and productivity in OECD economies. *European Economic Review 41*, 1479-1488.

European Bank for Reconstruction and Development. (1995). *Transition report update.* EBRD, London.

European Commission. (2000). The EU economy 2000 review. *European Economy*, No. 71.

Evenson, R.E., & Englander, A.S. (1994). *International growth linkages between OECD countries.* Economic Growth Center, Yale University, New Haven, CT. (Mimeograph),.

Evenson, R. E. (1997). Industrial productivity growth linkages between OECD countries, 1970-90. *Economic Systems Research9*(2), 221-231.

Evenson, R. E., & Singh, L. (1997). *Economic growth, technological spillovers and public policy: Theory and empirical evidence from Asia.* Center Discussion Paper No. 777, Economic Growth Center, Yale University.

Ganley, D., Kraemer, K.L., & Wong, P.K. (2002). Spillover effects of production of IT on use of IT. *Proceedings of the 26th Hawaii International Conference System Sciences* (HICSS'03)

Granville, B., Leonard, C., & Manning, J. (2000, October). Information technology and developing countries: Potential and obstacles. Tokyo Club Meeting, Munich, Germany, 19-20.

Greene, W.H. (2000). *Econometric analysis* (4th ed.). Prentice Hall.

Granger, C.W.J. (1969). Investigation causal relations by econometric models and cross-spectral method, *Econometrica 1969*, 37, 424-438.

Griliches, Z. (1979). Issues in assessing the contribution of research and development to productivity growth. *The Bell Journal of Economics10*, 92-116.

Griliches, Z. (1994). Productivity, R&D and data constraint. *American Economic Review84*(1), 1-23.

Grossman, G., & Helpman, E. (1991). *Innovation and growth in the global economy*. Cambridge, MA: MIT Press.

Johansen, S. (1988). Statistical analysis of co-integrating vectors, *Journal of Economic Dynamics and Control12*, 231-54.

Johansen, S. &Juselius, K. (1990). Maximum likelihood estimation and inference on co-integration with applications for the demand for money. *Oxford Bulletin of Economics and Statistics52*, 169-210.

Jorgenson, D. W., & Stiroh, K.J. (2000). Raising the speed limit: U.S economic growth in the information age. *Brookings Paper Economic Actions1*(1), 125-211.

Jorgenson, D. W. (2001). Information technology and the U.S economy (Presidential address to the American Economic Association). *American Economic Review 91*(1), 1-32.

Jussawalla, M., & Lamberton, D. (1982). Communication economics and development: An economics of information perspective. In M. Jussawalla, D. Lamberton. (Eds.) *Communications, economics and development*. Elmsford, NY: Pergamon Press.

Kraemer, K., & Dedrick, J. (2001). *IT-led development in Singapore: From Winchester Island to intelligent island*. Working paper #ITR-123, Center for Research on Information Technology and Organizations, Graduate school of Management, University of California, Irvine.

Kumaresan, N. & Miyazaki, K. (2002). Integrated technologies as spillover infrastructures—Understanding the hidden dynamics of knowledge distribution in an innovation system. *Information Journal of Innovation Management6*(1), 25-51.

Lee, S.Y., Gholami, R., & Tong, T.Y. (2005). Time series analysis in the assessment of ICT impact at the aggregate level–lessons and implications for the new economy. *Information and Management42*(7), 1009-1022.

Leeuwen, G. V., & Wiel, H. V. D. (2003). Spillover effects of ICT. *CPB Report 3*, 24-30.

Los, B. (1997, October). *The empirical performance of a new inter-industry technology spillover measure*. Working Paper, University of Twente, the Netherlands.

Loveman, G. W. (1994). An assessment of the productivity impact of information technologies. In T.J. Aleen & M.S. Scott Morton (Eds.). *Information technology and the corporation of the 1990s: Research studies*. Cambridge: Oxford University Press, 48-110.

Lucas, R.E.B. (1988). On the mechanics of economic development. *Journal of Monetary Economics22*(1), 3-42.

Luukkainen, S., & Niininen, P. (2000). *Technology intensive services and national competitiveness*. VTT Group for Technology Studies, Working Papers 46.

Nadiri, M.I. (1993). *Innovations and technological spillovers*. National Bureau of Economic Research Working paper No. 4423. NBER, Cambridge, MA.

Madden, G., & Savage, S. J. (2000). R&D spillover, information technology and telecommunications, and productivity in ASIA and the OECD. *Information Economics and Policy12*, 367-392.

Madden, G., Savage, S.J., & Bloxham, P. (2001). Asian and OECD international R&D spillovers. *Applied Economics Letters 8*, 431-435.

Mankiw, N.G.(2001). *Principles of economics* (2nd ed.). Harcourt College Publishers.

Meijl, H. V., & Tongeren, F. V. (1999). *Endogenous international technology spillover and biased technological change in the GTAP model.* GTAP Technical Paper No. 15.

Mun, S.B., & Nadiri, M.I. (2002, October). *Information technology externalities: Empirical evidence from 42 U.S industries.* Working paper 9272, National Bureau of Economic Research.

Roach, S. S. (1987, April). *American's technology dilemma: A profile of the information economy.* Morgan Stanley Special Economic Study.

Romer, P. M. (1986). Increasing returns and long-run growth, *Journal of Political Economy. 94*(5), 1002-37.

Scherer, F.M. (1982). Inter-industry technology flows and productivity measurement. *Review of Economics and Statistics64*, 627-634.

Shapiro, C., & Varian, H. R. (1999). *Information rules: A strategic guide to network economy.* Harvard Business School Press.

Solow, R.M. (1957). Technical change and the aggregate production function. *Review of Economics and Statistics 39*(3), 312-320.

Solow, R.M. (1987). We'd better watch out. *New York Times Book Review,*July 12, 36.

Spiller, P., & Cardilli, C. (1997). The frontier of telecommunications deregulation: Small countries leading the pack. *Journal of Economic Perspectives11*, 127-138.

Stiroh, K. J. (2001). What drives productivity growth? *Economic Policy Review7*(1), 37-59.

ENDNOTES

[1] The reason we use logarithm of the variables is to create a linear functional form for estimation. This equation is also consistent with the Coe and Helpman (1995) specification of TFP.

[2] We skip the details of ADF test procedure and Johansen Co-integration test procedure. Please refer to Dickey(1979) and Johansen and Juselius (1990), respectively.

This work was previously published in Journal of Global Information Management, Vol. 15, Issue 4, edited by F. B. Tan, pp. 64-78, copyright 2007 by IGI Publishing, formerly known as Idea Group Publishing (an imprint of IGI Global).

Chapter XXIII
ICT Based Learning:
A Basic Ingredient for Socio-Economic Empowerment

Hakikur Rahman
SDNP, Bangladesh

ABSTRACT

ICT mediated learning provides utilities for achieving the goal of education for all, and in turn acts as an enabler in reducing the digital divide, reducing poverty, and promoting social inclusion. However, the integration of ICTs in education deserves considerable investment in time and resources. Consequently, during planning to integrate ICTs in evidence-based information for making sound decisions by the end users incorporate extensive research and sharing of critical information along different phases of planning. Furthermore, implementation of ICT based learning demands in depth analysis and intelligent feedback of the processes. Technology does not improve learning in a straight way and the fundamental question remains always unanswered, in assessing the effectiveness of ICTs or assessing the effectiveness of instructional treatments that were initially (and effectively) less than perfect. This chapter has tried to critically analyze the effective role of ICT methods in learning and put forwards several success cases of learning mechanisms that assisted in socioeconomic empowerment and at the same time, provided a few futuristic recommendations in establishing similar endeavors in promising economies.

INTRODUCTION

ICTs can increase access to information and this information helps communities to work more productively as well as in new opportunities. Increasing common people's access to ICTs should involve increasing availability of ICT infrastructure where most of them live. The infrastructure should be highly subsidized for at least a number of years so that the investment costs are not passed on to the end users (Mijumbi, 2002).

ICT can improve the learning process by making it faster, cheaper, and wider reaching that were not possible before. This form of learning can be treated as an interactive process among many entities and supporting the improvement of this process is expected to produce better results. However, innovative processes have to be incorporated both in terms of pedagogy and technology. Pedagogy should be universal and technology should give ubiquitous access with ambient intelligence.

In the area of education and training several hundred projects with thousands of participants around the globe have produced acceptable results in the areas of general education, specialized skill development training, and life long learning and have contributed positively to horizontal issues such as standards, metadata, interoperability, and sustainability.

Among them in 2001, an ambitious project, Prometeus, was built to establish a forum for expert opinions where participants from a wide range of countries, activities, professions, cultures, and languages productively interact towards the establishment of a community of cooperation in the field of educational technology and applications. All those contributions were taken into consideration and the contributors referenced in a position paper. Its aim was to bridge the gap between research and actual use of learning technologies, content and services, through direct contribution in a open consultation process (Bottino, 2001).

In 2002, Appeal launched a project on ICT Application for Non-Formal Education Programs with the support of the Japanese Funds-in-Trust. During its first phase, five countries (Indonesia, Lao PDR, Sri Lanka, Thailand, and Uzbekistan) implemented programs and activities to empower communities through the effective use of ICT.

However, in 2003 a study in this area entitled "Quality and e-learning in Europe training" was conducted and found that through a survey among 433 teachers and trainers from public and private sectors, about 61% felt that the quality of e-learning was fair or poor (Attwell, 2005). So, investment in this sector will remain a fair trade for many investors, including the development partners.

Therefore, the shift to the information society throws new challenges for learning processes and acquisition of knowledge through learning. In a society where information is becoming a strategic raw material and knowledge a value added product, how this resource is used is critical to the performance potential of each entrepreneur. The information and communication media provide necessary technologies to make knowledge available worldwide and transform the information society into a knowledge society. However, in response to individual needs, it is becoming increasingly important to harness appropriate information and systematize knowledge. A falling "half-life" of knowledge formulates life-long learning and up-to-date information becomes critical. Hence, in times of increasing globalization and networking, flexible access to information must be guaranteed at any place and at any time (Massey, 2003).

In this context, economic freedom plays an important role, in addition to technology update and information management. The 2006 Index of Economic Freedom measures 161 countries against a list of 50 independent variables divided into 10 broad factors in terms of economic freedom. The higher the score on a factor, the greater the level of government interference in the economy and the less economic freedom a country enjoys. In the ranking the top five countries (with lower scores between 1.28 and 1.74) are Hong Kong, Singapore, Ireland, Luxembourg, and United Kingdom, whereas North Korea, Iran, Burma, Zimbabwe, Libya, and Venezuela are among the bottom five (with higher scores between 5.00 and 4.16)[1]. This shows the level of ICT improvement in those countries, especially applicable to Hong Kong and Singapore in Asia.

The European Union has taken a lead role in reforming its member countries, improving their ICT situation, and establishing enhanced learning processes through ICT. The diverse e-learning visions, experiments and programs launched by individuals, organizations, institutions, nation-states of EU are found to be potentially more efficient in fostering flexible learning than traditional methods. The dominant view of e-learning has been, therefore, purely instrumental in legitimizing its *raison d'etre* as an ideal method to match the learner's choice and demand with more autonomy (Apollon, 2005).

The process of integrating ICT in the lower level of the education system involves a paradigm shift with new insights and new challenge facilitating new forms of understanding through earlier understandings to create new perspectives and interpretations. Integration should also incorporate an embedding of ICT in the institute's organizational structures and the organization of teaching (Walsh, 2002).

With the development of ICT a new brand of leaders are emerging, in instructional and transformational forms through commitment and enthusiasm for learning, working in partnership with colleagues across the curriculum to embed ICT into the learning process. These leaders have often come up very quickly through their ranks and subsequently their ICT skills have been learned on the job (Walsh, 2002).

At the same time, there is a growing interest with regards to ICTs being used to extend educational opportunities in developing countries. While many governments paid specific attention to integrate ICTs into compulsory schooling during the 1990s, more recently the focus has been shifted to post-secondary (K12) education. In essence ICTs need to be encouraged to make post-secondary teaching and learning more effective and more equitable by offering a diverse range of learning opportunities to a diverse range of learners in a convenient and cost-effective manner (Selwynn, 2003).

Henceforth, the ability to continue to learn throughout life is seen as a prerequisite to the development and sustainability of knowledge economies as countries, corporations, and communities require workers and citizens with flexible, *just-in-time* skills, competencies, and knowledge. Particularly the need for diverse and accessible learning opportunities has drawn policy makers in many countries towards the use of ICT as an educational delivery mechanism (Selwynn, 2003).

ICT-based learning can be formal (institutionally sponsored and structured), non-formal (non-credential but still institutionally-based and structured) or informal (happens incidentally or during everyday activities). This form of learning can, therefore, take place in the office, institution, home, or community, at different times for different purposes (Selwynn, 2003).

Hence, attempting to encourage full and effective participation of all stakeholders in ICT based education now forms a central part of current educational and economic policymaking in most developed countries (Selwynn, 2003). ICT in learning processes should not merely be used to acquire knowledge and skills; the processes should be more interactive and self-directed uses of ICTs should be encouraged so that the learners can actively construct new ideas, concepts, and meaning while transforming their existing knowledge (Rosen, 1998).

BACKGROUND

Learning is the cognitive process of acquiring knowledge[2] or skill through study, experience, or teaching. It is a process that depends on experience and leads to long-term changes in behavior potential. Behavior potential describes the possible behavior of an individual (not actual behavior) in a given situation in order to achieve a goal[3].

ICT-mediated learning is a process used to acquire data, information, skills, or knowledge. It is a form of learning that enables learning in a virtual world where technology merges with human creativity to accelerate and leverage the rapid development and application of deep knowledge[4]. ICT-based learning covers a wide set of applications and processes such as Web-based learning, computer-mediated learning, virtual classrooms, and digital collaboration. It includes the delivery of content via Internet, intranet/extranet (LAN/WAN), audio and videotape, satellite broadcast, interactive TV, PDA, mobile phone, CD-ROM, and other available technologies[5]. This chapter, specifically focuses on ICT-based learning to enable empowerment and socioeconomic development.

Empowerment is the process and practice of deriving power from within the self, or assisting others to do so through power within[6]. It is the process of equipping communities with knowledge, skills, and resources in order to change and improve the quality of their own lives and their community. Empowerment may evolve from within or it may be facilitated and supported through external agencies[7]. However, in terms of knowledge acquisition, empowerment is a consequence of liberatory learning and created within the emerging praxis in which co-learners are also engaged. The theoretical basis of this process is provided by critical consciousness; its expression is collective action on behalf of mutually agreed upon goals. Empowerment through knowledge is distinct from building skills and competencies that are being commonly associated with conventional schooling. Education for empowerment differs from schooling both in its emphasis on collective participation (rather than individuals) and in its focus on cultural transformation (rather than social adaptation)[8].

Whereas, socioeconomics is the study of the social and economic impacts of any product or service offering, market promotion or other

Table 1. Initiatives taken by EC for ICT-based learning

Year	Groups/Councils	Strategies Taken
2000	Lisbon Council	To form the most competitive and dynamic knowledge-based economy
2001	Ministers of Education	To achieve coherent community cooperation in the fields of education and training
2001	Working Group on ICT in education and training	To work on indicators and benchmarks, exchanging good practices and peer review
2002	Standing Group on Indicators and Benchmarks	Indicators and benchmarks were developed to monitor the progress
2003	Working Group on ICT in education and training	Focused on policy practices aiming at better quality education through integration of ICT

activity on an economy as a whole and on the entrepreneurs, organization and individuals who are its main economic actors. These effects can usually be measured in economic and statistical terms, such as growth in the size of the economy, the number of jobs created (or reduced), or levels of home ownership or Internet penetration (or number of telephones per inhabitant); and in measurable social terms such as life expectancy or levels of education[9]. This chapter provides emphasis on raising socioeconomic capacity of the economic actors through learning: information, content and knowledge; to lead into a knowledge-based economy.

A dynamic knowledge-based economy is capable of sustainable economic growth, but to achieve it, the economy not only needs a radical transformation within it, but also a modernized education system. The Lisbon Council of European Commission (EC) envisioned this in their March 2000 meeting, while in 2002 the EC stated that by 2010 Europe would be the world leader in terms of the quality of its education and training systems. To achieve this, a fundamental transformation of education and training has been taking place throughout Europe (European Commission, 2004). ICT-based education always demands a longer term strategy which the EC has initiated in 2000[10]. This strategy has been taken with a 10-year work plan to be implemented through an open method of coordination aiming at coherent community strategic framework of cooperation in the field of education and training. To support the implementation of the shared objectives for education and training systems at the national level through exchanges of "good practices," study tours, peer reviews, and so forth[11], EC has been working through twelve working groups since 2000.

Table 1 (*above*) shows a few initiatives taken by the European Commission to enhance the ICT-based learning in Europe. To date, the whole work has been carried out in four stages:

- First, decide upon key issues on which to focus future work.
- Second, focused on good practices and sharing policies to develop better quality education through ICT.
- Third, gather good policies and formulate recommendations learning from their problems.
- Fourth, gather examples to map those recommendations on good policy practices[12].

Integrating ICT in learning can mean anything from complete online training, with specific learning platforms using virtual microworlds and laboratories, to online access to and control of distant physical set ups such as cyber kiosks, or telecenters, or physics laboratories. This form of learning may also include a face-to-face situation in a laboratory with digital controls and computer-based mathematical tools. However, the question will remain: How is ICT-mediated learning taken into account by current school architecture decisions, or what are the priorities in setting up costly permanent establishments that will include such ICT-based activities?

Hence, the objectives for ICT based learning should be "to develop technologies to empower individuals and organizations to build competencies to explicit the opportunities of tomorrow's knowledge society. This is achieved by focusing on the improvement of the learning process for individuals and organizations, and of the intertwined learning process between individuals and organizations" (The Learning Citizen, 2003, p. 2).

Table 2 (*above*) illustrates a few figures on non-capital investment of the European Union (EU) for learning purposes.

In this way, the ICT (specifically, the WWW, or the Internet) offers itself as a tool to increase formal education as well as "ambient" learning that may be treated as electronic-mediated learning, or e-learning. During a survey done by the

Table 2. Non-Capital investment for learning in EU countries (Source: The Learning Citizen, 2003)

Items	Increase in 2001	Increase in 2002
Spending on training products and services	7%	7%
Raise in e-learning content	70%	50%
Growth rate of e-learning products expenditure	17%	23%

Oxford Internet Institute (OII), 78% of users say they use the Internet to look up a fact, while 47% say they look up the definition of a word. Nearly 40% of the respondents say they use the Internet to find information for school, and 20% of them use it for distance learning (OII, 2005).

MAIN THRUST

Given the critical changes in education and given the potential of ICT, it is vital that policies and strategies in the area of ICT be driven by long-term educational objectives, such as:

- ICT supported learning provisions in the services sector.
- ICT inclusive educational policies.
- ICT conducive research programs incorporating solutions to problem locale.
- Optimal use of ICT for educational purposes.
- Integrating ICT in bringing fundamental transformations in education.

Transformations with ICT can be limited to learner-centered multimedia learning, without changing the school curriculum and progressively invalidating the changes. Thus, school reform is not a spontaneous consequence of the introduction of ICT in education. Furthermore, as learners enter into education system with a growing

ICT familiarity, the definition of basic skills, to be addressed by the educational integration of ICT, needs to embrace more and more higher-order thinking skills. Therefore, a global vision of ICT supported education has to be prepared for common citizens to actively take part in an increasing communication setting to improve their own values and thoughts. In this context, utilizing available utility software, exciting ICT-based e-learning materials can be developed with an absolute minimum of effort.

The main thrust of this chapter comprises of a few case studies that are being treated as success stories in the aspect of ICT mediated learning, and at the same time act as empowering tool in terms of socioeconomic development. Emphasis has been given to incorporate cases that involve ICT for community learning, and they have been portrayed with analytic approach. It is expected that these cases will be able to justify inclusion of ICTs in community learning and regional development.

CASE STUDIES

Case 1

Asia Pacific Information Network (APIN)
A regional network working to achieve information for all

Among key five areas of interests, one is to promote ICT literacy and the application of ICT in education, science, culture, and communication.

Broad aims are to:

- Encourage the development of strategies, policies, infrastructures, human resources, and tools for application of ICTs.
- Prepare policy advice to member states for use of ICT in national targets,especially for improvement of education, (APIN, 2004).

Specific focus areas are to:

- Promote ICT based learning opportunities for all.
- Enhance learning opportunities through access to diversified contents and delivery systems.
- Assist in establishing networks for learners and educators.
- Assist in promoting universal and equitable access to scientific knowledge.

Table 3. ICT based ABE courses during 1997-2002 (Adapted from Harris, 2002)

Year and Duration of Courses	Courses	Activities
1997-98, 4 hrs/week	Internet Club	• Web browsing and searching • email • HTML authoring
1998-99, 6 hrs/week	Internet Club2	• Web browsing and searching • Email • HTML authoring • Computer graphics • 3D Animation
1999-2000, 8 hrs/week	Internet Club3 under network	• Web browsing and searching • Email • HTML authoring • Computer graphics • 3D Animation
2000-01, 16 hrs/week	• Computer Club • Creative Computation • Web workshops	• Web browsing and searching • Email • HTML authoring • Computer graphics • Digital Video • Computer Programming
2001-02, 24 hrs/week	• Computer Club • Creative Computation • Web workshops • Film workshops • DTP workshops	• Web browsing and searching • Email • HTML authoring • Computer graphics • Digital Video • Computer Programming • Desk Top Publishing

- Support the development of code of practice involving scientific information chain by using ICT.
- Strengthen capacities for scientific research, information and knowledge sharing. (APIN, 2004)

Case 2

Adult Basic Education (ABE)
Integrates the use of ICT into teaching practices for organizational realignment and empowerment

Established in 1990, ABE provided ICT supported courses in the South Wales Valleys in UK that is a post-industrial area with low levels of education, widespread illiteracy and innumeracy in adult population and growing digital divide. The program has established community based Open Learning Centres (OLCs) dedicated to teaching basic literacy, communication, and numeric skills to adult groups. It introduced a network of personal computers with broadband Internet since 1997 and gradually led to the design and development of many innovative courses utilizing multimedia technologies. This has created increased participation of learners, tutors, and volunteers resulting in changes to the structure of learning content and techniques acting as a catalyst among the adult communities (Harris, 2002).

Table 3 shows the ICT based courses that evolved since its inception in 1997. This table not only shows the necessary modification of courses to meet the demand of the community throughout this period, but also adjusted contents that show the development trend of ICT based courses.

Case 3

Gateshead Testbed Learning Communities (GTLC)
Demonstrates how communities and individuals develop through learning and share good practices in UK[13].

Priority areas are to:

- Build on success.
- Listen to local demands and needs.
- Recognize all aspects and levels of community learning.
- Recognize barriers and address them properly.
- Improve quality of life, not just qualifications.
- Unlock national digital resources.
- Encourage establishment of remotely based stations with subsidies.

Case 4

EdComNet (Humanistic Urban Communal Educational Net)[14]
Aims to enhance the participant's sense of autonomy and dialogical belonging

Based on Autonomy Oriented Education (AOE) for personal empowerment and personal growth, users of this network actively utilize Internet content and features for their learning processes to reflect and explore elements of self and the alternatives available. According to AOE, gaining knowledge is to learn as per a personal plan that stems from one's self knowledge, and it portrays one's personal interests, performance styles, and capabilities. EdComNet incorporates AOE principles and offers an empowerment tool for the European Citizen.

Case 5

EducaNext[15]
Supports acquisition of high skills as per demand of the European industry and need of the global market

This program supports the creation and sharing of knowledge between educators. It also enables collaboration among the participants by providing a complete package of services to support the exchange and delivery of learning resources. EducaNext acts as a collaboration facilitator and at the same time as a marketplace. It is primarily considered as a business-to-business service and enables partnerships among institutes of higher education and industry to provide the right expertise at the right time.

Case 6

Pan Asia Network (PAN) in Bhutan[16]
Establishment of ICT supported distance education

In 2003, PAN started a project supporting Bhutan's National Institute of Education (NIE) to establish ICT based distance education programme for educators. The project developed and tested appropriate ICT based learning support system and assessed whether ICTs improve the quality of and access to learning. The project aims to implement 16 distance education courses, including development of online tutorials, support services, counseling services, and multimedia contents. This project also emphasized the development of key performance indicators for distance educators, especially for those that may be replicated across the PAN regions (PAN, 2005).

Case 7

Scottish Workforce Empowerment for Lifelong Learners (SWELL) Project[17]
Promotes lifelong learning for working people in Scotland

The project has successfully facilitated new learning opportunities to more than 700 learners till May 2005 across Scotland's urban and rural labor markets. SWELL support has enabled partners to develop and deliver innovative learning solutions, by empowering "non-traditional" learners through offering new opportunities to the disadvantaged communities; learners that are remotely located, with disability, not adequately literate, and jobless. The organizational leadership has been carried out efficiently through innovation, transnationality, mainstreaming, empowerment and equal opportunity. The most successful SWELL activities have involved mainstreaming education providers to deliver a wide ranging and high quality training provision. It has contributed to a "community of learning" by equality of learning opportunities through ICT (McQuaid & Lindsay, 2005).

Case 8

S2NET in EU Region[18]
ICT-based learning as a tool for social inclusion

The project prepared a guide to support the target groups in the design, delivery, and evaluation of training actions for disadvantaged individuals, provided directives to develop learners' meta-competencies and train them in order to sustain an empowered attitude towards their practical lives (Dondi, 2003).

Main objectives are to:

- Encourage use of e-learning for training educators and policy makers.
- Support innovation in training and education methods using ICT based learning.
- Promote good practices in the use of ICT for real life application.
- Raise awareness on e-learning to prevent social exclusion.

Case 9

e-learning for sustainable development by IGES (Institute for Global Environmental Strategies)
Promotes community-based learning for sustainability

This project provides community learning programme on sustainable development through ICT. E-courses are designed for teachers novice in computer-based learning and these courses act as stand alone training material replacing face-to-face trainings on community learning. The course content is built based on ten years experience of the Institute of Sustainable Communities, USA in Central and Eastern Europe, USA, and Japan[19].

FUTURE ISSUES

The question about the quality of ICT based learning remains opaque and fraught with difficulties. These difficulties further compounded when it comes to evaluate the quality of the use of ICT for learning en masse. However, the development of ICT based learning products and opportunities are rapidly expanding in areas of education and skill development. The media varies from intranet, Internet, multimedia, email, interactive TV, teleconferencing, video conferencing, or other computer mediated learning methods[20]. But, until now innovative approaches have been missing to evaluate the development, growth, impact, and potential of this form of education system. Despite global efforts in diversified platforms, distance education or e-learning, or ICT based learning has not attained a suitable state; governments remain hesitant (often mismanaged or misguided) in funding, private investors behave in unfamiliar ways, and development actors stay away from investing in this sector.

In the near future, education will be online or at least blended with online teaching and learning activities. However, the strategies should focus on constraints and normalization of educational interactions, without much restricting on initial investments. Similarly, standardization of education system should be object oriented and encouraging. Learning models should pass through technical and quality as standards, rather than just

industrialization or *professionalization* and focus on extensive research to achieve fundamental educational objectives.

The opening to higher education should ensure better links between education and research. Higher education has to be at the forefront of knowledge production, management, and dissemination. Moreover, the use of ICT in education at all levels requires new pedagogical and organizational settings. Therefore, cross-partnership among education, social science, pure science and within different fields of research is needed.

Innovative e-learning should aim to empower the lifelong learners and vocational trainees. This form of ambient learning provides access to high quality learning materials suiting individual's demand and pace. To achieve this, ICT based learning should utilize multimodal broadband access and content management. Furthermore, the provision of content integration will allow access to new e-learning materials, as well as existing resources from those repositories (Paraskakis, 2005). There is a need to develop policies and action plans in using technological and non-technological means to address the social, economic, and cultural factors underlying educational problems. There are also clear needs to redevelop educational and pedagogical understandings on effective ICT across life long learning in its many forms (Selwynn, 2003).

CONCLUSION

Looking at the success cases around the globe, it is apparent that educational policy makers are tempted to deal with ICT based learning as a potent bridging method used to flexibilize individuals and make them adequate to the needs of the community, thus empowering them to act as an element of socioeconomic development. The main educational, social, and economic discourse related to new professional, social, and learning needs tends, therefore, to relapse recurrently into the flexibilization rhetoric, according to which the adaptability of the new demand evolves, if one adopts this perspective to a new flexibility of individual's desire (Apollon, 2005).

The development of e-learning up to this point has been largely demand driven, the two principal players being the technology and the content. Perhaps for this reason the majority of products developed in this sector have followed two basic and well-tried business models, by providing:

- Distance education to individuals, which is a technologically enhanced continuation of the previous correspondence course model;
- Online environments to permit existing educational institutions in extending their services through the use of virtual classroom.

The technology driven and network intensive nature of these *virtual classrooms* however, restricts the number of users to those who have specialist, up to date equipment and broadband access, shutting out the majority of marginal learners. Furthermore, in both models e-learning approaches are based on assumptions about the pedagogical focus and organizational structure of existing educational institutions, rather than potentially validated research (PROMETEUS, 2003).

Many recommendations floated around focusing the potential for development of more appropriate ways of learning through ICT, but at the same time suffered the lack of a solid framework of learning theory in providing a more comprehensive and less anecdotic understanding. Only in this way can it be ensured that many positive experiences taking place already across the globe can be reproduced in other countries. There are thousands of handbooks on e-learning but they lack good validated research. In this context, intensive analysis of e-learning processes is needed and particularly there is a need for a conceptual framework for lifelong learning, and

for the development of models derived from non formal settings and self organizing communities of learners (PROMETEUS, 2003).

To realize that ICT is not another passing fad or innovation, which might or might not affect learning and to be able to change the way the institutions work accordingly, is perhaps one of the most important requisites for leaders in this field. Emphasis should be given in communicating the vision, and at the same time efforts should be given for skills development and involvement of all teaching and non teaching staff who might have come through the conventional system of learning (Walsh, 2002).

ICT based education and training leads to improved learning environment. However, as with most research on education and technology the effectiveness of ICT-based mass learning is still fragmented. It is also suggested that learning with ICT leads to a more reflective, insightful learning with more empowered and democratic diffusion amongst learners (Doubler, Harlen, Harlen, Paget & Asbell-Clarke, 2003; Jeris, 2002) as well as proving to be an attractive and motivating medium of learning with basic skills (Lewis & Delcourt, 1998). Furthermore, engagement in e-learning is also leading to wider educational outcomes, such as increases in learners' self-esteem and propensity to engage in further learning. Therefore, as Kennedy-Wallace (p. 49) reminds, "whether learning online in the workplace, in college or at home, e-learning is still about learning and culture, not just technology and infrastructure" is a true reflection of the transformation of communities in this respect.

REFERENCES

APIN. (2004). *Report of the first statutory meeting of the Asia Pacific Information Network*. Retrieved June 17, 2006, from http://irandoc.ac.ir/apin/constitution.html

Apollon, D. G. (2005, May 10-20). The shape of things to come in learning and e-learning. *Conference on e-learning*, European Commission, Brussels.

Attwell, G. (2005). *Quality and the use of ICT for learning in SMEs, The Wales-Wide Web*. Retrieved June 17, 2006, from http://www.theknownet.com/writing/weblogs/Graham_Atwell/

Bottino, R. M. (2001, September). *PROMETEUS position paper to the open consultation process of the European Commission.*

Chinien, C., & Boutin, F. (2005, July 7-9). Framework for strengthening research in ICT-mediated learning. In *Proceedings of the ITHET 6th Annual International Conference*, Juan Dolio, Dominican Republic.

Dondi, C. (2003). E-learning-me included: How to use e-learning as a tool for social inclusion. *Leornado da Vinci Programme 2000-2006*, European Commission.

Doubler, S., Harlen, W., Harlen, W., Paget, K., & Asbell-Clarke, J. (2003, April 21-25). *When learners learn on-line, what does the facilitator do?* Paper presented at the American Educational Research Association Annual Conference, Chicago, Illinois.

European Commission. (2004, November). *ICT in education and training. Progress Report of Working Group C on Implementation of Education and Training 2010 Work Programme*, Directorate-General for Education and Culture, European Commission.

Harris, S. R. (2002). PD in Ponty: Design-by-doing in adult basic education. In A. Dearden & L. Watts (Eds.), *Proceedings of HCI2004: Design for Life* (Vol.2, pp. 41-44). Bristol: Research Press International.

Jeris, L. (2002). Comparison of power relations within electronic and face-to-face classroom discussions: A case study. *Australian Journal of Adult Learning, 42*(3), 300-311.

Kennedy-Wallace, G. (2002, April 16). E-learning is booming but the UK still lags behind. *Guardian-Education Supplement*, p. 49.

The Learning Citizen. (2003, April-June). *The knowledge citizen* (Forward by J. Christensen, Issue No. 5, p. 2).

Lewis, L., & Delcourt, M. (1998). Adult basic education students' attitudes toward computers. In *Proceedings of the SCUTREA 1998 Conference*, University of Exeter, Devon, UK (pp. 238-242).

Massey, J. (2003). *Lifelong learning: A citizen's views: Quality and e-learning in Europe*. Luxembourg: Office for Official Publication of the European Communities.

McQuaid, R.W., & Lindsay, C. (2005, May). *Evaluating the Scottish Workforce Empowerment for Lifelong Learners (SWELL) Project*. Final evaluation report and quarterly progress report, Employment Research Institute, Edinburgh.

Mijumbi, R. (2002, November 11-14). ICTs as a tool for economic empowerment of women: Experiences from the use of a CD ROM by rural women in Uganda. In *Proceedings of the Expert Group Meeting on Information and Communication Technologies and Their Impact on and Use As an Instrument for the Advancement and Empowerment of Women*, Seoul, Korea. UN Division for the Advancement of Women (DAW).

OII. (2005). *The Internet in Britain: A survey report of the Oxford Internet Institute on the Oxford Internet Survey (OxIS)*. Oxford, UK: University of Oxford.

PAN. (2005, November). *Connecting people-changing lives in Asia: Pan Asia networking*. Retrieved June 17, 2006, from http://www.idrc.ca/IMAGES/ICT4D/PanAsia/PANASIAHTML/

Paraskakis, I. (2005). Ambient learning: A new paradigm for e-learning. In *Proceedings of Recent Research Developments in Learning Technologies*, Formatex 2005. Retrieved June 17, 2006, from http://formatex.org/micte2005/

PROMETEUS. (2003). *PROMETEUS position paper on pedagogical and organizational aspects*. Sixth Framework on Open Consultation Process, European Commission.

Rosen, D. (1998). Using electronic technology in adult literacy education. *The annual review of adult learning and literacy* (vol. 1). Cambridge, MA: NCSALL.

Selwynn, N. (2003, November 12-14). ICT in adult education: Defining the territory. In *Proceedings of the ICT in Non-formal and Adult Education: Supporting Out-of-School Youth and Adults, OECD/NCAL International Roundtable*, Philadelphia, Pennsylvania.

Walsh, K. (2002). *ICT's about learning: School leadership and the effective integration of information and communications technology*. UK: National College for School Leadership.

ENDNOTES

[1]   Index of Economic Freedom 2006, available at http://www.heritage.org/research/features/index/index.cfm

[2]   wordnet.princeton.edu/perl/webwn

[3]   en.wikipedia.org/wiki/Learning

[4]   www.mountainquestinstitute.com/definitions.htm

[5]   www.cybermediacreations.com/elearning/glossary.htm

[6]   www.soul-dynamics.com/glossary

[7]   www.quest-net.org/glossary.asp

[8]   http://www.trentu.ca/nativestudies/courses/nast305/keyterms.htm

[9]   http://en.wikipedia.org/wiki/socioeconomic

[10]   http://register.consillium.eu.int/pdf/en/01/st05/05980en1.pdf

[11]   http://europa.eu.int/comm/education/policies/2010/objectives_en.html

[12]   http://europa.eu.int/comm/education/policies/2010/objectives_en.html#information

[13]   http://www.gatesheadgrid.org/testbed/

[14]   http://learningcitizen.net/download/LCCN_Newsletter_N5.pdf; http://www.calt.insead.edu/project/EdComNet/; http://www.isoc.org.il/docs/eva_anex1.pdf

[15]   http://www.prolearn-project.org/links/list; http://projekte.l3s.uni-hannover.de/pub/bscw.cgi/d37280/nejdl_learntec_prolearn.final.ppt http://learningcitizen.net/download/LCCN_Newsletter_N5.pdf

[16]   http://www.pandora-asia.org/panprojects.php?main=panprojects_10.htm

[17]   http://www.sfeu.ac.uk/

[18]   http://www.menon.org/publications/HELIOS%20thematic%20report-%20Access.pdf

[19]   http://cmp.iges.net/learn/faculties/courses/index.php?CMS_Session.html

[20]   http://wiki.ossite.org/index.php?title=ICT_and_Learning_in_Small_and_Medium_enterprises._The_issue_of_learners_needs

This work was previously published in Information and Communication Technologies for Economic and Regional Developments, edited by H. Rahman, pp. 39-54, copyright 2007 by IGI Publishing, formerly known as Idea Group Publishing (an imprint of IGI Global).

Chapter XXIV
IT Implementation in a Developing Country Municipality:
A Socio–Cognitive Analysis

Clive Sanford
Aalborg University, Denmark

Anol Bhattacherjee
University of South Florida, USA

ABSTRACT

This article presents an interpretive analysis of the key problems and challenges to technology implementation in developing countries, based on a three-year case analysis of an IT project in a city government in Ukraine. We employ the concept of technological frames of reference as an analytical tool for articulating the group-level structures related to the implementation context from the perspectives of key stakeholders and examine the degree of conflict between these frames using a Fishbone diagram. We report that conflict between technological frames held by key stakeholders in large-scale system implementation projects often create an unexpected, dysfunctional, and politically charged implementation environment, ultimately leading to project failures, even if the project enjoys a high level of financial and management support. This, in turn, creates unique challenges for technology implementation projects in developing countries that are often overlooked in the traditional academic and practitioner literatures based on experiences from developed countries.

INTRODUCTION

Information technology (IT) has long been viewed by central planners in the developing world as an important tool for achieving rapid economic and wage growth, improving operational efficiency and effectiveness, and enhancing political participation and transparency. However, achievement of these objectives is often thwarted due to incentive structures that are based on existing rules and organizational structures. Improvements in administrative capacity can only be expected when there is a sound institutional base that is supported by operational, technical, and infrastructural facilities. Therefore, planning for the diffusion of IT into a developing country's administrative strategies presents a challenge that is significantly different from that encountered by developed countries.

The UN Secretary-General has stated, "information technologies can give developing countries the chance to leapfrog some of the long and painful stages of development that other countries had to go through" (Annan, 2002). In other words, IT has the potential to support the development strategy of bypassing some of the processes of the accumulation of human capabilities and fixed investment in order to narrow the gaps in productivity and output that separate industrialized and developing countries (Steinmueller, 2001). Recently, there is also the indication that the creation of an information society and, in particular, e-government implementation would lead to better (or good) governance (Ciborra & Navarra, 2005). However, the public and businesses in developing countries often have a mistrust of governments that are entrenched in hierarchical structures that are often politicized and corrupt, and are rife with cumbersome processes that stunt economic growth and discourage investment in productive business activities. Efforts to restructure government are either in direct conflict with institutional archetypes or have proven difficult for countries with unstable governments to adopt. In addition, government agencies in developing and transitional countries often try to install IT infrastructures that have been designed for private sector firms and/or for governments in other countries.

Globalization, democratization, and economic liberalization have prompted initiatives with IT as the primary lever to stimulate dramatic changes in the role of the state. New freedoms and opportunities, especially prevalent in developing countries, have raised the expectations of individual citizens, and emerging and increasingly vocal and proactive civil societies now do not hesitate to call governments to account. This is somewhat mitigated by the fact that IT in many public sectors has not delivered the value expected (Bellamy & Taylor, 1994; Lenk, 1990; Margetts, 1999; Margetts & Willcocks, 1993; Willcocks, 1994). The literature on IT in developing countries generally reports on planned systems, pilot studies, and failures, and seldom discusses the outcome of projects that are even partially functional (Cecchini & Raina, 2005). Further, even when systems are operational, sustaining operations in an ongoing manner is difficult (Frasheri, 2003).

This article presents a longitudinal case analysis of an IT initiative in the city government of L'viv, a municipality in western Ukraine, to improve governance and service quality for its citizens. The specific system under investigation is a Lotus Notes based document management system (DMS), intended to automate and streamline citizen services such as building construction permits, business license applications, and zoning clarifications. A similar project was rolled out in the Malaysian government Generic Office Environment (GOE) (Karim, 2003). Grant and Chau (2005) used the Malaysian GOE as a case example of service delivery in their strategic focus areas of their e-government framework. While a governmental DMS has an objective that is congruent with e-government to "enable effective constituent relationship management" (Grant & Chau, 2005, p. 9), and in general may qualify as a specific example of e-government, we prefer to orient the discussion of a DMS as an effort to improve e-administration. E-administrative initiatives deal particularly with projects that involve the re-engineering of internal structures and organizational activities. These initiatives include cutting process costs, managing process performance, making strategic connections in government, and "creating empowerment by transferring power, authority and resources for processes from their existing locus to new locations" (Heeks, 2002b, p. 99). This requires a fundamental restructuring of the public administration's organization and knowledge management practices by integrating work processes across departments and agencies in order to build a system that simplifies interactions and improves services.

We describe three years of the deployment history of the DMS project (2002-2005), by drawing on the experiences of one of the study's authors, who was a participant observer in this project at this time. The author was commissioned by the City Mayor as a consultant to provide user training for the DMS and related systems. Based on numerous personal interactions with people involved at all levels of this project, such as the Mayor's office, end users, the city's IT department, and external consultants, and direct involvement with the DMS and prior L'viv city projects, this was a unique opportunity to unravel the complex dynamics of the DMS project as it evolved over time. Our interpretive analysis of interview, observational, and documentary evidence revealed several interesting findings and implications about the politics of IT implementation projects in developing countries. Given the unprecedented nature of political, sociocultural and economic change witnessed in Ukraine and other new democracies of eastern Europe over the last decade, this context provided us an ideal testbed for studying the processes and impacts of e-administrative government projects in countries that are seeking to establish western-style democratic reforms.

The structure of the article proceeds as follows. The next section discusses the rationales behind the introduction of IT in developing countries. The third section describes a sociocognitive view of IT implementation, which serves as the theoreti-

cal backdrop for our research. The fourth section presents a background of the context of this case study, followed by a historical description of the events in the case. The fifth section describes our research methods, including data collection and analysis approaches. The sixth section presents our research findings, based on interpretive analysis of the case data. The seventh section provides a discussion of the key issues in the case and the final section proposes directions for future research and presents concluding remarks.

THE DIFFUSION OF IT TO DEVELOPING COUNTRIES

Information technology and associated organizational models, which form the basis of information systems and implementation methodologies, have originated and continue to be developed principally in western, developed countries. The unidirectional transfer of IT knowledge and skills from developed to developing countries is a process that characterizes most recent efforts at public sector reform (Minogue, 2001). However, in order to take advantage of technological knowledge of developed countries, developing countries must have acquired sufficient technological capabilities and institutional capacities to identify suitable technologies and to adapt, absorb, and improve the technologies imported from abroad (Ahrens, 2002). Often, they are not appropriate for use in countries that are in transition and have their own realities on the design of technologies that are used to automate and inform their internal and citizen-focused processes. Fountain (2001) addressed this issue in her differentiation between the deployment of already invented technologies that are available to practitioners and the need to recognize the importance of customizing the design to a specific locale.

A rationale that is often used for the introduction of IT is to automate, increase efficiencies, and cut costs. The cost of labor in developed countries is substantially higher than that in developing countries (Dewan & Kraemer, 2000), while the reverse is true with the cost of the IT (Heeks, 2002b). Therefore, replacing inexpensive civil servants with more expensive IT would not be justifiable for financial reasons alone. Consequently, the choice of projects and their ultimate success is dependent on careful consideration of the embedded web of relations and interactions within a particular socioeconomic context, and their design and implementation requires an understanding of this context (Sein & Harindranath, 2004).

Governmental and international development agencies (IDAs) in the developed world, such as the World Bank, the United Nations, and United States Agency for International Development (USAID), have spearheaded and provided resources for deploying governmental IT technologies in the developing world. Since nearly half the people of the world today are under 25 years old and 90% of these young people live in developing countries (World Bank, 2005), IDAs are seeking to optimize the deployment of their resources to parts of the world where they would have the potential to have the most enduring and significant impact. Their initiatives fit well with the western ideals of globalization, economic liberation, and democratization, with improved governmental functioning in developing countries helping to secure important sources for raw materials or low-cost labor for western businesses and opening up new or growing existing markets in these countries for western goods and services.

IDAs and others believe that the scarcity of IT in developing countries is one of the reasons for decreased opportunities for economic growth and social development in developing countries (Madon, 2004). However, such initiatives are challenged by the lack of integrated information and communication technology infrastructures, antiquated work practices, and perhaps most importantly, organizational obstacles such as conflicting objectives, lack of widespread sup-

port, and internal resistance to change within governmental agencies. Madon (2004) explored an alternative perspective of development where conditions are created to encourage individuals to realize their full potential by freely selecting their path to improvements in material, social, and spiritual lifestyles (Sen, 1999). The World Bank (2005) has encouraged such investments that empower people to participate in decisions about development projects that affect their lives and the lives of their families and have an enduring impact on their quality of life.

A Sociocognitive Perspective of Implementation

The sociocognitive perspective is based on the idea that reality is socially constructed through human beings' interpretation of social reality and negotiation of meaning among social entities (Berger & Luckmann, 1967). Like the cognitive perspective, the sociocognitive perspective emphasizes the role of one's personal knowledge structures in shaping her cognitive interpretation of the world and consequent actions. However, it differs from the cognitive perspective in the way it views the formation of individual knowledge structures. The cognitive perspective postulates information processing and learning as the key processes shaping individual knowledge structures, while sociocognitive research holds that shared knowledge and beliefs (group-level structures), imbibed through the processes of interaction, socialization, and negotiation within a larger social group, influence individual sense-making and interpretation. These shared knowledge structures, also called "frames" (Goffman, 1974) or "interpretive schemes" (Giddens, 1984), serve as templates or filters for individual sense-making and problem solving, filling information gaps with information that conforms with existing knowledge structures, and systematically rejecting inconsistent information (Fiske & Taylor, 1984).

Frames also provide a vehicle for organizing and interpreting complex and sometimes ambiguous social phenomena, reducing uncertainty under conditions of complexity and change, and justifying social actions.

The sociocognitive perspective has seen some applications in prior information systems research. In the context of information systems development, at least three studies (Bansler & Bodkar, 1993; Davidson, 2002; Newman & Nobel, 1990) have posited that requirements for IT applications do not exist *a priori* but are socially constructed through interactions among system developers, user groups, and other key stakeholders. The language used by participants and the nature of their interaction influences which requirements are identified and legitimized (Boland, 1978).

Drawing from the above research, Orlikowski and Gash (1994) proposed the concept of *technological frames of reference* as an analytical tool for understanding and articulating group-level structures that guide sense-making and action. Technological frames are defined as "assumptions, knowledge, and expectations, expressed symbolically through language, visual images, metaphors, and stories" that organizational members employ to interpret the role of technologies in organizations and understand the conditions and consequences of such use (Orlikowski & Gash, 1994, p. 176). Technological frames typically operate in the background, and have facilitating or constraining effects on the interpretations and actions of their intended users (Orlikowski & Gash, 1994).

Given the diversity of stakeholders often involved in large-scale IT implementation projects, such as system developers, senior management, and multiple user groups, it is likely that different stakeholder groups have different technological frames that may be partially or wholly incongruent with each other. For instance, technologists often view IT from an engineering perspective, as a tool specifically designed to accomplish a given task such as system development. In contrast, managers tend to take a more strategic view of IT, focusing on its return on investment and long-term value. End users may take a more instrumental view of the same technology, expecting specific work-related benefits from its use. Orlikowski and Gash (1994) suggest that when incongruent technological frames exist, organizations are likely to experience difficulties and conflicts in implementing IT, including breakdowns in communication, lack of user participation, and/or eventual suspension or failure of the project.

In his pioneering work on force-field analysis, social psychologist Kurt Lewin (1951) postulated that social systems such as organizations continuously seek equilibrium between forces favoring change and those opposing change, and that successful change rests on an organizations' ability to "unfreeze" the equilibrium by altering the dynamics of forces favoring and resisting change. Without explicit attention to and manipulation of the forces opposing change, organizational systems may tend to resist change and retain the status quo (similar to the concept of "homeostasis" in biological systems).

Lewin's ideas are applicable to understanding IT implementation because organizational introduction of IT is a social change process since it changes the way organizational members work, interact with each other, and make decisions. Given the natural behavioral resistance to change, technological frames once formed tend to be resistant to change. However, contextual changes, such as changes in key stakeholder groups, changes in resource distribution, or emergence of new emergent threats, can trigger shifts in frames by bringing new ideas, assumptions, and knowledge to the forefront of the group sense-making process, forcing the social group to reinterpret old information in new ways. El Sawy and Pauchant (1988) note that such "frame shifting" may be abrupt and of short duration; nonetheless they can engender long-term changes in the group's overall stance toward IT and IT-enabled work.

In summary, sociocognitive analysis can complement our traditional cognitive view of IT implementation by bringing into focus the role of group-based structures in individual sense-making and interpretation of social phenomena during the implementation process. We pursue such analysis using the concept of technological frames as an analytical lens to further explore the role of social structures during IT implementation.

CASE BACKGROUND AND DESCRIPTION

Given that technological frames are time- and context-dependent (Orlikowski & Gash, 1994), in this section, we first present a detailed picture of the social context within which the target IT was implemented, followed by a description of the actual implementation process.

The Sociopolitics of Ukraine

Ukraine is an eastern European country which became independent from the erstwhile Soviet Union in 1991. Limited exposure to free markets and state protection of enterprises from foreign competition since the Soviet days has led to an antiwestern sentiment among many Ukrainians, suspicion of western economic interests, an entrenched governmental bureaucracy, lack of corporate tax reforms, widespread organized crime, and corruption among many government officials. Transparency International (2004) ranks Ukraine as 122nd out of 145 countries on its corruption index. For instance, local elected officials often use their influence over water, electricity, and sanitation departments to force private enterprises to contribute to social programs and other less-productive ends.

Ukraine's IT infrastructure is ranked 78th out of 102 countries in the Networked Readiness Index (Dutta & Jain, 2004). A United Nations e-government readiness survey (2004) rated Ukraine a value of 0.53 on a 0-1 scale and an overall rank of 45 out of 191 UN member states. This ranking indicates the willingness and readiness among governments to employ the opportunities offered by IT to improve the access and quality of basic social services for sustainable human development. In 2004, Ukraine improved its ranking by nine positions, but further improvements are clearly needed to reduce poverty, unemployment, state control, and corruption, and to create an environment more conducive for private businesses.

Municipal government is an important element in Ukraine's public administration system. Each city is headed by a Mayor, who is elected by the entire city electorate. The Mayor is answerable to the municipal council (or city council), whose members are elected by the people to four-year terms. At the start of this project, city council members at L'viv were in office for about a year, with three years remaining in their term of office. The city administration consists of the Mayor and directors and division heads nominated by the Mayor for each of the city's subdivisions, pending confirmation by the city council.

At the time of the project, L'viv's information systems (IS) department consisted of 35 employees, responsible for supporting the city's IT infrastructure and application development and maintenance efforts. The director of this department reported to the Organization and Information Subdivision, which in turn, was accountable to the city council. However, like other city departments, the IS department was also highly compartmentalized with little interaction with other departments or awareness of others' needs. The IS director was often unaware of what software was used by other subdivisions, and therefore did not support its usage. This lack of coordination sometimes led to idiosyncratic IT implementations that were not coordinated across city departments, that lacked any plan for long-term maintenance, and that were sometimes not even useful.

Figure 1. *Timeline of Government IT Implementation at L'viv*

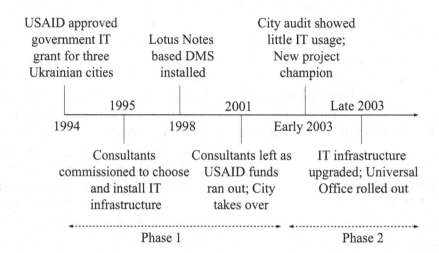

E-Administration at L'viv City Hall

The first phase of the e-administrative initiatives at L'viv started in 1994 as part of a $3 million USAID grant (see project timeline in Figure 1). The goal of this grant was to improve citizen service and government accountability by streamlining internal operations in three Ukrainian cities: L'viv (population: 850,000), Kharkiv (population: 1.6 million), and Ternopil (population: 230,000). Though no organizational analysis or needs assessment was conducted at Kharkiv and Ternopil prior to technology deployment, L'viv's IS deployment did follow a minimal analysis conducted by a local consultant group recruited and funded by USAID. The consulting group's main office is located in the United States, and operated from a branch office in Kyiv that employed local Ukrainians.

The primary directive of the consultant group was to install hardware and software infrastructures per USAID guidelines, leaving subsequent implementation activities, such as user support and training, and ultimate system usage to the grant recipients. Though technically proficient, the consultant group was not adequately experienced in large, complex process re-engineering initiatives

of this magnitude. Hence, the city's IS department was left out of the initial decisions regarding choice of hardware, software, and networking technology, and how they would be deployed. The internal IS department was assigned a role only after the consultant team left at the end of the year 2000. Disenchanted with their omission in key decision processes regarding the city's IT infrastructure, the IS department had little interest in supporting the city's IT initiatives.

In 1998, the consulting group designed a conceptual framework for improving internal workflow within the City Hall to serve as the foundation for a new document management system (DMS), and subsequently used the Lotus Notes software to customize the DMS to the city's needs. Lotus Notes was selected because of its compatibility with both Macintosh and PC operating systems. An internal audit of the DMS-enabled customer service by the Organization and Information Subdivision on a sample of three city departments during the first half of 2003 revealed some surprising inconsistencies in system use and usage outcomes. Though city departments were supposed to record all correspondence in the DMS, this mandate was not enforced and was widely ignored. Less than 20%

Table 1. Six-month document volume and dispositions

Department	On time (%)	Violation (%)*	No information (%)	Total
Housing	175 (21)	442 (53)	217 (26)	834
Architecture	8 (1)	563 (73)	200 (26)	771
Natural Resources	24 (3)	288 (36)	488 (61)	800
Total	184 (8)	1293 (54)	905 (38)	2405

of the filed requests were actually entered into the DMS, and the remaining requests were retained in article format for manual processing. Of the 2,405 citizen requests processed by the DMS during this six-month period, only 184 requests (8%) were completed within 30 days as required by city regulations, and an additional 905 requests (38%) were simply "lost in the system" in that no information was available regarding their final disposition (see Table 1).

Concerned with the above situation, the secretary to the city administration initiated new plans to enhance the levels and outcomes of DMS usage at L'viv City Hall. This second phase of IT implementation at L'viv focused more on change management and garnering user support, than on technology selection or installation. The secretary established a one-stop shop called the "Universal Office" at the city correspondence office to serve as a central clearinghouse for all citizen and business requests. The office was staffed with technically proficient people whose job was to enter and track all incoming user requests into the DMS system right at the source. Further, one of this study's authors was commissioned by the city at this time to provide technology training to the intended users of the DMS.

As of early 2005 (the end of the case analysis period), the status of DMS usage at L'viv was as follows. Most of about 8,300 citizen service monthly requests received by the City of L'viv were still being hand-delivered or mailed to the appropriate city department by citizens instead of being filed at the Universal Office as originally envisioned. The preferred methods of communication among citizens and city employees still remained telephone and face-to-face meetings. About 25% of city employees used the DMS's e-mail feature on a regular basis, and another 50% used it occasionally. The DMS was solely used by administrators to track documents, and other document lifecycle features such as version histories and audit trails were not being widely used. Each city department employed a staff member to handle internal correspondence electronically and exchange internal documents and files through a shared file system. Further, no interdepartmental correspondence was being tracked through the Notes system at the time.

DATA COLLECTION AND ANALYSIS

Case studies are particularly suitable for answering "how" and "why" questions, when multiple sources of evidence are needed, and when boundaries between the observable facts and the context are not clearly evident (Yin, 1994). It also enables researchers to use "controlled opportunism" to respond flexibly to new discoveries made while collecting new data (Eisenhardt, 1989). Such was the nature of this study, where the individual usage of frames was evident in the

Table 2. Informants interviewed

Role in DMS Project	Number of interviews	Role in DMS Project	Number of interviews
City Mayor	2	Departmental administrators	4
Secretary to the city administration	4	Staff personnel	4
Secretary to the city council	4	IS department administrator	5
Directors of subdivisions	5	Consultant	2
Informants interviewed	8	Total interviews	30

discourse that was related to IT requirements as well as written artifacts (Moch & Fields, 1985). In addition, a longitudinal case study design is desirable for observation and analysis of processes that change over time (Glick, Huber, Miller, Doty & Sutcliffe, 1990).

We therefore followed Walsham (1993) and Avgerou and Walsham (2000) in applying Pettigrew's (1985) methodology for examining the embedded web of relations and interactions between the choice of the IT and the context of its use. Thus, the research was conducted as an interpretive case study of the innovation provided by the technology as perceived by the IDA and other stakeholders where the primary purpose was to better understand the complexities of the subjective meanings of human subjects within cultural and contextual situations usually found in field studies (Orlikowski & Baroudi, 1991). Since in interpretive research the data and subsequent analysis are influenced by the researcher's own preconceptions and inquiry processes (Walsham, 1995, p. 376), the use of technology frames concept guided interpretation of the subjects' actions and the events in the DMS project. Throughout the study, key informants listed in Table 2 were interviewed and informal discussions about DMS project events were held.

Typical interviews ranged between 20 and 90 minutes, with an average duration of about 45 minutes. During the interviews, open-ended questions were asked with the intent of understanding the missions, goals, visions, and strategies being used, the expected and actual organizational impacts, and the influence of cultural factors in gaining acceptance and usage of the technology. In addition to the face-to-face personal interviews, nine group meetings with both city and departmental administrators were conducted at multiple stages of the project between 2002 and 2005. Given the sensitivity of government personnel and consultants to privacy issues, interviews were not tape recorded. However, the interviewer maintained extensive field notes for each interview, including actual quotes from interviewed personnel, which were used for subsequent data analysis.

Several additional forms of documentation were also employed for data collection. These included the city's vision statement and planning documents, internal memos, working papers, Powerpoint presentations, and USAID reports. Further, the researcher observed city employees at work at the city correspondence office and within individual departments, participated in several IT planning meetings, and had numerous informal interactions with key participants that were involved in the DMS project for over two years. This direct involvement provided a holistic understanding of the complex, multifaceted project as well as the individual behaviors, comments, and perspectives of the involved parties, by iterating between the parts and the whole in a "hermeneutic circle" (Klein & Myers, 1999).

The first step in our sociocognitive analysis was to identify the key frame domains. Orlikowski and Gash (1994) asserted that frames should be examined *in situ*, rather than assumed *a priori*, via an iterative examination of observed data and experiences. Hence, we analyzed our qualitative data to identify the assumptions, knowledge, or expectations (frames) of the DMS technology implicit in participants' direct or symbolic words (e.g., metaphors) or actions, and the implications of these frames for participants' work practices and City Hall's operations as a whole. Our qualitative data were first separated into groups based on whether it reflected the statements of end users (e.g., project managers or city administrators), executive management (e.g., Mayor's office, secretary of city administration, etc.), internal (city) IS department, and external consultants. Field notes and interview quotes for each group were coded into frame categories as suggested by the data using an open coding style typical of grounded theory research (Strauss, 1987). Following this exercise, we conducted cross-group analysis, where we compared the categories generated by each group to elicit common themes between groups, as recommended by Eisenhardt (1989).

The iterative examination of data described above resulted in the identification of four common themes or domains that are described here as technological frames. These domains were then examined for similarities and differences between different stakeholder groups. Higher dissonance between these frames was expected to lead to greater inconsistency and incoherence between activities by multiple stakeholder groups, thereby increasing the chances of project failure. The findings of our analysis are described next.

RESEARCH FINDINGS

Four dominant technological frames or common themes, representing the salient perceptions, assumptions, and interpretations of diverse stakeholder groups, emerged from our interpretive analysis of qualitative data from L'viv's DMS implementation project:

1. **Purpose of technology:** Stakeholders' perceptions of organizational motivation for implementing a specific IT and the reasonableness of such motivation.
2. **Technology features/capabilities:** Stakeholders' understanding of the IT's design, features, and functionalities, whether or not such perceptions were justified or realistic.
3. **Technology implementation process:** Stakeholders' perceptions of how the IT implementation process was managed, including such issues as user involvement, user training, and change management, and whether or not such implementation is reasonable or effective.
4. **Technology-induced changes:** Stakeholders' expectations of how IT implementation may change existing work practices, relationships, and responsibilities, and whether or not such changes are justified.

In the following subsections, we describe each of our four proposed frames from the perspectives of five key stakeholder groups involved in L'viv's DMS implementation project: the sponsor (USAID), the city management (Mayor's office and the city council), the external consultants, the internal IS department, and the targeted users (department administrators and staff members).

Purpose of Technology

Sponsor's Perspective

The sponsoring agency (USAID) had envisioned a western view of government functions, stressing the importance of citizen service quality, efficient organizational processes, and modern technologies. Government functions, such as business license processing or city zoning clarifications, were viewed as information processing activities that involved complex patterns of information sharing and collaboration among multiple governmental agencies. Such information processing activities were expected to benefit from the deployment and utilization of advanced IT such as a DMS. Additionally, automated e-administration was expected to indirectly increase the transparency of government functioning, enhance public accountability of city functions, and reduce corruption in city administration.

Consultants' Perspective

The external consultants did not play a significant role in shaping the purpose or motivation of IT implementation at City Hall. Their mandate was simply to take USAID's espoused goals as given and select and deploy a technological infrastructure (hardware, software, and network) within cost and schedule guidelines as specified by the sponsor, similar to the western norms of IT project management.

City Management's Perspective

IT initiatives at L'viv started in 1994, well before the current city administration was elected to office, and hence, the Mayor's office was not involved in early stages of the project. Initial work on the project was sponsored by USAID, with the support of the then city council. Post-Soviet western influence suggested that building appropriate IT systems were the best way to support cross-departmental data flow at the city hall for faster and accurate processing of customer requests. As stated by the secretary to the city council:

Our departments need to respond to citizen-centric views that involve cross agency data and

processes, and they will need to structure their systems, data and programs to be able to deliver on this objective.

Additionally, city council members also wanted to portray a protechnology and proreform image of themselves to their electorate in order to enhance their chances of re-election success. However, without strong leadership from the mayor and incentives to actually use the DMS, department heads were not motivated to use a system that they viewed to be a threat to their power. It was primarily the non-utilitarian considerations of citizen perceptions of the city council that amplified the city's motivation to deploy technologies that support e-administration.

IS Department's Perspective

Even though the city's IS department had expertise in areas such as needs analysis, technology identification, and technology deployment, it had no role during the initial phase of the project. The department was therefore disenfranchised from the city council's vision of improving their image to the electorate. Perhaps more importantly, they viewed the introduction of the technology to be incongruent with current workflows and were unprepared to assume responsibility for training city hall staff on its proper usage.

User Department's Perspective

The elected officials of the city had a shared goal of improving government functionalities and citizen service quality, but the administrators and staff personnel at the city departments did not share similar objectives. One administrator felt that the DMS system did not fit the face-to-face communication needs of his job and was more of an intrusion on his work, rather than benefiting it, though other IT systems such as office productivity software were more useful:

If the mayor tells us to use the system then I guess we will have to, but I really don't like it. Computers just get in the way of solving problems in face-to-face meetings. I don't think that I would want to trust my staff to follow my decisions through the system. These are always matters that I should be handling.

On rare instances, however, a small number of city administrators appeared to agree on the potential benefits of the DMS system and expressed some enthusiasm toward it. One of them commented:

This notes system is really interesting. It looks like it will help me do my work faster and make better decisions. With this kind of system it will be easy for me to find answers to my problems.

Technology Features/Capabilities

Sponsor's Perspective

USAID's goal was to improve government transparency and citizen service through the use of technology. However, being an IDA rather than a technology specialist, USAID was not familiar with different governmental solutions, their specific features or capabilities, or the technological infrastructure required to implement such solutions. Hence, it left technology selection and implementation decisions to the external consultants, who were familiar with the specific technologies as well as USAID policies and procedures for technology deployment in governmental agencies.

Consultants' Perspective

Based on their prior involvement with USAID projects (at other municipalities and cities) and their understanding of western procedures of IT implementation projects (e.g., tracking project costs and schedules), the consultants used a least-cost and shortest-route IT implementation process. Lotus Notes was deployed as the workflow system of choice because of its support for e-mail and file sharing capability, and its history of successful applications in document management tasks in western countries.

City Management's Perspective

The L'viv city administration was not involved in the technology selection process during early stages of the e-administration initiative, though they had approved the deployment of the technology at City Hall under the USAID grant. The city's administrators became more involved in the project only after the USAID grant expired and the consultants left, when the onus fell on the city to maintain and expand the infrastructure and technologies already installed.

IS Department's Perspective

The city's internal IS staff were not considered technology experts by other city departments, and were not consulted during key technology acquisition or deployment decisions. Hence, their opinions were of no consequence to the sponsor, the implementers (consultants), or the city, who planned to implement the DMS without the IS department's assistance. Since they were not participants in either the selection or installation of the technology, they were ambivalent about the technology changes both during and after deployment, and were not willing to actively engage in its implementation until instructed to do so by the city council.

User Departments' Perspective

Many of the user departments did not have the technology background or expertise to understand, appreciate, or critique the design elements of the implemented technologies. They viewed IT implementation as a technical process left best to domain experts such as the consultants.

Technology Implementation Process

Sponsor's Perspective

As noted earlier, USAID maintained a "hands-off" approach to the project. They entrusted the consultants with the task of planning and managing the implementation process.

City Management's Perspective

Like the sponsor, the city management also left the responsibility of managing initial stages of the project to the consultants. When USAID funding expired and the consultant team left, the city was left with complete ownership of the project and was forced to decide how to implement the rest of the project, upgrade necessary systems and the infrastructure, and enhance system usage among users.

Consultants' Perspective

The consultants did not understand or see the need for user support, process re-engineering, and change management that often accompany large IT implementation projects. They also failed to engage key stakeholders in the project, namely user departments and the city's IS department.

IS Department's Perspective

Excluded from key decisions involving the early planning and deployment of the IT, the city's IS department did not feel any ownership or obligation toward the project. They always felt that the project was "someone else's problem," and did not want to get involved during the second

phase of the project when invited to do so by the mayor's office.

User Departments' Perspective

Most city administrators and staff did not know much about the DMS, its purpose, or how it could benefit their work. Barring a few exceptions, most city administrators did not feel that the system was necessary to perform their job, and in some instances, when asked to do so, simply passed on the responsibility to their subordinates or secretaries. One departmental administrator commented:

They do not pay me enough for me to spend time learning computer skills. I will continue to do my job the same as always. Besides, nobody uses the Notes product anyway.

Technology-Induced Changes

Sponsor's Perspective

Though USAID viewed its role as only a funding agency and was not party to any implementation-related decisions, the fact that it allocated no resources for user training or any other change management process suggests that it may have viewed IT-induced changes that often accompany large IT projects as being less relevant or important, or a process that is best relegated to the user organization (City Hall).

City Management's Perspective

The city management was largely unaware of the complexities in large IT implementation projects and did not proactively plan for change management initiatives at the start of the project. However, when the low state of system use and usage outcomes were revealed during the 2003 audit, the city administration was forced to take notice. The secretary to the city administration, who had some prior exposure to large projects, commissioned an external trainer (one of the paper's authors) to train City Hall users. He also instituted a series of steps, such as expanding the Universal Office staff, to try to motivate DMS use among city employees.

Consultants' Perspective

Like the sponsors, the project consultants were not concerned with organizational changes induced by IT or the need to proactively plan for such changes. They were satisfied with the installation of the IT infrastructure and wrote glowing reports about themselves to USAID. They felt that their role in the project ended with system installation, and that they had fulfilled their objective and satisfied USAID's project requirements. When informed about problems of non-use and city administrators' resistance to DMS use in 2003, the director of the consulting group responded:

L'viv has a successfully integrated system of municipal information management which is sustainable at present and is unique for Ukraine. We have no more funding for this project and cannot justify any further need to assess the ICT infrastructure of City Hall.

IS Department's Perspective

The IS department's initial resentment toward the project and its key stakeholders continued into the implementation period, even after the departure of USAID and outside consultants. They were not convinced of the utility of the DMS system and associated organizational changes instituted by the city secretary, and were not unhappy to see it head toward failure. The IS director summarily rejected the idea of the Universal Office as:

This is a bad idea and will never work. Changing the way citizens submit their requests and training

new employees on how to process citizen requests will be impossible.

User Departments' Perspective

City Hall users demonstrated a general apathy toward the system and associated changes in workflows and organizational procedures, which were likely caused by low governmental wages and little opportunity for job growth or promotion. Most were subservient to their supervisors and were not interested in engaging in any critical thinking. They viewed the nature and substance of their tasks and activities at City Hall as being largely inconsequential, and were only intent in logging their work hours into the system to satisfy their supervisor. These users had no interest in any technology-induced changes that could potentially increase their workload, even if it promised improved service quality to the citizenry.

DISCUSSION

The sociocognitive analysis used in this study revealed the presence of dominant technological frames that existed prior to the project and persisted well after the installation and organizational implementation of the DMS system. In our study, we found four such frames—purpose of technology, technology features/capabilities, technology implementation process, and technology-induced changes—that were relevant to the context of DMS implementation at L'viv City Hall. Given the generic nature of these frames, and their conceptual overlap with similar frames reported in prior research (e.g., Davidson, 2002; Orlikowski & Gash, 1994), we can reasonably infer that these frames are not specific to government projects or to developing countries only, but may be generalizable to many large-scale IT implementation projects at large.

Technological frames act as a "sociocognitive lens" through which key stakeholders in an IT

Figure 2. Modified fishbone/force field diagram of technology frames

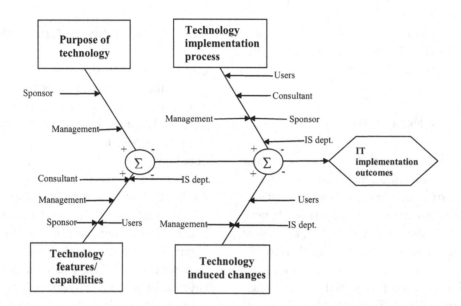

implementation project view and interpret reality, and thereby, also condition their responses and behaviors related to implementation processes and outcomes. Some of these frames may be based on pre-existing worldviews or biases that are extraneous to the project context, such as a typical Ukrainian distrust for western interests, lack of a culture of customer service, and limited opportunities of job growth and career enhancements within governmental bureaucracies. Nonetheless, such extraneous mindsets still play a powerful role in enabling or constraining their perceptions of and behaviors associated with IT implementation projects. Other frames may emerge as key stakeholders observe the process and/or outcomes of the IT implementation project. For instance, the IS department, despite being one of the stronger advocates of modern technologies at L'viv City Hall, decided to oppose the DMS implementation project because they were excluded from the planning and implementation phases of the project. In other words, they adopted a political stance to the project, in contrast to the economic stance

of improved customer service, faster processing times, and better document tracking espoused by the project sponsors.

What does the notion of technological frames imply for the process and outcome of IT implementation projects? If the frames of key stakeholders are somewhat convergent with each other, then the implementation process is likely to proceed more smoothly than if the frames were divergent to begin with. There may be challenges and difficulties faced during the implementation process, but the shared sociocognitive frame of key stakeholder groups will ensure the formulation of a coherent strategy that would address most implementation-related challenges and collective action to overcome these challenges. On the other hand, dissonant frames among key stakeholders will limit the amount of consensus building, shared interest in the project outcome, and collective action, thereby hindering the implementation process and outcomes. In the case of IT implementation at L'viv, the latter was clearly the case, which ensured an unfavorable project outcome despite financial sponsorship by an external agency and top management support from the city administration. In other words, large-scale IT implementation projects may fail despite financial and management support, if it engenders conflicts in dominant technological frames held by the major stakeholders. This assertion is consistent with prior academic studies on IT project failures such as Lyytinen and Hirschheim (1987), who contended that organizational politics is a key reason for IT project failures, and practitioner studies such as Heeks (2002a), who observed that government information systems projects often appear to be destined for failure.

We depict the conflict in technological frames in the L'viv case pictorially using a Fishbone diagram in Figure 2. This diagram has four branches, each dedicated to one of the four technological frames underscored in this study. In a sense, each branch represents the "force" of each key stakeholder group on the technological frames in this implementation project. Lewin (1951) posited that such "force-fields" depict a dynamic gestalt psychological environment created by multiple driving and restraining forces in the phenomenon of interest. The driving forces are those frames that positively impact the project's goals of enhancing citizen service quality, document processing efficiency, and transparent government functioning. Stakeholders' influence on these forces are indicated in our Fishbone diagram as arrows pointing to the right. Restraining forces act to restrain or inhibit the driving forces, either by negatively influencing the frame or by not being included at all, and are indicated by arrows pointing left. The length of each directional line is our qualitative assessment of the strength of the driving or restraining force held by each stakeholder group on a given technology frame.

As shown in the Fishbone diagram, the project sponsor and City Hall management had positive influences on the purpose of technology in the IT project by establishing the mission and goals of the project and by securing an external grant

to financially support the project. The consultant, management, and sponsor had positive influences on the technology features/capability of the DMS system in that they viewed the system as one that could contribute to productive ends and improve City Hall functioning. However, the IS department and user departments had a negative perception of the technology's capability, as evident from their remarks about the technology and the futility of its implementation. As stated before, such negative views may have been caused by their pre-existing biases against western agencies (the sponsor) or by virtue of their exclusion from key phases of the project. Nevertheless, this was a negative force that adversely influenced the project outcome. Only the management had a positive impression of how the technology implementation process was managed, while the remaining four stakeholder groups (sponsor, consultants, IS department, and user departments) had either no involvement or were negatively predisposed toward the implementation process. In particular, the disenfranchised IS department refused to accept the implementation process as legitimate, and the absence of support from the sponsor and consultant group during later stages of the project hurt its long-term sustainability, even with the overt support of officials in the mayor's office. Finally, the technology-induced changes were viewed as positive by the management, but negative by the IS department and user departments. The user departments refused to accept any changes in their existing work processes or the transparency of their work, despite the technology's promise of improved process performance.

The end result of the project was that the million-dollar USAID-sponsored governmental IT project at L'viv City Hall that promised to make government processing more efficient and transparent and improve the quality of citizen services, was headed for failure despite financial sponsorship and overt top executive support for the same. This failure was caused by the lack of buy-in and support of the key stakeholder groups during different stages of the implementation process. While it may be tempting to conclude that such failure may occur only in developing countries or with technologically-deficient governments, similar outcomes may also be observed for nongovernmental IT implementation projects (e.g., in universities, health care organizations) in developed countries as well.

What are the key lessons of this IT project? First, financial sponsorship and top executive support are necessary but not sufficient conditions for success of large-scale IT implementation projects. Indeed, IT projects may fail despite the above conditions if they fail to garner adequate support and buy-in from other key stakeholders. Second, the economic or rational perspective of technologies as a tool for improving organizational efficiency, service quality, and transparency may not be adequate for garnering the support of key stakeholder groups. Large IT implementation projects, or most organizational change initiatives for that matter, are often more dominated by sociopolitical considerations than economic considerations (Ewusi-Mensah & Przasnyski, 1991). Hence, mere communication of tangible benefits to stakeholder groups may be inadequate for obtaining their buy-in, and serious negotiations to understand and address issues of ownership, involvement, and power bases may be needed to enhance the chances of IT implementation success. Third, successful implementation requires intra-organizational policy coordination and implementation across stakeholder groups and organizational departments. Alienation or elimination of key departments such as information systems or circumventing key change management initiatives such as user training in order to expedite project goals, may eventually backfire and contribute to the ultimate demise of the project.

In addition to the conditions listed above, government IT implementation initiatives in developing countries such as Ukraine should devote adequate effort to understanding and overcoming sociocultural, legal, political, or other barriers to implementation. For instance, online documents were not officially recognized by the Ukrainian finance and tax system and only hard copy correspondence was recognized as admissible evidence in Ukrainian courts. Such statutes caused many City Hall employees to avoid electronic handling of business documents entirely, thus contributing to system non-usage. Until such restrictive rules were remedied, say by modifying appropriate legal statutes or governmental policies, electronic document management is likely to fail. Currently, a federal law endorsing the use of digital signatures as an acceptable alternative to signed paper documents is pending endorsement by L'viv's city government, which, when ratified may help reduce public concerns about electronic documents. In retrospect, it therefore appears that the DMS system at L'viv was implemented ahead of its time, and should have been considered after the passage of relevant city laws.

CONCLUSION

The interpretive power of technology frames becomes more apparent when dominant frames become dependent on the active involvement of influential individuals or groups during project activities. This perspective has been addressed through the lens of analyses of power in IT development projects (Brown, 1998; Markus, 1983). Future research that could further our understanding of the interpretive power of framing would involve the use of actor-network theory (cf., Latour, 1986; Law & Callon, 1988) concepts in order to provide a sense of power, direction, and causality. This would develop our understanding of how stakeholders influence others in their technology frames and thus engender more enduring support for their own interpretation (Lea, O'Shea & Fung, 1995).

The sociocognitive perspective used in this article supports the conclusion that the greatest constraints to e-administrative initiatives are nontechnical, such as political opposition, deeply ingrained policies and practices, and internal employee resistance. To overcome these constraints, governments require proactive, knowledgeable leaders who have an informed long-term vision of technology-induced organization change, who can help spur bureaucratic action, and who can implement strategies that promote and sustain change. In addition, implementers need to not only educate and motivate key stakeholder groups to use the systems, but also identify and redress political inequities and imbalances that hinder e-administrative acceptance among these groups.

REFERENCES

Ahrens, J. (2002). Governance and the implementation of technology policy in less developed countries. *Economics of Innovative New Technologies, 11*(4-5), 441-476.

Annan, K. (2002). *Kofi Annan's IT challenge to Silicon Valley.* Retrieved January 17, 2007, from http://news.com.com/2010-1069-964507.html?tab=1h

Avgerou, C., & Walsham, G. (2000). Introduction: IT in developing countries. In C. Avgerou & G. Walsham (Eds.), *Information technology in context: Studies from the perspective of developing countries.* Hants: Ashgate Publishing Limited.

Bansler, J., & Bodker, K. (1993). A reappraisal of structured analysis: Design in an organizational context. *ACM Transactions on Information Systems, 11*(2), 165-193.

Bellamy, C., & Taylor, J. (1992). Informatization and new public management: An alternative agenda for public administration. *Public Policy and Administration, 7*, 29-41.

Berger, P.L., & Luckmann, T. (1967). The social construction of reality. New York: Anchor Books.

Boland, R., Jr. (1978). The process and product of systems design. *Management Science, 24*, 887-898.

Brown, A. (1998). Narrative, politics and legitimacy in an IT implementation. *Journal of Management Studies, 35*(1), 35-58.

Cecchini, S., & Raina, M. (2005, Winter). Electronic government and the rural poor: The case of Gyandoot. *Information Technologies and International Development, 2*(2), 65–75.

Ciborra, C., & Navarra, D. (2005). Good governance, development theory, and aid policy: Risks and challenges of e-government in Jordan. *Information Technology for Development, 11*(2), 141–159.

Davidson, E. (2002). Technology frames and framing: A sociocognitive investigation of requirements determination. *MIS Quarterly, 26*(4), 329-358.

Dewan, S., & Kraemer, K.L. (2000, April). Information technology and productivity: Evidence from country-level data. *Management Science, 46*(4), 548-562.

Dutta, S., & Jain, H. (2004). The networked readiness index 2003–2004: Overview and analysis framework. Retrieved January 17, 2007, from http://www.weforum.org/pdf/Gcr/GITR_2003_2004/Framework_Chapter.pdf

Eisenhardt, K.M. (1989). Building theories from case study research. *Academy Management Review, 14*(4), 532–550.

El Sawy, O., & Pauchant, T. (1988). Triggers, templates and twitches in the tracking of emerging strategic issues. *Strategic Management Journal, 9*, 445-473.

Ewusi-Mensah, K., & Przasnyski, Z. (1991, March). On information systems project abandonment: An exploratory study of organizational practices. *MIS Quarterly,* 67-86.

Fiske, S., & Taylor, S. (1984). *Social cognition.* Reading, MA: Addison-Wesley.

Fountain, J. (2001). *Building the virtual state.* Washington, DC: Brookings Institution Press.

Frasheri, N. (2003). Critical view of e-governance challenges in developing countries. In S. Krishna & S. Madon (Eds.), *The digital challenge: Information technology in the development context* (pp. 183-201). Aldershot, UK: Ashgate.

Giddens, A. (1984). *The constitution of society: Outline of the theory of structure.* Berkeley, CA: University of California Press.

Glick, W., Huber, G., Miller, C., Doty, D., & Sutcliffe, K. (1990). Studying changes in organizational design and effectiveness: Retrospective event histories and periodic assessments. *Organization Science, 1*(3), 293-312.

Goffman, I. (1974). *Frame analysis.* New York: Harper & Row.

Grant, G., & Chau, D. (2005, January-March). Developing a generic framework for e-government. *Journal of Global Information Management, 13*(1), 1-30.

Heeks, R. (2002a). Information systems and developing countries: Failures, success and local improvisations. *Information Society, 18*(2), 101–112.

Heeks, R. (2002b). E-government in Africa: Promise and practice. *Information Polity, 7*, 97-114.

Karim, M. (2003). Technology and improved service delivery: Learning points from the Malaysian experience. *International Review of Administrative Sciences, 69*, 191-204.

Klein, H., & Myers, M. (1999). A set of principles for conducting and evaluating interpretive field studies in information systems. *MIS Quarerly, 23*(1), 67-93.

Latour, B. (1986). The powers of association. Power, action and belief. A new sociology of knowledge? *Sociological Review monograph, 32*, Law, J. (Ed). London: Routledge & Kegan, 264-280.

Law, J., & Callon, M. (1988). Engineering and sociology in a military aircraft project: A network analysis of technological change. *Social Problems, 35*(3), 284-297.

Lea, M., O'Shea, T., & Fung, P. (1995). Constructing the networked organization: Content and context in the development of electronic communications. *Organization Science, 6*(4), 462-478.

Lenk, K. (1990). How adequate are informatization strategies? In P. Frissen & I. Snellen (Eds.), *Informatization strategies in public administration* (pp. 7-20). Amsterdam: Elsevier.

Lewin, K. (1951). Field theory in social science. New York: Harper & Row.

Lyytinen, K., & Hirschheim, R. (1987). Information systems failures: A survey and classification of the empirical literature. *Oxford Surveys in Information Technology, 4*, 257-309.

Madon, S. (2004). Evaluating the developmental impact of e-governance initiatives: An exploratory framework. *Electronic Journal on Information Systems in Developing Countries, 20*(5), 1-13.

Margetts, H. (1999). *Information technology in government: Britain and America.* London/New York: Routledge.

Margetts, H., & Willcocks L. (1993, April-June). Information technology in public services: Disaster faster? In *Public Policy and Management,* (pp. 49-56). Public Finance Foundation.

Markus, M.L. (1983). Power, politics and MIS implementation. *Communications of the ACM, 26*, 430-444.

Minogue, M. (2001) The internationalization of new public management. In W. McCourt & M. Minogue (Eds.), *The internationalization of public management* (pp. 1-19). Cheltenham, UK: Edward Elgar.

Moch, M., & Fields, W.C. (1985). Developing a content analysis for interpreting language use in organizations. *Research in the Sociology of Organizations, 4*, 81-126.

Newman, M., & Nobel, F. (1990). User involvement as an interaction process: A case study. *Information Systems Research, 1*(1), 89-113.

Orlikowski, W., & Baroudi, J. (1991). Studying information technology in organizations: Research approaches and assumptions. *Information Systems Research, 2*(1), 1-28.

Orlikowski, W., & Gash, D. (1994). Technology frames: Making sense of information technology in organizations. *ACM Transactions on Information Systems, 12*(2), 174-207.

Pettigrew, A.M. (1985). Contextualist research and the study of organisational change processes. In E. Mumford, R. Hirschheim, G. Fitzgerald, & A.T. Wood-Harper (Eds.), *Research methods in information systems* (pp. 53–78). Amsterdam: North-Holland.

Sein, M., & Harindranath, G. (2004). Conceptualizing the ICT artifact: Toward understanding the role of ICT in national development. *The Information Society, 20*, 15–24.

Sen, A. (1999). *Development as freedom.* Oxford: Oxford University Press.

Steinmuller, W.E. (2001). ICTs and the possibilities for leapfrogging by developing countries. *International Labour Review, 140*(2), 193-210.

Strauss, A. (1987). *Qualitative analysis for social scientists.* Cambridge, UK: Cambridge University Press.

Transparency International (2004). *Transparency International corruption perceptions index 2004.* Retrieved January 17, 2007, from http://www.transparency.org/cpi/2004/dnld/media_pack_en.pdf

United Nations (2004). *Global e-government readiness report 2004: Towards access for opportunity.* Retrieved January 17, 2007, from http://unpan1.un.org/intradoc/groups/public/documents/un/unpan019207.pdf

Walsham, G. (1993). *Interpreting information systems in organizations.* New York: John Wiley & Sons, Inc.

Walsham, G. (1995). The emergence of interpretivism in IS research. *Information Systems Research, 6*(4), 376-394.

Walsham, G. (2000). Globalization and IT: Agenda for research. In R. Baskerville, J. Stage, & J.I. DeGross (Eds.), *Organizational and social perspectives on information technology.* Boston: Kluwer Academic Publishers.

Willcocks, L. (1994, Spring). Managing information systems in UK public administration: Issues and prospects. *Public Administration, 72*, 13-32.

World Bank (2005). *The World Bank annual report 2005.* Retrieved May 29, 2006, from http://siteresources.worldbank.org/INTANNREP2K5/Resources/51563_English.pdf

Yin, R. (1994). *Case study research: Design and methods* (2nd ed.). Thousand Oaks CA: Sage Publications.

This work was previously published in Journal of Global Information Management, edited by F. B. Tan, pp. 20-42, copyright 2007 by IGI Publishing, formerly known as Idea Group Publishing (an imprint of IGI Global).

Chapter XXV
Cultural Diversity Challenges:
Issues for Managing Globally Distributed Knowledge Workers in Software Development

Haiyan Huang
The Pennsylvania State University, USA

Eileen M. Trauth
The Pennsylvania State University, USA

ABSTRACT

This chapter discusses cultural diversity challenges in globally distributed software development and the implications for educating and managing the future global information technology workforce. It argues that the work practices of global software development are facing a variety of challenges associated with cultural diversity, which are manifested in and can be analyzed from three dimensions: the work environment of global software development, the globally distributed knowledge workers, and the global software development work. It further articulates how cultural diversity is manifested in these three dimensions. Furthermore, it highlights the importance of developing cultural awareness and cultural diversity understanding as important skills for the future information technology workforce.

INTRODUCTION

In this chapter, we explore the cultural diversity challenges of managing globally distributed knowledge workers who engage in global software development work practices. This topic is important to information technology personnel management and knowledge management for three reasons. First, there has been a significant increase in global software development work practices in recent years. Such work practices not only adopt the conventional characteristics of knowledge intensive work, but also generate a set of distinct features, which call special attention to managerial researchers and practitioners. Second, in global software development, the information technology (IT) professionals are globally distributed in the forms of global virtual teams and represent a wide range of nationalities and, thus cultures. Therefore, we should not only acknowledge the existence of cultural diversity of globally distributed knowledge workers, but also explore how such cultural diversity may affect global software development work, and how to explore, assess, and manage this cultural diversity. Third, although cross-cultural issues have been one of the major concerns of the global information systems discipline, there are still on-going debates about how to assess culture and cultural diversity. As a result, different views of culture and cultural diversity will have impacts on the related human resource strategies used in managing global IT personnel. Consequently, evaluation and reflection on those issues in global software development work environments are very important.

As knowledge work is increasingly outsourced globally, we would like to take the opportunity in this book chapter to consider the cultural diversity challenges of managing globally distributed knowledge workers. The objectives of this book chapter are: (1) to propose a framework to address the cross-cultural aspects of managing IT personnel in globally distributed software development work; and (2) to discuss some managerial implications that are derived from this framework. We believe both professionals and academics working in the field of global information technology and information systems (IS) management will benefit from these discussions.

The organization of the book chapter proceeds as follows. In the Background section, we introduce the concepts of global software development and virtual teamwork. Then we present our research framework, which focuses on articulating

how cultural diversity is manifested in global software development workplaces, workers, and work practices. In the following section on recommendations, we discuss how we may address the cultural diversity challenges in managing globally distributed knowledge workers who are engaged in global software development activities, particularly from the perspectives of IS/IT education and organizational human resource management.

BACKGROUND

Global Software Development

Global software development as one type of information technology offshore outsourcing activities (Lacity & Willocks, 2001), has become an established practice for software and information systems development (Carmel & Agarwal, 2002; Herbsleb & Moitra, 2001). Global software development can be defined as software and information systems development practices that are knowledge intensive and involve the work arrangements between two or more organizations across the national boundaries.

Software and information systems development has been widely conceived as knowledge-intensive work (Henninger, 1997; Swart & Kinnie, 2003) with three characteristics. First, knowledge as intellectual capital is an important input to a software development project, and an important output as well (Swart & Kinnie, 2003; van Solingena, Berghoutb, Kustersc, & Trienekensc, 2000). Second, Waterson, Clegg, and Axtell (1997) pointed out that software development work is "knowledge intensive" in the sense that building a complex software system demands selecting and coordinating multiple sources of knowledge (Shukla & Sethi, 2004). Drucker (2004) argued that the specialized knowledge in knowledge work indicates that knowledge workers need to access the organization—the collective that brings together a diversity of specialized knowledge workers to achieve a common goal. For example, a software development project may involve a variety of IT personnel such as designer, analyst, programmer, tester, implementer, and manager. Therefore, collaborations of team work are necessary and critical for software development projects. Third, knowledge associated with software development is rapidly changing as the complexity and diversity of the application domain is increasing (Henninger, 1997). Therefore, software development knowledge is not static but, rather, is evolving with the changing needs of the customers and business environments (Henninger, 1997). Drucker (2004) pointed out that knowledge workers not only need formal education to enable them to engage in knowledge work in the first place, but also need continuous learning opportunities through the work practice to keep the knowledge up-to-date. These three characteristics of software development work usually refer to the work practices within a single organizational domain. As software and information systems development work is increasingly outsourced globally, how to manage the knowledge workers to facilitate effective software development work practice in the cross-cultural context has become a great challenge.

Since the 1990s, software development and IT services have become dominant in global sourcing, which includes application packages, contract programming, and system integration (Lee, Huynh, Kwok, & Pi, 2002). And the global IT outsourcing market is continuously growing (Sahay, Nicholson, & Krishna, 2003; Trauth, Huang, Morgan, Quesenberry, & Yeo, 2006). It was projected that the IT outsourcing revenue would reach $159.6 billion by 2005 (Laplante, Costello, Singh, Bindiganaville, & Landon, 2004). The U.S. is the primary user of the global software and systems development market, followed by Western European countries such as the UK and Germany (Sahay et al., 2003). Countries such as India, Ireland, and Israel, have domi-nated the offshore outsourcing supplier market (Gopal, Mukhopadhyay, & Krishnan, 2002). A news release (*InformationWeek*, June 3, 2004) indicated that India's revenues from exports of software and back-office services is at $12.5 billion in the latest fiscal year and with growth of 30% compared with $9.6 billion in the previous year. Another news release (Friedman, 2005) reported that 7 out of 10 top software designers have operations in Ireland.

When compared to the traditional characteristics of software development work, globally distributed software development knowledge work has three additional characteristics. First, it is mainly conducted through a virtual environment that is supported to a great extent by networking technologies. Such virtual space is global by nature and transcends national and organizational boundaries. Second, it is situated within different complex, multi-leveled socio-cultural contexts. Walsham (2000, 2001) argued that the distinct cultures of different local contexts are critical factors in mediating the globalization process in the specific contexts. Therefore, the globally distributed workplace has a global-local duality. Third, the work practices of global software development are facing a variety of challenges associated with the difficulties of temporal and spatial distance, and cultural diversity.

Global Virtual Team

The globally distributed virtual team is the basic unit engaged in software development work. A global virtual team can be defined as a collection of individuals who are organizationally and globally dispersed, and culturally diverse, and who communicate and coordinate work activity asynchronously or in real time primarily through information and communication technologies (ICTs) (DeSanctis & Poole, 1997; Jarvenpaa & Leidner, 1999).

A variety of strategic and catalytic factors have contributed to the increasing trend of using globally distributed virtual teams for software and information systems development (Carmel, 1999; Herbsleb & Moitra, 2001). These include: 24/7 around-the-clock development activities, the desire to reduce development costs and have access to a global resource pool, and the proximity to the customer. In addition, some authors have further emphasized the contribution of diversity of heterogeneous teams to work performance brought about by globally dispersed team members (Adair, 1986; Harrison, McKinnon, Wu, & Chow, 2000; Hartenian, 2000; Maugain, 2003; Trauth et al., 2006). For example, Maugain (2003) argued that the different thinking modes and dissimilar problem solving methods brought in by diverse team members in multicultural R&D (Research & Design) teams will stimulate novel ideas and creativity. Hartenian (2000) pointed out that diverse groups have a tendency to make higher quality decisions, to be more creatively motivated, and have a higher productivity potential than less diverse groups.

However, research also shows that the absence of regular face-to-face interactions and the breakdown of traditional communication and coordination mechanisms are negatively associated with the effectiveness of globally distributed software development teams (Cameral, 1999; Herbsleb & Mockus, 2003). Systems development tasks, particularly front-end activities, require formal and informal communication and coordination (Audy, Evaristo, & Watson-Manheim, 2004) to facilitate knowledge exchange and learning (Curtis, Krasner, & Iscoe, 1988). According to Herbsleb and Mockus (2003), the change of communication patterns and the lack of effective communication channels (formal or informal) in globally distributed software development teams can lead to delays in global software development projects. The study by Cramton and Webber (2005) shows a negative relationship between geographic dispersion and perceived team performance with respect to complex and interdependent tasks.

The cultural difference may further exacerbate the communication problems (Herbsleb & Moitra, 2001). Carmel (1999) pointed out that the barri-

ers of time, space, and cultural distances may be detrimental to building trust and achieving team cohesiveness in global virtual teams. Nicholson and Sahay (2004) argued that the barriers of knowledge sharing among knowledge workers in offshore software development are related to the embeddedness of knowledge in the local cultural context, and should be investigated at the interconnected societal, organizational, and individual levels of analysis.

While cultural factors may influence global virtual teams engaged in a variety of activities in general, they are particularly important to software development work for three reasons. First, compared to other activities such as new product developments in manufacturing sectors, the processes of software development are more complexly interdependent and iterative, the products of software development are less tangible, and knowledge perspectives involved in software development are more tacit and fast changing in nature (Sahay et al., 2003). Second, a number of studies have shown that culture is a critical influential factor in global software development work and has impacts on a variety of issues. While some issues are general issues faced by global virtual teams engaged in other activities in general (e.g., managing conflicts—Damian & Zowghi, 2003), building trust (Zolin, Hinds, Fruchter, & Levitt, 2004), some issues are specific to software development, such as managing IT outsourcing relationships (Krishna, Sahay, & Walsham, 2004; Nicholson & Sahay, 2001; Sahay et al., 2003), preference of software development methods (Borchers, 2003; Hanisch, Thanasankit, & Corbitt, 2001), preference of computer supported collaborative technologies (Massey, Hung, Montoya-Weiss, & Ramesh, 2001), knowledge transfer and management related to software development (Baba, Gluesing, Rantner, & Wagner, 2004; Nicholson & Sahay, 2004; Sarker, 2003), and the process and performance of globally distributed software development teams (Carmel, 1999; Olson & Olson, 2003). Third, as more and more countries are now entering the IT outsourcing market, global software development work practices are facing more cultural diversity (Sahay et al., 2003; Trauth et al., 2006). Companies in

Figure 1. Research framework: Situating cultural diversity in global software development

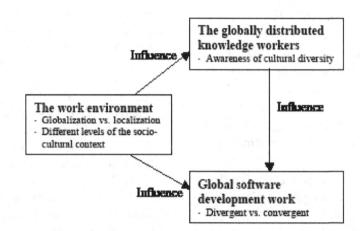

Japan and Korea join those of the U.S., Canada and other western European nations in outsourcing their software or information system development and services activities to other countries. Besides the current leading outsourced countries such as India, Ireland, and Israel, Russia and China are now establishing their capabilities as outsourcing providers (Sahay et al., 2003).

Globally distributed software development efforts, thus, must deal with trade-offs between taking advantage of the global resource pool and cultural diversity while managing the cultural and distance barriers to effective communication and coordination in a geographically dispersed environment. How to make sense of cultural diversity and its impact on managing globally distributed knowledge workers who are engaged in global software development work activities are becoming the primary concerns of global IT personnel management and knowledge management.

In the research framework (Figure 1), we propose that cultural diversity is situated and manifested in three interrelated dimensions of global software development activities: the virtual workplace, the workers, and the work (Trauth, 2000). These three main constructs reflect what dimensions of global software development may be affected by cultural diversity. And the bullets under each main construct further indicate how cultural diversity is manifested in each of these

dimensions. Trauth (2000) studied the information economy development in Ireland and pointed out that culture is one of the major influential factors. More specifically, she addressed the cultural influences from three perspectives: multinational workplaces, knowledge workers, and knowledge work. These three perspectives are interrelated and serve as our analytical lenses to study how the cultural factors influence IT work, and in this chapter, how cultural diversity is manifested in and affects global software development.

The virtual workplace of global software development is situated within a multi-leveled socio-cultural context with the global-local duality characteristic, which constitutes a unique work environment. Being engaged in global software development activities within such a work environment, globally distributed knowledge workers should be aware of the complexity and dynamics of cultural diversity, and constantly make sense of and negotiate meanings of such diversity. Global software development work, which includes both divergent and convergent perspectives is affected by the effectiveness of the sense-making processes and the management of cultural diversity. This framework adopts a situated approach and emphasizes the importance of studying globally distributed knowledge work as socially negotiated work practices by situating it within the both the global and local contexts (Avgerou, 2002; Trauth,

2000; Weisinger & Trauth, 2002, 2003). In the following sections, we discuss in detail how cultural diversity is manifested in each dimension of the framework, respectively.

THE WORK ENVIRONMENT

Globalization vs. Localization

Globally distributed software development work can be seen as a result of the globalization process—the IT industry is becoming more and more globally interconnected. According to Castells (1996), the globalization process involves the flows of capital, commodities, technology, cultural influences, and human resources across national boundaries, thereby creating a networked society. One stream of sociological and cultural research considers processes of globalization and flows of cultural elements across frontiers as a global "cultural homogenization" (Kellner, 2002; Schuerkens, 2003). Schuerkens (2003) criticized such "cultural homogenization" arguments of globalization by pointing out that they usually ignore the existence and active role of local cultural perspectives. Castells (1996) also pointed out that the globalization process is selective and segmented with many imbalances, and the networked society is both centralized and decentralized, which shows heterogeneous and global-local duality characteristics.

Sahay et al. (2003) argued against the "cultural homogenization" assumption of globalization and proposed that global software development work relationships can be seen as "models of" globalization process and "models for" globalization as well (p. 27). They emphasized the dynamic reciprocal relationships between the local cultural contexts and the globalization processes. Similarly, Walsham (2001) used Giddens' structuration theory (1990) and Castells' network society theory (1996) to study global IT development and stressed that the existing socio-cultural context of a country is a critical factor in mediating the globalization process in the specific context and, in turn, will have an impact on the complexity of globalization. They both acknowledge the uniqueness and importance of local contexts to globally distributed software development.

To illustrate the continuous interactions of local cultural elements and global cultural influences, Schuerkens (2003) cited Long's (1996) discussion: "Local situations are transformed by becoming part of wider global arenas and processes, while global dimensions are made meaningful in relation to specific local conditions and through the understandings and strategies of local actors" (p. 217).

Therefore, the local cultural context is neither a passive recipient of globalization and external cultural influences as indicated by the "global homogenization" argument, nor is it a static and deterministic factor that remains unchanged during the globalization process. The local cultural forms and meanings are constantly reconstructed (Schuerkens, 2003; Walsham, 2001).

We believe that such continuous interactions of globalization and localization processes have three implications for conceptualizing the cultural diversity of global software development work environments. First, global software development work is situated within a complex and dynamic global-local societal context. Second, cultural diversity is inherent in global software development and is a critical influential factor affecting global software development work practices. Third, the emergent nature of both the local cultural context and the globalization process indicates that we should focus on the appropriation and transformation of local cultural elements to address the dynamic perspectives of cultural diversity of the global software development work environment.

Different Levels of the Socio-Cultural Context

Another important feature of the cultural diversity of the virtual workplace of global software development is the multi-levels of analysis ranging from societal (national) to regional, organizational, professional, and team. Different cultural factors at different levels coexist, interact with each other, and together produce different work environments of globally distributed software development work practices. However, the influence of different cultural factors at different levels is not equal and varies across work environments. Some cultural factors may be more visible than others and some may seem trivial compared to the predominant factors depending on different cases.

For example, Robey, Gupta, and Rodriguez-Diaz (1988) studied one multinational company's efforts to implement an account system in its subsidiaries in two Latin American countries: Chile and Panama. Their findings showed that cultural and political differences between Chile and Panama could not explain the significant differences in the implementation outcomes. They believed that those differences were due to the organizational cultural differences of the two subsidiaries. This case is an example of the dominance of organizational cultural influences while national and organizational cultural differences coexist. Barrett and Walsham (1995) studied the global software development relationships between a Jamaican insurance company and an Indian software company. They pointed out that although the Indian and Jamaican team members of this joint venture development shared a similar professional culture, there were major differences between the local work culture at the Indian software company and the Jamaican insurance company. This case demonstrates the dominance of national and organizational cultural influences. The case study by Kaiser and Hawk (2004) on a long-term alliance outsourcing relationship between a U.S. company and an Indian company showed that the mutual understanding of ethnic and corporate cultures was an important factor to build stable and trust relationships.

In global IT outsourcing research, the focus tends to be on the national level of analysis. Therefore in most cultural studies of global software development, the national culture is predominant while other factors such as regional, organizational, and team cultures are in the background. This is probably due to the high visibility of cross-national cultural differences. Another reason may be that the cultural elements at different levels interact with each other and somehow diffuse into some inseparable influential factors.

Some studies (Cougar, Adelsberger, Borovits, Zviran, & Motiwalla, 1990; Constantine, 1995) pointed out that while the national culture may show divergent characteristics across national boundaries, the professionalism of the knowledge workers will share certain common cultural elements that constitute the professional culture. As a result, the team culture of the global virtual team may show a different pattern from either the national culture or the organizational or the professional culture. Earley and Gibson (2002) pointed out that through communications and interactions, the highly heterogeneous global team may appear to develop a common identity over the course of a long-term project, which they referred to as the team culture.

The contemporary work environment of global software development is situated within a complex multi-leveled socio-cultural context in which culture and its influences are emergent as the work practices evolve. The emergent perspective of cultural diversity indicates that it cannot be reduced to a set of variables and treated as unchanging inherited properties. In a sense, globally distributed knowledge workers are not passively embedded in their local context. Instead, they continuously and actively engage and negotiate with their work environment in everyday work practices.

The Globally Distributed Knowledge Workers

Brannen, Gómez, Peterson, Romani, Sagiv, and Wu (2004) pointed out that the concept of culture is by no means free of controversy. According to Worsley (1984), there are four ways of conceptualizing culture: the elitist view – culture implies superior power; the holistic view–culture implies the whole way of life; the hegemonic view – culture is a set of behaviors imposed by the majority; the relativist view – culture is localized and may bear different behaviors in different regions or communities from the same society.

There are two general doctrines of conceptualizing culture—the functionalist view and the interpretivist view (Schultz & Hatch, 1996). The functionalist view assumes that culture can be studied from several generalized dimensions and those dimensions are universal. As a result, the functionalist studies focus on categorizing cultural dimensions and predicting their influences. Hofstede's (1984) framework of five major national cultural dimensions is one example of the functionalist doctrine. The interpretivist doctrine, on the other hand, argues that culture may be ambiguous and unstable and should be studied within a specific local context instead of using general frames.

Schultz and Hatch (1996) studied the difference between the functionalist and interpretivist paradigms of cultural research. They proposed that these two paradigms can somehow interact to address the different perspectives of culture. To some extent, the mainstream of each of these doctrines can be integrated to a "multiparadigm" approach. They suggested that for example, to study national cultural patterns, the functionalist view uses predefined categories to provide a clear, generalizable and stable pattern, while the interpretivist view uses interpretation and symbolic representation to describe the ambiguous, situated and instable perspectives of culture. However, this approach may still be problematic since it assumes that there is a line between the stable and unstable elements of culture. In reality, the line itself may be ambiguous and dynamically changing.

The anthropological view of culture is a constructivist view which rejects the idea of culture as having hard and fast boundaries (Avison & Myers, 1995). On the contrary, culture is seen as contestable, temporal, and emergent, and is constantly interpreted and re-interpreted in social relations (Carrithers, 1992). Therefore, the anthropological cultural view rejects the notion of culture as a set of predefined variables peculiar to a certain society. In the information systems discipline, Walsham's notion of culture mediating the global process in specific local contexts (Walsham, 1993, 2000, 2001), Avegerou's proposal on relativism (2002), and the situated culture perspective suggested by Weisinger and Trauth (2002, 2003) are three approaches to studying culture through exploration, interpretation, and sense making, which reflect the anthropological perspective of conceptualizing culture.

We argue that when managing global software development practice, the functionalist approach may provide general guidance if cautiously adopted. However, it is lacking the capability to provide an in-depth understanding of cultural dynamics. Therefore, we take the following statement as a working definition of culture:

Culture is the sense making of different social structures and relations such as beliefs, values, and norms, attitudes, hierarchies by a group of people within a particular social context.

In this definition, we view culture as the "sense making" which actively strives for interpretation and re-interpretation of the relationships between the self-identity and the surrounding contexts. We believe that viewing culture as dynamic and emergent instead of static and predefined will provide the corresponding cross-cultural management the capability of accounting for the evolving and diversified nature of global software development phenomena.

Child (2002a, b) pointed out that the globalization trend and subsequent interconnectivity of networking technologies have pushed the traditional boundaries between nations and organizations to become somehow "borderless." At the same time, they enhance the people's awareness of their own identity and cultural distinctiveness as they have more and more opportunities to interact with a variety of cultural groups during the processes. In a sense, they interpret and reinterpret self-identity and the relationships between the self-identity and the surrounding contexts.

We argue that cultural awareness of globally distributed knowledge workers should have two levels—the self-awareness of their own identity and the mutual awareness of the existence of the cultural diversity and differences in others. Baba et al. (2004) pointed out that in order for team members of a globally distributed team to bring together and integrate the divergent knowledge, they should first develop the mutual awareness and shared cognition of the divergences. They further stressed (Baba et al., 2004) that the mutual awareness is not simply exchanging declarative or procedural knowledge—it requires: "…suspending our own judgment as we learn the cultural logic and rationality of others' divergent beliefs and values, while also allowing those others to call our own beliefs and values into question as they learn about us…" (p. 583).

The Global Software Development Work

Studies have shown that while cultural diversity may lead to advantages with respect to the divergent processes of knowledge work, it may also cause problems for the convergent processes (Miroshnik, 2002). Divergent knowledge work processes in software development refer to processes of generating and articulating different viewpoints by different team members,

as well as challenging the existing assumptions in requirement analyses and systems designs, which are important for surfacing and exploring alternatives, thus promoting creativity and innovation in software development (Kryssanov, Tamaki, & Kitamura, 2001; Nickerson, 1999). Convergent knowledge work processes refer to processes of developing shared understanding and building common ground among team members with respect to different perspectives of software development, which are important to decision-making and effectiveness of teamwork (Potts & Catledge, 1996).

Knowledge intensive work, such as design and development of new software and information systems is usually characterized as highly ambiguous, uncertain, equivocal, and interdependent (Curtis et al., 1988; Herbsleb & Grinter, 1999; Hoegl & Proserpio, 2004). The analysis of systems requirements, which is a critical task at the front-end of software and information systems development, is highly dynamic, complex, fluctuating, and evolutionary in nature (Audy et al., 2004; Curtis et al., 1988; Mathiassen & Stage, 1990). Cultural diversity may provide benefit to the front-end of software development work by providing different perspectives, ideas, and approaches. Dafoulas and Macaulay (2001) pointed out that cultural diversity may be beneficial to team performance, especially on tasks for which differing perspectives might increase team performance (Trauth et al., 2006). Miroshnik (2002) also argued that cultural diversity can be used as a resource to enhance creativity, flexibility and problem solving skills, all of which are important for knowledge-intensive work.

On the other hand, to bring the divergent perspectives into a convergent development practice, cultural diversity may become a barrier to knowledge sharing and transference since knowledge is contextually dependent and culturally contingent (Nicholson & Sahay, 2004). To a great extent, the convergent processes require both formal and informal communication and coordination mechanisms to exchange diverse knowledge perspectives and facilitate learning (Curtis et al., 1988), to surface conflicts and negotiate differences (Audy et al., 2004; Briggs & Gruenbacher, 2002; Curtis et al., 1988), and to build shared understandings and common ground regarding various issues such as how to represent the system requirements and which system development methodologies are more appropriate (Cramton & Webber, 2005; Damian & Zowghi, 2003). During these convergent processes, cultural diversity may create cultural distance and barriers to knowledge sharing and transference. Herbsleb and Moitra (2001) pointed out that while cultural diversity can be seen as an enriching factor by bringing together divergent bodies of knowledge, it can also lead to serious and chronic misunderstandings.

For example, in the case study of distributed software development between England and India, Nicholson and Sahay (2004) identified cultural difference in perceptions of time between India and England. In England, a 9 AM to 5 PM working routine and the separation of working life from personal life are encouraged. In India, the boundaries between working life and home life are less defined (Nicholson & Sahay, 2004). Thus, Indian employees may respond to personal or home needs during regular working hours and may spend extra time working later hours or on weekends (Nicholson & Sahay, 2004). Such cultural differences are implicitly embedded in each local cultural context. Without building corresponding mutual knowledge and awareness about these differences, team members from one site may have misconceptions about the availability of team members from the other site. Saunders, van Slyke, and Vogel (2004) argued that different global virtual team members may have different time visions, which may influence the management and performances of global virtual teams.

The interchange of benefits of cultural diversity and hindrance of cultural distance put forward special challenges of teaching cultural diversity to future IS/IT workforce and managing globally distributed knowledge workers. On one hand, we need to address issues related to bridging cultural distance to encourage knowledge sharing and transference across different cultures. On the other hand, we need to study how to cultivate and integrate cultural diversity in order to develop new organizational capabilities (Baba et al., 2004).

RECOMMENDATIONS FOR PRACTICE

As suggested by our research framework, it is very challenging to manage such a diverse workforce for global software development for three reasons. First, the culture of the virtual work environment is complex and dynamic. Second, the cultural diversity of globally distributed knowledge workers has the potential for both great accomplishments and great conflicts. Third, the cultural diversity of such a global workforce needs to be proactively managed, and cultivated in order to facilitate both the divergent and convergent perspectives of software development work activities.

To address these challenges, we recommend the following. First, treat cultural awareness and cultural diversity understanding as important and necessary skills for the future IS/IT workforce, provide IS/IT students opportunities to experience cultural diversity, and help them explore and develop a proper mind-set towards diversity. Second, adopt the sense-making approach in human resource practices to motivate and facilitate globally distributed knowledge workers' articulation of their self-identities and the identities of others during the social interactions of teamwork processes. Third, balance the tensions between the values and the conflicts of cultural diversity by encouraging contested, diverse thinking while building the trust and shared understanding among globally distributed team members. Finally, value cultural diversity knowledge as an important part of the organization's intellectual capital and strategic resources for competing in the global market.

IS/IT Education

The gap of critical skills and knowledge required for information technology professionals between academe and industry has been a major concern for IS/IT education (Lee, Trauth, & Farwell, 1995; Miller & Donna, 2002; Swanson, Phillips, & Head, 2003; Trauth, Farwell, & Lee, 1993). Academics and practitioners have called for assessing and expanding IT, IS, and MIS curricula to adapt to the needs of future global IS/IT workforces (Miller & Donna, 2002; Swanson et al., 2003). For example, Swanson, et al. (2003), and Noll and Wilkins (2004) discussed the growing needs for soft skills such as communication skills and teamwork skills in information technology professionals. Larsen and McInerney (2002) simulated the inter-organization virtual teamwork environment in course design to teach students certain skill sets needed in virtual work.

However, only a few of these programs specifically target the global IT environment and conceptualize diversity as one of the core elements in the global IT environment. One of those few examples is the online "IT Landscape in Nations" repository initiated by Carmel and Mann (2003) to facilitate students conducting comparative analyses of different nations and developing greater awareness of the global IT environment. Therefore, there is a great gap between current IS/IT education and the increasing demands of the global IS/IT workforce. Educators should focus on designing and implementing corresponding curricula, renovating and expanding current pedagogical approaches to bridge such a gap.

IS/IT Human Resource Management

Along with the focus shifting from capital resources to knowledge resources in modern eco-nomic development, the role of knowledge has been fundamentally changed (Drucker, 1994). As a result, the role of human resource management has become more and more important because "*people are the only sustainable asset in modern business*" (Schwarzkopf, Saunders, Jasperson, & Croes, 2004, p. 28). The strategies and implementations of human resource practices directly affect how knowledge workers will be continuously motivated and trained to perform their value creation tasks (Hill & Jones, 1998; Pfeffer, 1994). Trauth et al. (2006) pointed out that it is critical that researchers and practitioners take an active role in creating HR solutions and it is important to understand diversity issues in the global IT environment.

Kakabadse and Kakabadse (2000) pointed out that organizational outsourcing initiatives have both negative and positive effects on their employees. As more and more IT jobs shift off-shore, it may hamper the employment relationship of belonging and dedication when employees feel unsafe with respect to job security (Kakabadse & Kakabadse, 2000). The cultural diversity and the lack of trust and cohesiveness of global virtual teams may influence team members' working experiences (Carmel, 1999). It is also argued that outsourcing and global software development arrangements may provide career enhancement and learning opportunities for employees and organizations provided that special expertise and skills can be acquired and knowledge can be mutually shared and transferred across borders (Baba et al., 2004; Carmel, 1999; Kakabadse & Kakabadse, 2000). Therefore, one of the primary concerns of human resource management in global software development practices is how to mitigate the negative impacts and enhance the positive effects.

Given the complexity and dynamics of cultural diversity and its criticality in global software development work practices, it is important to emphasize the sense-making perspective in cultural training and provide employees proper and continuous cross-cultural training. When knowledge workers are involved in different virtual work environments, the stereotypically and culturally specific approach may fail to help them make sense of different cultural nuances from different cultural contexts (Goodall, 2002; Osland & Bird, 2004). Therefore, cross-cultural training should focus on how to develop and improve the cultural sense-making skills of employees.

Foster (2000) studied the cultural training for expatriates of multi-national companies and pointed out that most of those training programs focus on pre-departure training and fail to provide continuous training during the work processes. Krishna et al. (2004) pointed out that systematic cross-cultural training is less common than informal experience sharing in their case studies of global software development activities. And if in place, that cultural training is usually in one direction: for the outsourced companies to learn the culture of the outsourcing companies (Krishna et al., 2004). Osland and Bird (2004) advocated the sense-making approach for cultural training and stressed that there should be both formal and informal mechanisms for sharing cultural knowledge.

We believe that organizational human resource management together with knowledge management practices should value cultural diversity knowledge as an important part of the organizational intellectual capital and strategic resources for competing in the global IT market in the future. Cross-cultural sense making, understanding, and knowledge sharing are critical to develop flexible, competitive, and yet sustainable learning organizations (Garvin, 1998). In cross-cultural training and learning practices, we should allow distributed knowledge workers to have opportunities to continuously reflect on their cultural experiences in the course of accomplishing working processes and encourage them to take such reflections as learning opportunities.

CONCLUSION

To address the cultural diversity challenges of managing globally distributed knowledge workers in global software development, we proposed a research framework to articulate how cultural diversity is manifested in global virtual work environments and how the cultural diversity of distributed knowledge workers may influence global software development work practices. The main objective of the chapter is to promote the awareness of cultural diversity challenges to managing information technology professionals in the increasingly globalized IT environment. Our analyses show that we should critically examine the global-local context of the cross-cultural issues to overcome the obstacles of cultural diversity in convergent tasks of software development work and maximize its values in divergent tasks of the work activities.

As researchers and educators in academic settings, we believe that cultural awareness and cultural diversity understanding should be viewed as important skills for the future IS/IT workforce. We also believe that organizational human resource practices should adopt the sense-making approach for cross-cultural training and knowledge sharing. In order for organizations to compete in the global market in the future, cultural diversity knowledge should become an important part of the organization's intellectual capital and strategic resources.

REFERENCES

Adair, J. (1986). *Effective teambuilding: How to make a winning team.* London: Pan.

Avgerou, C. (2002). *Information systems and global diversity.* Oxford; New York: Oxford University Press.

Avison, D. E., & Myers, M. D. (1995). Information systems and anthropology: An anthropological perspective on IT and organizational culture. *Information Technology & People, 8*(3), 43-56.

Audy, J., Evaristo, R., & Watson-Manheim, M. B. (2004). Distributed analysis: The last frontier? *Proceedings of the 37th Hawaii International Conference on System Sciences.* IEEE.

Baba, M. L., Gluesing, J., Rantner, H., & Wagner, K. H. (2004). The contexts of knowing: Nature history of a globally distributed team. *Journal of Organizational Behavior, 25*(5), 547-587.

Barrett, M., & Walsham, G. (1995). Managing IT for business innovation: Issues of culture, learning, and leadership in a Jamaican insurance company. *Journal of Global Information Management, 3*(3), 25-33.

Borchers, G. (2003). The software engineering impacts of cultural factors on multi-cultural software development teams. *Proceedings of 25th International Conference on Software Engineering* (pp. 540-545).

Brannen, M. Y., Gómez, G., Peterson, M. F., Romani, L., Sagiv, L., & Wu, P. C. (2004). People in global organizations: Culture, personality, and social dynamics. In H. W. Lane, M. L., Maznevski, M. E., Mendenhall, & J. McNett (Eds.), *The Blackwell handbook of global management: A guide to managing complexity* (pp. 26-54). Malden, MA: Blackwell Publishing.

Briggs, R. O., & Gruenbacher, P. (2002). Easy winwin: Managing complexity in requirements negotiation with GSS. *Proceedings of 35th Annual Hawaii International Conference on Systems Science.* IEEE.

Carmel, E. (1999). *Global software teams: Collaborating across borders and time zones.* Upper Saddle River, NJ: Prentice Hall PTR.

Carmel, E., & Agarwal, R. (2002). The maturation of offshore sourcing of information technology work. *MIS Quarterly Executives, 1*(2), 65-77.

Carmel, E., & Mann, J. (2003). Teaching about information technology in nations: Building and using the "landscape of it" repository. *Journal of Information Technology Education, 2*, 91-105.

Carrithers, M. (1992). *Why human have cultures.* Oxford: Oxford University Press.

Castells, M. (1996). *The rise of the network society.* Oxford: Blackwell.

Child, J. (2002a). Theorizing about organization cross-nationally: Part 1 – An introduction. In M. Warner & P. Joynt (Eds.), *Managing across cultures: Issues and perspectives* (2nd ed., pp. 26-39). London: Thomson Learning.

Child, J. (2002b). Theorizing about organization cross-nationally: Part 2 – Towards a synthesis. In M., Warner & P. Joynt (Eds.), *Managing across cultures: Issues and perspectives* (2nd ed., pp. 40-56). London: Thomson Learning.

Constantine, L. (1995). *Constantine on Peopleware.* Englewood Cliffs, NJ: Yourdon Press.

Cougar, J. D., Adelsberger, H., Borovits, I., Zviran, M., & Motiwalla, J. (1990). Commonalities in motivating environments for programmer/analysts in Austria, Israel, Singapore, and the USA. *Information and Management, 18*(1), 41-46.

Cramton, C. D., & Webber, S. S. (2005). Relationships among geographic dispersion, team processes, and effectiveness in software development work teams. *Journal of Business Research, 58*(6), 758-765.

Curtis, B., Krasner, H., & Iscoe, N. (1988). A field study of the software design process for large systems. *Communications of the ACM, 31*(11), 1268-1287.

Dafoulas, G., & Macaulay, L. (2001). Investigating cultural differences in virtual software teams. *The Electronic Journal on Information Systems in Developing Countries, 7*(4), 1-14.

Damian, D. E., & Zowghi, D. (2003). An insight into the interplay between culture, conflict, and distance in globally distributed requirements negotiations. *Proceedings of the 36ᵗʰ Hawaii International Conference on System Sciences.* IEEE.

DeSanctis, G., & Poole, M. S. (1997). Transitions in teamwork in new organizational forms. In B. Markovsky (Ed.), *Advances in group processes* (Vol. 14, pp. 157-176). Greenwich, CT: JAI Press.

Drucker, P. F. (1994). The age of social transformation. *The Atlantic Monthly, 274*(5), 53-80.

Drucker, P. (2004). *The next workforce.* Retrieved on February 17, 2005, from http://207.36.242.12/data/html/pop/article3print.htm

Earley, P. C., & Gibson, C. B. (2002). *Multinational work teams: A new perspective.* Mahwah, NJ: Lawrence Erlbaum Associates Publishers.

Foster, N. (2000). Expatriates and the impact of cross-cultural training. *Human Resource Management Journal, 10*(3), 63-78.

Friedman, T. L. (2005, June 29). The end of the rainbow. *New York Times.* Retrieved January 26, 2006, from http://www.nytimes.com/2005/06/29friedman.html ?ex=1277 69700&en=a3f1a208e2617871&ei=5088 &partner=rssnyt&emc=rrs

Garvin, D. A. (1998). Building a learning organization. In *Harvard Business Review on Knowledge Management* (pp. 47-80). Boston: Harvard Business School Publishing.

Giddens, A. (1990). *The consequences of modernity.* Cambridge: Polity Press.

Goodall, K. (2002). Managing to learn: From cross-cultural theory to management education practice. In M. Warner & P. Joynt (Eds.), *Managing across cultures: Issues and perspectives* (2ⁿᵈ ed., pp. 256-268). London: Thomson Learning.

Gopal, A., Mukhopadhyay, T., & Krishnan, M. S. (2002). The role of software process and communication in offshore software development. *Communications of the ACM, 45*(4), 193-200.

Hanisch, J., Thanasankit, T., & Corbitt, B. (2001, June 27-29). Understanding the cultural and social impacts on requirements engineering processes–Identifying some problems challenging virtual team integration with clients. *Proceedings of the 9ᵗʰ European Conference on Information Systems* (pp. 11-22). Bled, Slovenia.

Harrison, G., McKinnon, J., Wu, A., & Chow, C. (2000). Cultural influences on adaptation to fluid workgroups and teams. *Journal of International Business Studies, 31*(3), 489-505.

Hartenian, L. (2000, December). Cultural diversity in small business: Implications for firm performance. *Journal of Developmental Entrepreneurship*, 209-219.

Henninger, S. (1997). Case-based knowledge management tools for software development. *Automated Software Engineering, 4*(3), 319-340.

Herbsleb, J. D., & Grinter, R. E. (1999). Splitting the organization and integrating the code: Conway's law revisited. *Proceedings of the 21ˢᵗ International Conference on Software Engineering* (pp. 85-95). Los Alamitos, CA.

Herbsleb, J., & Mockus, A. (2003). An empirical study of speed and communication in globally distributed software development. *IEEE Transactions on Software Engineering, 29*(6), 481-494.

Herbsleb, J. D., & Moitra, D. (2001). Global software development. *IEEE Software, 18*(2), 16-20.

Hill, C. W. L., & Jones, G. R. (1998). *Strategic management: An integrated approach* (4ᵗʰ ed.). New York: Houghton Mifflin.

Hoegl, M., & Proserpio, L. (2004). Team member proximity and teamwork in innovative projects. *Research Policy, 33*(8), 1153-1165.

Hofstede, G. (1984). *Culture's consequences: International differences in work-related values.* Beverly Hills, CA: Sage.

InformationWeek (2004, June 3). India's software exports reach $12.5 billion. Retrieved on December 10, 2005, from http://www.informationweek.com/story/showArticle.jhtml?articleID=21401198.

Jarvenpaa, S., & Leidner, D. (1999). Communication and trust in global virtual teams. *Organization Science, 10*(6), 791-815.

Kaiser, K. M., & Hawk, J. (2004). Evolution of offshore software development: From outsourcing to cosourcing. *MIS Quarterly Executive, 3*(2), 69-81.

Kakabadse, N., & Kakabadse, A. (2000). Critical review – Outsourcing: A paradigm shift. *Journal of Management Development, 19*(8), 670-728.

Kellner, D. (2002). Theorizing globalization. *Sociological Theory, 20*(3), 285-305.

Krishna, S., Sahay, S., & Walsham, G. (2004). Managing cross-cultural issues in global software development. *Communications of the ACM, 47*(4), 62-66.

Kryssanov, V. V., Tamaki, H., & Kitamura, S. (2001). Understanding design fundamentals: how synthesis and analysis drive creativity, resulting in emergence. *Artificial Intelligence in Engineering, 15*(4), 329-342.

Lacity, M., & Willcocks, L. (2001). *Global information technology outsourcing: Search for business advantage.* Chichester, UK: John Wiley & Sons.

Laplante, P. A., Costello, T., Singh, P., Bindiganaville, S., & Landon, M. (2004). The who, what, why, where, and when of IT outsourcing. *IT Professional, 6*(1), 19-23.

Larsen, K. R., & McInerney, C. R. (2002). Preparing to work in the virtual organization. *Information & Management, 29*, 445-456.

Lee, D. M., Trauth, E. M., & Farwell, D. (1995). Critical skills and knowledge requirements of IS professionals: A joint academic/industry investigation. *MIS Quarterly, 19*(3), 313-340.

Lee, J., Huynh, M., Kwok, R., & Pi, S. (2002). Current and future directions of IS outsourcing. In R. Hirschheim, A., Heinzl, & J. Dibbern (Eds.), *Information systems outsourcing: enduring themes, emergent patterns, and future directions* (pp. 195-220). Berlin, Germany: Springer-Verlag.

Massey, A. P., Hung, Y. T. C., Montoya-Weiss, M., & Ramesh, V. (2001). Cultural perceptions of task-technology fit. *Communications of the ACM, 44*(12), 83-84.

Mathiassen, L., & Stage, J. (1990). Complexity and uncertainty in software design. *Proceedings of the 1990 IEEE Conference on Computer Systems and Software Engineering* (pp. 482-489). Los Alamitos, CA: IEEE.

Maugain, O. (2003). *Managing multicultural R&D teams: An in-depth case study of a research project at CERN.* PhD thesis. Retrieved on January 26, 2006, from http://www.unisg.ch/www/edis.nsf/wwwDisplayIdentifier/2820/$FILE/dis2820.pdf

Miller, R. A., & Donna, D. W. (2002). Advancing the IS curricula: The identification of important communication skills needed by is staff during systems development. *Journal of Information Technology Education, 1*(3), 143-156.

Miroshnik, V. (2002). Culture and international, management: A review. *Journal of Management Development, 21*(7/8), 521-544.

Nicholson, B., & Sahay, S. (2004). Embedded knowledge and offshore software development. *Information and Organization, 14*(4), 329-365.

Nickerson, R. S. (1999). Enhancing creativity. In R. E. Sternberg (Ed.), *Handbook of creativity* (pp. 392-430). Cambridge: Cambridge University Press.

Noll, C. L., & Wilkins, M. (2004). Critical skills of IS professionals: A model for curriculum development. *Journal of Information Technology Education, 3*, 117-131.

Olson, J. S., & Olson, G. M. (2003). Culture surprises in remote software development teams. *QUEUE, 1*(9), 52-59.

Osland, J. S., & Bird, A. (2004). Beyond sophisticated stereotyping: Cultural sensemaking in contex. In S. M. Puffer (Ed.), *International management: Insights from friction and practice* (pp. 56-66). Armonk, NY: M.E. Sharpe.

Pfeffer, J. (1994). *Competitive advantage through people: Unleashing the power of the work force.* Boston: Harvard Business School Press.

Potts, C., & Catledge, L. (1996). Collaborative conceptual design: A large software project case study. *Computer Supported Cooperative Work, 5*(4), 415-445.

Robey, D., Gupta, S. K., & Rodriguez-Diaz, A. (1988). Implementing information systems in developing countries: organizational and cultural considerations. In S. C. Bhatnagar & N. BjØrn-Andersen (Eds.), *Information technology in developing countries* (pp. 41-50). New York: Elsevier Science Publishers.

Sahay, S., Nicholson, B., & Krishna, S. (2003). *Global IT outsourcing: Software development across borders*. Cambridge, UK: Cambridge University Press.

Sarker, S. (2003). Knowledge transfer in virtual information systems development teams: An empirical examination of key enables. *Proceedings of the 36ᵗʰ Annual Hawaii International Conference on System Sciences* (pp. 119-128).

Saunders, C., van Slyke, C., & Vogel, D. R. (2004). My time or yours? Managing time visions in global virtual teams. *Academy of Management Executive, 18*(1), 19-31.

Schuerkens, U. (2003). The sociological and anthropological study of globalization and localization. *Current Sociology, 51*(3/4), 209-222.

Schultz, M., & Hatch, M. J. (1996). Living with multiple paradigms: The case of paradigm interplay in organizational culture studies. *The Academy of Management Review, 21*(2), 529-557.

Schwarzkopf, A. B., Saunders, C., Jasperson, J., & Croes, H. (2004). Strategies for managing IS personnel: IT skills staffing. In M. Igbaria & C. Shayo (Eds.), *Strategies for managing IS/IT personnel* (pp. 37-63). Hershey, PA: Idea Group Publishing.

Shukla, M., & Sethi, V. (2004). An approach of studying knowledge worker's competencies in software development team. *Journal of Advancing Information and Management Studies, 1*(1), 49-62.

Swanson, D. A., Phillips, J., & Head, N. W. (2003, June 8-12). Developing growing need for soft-skills in IT professionals. *Proceedings of the 2003 ASCUE Conference* (pp. 263-269). Myrtle Beach, SC.

Swart, J., & Kinnie, N. (2003). Sharing knowledge in knowledge-intensive firms. *Human Resource Management Journal, 13*(2), 60-75.

Trauth, E. M. (2000). *The culture of an information economy: Influences and impacts in the Republic of Ireland*. Dordrecht, The Netherlands: Kluwer Academic Publishers.

Trauth, E. M., Farwell, D., & Lee, D. (1993). The IS expectation gap: Industry expectations versus academic preparation. *MIS Quarterly, 17*(3), 293-307.

Trauth, E. M., Huang, H., Morgan, A., Quesenberry, J., & Yeo, B. J. K. (2006). Investigating diversity in the global IT workforce: An analytical framework. In F. Niederman & T. Ferratt (Eds.), *Human resource management of IT professionals.* Hershey, PA: Idea Group Publishing.

van Solingena, R., Berghoutb, E., Kustersc, R., & Trienekensc, J. (2000). From process improvement to people improvement: Enabling learning in software development. *Information and Software Technology, 42*(14), 965-971.

Walsham, G. (1993). *Interpreting information systems in organizations.* New York: John Wiley & Sons.

Walsham, G. (2000). IT, globalization and cultural diversity. In C. Avgerous & G. Walshem (Eds.), *Information technology in context: Studies from perspective of developing countries* (pp. 291-303). Aldershot, UK: Shgate Publishing.

Walsham, G. (2001). *Making a world of difference: IT in a global context.* Chichester, UK: John Wiley & Son.

Waterson, P. E., Clegg, C. W., & Axtell, A. M. (1997). The dynamics of work organization, knowledge, and technology during software development. *International Journal of Human-Computer Studies, 46*(1), 79-101.

Weisinger, J. Y., & Trauth, E. M. (2002). Situating culture in the global information sector. *Information Technology and People, 15*(4), 306-320.

Weisinger, J. Y., & Trauth, E. M. (2003). The importance of situating culture in cross-cultural IT management. *IEEE Transactions on Engineering Management, 50*(1), 26-30.

Worsley, P. (1984). *The three worlds.* Chicago: The University of Chicago Press.

Zolin, R., Hinds, P. J., Fruchter, R., & Levitt, R. E. (2004). Interpersonal trust in cross-functional, geographically distributed work: a longitudinal study. *Information and Organization, 14*(1), 1-26.

Section VI
Emerging Trends

Chapter XXVI
E–Government Payoffs:
Evidence from Cross–Country Data

Shirish C. Srivastava
National University of Singapore, Singapore

Thompson S. H. Teo
National University of Singapore, Singapore

ABSTRACT

Using secondary data from 99 countries and IT impact literature as the guiding theoretical perspective; we examine the payoffs from e-government in the form of national performance. We do this by initially examining the relationship of e-government development with the first order government process efficiency parameters (resource spending efficiency and administrative process efficiency). Subsequently we examine the association of these first order efficiency outcomes with the two second order dimensions of national performance (reduction of social divide and business competitiveness). Our analysis reveals significant association of 'e-government development' with both the first order 'government efficiency parameters'. Further analysis reveals significant relationships of 'government efficiency parameters' with the dimensions of 'national performance'. Important role of 'national business competitiveness' in the reduction of 'social divide' is brought forth through post-hoc analysis. Through this research, we make some important contributions which have implications for researchers, practitioners, public administrators, and policy makers.

INTRODUCTION

E-government can be defined as the use of information and communication technologies (ICTs) and the Internet to enhance the access to and delivery of all facets of government services and operations for the benefit of citizens, businesses, employees, and other stakeholders. In recent times, e-government has generated a lot of interest among researchers. Studies on e-government can be roughly classified into three broad areas: e-government development and evolution (Kunstelj & Vintar, 2004; Layne & Lee, 2001; Srivastava & Teo, 2004; Tan & Pan, 2003), e-government adoption and implementation (Koh et al., 2005; Li, 2003; Melitski et al., 2005), and the impact of e-government on citizens and businesses (Banerjee & Chau, 2004; West, 2004). Though research in all the three identified areas is important, governments, policy makers, practitioners, and academics are often intrigued by the *payoffs* from e-government. The facts that research on e-government impact is still in a nascent stage, and its relationship with national performance has not been adequately addressed in previous research, are the prime motivators for this research.

The link between information technology (IT) investments and organizational performance, termed as IT payoffs, has been researched by numerous scholars (Brynjolfsson & Hitt, 1996; Devaraj & Kohli, 2003; Melville et al., 2004). The practical relevance of IT impact continues to motivate researchers to investigate the relationship between IT and performance (Srivastava & Teo, 2007). Although IT impact research continues to be a major component of information systems (IS) research, relatively few studies have been conducted to gauge the relationship of e-government with national performance. Past research on the e-government impact has highlighted some of the benefits it offers for citizens, businesses, and governments. E-government has not only helped in improving service delivery (Kibsi et al., 2001;

Von Haldenwang, 2004; West, 2004) and increasing democratization (Von Haldenwang, 2004; West, 2004), but has also helped in reducing corruption and increasing government transparency (Banerjee & Chau, 2004; Cho & Choi, 2004; Von Haldenwang, 2004; Wong & Welch, 2004). Most e-government payoff variables investigated in past studies are intermediate process variables, which may eventually impact the national performance (Barua et al., 1995). But this link has not been clearly examined in the current e-government literature. In our study, we address this gap by conceptualizing the relationship between e-government development and national performance, mediated through intermediary payoff variables. We construe national performance as consisting of two dimensions: *reduction of social divide* and *business competitiveness*. Further, we posit that e-government development impacts government process efficiency (*resource spending efficiency* and *administrative process efficiency*), which in turn impacts national performance on the two construed dimensions. Through our research, we investigate the relationship between e-government development and first order impacts, and consequently the linkage between first order efficiency variables and higher order performance variables (Barua et al., 1995; Melville et al., 2004).

Further, most e-government studies are either conceptual (Kibsi et al., 2001; Layne & Lee, 2001; Warkentin et al., 2002; Wimmer, 2002), or case studies (Heeks, 2002; Lee et al., 2005; Li, 2003; Srivastava & Teo, 2005). Though e-government literature also has some theoretically-grounded empirical survey studies (Phang et al., 2005; Bretschneider, 1990), such empirical studies are relatively few and are often limited to analyzing a particular e-government implementation within a country (Kaylor et al., 2001; Norris & Moon, 2005; McNeal et al., 2003; Moon, 2002; West, 2004). Cross-country and country level empirical studies are very few (for example, Wong & Welch, 2004; Singh et al., 2004). Moreover, empirical studies assessing the impact of e-government are even fewer (for example, Jain, 2003). In their review of IT impact research, Melville et al. (2004) have also stressed the paucity of IT impact research at national and cross-country levels. To fill these research gaps, we use data from 99 countries to analyze the relationship of e-government development with national performance mediated by the intermediate efficiency variables.

The rest of the article is organized as follows. First, using *IT impact* as the guiding theoretical framework, we explicate the relationship of e-government development with national performance. Next, conceptualizing IT impact as a mediated phenomenon, we posit that the relationship of e-government with national performance (reduction of social divide and business competitiveness) is mediated through efficiency-enhancing intermediary variables (resource spending efficiency and administrative process efficiency) as shown in the research model in Figure 1. Subsequently, using this data, we test the hypotheses so formulated and

finally end the discussion with a set of implications and conclusions arising out of this study.

THEORY AND HYPOTHESES

E-Government Impact

Previous research has shown that IT may contribute to the improvement of organizational performance (Brynjolfsson & Hitt, 1996; Melville et al., 2004; Mukhopadhay et al., 1995). To measure the impact of IT, researchers have used multifarious measures of organizational performance, like productivity enhancement, inventory reduction, cost reduction, competitive advantage, etc. (Devaraj & Kohli, 2003; Hitt & Brynjolfsson, 1996; Melville et al., 2004). Studies have used both intermediate-level measures as well as organizational performance measures for exhibiting the impact of IT. Barua et al. (1995) made a distinction between the intermediate mediating variables and

Figure 1. Research model: E-government payoffs

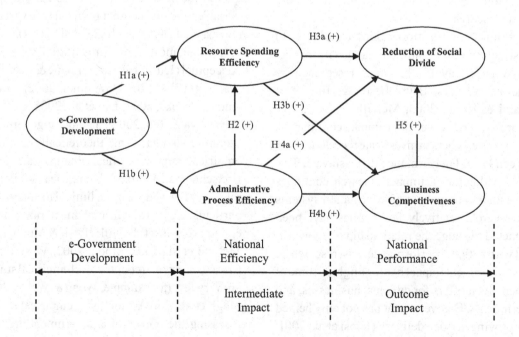

organizational outcome impact variables. In their research, they presented a model which incorporated both, that is, first order effects impacting operational variables like inventory turnover, as well as higher level variables (like market share) impacted by first order variables.

Researchers have conceptualized the intermediate variables mediating the impact of IT on firm performance in a number of ways. For example, Weill (1992) identified intermediate mediating variables as "conversion effectiveness factors" and Francalanci & Galal (1998) proposed managerial choices as the intermediary variables which mediate the relationship between IT and firm performance. In a similar vein, Soh and Markus (1995) conceptualized IT assets (IT conversion process) which mediate the relationship between IT investment and organizational performance. To have a fuller understanding of IT impact, it is imperative to conceptualize IT as having first as well as higher order effects (Melville et al., 2004). The first order effects are mostly related to process efficiency whereas higher order effects are the impacts of these processual efficiency enhancements on organizational performance measures (Barua et al., 1995; Brynjolfsson & Hitt, 2000; Subramani, 2004; Subramaniam & Shaw, 2002). Apart from creating value at the business unit and process level, IT may also impact performance at the country level of analysis by improving the efficiency as well as effectiveness of the country (Alpar & Kim, 1990; Dewan & Kraemer, 2000). In our research, we conceptualize the relationship of e-government development with the intermediate variables related to efficiency, which in turn are associated with the country performance measures.

Governments in countries have multifarious objectives, which can be broadly classified into two kinds. *First,* social objectives, which deal with improving the quality of life of their citizens by reducing poverty and removing social inequalities, which we refer to as reduction of social divide, and *second,* economic objectives of making the nation and its businesses more competitive which we name business competitiveness (Drazen, 2001; Mansoorian & Myers, 1997; Mok & Lau, 2002). Governments achieve these objectives through policy making, program administration, and ensuring compliance (U.S. Government, 2002). We posit that e-government may be instrumental in achieving these ultimate national performance objectives (reduction of social divide and business competitiveness) through intermediate efficiency-enhancing processes.

Mok and Lau (2002) highlighted the importance of efficient resource allocation by governments to achieve their social and economic objectives. In the current networked era, organizational linkages within and among organizations are opening up new ways in which firms not only acquire and convert factor inputs but also assimilate and use information from various sources for increasing their competitiveness (Hammer, 2001; Straub & Watson, 2001). In a similar vein, e-government may be helpful in getting more accurate information about citizens and businesses. In addition to this, e-government will improve the access of the government to its citizens and businesses and vice versa. This will help in a more accurate and efficient resource allocation and spending, implying that government spends its resources in an effective way thereby avoiding wastages. Thus, the level of e-government development in a nation should help governments plan their resource spending in a prudent way, thereby minimizing wastages and consequently directing spending on projects that create maximum value for the citizens and businesses. Hence we hypothesize:

H1a: E-government development in a country is positively associated with the nation's government resource spending efficiency.

Past studies have shown that IT has been instrumental in impacting the general working scenario in organizations and businesses by significantly reducing the costs of information dissemination, acquisition, and processing (Dern, 1992; Stewart, 1995). IT facilitates relatively smooth information flow, thereby considerably reducing information asymmetries (Alba et al., 1997; Kulkarni, 2000). This helps in making organizations more efficient. In a similar vein, e-government not only helps in providing more accurate information facilitating better decisions by the government but also helps in bringing down the processing time by reducing and simplifying the number of working procedures.

Some years ago, obtaining an import export license in Singapore required applicants to fill out 21 different forms and then wait for 15 to 20 days for the 23 government agencies to process the request. After the government launched TradeNet (an electronic data interchange network for trade administration), applicants have to submit only one online form, and they may receive a license as soon as 15 seconds later (Kibsi et al., 2001). In a fully integrated e-government system, vertical and horizontal integration, within and across various ministries and government offices, reduces the processing time for citizens and businesses drastically. In such a networked e-government scenario, citizens and businesses may interact with multiple government agencies through a one stop portal, resulting in an increased "administrative process efficiency" for the government through the reduction of bureaucratic red tape. Thus, we hypothesize,

H1b: E-government development in a country is positively associated with the administrative process efficiency of the nation's government.

E-government helps governments become more efficient in their processes by increasing their proficiency and responsiveness (Banerjee & Chau, 2004; West, 2004). Efficiency in administrative processes has a cascading effect on other aspects of government efficiency, e.g., shorter response time may help governments plan their resource allocation and spending in a more accurate fashion. Further, an enhanced administrative process efficiency coupled with the more accurate information (since the information is received directly and does not need retyping) that it receives through the e-government channels will help governments make "informed and timely decisions" related to their spending. Thus, an increase in administrative process efficiency will help enhance government's resource spending efficiency. Hence we have the next hypothesis,

H2: Government administrative process efficiency in a country is positively associated with the nation's resource spending efficiency.

To fulfil the social and economic objectives of the government, the intervening processes of service delivery and resource allocation should be efficient (Mok & Lau, 2002). We posit that the impact of e-government on the process efficiency variables will translate to national performance variables related to the two objectives of "reduction of social divide" and "business competitiveness." Efficient resource spending implies a better distribution of resources to the areas where it is really needed, thus helping citizens and businesses in the required proportions. Efficient resource spending by the government will help the nation not only in achieving social objectives (poverty and social inequality reduction) but also will help in improving business competitiveness by contributing efficiently to their development. Hence we hypothesize:

H3a: Government resource spending efficiency in a country is positively associated with the nation's reduction of social divide.

H3b: Government resource spending efficiency in a country is positively associated with the nation's business competitiveness.

In a similar vein, a government which has simple and quick administrative processes will not only process business proposals more efficiently but will also process the implementation of "reduction of social divide programs" in a shorter time. The reduction in red tape in the government coupled with increased information flow through e-government channels will not only help the government make faster decisions, but also more accurate and useful ones. Thus, government administrative process efficiency helps in the reduction of national social divide as well as assists enhancement of national business competitiveness.

H4a: Government administrative process efficiency in a country is positively associated with the nation's reduction of social divide.

H4b: Government administrative process efficiency in a country is positively associated with the nation's business competitiveness.

Increased business competitiveness in a nation results in multifarious benefits not only for businesses but also for citizens. An increase in business competitiveness implies an improvement in the micro-economic condition of the country, which is translated into increased wealth in the country (Porter, 2005). This increased wealth in the nation can be used by governments to achieve their social objectives. More so in the presence of e-government and increased administrative process and resource spending efficiencies, we posit that business competitiveness positively influences reduction of social divide. Thus, we hypothesize,

H5: A nation's business competitiveness is positively associated with its reduction of social divide.

METHODOLOGY

Data

For a meaningful testing of hypotheses, we require data from a large number of countries aggregated at the national level. Collecting large-scale primary data from over a hundred countries is constrained by the amount of resources and time available for conducting such research. Hence, for the purpose of testing our hypotheses, we explored numerous reliable secondary data sources which have been used in past research. Finally, for testing the formulated hypotheses, we used two secondary data sources: the United Nations Global e-government Readiness Report (UN Report, 2004) and the World Economic Forum Global Competitiveness Report (WEF, 2005). Data from United Nations Global e-government Readiness Reports have been used by past studies such as Siau & Long (2004, 2006), Srivastava & Teo (2006a, 2006b), and data from World Economic Forum Global Competitiveness Report have been used in studies such as Delios and Beamish (1999) and Gaur and Lu (2007).

The Global E-government Readiness Report (UN Report, 2004) and the World Economic Forum Global Competitiveness Report (WEF, 2005) were the two most recent reports available at the time of the study. Though WEF has been publishing global competitiveness reports for a number of years now, the UN started publishing the United Nations Global e-government Readiness Report only recently in 2003. Hence, we used cross-sectional data from two reports: the UN report (released late 2004) and the WEF Global Competitiveness Report (released early 2005) for our analyses. Both the data reports used in this study were released by the agencies within a period of few months, hence they are contemporary and comparable (although the years are different). The data from the UN e-government readiness report cover 191 countries and data from the Global Competitiveness Report cover 117 countries. As the variables used in this study were taken from both of these reports, it was essential to consider data only for those countries which were available in both reports. After analyzing the two reports for the common countries (data points), we had data from 99 countries for analyses. The list of these 99 nations (divided into high and low income nations[1]) is given in Appendix 1A. We also provide a continent-wise classification of the 99 countries in Appendix 1B.

Although using secondary data for research provides some advantages, such as easy reproducibility, ability to generalize the results arising from larger datasets, etc., it has some limitations (Kiecolt & Nathan, 1985; UIOWA, 2004). Secondary data research is often constrained by the kind of data available in the data sets (Atkinson & Brandolini, 2001; Rabianski, 2003). But considering the fact that secondary data research is an accepted norm in many of the important management disciplines like strategy, finance, international business, etc., and direct collection of large scale cross-country data by individual researchers may not be feasible, we decided to use the above mentioned secondary data sources for our cross-country research.

Constructs, Variables, and Measures

As depicted in our research model (Figure 1), there are five constructs in this study: *e-government development*, the two "government process efficiency constructs," namely, *resource spending efficiency* and *administrative process efficiency*, and the two "national performance constructs," namely, *reduction of social divide* and *business competitiveness*. In our research model, we conceptualize e-government impact translating to national performance (reduction of social divide and business competitiveness) through the effi-

ciency enhancements in resource spending and administrative process efficiency. The measures for various constructs have been directly taken from the two reports mentioned above. We next provide a brief description of the constructs and measures employed in this study.

E-Government Development

The construct of e-government development is indicated by the Web Measure Index from the UN e-government readiness report of 2004. The Web Measure Index is based upon a five-stage model, ascending in nature and building upon the previous level of sophistication, of a country's online presence. For countries which have established an online presence, the model defines stages of e-readiness according to a scale of progressively sophisticated citizen services (UN Report, 2004). Countries are coded in consonance with what they provide online and the stage of e-government evolution they are presently in. The five stages of e-government on which the country Web sites were coded were based on the UN's five stage e-government evolution model[2] in which the stages are: emerging presence, enhanced presence, interactive presence, transactional presence, and networked presence. The Web Measure Index is an indicator of the sophistication and development of the e-government Web sites of that particular country and has been used in past studies as a measure of e-government development (Siau & Long 2004, 2006; Srivastava & Teo, 2006a, 2006b).

Resource Spending Efficiency

Resource spending efficiency refers to a government's prudence in utilizing its funds. The construct of Resource Spending Efficiency is based on the indicator for "Wastefulness of Government Spending" taken from the Global Competitiveness Report of 2005. "Resource spending efficiency" indicates whether the public spending provides necessary goods and services not catered to by the market or whether the spending is done in wasteful propositions. High "resource spending efficiency" indicates that the government funds are being utilized for meeting the actual requirements of its citizens.

Administrative Process Efficiency

Administrative Process Efficiency refers to the government's efficiency in executing its routine operations. The construct of Administrative Process Efficiency is based on the indicator for "Extent of Bureaucratic Red Tape" taken from the Global Competitiveness Report of 2005. The measure as used in our research indicates the efficiency in government operations and the extent to which bureaucratic red tape is not impeding the processing time. High "administrative process efficiency" indicates that the government is efficient in conducting its routine administrative processes and there is less waiting time for citizens and businesses when dealing with government.

Reduction of Social Divide

Reduction of Social Divide is a measure of success of governments in their welfare objectives. Social upliftment, poverty alleviation, removal of social inequality, etc., appear as some of the most important welfare objectives of governments across the world. We posit that governments doing well on the social objectives succeed in having a significant reduction of social divide in the country. In our study, reduction of social divide is based on the indicator for "Government Effectiveness in Reducing Poverty and Inequality" taken from the Global Competitiveness Report of 2005.

Business Competitiveness

The Business Competitiveness of a nation is an indicator of the micro-economic capabilities of its constituents. Unless the micro-economic capabilities of the national constituents improve, macro-economic, political, legal, and social reforms will not bear full fruit in terms of the nation's prosperity. Competitiveness is thus related to a nation's standard of living and prosperity (Porter, 2005) and is measured by the GDP per capita adjusted for purchasing power parity, the values for which are taken from the Global Competitiveness Report 2005.

While forming the various indexes, the reporting agencies carried out suitable statistical procedures for ensuring their validity and reliability (UN Report, 2004; WEF, 2005). For example, in their report the reporting agencies have highlighted the use of multiple respondent expert surveys in each nation, where the responses from respondents within a nation were examined for internal consistency before being included in the index calculation. A brief description on their reliability and validity are given in Appendix 2.

RESULTS AND DISCUSSION

Before testing our research hypotheses, we present the descriptive statistics of the sampled nations in Table 1. We also divide the nations into two groups of high income and low income nations (as per the World Bank classification scheme) to have a better understanding of the differences that exist in the values of the research variables across the two sub-samples. From the figures in the table, we see that there is a significant difference in the level of e-government development between the high income and low income nations. This result is consistent with some of the past studies on e-government (e.g., Melitski et al., 2005), which suggests a difference in the digital government capabilities among the 30 developed nations belonging to the Organization for Economic Cooperation and Development (OECD) and lesser developed (non-OECD) nations. In

Table 1. Descriptive statistics: High and low income countries

	All Nations (n=99)		High Income Nations (n=52)		Low Income Nations (n=47)	
	Mean	Std. Dev.	Mean	Std. Dev.	Mean	Std. Dev.
E-Government development	0.446	0.255	0.602	0.204	0.274	0.186
Resource spending efficiency	3.289	0.870	3.637	0.854	2.904	0.717
Administrative process efficiency	5.180	0.417	5.350	0.367	4.994	0.391
Reduction of social divide	3.517	1.046	3.952	1.030	3.036	0.840

addition to e-government, we observe differences in other efficiency and performance figures for the two sub-groups.

For testing the hypotheses, we employed partial least squares (PLS) (Barclay, et al., 1995; Chin, 1998; Wold, 1989). The advantage of using PLS is that it enables us to examine complex theoretical models (having more than one level of theoretical linkage) as is the case in our study (Gefen et al., 2000). PLS imposes minimal demands in terms of sample sizes, measurement scales, and residual distributions to validate a model compared to other structural equation modeling techniques (Wold, 1989; Gefen et al., 2000; Mahmood et al., 2004). Another advantage is that the PLS analysis is distribution free and does not assume true independence of the variables, leading to more reliable results (Gefen et al., 2000; Tobias, 1999). PLS is also robust against other data structural problems such as skew distributions and omissions of regressors (Cassel et al., 1999). Many information systems (IS) studies have found it to be an effective method of analysis (Bock, et al., 2005; Subramani, 2004). Moreover, the exploratory theory development stage that e-government research is currently in makes PLS a suitable choice for analyzing the data in our study. The results of our analyses are presented in Figure 2.

From the results (Figure 2), Hypothesis 1a, which states that there is a positive association between e-government development and resource spending efficiency, received strong support (path = 0.38, t = 3.32, p<0.01). Hypothesis 1b, which states that e-government development is positively associated with administrative process efficiency, was also strongly supported (path = 0.46, t = 6.86, p<0.01). Hypothesis 2 was not supported (path = 0.05, t = 0.46, ns), indicating the lack of a significant relationship between administrative process efficiency and resource spending efficiency. One possible reason is that the resource spending may be more of an external-driven process rather than being influenced by internal administrative process efficiency. The result signifies the greater role of citizens and businesses in providing information and also influencing government for facilitating efficient resource allocation and spending.

Hypothesis 3a, which indicates a link between resource spending efficiency and reduction of social divide, was strongly supported (path = 0.78, t = 13.82, p<0.01). Hypothesis 3b was also strongly supported (path = 0.47, t = 7.00, p<0.01), establishing the association of resource spending efficiency with business competitiveness. These results establish the intermediate role of resource spending efficiency in the relationship between e-government development and national performance on both the dimensions of reduction of social divide as well as business competitiveness. It indicates the presence of intermediate variables in the e-government impact process,

Figure 2. Results of PLS analysis

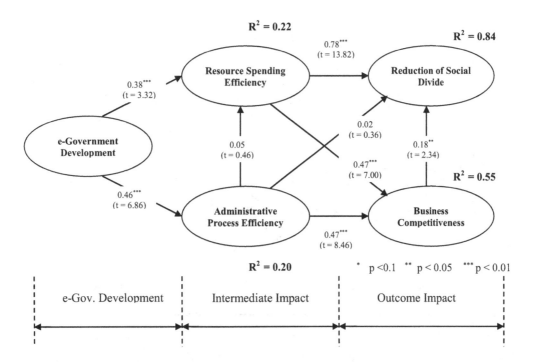

thus extending the work on IT impact in the e-government context. Surprisingly, Hypothesis 4a, which indicates a positive association between administrative process efficiency and reduction of social divide, was not supported (path = 0.02, t = 0.36, ns). Hypothesis 4b was strongly supported (path = 0.47, t = 8.46, p<0.01), indicating a strong link between administrative process efficiency and national business competitiveness. The relationship between business competitiveness and reduction of social divide was also significant (path = 0.18, t = 2.34, p<0.05), thus providing support for Hypothesis 5. Further, the proposed model explains a significant amount of variance (83.6%) in reduction of social divide and in business competitiveness (54.8%).

The lack of support for hypothesis 4a is interesting and also surprising as it apparently refutes past IS studies on IT impact which indicate that improvement in administrative process efficiency should create an impact on its performance parameters (Barua et al., 1995; Subramaniam

& Shaw, 2002). Studies on e-government in the past have also shown positive impacts on different performance metrics including those related to social objectives (Banerjee & Chau, 2004; Von Haldenwang, 2004; West, 2004). A result indicating nonassociation of administrative process efficiency with reduction of social divide no doubt raises an important counter-intuitive issue which needs further exploration. There can be two plausible reasons for this non-significant result. First, there is actually no relationship between administrative process efficiency and reduction of social divide. Second, the impact of administrative process efficiency on reduction of social divide is realized fully through business competitiveness (since in our model that is the only other significant path from administrative process efficiency to reduction of social divide). Some past studies on IT impact have shown the importance of understanding the path of impact realization through intermediate mediating variables (Barua, et al., 1995; Hitt & Brynjolfsson,

Figure 3. Testing for mediation of administrative process efficiency through business competitiveness for achieving social competitiveness

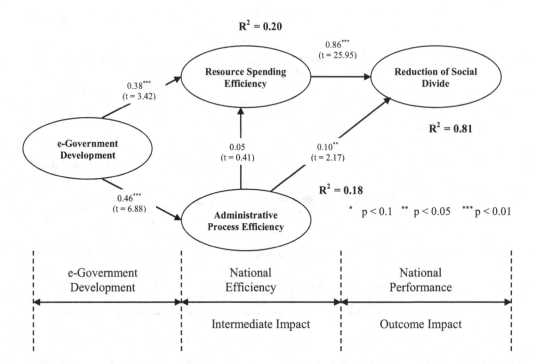

1996; Mukhopadhyay et al., 1995; Subramaniam & Shaw, 2002). To analyze this aspect, we did the PLS analysis again without the construct of business competitiveness in the structural model, the results of which are shown in Figure 3.

We observe that in the revised model, the path from administrative process efficiency to reduction of social divide becomes significant (path = 0.10, t = 2.17, p<0.05). This brings forth a very interesting finding about the relationship between administrative process efficiency and reduction of social divide. In the presence of the path between administrative process efficiency to reduction of social divide through business competitiveness, the direct path between administrative process efficiency and reduction of social divide becomes insignificant (Figure 2). This indicates that the relationship between administrative process efficiency and reduction of social divide is fully mediated through business

competitiveness. The result is interesting as it indicates that in our hypothesized model, even a second order impact (business competitiveness) serves as a mediating variable for another second order impact (reduction of social divide). The result makes an important contribution in enriching our understanding about the complex process of e-government impact assessment at the national level. Further, it brings forth the important role of business development in a nation, as it is not only related to enhancing national business competitiveness but also is instrumental in helping governments achieve social equity objectives.

LIMITATIONS

The key limitation of this study is the reliance on secondary data for our analyses. We analyze data only from those countries that were present in our secondary data sources; for example, we could not include countries like Hong Kong and Taiwan in our analyses, as data for these countries were not available in the UN report. Taking into consideration the fact that we have large-scale data from 99 countries, omitting some of the countries may not make a substantial difference in the results. Moreover, for an analysis such as ours, which aims to analyze data across nearly a hundred countries, we have to depend on established secondary sources of data, as collection of primary data would entail a huge amount of resources.

Another limitation of this study is the use of cross-sectional data for analyses. Although we hypothesize only for an *association* between the variables, there is an implicit causality embedded in the structural model. Analysis using longitudinal data would have provided us greater confidence for causality assumptions. Though the WEF has been publishing global competitiveness report for a number of years now, the UN started publishing the United Nations Global E-Government Readiness Report only recently since 2003. Hence, we do not currently have sufficient data to do a meaningful longitudinal time-series analysis. Future studies can conduct such an analysis. Moreover, cross-sectional data analysis has been used in similar e-government studies (e.g., Siau & Long 2004, 2006; Srivastava & Teo, 2006a, 2006b). Despite these limitations, our study is one of the first to understand the role of intermediate variables associated with e-government impact in a cross-country scenario.

IMPLICATIONS

Through this research, we make some important contributions which have implications for research as well as practice.

Implications for Research

First, most studies on e-government are either conceptual or case studies. There is a dearth of quantitative empirical studies on e-government (Norris & Moon, 2005). Moreover, there are relatively few studies on e-government which address issues from a global perspective. Our empirical study, which uses secondary data to analyze e-government development and its impact from a cross-country perspective, fills these gaps in the e-government literature. Future research can make use of other innovative sources of secondary data for better understanding of the role of e-government.

Second, there are few studies that analyze the impact of IT at the country level of analysis (Melville et al., 2003). Moreover, studies which address the relationship of e-government with national performance are even fewer (Banerjee & Chau, 2004; Wong & Welch, 2004). Through this research on the relationship between e-government and national performance on the two dimensions of reduction of social divide and business competitiveness, we enrich the IT impact literature by analyzing contexts not explicitly explored in the past.

Third, in our research we conceptualize an e-government impact model as having first order association with efficiencies (resource spending efficiency and administrative process efficiency), which in turn are related to reduction of social divide and enhancement of business competitiveness. Analyzing e-government payoffs through intervening mediating variables gives a more accurate and fuller understanding of the path through which e-government development is associated with national performance. Past IT impact studies have used models with intervening variables in various other contexts. Our study is one of the first to take a processual mediated view of e-government impact.

Fourth, there are very few studies on e-government which use rich sources of secondary data for cross-country studies. Our study is a case in point and exhorts future researchers to use other innovative cross-country secondary data sources to make inferences about e-government from a global perspective.

Fifth, another aspect that is brought out in our study is the non-significant role of government administrative process efficiency in enhancing resource spending efficiency. Future research can investigate the role and impact of administrative process efficiency as well as other intermediary variables like the actual usage and quality of e-government (Devaraj & Kohli, 2003) on national performance.

Implications for Practice

In addition to the implications for research, our study has several important implications for public administrators and policy makers. *First,* our study highlights the importance of considering intermediate process variables when considering the relationship of e-government with national performance. Specifically, our research suggests that the development of e-government is significantly associated with resource spending efficiency and administrative process efficiency of governments. Enhancement of these efficiencies in turn is positively associated with national performance on the two dimensions of reduction of social divide and business competitiveness. Thus, government efficiency mediates the relationship between e-government development and national performance. Instead of looking for direct benefits from e-government, public administrators and policy makers should make use of e-government in areas where they require an enhancement of efficiency.

Second, our results show that a second order impact on one dimension of national performance may impact the other dimension of national performance. Specifically, in this research we

see that the relationship between government administrative process efficiency and reduction of social divide is fully mediated by business competitiveness. This result reiterates the important role of business competitiveness in attaining social equity objectives. The result has implications for policy makers to encourage greater focus on the business development in a nation as it is not only related to the business competitiveness but is also associated with lesser social divide. Business competitiveness may thus help nations alleviate poverty and achieve social equality. Hence, concerted efforts should be made by governments in both directions.

Third, the study provides policymakers with a framework for conceptualizing and visualizing the impact of e-government. Consideration of multiple efficiency variables may help them to better understand and identify areas of critical importance for e-government implementation. The results of this study can also be helpful for public administrators in justifying investments in e-government projects.

CONCLUSION

The recent spur in e-government implementations by governments across the world is motivated by the expectations of anticipated payoffs. Accenture in its recent report mentioned:

Electronic government (e-government) enables high performance. It enables better outcomes for less cost—maximum value from every resource expended. In the process it helps governments transform service delivery, so that they meet their obligations to their stakeholders in the most efficient and cost-effective way possible. (Accenture, 2004, p.2)

Although, e-government promises a lot to the citizens, there are very few studies which analyze the relationship of e-government with the various performance parameters. Understanding the impact of e-government development by governments and policymakers is vital for the effective implementation and administration of government plans and policies (UN Report, 2004; Von Haldenwang, 2004). In this research using the IT impact perspective, we analyze the way in which e-government can help nations achieve their social and economic objectives. The study brings forth the significant relationships of e-government development with administrative and resource allocation efficiencies, which in turn are related to the social equity and business competitiveness of a nation.

REFERENCES

Accenture. (2005). E-Government leadership: High performance, maximum value. *Government Executive Series,* Accessed January 14, 2005, from http://www.egov.gov.sg

Alba, J., Lynch, J., Weitz, B. & Janiszewski, C. (1997). Interactive home shopping: Consumer, retailer, and manufacturer incentives to participate in electronic marketplaces. *Journal of Marketing, 61*(3), 38- 53.

Alpar, P., & Kim, M. (1990). A microeconomic approach to the measurement of information technology value. *Journal of Management Information Systems, 7*(2), 55-69.

Atkinson, A. B. & Brandolini, A. (2001). Promise and pitfalls in the use of 'secondary' data-sets: Income inequality in OECD countries as a case study. *Journal of Economic Literature, 39*(3), 771-799.

Banerjee, P., & Chau, P. Y. K. (2004). An evaluative framework for analysing e-government convergence capability in developing countries. *Electronic Government, 1*(1), 29-49.

Barclay, D., Thompson, R., & Higgins, C. (1995). The partial least squares (PLS) approach to causal modeling: Personal computer adoption and use, an illustration. *Technology Studies, 2*(2), 285–309.

Barua, A., Kriebel, C. H., & Mukhopadhyay, T. (1995). Information technologies and business value: An analytic and empirical investigation. *Information Systems Research, 6*(1), 3-23.

Bock, G. W., Zmud, R. W., Kim, Y. G., & Lee, J. N. (2005). Behavioral intention formation in knowledge sharing: Examining the roles of extrinsic motivators, social-psychological forces and organizational climate. *MIS Quarterly, 29*(1), 87-111.

Bretschneider, S. (1990). Management information systems in public and private organizations: An empirical test. *Public Administration Review, 50*(9), 536-545.

Brynjolfsson, E., & Hitt, L. (1996). Paradox lost? Firm-level evidence on the returns to information systems spending. *Management Science, 42*(4), 541-558.

Brynjolfsson, E., & Hitt, L. (2000). Beyond computation: Information technology, organizational transformation and business performance. *Journal of Economic Perspectives, 14*(4), 23-48.

Cassel, C., Westlund, A. H., & Hackl, P. (1999). Robustness of partial least squares method for estimating latent variable quality structures. *Journal of Applied Statistics, 26*, 435-448.

Chin, W. W. (1998). The partial least squares approach to structural equation modeling. In G. A. Marcoulides (Ed.), *Modern methods for business research* (pp. 295-336). Mahwah, NJ: Lawrence Erlbaum Associates.

Cho, Y. H., & Choi, B. (2004). E-government to combat corruption: The case of Seoul metropolitan government. *International Journal of Public Administration, 27*(10), 719-735.

Delios, A., & Beamish, P. W. (1999). Ownership strategies of Japanese firms: Transactional, institutional and experience influences. *Strategic Management Journal, 20*, 915-933.

Dern, D. (1992). Internet system experiencing meteoric growth. *Info World, 14*(38), 56.

Devaraj, S., & Kohli, R. (2003). Performance impacts of information technology: Is actual usage the missing link? *Management Science, 49*(3), 273-289.

Dewan, S., & Kraemer, K. L. Information technology and productivity: Evidence from country-level data. *Management Science, 46*(4), 548-562.

Drazen, A. (2001). *Political economy in macroeconomics.* Princeton: Princeton University Press.

Francalanci, C., & Galal, H. (1998). Information technology and worker composition: Determinants of productivity in the life insurance industry. *MIS Quarterly, 22*(2), 227-241.

Gaur, A.S., & Lu, J. (2007). Ownership strategies and subsidiary performance: Impact of institutions and experience. *Journal of Management, 33*(1), 84-110.

Gefen, D., Straub, D.W., & Boudreau, M. (2000). Structural equation modeling and regression: Guidelines for research practice. *Communications of the AIS, 4*(7), 2-76.

Hammer, M. (2001). The superefficient company. *Harvard Business Review, 79*(8), 82-91.

Heeks, R. (2002). E-Government in Africa: Promise and practice. *Information Polity, 7*, 97-114.

Hitt, L., & Brynjolfsson, E. (1996). Productivity, business profitability, and consumer surplus: Three different measures of information technology value. *MIS Quarterly, 20*(2), 121-142.

Jain, A. (2003). Performance paradox: Information technology investments and administrative performance in the case of the 50 U.S. state governments. *Proceedings of the Twenty-Fourth International Conference on Information Systems (ICIS 2003).* Seattle, Washington.

Kaylor, C., Deshazo, R., & Van Eck, D. (2001). Gauging e-government: A report on implementing services among American cities. *Government Information Quarterly, 18*, 293-307.

Kibsi, G., Boer, K., Mourshed, M., & Rea, N. (2001). Putting citizens online, not in line. *The McKinsey Quarterly, 2*, 65-73.

Kiecolt, K. J. & Nathan, L. E. (1985). *Secondary analysis of survey data.* Beverly Hills, CA: Sage.

Koh, C. E., Ryan, S., & Prybutok, V. R. (2005). Creating value through managing knowledge in an e-government to constituency (G2C) environment. *Journal of Computer Information Systems,* Summer, 32-41.

Kulkarni, S. P. (2000) The influence of information technology on information asymmetry in product markets. *Journal of Business & Economic Studies, 6*(1), 55-71.

Kunstelj, M., & Vintar, M. (2004). Evaluating the progress of e-government development: A critical analysis. *Information Polity, 9*, 131-148.

Layne, K., & Lee, J. (2001). Developing fully functional e-government: A four stage model *Government Information Quarterly, 18*, 122-136.

Lee, S. M., Tan, X., & Trimi, S. (2005). Current practices of leading e-government countries. *Communications of the ACM, 48*(10), 99-104.

Li, F. (2003). Implementing e-government strategy in Scotland: Current situation and emerging issues. *Journal of Electronic Commerce in Organizations, 1*(2), 44-65.

Mahmood, M. A., Bagchi, K., & Ford, T. C. (2004). On-line shopping behavior: Cross-country empirical research. *International Journal of Electronic Commerce, 9*(1), 9-30.

Mansoorian, A. and Myers G. M. (1997). On the consequences of government objectives for economies with mobile populations. *Journal of Public Economics, 63*(2), 265-281.

McNeal, R. S., Tolbert, C. J., Mossberger, K., & Dotterweich, L. J. (2003). Innovating in digital government in the american states. *Social Science Quarterly, 84*(1), 52-70.

Melitski, J., Holzer, M., Kim, S. T., Kim, C. G., & Rho, S. Y. (2005). Digital government worldwide: An e-government assessment of municipal websites. *International Journal of Electronic Government Research, 1*(1), 1-19.

Melville, N., Kraemer, K., & Gurbaxani, V. (2004). Review: Information technology and organizational performance: An integrative model of it business value. *MIS Quarterly, 28*(2), 283-322.

Mok, K. & Lau, M. (2002). Changing government role for socio-economic development in Hong Kong in the twenty-first century. *Policy Studies, 23*(2), 107-124.

Moon, M. J. (2002). The evolution of e-government among municipalities: Rhetoric or reality? *Public Administration Review, 62*(4), 424-433.

Mukhopadhyay, T., Kekre, S., & Kalathur, S. (1995). Business value of information technology: A study of electronic data interchange. *MIS Quarterly, 19*(2), 137-156.

Norris, D. F., & Moon, M. J. (2005). Advancing e-government at the grassroots: Tortoise or hare? *Public Administration Review, 65*(1), 64-75.

Phang, C. W., Sutanto, J., Yan, L., & Kankanhalli, A. (2005). Senior citizen's adoption of e-government: In quest of antecedents of perceived usefulness. *Proceedings Hawaii International Conference on Systems Sciences (HICSS 2005)*, Hawaii.

Porter, M. E. (2005). Building the micro-economic foundations of prosperity: Findings from the business competitiveness index. In *The global competitiveness report 2005-06*. Geneva, Switzerland: World Economic Forum

Rabianski, J. S. (2003). Primary and secondary data: Concepts, concerns, errors, and issues. *Appraisal Journal, 71*(1), 43-55.

Siau, K., & Long, Y. (2004). Factors impacting e-government development. *Proceedings Twenty-Fifth International Conference on Information Systems (ICIS 2004),Washington, D.C.*, 221-233.

Siau, K., & Long, Y. (2006). Using social development lenses to understand e-government development. *Journal of Global Information Management, 14*(1), 47-62.

Singh, H., Das, A., & Joseph, D. (2004). Country-level determinants of e-government maturity. *Proceedings 1st e-Government SIG Pre-ICIS Workshop. Washington D.C.*

Soh, C., & Markus, M. L. (1995). How IT creates business value: A process theory synthesis. *Proceedings 16th International Conference on Information Systems, Amsterdam, The Netherlands,* 29-41.

Srivastava, S. C., & Teo, T. S. H. (2004). A framework for electronic government: Evolution, enablers and resource drainers. *Proceedings Eighth Pacific Asia Conference on Information Systems (PACIS 2004), Shanghai, China.*

Srivastava, S. C., & Teo, T. S. H. (2005). Electronic government as a guided evolution in Singapore: Vision for the world in the 21st century. In M. Weaver (Ed.), *Proceedings Academy of Management Meeting Best Papers (AOM 2005), Honolulu, Hawaii,* E1-E6.

Srivastava, S. C., & Teo, T. S. H. (2006a). Is e-government development and e-participation related to business competitiveness? *Proceedings Academy of International Business Annual Meeting (AIB 2006),* Beijing, China.

Srivastava, S. C., & Teo, T. S. H. (2006b). Determinants and impact of e-government and e-business development: A global perspective. *Proceedings Twenty-Seventh International Conference on Information Systems (ICIS 2006).* Milwaukee, Wisconsin.

Srivastava, S. C., & Teo, T. S. H. (2007). Information systems research relevance. In M. Khosrow-Pour (Ed.), *Encyclopedia of information science and technology,*(2ⁿᵈ ed.).Hershey, PA: Idea Group (Forthcoming).

Stewart, T. A. (1995). What information costs? *Fortune, 132,* 119-121.

Straub, D. W., & Watson, R. T. (2001). Transformational issues in researching IS and net-enabled organizations. *Information Systems Research, 12*(4), 337-345.

Subramani, M. (2004). How do suppliers benefit from information technology use in supply chain relationships? *MIS Quarterly, 28*(1), 45-73.

Subramaniam, C., & Shaw, M. J. (2002). A study of the value and impact of b2b e-commerce: The case of web-based procurement. *International Journal of Electronic Commerce, 6*(4), 19-40.

Tan, C. W., & Pan, S. L. (2003). Managing e-transformation in the public sector: An e-government study of the inland revenue authority of Singapore (IRAS). *European Journal of Information Systems, 12,* 269-281.

Teo, T. S. H., & Too, B. L. (2000). Information systems orientation and business use of the Internet: An empirical study. *International Journal of Electronic Commerce, 4*(4), 105-130.

Tobias, R. D. (1999). *An introduction to partial least squares regression.* Cary, NC: SAS Institute.

UIOWA. (2004). *University of Iowa lecture series on secondary data analysis.* Accessed March

7, 2007, from http://www.uiowa.edu/~c07b176/SECONDARY_DATA_ANALYSIS_files/frame.htm

UN Report. (2004). *UN global e-government readiness report: Towards access for opportunity.* New York, United Nations.

US Government. (2002). *E-government strategy: Simplified service delivery to citizens.* Office of Management and Budget, Washington D.C.

Von Haldenwang, C. (2004). Electronic government (e-government) and development. *The European Journal of Development Research, 16*(2), 417-432.

Warkentin, M., Gefen, D., Pavlou, P. A., & Rose, G. M. (2002). Encouraging citizen adoption of e-government by building trust. *Electronic Markets, 12*(3), 157-162.

WEF. (2005). *Global competitiveness report 2005-2006.* Geneva, Switzerland: World Economic Forum.

Weill, P. (1992). The relationship between investment in information technology and firm performance: A study of the valve manufacturing sector. *Information Systems Research, 3*(4), 307-331.

West, D. M. (2004). E-government and the transformation of service delivery and citizen attitudes. *Public Administration Review, 64*(1), 15-27.

Wimmer, M. A. (2002). Integrated service modelling for online one-stop government. *Electronic Markets, 12*(3), 149-156.

Wold, H. (Ed.). (1989). *Introduction to the second generation of multivariate analysis.* New York: Paragon House.

Wong, W., & Welch, E. (2004). Does e-government promote accountability? A comparative analysis of website openness and government accountability. *Governance: An International Journal of Policy, Administration and Institutions, 17*(2), 275-297.

END NOTES

[1]   Classification of nations based on Gross National Income (GNI) per capita is given by the World Bank and is available at http://www.worldbank.org/ For our study, instead of using the four groups as defined by the World Bank, we grouped low income and lower middle income countries as *low income nations*, and high income and upper middle income countries as *high income nations.*

[2]   The full description of the model is available at http://www.unpan.org/egovernment3.asp

APPENDIX 1A: LIST OF COUNTRIES ANALYZED (HIGH AND LOW INCOME CLASSIFICATION)

High Income Countries: Argentina, Australia, Austria, Bahrain, Belgium, Botswana, Canada, Chile, Costa Rica, Croatia, Cyprus, Czech Republic, Denmark, Estonia, Finland, France, Germany, Greece, Hungary, Iceland, Ireland, Israel, Italy, Japan, Korea, Latvia, Lithuania, Malaysia, Malta, Mauritius, Mexico, Netherlands, New Zealand, Norway, Panama, Poland, Portugal, Russian Federation, Singapore, Slovakia, Slovenia, South Africa, Spain, Sweden, Switzerland, Trinidad and Tobago, Turkey, United Arab Emirates, United Kingdom, United States, Uruguay, Venezuela

Low Income Countries: Algeria, Bangladesh, Bolivia, Bosnia and Herzegovina, Brazil, Bulgaria, Chad, China, Colombia, Dominican Republic, Ecuador, Egypt, El Salvador, Ethiopia, Gambia, Georgia, Ghana, Guatemala, Honduras, India, Indonesia, Jamaica, Jordan, Kenya, Macedonia, Madagascar, Malawi, Mali, Morocco, Mozambique, Namibia, Nicaragua, Nigeria, Pakistan, Paraguay, Peru, Philippines, Romania, Serbia and Montenegro, Sri Lanka, Tanzania, Thailand, Tunisia, Uganda, Ukraine, Vietnam, Zimbabwe

Total Number of Countries Analyzed = 99

APPENDIX 1B: LIST OF COUNTRIES ANALYZED (CONTINENT-WISE)

Continents	Countries
Africa	Algeria, Botswana, Chad, Egypt, Ethiopia, Gambia, Ghana, Kenya, Madagascar, Malawi, Mali, Mauritius, Morocco, Mozambique, Namibia, Nigeria, South Africa, Tanzania, Tunisia, Uganda, Zimbabwe
Asia	Bahrain, Bangladesh, China, Cyprus, Georgia, India, Indonesia, Israel, Japan, Jordan, Korea, Malaysia, Pakistan, Philippines, Singapore, Sri Lanka, Thailand, Turkey, United Arab Emirates, Vietnam
Europe	Austria, Belgium, Bosnia and Herzegovina, Bulgaria, Croatia, Czech Republic, Denmark, Estonia, Finland, France, Germany, Greece, Hungary, Iceland, Ireland, Italy, Latvia, Lithuania, Macedonia, Malta, Netherlands, Norway, Poland, Portugal, Romania, Russian Federation, Serbia and Montenegro, Slovakia, Slovenia, Spain, Sweden, Switzerland, Ukraine, United Kingdom
North America	Canada, Costa Rica, Dominican Republic, El Salvador, Guatemala, Honduras, Jamaica, Mexico, Nicaragua, Panama, Trinidad and Tobago, United States
South America	Argentina, Bolivia, Brazil, Chile, Colombia, Ecuador, Paraguay, Peru, Uruguay, Venezuela
Oceania	Australia, New Zealand

APPENDIX 2: NOTE ON RELIABILITY AND VALIDITY OF DATA USED

The Global Competitiveness Report (2005) and the UN e-Government Readiness Report (2004) have been prepared by two leading agencies (namely, the World Economic Forum and the United Nations) which have long experience and expertise in collecting and interpreting global data. The data from both reports had two components, hard data and survey data. Some indices, like business competitiveness, rely completely on hard data while others, like e-Government development, resource spending efficiency, administrative process efficiency, and reduction of social divide are based on an expert survey conducted by the UN and the WEF. For ensuring reliability and validity of all the constructs, it is important to have an overview of the methods undertaken by the two agencies.

The country-level data was collected by the WEF through a number of partner institutes who were given a uniform set of guidelines which were strictly adhered to. Some of these guidelines included taking responses only from CEOs or equivalent rank company officials, facility for the respondents to answer in their preferred language (30 language versions were presented; the reliability of expression was ensured by the partner institutes), etc. A stratified random sampling procedure was adopted to ensure representation of the spectrum of companies in the country. In all, 10,993 respondents participated in the survey which corresponds to an average of 94 respondents from each country. A renowned leader in the field of survey research, Gallup International, was consulted with at the early stages and all suggestions given by them were adhered to. The data from respondents within countries were checked for internal consistency by analyzing the standard deviation of the responses. Apart from ensuring internal consistency, it was important to tackle the issue of perception bias, that is, "a systematic positive or negative bias found among all respondents in a given country; for example, some might believe that people in a certain country are generally more positive about their own economic environment than people in another country, who might be pessimistic" (WEF, 2005). To minimize chances of perception bias, two techniques were adopted. First, the questions were framed in a way that asks the respondents to compare their own country to world standards, rather than thinking in absolute national terms. Secondly, wherever possible, the survey data were compared with hard data on similar issues.

The UN also followed similar procedures for ensuring validity and reliability for their survey. The most important issue in the case of the UN survey was the training of the researchers who actually carried out the Web survey. Multiple researchers were used to rate the Web sites according to the stages of e-Government Web development. Detailed guidelines were provided for choosing the Web sites and features for classification and analysis. In all, a total of over 50,000 online features and services from 178 countries across six sectors were assessed, ensuring a wide coverage with reliable and consistent methods (UN Report, 2004). Since the two agencies (namely, the World Economic Forum and the United Nations) followed rigorous procedures as described above for ensuring the reliability and validity of the indices, data from these reports were used directly for analyses.

This work was previously published in Journal of Global Information Management, Vol. 15, Issue 4, edited by F. B. Tan, pp. 20-40, copyright 2007 by IGI Publishing, formerly known as Idea Group Publishing (an imprint of IGI Global).

Chapter XXVII
Going Global:
A Technology Review

Mahesh S. Raisinghani
Texas Woman's University, USA

Denise Taylor
University of Dallas, USA

ABSTRACT

The World Wide Web opened the door for many organizations with international ambitions to go global. Organizations that did not have a global presence or access to international markets could create Web sites to offer products/services to a new customer base, and companies that were already internationally entrenched could make their products easily accessible. However, developing a process to deliver products in a timely fashion and ensuring availability of items is still a challenge. This chapter explores the impact of telecommunications, customer relationship management (CRM), and supply chain management (SCM) and its impact on meeting customers' expecta-tions, regardless of location. We also address the challenges, advantages, and future trends in each of these areas. Finally, this chapter provides suggestions to help companies implement strategies that will effectively overcome the challenges of globalization.

INTRODUCTION

With the rapidly evolving telecommunications industry, especially in the US, it is becoming all the more challenging for companies to innovate and integrate. This is more so with businesses that choose to globalize, since even with the right telecommunications solution technologically, companies still need to ensure that they are communicating effectively with customers and providing them with detailed product information. This is where the supply chain systems become extremely important in modern globalization scenarios. An effective customer relationship management (CRM) solution will allow companies to provide timely and accurate data on customer orders and/or demand that can be used by the supply chain management (SCM) system to plan and schedule the manufacture of goods with minimal overruns. However, there is concern about whether domestic and/or global sourcing can effectively manage CRM, SCM, and telecommunications. These concerns arise from the fact that, although technology has evolved, the question of whether it is possible to improve the process of globalization by merely improving functionality of the technology in the areas of CRM, SCM, and telecommunications still remains. Before reviewing the technology components needed for globalization, it is imperative that a discussion occur on the means of communication. Implementation of a correct telecommunications solution is a key element in successfully managing and meeting customer demand. Therefore, a review of telecom technology and strategies will follow in order to understand the role it plays in the supply chain management process as well as the effect it has on meeting customer expectations. Later in this chapter, we provide an overview of the steps that companies can follow to review the customer needs and processes and develop a strategy that will help them achieve globalization.

BACKGROUND

The introduction of the World Wide Web opened the door for many companies seeking to go global and made it easy for companies to create a way to view their products online. However, developing a process to deliver products in a timely fashion and ensure availability of items is the challenge.

As companies strive to reduce expenditures by outsourcing jobs to locations beyond the US, they also want to grow revenues by attracting international business. This chapter explores the impact of telecommunications, customer relationship management (CRM), and supply chain management (SCM) and its impact on effectively meeting customers' expectations, regardless of the customers' locales. It addresses the challenges, advantages, and future trends in each of these areas. Finally, this chapter will provide suggestions to help companies implement strategies that will effectively help them overcome the challenges of globalization. Taking a closer look at all of these components will enable a review of the full cycle of customer processes, which will aid in developing a comprehensive global software strategy.

ROLE OF TELECOMMUNICATIONS IN THE GLOBALIZATION PROCESS

Telecommunications plays a significant role in globalization. Even with the implementation of good CRM and SCM systems, it is not likely that a company will realize the full potential of its business endeavors if the correct telecommunications strategy is not developed. The following section discusses the challenges and opportunities organizations face when embarking on global markets.

Telecommunications Challenges and Opportunities

When discussing global telecommunications' challenges, it is important to note that they differ from one country to another. While organizations in developed countries have stable infrastructures that are continuously enhanced by innovative technologies to manage electronic processing, in developing countries they do not have this luxury; rather, they tend to focus on how to exploit their in-house existing resources. Furthermore, unlike organizations in developed countries that can pick among giant telecommunications providers, in developing countries, organizations have been known to rely on a single source (usually owned by the government) for its telecommunications needs and support.

One of the ways developing countries have countered the telecomm obstacles is by using international host services to enter the market. Lake (2000) points out that an international hosting service raises the credibility of the enterprise and reduces fears that some consumers may have about purchasing from distant lands.

In the research conducted by Wresch (2003), the US hosted about half of the Web sites of nine developing countries. Another way organizations in developing countries are overcoming the reliability issues in telecomm is by developing the talent within the organization and by exchanging the knowledge and expertise with fellow organizations in the country.

In a study conducted by Kaarst-Brown and Wang (2003), respondents in the Turks and Caicos Islands (TCI) in the British West Indies of the Caribbean indicated that customer service is negatively impacted by sporadic outages. In

Table 1. Telecomm solutions (Passmore, 2003)

Service	Telecomm Solution
Single Service Provider	Find someone who can do everything, which is difficult. They assume end-to-end responsibility for meeting service level agreements. The Multiprotocol Label Switching-based backbone can deliver IP virtual private network services at Layer 3, ATM/frame relay services are provided at Layer 2 and circuit emulation or clear-channel bandwidth also may be available. But communications to some places is still restricted to lower-speed frame relay or X.25, and availability of specific services cannot be assumed.
Roll your own	Some large enterprises build their own private network to link global sites together. Because a private network potentially can be extended to wherever connectivity is needed, this approach usually solves the problem of reaching remote sites.

The largest enterprises can leverage the same economies of scale that would apply to a carrier network. Because of the current worldwide glut of fiber on certain long-haul routes (especially in North America), companies may be able to obtain a great deal of bandwidth economically. However, such savings may be offset by the relatively high cost in many countries associated with leasing private network access circuits. |
Stitch together multiple service provider clouds	Since a single service provider may not be able to deliver the desired network services to all of an enterprise's sites, an enterprise could try to combine different provider networks, either to extend geographic coverage, or to create multiple carrier paths in the backbone for redundancy and higher availability. The enterprise would obtain IP-VPN, frame relay, ATM or other services from each carrier, and maintain a few peering points where traffic would be handed off (routed) from one cloud to another.
Use a Virtual Network Organization (VNO)	VNO's offer more sophisticated services than traditional resellers, and there are currently two different models. 1) One type of VNO provides peering points between other carrier clouds, concatenating carrier services to provide end-to-end service across geographies. The peering points include performance-monitoring tools to enable the VNO to determine which carriers are meeting SLAs (or not). The result should be end-to-end service that meets SLAs on a global scale. 2) The other type uses IP-VPN services across provider networks. This cannot guarantee end-to-end performance, but they provide truly global reach. They leverage internet connectivity and use the same access facilities for both site-to-site and extranet access.
Hybrid	Hybrid system could be developed allowing a company to build a private network to gain economies of scale, and exploit cheap fiber runs to higher density locations or sites where transmission facilities are reasonable priced. This network could be extended via a provider's IP-VPN or frame relay to reach remote sites.

addition, the cost of maintaining adequate tele-comm service was expensive, as Kaarst-Brown and Wang (2003) explained:

The major complaints over the quality of phone service reflect the impact of the telecommunications systems on customer service. How to find inexpensive vehicles to communicate with the customers has been an important issue in CRM in TCI. (Kaarst-Brown & Wang, 2003)

The weather was also a challenge for this set of respondents. Since TCI is an island nation, it had to find ways to maintain the infrastructure in spite of hurricanes and the salt in the air. TCI Cable & Wireless indicated:

Fiber optics, heavy duty towers, bite the bullet and maintain, maintain, maintain. Remote sites will help because we will put fiber between the remote sites and the exchange and the fiber is impervious to water. It reduces the propensity for error and faults. (Kaarst-Brown & Wang, 2003)

On the other hand, developed countries face a different set of challenges. While the infrastructure is developed, companies seeking to do business globally must find ways to reach austere regions of the world. Companies must enhance their telecommunications strategy to ensure swift and secure communications, regardless of where the transaction is delivered.

As companies move their operations to less-developed countries in search of cheap labor, they quickly discover that in these (often rural) locations, few carriers offer service. (Passmore, 2003)

Some solutions that companies can use to enhance their service are listed in Table 1.

These solutions assist organizations in creating good telecommunications strategies. Since each option has its strengths and weaknesses, an organization must choose the option that works best in the context of its own. For example, a single service provider may work for smaller organizations that do not have the expertise or the resources to build its own telecomm infrastructure. However, one of the fallacies of obtaining a single source provider is that it may not be able to provide the required telecomm services needed by an organization. Therefore, organizations are forced to stitch together multiple service providers to ensure that all of their telecommunications needs are met.

An alternative strategy is that some companies may choose to roll their own telecommunications systems. There are cases when local exchange carriers are progressing slowly and are not up to speed with current market demands to make progress and improve performance on their networks. Reardon (2004) wrote:

For a total cost of $2.2 million and a year's worth of work, Douglas County traded its old 1.5 megabit per second leased system for a brand-new 10 gigabit per second network—enough capacity to consider selling the excess for a profit. The new network, which is capable of carrying everything from voice to video to data, has also eliminated roughly $320,000 per year in recurring data communications charges... (Reardon, 2004)

This option is expensive and requires considerable knowledge of telecommunications technology.

For companies that do not want to build their own network, working with other telecommunications companies to build/bridge a system is another option. The key is to link with providers that are reliable and to fully understand their capabilities and the extent of their footprint. However, a hybrid solution that employs a peer-to-peer concept using satellite transmission to communicate information, using wireless technology in remote areas and working with a single source in metropolitan areas, provides the most flexibility and allows organizations to develop a global strategy that best fits the need of that particular region.

FUTURE TRENDS IN TELECOMMUNICATIONS

Voice Over IP (VOIP)

VOIP has positive attributes that make it the wave of the future for global businesses. It can substantially cut telecom costs by allowing access to voice and data using the same line, reduce long distance costs, and improve productivity. In a survey conducted by *InformationWeek* of 300 business-technology executives, more than 80% said their companies are using 29%, testing 18%, or planning to deploy 34% of the technology (Ewalt, 2004).

The most common VOIP applications in use are IP-based phone systems (71%); connections with satellite offices (68%); remote access to telephone features (63%); and phone-based productivity apps, including IP conferencing, unified messaging, and multimedia training (62%) (Ewalt, 2004). Although the use of VOIP is becoming more popular, there are concerns. Companies are concerned with the cost of installation, reliability of the voice component, and security. The handsets tend to fail more frequently than conventional telephones, and additional care must be taken to ensure that security patches and upgrades are applied across the VOIP system.

Wireless Implementation

Using wireless technology is another option for global communications. The Institute of Electronics and Electrical Engineers (IEEE) and Wireless Fidelity (Wi-Fi) alliance has completed the Robust Security Network that is designed to dramatically decrease attacks (Dornan, 2003). In addition, VISIONng, a non-profit consortium of telecom operations and Internet service providers (ISPs)

promoting the creation of a global, multi-vendor IP telephony network has requested the International Telecommunications Union to establish a permanent global area code and prefix (878-10) for VOIP phone numbers registered with an electronic numbering service (Greenfield, 2003).

However, even with the right telecommunications solution, companies need to ensure that they are communicating effectively with the customer and providing product information back to the supply chain. An effective CRM enables companies to obtain order information while analyzing the trends and determining where the company's sales should be focused. Within the US, this process is challenging, because the correct solution is not always implemented, and stand-alone applications are used to evaluate this information. Developing a CRM solution that can be used globally is difficult. The subsequent section will review CRM, its challenges, advantages, and future trends in order for CRM to facilitate globalization.

Role of CRM in SCM Process

With the World Wide Web growing as a channel for global commerce, companies are trying to improve the way they communicate with their customers, obtain valuable marketing information, and increase customer loyalty. In the past, companies focused their marketing strategies on the areas of the world where they have a presence. In an effort to increase return on investment, companies use CRM software to identify target audiences and gather information about their spending habits and product use. The discussion that follows will focus on the challenges and opportunities of CRM in customer service, data management, and partnership management.

CRM Challenges and Opportunities

For companies globally marketing products on the Internet, the objective is to ensure that the company satisfies the three tenets of the customer relationship model (i.e., understanding consumer behavior, delivering personalized services, and earning customers' loyalty) (Hamid et al., 2004). Achieving each of these three tenets for global companies is a challenge. Although there are software vendors that provide customer relationship management software, additional developments are needed to increase effectiveness across the cultural markets and between the business-to-business (B2B) and business-to-consumer (B2C) customer relationships. An effective CRM is more than a software solution; it is about how customer information is used to create an ongoing relationship with the customer (Ragins et al., 2003). Companies are now seeking packages that can do the following:

- Allow for a multilingual order entry interface.
- Automate multilingual customer services.
- Allow for flexibility, depending on the way the customer prefers to shop (i.e., personal computer, wireless service, personal digital assistant (PDA), etc.).

Sergey Aityan, president of Huntington Beach Division, Paramon Technologies, said, "In a number of years, English will become the minority in the Internet world because the Internet is moving globally towards Asia and Europe" (Aityan, 2002). The US Census Bureau confirms Aityan's findings. There are more than 2.4 million Chinese-speakers, and four out of five of them prefer to speak Chinese at home. The number of Korean and Vietnamese speakers is also on the rise (Aityan, 2002). With B2C sales predicted to reach $100 billion in 2004 (Ragins et al., 2003), companies must find the right CRM solutions to fit their needs.

Business-to-Consumer Market

For B2C markets, the first challenge is to provide an interface that can be used universally across all ethnic channels and to ensure that accurate data is captured for market analysis. Second, businesses also will have to focus on providing B2C access services in the customer's preferred method of communication. Regardless of how a customer wants to access the Internet, the format must fit the various communication devices that are available. Finally, companies must ensure not only multilingual access to customer service, but also multilingual and multiple channels, such as customer initiated online chats, wireless access, or Web pages that provide the information the customer needs. Techniques that can foster ongoing dialog between marketers and their customers include CRM software, which integrates data from call centers and suggestion lines and develops customer profiles, personalized messages loyalty programs, special offerings, personalized Web pages, quarterly newsletters, and the formation of customer advisory councils. Other techniques might include chat-based online focus groups, Internet-based conferences, e-mail or Web-based customer surveys, and online customer panels (Ragins et al., 2003).

Business-to-Business Market

For companies whose primary customer base is the B2B market, finding the right CRM strategy is even more challenging, because the potential revenue loss an organization could experience from a substandard CRM strategy could negatively impact the relationship and discourage new customers from seeking their services. The CRM must allow sales representatives around the globe to access inventory from wherever they are in the world. The data must be updated in real time, and it must be converted easily from one language to another, allowing users to access the data in their preferred language. Gary Moore, vice-president of Global Business Development for mySAP, said, "If you've got a guy in Japan, and entering a (sales) opportunity and he's entering the text all in Japanese, it's not much use to anyone outside of Japan" (Aityan, 2002). Companies also can use future trends in CRM to meet their customers' demands and to help them achieve globalization. For companies that have B2C and B2B customers, there may be a need to have different software for the different relationships. "Effective CRM is more than a software solution; it is about how customer information is used to create an ongoing relationship with the customer" (Ragins et al., 2003).

FUTURE TRENDS IN CRM

Hosted CRM Solution

Although CRM software implementations are occurring within companies, several companies are turning to hosted customer relationship management solutions. For example, Polaroid has subscribed to CRM software from Right-Now Technologies Inc. (McDougall, 2004). The hosted CRM solution approach has proven to be less expensive for companies than those that run CRM applications in-house. Hosted software allows companies to reduce IT complexity and to improve delivery and integration technologies. With the use of Web services, this concept is seriously being considered, because integration can be accomplished easily.

An effective CRM solution will enhance the ability of the supply chain management system by providing order data that the SCM can use to plan and schedule the manufacture of goods with minimal overruns. A global SCM uses data from every region of the world in the planning process, making it possible for companies to significantly reduce backorder occurrences. To achieve this, an organization should have a good telecomm strategy, along with an effective CRM solution to back it up.

Supply Chain Management

The process of implementing supply chain management solutions is slowly progressing among businesses. Major corporations such as Wal-Mart, Boeing, and Intel are investing in the tools because they recognize the fact that SCM solutions enable businesses to collaborate with their customers in

Table 2. Logistics software implementation (Poirer et al., 2003)

Enterprise Resource Planning	63%
Inventory Planning and Optimization	53%
Web-based Applications	52%
Advanced Planning and Scheduling	48%
e-Procurement Systems	47%
Warehouse Management Systems	42%
Business-to-Business	41%
Transportation Management Systems	30%
Customer Relationship Management	26%
CPFR	24%
Event management	21%
Supplier Relationship Management	21%
Collaborative Product Design	13%
Enterprise Application Integration	13%

order to meet their demands as well as to minimize the unnecessary production of goods. In short, the return on investment is greatly increased, once the proper SCM is implemented.

SCM Challenges and Opportunities

The companies that are implementing SCM solutions are implementing stand-alone components with the hope of integrating the software, once it is incorporated into their process. "All too often, they buy supply chain software on an ad hoc basis, gambling that each purchase will integrate with their prior acquisitions and deliver the promised benefits. This practice often creates more problems than it solves—and it generally leads to a poor return on investment (ROI)" (Taylor, 2004).

The major reasons why companies are not aggressively moving toward SCM process are:

- The pace of adopting new ways of doing business is slow.
- Demand information supplied by customers is not integrated into corporate planning.
- Demand management and supply management processes are not integrated and, hence, are unable to synchronize demand and supply.
- Lack of trust among trading partners to share pertinent information and to collaborate on decision making.
- The desire to partner but not to commit to executing the communicated plans.
- A common view that demands collaboration is a technology solution, and that current technology is too complex. (Crum et al., 2004)

Even though companies are not quick to use technology, a survey conducted by Computer Sciences Corporation and Supply Chain Management Review of 142 businesses (Poirer et al., 2003) revealed that the companies that are using

technology are implementing the following kinds of software listed in Table 2.

With the slow implementation of SCM software, companies realize the need for technology. However, they are reluctant to change processes, because they perceive that the cost and time associated with change is too great. Companies now are demanding that suppliers change their processes. This requires a paradigm shift where suppliers and customers have to share information, and each entity is truly a trading partner. Even if partnerships are developed, every discrete organization must select the software that best fits its needs. Taylor (2004) recommends one of the following four approaches:

- **Enterprise Resource Planning (ERP):** This approach focuses on planning and operations. It allows companies to feed the system with demand forecast and schedule production as late as possible. It does not assist in deciding where to place production facilities and warehouses and how to transport goods.
- **Advance Planning and Scheduling Systems (APS):** This approach focuses on managing a network of facilities and also scheduling production using mathematical equations.
- **Simulation Systems:** This approach focuses on predicting production and planning outcomes, based on the variables supplied by the end user. It enables companies to evaluate outcomes on a bell curve distribution and allows companies to plan accordingly.
- **Supply Chain Execution Packages:** This approach focuses on the integration of APS, simulation tools, ERP, CRM, supplier relationship management, and event management. (Taylor, 2004)

To increase the use of SCM software, vendors now are incorporating ERP software into their packages. This enables companies to streamline their processes, and it will provide them with the capability to manage sales activities as well as inventory planning. For example, Whirlpool is working with a single vendor that supplies ERP and SCM software in hopes that the software will ensure nearly every time a customer walks into a store to buy a Whirlpool product that the product is ready and waiting on the retailer's floor (Bacheldor, 2004).

FUTURE TRENDS IN SCM

Collaborative Relationships and Federated Approach

When discussing future trends for supply chain management, it is important to note that, while technology is evolving, most companies still lag behind in implementing it. Many SCM research findings confirm that a good SCM process will yield ROI, but this only comes if the proper software selection is made and implemented. It is important for companies to understand thoroughly their processes before they can use software to enhance them and/or build collaborative relationships with customers to optimize results. "The most successful demand collaborative relationships are not brokered at the buyer-salesperson level but at the senior executive level of the trading partner organizations" (Crum, 2004). Both the supplier and the customer must agree to share information in order for both organizations to obtain what they need. "Reaching consensus on a single demand plan that is used by both the customer and supplier organizations to drive management and financial planning is a best practice. However trust is an issue here. Today, demand plans communicated between trading partners are usually just numbers. As a result, the demand plans are not well understood and thus lack credibility" (Crum, 2004).

For companies that have settled on an SCM strategy, they are striving to find ways to continue to reduce costs. One of the ways companies are achieving this is by providing customers with data regarding suppliers and subcontractors. These coordination efforts allow the customer, the supplier, and the supplier's supplier to plan resources more efficiently. Supply chain coordination is not new to leading companies like Wal-Mart and McDonald's. Their influence in the marketplace gives them a great advantage over their suppliers. For companies that may not have the same influence but want to achieve the same results, the federated approach to planning may be best. "The federated planning model does not depend upon a utopian dream that ignores the inherent conflicts between supply chain partners (such as the need to maximize returns to their separate shareholders). ... federated planning accepts that each will ultimately optimize alone which allows supply chain partners to collaborate"(Laseter et al., 2004). For example, if a group of companies combined its warehousing for like items, it could reduce warehousing and production costs by having the supplier provide services to all of the companies under one organization.

SCM Standards

Software will allow businesses to better plan their resources and reduce costs. With the use of standards, Jones et al. (2002) believe that it will improve communications among trading partners. In their study of the retail industry, they found that standardizing the processes would improve globalization. In fact, there is a global commerce initiative that endorsed standards that were developed to facilitate national and international communication among all trading partners participating in any supply chain, including raw material suppliers, manufacturers, wholesalers, distributors, retailers, hospitals, and final clients or consumers.

Implementing standards will assist in the following processes:

- A global approach will result in less diversity in communication among existing trading partners and thereby reduce overhead and facilitate cross-regional trading. This uniformity will enable better collaboration on non-competitive processes.
- A global approach will provide synergies within organizations that operate across regions. Reporting and information sharing will be more consistent, and certain services can be centralized.
- Currently, there are local standards and proprietary systems. Providing uniform standards improves the processes (Jones et al., 2002).

Peoplesoft has assisted the health care industry to implement standards by incorporating three initiatives from the Coalition for Healthcare Standards (CHeS) into its enterprise resource planning system in order to help health organizations automate supply chain functionality (Berman, 2003). With approximately 80% of the health care providers represented by CHeS, this software implementation will allow suppliers and distributors to transact business online and in a unified manner.

Recommendations

The following recommendations will help the organization achieve globalization:

- Create an SCM system that encompasses the required components and produces reports that are useful to all functional areas.
- Ensure the system is dynamic enough to allow for quick modifications (e.g., adding suppliers, changing portal information, product configurations, etc.).

- Use Web services to communicate information in real time.
- Create a hybrid telephony system that will enable the company to use carriers where they exist and develop wireless means of communications where there is no fiber.
- Consider hosted CRM services in regions where cultural differences exist.

With the integration of ERP applications into SCM software packages, vendors are recognizing that they can provide an integrated solution that will allow companies to achieve their supply chain goals. Companies that are using this software or creating their own processes and systems to address both global and domestic market needs also are realizing that they may need assistance and are outsourcing parts of the business that are too expensive to maintain. Regardless of the model used, as long as companies determine their strategy and work toward achieving or exceeding customer and supplier expectations, it is likely that whichever software or telecommunications solution is selected, it will enable the company to acquire global markets.

CONCLUSION

In this chapter, we have attempted to describe the steps needed to achieve globalization. We have also demonstrated that it is possible for companies to develop systems that will meet customer expectations, regardless of the customer's locale. The real challenge for organizations is how to create a system that streamlines operations and delivers, based on customer and supplier expectations while ensuring ROI in the shortest amount of time. Since functional departments within organizations traditionally have worked in isolation to create systems that work best for their area of expertise, it is necessary to consider key factors and prerequisites, if an organization wants to effectively penetrate global markets. First, organizations need to identify their strategic objectives. If the goal is to globalize, then an organization needs to develop a technology that supports this vision. Second, an organization needs to assess its current software capabilities and begin to meet with the various departments in the organization in order to understand their current demands and future needs. Third, it is imperative that an organization map all processes to show the interdependencies of each functional area in order to include the role each trading partner plays in the process. Finally, an organization must ensure buy-in from senior level management about the technological model that will be pursued. Once these steps have been implemented, the following recommendations will help the company achieve globalization.

- Create an SCM system that encompasses the following components and produces reports that are useful to all functional areas of the organization:
  - CRM
  - ERP
  - APS
  - Supplier Relationship Management (SRM)
  - WHMS (Warehouse Management System)
  - Event Management
  - Simulation Tools
- Ensure the system is dynamic enough to allow for quick modifications (e.g., adding suppliers, changing portal information, product configurations, etc.).
- Use Web services to communicate information in real time.
- Create a hybrid telephony system that will enable the company to use carriers where they exist and develop wireless means of communications where there is no fiber.
- Consider hosted CRM services in areas where cultural differences exist.

With the integration of ERP applications into SCM software packages, vendors are recognizing that they can provide an integrated solution that will allow companies to achieve their supply chain goals. Companies that are using software or creating their own processes and systems to address both global and domestic market needs also are realizing that they may need assistance and are outsourcing parts of the business that are too expensive to maintain. Regardless of the model used, as long as organizations plan and implement their strategy that meets or exceeds customer/supplier/stakeholder expectations, it is most likely that the software or telecommunications solution selected will serve as a catalyst and/or facilitate its globalization initiatives.

REFERENCES

Aityan, S. (2002). CRM must speak many tongues. *Computing Canada.*

Bacheldor, B. (2004). Supply-chain economics. *Information Week, 979,* 32-42.

Berman, J. (2003). Peoplesoft adds CHeS standards for supply chain efficiency. *HealthŸIT World.* Retrieved April 5, 2004, from *http://www.health-itworld.com/enewsarchive/e_article000181909.cfm*

Choudrie, J., Papazafeiropoulou, A., & Lee, H. (2003). A web of stakeholders and strategies: A case of broadband diffusion in South Korea. *Journal of Information Technology, 18,*(4).

Crum, C., & Palmatier, G. (2004). Demand collaboration: What's holding us back? *Supply Chain Management Review, 8*(1), 54-61.

D'Avanzo, R. (2003). The reward of supply-chain excellence. *Optimize.* Retrieved January 26, 2004, from *http://www.optimizemag.com/printer/026/pr_financial.html*

Dolinov, M.L. (2003). Wi-Fi: Questions and answers for execs. *Forrester Research Inc.* Wholeview TechStrategy Research.

Dornan, A. (2003). Emerging technology: Wireless security—Is protected access enough? Retrieved March 10, 2004, from *http://www.networkmagazine.com/shared/article/showArticle.jhtml?articleID=15201417*

Ewalt, D.M. (2004). The new voice choice. *InformationWeek, 978,* 34-44.

Greenfield, D. (2003). Global Watch. *Network Magazine.* Retrieved March 10, 2004, from *http://www.networkmagine.com/shared/article/showArticle.jhtml? articleID=15201423*

Hamid, N.R.A., & Kassim, N. (2004). Internet technology as a tool in customer relationship management. *The Journal of American Academy of Business,* 4(1/2), 103-108.

Jones, R.H, & Green, M.D. (2002). Streamlining the supply chain. *Chain Store Age, 78*(12), 47-54.

Kaarst-Brown, M., & Wang, C. (2003). Doing business in paradise: How small, information intensive firms cope with uncertain infrastructure in a developing island nation (TCI). *Journal of Global Information Management, 11*(4), 37-57.

Laseter, T., & Oliver, K. (2003). When will supply chain management grow up? *strategy+business.* Retrieved April 6, 2004, from *http://www.strategy-business.com/press/article/03304?pg=0*

McDougall, P.(2004). Hosted software gains more converts. *Informationweek, 979,* 30.

Pankaj, M. (2003). *Asia Computer Weekly.*

Passmore, D. (2003). Network architect. *Business Communications Review, 33*(10), 14.

Poirier, C., & Quinn, F. (2003). A survey of supply chain progress. *Supply Chain Management Review.* Retrieved March 8, 2004, from *http://www.manufacturing.net/scm/index.asp?layout=articlePrint&articleID=CA323602*

Ragins, E.J., & Greco, A.J. (2003). Customer relationship management and e-business: More than a software solution. *Review of Business, 24*(1), 25-31.

Reardon, M. (2004). A network of one's own. *C\net News.com.* Retrieved April 13, 2004, from *http://news.com.com/2100-1033_3-5166813.html?tag=st_pop*

Taylor, D.A. (2004). A master plan for software selection. *Supply Chain Management Review, 8*(1), 20-27.

Thought Leadership Summit on Digital Strategies. (2002). Real-time profit optimization: Coordinating demand and supply chain management.

Wresch, W. (2003). Initial e-commerce efforts in nine least developed countries: A review of national infrastructure, business approaches and product selection. *Journal of Global Information Management, 11*(2), 67-78.

This work was previously published in Global Integrated Supply Chain Systems, edited by Y. Lan and B. Unhelkar, pp. 14-28, copyright 2006 by Information Science Publishing (an imprint of IGI Global).

Chapter XXVIII
Indigenous Knowledges and Worldview:
Representations and the Internet

Judy Iseke-Barnes
University of Toronto, Canada

Deborah Danard
University of Toronto, Canada

ABSTRACT

This chapter explores how representations of indigenous peoples on the Internet and other media are contextualized according to an outsider worldview, and that much of the information about indigenous peoples accessed through virtual media lack the original context in which to position the information. This means that the information is completely distanced from the indigenous peoples whom the information is purported to represent. This is problematic when representations of indigenous peoples are defined by dominant discourses which promote bias and reinforce stereotypes. With the increase of technology and the race to globalization, symbols are being reconstructed and redefined to connect and create a global identity for indigenous peoples. The consequences of this further the current practices of erasing and reconstructing indigenous history, language, culture and tradition through control and commodification of representations and symbols. This removal from history and community ensures continued silencing of indigenous voices. Although these misrepresentations continue to frame the discourse for indigenous peoples in Canada, it is time for indigenous peoples to reclaim and resist these representations and for outsiders to stop creating social narratives for indigenous peoples which support western hegemony.

INTRODUCTION

Indigenous representations based on an indigenous worldview have historically been under the control of indigenous peoples; for example, picture writings or pictographs, recorded histories on skins, birch bark, pottery and rocks reflecting oral histories. Story-telling, myths, legends, songs and ceremonies are the means of ensuring indigenous knowledges are passed from one generation to the next. Recorded histories of indigenous peoples are found throughout the world (Mallery, 1972). Today, contemporary indigenous artists continue to engage in representational practices not only to record current and historic events but to critique political realities and as forms of personal expression. Artists use many modern means of expression such as canvas, paper, sculpture, film, photography, radio, music, electronic media and the Internet. Other indigenous artists continue to use more traditional art forms (beading, leather work, porcupine quill work, etc.) as forms of healing and expression.

However, others, both indigenous and non-indigenous, use these potentially expressive forms to supply a trade market in more imitative practices. This result is in the loss of control of representation of distinct indigenous nations across North America and globally. These representational practices may impact public perceptions of what it means to "be Indian," and project images that have been broadly adopted to generalize misrepresentations of all indigenous peoples. Consequences of these representational practices, which are ongoing in Canada, include erasure or reconstruction of indigenous histories, languages, cultures and traditions. Canada has continued to use romanticized representations of "Indians" as commodities of entertainment (Iseke-Barnes, 2005) and to support the Canadian national identity of being connected to the land (Mackey, 2002). This has been primarily systemic and rooted in all levels of society (vertical and horizontal, internal and external as well as within and outside communities and nations), including the national government (Adams, 1999). In media and popular discourse, indigenous peoples have been represented by non-indigenous peoples as culturally inferior and unable to provide for themselves. These representations function to strengthen Canada's right to define who is and is not Canadian and to control what can and cannot be considered indigenous (Doxtator, 1988).

Representations of indigenous peoples and practices are being reconstructed and redefined to create a global identity through the increased use of technology and in the race to globalization. Systemic representational practices, such as those described above, may be accelerated and their destructive outcomes broadened through the Internet (Iseke-Barnes, 2002; Iseke-Barnes & Sakai, 2003; Iseke-Barnes, 2005).

This chapter provides examples of resistance to colonial discourses by indigenous peoples but cautions that there are risks, with the increasing commercialization of the Internet, that dominant discourses might prevail. Readers are challenged to consider how representational practices contribute to growing problems, and also how they might be transformed in order to contribute to solutions.

COMMODIFICATION

When indigenous representations are taken out of their cultural context and interpreted through the dominant culture, interpretations will inevitably support the beliefs and biases in which the dominant culture communicates. This means that when one culture interprets another it generally obscures rather than clarifies meaning. "Native reality is grounded in the kaleidoscopic experience of being inscribed as subaltern in the history of others and as subject to one's own heritage. For Indians, these are placements built upon contradictory social imaginaries, representation of otherness prescribed by the missionary, the merchant, the military" (Valaskakis, 1993, p. 158).

This has led to the appropriation of indigenous symbols for the purpose of wealth accumulation, both historically within the tourist and commercial art markets and today through the Internet. Indigenous symbols and representations in this new world order become commodities. For example, dream catchers, which were specific to indigenous peoples in North America, are now produced in other countries by peoples who have no historical or cultural context to make this product (e.g., http://www.sacredart.com/dreamcatchers.html; http://www.native-languages.org/dreamcatchers.htm; http://www.dreamcatcher.com; http://allclassifieds.com.au; http://www.crystalinks.com/dreamcatcher.html; or just search for dream catchers for sale through a Web search engine to find hundreds of thousands of sites). This mass production and marketing via the Internet creates exploitation of cultural symbols and practices. The cultural significance of the dream catcher is erased. It simply becomes a commodity.

An earlier version of this process engaged indigenous women in making standardized products for sale in markets overseas — for example moccasins had to be produced in a standard design and structure so they could be mass marketed in the early 1900s. Today, however, there is no longer a desire or need for these indigenous women artists as these items are mass produced and marketed by companies who replicate indigenous designs through the labor of non-indigenous workers or, ironically, indigenous workers from another country. Marketing has extended to the Internet (e.g., http://www.minnetonkamoccasinshop.com; http://www.sofmoc.com; http://www.native-languages.org/moccasins.htm; http://shopping.yahoo.com; http://www.trademe.co.nz), and this further removes the goods from the women who created them for their own people.

Moreover, there is a trend amongst popular culture celebrities in the United States of America to wear mukluks — a type of leather boot originally made by indigenous peoples in Canada. These are also available on the Internet (http://www.focusonstyle.com/style-pack/mukluks.htm; http://www.harperlee.co.uk/ourproducts.html). Some of these Web sites describe mukluks as "made by Canadian Indians," with substantially increased prices when these "authenticity" claims are attached. These Web sites further exploit the productions and creativity of indigenous peoples in Canada.

This control of representations of indigenous cultures limits the expression and perception of indigenous symbols, designs and history and indigenous worldviews and knowledges. It creates a negative cycle where indigenous peoples may adapt their art to comply with tourist and commercial markets in order to receive "fair" market value, or indeed *any* market value for their products. However, this practice constitutes another control of indigenous representations of indigenous culture and limits expression. Significantly, indigenous peoples' worldviews become shaped by what the external society expects and demands of them. For indigenous survival, indigenous peoples must adapt, assimilate and accommodate. Furthermore, these controlled representations do not afford copyright to the indigenous peoples whose symbols and designs are incorporated into products such as moccasins and mukluks made in other countries and sold in tourist markets.

The use, misuse and abuse of indigenous representation are also created through trademarks. These trademarks are used to sell non-indigenous commodities, such as butter sold by Land O Lakes using the image of an "Indian maiden" (http://www.landolakes), Indian Motorcycles (http://www.indianmotorcycle.com) and high school, professional and college sports teams such as the Red Skins and Braves (http://www.aistm.org/1indexpage.htm). Trademark abuse instituted in the pre-Internet era has since been transferred to the Internet via Web sites promoting these products.

Medicines are now currently marketed through the use of indigenous actors in "traditional" attire suggesting natural products are associated with indigenous peoples, e.g., Lakota products sold at http://www.aworldofgoodhealth.com/american-indian-lakota-prostate.htm. These appropriated and grossly misrepresented images promote racial stereotypes and may disrupt valid perceptions of indigenous peoples and worldviews that are rooted in indigenous histories, cultures and languages.

Stuart Hall (1997) explains that meaning is produced through representational systems we refer to as languages. He explains that we use "signs to symbolize, stand for or reference objects, people and events" as well as "reference imaginary things and fantasy worlds or abstract ideas which are not in any obvious sense part of our material world" (Hall, p. 28). Hall further explains that within mainstream articulations of representational practices, "commodity racism" (Hall, p. 239) engages representations of the "other" in order to define and market a product based on a reduction of the "other cultural group" to a few essential characteristics which are fixed in meaning — a stereotype. The stereotypes produced are then associated with a product. Dominant culture retains the right and holds the power to define, classify and reduce cultural groups to stereotypes and to use these reductions to market and sell products. Stereotypes are often based on "binary oppositions" which polarize "extreme opposites" producing "absolute difference between human "types" or species" (Hall, p. 243). For example, indigenous peoples may be perceived as "nature" to dominant society's "culture/civilization." These practices split what is acceptable from what is unacceptable and externalize what is unacceptable. Differences between varying groups are naturalized, which

functions to fix difference and ensure that these differences are closed to change or reinterpretation (Hall, p. 245). This commodity racism and stereotyping of indigenous culture is evident in the Internet examples previously cited.

THE POWER TO CONTROL REPRESENTATIONS

The desire to control representations of indigenous peoples lies in the need of the dominant society to maintain its power. Edward Said (1978) describes this process as it applies to the production and maintenance of ideas about Asia in his discussion of "Orientalism." Similarly, Gerald Vizenor (1972), a mixed-blood Ojibway scholar, describes the term Indian as an invention. One of Vizenor's acts of resistance to this invention and the dominant stereotype associated with it is his substitution of "indian" for Indian and his use of *oshki anishinabe*, which is an Ojibway expression meaning roughly "we the people of mother earth," and either refers specifically to the Ojibway people or to all indigenous peoples. He explains that:

The dominant society has created a homogenized history of tribal people for a television culture. Being an indian is a heavy burden to the oshki anishinabe *because white people know more about the* indian *they invented than anyone. The experts and cultural hobbyists never miss a chance to authenticate the scraps of romantic history dropped by white travelers through* indian country *centuries ago. White people are forever projecting their dreams of a perfect life through the invention of the indian — and then they expect an* oshki anishinabe *to not only fulfill an invention but to authenticate third-hand information about the tribal past.* (Vizenor, 1972, pp. 15-16)

Stereotypes of indigenous peoples, which have been promoted around the world, are maintained to support the beliefs and biases of western society and exercise control. Galleries and museums that have "acquired" (stolen) indigenous objects maintain the power to interpret them. For example, ceremonial objects, such as a bison hide pictograph robe, are displayed and interpreted on the Web site of the Glenbow Museum in Calgary, Alberta, Canada (http://pages.prodigy.net/jzeller/storyrobe/srobe.htm#robe). The museum says it is "of the Plains First Nations" (something like describing the words of a great French scholar as European), rather than naming the national affiliation of the stories and people recorded in this document.

The Story Robe uses pictograph images like written words to record specific times and community events, no less so than the written words of English-speaking nations. Story Robes are historical recordings of patterns of social relationships to the land and between people. Wars, deaths, negotiations and treaties were documented. The indigenous historians recorded hunting success, weather patterns, droughts and interrelationships. Indigenous leadership used this information to make community and indigenous nation decisions.

As visitors to the Web site, we can read about these Story Robes, but we cannot enter the community of origin. We cannot know the ways that this history continues to live in the lives of the present generations and those of the future. The historical knowledge is portrayed as belonging *only* to the past (the vanishing Indian) rather than belonging to the present and future survival of indigenous peoples. To avoid this, it is important on museum Web sites to "integrate what native people write about their past ... [W]hat native people currently believe about their history may provide valuable insights into the significance of that history" (Trigger, 1988, p. 35). It is important that indigenous peoples are not denied their traditional roles of taking care of these items and being responsible for protecting and transmitting the history and the stories for the next generation

"and for seven generations into the future." On this Web site there is no evidence of this occurring.

DISTANCE

What happens when the need to control and exploit indigenous peoples is translated into cyberspace and information technology? Loretta Todd, a Cree filmmaker and theorist, explains that:

Western culture seems to want everything, to go everywhere. Wants that seem endless ... The desire to know, seek new experience, take new journeys, create light, has somehow grown from a flame to a forest fire that burns everything in its way ... Of course, in a world with a legacy of colonialism, the hunger of Western culture is threatening and frightening. We have had to feed that hunger, with the furs of animals and flesh of fish and the gold and silver of our lands and ourselves as fearsome mysteries in the West's drama of itself. (Todd, 1996, p. 184)

There appear to be no boundaries to the need of the West to conquer and control.

Cyberspace and information technology are limitless in their potential as the modes of transmission for the dominant society to continue colonization practices. Information accessed through the Internet has no context in which to position it and is distanced from the indigenous peoples that it purports to represent. Linda Smith (1999), a Maori indigenous scholar, describes distance as an ongoing part of colonization. She explains that it is "one of the concepts through which Western ideas about the individual and community, about time and space, knowledge and research, imperialism and colonialism can be drawn together" (p. 55). She explains that through colonization, "the individual can be distanced, or separated, from the physical environment, the community. Through the controls over time and space the individual can also operate at a distance from the universe"

(p. 55). In this way the individual is separated from his/her self, family, community, nation, land and universe. They are further separated from their history, culture, language and traditions. This complete separation of the self—physically, mentally, emotionally and spiritually — is the true nature of the colonial process.

The fragmentation of indigenous peoples' worldview and existence continues in cyberspace at a distance from those who are being represented. This distance encourages alienation and separation, rather than unifying and connecting people together. "The alienated psyche of western man and woman cannot find relief in cyberspace and virtual reality. You can go anywhere, be anyone — but you are still alone" (Todd, 1996, p. 193). Indigenous peoples have always seen themselves as connected to all of life and all of our relations. In contrast, rather than recognizing our natural connection to all life, cyberspace fabricates connections, further alienating our connection to the universe. The artificial structure of cyberspace reflects western thought, which is fragmented and disconnected, yet strives for dominance over humanity to find meaning. "A fear of the body, aversion of nature, a desire for salvation and transcendence of the earthly plane has created a need for cyberspace" (Todd, 1996, p. 182). "The Web" embodies this alienation of western thought.

Fragmenting and distancing colonial thought from colonial practices ensured that "crimes" committed against humanity were justified as necessary for colonization and, ultimately, civilization to prevail. Smith explains that "both imperial and colonial rule were systems of rule which stretched from the centre outwards to places which were far and distant. Distance again separated the person in power from the subjects they governed. It was all so impersonal, rational and extremely effective" (pp. 55-56). In such a process, distance also implies separation of those in control and who have power from those without the means to control their own realities. The Internet, in encouraging distance, also encourages power

and separation of those who are represented from the very representations which "write" them/us. Globalization is the ultimate expression of this colonial process. The Internet is powerful and instrumental in carrying this out.

Information represented on the Internet is distanced from its context. Perhaps this lack of context makes it appear neutral. This supposed neutrality may make the information seem more acceptable. But for indigenous peoples, who are represented and defined by non-indigenous peoples on the Internet, the information is not neutral or acceptable when it is filtered through perspectives which promote bias and reinforce stereotypes.

CONCLUSION

Representational practices generated in mainstream discourse produce destructive outcomes for indigenous peoples. These practices—associated with colonization—continue through the Internet today, furthering the destructive process (Iseke-Barnes, 2002; Iseke-Barnes & Sakai, 2003; Iseke-Barnes, 2005). Commercialization and its associated commodification and stereotyping continue to assail indigenous peoples. Dominant society continues to use the Internet to exert its control over images of indigenous peoples, art, production and creativity.

Colonization, and its ongoing practice in society and through information technology, produces distance—between the individual and their environment, between those doing the representing (mainstream) and those being represented (indigenous people), between indigenous peoples and their communities, between indigenous peoples and their knowledge and art, and between indigenous peoples and their sense of self n all aspects including physical, emotional, mental and spiritual. The outcome is that the history, culture, identity and tradition of indigenous peoples are being eroded, erased and reconstructed. The genuine loss of indigenous knowledge and diversity of thought is shifting the world towards a singular hegemonic structure, and towards globalization of thought, control and a singular world order. The value of life is being replaced by the value of commodities and resource accumulation for the dominant society.

How will indigenous peoples ever restore their rightful place in a world they are custodians of if this symbolic violence and colonial power is not challenged? How will we ensure that the race for globalization does not mean erasure and rewriting of indigenous peoples' knowledge and worldviews? According to Valaskakis (1993):

We stand apart, living together in an increasingly hostile and distrustful social reality in which land, sovereignty and self-determination are ever more urgent in the lived experience of native people. We stand opposed, unaware that we are all rooted to each other in the construction and the appropriation of the contradictory Indian social imaginaries which make native sovereignty and self-determination so important to understand and so difficult to achieve. (p. 167)

Shannon Thunderbird, a member of the Coast Tsimshian First Nation and a significant indigenous artist and educator in Canada, explains on her Web site that:

Once great and vibrant indigenous cultures are now being embraced through a rebirth of ancient art and music. ... This is what pride in indigenous culture is all about, beautiful art works, music and dance produced in a sacred and respectful manner that celebrates the vibrancy and texture of an ancient civilization that still resonates today in the care and trust of those who have followed in the footsteps of their ancestors and learned the old ways in order to produce works that speak to a contemporary world. (All My Relations, www.shannonthunderbird.com/indigenous_art.htm)

Thunderbird, like many other indigenous artists, uses her Web site for anti-colonial education and to promote indigenous art used for its true intention. She challenges the role of museums in relegating indigenous art into seclusion and creating "artifacts" from indigenous productive activities, noting that "many tribal groups were looted of their precious items by over-zealous collectors." In addition, she advocates for the recognition and acknowledgement of native art as "fine art and not just craft or artefact," and notes that newer exhibits in regional and national museums are starting to change the way indigenous peoples are represented. Further, Thunderbird's discussion brings to light the questions: How will we be remembered? By whom? Or is it worse not to be remembered? And, who will control how we are remembered?

It is not the sole responsibility of indigenous peoples to continually inform western society of their colonial narratives. It must become the responsibility of western society to (1) transform themselves; (2) begin to decolonize their own structures and systems; (3) look closely at themselves; and (4) find other ways to construct their identities rather than through attempts to control and define indigenous peoples.

Indigenous peoples have always seen themselves as connected to all of life, engaging the past, present and future simultaneously. Is information technology a competent resource to ensure our natural connection to life, a life to be experienced, shared and recorded by indigenous people; bringing knowledge from the past, building on the present and creating a solid foundation for the seven generations into the future?

Through the creativity of indigenous peoples, new ways of using information technology can and will be generated which result in the support of our identities and communities. Perhaps there are examples of this creativity and these positive outcomes in the remainder of this volume.

REFERENCES

Adams, H. (1999). *Tortured people: The politics of colonization*. Penticton, BC: Theytus.

Doxtator, D. (1988). *Fluffs and feathers: An exhibit of the symbols of Indianness: A resource guide*. Brantford, ON: Woodland Cultural Centre.

Hall, S. (1997). *Representation: Cultural representations and signifying practices*. London: Sage Books.

Iseke-Barnes, J. (2002). Aboriginal and indigenous peoples' resistance, the Internet, and education. *Race, Ethnicity, and Education*, *5*(2), 171-198.

Iseke-Barnes, J. (2005). Misrepresentations of indigenous history and science: Public broadcasting, the Internet, and education. *Discourse: Studies in the Cultural Politics of Education*, *26*(2), 149-165.

Iseke-Barnes, J., & Sakai, C. (2003). Indigenous knowledges, representations of indigenous peoples on the Internet, and pedagogies in a case study in education: Questioning using the Web to teach about indigenous peoples. *Journal of Educational Thought*, *37*(2), 197-232.

Mackey, E. (2002). *The house of difference: The cultural politics and national identity in Canada*. Toronto: University of Toronto.

Mallery, G. (1972). *Picture-writing of the American Indians* (2 vols). Canada: General Publishing.

Said, E. (1978). *Orientalism*. New York: Random House.

Smith, L. T. (1999). *Decolonizing methodologies: Research and indigenous peoples*. London: Zed Books.

Todd, L. (1996). Aboriginal narratives in cyberspace. In M. A. Moser & D. Macleod (Eds.), *Immersed in technology: Art and virtual environments* (pp. 179-194). Cambridge, MA: MIT Press.

Trigger, B. (1988). The historian's Indian: Native Americans in Canadian historical writing from Charlevoix to the present. In R. Fisher & K. Coates (Eds.), *Out of the background: Readings on Canadian native history*. Toronto: Copp Clark Pittman.

Valaskakis, G. G. (1993). Postcards of my past: The Indian as artefact. In V. Blundell, J. Shepherd, & I. Taylor (Eds.), *Relocating cultural studies: Developments in theory and research* (pp. 155-170). London: Routledge.

Vizenor, G. (1972). *The everlasting sky: New voices from the people named the Chippewa*. New York: Crowell-Collier Press.

Index

A

activity theory 278
administrative process efficiency 445
ADSL/VDSL 31
Africa 200
African education 194, 198
antiglobalization 66

B

broadband Internet 394
Business-to-Business Market 463
Business-to-Consumer Market 463
Business intelligence 77

C

CAPITA framework 159–160, 162
Collaborative Relationships 466
collaborative tools 77
color 234
communities of practice (CoPs) 77
community 78
computer-mediated learning 390
content management 77
CoPs (see communities of practice) 77
core indicators (CIs) 32
CRM 462
CRM Challenges 462
cross-cultural communication 207
cross-cultural differences 79
cultural diversity 420
culturally
  aware systems (CAWAS) 169–181
    architecture of 172
    authoring tool to produce cultural templates 174
    cultural adaptation of multimedia content 175
    cultural intelligence 171
    cultural representations 176

dual representation of cultural rules 171
culture 182, 183, 184, 185, 186, 189, 190, 191, 192
culture, U.S. and Canada 248
culture-centric Web site 230
culture network 210
currency 237
curriculum 392
customer relationship management (CRM) 458
cybercafé 232
cyber kiosks 391

D

Dallmayr, Jeff 41
date format 237
developing countries 379
developing countries, and e-government 327–346
developing countries, vs. developed 329–346
developing country, and e-medicine 306–326
developing country, and IT implementation 400–419
digital-divide 21
digital-divide reduction 29
digital-inequality 29
digital collaboration 390
digital divide 21, 51, 52, 53, 56, 60, 61, 65, 68, 387, 394
digital division 24
digital economy 18
digital exclusion 52, 55, 56, 60
digital exclusion, mediation of 55, 57, 60, 61, 64, 65, 67, 69
digital gap 23
digital inclusion 51, 52, 53, 54, 55, 56, 57, 60, 61, 62, 63, 64, 66, 67, 68, 69, 72, 73
digital inequality 23
digital literacy 3, 51, 52, 53, 55, 57, 58, 59
digitally illiterate 52
digitally literate 52, 68